CW00545267

CZECH & SLOVAK RAILWAYS

LOCOMOTIVES, MULTIPLE UNITS, METROS & TRAMS

FIRST EDITION

The complete guide to all Locomotives, Multiple Units, Metros & Trams of the Czech Republic and Slovakia

Robert Pritchard

Published by Platform 5 Publishing Ltd,
52 Broadfield Road, Sheffield, S8 0XJ, England.

Printed in England by The Lavenham Press, Lavenham, Suffolk.

ISBN 978 1 902336 71 8

▲ ČD 810.036 and four-wheel BDtax trailer 50 54 93-29 089 arrive at Příbor, Moravia (passing the gothic Church of Nativity of the Virgin Mary) working train Os23132, the 11.11 Studénka–Štramberk, on 9 July 2013.   **Robert Pritchard**

CONTENTS

Front Cover: Carrying the latest ČD livery, 362.084 approaches Praha Vršovice with train R1543, the 09.21 Praha Holešovice–Linz (Austria) via České Budějovice on 7 May 2015.   **Robert Pritchard**

Back Cover Top: Škoda EMU 671.010 leaves Trenčín with ZSSK train Os3314, the 14.44 Žilina– Nové Mesto nad Váhom on 10 June 2014.   **Robert Pritchard**

Back Cover Bottom: New Košice Vario LF2+ tram 806 arrives at VSS, križovatka with a Line 9 service from Havlíčkova to Važecka on 16 March 2015.   **Robert Pritchard**

FOREWORD

Welcome to this new volume in the Platform 5 European handbook series, covering the railways of the Czech Republic and Slovakia. This book bridges a gap between the Germany and Austria handbooks to link the railways of this historically connected region of Central and Eastern Europe. As our German handbook explained the merged renumbered fleets of the former East and West Germany, this book shows the opposite. Czechoslovakia divided into the separate states of the Czech Republic and Slovakia in 1993, with the railway ČSD splitting into ČD and ŽSR without any renumberings.

In the last ten years or so, since both countries became members of the EU, there has been a remarkable amount of investment in new or rebuilt trains and also in infrastructure and station improvements (such as line realignments and station rebuilds, particularly on the main pan-European lines). Despite this rate of change, particularly noticeable in the Czech Republic, both countries are still fantastic destinations for railfans. There are plenty of locomotive-hauled trains, heavy freight traffic on the core routes and some fantastic scenery. The increase in the number of private freight operators has also led to a very interesting and colourful freight scene, with some operators using refurbished electric locomotives dating from the 1950s and 1960s. Both countries are very affordable destinations, particularly when compared to western Europe.

The Czech Republic is a relatively small country, about the size of Ireland, but packs a lot in. It boasts one of the densest rail networks in Europe which includes many rural branch lines, and in some parts quite a bit of heavy industry and coal mining. Slovakia is slightly smaller and more rural, with around half the population and a much less dense rail network, plus slightly fewer lines that are electrified.

This book has taken somewhat longer to compile than I expected when I first took the project on, the sheer number of private operators today taking some time to "untangle". As someone who believes in extensive work "on the ground" I've spent more than 150 days in the two countries over the last four years, travelling on most lines and visiting all of the depots. Thanks to everyone for their help and patience and I hope you enjoy travelling the rails of the Czech and Slovak Republics as much as I have enjoyed researching this book.

Robert Pritchard, April 2016.

▲ There has been significant investment in new and rebuilt trains in both countries. The latest new units for ČD are the excellent Škoda "InterPanter" express EMUs. On 25 February 2016 660.105 arrives at Praha Vršovice empty stock, after working train R872, the 08.57 Brno–Praha hl.n.

Quintus Vosman

HISTORICAL BACKGROUND

In the 5th century AD, migrating Slavs from the Black Sea settled in the region, establishing kingdoms by the 7th to 9th centuries, later falling to Hapsburg (from 1867 Austro-Hungary Empire rule). An independent Czechoslovakia came into being in 1918 – uniting Bohemia, Moravia, Slovakia and Ruthenia following the collapse of the monarchy after World War I. Nazi Germany took direct occupation first of Sudentenland in 1938 and then the rest of the Czech region in 1939, Slovakia gaining nominal independence but also under Nazi control. The countries reunited into Czechoslovakia after World War II, but without the eastern area of Ruthenia which was lost to Soviet Russia. However Stalin's Soviet Union and the Communists soon seized power in 1948, and in 1969 Czechoslovakia became the Federation of Czech Socialist and Slovak Socialist Republics but keeping the 1960 name CSSR (Czech Slovak Socialist Republic).

1989 was a momentous year in Eastern Europe as Communist Governments fell in countries like East Germany, Poland and Bulgaria. Czechoslovakia joined them in November of that year when the famous "Velvet Revolution" saw mass, mainly peaceful, demonstrations in Praha, ultimately leading to the collapse of the communist Government.

On 1 January 1993 the country divided into separate Czech and Slovak Republics, both becoming European Union members in 2004. Slovakia adopted the Euro currency in 2009. The Czech Republic had been planning the same for 2010 but the global recession of this time put this on hold, and there are no current plans by the Czech Republic to adopt the Euro.

Since the fall of communism tourism has flourished in both countries, especially in the Czech Republic, where Praha is now the fifth most visited city in Europe. Much of the west and south of the country, including the spa towns, are popular with German and Austrian tourists. By contrast quite a bit of Moravia and also much of Slovakia are further off the tourist trail, but the High Tatra mountains are very popular with walkers and hikers.

Today the Czech Republic has a population of just over 10 million people, with Slovakia having a population of around 5.5 million. Both countries are very safe destinations for visitors, although tourists should be aware of pickpockets in operation in Praha, especially on the Metro. The Czech and Slovak languages are very similar, both belonging to the Slavic group of languages. Visitors to Praha and the other major cities should have no trouble finding someone who speaks English, and since the early 1990s English has been taught as the second language in schools, so younger people can often speak at least some English wherever you are in the two countries.

CZECH & SLOVAK RAILWAYS

Czechoslovak State Railways (Československé Státní Dráhy, or ČSD) came into being in 1918, taking over the parts of Imperial Austrian State Railways (kkStB) lying within the new state. kkStB took in early railways including the 1832 horse railway between České Budějovice and Linz, and the 1837 Wien–Krakow Kaiser Ferdinands Nordbahn. By 1884 the Austro-Hungary network totalled 5103 km when the Imperial General Directorate of State Railways was founded, later kaiserlich-königlichen Staatsbahnen (kkStB). By 1914, kkStB extended to some 18 859 km. ČSD initially lasted until 1939 when the Nazi controlled Protectorate of Bohemia and Moravia formed the Bohemian Moravian Railway (Českomoravska Dráha, or Böhmisch-Mährische Transversalbahn) under Deutsche Reichsbahn direction. In the Slovak region, Slovak Railways (Slovenske Železnice) was formed.

ČSD reformed in 1945, and ceased to exist at the close of 1992. České Dráhy (ČD) and Železnice Slovenskej Republiky (ŽSR) were formed out of the 1993 division of ČSD. Railway UIC/EVN codes are 54 for the Czech Republic (previously used for ČD and originally ČSD) and 56 for the Slovak Republic (previously used for ŽSR). Both railways took the infrastructure within each border, and motive power already allocated to each depot, but other rolling stock was assigned on a two-to-one ČD-ŽSR ratio.

Czechoslovakia had been self-sufficient in motive power with ČKD building the majority of diesel locomotives, Škoda electric locomotives, and MSV multiple units. ČKD and Škoda also built huge numbers of everything for the Eastern Bloc. Imported stock included carriages from East Germany, diesels and metro cars from the Soviet Union. At the turn of the political tide in 1989 building ceased, and the 1990s saw the traction sector collapse. Into the 21st century a refinanced Škoda has managed to keep its major plant in Plzeň, and it now constructs trains and trams both for the home market and for export. Siemens acquired the goodwill of some parts of ČKD with a new EMU factory at Praha Zlicín. However this closed in 2009.

The present day operating divisions (ČD and ČD Cargo and ZSSK and ZSSK Cargo (ŽSCS)), all generally continue the time-honoured practice of allocating small pools of locomotives, multiple units and rolling stock to particular diagrams, often outbased at sub-depots for extended periods. Each pool has specific locomotives or motor coaches, typically covering a four or five day plan, or set of diagrams. The main depots have reserves if dedicated stock is unavailable. Depots can heavily cannibalise stopped locomotives or railcars, with months or even years out of traffic.

ELECTRIFICATION

Main line electrification started in the mid-1950s using 3000 V DC with the Praha–Ostrava–Košice corridor wired between 1955 and 1960. In line with technical developments elsewhere, 25 kV AC 50 Hz was installed around Plzeň in 1962, reaching Bratislava by 1969. AC is supplied from national power grids through 110/25 kV substations, DC from 110/22 kV feeders through 22 kV AC lineside cables to rectifier substations. Thus both Czech and Slovak railways were bequeathed DC and AC systems, single and dual voltage motive power, and system changeover points. There is also the isolated 1500 V DC Tábor–Bechyně branch in the Czech Republic.

Generally speaking in the Czech Republic, the lines to the north and east of Praha are 3000 V DC, and those to the west and south of Praha are 25 kV AC. Czech DC/AC changeover points are at Kutná Hora (Kolín–Brno line), between Svitavy and Lany (Brno–Česká Třebová), Nezamyslice (Brno–Přerov), Nedakonice (Přerov–Břeclav), Benešov u Prahy (Praha–České Budějovice), between Beroun and Králův Dvůr (Praha–Plzeň line), and Kadaň-Prunéřov (Chomutov–Karlovy Vary). Slovak railways has just one AC/DC change point at Púchov. In 2015 the Czech Ministry of Transport, in association with SŽDC, started a feasibility study into converting the country's 3000 V DC network into 25 kV AC.

Being surrounded by German and Austrian 15 kV AC, Hungarian 25 kV AC and Polish 3000 V DC, the region seems ideal for the 21st century multi-system products of Bombardier, Siemens or Alstom, but due to traction interference with the unique local signalling systems, the introduction of these types has been slow. However by the time of going to press all three of the TRAXX, Vectron and Eurosprinter family are finally a regular sight, albeit so far only with private operators rather than the state passenger or freight operators.

DIESEL TRACTION

Main line steam working ceased in 1980, and there is no doubt that Škoda and ČKD had been constructing some of the world's most advanced machines. However, main line diesel locomotives were slow to develop, despite a history and large quantity of four-wheel railbuses dating back to the mid 1920s, and a long run of 549 M131.1 (Class 801) mainly built 1948–56, M262.0 (Class 820) bogie railcars of the same period, and pre-war four wheel shunters evolving into post-war T211.0 and successors (Class 700 etc).

Fitted with the ČKD 310 series six-cylinder engine, the first main line locomotive was T434.001 of 1953. The pre-series of eight machines (later T436.0) led to T435.0 (Class 720), built 1958–62. But their 551 kW was eclipsed in 1958 by three T658.0/T698.0 Co-Co prototypes for freight, passenger and export. Powered by 1214 kW eight-cylinder turbocharged 310 series engines, 44 T678.0/T679.0 (Classes 775/776) initially at 1325 kW then 1470 kW followed from 1961. Further development was suppressed by the Soviets who in 1963 ruled only they could build such large Co-Co diesel-electrics. In 1964 ČSD and ČKD therefore developed the 1103 kW T478.1/T478.2 (Classes 751/752) Bo-Bo using a turbocharged six-cylinder 310 series engine, while importing from 1966 the Lugansk built M62 model as Class T679.1 (Class 781). In parallel a number of prototype diesel hydraulics appeared from ČKD and TSM (Martin) mostly with ČKD 170 series engines, none of which led to anything except the various 515 kW T444.x machines (Classes 725/726).

Soviet agreements also evolved into the 1963 T669.0 prototypes that eventually led to a massive production run (see Classes 770/771 details), also using the 310 series engine. While ČSD was importing T679.1s, and Libeň was churning out export T669.0s, ČKD developed its 230 series engine appearing in vee-12 form from 1968 in the T478.3 "Goggle" (later Class 753) and straight form from 1973 in the assorted T475.15/T476.0 prototypes leading to T448.0/T466.2 (Classes 740/742).

DMUs continued to develop along the power tractor plus loose trailer line with ČSD seeming unable to decide on transmission. Using the current class numbers, Classes 830/831, 820/85x, 860, 842, 843 from the 1950s through to the 1980s alternated between electric and hydraulic transmission. Into the 1990s unreliability and fuel inefficiency of 230 series engines led to Class 750/753 withdrawals before the older Classes 751/752/749.

In more recent years various diesel locomotive types, such as Classes 735, 740 and 753, have been extensively rebuilt by some of the major workshops, essentially creating a new locomotive fit for another 20 years or more service. Most rebuilds are fitted with Caterpillar engines.

TRAIN SERVICES

Passenger train categories operated by ČD and ZSSK are similar and are classified as follows:

EC: EuroCity. International express; high standard First and Second Class accommodation. Air conditioned.
IC: InterCity. Connecting major centres; high standard First and Second Class accommodation. Air conditioned.
EN: EuroNight. Long distance, cross-border overnight trains offering First and Second Class accommodation and sleeping cars.
Ex: Express. Connecting major centres; First and Second Class.
railjet: Railjet train (ČD only). Train worked by one of the ČD/ÖBB Railjet push-pull sets.
R: Fast train (Rychlík). First and Second Class, often without catering.
Rx: Higher-quality Fast train (Rychlíky vyšší kvality) (ČD only). First and Second Class. At least part of the train has air-conditioning and level access.
REX: Regional Express limited stop train (ZSSK only).
SC: SuperCity (ČD only). Limited stop train usually operated by a Pendolino EMU, special fare structure with supplement payable, mandatory reservation.
Sp: Regional fast train (Spěšné vlak) (ČD only).
Os: Osobní vlak. All other passenger trains (including slow trains, regional and branch line services). Not used in timetable books but displayed on station notices.

Traditionally, in both countries, long distance trains have been mainly formed of coaches with compartments. The recent trend, on refurbishment, has been to convert coaches to open accommodation, although some recent refurbishments have retained compartments. Another growing trend is air conditioned carriages, which are now used on many long distance routes. Facilities for passengers have also improved in recent years, with wi-fi internet access now provided on many new and refurbished trains. ZSSK in particular is very good at providing wi-fi on its InterCity trains, which for visitors from abroad can be a good way to catch up on emails and news etc on their smartphones without having to pay roaming charges!

LOCOMOTIVE & RAILCAR NUMBERING SYSTEM

The 1988 ČSD numbering system remains in use in both countries, using the UIC six digits and computer check digit format. There is a formal definition stating number marking on vehicles shall consist of class number (three digits), space, inventory number (three digits), dash, check digit, but in written documents a dot should take the place of the space. Registered private and industrial locomotives use the same system. Number groups are:

100.000 DC electric locomotives
200.000 AC electric locomotives
300.000 Multi-system electric locomotives
400.000 DC Electric Multiple Units
500.000 AC Electric Multiple Units
600.000 Multi-system electric multiple units
700.000 Diesel locomotives
800.000 Diesel tractor and multiple units
900.000 Unpowered driving trailers
000.000 Unpowered intermediate trailers

The fourth digit can be used to denote a sub class or special characteristics. "5" or "6" usually denotes non-capital or industrial stock, "8" broad gauge and "9" narrow gauge. There are several anomalies and exceptions to the general numbering rules e.g. in some cases, the fifth digit indicates the sub-class.

EUROPEAN VEHICLE NUMBER & VEHICLE KEEPER MARKING

A more recent development is the 12-digit European Vehicle Number, a refinement of the former UIC full identification number. Because of open access across Europe it is essential that all traction and rolling stock has a European number. The Vehicle Keeper Marking (VKM) is also necessary because of the large number of railway operators across Europe.

Taking ZSSK Cargo electric locomotive 131.025 as an example, as can be seen from the photo below the full EVN is 91 56 6 131 025-9. This breaks down as follows:

The first two digits are the Type Code. The different types used in the Czech Republic and Slovakia relevant to this book are as follows:

50: Passenger vehicles for domestic use.
60: Battery vans (Slovakia only).
90: Miscellaneous traction – mostly used for steam locomotives.
91: Electric locomotives faster than 80 km/h.
92: Diesel locomotives faster than 80 km/h.
93: High Speed EMUs.
94: All other EMUs.
95: All DMUs.
96: DMU or EMU trailers or driving trailers (Slovakia only).
97: Electric locomotives with speed lower than 80 km/h (Slovakia only).
98: Diesel shunting locomotives.
99: Departmental self-powered vehicles.

The next two digits indicate the country code in which that vehicle is registered:

54: Czech Republic.   56: Slovakia.

The next digit is allocated by the operator, and a number has to be selected here to ensure that the previous (six digit) running number could continue to be used without having to change the check digit. It should be noted that in Slovakia some check digits did change on DMUs with the introduction of EVNs.

The next six digits are the locomotive or vehicle number (see above).

These are followed by the computer check digit which is arrived at by multiplying the 11 digits of the full EVN number alternatively by 2 and 1. The resulting digits are successively added together, and the total deducted from the next whole multiple of ten to give the check digit.

For example 91 56 6 131 025 can be calculated as follows:

9	1	5	6	6	1	3	1	0	2	5
x2	x1	x2	x1	x2	x1	x2	x1	x2	x1	x2
1+8	+1 +	1+0	+6 +	1+2	+1 +	6 +	1+	0 +	2 +	1+0

Total = 31
40 – 31 = 9.

Two examples of full EVN numbers in the Czech Republic and Slovakia. This is BF Logistics locomotive 742.627. Before the EVN is "CZ", indicating the locomotive is registered in the Czech Republic. This is followed by the Vehicle Keeper Marking, in this case "BFL".

The full EVN on ZSSK Cargo double-locomotive 131.025. In this case "SK" indicates the locomotive is registered in Slovakia. This is followed by the operator – "ZSSKC" standing for ZSSK Cargo. Underneath is the Škoda works plate. **Robert Pritchard (2)**

NUMBERING & NAMING NOTES

No general renumbering has taken place in either country, but rebuilds and conversions have duplicated some numbers between the two countries. In particular, Classes 752 and 755, 811, 812, 813, 840 and 010, 011, 012, 071 and 971 have different meanings to ČD and ZSSK. Following the recent renumbering of electric locomotive 363.001 by ČD there is also now a 362.001 operating in both countries, as well as a DMU 810.674 in both countries! During ČSD times, a handful of industrial number series were duplicated.

Track machines and on-track plant have alphanumeric prefixes indicating function and/or capacity followed by the unique number e.g. diesel railcar based MVTV (overhead electrified line maintenance cars), MPV (powered trolleys), PA (site work and traction generator), EDK (crane), and so on. MVTV were renumbered from the 890.000 series. MVTV2 and MVTV3 now duplicate numbers between Czech and Slovak railways.

The pre-1988 numbering system helps identify museum items as well as understand current stock. In 1921, engineer Kryspin devised a system to convey certain characteristics. Steam locomotives had no prefix letter e.g. 464.123; electric and diesel locomotives were prefixed "E" or "T" e.g. E469.234 or T679.1234; and motor coaches prefixed "M" or "EM", e.g. M240.0123 or EM475.0123. Other prefixes were driving trailer "R", battery "A", narrow gauge "U", and combined letters such as TU, TA, EMU and so on. The system was extended with S for AC electric; E then meaning DC; ES dual system; and TL gas turbine.

The first digit is the number of powered axles, 5 for ten coupled steam, and 4 or 6 for Bo-Bo or Co-Co as well as eight or 12 coupled steam. The second digit indicates maximum speed. Always add three and multiply by ten, hence 7 = 100 km/h (7+3 =10, 10x10 =100). The third digit denotes axle loading. Always add ten, hence 8 = 18 tonne. The first digit following the dot must always be used as this is a class as well as sub-class discriminator i.e. different designs with similar characteristics such as T478.1 and T478.3 (Classes 751/753) or similar basic type such as S669.2 and S669.3 (todays Classes 182/183) or T669.0 and T669.1 (Classes 770/771). There may be two, three or four digit numbers following the dot.

There are no officially named locomotives but many units have been given unofficial "stick-on" names, often girls names. These are not shown, but officially applied names, such as those given to the Děčín-allocated Class 440 EMUs, are shown.

BUILDERS NAMES

ČKD, Škoda and MSV are generally used throughout irrespective of alternate names used at certain times for political purposes i.e. ČKD includes Českomoravská Kolben-Daněk Praha, ČKD závod Lokomotivka Sokolovo Praha, ČKD Lokomotivka Praha. Škoda includes Škodovy závody Plzeň, Leninovy závody Plzeň, Škoda Plzeň; and MSV includes Vagonka Studénka, Moravskoslezska Vagonka and ČKD Studénka.

HOW TO GET TO THE CZECH REPUBLIC & SLOVAKIA

BY AIR

There are a number of different airports and airlines to choose from. The most popular airport is Praha, where flights arrive from all over Europe. In the Czech Republic there are also airports at Brno and Ostrava. Ostrava is the only one of the three airports to be linked by rail, a new link opening in 2015: there are direct trains to Studenka, Ostrava and Bohumín. Brno and Praha rely on bus connections. At Praha there is the Airport Express bus run by ČD which runs to hlavní nádraží. Alternatively regular service bus 119 runs to Nádraží Veleslavín which is the terminus of Metro Line A (and also has a tram stop). Transfer to the centre of Praha via bus 119 and the Metro generally takes 35–40 minutes.

In Slovakia there are airports at Bratislava, Poprad-Tatry and Košice. For those travelling to the Bratislava area, flights to Wein could also be considered.

Whilst new routes are starting all the time, the following is a list of the main routes in operation at the time of going to press. Note that not all run daily and some are more infrequent in the winter. For more details see the various airlines, websites or the price comparison website www.skyscanner.net.

British Airways: Heathrow–Praha.
Czech Airlines: Gatwick–Praha, Birmingham–Praha, Liverpool–Praha.
Easyjet: Gatwick–Praha, Stansted–Praha, Bristol–Praha, Manchester–Praha, Edinburgh–Praha.
Jet2: Manchester–Praha, East Midlands–Praha, Leeds/Bradford–Praha, Newcastle–Praha, Glasgow–Praha.
Ryanair: Stansted–Praha, Stansted–Brno, Stansted–Ostrava, Luton–Bratislava, Birmingham–Bratislava, Manchester–Bratislava, Liverpool–Bratislava, Edinburgh–Bratislava.
Smartwings: Gatwick–Praha, Birmingham–Praha, Liverpool–Praha.
Wizzair: Luton–Praha, Luton–Brno, Luton–Košice, Luton–Poprad-Tatry, Doncaster–Košice.

BY RAIL

There are direct trains to the Czech Republic and Slovakia from across mainland Europe. The main line from Germany to the Czech Republic brings you to Děčín and there are international trains from Hamburg and Berlin to Praha, some continuing via Brno and Bratislava to Budapest in Hungary. There are also direct trains from München to Praha via Plzeň and from Linz (Austria) to Praha via České Budějovice. There is also an international service linking Praha and Brno with Wien and Graz in Austria. From Poland the main link comprises services from Warszawa and Katowice to Bohumín, Ostrava and Praha.

In Slovakia, Bratislava is linked to Wien via two different routes (Marchegg and Kittsee). The aforementioned Germany–Praha–Budapest service runs via Štúrovo to Szob in Hungary and there are also limited international services between Košice and Budapest via Hidasnémeti and a local service from Čadca to Zwardoń (Poland). Finally, there is an international shuttle service linking Čierna nad Tisou and Chop (Ukraine).

There are a number of options available for travelling to and from the Czech Republic and Slovakia by rail from Britain, although almost all require an overnight stay en route. If you travel on an early morning Eurostar from London it is possible to reach Praha in a day (14 hours via Brussels, Frankfurt, Leipzig and Dresden), but this isn't possible in the opposite direction. Obvious places to break journeys include Brussels or somewhere in the west of Germany such as Köln. The CityNightLine overnight train from Praha to Köln is also a good option. The German Railways journey planner at www.db.de can be used to work out times and fares. Additional information is available on the excellent "Man in Seat 61" rail travel website at www.seat61.com.

FARES & ROVER TICKETS

Train travel in both countries is very reasonably priced compared to Britain, and thankfully there are no complicated time restrictions! While slightly cheaper advance purchase tickets do exist for certain routes, "walk up" tickets are not expensive, for example a Praha to Brno single is, at the time of writing, just 224czk (around £6.50) for 255 km. Returns are twice the single fare. Ticket prices can be checked on the ČD (www.cd.cz) or ZSSK (www.zssk.sk) websites. Tickets should be purchased before boarding the train where a ticket office is available. When boarding at unstaffed stations tickets can be purchased on board the train (on Driver Only Operated rural branch line services the driver sells tickets).

ČD also offers a range of well-priced rover tickets. There is one covering the whole network, valid on any day with no time restrictions ("Celodenní Jízdenka"). At the time of writing this costs 579czk (around £17) or slightly less if purchased via the internet and printed as an "e-ticket". It is valid on private operator GWTR but not on JHMD, RegioJet or Leo Express. Tickets bought via the internet are valid on ČD trains only.

There is also an extensive selection of 13 regional one day rover tickets covering all the regions, including one for Praha and the surrounding area. These are priced at between 159czk and 239czk. Depending where you are travelling it can be cheaper to buy two of these rather than a Celodenní Jízdenka. Another ticket worth considering for more than one person travelling at weekends is the Group Weekend ticket (Skupinová víkendová jízdenka). This allows travel on a Saturday, Sunday or Bank Holiday for 2 adults and up to 3 children for 679czk. Regional versions are again available as well. For more details of these rover tickets see the English version of the ČD website (under "Domestic Travel" / "Tickets" / "Discounts").

Every summer since 2012 ČD has offered its Ticket for Summer ("Jízdenka na léto") to encourage travel at this slightly quieter time of year (as many Czechs themselves are away on holiday). For 1190czk (or 990czk with InKarta card, see below) this offers 14 days unlimited travel during the months of July and August – outstanding value for money even if you can't use it for the full 14 days!

For regular travellers the "InKarta" loyalty card is worth a mention. There are three versions offering 25% off, 50% off or unlimited travel. It is presumed that the latter two wouldn't be suitable to visitors, but the IN25 card is worth considering for regular visitors – at 990czk for 3 years it is good value and also gives a 200czk discount on the "Ticket for Summer".

Unfortunately, by contrast, ZSSK offers little in the way of rover tickets for travel in Slovakia, apart from for travel on the High Tatra mountain railways in the Poprad-Tatry area, where 1 day, 3 day and 7 day tickets are available for €4, €8 and €14 respectively.

Interrail one-country passes are also available for both countries, and for Slovakia this is the only option for a rover ticket. 3, 4, 6 and 8 days travel in 1 month are available. For prices see the www.interrail.eu website. Interrail Global passes allow travel in both countries. With an Interrail pass travel is only allowed on the state operators (ČD and ZSSK) services.

LAYOUT OF INFORMATION & OTHER CODES

For each class of vehicle technical and historical information is given, followed by a list of individual vehicles arranged as follows:

(1) Number.
(2) Previous number (if any).
(3) Livery code (if applicable) in **bold condensed** type.
(4) Operating division sector code (if applicable) – an *F* in italics indicates the locomotive is operated by ČD Cargo or ZSSK Cargo.
(5) Detail difference notes (of applicable).
(6) Depot allocation code.
(7) Note (S) denoting a stored or withdrawn vehicle (if applicable). The actual location for stored vehicles is shown.

The following abbreviations and ISO standard symbols are used for vehicle technical data:

AC	Alternating Current	DM	Diesel Mechanical	kW	kilowatts
BE	Battery Electric	Hz	hertz	m	metres
DC	Direct Current	km/h	kilometres per hour	mm	millimetres
DE	Diesel Electric	km	kilometres	V	Volts
DH	Diesel Hydraulic	kN	kilonewtons		

Multiple unit control is usually within own class where fitted. Electric train heating is 3000 V DC (including Class 749/750/754 diesel locomotives). Multiple units are generally loose single vehicles and Second Class open accommodation only. Unpowered trailers used with diesel motor coaches are self-heated burning liquid fuel.

Seating accommodation:
The information given in class headings and sub-headings is in the form of First Class/Second Class, xT (or TD), xW, where T stands for Toilet, TD a universal access toilet and W wheelchair spaces. A number in brackets (ie +2) denotes tip-up seats in that vehicle (in addition to the fixed seats). So for example 9/44(+12) 1TD 2W indicates that vehicle has 9 First Class and 44 Second Class seats, plus 12 tip-up seats, one universal access toilet and spaces for two wheelchairs.

Multiple unit type codes: For multiple units the following type codes are used:

DMBSO	Driving Motor Brake Second Open	MCO	Motor Composite Open
DMCO	Driving Motor Composite Open	MSO	Motor Second Open
DMSO	Driving Motor Second Open	TSO	Trailer Second Open
DTSO	Driving Trailer Second Open		

Wheel arrangements:
The standard Whyte notation is used for steam locomotives and diesel shunting locomotives with coupled driving wheels. The number of leading wheels are given, followed by the number of driving wheels and then the trailing wheels. Suffixes are used to denote tank locomotives as follows: RT – rack tank, T – side tank, WT – well tank. F denotes a fireless locomotive.

For other shunting and main line diesel and electric locomotives, the system whereby the number of powered axles on a bogie or frame is denoted by a letter (A = 1, B = 2, C = 3 etc) and the number of unpowered axles is denoted by a number if used. The letter "o" after a letter indicates that each axle is individually powered and a + sign indicates that the bogies are intercoupled.

The following other notes are used in this book:

Suffix [II] denotes a vehicle that has been constructed to replace another ʹvehicle following accident damage and carries the same number as the original vehicle.

† (after "Total No. Built" in class headings) – indicates some of that specific class is also in operation in the other country (i.e. either the Czech Republic or Slovakia).

+ A locomotive or railcar that forms part of, or is designated for, the National Museum fleet of either the Czech Republic or Slovakia.

r after a date indicates when that vehicle was rebuilt.

GENERAL ABBREVIATIONS & BUILDERS

Spelling and wording vary between Czech and Slovak railways and languages. This list of manufacturers and other general abbreviations should be read for basic guidance only. In common with most European railways systems, ČD and ZSSK passenger coach codes are prefixed "A" for First and "B" for Second Class.

Adam	Adamovské Strojírny, Adamov.
BMB	Bohemian Moravian Railway (Českomoravská dráha) Bohmisch Mahrische Bahn 1939–45.
BMM	Erste Böhmisch-Mährische Maschinenfabrik, Praha.
BrDa	Breitfeld-Daněk, Slany (became part of ČKD).
ÇAT	Çaterpillar – American diesel engine manufacturer.
ČD	České Dráhy or Czech Railways.
ČKD	Českomoravská-Kolben-Daněk – steam and diesel locomotive builder ČKD.
ČSD	Československé Státní Dráhy – Czechoslovak State Railways.
ČSFR	Česko Slovak Republika – Czech & Slovak Federative Republic (1990–93 name).
ČSSR	Československá Socialistická Republika – Czechoslovak Socialist Republic (1960–90 name).
Chrz	Pierwsza Fabryka Lokomotyw w Polsce, Chrzanów, Poland.
czk	Česká koruna – Czech Crown (currency).
DAKO	Czech manufacturer of train air braking equipment
DB	Deutsche Bahn – German Railways.
DPOV	Dílny Pro Opravy Vozidel – Czech railway workshop company.
DR	Deutsche Reichsbahn – former East German Railways.
EDB	Electric dynamic braking.
ETH	Electric train heating (3000 V DC for all ŽSR and ČD domestic stock).
Hags	Christian Hagans Engineering Works, Erfurt, Germany.
Hart	Sächsische Maschinenfabrik vormals Richard Hartmann, Chemnitz, Germany.
Hens	Hensche & Sohn, Kassel, Germany.
hl.n.	hlavní nádraží – Czech main station.
hl.st.	hlavná stanica – Slovak main station.
HoHe	Hohenzollern Aktiengesellschaft für Lokomotivbau, Düsseldorf, Germany.
IMC	Iron Monument Club, Plzeň (Plzeň preservation club).
Kal	Kuluzhskii Mashinostroitel'nyi Zvod, Kaluga, Russia.
KFNB	Kaiser Ferdinands-Nordbahn.
kkStB	kaiserlich königliche österreichische Staatsbahnen – Imperial Austrian State Railways.
KOB	Kaschau-Oderberger Bahn – Košice–Bohumín railway.
Kolín	Privni Kolínská, Továrna na Lokomotivy, Kolín (workshops at Žamberk).
Křiž	Ceskomoravské Elektrotechnické Závody František Křižík, Praha.
KrLi	Lokomotivfabrik Krauss & Co, Linz, Austria.
KrMu	Lokomotivfabrik Krauss & Co, Linz, München, Germany.
LEW	Lokomotivbau und Elektrotechnische Werke, Hennigsdorf, Germany
LIAZ	LIberecké Automobilové Závody – Diesel engine manufacturer, now Tedom.
Luhan	Luhanskteplovoz locomotive works, Lugansk, USSR (now Ukraine).
MÁV	Magyar Államvasutak – Hungarian Railways.
MDC	Museum Dokumentačné Centrum – Slovak national museum collection.
Mein	Meiningen Steam Locomotive Works, Meiningen, Germany
MSV	Studénka Vagonka/Studénka – Carriage multiple unit manufacturer.
MTH	MTH Praha Mechanizace traťového hospodářství, Hranice na Moravě
MTU	MTU Friedrichshafen – German diesel engine manufacturer.
NTM	Národní Technické Muzeum – Czech national museum collection.
ÖBB	Österreichische Bundesbahnen – Austrian Railways.
O&K	Orenstein & Koppel, Berlin, Germany.
PKP	Polskie Koleje Państwowe – Polish Railways.
Res	Uzinele de Fier și Domeniile Reșița, Reșița, Romania.

Ring	Ringhoffer-Werke, Waggon-und Tenderfabrik, Praha.
RZD	Ruské Železnice – Russian Railways.
SA3	Automatic coupler used on all Russian Railways rolling stock, similar to a buck-eye.
ŞGP	Şimmering-Graz-Pauker, Austria.
Škoda	Škoda – steam and electric locomotive and EMU manufacturer.
Smo	Gesellschaft für Feldbahn Industri Smoschewer & Co, Beslau-Schmiederfeld, Germany
SMZ	Ştrojárske a Metalurgické Závody – locomotive builder at Dubnica nad Vahom, Slovakia.
SRT	Širokorozchodná trať – Slovak broad gauge (1520 mm) line.
StEG	Maschinen-Fabrik der KK priv Österreichisch Staatseisenbahn Gesellschaft, Wien.
SZD	Sovjetske Železnice – Soviet Railways.
SZDC	Správa Železniční Dopravní Cesty – Czech infrastructure authority.
TEŽ	Tatranských Elektrických Železníc – Tatra electric railway.
TREŽ	Trenčianska elektrická železnica – Trenčianska Teplá electric railway.
TSM	Ţurčianske Strojárne Martin – Slovak locomotive builder based in Martin.
URŽD	Úrad pre Reguláciu Železničnej Dopravy – Slovak railway regulatory body.
UŽ	Ukrajinské Železnice – Ukraine Railways.
VUŽ	Výzkumný Ústav Železniční – Railway research institute (Velim).
WLF	Wiener Lokomotiv Fabrik, Wien-Floridsdorf, Austria.
WNL	Aktien Gesellschaft der Lokomotiv-Fabrik vormals G. Sigl, Wien, Austria.
Zas	Zastal Zielona Góra, Zielona Góra, Poland
ŽOS	Železniční Opravny a Strojírny – Railway workshops (mainly Slovakia).
ŽSCS	Železničná spoločnosť Cargo Slovakia – Slovak railway cargo company (ZSSK Cargo).
ŽSR	Železnice Slovenskej republiky – Slovak Republic Railways.
ZSSK	Železničná Spoločnosť Slovensko – Slovak passenger railway company.

MAPS

The Czech Republic is made up of two areas – Bohemia to the west and Moravia to the east. Slovakia is a single entity. The map below shows the location of the two countries in Europe, whilst the maps over the following pages show the railway networks in more detail.

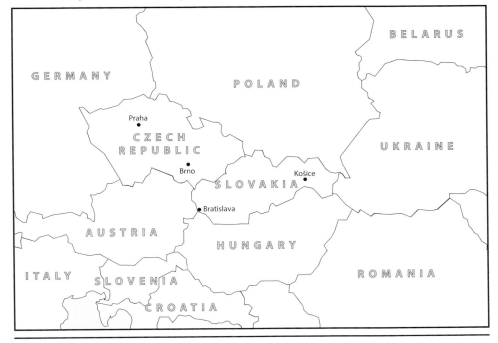

MAP 1

V Vojtanov
P Postoloprty
FL Františkovy Lázně
J Johanngeorgenstadt
KV **KARLOVY VARY**

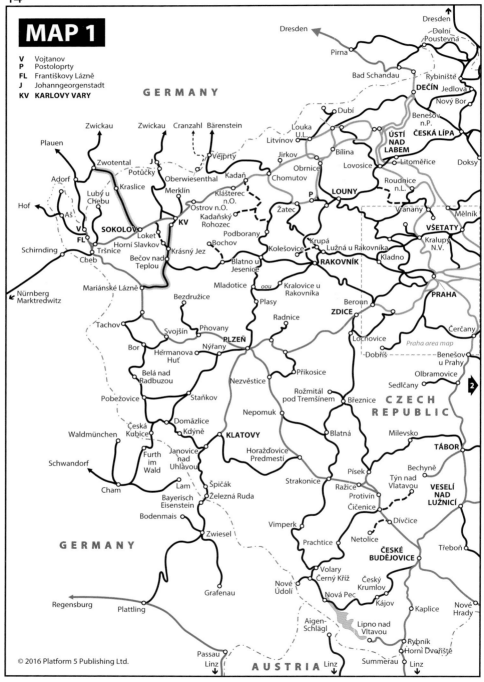

© 2016 Platform 5 Publishing Ltd.

MAP 2

© 2016 Platform 5 Publishing Ltd.

MAP 3

KEY TO MAPS:

Electrification of Lines:

	Non-electrified
	Electrified 3000 V DC
	Electrified 1500 V DC
	Electrified 25 kV AC 50 Hz
	Electrified 15 kV AC 16.7 Hz
	Electrified 600 V DC

Types of Lines:

	Passenger or Passenger and Freight
	Normally Freight Only
	Operated by companies other than ČD/ZSSK
	Broad gauge (1520 mm)
	Narrow gauge lines
	Country Borders
	Areas covered by local passes (Praha area map)

Place names in **BOLD** show major towns/cities

© 2016 Platform 5 Publishing Ltd.

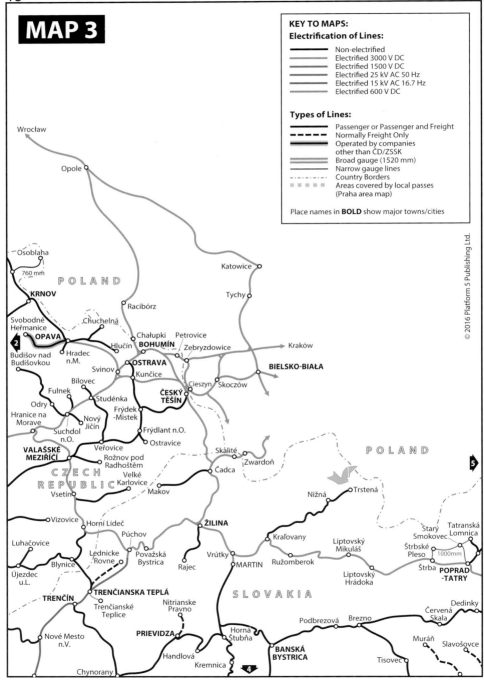

Wrocław
Opole
Osoblaha
760 mm
P O L A N D
KRNOV
Katowice
Svobodné Heřmanice
Chuchelná
Racibórz
Tychy
OPAVA
Chałupki
Petrovice
Budišov nad Budišovkou
Hradec n.M.
Hlučín
BOHUMÍN
Zebrzydowice
Kraków
Svinov
OSTRAVA
Bílovec
Kunčice
Cieszyn
Skoczów
BIELSKO-BIAŁA
Fulnek
Studénka
ČESKÝ TĚŠÍN
Odry
Frýdek -Místek
Hranice na Morave
Nový Jičín
Suchdol n.O.
Frýdlant n.O.
VALAŠSKÉ MEZIŘÍČÍ
Veřovice
Ostravice
Skalité
P O L A N D
Rožnov pod Radhoštěm
Zwardoň
C Z E C H
R E P U B L I C
Velké Karlovice
Čadca
Vsetín
Makov
Nižná
Trstená
Vizovice
Horní Lideč
ŽILINA
Luhačovice
Púchov
Kraľovany
Liptovský Mikuláš
Starý Smokovec
Tatranská Lomnica
Lednické Rovne
Považská Bystrica
Vrútky
Ružomberok
Štrbské Pleso
1000mm
Blynice
Rajec
MARTIN
Štrba
POPRAD -TATRY
Újezdec u.L.
Liptovský Hrádoka
TRENČIANSKA TEPLÁ
TRENČÍN
Trenčianske Teplice
Nitrianske Pravno
S L O V A K I A
Dedinky
Červená Skala
Nové Mesto n.V.
PRIEVIDZA
Horná Štubňa
Podbrezová
Brezno
Muráň
Slavošovce
Handlová
Kremnica
BANSKÁ BYSTRICA
Tisovec
Chynorany

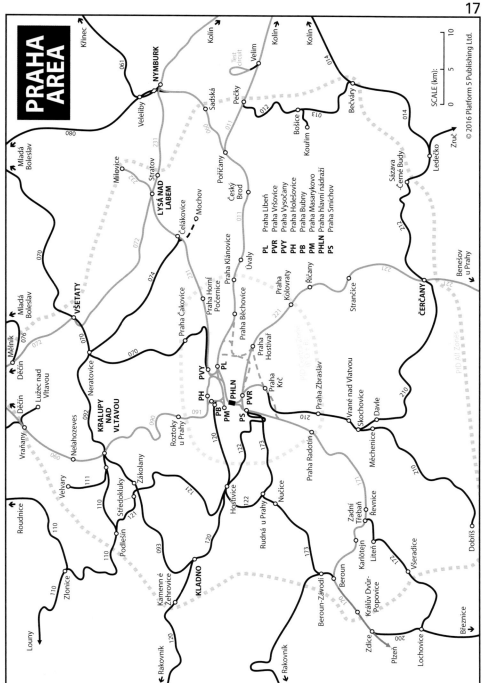

PRAHA AREA

Křinec

Mladá Boleslav

080

061

NYMBURK

Veleliby

Kolín

Kolín

Kolín

Velim

Test circuit

014

Sadská

Pečky

012

013

Bošice

Bečváry

Kouřim

Zruč

Ledečko

014

SCALE (km):

0   5   10

© 2016 Platform 5 Publishing Ltd.

Mladá Boleslav

070

231

Milovice

Stratov

231

LYSÁ NAD LABEM

Mochov

Celákovice

072

Poříčany

090

011

Český Brod

011

Sázava Černé Budy

212

Benešov u Prahy

221

VŠETATY

074

231

Praha Čakovice

Praha Horní Počernice

Praha Klánovice

Uvaly

Praha Kolovraty

Říčany

Strančice

221

PL   Praha Libeň
PVR   Praha Vršovice
PVY   Praha Vysočany
PH   Praha Holešovice
PB   Praha Bubny
PM   Praha Masarykovo
PHLN   Praha hlavní nádraží
PS   Praha Smíchov

ČERČANY

Mělník

Děčín

Lužec nad Vltavou

Děčín

076

072

070

Neratovice

092

070

070

Praha Běchovice

Praha Hostivař

221

210

Vrané nad Vltavou

Skochovice

Davle

Měchenice

210

KRALUPY NAD VLTAVOU

Nelahozeves

060

Vraňany

Velvary

111

Zákolany

Roztoky u Prahy

091

090

Praha Čakovice

PVY

PL

PH

PB

PM

PHLN

PS

PVR

Praha Krč

Praha Zbraslav

Praha Radotín

120

122

173

210

Roudnice

110

Zlonice

110

Středokluky

121

Podlešín

093

Kamenné Žehrovice

KLADNO

120

121

Hostivice

122

Nučice

Rudná u Prahy

173

Zadní Třebaň

Řevnice

171

Dobříš

Louny

120

Rakovník

Rakovník

Beroun-Závody

Beroun

Králův Dvůr-Popovice

Zdice

200

Plzeň

Lochovice

Březnice

Karlštejn

Liteň

Všeradice

172

200

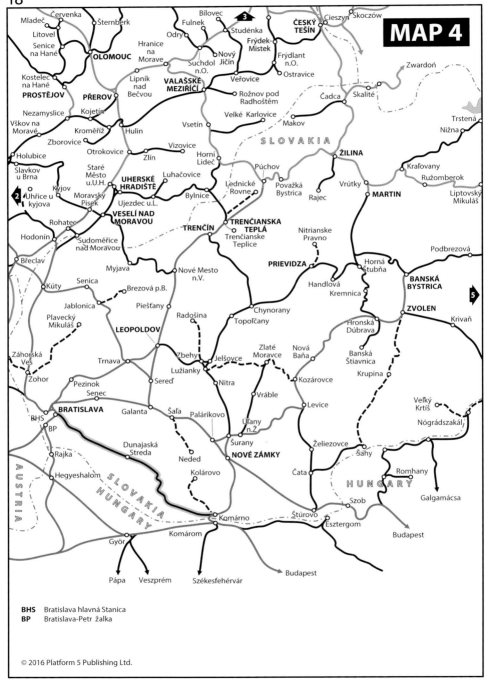

MAP 4

BHS Bratislava hlavná Stanica
BP Bratislava-Petr žalka

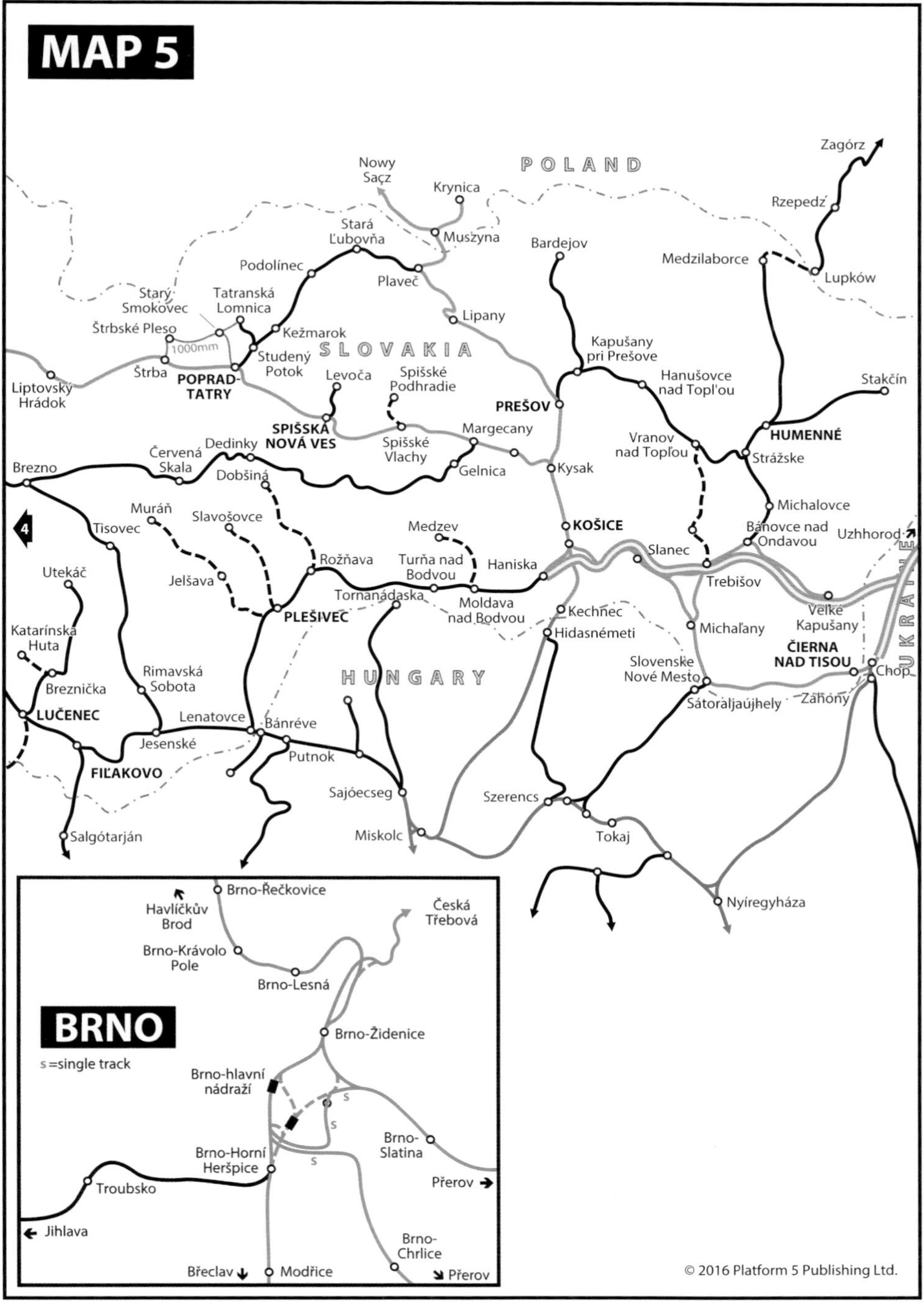

MAP 5

POLAND

Zagórz

Nowy
Sącz
Krynica
Rzepedź
Stará
Ľubovňa
Muszyna
Bardejov
Medzilaborce
Lupków
Podolínec
Plaveč
Starý
Smokovec
Tatranská
Lomnica
Lipany
Štrbské Pleso
Kežmarok
Kapušany
pri Prešove
Hanušovce
nad Topľou
Stakčín
1000mm
Studený
Potok
SLOVAKIA
Štrba **POPRAD-
TATRY**
Levoča
Spišské
Podhradie
Liptovský
Hrádok
PREŠOV
HUMENNÉ
**SPIŠSKÁ
NOVÁ VES**
Margecany
Vranov
nad Topľou
Strážske
Brezno
Červená
Skala
Dedinky
Spišské
Vlachy
Kysak
Dobšiná
Gelnica
Michalovce
Muráň
Slavošovce
Medzev
KOŠICE
Báňovce nad
Ondavou
Uzhhorod
Tisovec
Rožňava
Turňa nad
Bodvou
Haniska
Slanec
Trebišov
Utekáč
Jelšava
Tornaľadaska
Moldava
nad Bodvou
Kechňec
Michaľany
Veľké
Kapušany
Katarínska
Huta
PLEŠIVEC
Hidasnémeti
**ČIERNA
NAD TISOU**
Chop.
Breznička
Rimavská
Sobota
HUNGARY
Slovenské
Nové Mesto
LUČENEC
Lenatovce
Bánréve
Sátoraljaújhely
Záhony
Jesenské
Putnok
FIĽAKOVO
Sajóecseg
Szerencs
Salgótarján
Miskolc
Tokaj
Nyíregyháza

UKRAINE

BRNO

s = single track

Brno-Řečkovice
Havlíčkův
Brod
Česká
Třebová
Brno-Krávolo
Pole
Brno-Lesná
Brno-Židenice
Brno-hlavní
nádraží
s
s
Brno-
Slatina
Brno-Horní
Heršpice
s
Troubsko
Přerov
Jihlava
Brno-
Chrlice
Břeclav
Modřice
Přerov

ACKNOWLEDGEMENTS

Firstly I must acknowledge Nick Lawford for laying the groundwork of the original book. Between Nick and myself, data has been collected over more than two decades from many sources and during extensive research trips to the two countries. As far as practical, all information is updated to early April 2016.

I would like to thank the helpful staff at depots visited, and also in particular the excellent annual "STARS" enthusiast tours to these countries, which not only give behind the scenes access to running depots but also to private and industrial installations. See www.stars-tours.org.uk for more details.

Thanks in particular are due to the following individuals for their help: Keith Fender, Quintus Vosman, Brian Garvin, Nick Kelly, David Haydock, Shaun Wallace, Gary Jones, Adrian Norton, Stuart Hicks, Andrew Thompson, Tony Bartlett, Russell Sedgwick, Michael Malek, Mike Reynolds, Geoff Kelsey, Colin Dingley, Michal Pospíšil, Jan Petrás and Marek Fabian.

The private operators were each sent their respective sections. Many thanks to those who responded with further information and corrections, in particular to ArcelorMittal Ostrava, AWT, Coal Services (Most), EŽ, JHMD, METRANS, PSŽ, RegioJet and also the tramways of Brno, Praha, Plzeň and Košice plus DPP Praha Metro. Thanks also to ŽOS Zvolen and ŽOS Vrútky for organising works visits.

As well as on the ground research, a number of resources have been consulted during research for this book. Mention should be made of the useful "Malý Atlas Lokomotiv 2013" book published by Gradis Bohemia and also Czech language magazines "Dráha" and "Železniční magazín".

The following Czech and Slovak websites have yielded data from their many news pages and discussion forums: www.k-report.net (extensive Czech language railway and tramway forum), www.vlaky.net (a mainly Slovak news site, but also containing Czech news and Slovak fleetlists), www.zelpage.cz (Czech news and photo site also containing formation information for ČD and ZSSK trains), www.railpage.net (photo website), www.spz.logout.cz (Czech news site), www.alanbutschek.cz (site about Czech rolling stock, particularly focussed on the Brno allocation), www.imhd.sk (Slovak tram and trolleybus fansite), www.lokomotivy.net (photo website), www.prototypy.cz (extensive Czech language site giving technical details of rolling stock), www.mamba754.wz.cz ("Goggle" diesel locomotive fansite), https://uk.groups.yahoo.com/neo/groups/CDGEN/info (CD Gen yahoo newsgroup) and http://sledovanihv.blogspot.co.uk (link to spreadsheets giving locomotive allocations for each depot).

Technical data has mostly come from official ČD and ZSR documentation or from ČKD and Škoda material.

UPDATES

Updates to this book can be found in the monthly Platform 5 magazine **Today's Railways Europe**, which also contains regular news and features from both the Czech Republic and Slovakia. For more details see the advert on the inside front cover of this book.

PROVISION OF INFORMATION

This book has been compiled with care to be as accurate as possible, but in many cases information is not officially available and the publisher cannot be held responsible for any errors or omissions.

The author of this book would be very pleased to receive any observations or sightings from the Czech Republic and Slovakia that readers may think would enhance future editions. In particular any additional information on the private freight operators' fleets or preserved locomotives and railcars would be most welcome.

Please send any comments to: Robert Pritchard, Platform 5 Publishing Ltd, 52 Broadfield Road, Sheffield S8 0XJ, England.

e-mail: robert.pritchard@platform5.com   **Tel:** (+44) 0114 2552625.

1. CZECH RAILWAYS

Česke Drahy (ČD) came into being on 1 January 1993 at the same time as the independent Czech Republic. In 2003, Správa Železniční Dopravní Cesty (SŽDC) was established for management of Czech Railways infrastructure but still under ČD control, while independent Drážní Úřad (DÚ) regulates the market and rolling stock approval. In 2007 the freight sector was separated as ČD Cargo, and in 2008 SŽDC was split away, leaving ČD operating just passenger trains.

Since 2005, local passenger train funding has been the responsibility of regional authorities. ČD passenger services became fully independent during 2009. Czech metallurgical, petrochemical, mining and energy utilities are largely privatised, and compete with ČD Cargo for freight. At the same time, ČD Cargo hires locomotives to Polish and Slovak freight operators competing with PKP Cargo and ZSSK Cargo.

The ČD public timetable ("Jízdní řád") runs annually from December to December. Unfortunately from the 2015–16 edition ČD chose to remove the services of competing open access operators RegioJet and Leo Express, the space where these services had been shown now simply being white space. Other private operators which operate rural services (like GW Train Regio and JHMD) are still shown. The full tables with details of the main line open access operators services are still downloadable from the SŽDC website. The crossed hammers timetable symbol used by Czech Railways means Mondays–Fridays not Mondays–Saturdays.

ČD has invested heavily in new and refurbished rolling stock in recent years, and introduced new ticket offers, in particular to compete with the new open access operators on the key Praha–Ostrava route. The company has some 24 000 employees and operates over more than 9400 km of track, a third of which is electrified. The company carried 176.6 million passengers in 2015, with the number of passenger kilometres being the highest for 20 years.

ČD CARGO

Despite the recent influx of private freight operators, the vast majority of freight traffic in the Czech Republic is still operated by ČD Cargo, which employs some 7500 staff. ČD Cargo locomotives are indicated by the letter *F* in class listings. The company has received some modernised locomotives in recent years (such as the rebuilt Class 753.7), but generally operates a mixed and somewhat ageing fleet, although it has recently issued tenders for some new electric locomotives. Subsidiary Koleje Czeskie operates trains in Poland, using a number of former ČD Cargo electric locomotives (such as Class 181).

DEPOTS – ČD

For ČD there are five distinct motive power regions – Brno, Česká Třebová, Olomouc, Plzeň and Praha, with ČD also sharing space with ČD Cargo at České Budějovice and Břeclav. In recent years a number of smaller depots have closed and their allocations have been transferred elsewhere. Others have closed as maintenance locations but remained for stabling and fuelling.

The depot codes used in this book for ČD depots are based on the first two letters of the code indicating the motive power region – for major work or overhauls the locomotive or railcar is likely to return to its mother depot for attention. So it's BR for Brno Maloměřice, CT for Česká Třebová, OL for Olomouc, PL for Plzeň and PR for Praha Vršovice. The third letter reflects the actual depot the locomotive or railcar is based at. For example **BRM** is Brno **M**aloměřice and **BRV** is **V**eselí nad Moravou. The full list of codes is shown below (with the "mother depot" shown first):

BRNO

BRM Brno Maloměřice	BRO Havlíčkův Brod	BRZ Znojmo
BRH Brno Horní Heršpice	BRV Veselí nad Moravou	

There are also smaller depots at Telč and Tišnov. ČD also uses the ČD Cargo depot at Břeclav.

ČESKÁ TŘEBOVÁ

CTC Česká Třebová	CTL Liberec	CTT Trutnov
CTH Hradec Králové	CTP Pardubice	

There are also smaller depots at Meziměstí and Stará Paka.

OLOMOUC

OLO Olomouc	OLH Osoblaha (760 mm)	OLS Šumperk
OLB Bohumín	OLP Opava	OLV Valašské Meziříčí

There are also smaller depots at Frýdek-Místek, Kroměříž and Otrokovice.

PLZEŇ

PLZ Plzeň	PLC Cheb	PLR Rakovník
PLA Blatná	PLL Louny	PLT Tábor
PLB České Budějovice	PLK Klatovy	PLV Volary

There are also smaller depots at Bělá nad Radbuzou, Bezdružice and Domažlice.

PRAHA

PRG Praha Vršovice	PRD Děčín	PRL Praha Libeň
PRC Čerčany	PRO Praha Odstavné Nádraží Jih (ONJ)	PRK Kolín

There are also smaller depots at Česká Lípa, Kladno, Kralupy nad Vlatavou, Mladá Boleslav and Rumberk.

DEPOTS – ČD CARGO

ČD Cargo locomotives are allocated to the three main "SOKV" (Střediska Oprav Kolejových Vozidel, or "rolling stock repair centre") sites at České Budějovice, Ostrava and Ústí nad Labem. České Budějovice also includes Plzeň, Ostrava includes Brno Maloměřice and Břeclav and Ústí nad Labem includes Nymburk, Most and Praha Vršovice (depot space is shared with ČD at Plzeň, Brno Maloměřice, Břeclav and Praha). Codes used are:

FSC SOKV České Budějovice
FSO SOKV Ostrava
FSU SOKV Ústí nad Labem

▲ Most depots are converted steam sheds or roundhouses with turntables. One of the author's favourites is the ČD Cargo depot at Ústí nad Labem. On a visit on 14 July 2014 classic Škoda electric locomotives (left to right) 122.022, 122.005, 123.006, 122.015, 122.023 and 122.027 were positioned in the shed awaiting maintenance or their next duties. **Robert Pritchard**

MAIN WORKS

ČD no longer has its own dedicated locomotive works, having sold them during the 1990s, although a number of ČD and ČD Cargo depots undertake full locomotive overhauls. DPOV (Dílny Pro Opravy Vozidel or "Railway Rolling Stock Repair Works"), part of the Czech Railway Group, operates heavy works at Nymburk, Přerov and Veselí nad Moravou, with a smaller facility at Valašské Meziříčí. The works at Nymburk and Přerov handle heavy overhauls for both ČD and other companies, using former ČD depots (the site at Veselí is alongside the ČD running depot).

A second works at Přerov is the unconnected ČMŽO (Českomoravská Železniční Opravna) facility, whilst the major CZ LOKO works at Česká Třebová is the largest in the country, specialising in diesel locomotive rebuilds, as well as electric locomotive overhauls. CZ LOKO has a second site at Jihlava (the former JLS Jihlava workshops).

A summary of the major works sites and what rolling stock they mainly deal with is given below.

ČMŽO Přerov: All electric locomotives, RegioJet Class 162.

CZ LOKO Česká Třebová/Jihlava: Diesel and electric locomotive rebuilds, overhauls on most types of rolling stock.

DPOV Nymburk (code DPNY): Diesel locomotives, DMU Class 854, trailer cars Class 021, 050, 053.

DPOV Přerov: All electric locomotives, EMU Class 471.

DPOV Veselí nad Moravou: DMU Class 809, 810, 814, 842, 843, trailer cars Class 010–015, 042, 043, 943.

KOS Krnov: Locomotive-hauled coaches and wagons.

Pars nova Šumperk (part of Škoda): Classes 362/363, 380, EMU Classes 460 and 560 and DMU Class 854, loco-hauled coaches.

LIVERIES

In times past Czech railways have at times been quite colourful. In recent years a lot of non-standard liveries have been swept away in favour of the corporate blue livery, introduced by ČD Cargo in 2008 and by ČD in 2009. The style of this scheme has changed several times, but the ČD Cargo version is two-tone blue whereas the various ČD version has white and multiple-shades of blue. However some special liveries remain.

The standard pre ČD blue liveries still survive on many classes as well. In simple terms most liveries were based on the original as-built type-by-type schemes. Electric locomotives in general followed green, red and blue colours for DC, AC and dual voltage respectively, relieved with assorted yellow or cream or silver bands or stripes or two-tone shades of the base colour.

ČSD 1980s standard diesel locomotive livery was maroon with no relief. Yellow bands or cab surrounds or other markings were then applied – these can vary considerably. There was a phase in the early 1990s of depot-by-depot or locomotive-by-locomotive colours and styles. More recent diesel repaints were permutations of reds, blues, dark greens and light greys applied in different ways to cabs and window surrounds or upper and lower body panels. Classes 704/708/714 were generally bright red and blue, Class 742 deep red, Classes 749/751 red & grey, and Classes 750 & 754 green/grey. Diesel motors and trailers were bright red and white. Older EMUs were blue & grey and newer EMUs more white & blue.

The livery of each class is as indicated in the class headings unless shown as one of the following codes:

A   Advertising Livery (see class heading for details).
B   New ČD or ČD Cargo blue livery.
0   Non-standard livery (see class heading for details).

1.1. ČD & ČD CARGO ELECTRIC LOCOMOTIVES

CLASS 110   Bo-Bo

Class 110 is a centre-cab locomotive with a low bonnet and a single cab roof-mounted pantograph for shunting, empty stock pilot work and light freight duties. Most of the class have now been stored and there are no booked passenger turns.

Livery for Classes 110/111 is deep orange with a cream stripe or dark green with a yellow stripe, unless stated.

System: 3000 V DC.
Built: 1971–73.
Former ČSD Class: E458.0.
Builder: Škoda, model 33E.
Continuous Rating: 800 kW (1070 hp).
Maximum Tractive Effort: 160 kN.

Total No. Built: 52†.
Wheel Diameter: 1050 mm.
Weight: 72 tonnes.
Length over Buffers: 14.40 m.
Maximum Speed: 80 km/h.
EVN: 91 54 7 110 0xx-c.

110.001-5	F	FSO	110.029-6	F	Břeclav (S)	110.039-5		OLV
110.006-4	F	FSO (S)	110.030-4		PRG (S)	110.044-5	F	FSO (S)
110.007-2	F	FSO	110.032-0		PRG (S)	110.045-2		CTC (S)
110.017-1	F	Břeclav (S)	110.037-9	F	FSC (S)	110.046-0	F	FSO (S)
110.019-7	F	FSO	110.038-7	F	FSO (S)	110.051-0	F	Břeclav (S)
110.024-7	F	Břeclav (S)						

CLASS 111   Bo-Bo

Class 111 is an updated version of Class 110 with thyristor control and a higher tractive effort. The class was developed from the prototype conversion of E458.0012 (which would have become 110.012).

System: 3000 V DC.
Built: 1981–82.
Former ČSD Class: E458.1.
Builder: Škoda, model 78E.
Continuous Rating: 760 kW (1020 hp).
Maximum Tractive Effort: 186 kN.

Total No. Built: 35.
Wheel Diameter: 1050 mm.
Weight: 70.4 tonnes.
Length over Buffers: 14.48 m.
Maximum Speed: 80 km/h.
EVN: 91 54 7 111 0xx-c.

111.001-4			PRG	111.015-4		F	FSU	111.026-1	B F	FSO
111.002-2			PRG	111.016-2		F	FSO	111.027-9	F	FSU
111.003-0	B	F	FSO	111.017-0		F	FSO	111.028-7		OLB
111.006-3			PRG	111.018-8		F	FSO	111.029-5		CTC (S)
111.007-1		F	FSO	111.019-6	B		CTC	111.030-3		OLB
111.008-9		F	FSO	111.020-4	B	F	FSU	111.031-1		PRG
111.009-7		F	FSU	111.021-2	B	F	FSU	111.032-9		PRG
111.010-5	B		PRG	111.022-0	B	F	FSO	111.033-7	F	FSU
111.011-3			PRG	111.023-8			PRG	111.034-5	F	FSU
111.012-1			PRG	111.024-6		F	FSU	111.035-2		PRG
111.013-9		F	FSU	111.025-3		F	FSU			

CLASS 113 Bo-Bo

Class 113 was built as a half-power version of Class 110 for the 1500 V DC Tábor–Bechyně and Rybník–Lipno nad Vltavou branch lines. The latter was converted to 25 kV AC in 2004 and two of the class, 113.005/006 were converted to Class 110.2 (they have since been scrapped). The power of Class 113 was later increased to 800 kW and the maximum speed increased from 50 to 80 km/h.

The remaining three serviceable locomotives (113.004 has been scrapped) now share services on the Tábor–Bechyně line (the oldest electrified railway in the Czech Republic) with Class 814 DMUs. In 2014 Class 113s were working most trains, but from December 2014 this was reduced to just one diagram, working mainly peak-hour trips (weekday trains Os28401/402/405/418).

Fitted with door control cables for operating with Class 010 and 021 DMU trailers.

Livery is green with a yellow stripe.

System: 1500 V DC.
Built: 1973.
Former ČSD Class: E426.0.
Builder: Škoda, model 33E.
Continuous Rating: 800 kW (1070 hp).
Maximum Tractive Effort: 160 kN.

Total No. Built: 6.
Wheel Diameter: 1050 mm.
Weight: 64 tonnes.
Length over Buffers: 14.40 m.
Maximum Speed: 80 km/h.
EVN: 91 54 7 113 00x-c.

113.001-2	PLT	113.002-0	PLT	113.003-8	PLT

CLASS 121 Bo-Bo

Once electrification was adopted for main lines, 90 km/h four and six-axle locomotives were developed for freight traffic. Class 121 was the first of the Bo-Bos, ČSD examples being built for the first stages of electrification from Praha to Česká Třebová and eastwards to Žilina and Košice. As wires were extended through the 1960s, Class 121s were joined by Classes 122/123 in northern Bohemia, with all three classes working side by side on similar duties. Classes 121–123 may be distinguished by side windows: Class 121 has four deep rectangular windows, but on Classes 122/123 the right hand side window is replaced by shallow glazing above a blanked out panel.

Some 121s have been preserved (see Preserved Locomotives section) and a number are also operated by open access private operators in both the Czech Republic and Slovakia (see Private Freight Operators section). The four remaining ČD Cargo locomotives listed here are in store at the dump at Ústí nad Labem depot and are awaiting disposal.

Livery for Classes 121–123 and 130 is a light green upper bodyside and darker green lower bodyside, unless stated.

System: 3000 V DC.
Built: 1960–61.
Former ČSD Class: E469.1.
Builder: Škoda, model 43E.
Continuous Rating: 2032 kW (2725 hp).
Maximum Tractive Effort: 234 kN.

Total No. Built: 85.
Wheel Diameter: 1250 mm.
Weight: 88 tonnes.
Length over Buffers: 16.14 m.
Maximum Speed: 90 km/h.
EVN: 91 54 7 121 0xx-c.

121.019-4	F	FSU (S)	121.055-8	F	FSU (S)	121.083-0	F	FSU (S)
121.028-5	F	FSU (S)						

▲ Praha hl.n station pilot 111.010 is pictured shunting a single coach on 15 May 2013. **Robert Pritchard**

▼ A typical duty for a Class 122/123 as 123.029 hauls a train of brown coal south through Libochovany on Line 072 on 3 September 2012. The locomotive is still in the traditional green livery. This line is a great place to see Classes 122/123 in action. **Robert Pritchard**

CLASS 122 — Bo-Bo

Class 122 is an updated version of Class 121 with a one tonne lighter axle load and home-produced DAKO braking replacing the Westinghouse system. Class 122s arrived with electrification from Praha and Kolín northwards along the Labe (Elbe) river valley to Ústí nad Labem, connecting the northern Bohemia brown coal mines around Chomutov and Most with the power stations further south. The class are now all based at Ústí nad Labem depot and used on freight, including brown coal and automotive traffic, on the Kadan, Most and Ústí corridor and in the Labe Valley.

A number of Class 122s have already been withdrawn and scrapped and with ČD Cargo acquiring 23 redundant ČD Class 163s in 2015, 23 Class 122 were stored as a result. 122.019 and 122.023 were already stored after being badly damaged in an accident near Litoměřice in March 2015.

System: 3000 V DC.
Built: 1967.
Former ČSD Class: E469.2.
Builder: Škoda, model 57E1.
Continuous Rating: 2040 kW (2735 hp).
Maximum Tractive Effort: 224 kN.
Total No. Built: 55.
Wheel Diameter: 1250 mm.
Weight: 85 tonnes.
Length over Buffers: 17.21 m.
Maximum Speed: 90 km/h.
EVN: 91 54 7 122 0xx-c.

No.				No.				No.			
122.001-1		F	FSU	122.016-9	B	F	FSU	122.034-2		F	FSU (S)
122.002-9	B	F	FSU	122.018-5		F	FSU (S)	122.035-9	B	F	FSU
122.004-5		F	FSU (S)	122.019-3		F	FSU (S)	122.036-7		F	FSU (S)
122.005-2		F	FSU (S)	122.021-9	B	F	FSU	122.037-5		F	FSU (S)
122.006-0	B	F	FSU	122.022-7		F	FSU (S)	122.039-1		F	FSU (S)
122.007-8	B	F	FSU	122.023-5	B	F	FSU (S)	122.043-3		F	FSU (S)
122.008-6		F	FSU (S)	122.024-3		F	FSU (S)	122.044-1		F	FSU (S)
122.009-4		F	FSU (S)	122.025-0	B	F	FSU	122.045-8		F	FSU (S)
122.010-2		F	FSU (S)	122.026-8		F	FSU (S)	122.046-6		F	FSU (S)
122.011-0	B	F	FSU	122.027-6		F	FSU	122.047-4		F	FSU (S)
122.012-8		F	FSU (S)	122.028-4	B	F	FSU	122.049-0		F	FSU (S)
122.013-6	B	F	FSU	122.029-2	B	F	FSU	122.051-6	B	F	FSU
122.014-4		F	FSU (S)	122.031-8		F	FSU	122.053-2	B	F	FSU (S)
122.015-1		F	FSU (S)	122.032-6		F	FSU	122.055-7		F	FSU

CLASS 123 — Bo-Bo

Class 123 is the final development of Classes 121/122, with modernised electronics, and again are concentrated at Ústí nad Labem. Škoda continued to use the traditional body style for DC locomotives, at the same time using the less conventional design for AC Classes 230/240. Class 123s are generally employed on intensive diagrams of block coal trains between the lignite mines off the Ústí nad Labem–Chomutov line and power stations in northern Bohemia. Despite being 45 years old, all 29 Class 123s built are still in traffic (and also still receiving heavy overhauls), a testament to the success of this classic Škoda design.

See VUZ Velim under Private Operators for the departmental high speed locomotive 124.601, which was a more powerful Class 123 designed for 200 km/h test running.

System: 3000 V DC.
Built: 1971.
Former ČSD Class: E469.3.
Builder: Škoda, model 57E2.
Continuous Rating: 2040 kW (2735 hp).
Maximum Tractive Effort: 224 kN.
Total No. Built: 29.
Wheel Diameter: 1250 mm.
Weight: 85 tonnes.
Length over Buffers: 17.21 m.
Maximum Speed: 90 km/h.
EVN: 91 54 7 123 0xx-c.

No.				No.				No.			
123.001-0	B	F	FSU	123.011-9		F	FSU	123.021-8		F	FSU
123.002-8	B	F	FSU	123.012-7		F	FSU	123.022-6	B	F	FSU
123.003-6	B	F	FSU	123.013-5	B	F	FSU	123.023-4	B	F	FSU
123.004-4	B	F	FSU	123.014-3		F	FSU	123.024-2		F	FSU
123.005-1		F	FSU	123.015-0	B	F	FSU	123.025-9	B	F	FSU
123.006-9	B	F	FSU	123.016-8	B	F	FSU	123.026-7		F	FSU
123.007-7	B	F	FSU	123.017-6		F	FSU	123.027-5	B	F	FSU
123.008-5		F	FSU	123.018-4	B	F	FSU	123.028-3	B	F	FSU
123.009-3	B	F	FSU	123.019-2	B	F	FSU	123.029-1		F	FSU
123.010-1		F	FSU	123.020-0	B	F	FSU				

CLASS 130 Bo-Bo

Class 130 was built as a mixed-traffic locomotive, and was the first to use power electronics. It was the last new DC type with the early style bodywork. In total 54 were built, the first 40 of these for ČSD. A further 14 went new to industrial service and carry running numbers following on from the ČSD main series – see the Private Freight Operators section. 130.042 was subsequently transferred to ČD in 2004 whilst 130.043 is the only class member that has been scrapped to date.

Before ČD sectorisation the class were used on passenger, parcels and lighter freight traffic around their home depots of Česká Třebová, Pardubice and Hradec Králové. Since 2006 all have been ČD Cargo owned and based at Ostrava. They can be found on a variety of freight traffic, especially on the main east-west line, but also reaching as far as North Bohemia.

System: 3000 V DC.
Built: 1977.
Former ČSD Class: E479.0.
Builder: Škoda, model 79E.
Continuous Rating: 2040 kW (2735 hp).
Maximum Tractive Effort: 228 kN.

Total No. Built: 40 for ČD+14 for private operators.
Wheel Diameter: 1250 mm.
Weight: 84.8 tonnes.
Length over Buffers: 17.21 m.
Maximum Speed: 100 km/h.
EVN: 91 54 7 130 0xx-c.

130.001-1	**B**	*F*	FSO	130.015-1	**B**	*F*	FSO	130.029-2		*F*	FSO
130.002-9	**B**	*F*	FSO	130.016-9	**B**	*F*	FSO	130.030-0	**B**	*F*	FSO
130.003-7	**B**	*F*	FSO	130.017-7		*F*	FSO	130.031-8	**B**	*F*	FSO
130.004-5		*F*	FSO	130.018-5	**B**	*F*	FSO	130.032-6		*F*	FSO
130.005-2	**B**	*F*	FSO	130.019-3	**B**	*F*	FSO	130.033-4	**B**	*F*	FSO
130.006-0		*F*	FSO	130.020-1		*F*	FSO	130.034-2		*F*	FSO
130.007-8		*F*	FSO	130.021-9	**B**	*F*	FSO	130.035-9		*F*	FSO
130.008-6		*F*	FSO	130.022-7	**B**	*F*	FSO	130.036-7	**B**	*F*	FSO
130.009-4	**B**	*F*	FSO	130.023-5		*F*	FSO	130.037-5	**B**	*F*	FSO
130.010-2		*F*	FSO	130.024-3	**B**	*F*	FSO	130.038-3	**B**	*F*	FSO
130.011-0	**B**	*F*	FSO	130.025-0	**B**	*F*	FSO	130.039-1	**B**	*F*	FSO
130.012-8		*F*	FSO	130.026-8	**B**	*F*	FSO	130.040-9	**B**	*F*	FSO
130.013-6	**B**	*F*	FSO	130.027-6		*F*	FSO	130.042-5	**B**	*F*	FSO
130.014-4	**B**	*F*	FSO	130.028-4	**B**	*F*	FSO				

CLASS 141 Bo-Bo

Developed from Class 140 (all now withdrawn, although some are used by private freight operators or have been preserved) to a home-built design, this class was used on express passenger trains until replaced by Classes 162/163 from the mid 1980s. They were then transferred to secondary passenger work. 30 of similar Škoda model 46E went to Polish Railways as Classes EU05/EP05.

Two serviceable Class 141s remain on ČD's books, and are designated historical locomotives. Both can see occasional use from Praha Vršovice or Děčín depots, sometimes even on normal passenger work if there is a shortage of other locomotives.

Livery is two tone-green like Classes 121–123/130, but the lower bodyside green is darker.

System: 3000 V DC.
Built: 1959–60.
Former ČSD Class: E499.1.
Builder: Škoda, model 30E.
Continuous Rating: 2032 kW (2725 hp).
Maximum Tractive Effort: 225 kN.

Total No. Built: 61.
Wheel Diameter: 1250 mm.
Weight: 84 tonnes.
Length over Buffers: 16.14 m.
Maximum Speed: 120 km/h.
EVN: 91 54 7 141 0xx-c.

141.012 carries its original number E499.112.

141.004-2	+	PRG	141.012-5	+	PRD	141.054-7	CTC (S)
141.009-1		CTC (S)				

▲ ČD Cargo 130.040 passes the popular vantage point by Hrad Střekov, south of Ústí nad Labem, with empty cartics for the Škoda factory at Mladá Boleslav (via Kolín) on 10 March 2015. **Robert Pritchard**

▼ Carrying the latest version of the ČD passenger livery, 150.205 arrives at Česká Třebová with train EC122, the 13.38 Žilina–Praha hl.n on 11 May 2015. **Robert Pritchard**

CLASSES 150 & 151   Bo-Bo

These distinctive and popular classes were introduced onto express passenger work in the late 1970s and quickly earned the nickname "Gorilla". DC Class 150 and AC/DC Class 350 (the latter now all with ZSSK in Slovakia) raised express train speeds to 140 km/h.

Between 1996 and 2002 Škoda rebuilt 14 of the Class 150s to Class 151 for 160 km/h operation by altering gear ratios and shifting the continuous rating from 138 kN at 101.2 km/h to 123.3 kN at 113.9 km/h. Rebuilt locomotives kept the former Class 150 serial numbers. The two missing locomotives were both written off in serious accidents and have been scrapped: 150.017 was destroyed in an accident near Spišská Nová Ves in January 1981. Meanwhile, in the worst accident in recent years in the country, 151.018 was working a EuroCity train from Kraków to Praha on 8 August 2008 when it crashed into part of a motorway bridge that fell onto the main line during a construction project at Studénka – eight people were killed and more than 60 injured in the accident.

At the time of writing there are five diagrams for the Praha-based Class 150.2s, mainly working Praha–Staré Město u Uherského Hradiště portions of Praha–Luhačovice trains and some trains on the Praha–Vsetín route.

The home depot of the Class 151s is now Bohumín. With nine diagrams, the class is used on express trains on the Praha–Bohumín/Žilina (Slovakia) route and also on "R" trains between Praha and Ústí nad Labem (normally taken forward to Cheb by a Class 362). They also work a new return train between Praha and Opava. The Bohumín-based Class 150.2s provide back-up for the Class 151s.

Although ZSSK is actively looking to replace its similar Class 350s, ČD currently has no plans to replace its Classes 150/151.

Compared to other DC electric locomotive liveries, Classes 150/151 had more cream and less green than other types, although in recent years the ČD blue livery has been applied, and is now carried by most members of the class.

System: 3000 V DC.
Built: 1978.
Former ČSD Class: E499.2.
Builder: Škoda, models 65E or 65Em.
Continuous Rating: 4000 kW (5360 hp).
Maximum Tractive Effort: 227 kN.

Total No. Built: 27.
Wheel Diameter: 1250 mm.
Weight: 82.4 tonnes (* 82 tonnes).
Length over Buffers: 16.74 m.
Maximum Speed: 140 km/h or * 160 km/h.
EVN: 91 54 7 150 2xx-c or
       91 54 7 151 0xx-c.

Non-standard and Advertising Liveries: 151.019: ČEZ (orange & grey).
                                              151.023: Original cream & green livery.

Class 150.2. Rebuilt 2008–10 from Class 150.0 with modified electronic speed control system. 140 km/h. Škoda model 65E.

150.202-0	(150.002)	B	PRG	150.215-2	(150.015)	B	PRG
150.203-8	(150.003)	B	PRG	150.221-0	(150.021)	B	OLB
150.205-3	(150.005)	B	PRG	150.222-8	(150.022)	B	OLB
150.209-5	(150.009)		PRG	150.224-4	(150.024)	B	PRG
150.210-3	(150.010)	B	PRG	150.225-1	(150.025)	B	OLB
150.213-7	(150.013)	B	PRG	150.226-9	(150.026)	B	OLB

Class 151. * Rebuilt 1996–2002 and modified for 160 km/h. Škoda model 65Em.

151.001-5	(150.001)	B	OLB	151.014-8	(150.014)	B	OLB
151.004-9	(150.004)	B	OLB	151.016-3	(150.016)	B	OLB
151.006-4	(150.006)	B	OLB	151.019-7	(150.019)	A	OLB
151.007-2	(150.007)	B	OLB	151.020-5	(150.020)	B	OLB
151.008-0	(150.008)	B	OLB	151.023-9	(150.023)	O	OLB
151.011-4	(150.011)	B	OLB	151.027-0	(150.027)	B	OLB
151.012-2	(150.012)	B	OLB				

CLASS 162 Bo-Bo

The most numerous type of electric locomotive operating in both in the Czech Republic and Slovakia are the Class 162/163/263/361/362/363/371/372 types, respectively 140 km/h DC, 120 km/h DC, 120 km/h AC and 120 km/h, 140 km/h or 160 km/h AC/DC thyristor-controlled locomotives (Class 361 is only operated by ZSSK).

All classes of this hugely successful design have fully interchangeable mechanical parts and are known as "Pershing" ("Peršing" in Czech) after the missile. As single locomotives (not including the 50 Slovak Class 131 double-locomotives), in total 408 were constructed by Škoda between 1980 and 1992. This includes 20 built for German Railways as Class 180 (DR Class 230), most of which have now been sold to private Czech freight operator TSS Cargo. To date only one ČSD machine (363.153) has been scrapped, after accident damage, whilst DB 180 004/005 have also been scrapped.

Class 162 is an updated 140 km/h version of Class 163. All are fitted with 3000 kW dynamic braking. Compared to Class 163 continuous tractive effort of 186 kN at 66 km/h, a Class 162 is 160 kN at 76 km/h. The original number series was 162.001–060 but bogie swaps with Class 363s over a long period of time have created more Class 362/163 and fewer Class 162/363 (see Class 163 for renumbering details).

Now all Děčín based, the remaining Class 162s are favoured for express services on the main routes north and east from Praha, where their maximum speed is used to advantage along these upgraded corridors. They work "R" trains between Praha and Děčín on Mondays–Fridays (these trains are mainly Class 471 EMUs at weekends) and between Ústí nad Labem and Kolín (Line 072, via Všetaty) with push-pull sets. They can also cover for shortages of Classes 150/151/163, which can take them into Slovakia, as far as Žilina.

Nine Class 162s (formerly Class 163) are also used by private operator RegioJet – see Private Passenger Operators section for details.

System: 3000 V DC.
Built: 1991.
Former ČSD Class: Not applicable.
Builder: Škoda, model 98E.
Continuous Rating: 3480 kW (4665 hp).
Maximum Tractive Effort: 258 kN.

Total No. Built: 60†.
Wheel Diameter: 1250 mm.
Weight: 85 tonnes.
Length over Buffers: 16.80 m.
Maximum Speed: 140 km/h.
EVN: 91 54 7 162 0xx-c.

Advertising Livery: 162.011: www.cdmuseum.cz (white & blue).

p   modified for operation in push-pull mode with Type Bfhpvee295 driving trailers.

162.011-1	**A**	p	PRD	162.020-2	**B**		PRD	162.039-2	**B**		PRD
162.012-9	**B**		PRD	162.035-0	**B**		PRD	162.040-0	**B**	p	PRD
162.013-7	**B**		PRD	162.036-8	**B**		PRD	162.046-7	**B**		PRD
162.014-5	**B**	p	PRD	162.037-6	**B**		PRD	162.053-3	**B**		PRD
162.018-6	**B**	p	PRD	162.038-4	**B**		PRD	162.054-1	**B**		PRD
162.019-4	**B**		PRD								

CLASS 163   Bo-Bo

Class 163 was built in two batches of 60 with a five year gap between production – the two batches have slightly different performance characteristics. The original batch, 163.001–060, has a lower continuous tractive effort than the second batch. Intended as 163.061–120, the second batch had an interesting start, being completed by Škoda in the early 1990s to ČSD order, but then neither ČD nor ŽSR could afford them. ČD eventually took 163.061–100 and ŽSR 163.101–111. Following a period in storage, in 1995 Škoda sold the remaining nine locomotives (163.112–120) to Italian railway company FNM. These locomotives were later sold to private operator Regiojet and are now back in the country for which they were originally intended, operating as 162.112–120.

Between 1993 and 2001, 14 Class 162s swapped bogies with 140 km/h Class 363s to create Class 362s. The Class 162s were renumbered the last two digits of their serial numbers, becoming 163.241–245/248–252/255–260. 163.215–217/233/234/247 followed in 2006–08. Between 2010 and 2013 all 30 of the ČD Cargo Class 163s were rebuilt as Class 363.5 (363.501–530), so all of the remaining Class 163s in the Czech Republic were, in 2013, then operated by ČD.

Class 163s can be found on lower speed passenger or stopping trains more-or-less anywhere in the DC area. Česká Třebová has by far the largest allocation and there are 33 diagrams. Hradec Králové is a good base to see Class 163s in action. They work the Praha–Hradec Králové trains, and also local services between Choceň, Týniště nad Orlicí and Hradec Králové/Chlumec nad Cidlinou. Push-pull modified locomotives operate stopping services on the main line between Česká Třebová and Pardubice/Kolín, and Ústí nad Orlicí–Lichkov loco-hauled trains are also hauled by Class 163s. There is also work deep into Moravia, including Olomouc–Prostějov, Přerov–Vsetín/Bohumín, Přerov–Nezamyslice and Šumperk–Olomouc–Nezamyslice.

The Děčín-based locomotives (most have been modified for push-pull operation) work alongside Class 162s on Line 072 passenger trains.

In late 2015, the introduction of new EMUs and the return of Class 163s from hire to PKP enabled ČD to sell 23 locomotives (a mix of Class 163 and 163.2) to sister company ČD Cargo, once again giving ČD Cargo some locomotives of this type. The newly acquired ČD Cargo Class 163s are based at Ostrava (for operation on services into Poland) or Ústí nad Labem, and their introduction led to the withdrawal of a number of ageing Class 122s.

Livery is the DC green livery with a yellow stripe, unless stated.

System: 3000 V DC.
Built: 1984–86 and 1991–92.
Former ČSD Class: E499.3.
Builder: Škoda, model 71E or 99E.
Continuous Rating: 3480 kW (4665 hp).
Maximum Tractive Effort: 250 kN.
Total No. Built: 120 (9 now with Regiojet)†.
Wheel Diameter: 1250 mm.
Weight: 85 tonnes.
Length over Buffers: 16.80 m.
Maximum Speed: 120 km/h.
EVN: 91 54 7 163 xxx-c.
Advertising Liveries: 163.030/093: ČEZ (orange & grey).
                                     163.043: Euro 2012 (blue, red & white).
                                     163.065: www.cd.cz/www.cdprovas.cz (white & blue).
                                     163.094: InKarta card (white & blue).

k   Fitted with PKP safety systems and modified pantographs for through working to Poland.
p   modified for operation in push-pull mode with type Bfhpvee295 driving trailers.

Class 163. Original build, Škoda model 71E (163.001–060), lower continuous tractive effort of 176.1 kN at 66.5 km/h.

163.021-9	B	*F*	k	FSO	163.034-2	B	*F*	k	FSO	163.043-3	A	*F*	k	FSO
163.022-7	B	*F*	k	FSO	163.035-9		*F*	k	FSO	163.044-1		*F*	k	FSO
163.025-0	B		p	CTC	163.039-1	B		p	PRD	163.045-8		*F*	k	FSO
163.026-8	B	*F*	k	FSO	163.040-9	B		k	CTC	163.046-6		*F*	k	FSO
163.029-2	B		k	CTC	163.041-7		*F*	k	FSO	163.047-4	B	*F*	k	FSO
163.030-0	A	*F*	k	FSO	163.042-5	B	*F*	k	FSO	163.048-2	B		k	CTC

Class 163. Second build, Škoda model 99E (163.061–120), higher continuous tractive effort of 186 kN at 66 km/h.

163.061-5	B	p	CTC	163.075-5			CTC	163.088-8	B	p	CTC	
163.062-3			CTC	163.076-3	B		CTC	163.089-6	B		CTC	
163.063-1	B		CTC	163.077-1	B	p	PRD	163.090-4	B		CTC	
163.064-9	B		CTC	163.078-9			CTC	163.091-2			CTC	
163.065-6	A	p	CTC	163.079-7	B	p	PRD	163.092-0			CTC	
163.066-4	B	p	CTC	163.080-5	B		CTC	163.093-8	A		CTC	
163.067-2	B		CTC	163.081-3			CTC	163.094-6	A	p	PRD	
163.068-0	B	p	CTC	163.082-1			CTC	163.095-3			CTC	
163.069-8	B		CTC	163.083-9	B		CTC	163.096-1			CTC	
163.070-6			CTC	163.084-7			CTC	163.097-9	B	p	CTC	
163.071-4	B		CTC	163.085-4	B		CTC	163.098-7			CTC	
163.072-2			CTC	163.086-2			CTC	163.099-5	B		CTC	
163.073-0	B	p	PRD	163.087-0	B		CTC	163.100-1	B	p	CTC (S)	
163.074-8	B		CTC									

Class 163.2. Class 162 fitted with bogies from Class 363. Converted 1993–2008.

163.215-7	(162.015)	F	FSU	163.248-8	(162.048)	F	FSU
163.216-5	(162.016)		PRD	163.249-6	(162.049)	B	PRD
163.217-3	(162.017)	F	FSU	163.250-4	(162.050)		CTC
163.233-0	(162.033)	F	FSU	163.251-2	(162.051)	F	FSU
163.234-8	(162.034)		CTC	163.252-0	(162.052)	F	FSU
163.241-3	(162.041)		CTC	163.255-3	(162.055)	F	FSU
163.242-1	(162.042)		CTC	163.256-1	(162.056)	F	FSU
163.243-9	(162.043)	F	FSU	163.257-9	(162.057)	B	PRD
163.244-7	(162.044)	B	CTC	163.258-7	(162.058)	B	CTC
163.245-4	(162.045)	F	FSU	163.259-5	(162.059)		CTC
163.247-0	(162.047)		CTC	163.260-3	(162.060)	B	PRD

CLASS 181   Co-Co

Class 181 was the first production six-axle electric locomotive, which followed two Class 180 prototypes (both of which are now in preservation). Class 181 was introduced from 1961 as freight traffic increased eastwards from Praha towards Ostrava and Žilina. 181.081 upwards are slightly more powerful with improved traction motors. Nearly 1000 similar Škoda model 34E locomotives were built for the Soviet Union as SZD Class ChS2.

Only a handful of these locomotives remain serviceable with ČD Cargo, all based at Ostrava. Freight work from the east of the Czech Republic for both Classes 181 and 182 can take them into Slovakia.

In recent years a large number of Class 181s and 182s have been exported for use with private freight operators in Poland (some with ČD Cargo's subsidiary Koleje Czeskie) and these may sometimes be seen returning to the Czech Republic (often at DPOV Přerov) for overhaul. Some locomotives of these classes are also operated by Czech and Slovak private operators.

Livery for Classes 181/182 is two tone-green, like Class 141, unless stated.

System: 3000 V DC.
Built: 1961–62.
Former ČSD Class: E669.1.
Builder: Škoda, model 31E.
Continuous Rating: 2610 kW (3500 hp) or 2790 kW (3740 hp).
Maximum Speed: 90 km/h.
Maximum Tractive Effort: 345 kN.

Total No. Built: 150.
Wheel Diameter: 1250 mm.
Weight: 124.2 tonnes.
Length over Buffers: 18.80 m.

EVN: 91 54 7 181 xxx-c.

Class 181. Škoda model 31E1: 2610 kW, original traction motors.

181.008-4	B	F	FSO	181.069-6	B	F	FSO

Class 181. Škoda model 31E2: 2790 kW, improved traction motors.

181.084-5		F	FSO	181.115-7		F	FSO	181.150-4	B	F	FSO

CLASS 182 Co-Co

Class 182 is an improved Class 181 with similar characteristics but one tonne per axle lighter. There are three sub-versions with detail differences: 182.001–038 are Škoda model 59E1, 182.039–138 are model 59E2, and 182.139–168 are model 59E3. Like Class 181, the Class 182s are approaching the end of their working lives and likewise many have been overhauled for lease or export to Slovakia and Poland. A large number are operated by ČD Cargo's Polish subsidiary Koleje Czeskie. 182.080/099 are currently leased to private freight operator ODOS.

System: 3000 V DC.
Built: 1963–65.
Former ČSD Class: E669.2.
Builder: Škoda, model 59E.
Continuous Rating: 2790 kW (3740 hp).
Maximum Tractive Effort: 345 kN.

Total No. Built: 168.
Wheel Diameter: 1250 mm.
Weight: 120 tonnes.
Length over Buffers: 18.80 or * 18.94 m.
Maximum Speed: 90 km/h.
EVN: 91 54 7 182 xxx-c.

182.038-0	**B**	*F*	FSO	182.099-2	**B**	*F*	FSO	182.168-5		*F* + * FSO
182.080-2	**B**	*F*	FSO	182.134-7	**B**	*F*	* FSO			

CLASS 210 Bo-Bo

Class 210 has the same body style as DC Classes 110/111/113, and collectively these are known as "Žehlička" ("flat iron"). The 74 Class 210s were built in two batches, 210.001–031 in 1972–73 and 210.032–074 in 1979–83. They were the first thyristor controlled locomotives to be owned by ČSD.

Škoda also built similar locomotives for export – 20 Class 61s were built for BDŽ in Bulgaria and ten of the type were built as Class 443 for industrial use at the TPP Nikola Tesla power plant in Serbia. Numbered E443.01–10 these can sometimes be seen back in the Czech Republic at CZ LOKO Česká Třebová for overhaul.

Class 210 is now split between ČD and ČD Cargo and is generally used on station pilot, shunting and empty coaching stock duties. There is still diagrammed passenger work in the summer on the Rybník–Lipno nad Vltavou branch in south Bohemia (hauling DMU trailers). Others may occasionally be found on ad-hoc passenger work as required and there is a Mondays Only peak-hour turn from Brno.

Two ČD Cargo locomotives have been fitted with an auxiliary diesel engine and renumbered Class 218 (see below).

Livery is dark blue with cream stripe, or the deep orange scheme, unless stated.

System: 25 kV AC 50 Hz.
Built: 1972–73 and 1979–83.
Former ČSD Class: S458.0.
Builder: Škoda, model 51E.
Continuous Rating: 880 kW (1180 hp).
Maximum Tractive Effort: 164 kN.

Total No. Built: 74†.
Wheel Diameter: 1050 mm.
Weight: 72 tonnes.
Length over Buffers: 14.40 m.
Maximum Speed: 80 km/h.
EVN: 91 54 7 210 0xx-c.

d   Fitted with door control cables for operating with Class 010 and 021 DMU trailers.
x   Equipped with electrical connectors for working with auxiliary battery power wagons.

210.003-0			CTC (S)	210.036-0	**B**	*F*	FSC	210.055-0			PLZ
210.014-7		*F*	FSC (S)	210.037-8		d	PLB	210.056-8	*F*		FSC (S)
210.015-4		*F*	FSC (S)	210.038-6		*F*	FSC (S)	210.057-6		d	PLB
210.021-2			PLB	210.039-4		d	PLB	210.058-4		d	PLB
210.023-8			BRM	210.045-1		d	PLB	210.059-2			PLB
210.024-6	**B**	*F*	FSC	210.046-9		*F* x	FSC	210.066-7	*F*		FSC
210.025-3		*F*	FSC (S)	210.047-7	**B**	*F*	FSC	210.067-5	*F* x		FSC (S)
210.026-1		xd	CTC (S)	210.052-7			BRM	210.072-5	*F*		FSC (S)
210.027-9		*F* x	FSC	210.053-5		*F*	FSC (S)	210.073-3	*F*		FSC
210.029-5		*F*	FSC (S)	210.054-3		*F*	FSC	210.074-1	*F* x		FSC

CLASS 218   Bo-Bo

Class 218 is Class 210 rebuilt as hybrid locomotives, with an auxiliary Caterpillar diesel engine and Siemens alternator for working freights on short sections of non-electrified lines (or shunting in non-electrified sidings). The renumbering is confusing, as the first conversion kept its serial number, whilst the second was renumbered into a completely new series as 218.102 (the first conversion hasn't yet become 218.101!).

System: 25 kV AC 50 Hz, plus diesel engine.
Built: Rebuilt 2008/2014 from Class 210.
Former ČSD Class: Not applicable.
Builder: Škoda, model 51E.
Continuous Rating: Electric: 880 kW (1180 hp); Diesel: 384 kW (515 hp) or 520 kW (700 hp).
Maximum Speed: 80 km/h.
Maximum Tractive Effort: 164 kN.

Total No. Built: 2.
Wheel Diameter: 1050 mm.
Weight: 72 tonnes.
Length over Buffers: 14.40 m.

EVN: 91 54 7 218 xxx-c.

Class 218.0. Converted by ČD Cargo České Budějovice in a protracted project started in 2001 but not completed until 2008. Caterpillar 3406 engine of 384 kW.

218.028-9   (210.028) **B** *F*   FSC

Class 218.1. Converted by CZ LOKO Česká Třebová 2014 with a more powerful Caterpillar C18 engine of 520 kW.

218.102-2   (210.016) **B** *F*   FSC

▲ One of the few lines that still has centre cab electric locomotives hauling trailers is Line 195 (loco-hauled trains summer only). At the end of the line at Lipno nad Vltavou, 210.057 has just arrived with train Os18808, the 13.02 from Rybník on 10 May 2014, hauling Btx763 trailer 28-29 055 and Bdtx766 trailer 84-29 006.   **Robert Pritchard**

CLASS 230   Bo-Bo

The fibreglass cab design of the Class 230, which resembles some kind of science fiction underwater monster, won a number of design awards in the 1960s. The material used earned the class the nickname "Laminatka". The prototype locomotive used for the 1963 launch was the unique Co-Co S699.001 (later 280.001), now preserved at the Techmania museum, Plzeň. Škoda and ČSD had earlier proved 25 kV with 1960 development prototypes S479.0/S479.1 (but unusually none of these four pioneers are preserved). Classes S489.0/S489.1 (230/240) were the first introduced for regular service.

Today the remaining Class 230s are owned by ČD Cargo and based at České Budějovice or Ostrava (the latter outbased at Břeclav). They can be found throughout the arc of AC electrification. They work in multiple south of Kutná Hora through Brno and over the Slovak border at Kúty, heading to the Bratislava area on heavy freights. Some are also cleared for operation into Hungary. Some Class 230s operate in semi-permanently coupled pairs.

In 1965–70 Škoda built 90 similar locomotives under the same model number for Bulgaria as BDŽ Class 42.

Livery for Classes 230 and 240 is orange & cream, unless stated.

System: 25 kV AC 50 Hz.   **Total No. Built:** 110.
Built: 1966–67.   **Wheel Diameter:** 1250 mm.
Former ČSD Class: S489.0.   **Weight:** 88 tonnes.
Builder: Škoda, model 47E.   **Length over Buffers:** 16.44 m.
Continuous Rating: 3080 kW (4130 hp).   **Maximum Speed:** 110 km/h.
Maximum Tractive Effort: 320 kN.   **EVN:** 91 54 7 230 xxx-c.
Non-Standard Livery: 230.065: All over blue with a white stripe.

230.001 has been restored to original condition and carries original No. S489.0001.

v   Fitted with MAV Mirel equipment for operation into Hungary.

Number	B	F	v	Depot	Number	B	F	v	Depot	Number	B	F	v	Depot
230.001-0		F	+	FSO	230.054-9		F		FSO	230.085-3		F		FSC (S)
230.003-6	B	F		FSO	230.055-6		F		FSC	230.087-9		F		FSC
230.006-9	B	F		FSO	230.056-4	B	F		FSO	230.088-7	B	F		FSO
230.009-3		F		FSO	230.057-2	B	F		FSC	230.089-5		F		FSC
230.018-4		F		FSO	230.058-0		F		FSO	230.090-3	B	F	v	FSO
230.019-2	B	F	v	FSO	230.059-8		F		FSC	230.091-1	B	F		FSC
230.024-2		F		FSC (S)	230.061-4	B	F		FSC	230.092-9	B	F	v	FSO
230.025-9	B	F		FSO	230.063-0	B	F		FSC	230.094-5		F		FSC
230.028-3		F		FSO	230.064-8	B	F		FSO	230.095-2	B	F	v	FSO
230.029-1		F		FSO	230.065-5	0	F		FSC	230.096-0	B	F		FSO
230.031-7	B	F		FSO	230.067-1	B	F	v	FSO	230.097-8		F		Břeclav (S)
230.035-8		F		FSO	230.069-7	B	F		FSC	230.100-0	B	F		FSO
230.036-6		F		FSC	230.070-5	B	F		FSO	230.101-8	B	F		FSO
230.040-8	B	F		FSO	230.072-1		F		FSC	230.102-6		F		FSO
230.041-6		F		FSC	230.073-9	B	F		FSO	230.103-4		F		FSO
230.042-4		F		FSC	230.075-4	B	F		FSC	230.105-9	B	F		FSO
230.044-0		F		Břeclav (S)	230.079-6	B	F		FSC	230.107-5		F		FSC (S)
230.047-3	B	F	v	FSO	230.081-2		F		FSC (S)	230.108-3		F		FSC
230.048-1	B	F	v	FSO	230.082-0		F		FSO	230.109-1	B	F		FSO
230.051-5	B	F		FSO	230.083-8		F		FSC (S)	230.110-9	B	F		FSO
230.053-1		F		FSC	230.084-6		F		FSC (S)					

CLASS 240   Bo-Bo

The main difference between Class 230 and Class 240 is their 110 km/h and 120 km/h maximum speeds, Class 240 having modified gearing to allow the 120 km/h maximum. 27 Class 240s were built for 140 km/h running (as Class S499.1, later designated Class 241) but between 1978 and 1986 these were returned to the standard 120 km/h maximum speed.

The Czech Class 240s are all operated by ČD Cargo (whereas more than half of the Slovak examples are with the passenger sector) and most are based at České Budějovice. They can be found on freights, often in pairs, throughout the AC electrified area.

System: 25 kV AC 50 Hz.
Built: 1968–70.
Former ČSD Class: S499.0 or S499.1.
Builder: Škoda, model 47E.
Continuous Rating: 3080 kW (4130 hp).
Maximum Tractive Effort: 255 kN.
Total No. Built: 145†.
Wheel Diameter: 1250 mm.
Weight: 85 tonnes.
Length over Buffers: 16.44 m.
Maximum Speed: 120 km/h.
EVN: 91 54 7 240 xxx-c.

v   Fitted with MAV Mirel equipment for operation into Hungary.

240.007-5		*F*	FSC	240.044-8	**B**	*F*	FSC	240.065-3		*F*	FSC
240.008-3	**B**	*F*	FSC	240.045-5	**B**	*F*	FSC	240.066-1	**B**	*F*	FSC
240.010-9		*F*	FSC	240.047-1		*F*	FSC	240.086-9		*F*	FSC
240.011-7		*F*	FSC	240.048-9		*F*	FSC	240.094-3		*F*	FSC
240.014-1	**B**	*F*	FSC	240.050-5	**B**	*F*	FSC	240.106-5	**B**	*F* v	FSO
240.021-6	**B**	*F*	FSC	240.053-9	**B**	*F*	FSC	240.107-3	**B**	*F* v	FSO
240.023-2	**B**	*F*	FSC	240.057-0	**B**	*F*	FSC	240.108-1		*F*	FSC
240.025-7	**B**	*F*	FSC	240.060-4	**B**	*F*	FSC	240.109-9		*F*	FSC
240.026-5	**B**	*F*	FSC	240.063-8		*F*	FSC	240.139-6		*F*	FSC
240.035-6	**B**	*F*	FSC	240.064-6	**B**	*F*	FSC				

CLASS 242   Bo-Bo

Class 242 is a more conventional looking, updated version of Classes 230/240, using the earlier body style. Built as mixed-traffic locomotives, when ČD and ČD Cargo were split all of the class transferred to ČD for passenger work. For technical purposes Class 242 is no more than a sub-class of Class 240, and in common features weight transfer beams underslung from the body to each bogie (none of the DC electrics have these). A quirk of the old numbering system made them Class S499.02, hence the 242.201–286 number series. Whilst DC Class 130 was the last new type to feature the classic body style, Class 242 was the last actually built to this style, up to 1981 (after the first prototype Class 363s had been built). The class was constructed in two batches: Series I 242.201–230 in 1975 and Series II 242.231–286 in 1979–81.

Škoda built very similar model 68E machines for Bulgaria as BDŽ Class 43, several of which are now used by private operators in the Czech Republic and Slovakia (see Private Freight Operators section) and also in Hungary. Confusingly the ex-BDŽ Class 43s in Slovakia are numbered in the 242.2 series at the end of the Czech series, while other ex-BDŽ Class 43s in the Czech Republic and Slovakia are numbered in the 242.5 series, retaining the last two digits of their BDŽ serial number.

Whilst general withdrawals only started in 2013, four of the class (242.225/232/257/270) had already been scrapped after suffering accident damage. In 2014 and 2015 a number of ČD locomotives were sold to private freight operators of various countries, and the class is now increasingly seen on freight duties.

Class 242s still work all categories of passenger train throughout the AC area, from Karlovy Vary in an anti-clockwise arc through Cheb, Plzeň, České Budějovice, Jihlava, Brno and Břeclav.

Brno based locomotives are mainly used on the Žďár nad Sázavou/Tišnov–Brno–Vranovice/Břeclav route, along with some services around Havlíčkův Brod, such as to Jihlava and Počátky. Plzeň based locomotives are mainly used on the following routes: Plzeň–Horažďovice předměstí–České Budějovice–Jihlava (portions of Brno "R" trains), and also stopping trains between Plzeň, Horažďovice předměstí and Nepomuk), Havlíčkův Brod–Jihlava, Cheb/Mariánské Lázně–Plzeň–Zdice and Plzeň–Klatovy.

Although the introduction of new RegioPanter EMUs, and even DMUs in North Bohemia, have seen some diagrams withdrawn, the class would seem to have at least a medium-term future, with overhauls and repaints into the new blue livery continuing.

Livery is a unique cream and deep orange style, unless stated.

System: 25 kV AC 50 Hz.
Built: 1975–81.
Former ČSD Class: S499.02.
Builder: Škoda, model 73E.
Continuous Rating: 3080 kW (4130 hp).
Maximum Tractive Effort: 240 kN.
Non-Standard Livery: 242.239: Deep red with a grey lower bodyside band.
Total No. Built: 86.
Wheel Diameter: 1250 mm.
Weight: 84 tonnes.
Length over Buffers: 16.44 m.
Maximum Speed: 120 km/h.
EVN: 91 54 7 242 2xx-c.

p   modified for operation in push-pull mode with Type Bfhpvee295 driving trailers.

▲ Carrying the latest version of the ČD livery, 242.211 leaves Plzeň hlavní nádraží with train Os7522, the 18.12 Plzeň–Klatovy on 12 July 2014. Class 242s work most passenger services on this route. Station pilot 742.087 (now stored) can be seen alongside. **Robert Pritchard**

▼ Dual-voltage 340.055 is seen stabled at České Velenice, close to the Austrian border, on 16 August 2011. The adjacent locomotive is 218.028. **Paul Abell**

242.201-2	B	PLZ	242.231-9	B		PLZ	242.255-8				CZLC (S)
242.204-6		BRM	242.233-5	B		BRM	242.258-2				PLZ
242.205-3		PLZ	242.234-3			BRM	242.259-0				PLZ
242.207-9		PLZ	242.235-0			BRM	242.260-8				BRM
242.208-7	B	PLZ	242.236-8	B		BRM	242.261-6				BRM
242.209-5	B	BRM	242.237-6	B		PLZ	242.263-2				PLZ
242.210-3		CZLC (S)	242.238-4	B		BRM	242.264-0	B		p	BRM
242.211-1	B	PLZ	242.239-2	0		PLZ	242.265-7				PLZ
242.212-9		PLZ	242.240-0	B	p	BRM	242.266-5				PLZ (S)
242.213-7		PLZ	242.241-8	B		PLZ	242.267-3	B			PLZ
242.214-5		BRM	242.242-6	B	p	BRM	242.268-1				BRM
242.215-2	B	PLZ	242.243-4			BRM	242.269-9	B			PLZ
242.216-0		PLZ	242.244-2	B		PLZ	242.272-3				BRM
242.217-8		BRM	242.245-9			PLZ	242.273-1				BRM
242.218-6		PLZ	242.246-7	B		BRM	242.274-9				BRM
242.220-2	B	PLZ	242.247-5			BRM	242.276-4				PLZ
242.221-0	B	BRM	242.248-3	B		BRM	242.277-2	B			PLZ
242.222-8		PLZ	242.249-1	B		PLZ	242.278-0	B			BRM
242.223-6		BRM	242.250-9	B		PLZ	242.279-8				PLZ
242.226-9		PLZ	242.251-7			PLZ (S)	242.281-4				PLZ
242.227-7		BRM	242.252-5			BRM	242.283-0				PLZ (S)
242.228-5		BRM	242.253-3			BRM	242.285-5				BRM
242.229-3		BRM	242.254-1			PLZ	242.286-3				PLZ
242.230-1		PLZ									

CLASS 263   Bo-Bo

These two pre-series 25 kV "Pershing" locomotives are used by ČD and are slightly less powerful than the production machines, all of which are operated by ZSSK. 263.001/002 are normally used on two diagrams on the Žďár nad Sázavou–Tišnov–Brno–Vranovice–Břeclav route, with a Class 242 covering if one is unavailable.

System: 25 kV AC 50 Hz.
Built: 1984.
Former ČSD Class: S499.2.
Builder: Škoda, model 70E.
Continuous Rating: 3060 kW (4100 hp).
Maximum Tractive Effort: 250 kN.

Total No. Built: 12†.
Wheel Diameter: 1250 mm.
Weight: 85 tonnes.
Length over Buffers: 16.80 m.
Maximum Speed: 120 km/h.
EVN: 91 54 7 263 00x-c.

263.001-0	B	BRM		263.002-8	B	BRM

CLASS 340   Bo-Bo

These three dual-voltage locomotives were converted at ČD České Budějovice from single voltage 25 kV AC Class 240s in 2001–04 for cross-border work between the Czech Republic and Austria (via the České Budějovice–Horní Dvořiště–Summerau line which was electrified in 2004 and also later between České Budějovice, České Velenice and Gmünd, which was electrified in 2012).

Performance is much reduced to only 1200 kW under 15 kV AC making the locomotives suitable only for local movements. They were for a time used on passenger trains on this route but are now limited to freights.

Livery is blue, cream & orange.

System: 25 kV AC 50 Hz and 15 kV AC 16.7 Hz.
Built: Rebuilt 2001–04 from Class 240.
Former ČSD Class: S499.0 or S499.1.
Builder: Škoda, model 47E.
Continuous Rating: 25 kV AC 3080 kW (4130 hp); 15 kV AC 1200 kW (1610 hp).
Maximum Speed: 120 km/h.
Maximum Tractive Effort: 255 kN.

Total No. Built: 3 (converted from Class 240).
Wheel Diameter: 1250 mm.
Weight: 85 tonnes.
Length over Buffers: 16.44 m.

EVN: 91 54 7 340 0xx-c.

340.049-6	(240.049)	F	FSC		340.062-9	(240.062)	F	FSC
340.055-3	(240.055)	F	FSC					

CLASS 362 Bo-Bo

Class 362 (and the remaining Class 363 still operating with the passenger sector) is the standard type of dual-voltage electric locomotive used on routes between DC Praha and AC Plzeň, České Budějovice and Brno. All Class 362 and 363 are fitted with 3000 kW electric dynamic brakes. Originally 181 Class 363s were built but since the early 1990s an ongoing programme has seen their original 120 km/h bogies exchanged with 140 km/h bogies from Class 162s, to create Class 362. All renumbered ČD locomotives have kept their original Class 363 serial numbers, but this wasn't the case for the ZSSK rebuilds (see Slovakia section).

362.001 and 363.002 are the original Class 363 prototype locomotives (362.001 is ex-363.001), not to be confused with ZSSK 362.001, which is a different prototype locomotive, built some ten years later.

Brno-based Class 362s work express passenger services on the Brno–Česká Třebová–Praha, Brno–Havlíčkův Brod–Praha, Brno–Přerov–Bohumín and Brno–Olomouc–Šumperk routes plus some stopping or semi-fast trains on the Tišnov–Břeclav and Havlíčkův Brod–Čáslav/Kolín routes. Work on the Brno–Česká Třebová–Praha route was being progressively taken over by new InterPanter EMUs during 2016.

Plzeň based Class 362s are mainly used on express trains on the Cheb/Plzeň–Beroun–Praha, Praha–České Budějovice and Cheb–Most–Ústí nad Labem (trains continue to Praha via Kralupy) routes, plus some trains between Plzeň and Klatovy.

Although most Class 362s have been now painted in the new ČD blue livery they are still quite a colourful class, with a number of different advertising liveries, some of these being advertising for ČD itself. Those Class 362s and 363s not in the new ČD or ČD Cargo blue liveries or advertising liveries carry the old dual-voltage dark blue with a cream stripe livery.

System: 3000 V DC and 25 kV AC 50 Hz.
Built: * 1980; 1984–90; rebuilt 1993–2015.
Former ČSD Class: ES499.1.
Builder: Škoda, model 69E (u 69Em).
Continuous Rating: DC 3480 kW (4665 hp); AC 3060 kW (4100 hp).
Maximum Speed: 140 km/h.
Maximum Tractive Effort: 258 kN.
Non-Standard and Advertising Liveries:

Total No. Built: 77 (converted from Class 363).
Wheel Diameter: 1250 mm.
Weight: 87 tonnes.
Length over Buffers: 16.80 m (* 16.74 m).

EVN: 91 54 7 362 xxx-c.

362.001: Original prototype livery of orange, blue & white. Carries original number ES499.1001.
362.027: www.runczech.com (white & blue).
362.081/110: www.cd.cz e-shop (white & blue).
362.086: Euro 2012 (red & white).
362.119/121: www.postovnisporitelna.cz – the Czech post office (red & yellow).

p   Modified for operation in push-pull mode with Type Bfhpvee295 driving trailers.
u   Built new with updated power electronics and control systems and an increased tractive effort of 292 kN.

362.001-0	(363.001)	0	*	BRM	362.068-9	(363.068)	B		PLZ
362.017-6	(363.017)	B	p	BRM	362.070-5	(363.070)	B	p	BRM
362.019-2	(363.019)	B		BRM	362.071-3	(363.071)	B		PLZ
362.021-8	(363.021)	B		BRM	362.076-2	(363.076)	B		BRM
362.023-4	(363.023)	B	p	BRM	362.077-0	(363.077)	B		PLZ
362.024-2	(363.024)	B		BRM	362.078-8	(363.078)			PLZ
362.027-5	(363.027)	A	p	BRM	362.079-6	(363.079)	B		PLZ
362.033-3	(363.033)	B	p	BRM	362.080-4	(363.080)	B	p	BRM
362.039-0	(363.039)	B		BRM	362.081-2	(363.081)	A		PLZ
362.040-8	(363.040)	B		BRM	362.082-0	(363.082)	B	p	BRM
362.042-4	(363.042)	B		BRM	362.083-8	(363.083)	B		PLZ
362.046-5	(363.046)	B		PLZ	362.084-6	(363.084)	B		PLZ
362.052-3	(363.052)			PLZ	362.085-3	(363.085)	B		PLZ
362.053-1	(363.053)	B		PLZ	362.086-1	(363.086)	A		PLZ
362.055-6	(363.055)	B		PLZ	362.087-9	(363.087)	B	p	BRM
362.056-4	(363.056)	B	p	BRM	362.108-3	(363.108)	B		PLZ
362.057-2	(363.057)	B		PLZ	362.109-1	(363.109)	B		BRM
362.060-6	(363.060)			BRM	362.110-9	(363.110)	A		PLZ
362.062-2	(363.062)	B		PLZ	362.111-7	(363.111)	B		BRM

362.112-5	(363.112)	B		BRM	362.132-3	(363.132)	B	PLZ
362.113-3	(363.113)	B		BRM	362.158-8	(363.158)	B	BRM
362.114-1	(363.114)	B		PLZ	362.159-6	(363.159)	B	BRM
362.115-8	(363.115)	B		PLZ	362.160-4	(363.160)	B	BRM
362.116-6	(363.116)	B		PLZ	362.161-2	(363.161)	B	BRM
362.117-4	(363.117)	B		PLZ	362.162-0	(363.162)	B p	BRM
362.118-2	(363.118)	B		BRM	362.163-8	(363.163)	B	BRM
362.119-0	(363.119)	A		BRM	362.164-6	(363.164)	B	BRM
362.120-8	(363.120)	B		PLZ	362.165-3	(363.165)	p	BRM
362.121-6	(363.121)	A		BRM	362.166-1	(363.166)	B	BRM
362.122-4	(363.122)			BRM	362.167-9	(363.167)	B	BRM
362.123-2	(363.123)	B		BRM	362.168-7	(363.168)		BRM
362.124-0	(363.124)			BRM	362.169-5	(363.169)	B	BRM
362.125-7	(363.125)			PLZ	362.170-3	(363.170)		BRM
362.126-5	(363.126)	B		PLZ	362.171-1	(363.171)		BRM
362.127-3	(363.127)	B		PLZ	362.172-9	(363.172)		BRM
362.128-1	(363.128)	B	p	BRM	362.173-7	(363.173)	B	BRM
362.129-9	(363.129)	B		PLZ	362.174-5	(363.174)	B u	BRM
362.130-7	(363.130)			PLZ	362.175-2	(363.175)	B u	BRM
362.131-5	(363.131)	B		PLZ				

CLASS 363   Bo-Bo

Following the conversion of most ČD passenger Class 363s to Class 362s, the Class 363s are now mostly used by ČD Cargo. The ČD Cargo Class 363 and 363.5 (the latter were rebuilt from Class 163), are used on freight trains (in pairs on heavier trains) on all main lines radiating to and from Praha.

As this book closed for press six unmodified Class 363s remained on ČD's books, although the four push-pull fitted Plzeň-based Class 363s are not currently planned to be rebuilt as Class 362s. These have been modified for push-pull operation and can generally be found on stopping trains between Plzeň and Beroun.

System: 3000 V DC and 25 kV AC 50 Hz.
Built: * 1980; 1984–90.
Former ČSD Class: ES499.1.
Builder: Škoda, model 69E.
Continuous Rating: DC 3480 kW (4665 hp); AC 3060 kW (4100 hp).
Maximum Speed: 120 km/h.
Maximum Tractive Effort: 285 kN.
Advertising Livery: 363.015: ČD Cargo blue & white.

Total No. Built: 181†.
Wheel Diameter: 1250 mm.
Weight: 87 tonnes.
Length over Buffers: 16.80 m.

EVN: 91 54 7 363 0xx-c.

p   Modified for operation in push-pull mode with Type Bfhpvee295 driving trailers.

363.002-7		*	BRM	363.025-8	B	F	FSO	363.049-8	B	F	FSU
363.003-5	B	F	FSO	363.026-6	B	F	FSO	363.050-6	B	F	FSO
363.004-3	B	F	FSO	363.028-2	B	F	FSO	363.051-4	B	F	FSO
363.005-0	B	F	FSO	363.029-0	B	F	FSO	363.054-8	B	p	PLZ
363.006-8		F	FSO	363.030-8	B		BRM	363.058-9	B	F	FSO
363.007-6	B	F	FSO	363.031-6	B	F	FSO	363.059-7	B	F	FSO
363.008-4	B	F	FSO	363.032-4	B	F	FSO	363.061-3	B	p	PLZ
363.009-2	B	F	FSO	363.034-0	B	F	FSO	363.063-9	B	F	FSO
363.010-0	B	F	FSO	363.035-7	B	F	FSO	363.064-7	B	p	PLZ
363.011-8	B	F	FSO	363.036-5	B	F	FSO	363.065-4		F	FSO
363.012-6	B	F	FSO	363.037-3	B	F	FSO	363.066-2	B	F	FSU
363.013-4	B	F	FSO	363.038-1	B	F	FSO	363.067-0	B	F	FSO
363.014-2	B	F	FSO	363.041-5	B	F	FSO	363.069-6	B	p	PLZ
363.015-9	A	F	FSO	363.043-1	B	F	FSU	363.072-0	B	F	FSU
363.016-7	B	F	FSO	363.044-9	B	F	FSU	363.073-8	B	F	FSU
363.018-3	B	F	FSO	363.045-6	B	F	FSU	363.074-6	B	F	FSU
363.020-9	B	F	FSO	363.047-2	B	F	FSU	363.075-3	B	F	FSU
363.022-5	B	F	FSO	363.048-0	B	F	FSO				

CLASS 363.5   Bo-Bo

Class 363.5s is a major rebuild of ČD Cargo Class 163, carried out by Pars nova, Šumperk (a Škoda subsidiary) between 2010 and 2013. All 30 are based at České Budějovice but can be seen on freight duties across much of the country, and also on cross-border traffic into Slovakia.

System: 3000 V DC and 25 kV AC 50 Hz.
Built: 1984–86; rebuilt 2010–13.
Former ČSD Class: ES499.1.
Builder: Škoda, model 71Em.
Continuous Rating: 3700 kW (4960 hp).
Maximum Tractive Effort: 282 kN.

Total No. Built: 30 (rebuilt from Class 163).
Wheel Diameter: 1250 mm.
Weight: 87.1 tonnes.
Length over Buffers: 16.80 m.
Maximum Speed: 120 km/h.
EVN: 91 54 7 363 5xx-c.

363.501-8	(163.031)	**B**	*F*	FSC		363.516-6	(163.024)	**B**	*F*	FSC
363.502-6	(163.004)	**B**	*F*	FSC		363.517-4	(163.013)	**B**	*F*	FSC
363.503-4	(163.011)	**B**	*F*	FSC		363.518-2	(163.019)	**B**	*F*	FSC
363.504-2	(163.006)	**B**	*F*	FSC		363.519-0	(163.017)	**B**	*F*	FSC
363.505-9	(163.018)	**B**	*F*	FSC		363.520-8	(163.015)	**B**	*F*	FSC
363.506-7	(163.005)	**B**	*F*	FSC		363.521-6	(163.032)	**B**	*F*	FSC
363.507-5	(163.037)	**B**	*F*	FSC		363.522-4	(163.007)	**B**	*F*	FSC
363.508-3	(163.002)	**B**	*F*	FSC		363.523-2	(163.027)	**B**	*F*	FSC
363.509-1	(163.036)	**B**	*F*	FSC		363.524-0	(163.020)	**B**	*F*	FSC
363.510-9	(163.003)	**B**	*F*	FSC		363.525-7	(163.016)	**B**	*F*	FSC
363.511-7	(163.014)	**B**	*F*	FSC		363.526-5	(163.028)	**B**	*F*	FSC
363.512-5	(163.012)	**B**	*F*	FSC		363.527-3	(163.010)	**B**	*F*	FSC
363.513-3	(163.038)	**B**	*F*	FSC		363.528-1	(163.023)	**B**	*F*	FSC
363.514-1	(163.009)	**B**	*F*	FSC		363.529-9	(163.001)	**B**	*F*	FSC
363.515-8	(163.033)	**B**	*F*	FSC		363.530-7	(163.008)	**B**	*F*	FSC

CLASSES 371 & 372   Bo-Bo

Class 372 was built as a dual-voltage 15 kV AC and 3000 V DC locomotive for use on express services between the Czech Republic and Germany. 20 similar Class 230s (later Class 180) were built for German Railways at the same time for bridging the Děčín–Bad Schandau traction gap. In 1988 one prototype went to ČSD (372.001) and one to DR (230 001). Series locomotives, built 1991, were Škoda model 80E (Knorr air braking), later DB Class 180, and ČD 372.002–015, Škoda model 76E (DAKO air braking).

In 1994 372.001 was rebuilt by Škoda as 371.001 for 160 km/h operation by changing the traction motor gear ratios, decreasing tractive effort from 140 kN at 77 km/h to 104 kN at 103 km/h – a further five locomotives followed between 1997 and 2001, all retaining their serial numbers on renumbering from Class 372 to 371. In 2003, already withdrawn DB 180 001 was transferred to ČD in compensation for accident damage to 372.006 (later repaired) in Dresden. 180 001 had also been adapted by DB for 160 km/h operation, so ČD renumbered it 371.201.

At the time of writing Class 371s are almost exclusively used on the scenic Line 090 north from Praha to Ústí nad Labem, Děčín and then into Germany, on EuroCity (EC) or EuroNight (EN) trains. There are five diagrams, and Class 371s normally operate as far as Dresden, from where a DB locomotive (usually a Class 101) works forward to Berlin or Hamburg. On the nightly EN train the Class 371 reaches Leipzig. Some of the trains are very long distance services taking in as many as four countries with more than one locomotive change. For example the EC173 Hamburg–Budapest "Hungaria" is a DB Class 101 as far as Dresden, then a Class 371 to Praha and then a Class 380 to Budapest (via Brno and Bratislava).

A Class 371 is also used on an overnight/early morning return train from Praha to Přerov.

The ČD Cargo Class 372s can be found on cross-border Czech-Germany freights.

Those locomotives not in the new blue livery are in a red & cream scheme, with yellow stripe.

System: 3000 V DC and 15 kV AC 16.7 Hz.
Built: 1988 or 1991.
Former ČSD Class: ES499.2.
Builder: Škoda, model 76E (* 80E) or 76Em.
Continuous Rating: 3080 kW (4130 hp).
Maximum Tractive Effort: 243 kN.
Non-Standard Livery: 371.201: The Czech national flag colours – blue, red & white.

Total No. Built: 15 (plus one ex-DB Class 180).
Wheel Diameter: 1250 mm.
Weight: 83 (Class 371) or 84 (Class 372) tonnes.
Length over Buffers: 16.80 m.
Maximum Speed: 120 km/h or 160 km/h.
EVN: 91 54 7 371 xxx-c or 91 54 7 372 0xx-c.

▲ At the time of writing a couple of Class 371s are still in the original livery. On 10 March 2015 371.005 passes Roztoky u Prahy with train EC171, the 06.46 Berlin Hbf–Budapest-Keleti.
Robert Pritchard

▼ With the city of Praha forming a backdrop, 380.004 leaves the Czech capital behind at Krejcárek with train R606, the 07.29 Praha hl.n–Cheb on 14 July 2013. **Robert Pritchard**

Class 371.0. Class 372 modified for 160 km/h. Built 1988 (371.001) or 1991.

371.001-9	(372.001)	**B**	*	PRG	371.004-3	(372.004)		PRG
371.002-7	(372.002)	**B**		PRG	371.005-0	(372.005)		PRG
371.003-5	(372.003)	**B**		PRG	371.015-9	(372.015)	**B**	PRG

Class 371.2. The former DB 180 001, retaining Knorr brakes and modified for 160 km/h. Built 1988.

371.201-5　(DB 180 001) **0** *　PRG

Class 372. Original version now used by ČD Cargo; 120 km/h. Built 1991.

372.006-7		*F*	FSU	372.009-1	**B**	*F*	FSU	372.012-5	**B**	*F*	FSU
372.007-5	**B**	*F*	FSU	372.010-9	**B**	*F*	FSU	372.013-3		*F*	FSU
372.008-3	**B**	*F*	FSU	372.011-7		*F*	FSU	372.014-1	**B**	*F*	FSU

CLASS 380   Bo-Bo

The idea of the home-built Class 380 was first conceived in 2004 as a 200 km/h tri-series IGBT inverter asynchronous motor locomotive capable of operating on three voltages across multiple countries (the Czech Republic, Slovakia, Germany, Austria, Hungary and Poland). Devised as the third generation of Škoda electric locomotives, in 2005 ČD ordered 20 machines, but the first wasn't delivered until 2010, entering service initially between Praha and Brno.

Inevitable acceptance problems, as well as issues with reliability, initially saw the class largely confined to domestic ČD services, and during their short life they have been used on a number of different routes. At the time of writing in 2016 the class have finally been approved for operation in all of the countries listed above, the most recent being Germany. However, as yet there is no regular work into either Poland or Germany. It was planned that Class 380 would take over some Class 371 diagrams on the Praha–Dresden route, removing the need for a locomotive change at Praha. However this has yet to happen, and it is understood that ČD is now considering hiring Siemens Vectrons for this route instead. The Class 380 200 km/h top speed is also not yet utilised on the Czech network as no lines have yet been upgraded for speeds higher than 160 km/h.

There are now 17 diagrams for the class, on three main routes: Praha–Brno–Bratislava–Budapest Keleti portions of "EC" trains from Germany to Budapest, Wien–Břeclav–Bohumín portions of "EC"/"Ex" trains (some of which continue through to Poland behind a PKP Class 370) and Praha–Žilina "EC" trains. An exception is one turn from Staré město u Uherského Hradiště to Praha and return.

In 2015 ČD awarded Škoda subsidiary Pars nova, Šumperk a maintenance contract for the class.

Two similar Class 381s were built for ZSSK in Slovakia (but geared for 160 km/h) and Škoda is now constructing six further locomotives of this type for DB Regio for Nürnberg–München trains (to be designated DB Class 102).

The Class 380 livery is a unique silver & blue scheme.

System: 3000 V DC, 15 kV AC 16.7 Hz and 25 kV AC 50 Hz.　**Total No. Built:** 20.
Built: 2008–11.　**Wheel Diameter:** 1250 mm.
Former ČSD Class: Not applicable.　**Weight:** 86 tonnes.
Builder: Škoda, model 109E1.　**Length over Buffers:** 18.00 m.
Continuous Rating: 6400 kW (8580 hp).　**Maximum Speed:** 200 km/h.
Maximum Tractive Effort: 274 kN.　**EVN:** 91 54 7 380 0xx-c.
Advertising Liveries: 380.002: Športuj s námi (various colours).
　　　　　　　　　　380.011: ČD Nostalgie (various colours).

380.001-8		PRG	380.008-3		PRG	380.015-8	PRG
380.002-6	**A**	PRG	380.009-1		PRG	380.016-6	PRG
380.003-4		PRG	380.010-9		PRG	380.017-4	PRG
380.004-2		PRG	380.011-7	**A**	PRG	380.018-2	PRG
380.005-9		PRG	380.012-5		PRG	380.019-0	PRG
380.006-7		PRG	380.013-3		PRG	380.020-8	PRG
380.007-5		PRG	380.014-1		PRG		

1.2. ČD ELECTRIC MULTIPLE UNITS & TRAILERS

Until recent years ČD EMUs have been largely confined to suburban and inter-urban work around the large cities of Praha, Brno, Ostrava and Olomouc. However the new RegioPanter units have brought EMUs to regional services, and similar "InterPanter" units entered service in 2015–16 on longer distance "R" and "Rx" trains.

ČD EMUs are numbered as follows: 4xx series units are 3000 V DC only; 5xx series units are 25 kV AC 50 Hz only whilst 6xx series are dual-voltage, equipped for operating on 3000 V DC and 25 kV AC. The Class 680 Pendolinos are also equipped for operation on German and Austrian 15 kV AC 16.7 Hz.

Formations: Classes 440, 471, 640, 650, 660 and 680 were built to operate in fixed formation sets (although Class 471s sometimes run in misformed formations). Others are classed as separate motor coaches and trailers, but in practice operate in semi-permanent formations, so formations for these (Classes 451, 452, 460 and 560; serviceable units only) are listed below each class.

Unlike most of the unwired trailer coaches used with diesel units, EMU trailers are fully compatible as proper multiple unit cars, and have never been numbered in the locomotive-hauled carriage series. Class 051/052, 060 and 063 trailers are listed here after the EMU Class that they are used with. Class 064 trailers form part of the new fixed formation Class 660 units and Class 071 trailers form part of the Class 471 double-deck units.

CLASS 440   REGIOPANTER   3-CAR UNITS

Škoda's first new regional EMU for ČD entered service in 2012, branded "RegioPanter" ("Panter" = "Panther" in English). With 65% of the floor space classed as "low floor", much of the electrical equipment is housed in the roof space. Air-conditioned and featuring a small First Class area and wi-fi, the RegioPanters can be found in the Hradec Králové, Ústí nad Labem, Brno, Olomouc and České Budějovice areas. They have been well received and a similar design is now being delivered for longer distance services (Class 660) – more Class 650 RegioPanters are on order as well. Škoda is hopeful that this design will continue to be built for ČD (and for the export market as well) for some years to come. The units are assembled by Škoda Vagónka at its Ostrava-Vítkovice or Plzeň plants.

The RegioPanters are numbered in Classes 440, 640 or 650 depending on whether they are single voltage or dual voltage and 2- or 3-cars. Class 440s are 3-car 3000 V DC only units, operating out of Děčín and Hradec Králové depots. The Děčín-based units are used on stopping services between Děčín, Ústí nad Labem, Most, Chomutov and Kadaň and also between Ústí nad Labem and Louka u Litvínova. All of these units have also received official names after the towns and cities they serve. The Hradec Králové-based units are used exclusively on the busy Jaroměř–Hradec Králové–Pardubice corridor.

System: 3000 V DC.
Built: 2012–14.   **Total No. Built:** 12 x 3-car sets.
Builder: Škoda, model 7Ev.
Accommodation: 9/44(+12) 1TD 2W + –/90(+4) 1T + –/78(+4).
Traction Motors: 6 x Škoda ML 3942 K/4 asynchronous of 340 kW (455 hp); total 2040 kW (2730 hp).
Weight: 49.8 + 45.3 + 48.2 tonnes.   **Length over Couplers:** 26.45 + 26.50 + 26.45 m.
Wheel Arrangement: Bo-2 + Bo-2 + 2-Bo.   **Maximum Speed:** 160 km/h.
Formation: DMCO–MSO–DMSO.
EVN: 94 54 1 440 0xx-c + 94 54 1 442 0xx-c + 94 54 1 441 0xx-c.

440.001-6	442.001-4	441.001-5	B	PRD	Ústí nad Labem
440.002-4	442.002-2	441.002-3	B	PRD	Děčín
440.003-2	442.003-0	441.003-1	B	PRD	Most
440.004-0	442.004-8	441.004-9	B	PRD	Chomutov
440.005-7	442.005-5	441.005-6	B	PRD	Teplice
440.006-5	442.006-3	441.006-4	B	PRD	Litvínov
440.007-3	442.007-1	441.007-2	B	PRD	Kadaň
440.008-1	442.008-9	441.008-0	B	CTH	
440.009-9	442.009-7	441.009-8	B	CTH	
440.010-7	442.010-5	441.010-6	B	CTH	
440.011-5	442.011-3	441.011-4	B	CTH	
440.012-3	442.012-1	441.012-2	B	CTH	

CLASSES 451 & 452   MOTOR COACHES

These distinctive suburban multiple units have been a familiar sight around Praha for many years, but have been in decline in the last few years as Class 471s have taken over many of their diagrams. The units have low platform height floors and run formed with Class 051 or 052 trailers, usually as 3- or 4-car sets. Units can run in pairs to form longer trains. A total of 51 Class 451 units and 11 Class 452 were built, the Class 452s following four years after the last Class 451s were constructed. The two classes are almost identical, Class 452s having minor technical detail differences, such as different compressors.

The remaining ten serviceable units still find use on five diagrams north of Praha: between Praha Masarykovo and Kralupy nad Vltavou (4-car sets) and Praha Libeň and Roztoky u Prahy (3-car sets). A number of Class 451/452s can be found stored in the dump close to Praha ONJ depot. At the time of writing the last remaining units were expected to be withdrawn by 2017, replaced by push-pull loco-hauled formations with double deck stock. Unit 451.045/046 has been preserved at Pars nova Šumperk (see Preserved EMU section). Livery is light blue & grey unless stated.

System: 3000 V DC.
Built: 1964–68 and 1972–73.
Builder – Mechanical Parts: MSV Studénka.
Builder – Electrical Parts: Škoda.
Traction Motors: 4 x 165 kW (220 hp) DC.
Former ČSD Class: EM475.1 or EM475.2.
Wheel Arrangement: Bo-Bo.
Formation: DMBSO.
Non-Standard Livery: Original all-over blue with a red stripe.

Total No. Built: 451: 102; 452; 22 (motor cars).
Accommodation: –/61.
Weight: 59 tonnes.
Length over Couplers: 24.60 m.
Maximum Speed: 100 km/h.
EVN: 94 54 1 451 xxx-c or 94 54 1 452 xxx-c.

Class 451. Built 1964–68.

451.001-2	**0** +	PRO	451.034-3		PRO (S)	451.080-6	PRO
451.002-0	**0** +	PRO	451.052-5		PRO	451.084-8	PRO (S)
451.013-7		PRO (S)	451.054-1		PRO (S)	451.087-1	PRO
451.014-5		PRO (S)	451.056-6	**B**	PRO	451.088-9	PRO
451.015-2		PRO	451.057-4		PRO (S)	451.091-3	PRO
451.017-8		PRO (S)	451.059-0		PRO	451.092-1	PRO
451.018-6		PRO (S)	451.060-8		PRO	451.094-7	PRO (S)
451.025-1	**0**	PRO	451.069-9		PRO (S)	451.095-4	**B** PRO
451.026-9	**0**	PRO	451.070-7		PRO (S)	451.096-2	**B** PRO
451.033-5		PRO (S)	451.079-8		PRO	451.098-8	**B** PRO

Class 452. Built 1972–73.

452.001-1	PRO	452.012-8	PRO (S)	452.016-9	PRO (S)
452.002-9	PRO	452.015-1	PRO (S)	452.022-7	PRO (S)

CLASSES 051 & 052   INTERMEDIATE TRAILERS

Intermediate trailers used between Class 451/452 motor coaches (see above) in 3- or 4-car sets.

Built: 1964–68 and 1972–73.
Builder: MSV Studénka.
Former ČSD Class: N475.1 and N475.2.
Accommodation: –/105.
Non-Standard Livery: Original all-over blue with a red stripe.

Weight: 32 tonnes.
Length over Buffers: 23.35 m.
Maximum Speed: 100 km/h.
EVN: 94 54 1 051 xxx-c or 94 54 1 052 xxx-c.

Class 051. Built 1964–68.

051.001-6	**0** +	PRO	051.044-6		PRO (S)	051.073-5	PRO (S)
051.002-4	**0** +	PRO	051.053-7		PRO (S)	051.079-2	PRO
051.004-0		PRO	051.055-2	**B**	PRO	051.081-8	PRO (S)
051.013-1		PRO (S)	051.056-0	**B**	PRO	051.087-5	PRO
051.014-9		PRO (S)	051.057-8		PRO (S)	051.088-3	PRO
051.017-2		PRO (S)	051.058-6		PRO (S)	051.092-5	PRO
051.025-5	**0**	PRO	051.060-2		PRO	051.095-8	**B** PRO
051.026-3	**0**	PRO	051.061-0		PRO (S)	051.096-6	**B** PRO
051.036-2		PRO					

Class 052. Built 1972–73.

052.002-3	PRO	052.016-3	PRO (S)	052.018-9	PRO (S)
052.015-5	PRO (S)	052.017-1	PRO (S)	052.022-1	PRO (S)

Class 451 and 452 formations:

451.001+051.001+051.002+451.002	451.079+051.092+451.092
451.025+051.025+051.026+451.026	451.080+051.036+051.079+451.091
451.015+051.004+451.052	451.087+051.087+051.088+451.088
451.056+051.056+051.055+451.098	451.095+051.095+051.096+451.096
451.059+051.060+451.060	452.001+052.002+452.002

CLASS 460   MOTOR COACHES

Class 460 motor coaches are based in Moravia and used in 4-car or 5-car formations with Class 063 trailers. All have normal platform-height floors for use on regional services. 3000 V DC prototype 460.001/002 and the first three trailers were built in 1971, with the production batch of 84 motor coaches and 126 further trailers following three years later (to create a fleet of 43 5-car sets). Ten Class 063 trailers were later converted to work with Class 560 and renumbered in the 060.xxx series.

The Class 460s operate from either Olomouc or Bohumín depots and are mainly used on the Čadca (Slovakia)/Mosty u Jablunkova–Český Těšín–Bohumín–Ostrava, Olomouc–Přerov–Nezamyslice and Olomouc–Přerov–Hranice na Moravě–Valašské Meziříčí–Horní Lideč routes.

At the time of writing there are 19 serviceable units to cover 13 diagrams. The introduction of a small number of Class 640 "RegioPanter" units around Olomouc has seen a few Class 460s withdrawn but the class can substitute for unavailable Class 640s (Olomouc) or Class 471s (Bohumín). Most of those still in traffic are now in the ČD blue livery, otherwise the livery is light blue & grey. A number of Class 460s are also used by ZSSK in Slovakia.

System: 3000 V DC.
Built: 1974–78.
Builder – Mechanical Parts: MSV Studénka.
Builder – Electrical Parts: Škoda.
Traction Motors: 4 x 250 kW (335 hp) DC.
Former ČSD Class: EM488.0.
Wheel Arrangement: Bo-Bo.
Formation: DMBSO.

Total No. Built: 86 motor cars†.

Accommodation: –/48 1T.
Weight: 64 tonnes.
Length over Couplers: 24.50 m.
Maximum Speed: 110 km/h.
EVN: 94 54 1 460 0xx-c.
Non-Standard Livery: 460.079/080 original ČSD EMU livery of green & cream.

460.004-5		OLO	460.019-3		OLO	460.064-9		OLO
460.005-2		OLO	460.020-1		OLO	460.065-6		OLO
460.006-0		OLO	460.023-5	B	OLO	460.066-4		OLO
460.007-8		OLO	460.024-3	B	OLO	460.069-8	B	OLO
460.008-6		OLO	460.025-0	B	OLO	460.070-6	B	OLO
460.009-4	B	OLO	460.026-8	B	OLO	460.071-4		OLO
460.010-2	B	OLO	460.027-6	B	OLO	460.072-2		OLO
460.011-0	B	OLO	460.028-4	B	OLO	460.075-5	B	OLO
460.012-8	B	OLO	460.059-9	B	OLO	460.076-3	B	OLO
460.013-6		OLO	460.060-7	B	OLO	460.079-7	O +	OLO
460.014-4		OLO	460.061-5	B	OLO	460.080-5	O +	OLO
460.015-1	B	OLO	460.062-3	B	OLO	460.082-1		OLO
460.016-9	B	OLO	460.063-1		OLO			

CLASS 063   INTERMEDIATE TRAILERS

Intermediate trailers used with Class 460 EMU motor coaches (see above) in 4- or 5-car sets.

Built: 1974–78.
Builder: MSV Studénka.
Former ČSD Class: N488.03.
Accommodation: –/72(+8) 2T.

Weight: 55.3 tonnes.
Length over Buffers: 24.50 m.
Maximum Speed: 110 km/h.
EVN: 94 54 1 063 xxx-c.
Non-Standard Livery: 063.352/353/362/365/420/421 original ČSD EMU livery of green & cream.

063.308-1		OLO	063.329-7		OLO	
063.309-9		OLO	063.330-5		OLB (S)	
063.310-7		OLO	063.334-7	B	OLO	
063.311-5		OLO	063.335-4	B	OLO	
063.312-3	B	OLO	063.336-2	B	OLO	
063.313-1	B	OLO	063.337-0	B	OLO	
063.314-9	B	OLO	063.338-8	B	OLO	
063.316-4	B	OLO	063.339-6	B	OLO	
063.317-2	B	OLO	063.340-4	B	OLO	
063.318-0	B	OLO	063.341-2	B	OLO	
063.319-8		OLO	063.342-0	B	OLO	
063.320-6		OLO	063.352-9	0	CTC (S)	
063.321-4		OLO	063.353-7	0	CTC (S)	
063.322-2	B	OLO	063.362-8	0	CTC (S)	
063.323-0	B	OLO	063.365-1	0	CTC (S)	
063.324-8	B	OLO	063.388-3	B	OLO	
063.327-1		OLO	063.391-7	B	OLO	
063.328-9		OLO				

063.392-5	B	OLO
063.393-3	B	OLO
063.394-1		OLO
063.395-8		OLO
063.396-6		OLO
063.398-2		OLO
063.399-0		OLO
063.404-8	B	OLO
063.405-5	B	OLO
063.408-9		OLO
063.409-7		OLO
063.415-4	B	OLO
063.416-2	B	OLO
063.420-4	0 +	OLO
063.421-2	0 +	OLO
063.426-1		OLO
063.428-7	B	OLO

Class 460 formations:

460.004+063.327+063.426+460.082
460.005+063.308+063.309+460.006
460.007+063.310+063.311+460.008
460.009+063.314+063.313+460.010
460.011+063.317+063.318+460.012
460.013+063.319+063.320+063.321+460.014
460.015+063.322+063.323+063.324+460.016
460.019+063.328+063.329+460.020
460.023+063.334+063.335+063.336+460.024
460.025+063.339+063.338+063.337+460.026

460.027+063.340+063.341+063.342+460.028
460.059+063.388+063.312+460.060
460.061+063.393+063.392+063.391+460.062
460.063+063.394+063.395+063.396+460.064
460.065+063.399+063.398+460.066
460.069+063.404+063.405+460.070
460.071+063.408+063.409+460.072
460.075+063.415+063.416+460.076
460.079+063.420+063.421+460.080

▲ In the ČD blue & white livery, 5-car Class 460 set 460.061/063.393/063.392/063.391/460.062 is seen near Ostrava Mariánské Hory on 15 May 2013 with train Os2933, the 10.04 Studénka–Mosty u Jablunkova. **Robert Pritchard**

CLASS 471+071+971   CITYELEFANT   3-CAR UNITS

These 3-car, IGBT asynchronous-motored double-deck "CityElefant" multiple units operate as Class 471 power cars, with Class 071 intermediate trailers and Class 971 driving trailers, formed 471+071+971. The units were assembled at Škoda's Plzeň works and the production period stretched to 16 years, as ČD ordered units in small batches when it could afford them. They were used to replace Class 451/452 EMUs around Praha and also to introduce new and lengthened services from the capital.

The majority of the fleet are based at Praha ONJ and are used on outer suburban work from Praha hlavní nádraží and Praha Masarykovo, running in pairs on busy trains (9-car formations are sometimes seen on empty stock moves). They regularly work to Kolín via Nymburk or Poříčany, Milovice, Benešov u Prahy and Beroun and they are also used on longer distance stopping trains – reaching destinations such as Ústí nad Labem and Letohrad. They are also used on "R" trains from Praha to Děčín at weekends. 12 units are based at Bohumín and used on commuter and regional trains on the Český Těšín–Havířov–Ostrava–Opava východ and Mosty u Jablunkova–Bohumín–Ostrava routes.

Seating is 2+2 in Second Class (with some longitudinal seating) and 2+1 in First Class, which is located on the upper level of the 471 car (also unusually featuring a top-deck toilet).

Four different liveries are carried, reflecting the long period of introduction and changing ČD policy on liveries. The first units were delivered in a mainly off-white livery, offset by a light blue stripe – this is still carried by 471.003/005–021. Most units – 471.001/002/004/022–059 (but not 028–030 which were delivered later, out of sequence) – carry the second version of this livery, which is mostly blue and red with light grey ends. The first version of the new ČD blue & white livery is carried by 471.028–030/061–075, whilst the later version of the ČD blue livery (featuring more dark blue than white) is carried by 471.076–083.

Two serious accidents have seen two vehicles written off and replacements delivered: Vehicle 471.003 was damaged in an accident near Praha Libeň in August 2011 and vehicle 971.005 was damaged in an accident near Ústí nad Labem in June 2010.

Class 471s can sometimes be found operating as mixed sets. Therefore it is recommended that the full formation of each set seen is always checked.

Škoda has also won export orders for the type, for ZSSK in Slovakia (Class 671) and also for Ukraine and Lithuania.

System: 3000 V DC.
Built: 1997–2013.   **Total No. Built:** 83 x 3-car sets.
Builders – Mechanical Parts: MSV/Škoda.
Builders – Electrical Parts: Škoda Ostrava.
Accommodation: 23/28(+8) 1TD 1T + –/134 2T + –/117 1TD 1T.
Traction Motors: 4 x 500 kW (670 hp) AC.   **Weight:** 62.7 + 46 + 46.5 tonnes.
Wheel Arrangement: Bo-Bo + 2-2 + 2-2.   **Maximum Speed:** 140 km/h.
Formation: DMCO–TSO–DTSO.   **Length over Couplers:** 26.40 + 26.40 + 26.40 m.
EVN: 94 54 1 471 0xx-c + 94 54 1 071 0xx-c + 94 54 1 971 0xx-c.
Advertising Livery: 471.011 – PID (Praha Integrated Transport) (blue, white & red).

471.001-8	071.001-2	971.001-3	PRO	471.018-2	071.018-6	971.018-7		PRO
471.002-6	071.002-0	971.002-1	PRO	471.019-0	071.019-4	971.019-5		PRO
471.003-4[II]	071.003-8	971.003-9	PRO	471.020-8	071.020-2	971.020-3		PRO
471.004-2	071.004-6	971.004-7	PRO	471.021-6	071.021-0	971.021-1		PRO
471.005-9	071.005-9	971.005-4[II]	PRO	471.022-4	071.022-8	971.022-9		PRO
471.006-7	071.006-1	971.006-2	PRO	471.023-2	071.023-6	971.023-7		PRO
471.007-5	071.007-9	971.007-0	PRO	471.024-0	071.024-4	971.024-5		OLB
471.008-3	071.008-7	971.008-8	PRO	471.025-7	071.025-1	971.025-2		OLB
471.009-1	071.009-5	971.009-6	PRO	471.026-5	071.026-9	971.026-0		PRO
471.010-9	071.010-3	971.010-4	PRO	471.027-3	071.027-7	971.027-8		PRO
471.011-7	071.011-1	971.011-2 **A**	PRO	471.028-1	071.028-5	971.028-6	**B**	PRO
471.012-5	071.012-9	971.012-0	PRO	471.029-9	071.029-3	971.029-4	**B**	PRO
471.013-3	071.013-7	971.013-8	PRO	471.030-7	071.030-1	971.030-2	**B**	PRO
471.014-1	071.014-5	971.014-6	PRO	471.031-5	071.031-9	971.031-0		PRO
471.015-8	071.015-2	971.015-3	PRO	471.032-3	071.032-7	971.032-8		PRO
471.016-6	071.016-0	971.016-1	PRO	471.033-1	071.033-5	971.033-6		PRO
471.017-4	071.017-8	971.017-9	PRO	471.034-9	071.034-3	971.034-4		PRO

471.035-6	071.035-0	971.035-1		OLB	471.060-4	071.060-8	971.060-9		PRO
471.036-4	071.036-8	971.036-9		PRO	471.061-2	071.061-6	971.061-7	B	PRO
471.037-2	071.037-6	971.037-7		PRO	471.062-0	071.062-4	971.062-5	B	PRO
471.038-0	071.038-4	971.038-5		PRO	471.063-8	071.063-2	971.063-3	B	PRO
471.039-8	071.039-2	971.039-3		PRO	471.064-6	071.064-0	971.064-1	B	PRO
471.040-6	071.040-0	971.040-1		PRO	471.065-3	071.065-7	971.065-8	B	PRO
471.041-4	071.041-8	971.041-9		PRO	471.066-1	071.066-5	971.066-6	B	PRO
471.042-2	071.042-6	971.042-7		PRO	471.067-9	071.067-3	971.067-4	B	PRO
471.043-0	071.043-4	971.043-5		PRO	471.068-7	071.068-1	971.068-2	B	PRO
471.044-8	071.044-2	971.044-3		PRO	471.069-5	071.069-9	971.069-0	B	PRO
471.045-5	071.045-9	971.045-0		PRO	471.070-3	071.070-7	971.070-8	B	PRO
471.046-3	071.046-7	971.046-8		PRO	471.071-1	071.071-5	971.071-6	B	PRO
471.047-1	071.047-5	971.047-6		PRO	471.072-9	071.072-3	971.072-4	B	PRO
471.048-9	071.048-3	971.048-4		PRO	471.073-7	071.073-1	971.073-2	B	PRO
471.049-7	071.049-1	971.049-2		PRO	471.074-5	071.074-9	971.074-0	B	PRO
471.050-5	071.050-9	971.050-0		PRO	471.075-2	071.075-6	971.075-7	B	PRO
471.051-3	071.051-7	971.051-8		PRO	471.076-0	071.076-4	971.076-5	B	PRO
471.052-1	071.052-5	971.052-6		PRO	471.077-8	071.077-2	971.077-3	B	PRO
471.053-9	071.053-3	971.053-4		PRO	471.078-6	071.078-0	971.078-1	B	PRO
471.054-7	071.054-1	971.054-2		OLB	471.079-4	071.079-8	971.079-9	B	PRO
471.055-4	071.055-8	971.055-9		OLB	471.080-2	071.080-6	971.080-7	B	OLB
471.056-2	071.056-6	971.056-7		OLB	471.081-0	071.081-4	971.081-5	B	OLB
471.057-0	071.057-4	971.057-5		OLB	471.082-8	071.082-2	971.082-3	B	OLB
471.058-8	071.058-2	971.058-3		OLB	471.083-6	071.083-0	971.083-1	B	OLB
471.059-6	071.059-0	971.059-1		PRO					

Names:

471.024	Opava		471.056	ČESKÝ TĚŠÍN
471.025	OSTRAVA		471.057	STUDÉNKA
471.035	Moravskoslezský kraj		471.058	MORAVSKOSLEZSKÝ KRAJ
471.054	BOHUMÍN		471.080	TŘINEC
471.055	HAVÍŘOV		471.081	KARVINA

▲ A pair of Class 471s in the first version of the new CD blue & white livery, 471.068+471.061, leave Praha Smíchov with train Os8850, the 17.19 Praha hl.n–Beroun on 10 May 2015.   **Robert Pritchard**

CLASS 560 — MOTOR COACHES

Two 1966 prototypes were the first of this type of EMU constructed (that later led to the successful Class 560/460 designs). The two prototypes were 3-car units, each formed Bo-Bo motor coach+intermediate trailer+driving trailer (Class SM488.0+N488.0+R488.0). This led to a production run in 1970–71 of a further 16 5-car units, with two motor coaches and three trailers each. More recently, following the disbanding of a couple of units and the conversion of ten Class 460 trailers from Class 063 to Class 060, Class 560s have been running as 6-cars. In more recent years the two original prototype motor coaches 560.001/002 have been formed in a standard 6-car unit. The driving trailers were abolished, one was converted to an intermediate trailer (060.054, now scrapped) and the other remains in use as a test car at VUZ Velim.

All ČD Class 560s are based at Brno Maloměřice and at the time of writing there were four diagrams for suburban services on the Vyškov na Moravě/Křenovice horní nádraží–Brno hlavní nádraží–Skalice nad Svitavou/Březová nad Svitavou route. There have been some withdrawals and disposals as a result of the introduction of new Class 650s. 560.015/019 were acquired from ZSSK in 2008 for spares. A number of Class 560s were also used by ZSSK in Slovakia, but all have now been stored.

Livery is light blue & grey unless stated.

System: 25 kV AC 50 Hz.
Built: * 1966; 1970–71.
Builder – Mechanical Parts: MSV Studénka.
Builder – Electrical Parts: Škoda.
Traction Motors: 4 x 210 kW (280 hp) DC.
Former ČSD Class: SM488.0.
Wheel Arrangement: Bo-Bo.
Formation: DMBSO.

Total No. Built: 34 motor cars†.

Accommodation: –/48 1T.
Weight: * 70 tonnes; 64 tonnes.
Length over Couplers: 24.50 m.
Maximum Speed: 110 km/h.
EVN: 94 54 1 560 0xx-c.

Non-Standard Liveries: 560.015/019 – ZSSK red & cream.
560.023/024 – Original red & cream. Carry original numbers SM488.0023 and SM488.0024.

560.001-0	*	CTC (S)	560.007-7	B	BRM	560.023-4	O	BRM
560.002-8	*	BRM (S)	560.008-5	B	BRM	560.024-2	O	BRM
560.003-6		BRM	560.015-0	O	BRM (S)	560.025-9		BRM
560.004-4		BRM	560.019-2	O	BRM (S)	560.026-7		BRM
560.005-1		BRM	560.021-8	B	BRM	560.027-5		BRM
560.006-9		BRM	560.022-6	B	BRM	560.028-3		BRM

CLASS 060 — INTERMEDIATE TRAILERS

Intermediate trailers used with Class 560 motor coaches, normally in 6-car sets. Vehicles 060.301–423 were converted from Class 063 trailers in 2002, retaining their last three numbers.

Built: 1970–71; † 1975–78.
Builder: MSV Studénka.
Former ČSD Class: N488.0.
Accommodation: –/80 2T.

Weight: 55.3 tonnes.
Length over Buffers: 24.50 m.
Maximum Speed: 110 km/h.
EVN: 94 54 1 060 xxx-c.

Non-Standard Livery: 060.032/033/034/035 – Original red & cream.

060.003-1		BRM	060.016-3	B	BRM	060.042-9		BRM
060.004-9		BRM	060.032-0	O	BRM	060.043-7		BRM
060.007-2		BRM	060.033-8	O	BRM	060.301-9		BRM
060.008-0		BRM	060.034-6	O	BRM	060.302-7		BRM
060.009-8	B	BRM	060.035-3	O	BRM	060.331-6	†	BRM
060.010-6	B	BRM	060.036-1		BRM	060.332-4	†	BRM
060.011-4	B	BRM	060.037-9		BRM	060.403-3	†	BRM
060.012-2	B	BRM	060.038-7		BRM	060.419-9	†	BRM
060.013-0	B	BRM	060.039-5		BRM	060.422-3	†	BRM (S)
060.014-8	B	BRM	060.040-3		BRM	060.423-1	†	BRM (S)
060.015-5	B	BRM	060.041-1		BRM			

Class 560 formations:

```
560.003+ 060.004+ 060.007+ 060.008+ 060.302+560.004
560.005+ 060.331+ 060.332+ 060.403+ 060.419+560.006
560.007+ 060.013+ 060.014+ 060.015+ 060.016+560.008
560.021+ 060.009+ 060.010+ 060.011+ 060.012+560.022
560.023+ 060.032+ 060.033+ 060.034+ 060.035+560.024
560.025+ 060.036+ 060.037+ 060.038+ 060.039+560.026
560.027+ 060.040+ 060.041+ 060.042+ 060.043+560.028
```

CLASS 640   REGIOPANTER   3-CAR UNITS

These dual-voltage 3-car RegioPanter sets are based at Olomouc and Brno. Those based at Olomouc have replaced locomotive-hauled trains or Class 460s on the Šumperk–Olomouc–Prostějov–Nezamyslice route. The Brno-based units work alongside Class 560 EMUs on suburban services around Brno on the Vyškov na Moravě/Křenovice horní nádraží–Brno hlavní nádraží–Skalice nad Svitavou/Březová nad Svitavou route (operating in pairs on busy trains).

Systems: 3000 V DC and 25 kV AC 50 Hz.
Built: 2012–14.   **Total No. Built:** 8 x 3-car sets.
Builder: Škoda, model 7Ev.
Accommodation: 9/44(+12) 1TD 2W + –/90(+4) 1T + –/78(+4).
Traction Motors: 6 x Škoda ML 3942 K/4 asynchronous of 340 kW (455 hp); total 2040 kW (2730 hp).
Weight: 54.5 + 45.5 + 52.2 tonnes.   **Length over Couplers:** 26.45 + 26.50 + 26.45 m.
Wheel Arrangement: Bo-2 + Bo-2 + 2-Bo.   **Maximum Speed:** 160 km/h.
Formation: DMCO–MSO–DMSO.
EVN: 94 54 1 640 0xx-c + 94 54 1 642 0xx-c + 94 54 1 641 0xx-c.

640.001-4	642.001-2	641.001-3	B	OLO
640.002-2	642.002-0	641.002-1	B	OLO
640.003-9	642.003-8	641.003-9	B	OLO
640.004-8	642.004-6	641.004-7	B	BRM
640.005-5	642.005-3	641.005-4	B	BRM
640.006-3	642.006-1	641.006-2	B	BRM
640.007-1	642.007-9	641.007-0	B	BRM
640.008-9	642.008-7	641.008-8	B	BRM

CLASS 650   REGIOPANTER   2-CAR UNITS

These dual-voltage 2-car RegioPanter sets are based at České Budějovice, Brno and Bohumín. Those based at České Budějovice mainly operate services on the Ceske Velenice–České Budějovice–Strakonice route, as well as some trains on Line 225 to Jindřichův Hradec/Počátky. Those based at Brno are used alongside the 3-car Class 640s on suburban services. The two Bohumín units entered traffic in late 2015 on the Bohumín–Mošnov Ostrava Airport route.

ČD and Škoda have a framework deal in place for the supply of a further nine sets, to be numbered 650.009–017, but it has not yet been confirmed when these will be delivered.

Systems: 3000 V DC and 25 kV AC 50 Hz.
Built: 2011–15.   **Total No. Built:** 8 x 2-car sets (+ 009–017 on order).
Builder: Škoda, model 7Ev.
Accommodation: 9/44(+12) 1TD 2W + –/78(+4).
Traction Motors: 4 x Škoda ML 3942 K/4 asynchronous of 340 kW (455 hp); total 1360 kW (1825 hp).
Weight: 54.3 + 48.5 tonnes.   **Length over Couplers:** 26.45 + 26.45 m.
Wheel Arrangement: Bo-2 + 2-Bo.   **Maximum Speed:** 160 km/h.
Formation: DMCO–DMSO.   **EVN:** 94 54 1 650 0xx-c + 94 54 1 651 0xx-c.

650.001-1	651.001-0	B	PLB		650.009-4	651.009-3
650.002-9	651.002-8	B	PLB		650.010-2	651.010-1
650.003-7	651.003-6	B	PLB		650.011-0	651.011-9
650.004-5	651.004-4	B	PLB		650.012-8	651.012-7
650.005-2	651.005-1	B	BRM		650.013-6	651.013-5
650.006-0	651.006-9	B	BRM		650.014-4	651.014-3
650.007-8	651.007-7	B	OLB		650.015-1	651.015-0
650.008-6	651.008-5	B	OLB		650.016-9	651.016-8
					650.017-7	651.017-6

▲ One of the three 3-car "RegioPanter" units based at Olomouc, 640.001, leaves Zábřeh na Moravě with train Os3715, the 07.30 Šumperk–Olomouc hl.n on 7 July 2014. **Robert Pritchard**

▼ CD's seven tilting Pendolinos are mostly used on the Praha–Ostrava–Bohumín main line. On 8 September 2012 680.006 passes Žichlínek with train SC30, the 14.03 Žilina–Praha hl.n. **Robert Pritchard**

CLASS 660.0   INTERPANTER   3-CAR UNITS

Express version of the Skoda "RegioPanter" EMU configured for long distance operation, with one set of double doors per vehicle.

The first units entered traffic in late 2015 on the Brno–Břeclav–Hulín–Olomouc route, the 3-car sets usually operating in pairs.

System: 3000 V DC and 25 kV AC 50 Hz.
Built: 2015–16.   **Total No. Built:** 4 x 3-car sets.
Builder: Škoda, model 10Ev.
Accommodation: –/58(+10) 1TD 2W + 17/58 1T + 8/46(+3).
Traction Motors: 6 x Škoda asynchronous of 340 kW (455 hp); total 2040 kW (2730 hp).
Weight: 55.3 + 46.6 + 53.0 tonnes.
Length over Couplers: 26.45 + 26.50 m + 26.45 m.
Wheel Arrangement: Bo-2 + Bo-2 + 2-Bo.   **Maximum Speed:** 160 km/h.
Formation: DMSO–MCO–DMCO.
EVN: 94 54 1 660 0xx-c + 94 54 1 662 0xx-c + 94 54 1 661 0xx-c.

660.001-9	662.001-7	661.001-8	B	BRM
660.002-7	662.002-5	661.002-6	B	BRM
660.003-5	662.003-3	661.003-4	B	BRM
660.004-3	662.004-1	661.004-2	B	BRM

CLASS 660.1   INTERPANTER   5-CAR UNITS

Express version of the Skoda "RegioPanter" EMU configured for long distance operation, with one set of double doors per vehicle. Formed with four motor cars either side of a centre trailer car.

The 5-car units were introduced in November 2015, initially working trains on the Brno–Břeclav–Hulín–Olomouc route (replacing locomotive-hauled push-pull sets). In early 2016 they were introduced onto the Brno–Česká Třebová–Praha route, where they are operating the "R" semi-fast trains.

System: 3000 V DC and 25 kV AC 50 Hz.
Built: 2015–16.   **Total No. Built:** 10 x 5-car sets.
Builder: Škoda, model 10Ev.
Accommodation: –/58(+10) 1TD 2W + 17/58 1T + –/75 + 17/58 1T + 8/46(+3).
Traction Motors: 8 x Škoda asynchronous of 340 kW (455 hp); total 2720 kW (3640 hp).
Weight: 55.3 + 46.6 + 41.3 + 46.5 + 53.0 tonnes.
Length over Couplers: 26.45 + 26.50 + 26.50 + 26.50 + 26.45 m.
Wheel Arrangement: Bo-2 + Bo-2 + 2-2 + Bo-2 + 2-Bo.
Maximum Speed: 160 km/h.
Formation: DMSO–MCO–TSO–MCO–DMCO.
EVN: 94 54 1 660 1xx-c + 94 54 1 662 1xx-c + 94 54 1 064 1xx-c + 94 54 1 662 2xx-c + 94 54 1 661 1xx-c.

660.101-7	662.101-5	064.101-9	662.201-3	661.101-6	B	BRM
660.102-5	662.102-3	064.102-7	662.202-1	661.102-4	B	BRM
660.103-3	662.103-1	064.103-5	662.203-9	661.103-2	B	BRM
660.104-1	662.104-9	064.104-3	662.204-7	661.104-0	B	BRM
660.105-8	662.105-6	064.105-0	662.205-4	661.105-7	B	BRM
660.106-6	662.106-4	064.106-8	662.206-2	661.106-5	B	BRM
660.107-4	662.107-2	064.107-6	662.207-0	661.107-3	B	BRM
660.108-2	662.108-0	064.108-4	662.208-8	661.108-1	B	BRM
660.109-0	662.109-8	064.109-2	662.209-6	661.109-9	B	BRM
660.110-8	662.110-6	064.110-0	662.210-4	661.110-7	B	BRM

CLASS 680   PENDOLINO   7-CAR HIGH SPEED UNITS

These 7-car tri-voltage 230 km/h tilting units are formed of alternate motors and trailers in sequence as Class 681+081+683+084+684+082+682 (no vehicles are actually numbered as Class 680). Effectively each train is two sets of three cars which are linked to form two independent units, with a centre trailer car in the middle. The units may not run in other formations as equipment essential to the whole train is distributed between cars. Class 681/682 are driving motor cars carrying DC pantographs, while Class 683/684 are intermediate motor cars. AC pantographs and transformers are on the Class 081/082 trailers. Although they have a top speed of 230 km/h, operation has so far been limited by infrastructure and signalling to 160 km/h.

From conception, Class 680 took more than 12 years to enter service. Originally a ČKD/Škoda project, then Siemens, then finally Alstom who hived it out to its subsidiary, the former Fiat, Ferroviaria – the new trains would be based on the Italian ETR 470 "Cisalpino" units and built at Savigliano. Class 680, branded "Pendolino", finally obtained approval for full operation in 2006 although units had been used on route specific services from the end of 2005.

The class is now mainly used on the premium SuperCity (SC) services between Praha and Ostrava/Bohumín. However in recent years their sphere of operation has been expanded to include a couple of trains starting back from west Bohemia: one train starts back from Cheb and another from Františkovy Lázně, running via Plzeň to Praha. The most significant service development was the extension of one of the trains to Košice in east Slovakia in 2014: A Pendolino is used on the 06.43 Praha–Košice, returning at 14.47.

Apart from when operating west of Plzeň, a supplement is payable for travelling in a SC train, and a reservation must be made. Internally the trains are laid out to a very high standard, with all seating arranged in a 2+1 layout: First and Second Class saloons are almost identical apart from the fact that red upholstery is used in First Class, compared to blue in Second.

On 22 July 2015 680.003 was involved in a fatal crash at Studénka when it hit a lorry on a level crossing. Three passengers were killed in the worst accident in the country since the previous crash at almost the same location in 2008 (see Classes 150/151 details). The unit was badly damaged, but repairs have been sanctioned and should be complete by late 2017. A new aluminium bodyshell is to be constructed to replace the damaged vehicle 682.003. As six Class 680s are diagrammed daily, while 680.003 is out of traffic the fleet is stretched. A locomotive-hauled set can substitute (usually on the Košice turn) if not enough Class 680 are available.

Livery is a unique silver and light blue, with black window surrounds.

System: 3000 V DC, 25 kV AC 50 Hz, 15 kV AC 16.7 Hz.
Built: 2002–05.
Total No. Built: 7 x 7-car sets.
Builder – Mechanical Parts: Alstom Ferroviaria, Savigliano, Italy.
Builder – Electrical Parts: Alstom.
Accommodation: 105/226 per unit (see table).
Traction Motors: 8 x 500 kW (670 hp) AC per unit.
Weight: 384 tonnes per unit (see table).
Length over Couplers: 184.7 m per unit (see table).
Maximum Speed: 230 km/h.
Wheel Arrangement: 1-A-A-1 + 2-2 + 1-A-A-1 + 2-2 + 1-A-A-1 + 2-2 + 1-A-A-1.

Vehicle EVN	Vehicle type	Seating	tonnes	Length
93 54 6 681 00x-c	Driving Motor First	53/– 1T	57.2	27.60 m
93 54 6 081 00x-c	Trailer Pantograph First	52/– 2T	57.1	25.90 m
93 54 6 683 00x-c	Non Driving Motor Buffet Standard	–/24	55.6	25.90 m
93 54 6 084 00x-c	Trailer Standard	–/44 1TD 2W	44.1	25.90 m
93 54 6 684 00x-c	Non Driving Motor Standard	–/53 2T	56.1	25.90 m
93 54 6 082 00x-c	Trailer Pantograph Standard	–/52 2T	57.2	25.90 m
93 54 6 682 00x-c	Driving Motor Standard	–/53 1T	57.2	27.60 m

681.001-4	081.001-0	683.001-2	084.001-7	684.001-1	082.001-9	682.001-3	PRO
681.002-2	081.002-8	683.002-0	084.002-5	684.002-9	082.002-7	682.002-1	PRO
681.003-0	081.003-6	683.003-8	084.003-3	684.003-7	082.003-5	682.003-9	PRO (S)
681.004-8	081.004-4	683.004-6	084.004-1	684.004-5	082.004-3	682.004-7	PRO
681.005-5	081.005-1	683.005-3	084.005-8	684.005-2	082.005-0	682.005-4	PRO
681.006-3	081.006-9	683.006-1	084.006-6	684.006-0	082.006-8	682.006-2	PRO
681.007-1	081.007-7	683.007-9	084.007-4	684.007-8	082.007-6	682.007-0	PRO

1.3. ČD & ČD CARGO DIESEL LOCOMOTIVES

CLASS 703 B

Class 703 is a four-wheel diesel-hydraulic shunter with cardan shaft transmission. The first locomotive appeared as a prototype in 1969. They were the final development of mechanical transmission Classes 700/701/702, which can today be found in preservation and extensively with industrial and departmental users. Many Class 700–703 underframes have been reused as platforms for "new" industrial types as well as ČD Class 799 and ŽSR Class 199 depot shunting tractors. The remaining Class 703s are mainly used for shunting within depots.

Built: 1977–79.
Former ČSD Class: T212.1.
Builder: TSM.
Engine: Tatra 930-54.
Power: 169 kW (225 hp).
Transmission: Hydraulic.
Maximum Tractive Effort: 83 kN.

Total No. Built: 52 (Class 703.0).
Wheel Diameter: 1000 mm.
Train Heating Equipment: None.
Weight: 24 tonnes.
Length over Buffers: 7.22 m.
Maximum Speed: 40 km/h.
EVN: 98 54 4 703 0xx-c.

703.029-9		CTC	703.037-2	**B**	*F*	FSU	703.045-5		CTC (S)
703.031-5		PLL	703.042-2			PRD	703.046-3	*F*	FSU

CLASS 704 Bo

These are small four-wheel diesel electrics known as "male lego" (small lego bricks) from their very angular construction. Originally they had occasional passenger work, but today they are used for station pilot, shunting and light trip freight work. Also found with industrial users and private operators as model T238.0, numbered as Class 704.4/704.5.

Livery for Classes 704 and 708 is dark blue with red cabs and front ends unless stated.

Built: *1988; 1992.
Former ČSD Class: Not applicable.
Builder: ČKD, model T234.0.
Engine: M1-655 (* Liaz M2-650, † Liaz M 1.2C).
Power: 250 kW (335 hp) (* 220 kW (295 hp)).
Transmission: Electric.
Maximum Tractive Effort: 103 kN.

Total No. Built: 20 (plus 57 for industry).
Wheel Diameter: 1000 mm.
Train Heating Equipment: None.
Weight: 29 tonnes (* 28 tonnes).
Length over Buffers: 7.50 m (* 7.30 m).
Maximum Speed: 65 km/h (* 60 km/h).
EVN: 98 54 4 704 0xx-c.

704.001-7		*	BRM	704.008-2		†	PRD	704.015-7		OLS
704.002-5	**B**	*	CTH	704.009-0	**B**		PRG	704.016-5		PLB
704.003-3	*F*	†	FSC	704.010-8	**B**		OLB	704.017-3	*F*	FSO
704.004-1	**B**		CTH	704.011-6	*F*	†	FSC	704.018-1		PRL
704.005-8	**B**		PRD	704.012-4	**B**		PRG	704.019-9	**B** *F*	FSC
704.006-6	*F*	†	FSC	704.013-2			PLT	704.020-7		BRM
704.007-4			BRO	704.014-0			PLZ			

CLASS 708 Bo

Class 708 is another four-wheel diesel-electric but longer, heavier and faster than Class 704, and fitted with a 470 kW electric dynamic brake. Class 708s are known as "lego", fitting between Class 704s "male" (small) and Class 714s "velke" (big) "lego". All are now operated by ČD Cargo; they are used for light trip freight work or shunting. 708.001–003 have been rebuilt as 708.701–703 with new Caterpillar engines.

Built: 1995–97.
Former ČSD Class: Not applicable.
Builder: ČKD, model T239.0.
Engine: Liaz M1.2C M640D.
Power: 300 kW (400 hp).
Transmission: Electric.
Maximum Tractive Effort: 110 kN.

Total No. Built: 13 (plus 1 for industry).
Wheel Diameter: 1000 mm.
Train Heating Equipment: None.
Weight: 34 tonnes.
Length over Buffers: 9.45 m.
Maximum Speed: 80 km/h.
EVN: 92 54 2 708 xxx-c.

708.004-7	F	FSC	708.008-8	F	FSU	708.011-2	F	FSC
708.005-4	F	FSC	708.009-6	F	FSC	708.012-0	F	FSU
708.006-2	F	FSC	708.010-4	F	FSU	708.013-8	F	FSC
708.007-0	F	FSC						

Class 708.7. Rebuilt 2010–12 by CZ LOKO and DPOV. Details as above except:

Engine: CAT C13 of 300 kW (400 hp).

| 708.701-8 | (708.001) | **B** | F | FSC | 708.703-4 | (708.003) | **B** | F | FSC |
| 708.702-6 | (708.002) | **B** | F | FSC | | | | | |

CLASS 709   Bo

These shunters were manufactured by CZ LOKO for ČD Cargo and marketed as "Effishunter". A parallel version for industry and export was also built and numbered in the Class 709.7 series.

Built: 2006–07.
Former ČSD Class: Not applicable.
Builder: CMKS.
Engine: Caterpillar C15.
Power: 403 kW (540 hp).
Transmission: Electric.
Maximum Tractive Effort: 110 kN.

Total No. Built: 2.
Wheel Diameter: 1000 mm.
Train Heating Equipment: None.
Weight: 36 tonnes.
Length over Buffers: 9.45 m.
Maximum Speed: 80 km/h.
EVN: 92 54 2 709 00x-c.

709.001-2 **B** F   FSC | 709.002-0 **B** F   FSC

CLASS 714   Bo-Bo

Class 714 is a drastic rebuild of Class 735, mainly designed for light passenger and station pilot work. They are powered by two automotive diesel engines, similar to those fitted to Class 704. Little remains of the original locomotive apart from the underframe and bogies. There were two prototypes (714.001/002 – 714.002 is now converted to natural gas operation as 714.811 with private operator Vítkovice Doprava) and these kept the original angled cabs; others have new square cabs. 714.001/002 were briefly numbered 714.117/170; these and 714.003/004 were slightly less powerful than the rest of the fleet.

There are two axle load versions; Class 714.0 is 16 tonnes and Class 714.2 is 15 tonnes. All have door controls for operation with Class 021 trailers. A further 18 (Class 714.3) were planned to be converted but the order was cancelled; their donor locomotives were set aside but later scrapped.

Passenger work for Class 714 has declined in recent years and many diagrams have been replaced by Class 814 DMUs. At the time of writing passenger diagrams include peak-hour workings from Praha Masarykovo to Kladno/Rakovník and Praha Vršovice–Jílové u Prahy–Čerčany and also certain trains between Břeclav and Znojmo (on Line 246, recently reduced to just one diagram) and Opava and Hlučín, hauling Class 021 or 010 DMU trailers. Other locomotives are used for shunting and as station or depot pilots. Those locomotives shown as allocated to Praha Vršovice may also be found at Praha ONJ or Praha Libeň depots.

Livery is dark blue with red cabs and front ends unless stated.

Built: * 1993; 1994–97.
Former ČSD Class: Not applicable.
Builder: ČKD.
Engine: Two Liaz M1.2C.
Power: 2 x 300 kW (805 hp).
Transmission: Electric.
Maximum Tractive Effort: 190 kN.
Non-Standard Livery: 714.801: dark blue & green.

Total No. Built: 60.
Wheel Diameter: 1000 mm.
Train Heating Equipment: None.
Weight: 64 or 60 tonnes.
Length over Buffers: 14.24 m.
Maximum Speed: 80 km/h.
EVN: 92 54 2 714 xxx-c.

▲ ČD depot pilot 704.012 at Praha Vršovice depot on 12 May 2013.   **Robert Pritchard**

▼ Class 714s can be found on peak-hour trains from Praha Masarykovo along Line 120. On 9 May 2014 714.218 leaves Praha-Veleslavín with train Sp1892, the 17.17 Praha Masarykovo–Kladno with Btx763 (ex-Class 021) trailers 28-29 054, 28 29-046 and 28 29-013.   **Robert Pritchard**

Class 714. Prototype 714.001 (now classed as preserved, see Preserved Locomotives section) and 714.004 were fitted with less powerful engines than the rest of the fleet. Details as above except:

Engine: Two Liaz M2.
Power: 2 x 250 kW (670 hp).
Maximum Tractive Effort: 154 kN.

Weight: 64 tonnes.
Maximum Speed: 90 km/h.

714.004-9   (735.169)   *   BRM

Class 714.0. Weight 64 tonnes.

714.006-4	(735.232)		BRM	714.019-7	(735.096)	PRG
714.007-2	(735.281)		OLV	714.020-5	(735.075)	PRG
714.008-0	(735.099)		OLB	714.021-3	(735.114)	PLR
714.009-8	(735.037)		PRG	714.022-1	(735.171)	PRG
714.011-4	(735.290)		PRG	714.023-9	(735.128) **B**	PRG
714.012-2	(735.133)		PRG	714.024-7	(735.259)	OLO
714.013-0	(735.106)		PRD	714.025-4	(735.138)	OLB
714.014-8	(735.048)		OLO	714.026-2	(735.104)	OLB
714.015-5	(735.274) **B**	OLO	714.027-0	(735.033)	PRD
714.016-3	(735.097)		OLP	714.028-8	(735.206)	BRM
714.017-1	(735.115)		PRG (S)	714.029-6	(735.272)	OLO
714.018-9	(735.090) **B**	OLB			

Class 714.2. Weight 60 tonnes.

714.201-1	(735.199) **B**	CTH	714.217-7	(735.214)		CTL
714.202-9	(735.164) **B**	PLR	714.218-5	(735.131)		PLR
714.203-7	(735.279)		OLP	714.219-3	(735.215) **B**	CTH
714.204-5	(735.039)		BRM	714.220-1	(735.221)		PLZ
714.205-2	(735.085) **B**	CTH	714.221-9	(735.257)		PLZ
714.206-0	(735.070)		PLR	714.222-7	(735.082) **B**	CTP
714.207-8	(735.139)		OLO	714.223-5	(735.187)		BRM
714.208-6	(735.294)		CTL	714.224-3	(735.102)		PLZ
714.209-4	(735.297)		OLB	714.225-0	(735.068)		PLC
714.210-2	(735.179) **B**	BRZ	714.226-8	(735.126)		BRZ
714.211-0	(735.212) **B**	BRZ	714.227-6	(735.027)		PLR
714.212-8	(735.250) **B**	PLC	714.228-4	(735.205)		PLR
714.213-6	(735.074)		CTP (S)	714.229-2	(735.144)		PLB
714.214-4	(735.046)		PLR	714.230-0	(735.213)		BRZ
714.215-1	(735.010)		PLR	714.231-8	(735.158)		PLR
714.216-9	(735.132)		PLR			

Class 714.8. Converted 2011 to operate on Compressed Natural Gas (CNG) as part of joint project between Vítkovice Doprava and ČD.

The fuel tank has been replaced by 360 mm diameter gas cylinders with a total capacity of 3430 litres, or 479 kg of CNG pressurised at 200 bar, which gives a range of 510 km without refuelling.

At the time of writing the locomotive is based at Opava for working the weekday loco-hauled diagram between Opava and Hlučín on a trial basis. Details as above except:

Engine: Two Tedom TG 250 AV of 260 kW (350 hp).
Power: 2 x 260 kW (700 hp).
Weight: 64 tonnes.

714.801-8   (735.167, 714.010)   **0**   OLP

CLASS 730 Bo-Bo

Class 730 were built as mixed-traffic and heavy shunting locomotives, one of their main duties being hump shunting in large marshalling yards. 730.002 is one of two prototypes built for ČSD in 1978; a further prototype was built for industrial use (730.501). Class 730s are similar in performance to the later Class 731s but have angled cabs and bonnet tops. 17 were delivered to ČSD capital stock, and then more for departmental service and military use (numbered in the 730.6xx series). 730.018/019 were previously departmental 730.620 and 730.607 respectively. All except two locomotives in this class have been stored at the time of writing.

Livery for Classes 730, 731 and 742 is ČSD red & cream unless stated.

Built: *1978; 1985–88.
Former ČSD Class: T457.0.
Builder: ČKD, model T457.0.
Engine: ČKD K6S230DR.
Power: 600 kW (805 hp).
Transmission: Electric.
Maximum Tractive Effort: 205 kN.
Non-Standard Liveries: 730.002: Yellow.
730.018: Green & yellow.

Total No. Built: 17 (plus 42 for industry).
Wheel Diameter: 1000 mm.
Train Heating Equipment: None.
Weight: 70 tonnes (* 69 tonnes).
Length over Buffers: 14.00 m.
Maximum Speed: 80 km/h.
EVN: 92 54 2 730 0xx-c.

730.002-3	**0**	*F*	*	Břeclav (S)	730.008-0	*F*	Břeclav (S)	730.014-8	*F*	FSU (S)
730.003-1		*F*		FSU (S)	730.009-8	*F*	Břeclav (S)	730.015-5 **B**	*F*	FSU
730.004-9		*F*		FSU (S)	730.010-6	*F*	Břeclav (S)	730.016-3 **B**	*F*	FSU
730.005-6		*F*		Břeclav (S)	730.011-4	*F*	Břeclav (S)	730.017-1	*F*	Břeclav (S)
730.006-4		*F*		Břeclav (S)	730.012-2	*F*	Břeclav (S)	730.018-9 **0**	*F*	Břeclav (S)
730.007-2		*F*		FSU (S)	730.013-0	*F*	FSU (S)	730.019-7	*F*	Břeclav (S)

CLASS 731 Bo-Bo

Class 731 looks very similar to Class 730. It was developed as a replacement for Classes 720/721 and known as "Favorit" after the contemporary Škoda car. 731.001 was noteworthy as being the 15000th locomotive built by ČKD, and still carries the large numbers "15000" on its bodyside. Class 731 was the last new main line diesel locomotive built for ČSD before its demise. They are fitted with AC/DC transmission and electric dynamic braking.

Industrial equivalents are numbered in the 729.5xx and 729.6xx series', ballasted to a weight of 80 and 84 tonnes for the steel industry (see Private Freight Operators section).

Class 731s are all owned by ČD Cargo and based at either Ostrava and Ústí nad Labem. They can be found on general freight traffic, operating singly and in pairs, and for yard or hump shunting.

Built: 1988–92.
Former ČSD Class: T457.1.
Builder: ČKD, model T457.1.
Engine: ČKD K6S230DR.
Power: 600 kW (805 hp), *800 kW (1070 hp).
Transmission: Electric.
Maximum Tractive Effort: 205 kN.
Non-Standard Livery: 731.031: lilac & cream.

Total No. Built: 62†.
Wheel Diameter: 1000 mm.
Train Heating Equipment: None.
Weight: 68 tonnes.
Length over Buffers: 15.28 m.
Maximum Speed: 80 km/h.
EVN: 92 54 2 731 0xx-c.

731.001-4	**B**	*F*	FSO	731.015-4		*F*	FSO	731.029-5		*F*	FSO
731.002-2		*F*	FSO	731.016-2		*F*	FSO	731.030-3		*F*	FSO
731.003-0	**B**	*F*	FSO	731.017-0	**B**	*F*	FSU	731.031-1 **0**	*F*	* FSU
731.004-8		*F*	FSO	731.018-8		*F*	FSU	731.032-9		*F*	FSU
731.005-5		*F*	FSU	731.019-6		*F*	FSO	731.039-4		*F*	FSO
731.006-3		*F*	FSU	731.020-4		*F*	FSO	731.040-2		*F*	FSO
731.007-1		*F*	FSU	731.021-2		*F*	FSO	731.041-0		*F*	FSU
731.008-9		*F*	FSO	731.022-0		*F*	FSO	731.042-8 **B**	*F*	FSO
731.009-7		*F*	FSO	731.023-8	**B**	*F*	FSO	731.043-6		*F*	FSO
731.010-5		*F*	FSU	731.024-6		*F*	FSO	731.044-4		*F*	FSO
731.011-3		*F*	FSU	731.025-3		*F*	FSO	731.045-1		*F*	FSO
731.012-1		*F*	FSU	731.026-1		*F*	FSO	731.046-9		*F*	FSO
731.013-9	**B**	*F*	FSU	731.027-9	**B**	*F*	FSO	731.047-7		*F*	FSO
731.014-7		*F*	FSO	731.028-7		*F*	FSU	731.048-5		*F*	FSO

731.049-3	F	FSO	731.057-6	F	FSU	731.060-0	F		FSO
731.050-1	F	FSO	731.058-4	F	FSU	731.061-8	F		FSO
731.056-8	F	FSU	731.059-2	F	FSO	731.062-6	B	F *	FSO

CLASS 742   Bo-Bo

Class 742 was built as a light freight equivalent of Class 740 (Class 740 was heavier, ballasted, lower geared and with a higher tractive effort). Collectively Class 740s (none of which are still used by ČD or ČD Cargo) and Class 742s are the most numerous main line diesels in the country, 953 examples having been built.

Class 742 still forms an important part of the Czech scene, with more than half of the original build still active, although in recent years many ČD locomotives have been sold to private operators or exported, to the extent that there are fewer than 20 serviceable locomotives still operated by ČD. While at the time of writing there is only one booked passenger diagram for the class (on Line 142 between Karlovy Vary and Johanngeorgenstadt) they are still used as reserve traction for out of service DMU motor coaches (mainly Classes 842 and 843) and also for additional or special ad-hoc trains. ČD locomotives are also used for depot shunting and station pilot duties. Unlike ČD Cargo, ČD hasn't repainted any of its 742s into the new blue livery.

ČD Cargo freight duties range from station pilot and pick-up trips (many branch lines still have pick-up freights) to heavy block train work in pairs, including some work into Germany and Poland. Multiple working connections are only on the short nose, hence pairs are usually coupled in this way. Some ČD Cargo machines have been rebuilt to give better visibility from the cabs.

The history of the Czech fleet is complex, with departmental 742.6xxs, some ex-742.6xxs in the main 742.000 series, and some 742.000s permanently assigned to departmental work or now in use with private operators having been sold by ČD or ČD Cargo.

The 742s were built in nine sub-series with some minor technical differences: Series I 742.001–060, Series II 742.061–120, Series III 742.121–180, Series IV 742.181–228, Series V 742.229–288, Series VI 742.289–361, Series VII 742.362–410, Series VIII 742.411–425 and Series IX 742.426–453. 742.501–541 were built for industrial users.

Built: 1977–86.
Former ČSD Class: T466.2.
Builder: ČKD, model T466.2.
Engine: ČKD K6S230DR.
Power: 883 kW (1185 hp).
Transmission: Electric.
Maximum Tractive Effort: 193 kN.
Non-Standard Liveries: 742.129/156/254/452: Green & yellow.
         742.007/026/064/141: Blue & white.
         742.454: Blue & yellow.

Total No. Built: 453 (plus 41 for industry)†.
Wheel Diameter: 1000 mm.
Train Heating Equipment: None.
Weight: 64 tonnes.
Length over Buffers: 13.60 m.
Maximum Speed: 90 km/h.
EVN: 92 54 2 742 xxx-c.

*   Rebuilt ČD Cargo locomotives with a reduced height front end (at the cab end), to aid visibility.

742.201 carries its original number T466.2201.

742.370 is ex-742.503 (a frame swap).

742.007-8	0	F		FSO	742.043-3				CTC (S)	742.069-8	B	F		FSC
742.008-6		F		FSU	742.044-1				BRM	742.070-6				PRG
742.009-4		F		Břeclav (S)	742.045-8				CTC (S)	742.073-0	B	F		FSU
742.013-6		F		FSU	742.046-6				CTC (S)	742.074-8				CTC (S)
742.015-1		F		FSU (S)	742.048-2	B	F	*	FSO	742.075-5	B	F		FSO
742.016-9		F		FSU (S)	742.049-0		F		Břeclav (S)	742.076-3				CTC (S)
742.018-5		F		FSU	742.058-1		F		FSO	742.077-1	B	F	*	FSO
742.025-0	B	F		FSO	742.059-9				CTC (S)	742.079-7		F		FSO
742.026-8	0	F		Břeclav (S)	742.061-5		F		FSU (S)	742.080-5		F		FSO
742.029-2	B	F		FSO	742.062-3		F		FSO	742.081-3		F		FSU
742.030-0		F		FSO	742.063-1		F		FSU (S)	742.082-1		F		FSO
742.031-8		F		FSU (S)	742.064-9	0	F		Břeclav (S)	742.083-9	B	F		FSC
742.032-6		F		FSU (S)	742.065-6	B	F	*	FSO	742.084-7	B	F	*	FSO
742.033-4	B	F		FSC	742.066-4				CTC (S)	742.085-4		F		FSO
742.034-2		F		FSC	742.067-2		F		FSC (S)	742.086-2				PRG
742.035-9				CTC (S)	742.068-0	B	F		FSC	742.087-0				CTC (S)

Number					Code
742.088-8			F		FSU (S)
742.090-4	B		F	*	FSO
742.091-2	B		F	*	FSO
742.092-0	B		F		FSO
742.093-8	B		F		FSO
742.094-6	B		F		FSU
742.095-3			F		FSO
742.096-1			F		FSO
742.098-7			F		FSC (S)
742.099-5			F		FSU (S)
742.100-1					CTC (S)
742.101-9			F		FSU
742.102-7			F		FSO
742.104-3			F		FSO
742.105-0			F		FSU
742.106-8			F		FSC
742.107-6			F		FSO
742.108-4			F		FSO
742.109-2	B		F		FSU
742.110-0			F		FSO (S)
742.111-8	B		F	*	FSC
742.113-4					CTP
742.114-2			F		FSO
742.115-9					CTC (S)
742.116-7			F		FSU
742.117-5			F		FSO
742.126-6			F		FSC
742.129-0		0	F		FSU
742.130-8			F		FSU
742.133-2	B		F	*	FSU
742.134-0			F		FSO
742.135-7			F		FSU
742.136-5			F		FSC
742.137-3	B		F	*	FSC
742.138-1			F		FSU (S)
742.139-9			F		FSO
742.140-7			F		FSU
742.141-5		0	F		FSO
742.142-3			F		FSO
742.143-1			F		Břeclav (S)
742.144-9			F		FSO
742.146-4	B		F	*	FSO
742.147-2	B		F		FSO
742.148-0	B		F		FSO
742.149-8					CTC (S)
742.150-6			F		FSC
742.151-4			F		FSU
742.153-0			F		FSC
742.154-8			F		FSC (S)
742.156-3		0	F		FSO
742.157-1			F		FSU
742.158-9			F		FSO
742.160-5			F		FSO (S)
742.165-4					PLT
742.166-2	B		F		FSU
742.167-0					PLB
742.169-6	B		F		FSU
742.170-4			F		FSU
742.171-2	B		F		FSC
742.172-0	B		F		FSC
742.173-8	B		F		FSU
742.174-6	B		F		FSO
742.175-3	B		F		FSO
742.176-1			F		FSO
742.178-7			F		FSO
742.179-5	B		F		FSO
742.180-3			F		FSO
742.184-5			F		FSC
742.185-2			F		FSO
742.186-0			F		FSO
742.187-8			F		FSU
742.188-6	B		F		FSC
742.189-4	B		F	*	FSO
742.190-2			F		FSU
742.191-0	B		F		FSO
742.192-8	B		F		FSU
742.194-4			F		FSU
742.196-9					CTC
742.198-5			F		FSU (S)
742.199-3			F		FSU (S)
742.200-9			F		FSU
742.201-7		+			PLZ
742.202-5			F		FSO
742.203-3			F		Břeclav (S)
742.204-1	B		F		FSC
742.206-6			F		FSC
742.208-2			F		FSO
742.209-0	B		F		FSO
742.210-8					CTT
742.211-6			F		FSC (S)
742.212-4			F		FSC (S)
742.214-0	B		F	*	FSO
742.215-7	B		F		FSU
742.216-5			F		FSU
742.217-3			F		FSU
742.219-9			F		FSC
742.220-7			F		FSO (S)
742.224-9			F		FSO
742.225-6			F		FSU
742.226-4			F		FSO
742.229-8			F		FSC (S)
742.230-6	B		F	*	FSO
742.231-4			F		FSC (S)
742.236-3			F		FSU
742.238-9	B		F		FSC
742.239-7			F		FSU
742.241-3			F		Hradec Kr (S)
742.242-1			F		FSU
742.243-9	B		F	*	FSC
742.247-0			F		Břeclav (S)
742.248-8			F		FSC
742.250-4			F		Břeclav (S)
742.251-2			F		Břeclav (S)
742.252-0			F		FSO
742.253-8			F		FSU
742.254-6		0	F		FSC
742.261-1			F		FSU
742.262-9	B		F	*	FSO
742.263-7			F		FSO
742.264-5					PLZ
742.265-2			F		FSC
742.270-2	B		F	*	FSU
742.271-0			F		FSO
742.272-8			F		FSO
742.273-6	B		F		FSO
742.274-4	B		F	*	FSO
742.279-3					OLV
742.280-1					OLV
742.281-9			F		FSC
742.282-7			F		FSC
742.283-5			F		FSC
742.284-3			F		FSC
742.285-0			F		FSU
742.289-2	B		F		FSC
742.291-8			F		FSU
742.292-6			F		FSO
742.293-4			F		FSO
742.294-2			F		FSO
742.295-9	B		F		FSO
742.300-7	B		F		FSC
742.301-5			F		FSC (S)
742.302-3			F		FSC (S)
742.303-1			F		FSO
742.304-9			F		FSO (S)
742.305-6			F		FSU
742.307-2			F		FSU (S)
742.308-0	B		F	*	FSO
742.309-8			F		FSO
742.314-8	B		F		FSO
742.316-3	B		F	*	FSO
742.317-1			F		FSU
742.318-9					CTP (S)
742.319-7			F		FSC (S)
742.320-5					BRV
742.322-1			F		FSO
742.323-9			F		FSC
742.328-8	B		F		FSO
742.329-6	B		F	*	FSC
742.331-2			F		FSO
742.332-0			F		FSU
742.333-8			F		FSU
742.334-6			F		FSO
742.336-1			F		FSO
742.341-1			F		Břeclav (S)
742.343-7					PLC
742.344-5			F		FSU
742.345-2			F		FSO
742.346-0			F		FSO
742.347-8			F		FSC
742.349-4	B		F		FSU
742.350-2			F		FSU
742.353-6			F		FSO
742.354-4			F		FSC (S)
742.355-1			F		FSU (S)
742.357-7			F		FSU
742.358-5			F		FSU
742.362-7	B		F		FSC
742.365-0			F		FSU (S)
742.366-8					OLB
742.367-6					OLV
742.369-2	B		F		FSC
742.370-0			F		FSC
742.371-8			F		FSC (S)
742.372-6			F		FSU
742.377-5			F		FSU
742.378-3			F		FSC (S)
742.379-1			F		FSO
742.380-9			F		FSU
742.381-7	B		F		FSC
742.382-5			F		FSC
742.383-3					PRG
742.385-8	B		F		FSC

742.390-8		*F*	FSO	742.420-3		*F*	FSC	742.437-7	*F*	FSC
742.391-6	**B**	*F*	* FSO	742.421-1		*F*	FSU	742.438-5	*F*	FSU
742.392-4		*F*	FSO (S)	742.422-9		*F*	FSU	742.439-3	*F*	FSC
742.393-2		*F*	FSC	742.424-5		*F*	FSU	742.440-1	**B** *F*	FSC
742.394-0	**B**	*F*	FSU	742.425-2		*F*	FSO	742.441-9	*F*	FSC
742.395-7		*F*	FSU	742.426-0		*F*	FSO	742.442-7	**B** *F*	FSC
742.396-5		*F*	FSU	742.427-8	**B**	*F*	FSO	742.443-5	*F*	FSU
742.397-3		*F*	FSC	742.428-6		*F*	FSO	742.445-0	*F*	FSO
742.399-9		*F*	FSC	742.429-4		*F*	FSC	742.446-8	**B** *F*	FSC
742.402-1			CTC (S)	742.430-2	**B**	*F*	FSO	742.447-6	*F*	FSO
742.403-9		*F*	FSC	742.431-0		*F*	FSU	742.449-2		CTC (S)
742.404-7		*F*	FSC	742.432-8		*F*	FSO	742.451-8		CTC (S)
742.405-4		*F*	FSC	742.433-6		*F*	FSO	742.452-6	**0**	BRO
742.406-2		*F*	FSU (S)	742.434-4		*F*	FSU	742.453-4	*F*	FSO
742.409-6		*F*	FSU	742.435-1		*F*	FSO	742.454-2	**0** *F*	FSU
742.419-5		*F*	FSU	742.436-9		*F*	FSC			

CLASS 742.7   Bo-Bo

This is a drastic rebuild of Class 742 to extend the operating life by CZ LOKO at Česká Třebová. The locomotive has been fitted with a new Caterpillar engine that meets EU Stage 3A emissions targets and also has reduced height front and rear ends and AC/DC transmission. The locomotive is more powerful than the originals and the top speed has been increased from 90 to 100 km/h. Other Class 742.7s have been rebuilt for private operators.

Built: Rebuilt 2010–12 by CZ LOKO.
Former ČSD Class: T466.2.
Builder: ČKD, model T466.2.
Engine: Caterpillar 3508C.
Power: 1000 kW (1340 hp).
Transmission: Electric.
Maximum Tractive Effort: 189 kN.

Total No. Built: 1 for ČD Cargo.
Wheel Diameter: 1000 mm.
Train Heating Equipment: None.
Weight: 64 tonnes.
Length over Buffers: 13.82 m.
Maximum Speed: 100 km/h.
EVN: 92 54 2 742 701-6.

742.701-6   (742.306)   **B**   *F*   FSO

▲ 742.343 leaves Karlovy Vary with the booked loco-hauled turn on Line 142 – train Os17110, the 14.30 Karlovy Vary dolní nádraží–Johanngeorgenstadt, on 12 July 2014. In 2016 the booked weekday daytime loco-hauled turn is the 12.55 from Karlovy Vary, returning at 14.45.   **Robert Pritchard**

CLASS 743 Bo-Bo

Class 743 was built as a modified Class 742 with the engine derated to 800 kW and fitted with 1020 kW dynamic brakes. Originally they were designed for the severely graded Tanvald–Kořenov–Harrachov route, formerly rack operated but adhesion worked by Class 743 from 1988. Displaced from those duties, six Class 743s were transferred south to České Budějovice in 2013; some of these are outbased at Volary for local freight work on the steeply-graded lines in the area. The remaining Ústí nad Labem allocated locomotives can mainly be found on trip freights around Liberec, Most and Turnov.

The class were delivered in a green & yellow livery, unlike the red & cream of Class 742, and most still carry this livery.

Built: 1987–88.
Former ČSD Class: T466.3.
Builder: ČKD, model T466.3.
Engine: ČKD K6S230DR.
Power: 800 kW (1070 hp).
Transmission: Electric.
Maximum Tractive Effort: 205 kN.
Non-Standard Liveries: 743.002/010: Blue & white
743.003/005/006/007/008/009: Green & yellow.

Total No. Built: 10.
Wheel Diameter: 1000 mm.
Train Heating Equipment: None.
Weight: 66 tonnes.
Length over Buffers: 13.60 m.
Maximum Speed: 90 km/h.
EVN: 92 54 2 743 0xx-c.

743.001-0	**B**	*F*	FSU	743.005-1	**0**	*F*	FSC	743.008-5	**0**	*F*	FSC
743.002-8	**0**	*F*	FSU	743.006-9	**0**	*F*	FSC	743.009-3	**0**	*F*	FSC
743.003-6	**0**	*F*	FSC	743.007-7	**0**	*F*	FSU	743.010-1	**0**	*F*	FSU
743.004-4		*F*	FSC								

CLASS 749 Bo-Bo

Class 749s are Class 751 or Class 752 that have been fitted with electric train heating for passenger work. A programme of 60 conversions started in 1992 with 749.039. 34 locomotives were rebuilt from Class 751 and retained their serial numbers. The remaining 26 locomotives were rebuilt from Class 752 and received a completely new number series in order of conversion, numbered 749.240–265 (752.083 and 752.084 were themselves ex-751.215 and 751.048).

Withdrawals started to take place in the late 2000s and scheduled passenger work ceased at the end of 2013. However, at the time of writing, the class are still used as reserve motive power in the Praha and Olomouc areas: Praha-Vršovice based locomotives are used as cover for unavailable Class 754s on the weekend Praha–Čerčany and Praha–Tanvald lines and also occasionally on other routes. Similarly there are two locomotives based at Olomouc and Šumperk as cover for Class 750.7 or Class 754 on the Jeseník line or Olomouc–Šumperk trains. All other locomotives have been stored, and many moved to the dump at Česká Třebová.

On a more positive note several of this popular class have been preserved and some also sold for use by private companies – see sections at the rear of this book. ČD Cargo also owns several locos, but most are now stored, having been replaced on duties around Volary by Class 743.

The Class 749 (and the Class 751 before them) attracted a cult following amongst British enthusiasts due to their load engine noise being reminiscent of a BR Sulzer Type 2, with many enthusiasts travelling to Praha to sample the class on steeply graded and scenic lines during the last years of scheduled passenger service. Some locomotives (marked *) are silenced, although it should be noted that in the past silencers have been transferred between locomotives.

Normal livery is basic grey with side panels and/or cab ends in assorted reds. At one time there were around 20 colourful paint schemes shared with Class 751.

Built: Rebuilt 1992–96 from Classes 751 or 752.
Former ČSD Class: Not applicable.
Builder: ČKD.
Engine: ČKD K6S310DR.
Power: 1103 kW (1480 hp); e 1215 kW (1630 hp).
Transmission: Electric.
Maximum Tractive Effort: 185 kN.

Total No. Built: 60.
Wheel Diameter: 1000 mm.
Train Heating Equipment: Electric.
Weight: 75 tonnes.
Length over Buffers: 16.50 m.
Maximum Speed: 100 km/h.
EVN: 92 54 2 749 xxx-c.

Non-Standard Liveries: 749.051: Red & blue.
749.102: Maroon & yellow.
749.121: Dark blue & red.
749.251: Red.
749.252: Orange.
749.260: Red with a broad blue bodyside stripe.
749.264: Green & cream.
749.265: All over blue with red ends.

*   Fitted with silencer.
e   Fitted with electronic engine control system.

Class 749. Rebuilt from Class 751 series 0 pre-production type with earlier curved body styling.

749.006-3	(751.006)				PRG

Class 749. Rebuilt from Class 751 production series with more angular styling.

749.018-8	(751.018)	**B**	*F*		FSC	749.107-9	(751.107)			OLO
749.019-6	(751.019)		*F*	*	FSC	749.121-0	(751.121)	**0**		PRG
749.051-9	(751.051)	**0**			CTC (S)	749.187-1	(751.187)		*F* *	FSC
749.102-0	(751.102)	**0**			CTC (S)					

Class 749. Rebuilt from Class 752.

749.241-6	(752.001)				CTC (S)	749.254-9	(752.084)		*	PRG (S)
749.247-3	(752.081)		*F* *		FSC (S)	749.260-6	(752.077)	**0**	*	CTC (S)
749.251-5	(752.073)	**0**	*F* *		FSC (S)	749.264-8	(752.058)	**0**	*	PRG
749.252-3	(752.080)	**0**	*		CTC (S)	749.265-5	(752.055)	**0**	*e	OLS

CLASS 750   Bo-Bo

In 1989 a pilot conversion of 753.242 from steam to electric heat led to the conversion of further Class 753s to Class 750. The prototype initially carried the number 750T242. ČSD started and ČD continued to convert 117 locomotives by 1995 whilst ZSR rebuilt 46 locomotives.

In recent years further rebuild programmes have reduced the numbers of Class 750, and there are now just a handful of serviceable machines in traffic with ČD Cargo, with all remaining ČD locomotives having been stored. ČDC 750s are still used on general freight traffic, like the rebuilt Class 753.7s often operating in pairs. Most of the Ostrava based locos are sub-based at Brno.

750.063/116/380 and 753.265 are stored in Česká Třebová yard but have been sold to CZ LOKO for possible future rebuilding (see Private Freight Operators section).

Livery for Classes 750 and 753 is light grey and green unless stated.

Built: Rebuilt 1991–95 from Class 753.
Former ČSD Class: Not applicable.
Builder: ČKD.
Engine: ČKD 12V230DR.
Power: 1325 kW (1775 hp).
Transmission: Electric.
Maximum Tractive Effort: 185 kN.

Total No. Built: 163†.
Wheel Diameter: 1000 mm.
Train Heating Equipment: Electric.
Weight: 74 tonnes.
Length over Buffers: 16.50 m.
Maximum Speed: 100 km/h.
EVN: 92 54 2 750 xxx-c.

Non-Standard Liveries: 750.302: Red & yellow.
750.333: Blue & white with a yellow stripe.
750.346: Dark blue.

750.013-5	(753.013)	**B**	*F*	FSO	750.252-9	(753.252)	**B**	*F*	FSU
750.042-4	(753.042)	**B**		CTC (S)	750.275-0	(753.275)		*F*	FSO
750.061-4	(753.061)	**B**	*F*	FSU	750.277-6	(753.277)		*F*	FSO
750.079-6	(753.079)	**B**	*F*	FSU	750.287-5	(753.287)	**B**	*F*	FSO
750.103-4	(753.103)		*F*	FSO	750.302-2	(753.302)	**0**	*F*	CTC (S)
750.118-2	(753.118)			PLZ (S)	750.326-1	(753.326)	**B**	*F*	FSU
750.163-8	(753.163)	**B**	*F*	FSO	750.330-3	(753.330)	**B**	*F*	FSU
750.195-0	(753.195)		*F*	CTH (S)	750.333-7	(753.333)	**0**	*F*	FSO
750.213-1	(753.213)		*F*	FSO	750.338-6	(753.338)	**B**	*F*	FSO
750.222-2	(753.222)	**B**	*F*	FSO	750.346-9	(753.346)	**0**		CTC (S)
750.235-4	(753.235)	**B**	*F*	FSO					

CLASS 750.7   Bo-Bo

Class 750.7 was rebuilt by CZ LOKO at Česká Třebová for use by ČD on passenger trains. Like the ZSSK Class 757 rebuilds, these are effectively new locomotives with all that remains of the original locomotive being the frame. The new Caterpillar engines are more powerful and fuel efficient and the cabs have been redesigned.

Although some official lists show 750.719 as being rebuilt from 750.312, it is understood that 750.719 is actually a rebuild of ex-ZSSK 750.096. Similarly 750.701 is understood to have been rebuilt from 750.368, not 750.314 as shown in some official lists.

The locomotives were sold to Impuls-Leasing AUSTRIA for rebuilding, before being leased back to ČD. Diagrams are mainly shared with Class 754. In addition Rakovník based locomotives work two all-day diagrams between Praha Masarykovo and Rakovník using push-pull stock.

Built: Rebuilt 2010–12 from Classes 750 and 753.   **Total No. Built:** 19.
Former ČSD Class: Not applicable.   **Wheel Diameter:** 1000 mm.
Builder: CZ LOKO.   **Train Heating Equipment:** Electric.
Engine: Caterpillar 3512C.   **Weight:** 72 tonnes.
Power: 1550 kW (2080 hp).   **Length over Buffers:** 16.60 m.
Transmission: Electric.   **Maximum Speed:** 100 km/h.
Maximum Tractive Effort: 202 kN.   **EVN:** 92 54 2 750 7xx-c.

750.701-5	(750.368)	B	CTT	750.711-4	(750.409)	B	BRM
750.702-3	(750.121)	B	CTT	750.712-2	(750.410)	B	BRM
750.703-1	(753.192)	B	CTT	750.713-0	(750.162)	B	BRM
750.704-9	(750.119)	B	BRM	750.714-8	(750.022)	B	CTT
750.705-6	(750.078)	B	BRM	750.715-5	(750.236)	B	OLS
750.706-4	(750.144)	B	PLR	750.716-3	(750.253)	B	OLS
750.707-2	(750.243)	B	PLR	750.717-1	(750.258)	B	OLS
750.708-0	(750.143)	B	PLR	750.718-9	(750.160)	B	OLS
750.709-8	(750.259)	B	BRM	750.719-7	(750.096)	B	BRM
750.710-6	(750.285)	B	BRM				

▲ All 19 Class 750.7 are in ČD blue livery, but 750.712–719 carry the second version of this livery. Šumperk based locomotives work trains on the scenic Line 292. On 7 July 2014 750.718 approaches Nové Losiny with train R1410, the 08.54 Jeseník–Zábřeh na Moravě.   **Robert Pritchard**

CLASS 751   Bo-Bo

Mixed-traffic locomotive prototypes T478.1001–1002 of 1964, and pre-series T478.1003–1007 of 1966 are known as "Bardotka" after Brigitte Bardot and feature curvaceous front ends. None of these machines are still in normal service, but four have been preserved (see Preserved Locomotives section). A third prototype (diesel-hydraulic) numbered T478.2001 (later T478.4501) was scrapped in the 1980s.

In total 312 T478.1 and T478.2 (later Classes 751/752) were built. ZSSK still uses Class 752s (of which 82 were built as a no train heat version). Series machines were built 1967–71 and are more angular and known as "Zamračená" ("Grumpy" or "frowner"). They were constructed in three builds: Series I originally T479.1008–1092, Series II T478.1093–1170 and T478.2001–2052, and Series III T478.2053–2082 and T478.1171–1230. T478.1 were originally all steam-heat fitted (Class 751) and T478.2 no boiler (Class 752). Series III have bodyside corrugations extending to the roof line (751.107, now 749.107, is the same). Earlier machines have plain upper side panels. 751.231–239 were renumbered from 752.003/004/008/005/007/006/062/017/059 in the 1990s. Series III locomotives T478.1171–1230 and T478.2053–2082 were originally built with silencers but not all are still fitted.

After some locomotives were rebuilt as Class 749, with electric train heating in the early-to-mid 1990s, the remaining ČD Class 752s were renumbered in the Class 751.3 sub-series, retaining the last two digits of the serial number (the Class No. 752 was then reused for a Class 753 rebuild). Two Class 751s (751.141/316) were modified in 1996–97 with auxiliary diesel engines for yard and depot light movements.

Withdrawals started in earnest in the mid 2000s and at the time of writing only two Class 751s are still serviceable with ČD Cargo, although ZSSK Cargo in Slovakia still operates much larger numbers of the class and several machines have been preserved. All of the remaining locomotives listed here are owned by ČD Cargo; most are now stored at České Budějovice, Ostrava or Břeclav.

Normal livery is basic grey with side panels and/or cab ends in assorted reds.

Built: 1964–71.	**Total No. Built:** Class 751:230†; (Class 752: 82).
Former ČSD Class: T478.1.	**Wheel Diameter:** 1000 mm.
Builder: ČKD.	**Train Heating Equipment:** Steam.
Engine: ČKD K6S310DR.	**Weight:** 75 tonnes.
Power: 1103 kW (1480 hp).	**Length over Buffers:** 16.50 m.
Transmission: Electric.	**Maximum Speed:** 100 km/h.
Maximum Tractive Effort: 185 kN.	**EVN:** 92 54 2 751 xxx-c.

Non-Standard Liveries: 751.089/105/210/228/374: Red & yellow.
                              751.144/149/316/338: Blue & red.
                              751.335: Green & blue.

*   Fitted with silencer.
k   Fitted with 72 kW auxiliary engine.

751.232 also carries its original number T478.2004.

Class 751. Production type with more angular body styling.

751.031-6		F	*	FSC (S)	751.137-1		F	*	FSC (S)	751.210-6	**0**	F			FSC (S)
751.053-0		F		FSO (S)	751.141-3		F	k	Břeclav (S)	751.219-7	**B**	F	*		FSC
751.066-2		F		FSC (S)	751.144-7	**0**	F		FSO (S)	751.220-5		F	*		FSO (S)
751.089-4	**0**	F		FSC (S)	751.145-4		F		FSO (S)	751.223-9		F	*		FSC (S)
751.094-4		F	*	FSO (S)	751.149-6	**0**	F		Břeclav (S)	751.228-8	**0**	F	*		FSC (S)
751.101-7		F		FSO (S)	751.154-6		F		FSC (S)	751.232-0		F			FSC (S)
751.105-8	**0**	F	*	FSC (S)	751.167-8		F		FSC (S)	751.233-8		F			FSC (S)
751.119-9		F	*	Břeclav (S)	751.176-9		F	*	FSO (S)	751.236-1		F	*		FSC (S)

Class 751.3. Renumbered from Class 752.

751.316-1	(752.016)	**0**	F	k	FSC	751.354-2	(752.054)		F	*	FSC (S)
751.335-1	(752.035)	**0**	F		FSO (S)	751.364-1	(752.064)		F		FSC (S)
751.338-5	(752.038)	**0**	F		FSO (S)	751.374-0	(752.074)	**0**	F	*	FSC (S)

CLASS 753   Bo-Bo

This large mixed-traffic class, which started to appear from the late 1960s, soon earned the nickname "Brejlovec" (meaning "Goggles" or "Spectacles") as a result of their unorthodox cab styling. Two Class T478.3 prototypes in 1968 (T478.3001/3002) were followed by ten pre-series locomotives, then production of a further 396 locomotives between 1971 and 1977. Officially 408 were built, but "new" T478.3396 reused the underframe recovered from 1971 accident damaged T478.3004.

As originally built for ČSD, after the prototypes T478.3001/3002 and pre-series T478.3003–3012, successive batches were built as Series I T478.3013–3072, Series II T478.3073–3132, Series III T478.3133–3252, Series IV T478.3253–3300, Series V T478.3301–3360, Series VI T478.3361–3390 and Series VII T478.3391–3408. All locomotives were fitted with silencers.

One external difference between the locomotives is that 753.003–081 had single lamp clusters, the remainder having double lamps. Many were converted to Class 750 with electric train heating, with the remaining Class 753s cascading to freight work.

More than 100 Class 750 and Class 753 have been rebuilt as private Classes 752.6, 753.7, ČD Class 750.7, 753.7 or 755 and a number were also exported to Italy or Hungary. The small number of remaining original Class 753s are now stored at Ústí nad Labem depot awaiting disposal or possible rebuilding, whilst a small number have also been preserved.

Built: 1968–77.
Former ČSD Class: T478.3.
Builder: ČKD.
Engine: ČKD 12V230DR.
Power: 1325 kW (1775 hp).
Transmission: Electric.
Maximum Tractive Effort: 185 kN.
Non-Standard Liveries: 753.006/263: Red & cream.
                         753.073/141/211/212/352: Red & yellow.
                         753.187: Red.

Total No. Built: 408†.
Wheel Diameter: 1000 mm.
Train Heating Equipment: Steam.
Weight: 76.8 tonnes.
Length over Buffers: 16.50 m.
Maximum Speed: 100 km/h.
EVN: 92 54 2 753 xxx-c.

Class 753. Prototype and series 0 pre-production version.

753.006-6	**0** *F*	FSU (S)

Class 753. Production series locomotives.

753.073-6	**0** *F*	FSU (S)	753.212-0	**0** *F*	FSU (S)	753.301-1	*F*	FSU (S)
753.141-1	**0** *F*	FSU (S)	753.229-4	*F*	FSU (S)	753.352-4	**0** *F*	FSU (S)
753.187-4	**0** *F*	FSU (S)	753.263-3	**0** *F*	FSU (S)	753.372-2	*F*	FSU (S)
753.211-2	**0** *F*	FSU (S)						

CLASS 753.7   Bo-Bo

In 2008 ČD Cargo ordered 30 Class 753.7 rebuilds from CZ LOKO to similar specification as those with private operators. The number series used, 753.751–780, follows on from the private operator batch, whilst 753.781–784 were subsequently rebuilt for TSS. The Class 753.7s use many new components, including new more fuel efficient Caterpillar engines. The locomotives are leased from ING Lease to ČD Cargo. There has been some confusion surrounding the donor locomotives for some conversions, with official documentation not matching what actually happened in many cases.

Most of the Class 753.7s are based at Ústí nad Labem, and can be found double-heading heavy freights in north Bohemia, such as car trains from Mladá Boleslav to Poland (via Liberec, where several of the class can often be found stabled). Ostrava and České Budějovice also have smaller allocations of the class for use on bulk freight work on local non-electrified lines.

Built: Rebuilt 2008–10 from Classes 750 & 753.
Former ČSD Class: Not applicable.
Builder: CZ LOKO, Česká Třebová.
Engine: Caterpillar 3512B.
Power: 1500 kW (2010 hp).
Transmission: Electric.
Maximum Tractive Effort: 202 kN.

Total No. Built: 30 (plus 43 for other operators).
Wheel Diameter: 1000 mm.
Train Heating Equipment: None.
Weight: 72 tonnes.
Length over Buffers: 16.60 m.
Maximum Speed: 100 km/h.
EVN: 92 54 2 753 7xx-c.

753.751-7	(750.156)	B	F	FSU
753.752-5	(750.329)	B	F	FSU
753.753-3	(750.209)	B	F	FSU
753.754-1	(750.223)	B	F	FSU
753.755-8	(750.224)	B	F	FSU
753.756-6	(750.240)	B	F	FSU
753.757-4	(750.292)	B	F	FSU
753.758-2	(750.311)	B	F	FSU
753.759-0	(750.313)	B	F	FSU
753.760-8	(750.322)	B	F	FSU
753.761-6	(750.334)	B	F	FSU
753.762-4	(750.335)	B	F	FSU
753.763-2	(750.336)	B	F	FSU
753.764-0	(750.341)	B	F	FSO
753.765-7	(750.348)	B	F	FSO
753.766-5	(750.356)	B	F	FSO
753.767-3	(750.358)	B	F	FSO
753.768-1	(750.364)	B	F	FSO
753.769-9	(750.368)	B	F	FSO
753.770-7	(753.122)	B	F	FSO
753.771-5	(753.171)	B	F	FSC
753.772-3	(753.208)	B	F	FSC
753.773-1	(753.233)	B	F	FSU
753.774-9	(753.278)	B	F	FSO
753.775-6	(753.337)	B	F	FSU
753.776-4	(753.340)	B	F	FSO
753.777-2	(753.344)	B	F	FSU
753.778-0	(753.390)	B	F	FSU
753.779-8	(753.391)	B	F	FSU
753.780-6	(753.405)	B	F	FSO

▲ ČD Cargo Class 753.7s are often used in pairs. On 5 September 2014 753.760 and 753.761 pass Mojžíř, near Ústi nad Labem, with a train of sand from Libuň to Řetenice. **Quintus Vosman**

CLASS 754 Bo-Bo

Following two 1975-built prototypes (T478.4201/4202, later 754.201/202, then 750.409/410 and now 750.711/712!), 84 Class T478.4s were built in 1979–80 as T478.4003–4086, renumbered in 1988 to 754.003–086. These locomotives used the same bodyshell as Class 753, and all had electric train heating from new for use on passenger services. Batches were Series I T478.4003–4026, Series II T478.4027–4065 and Series III T478.4066–4086. Class 754 is still nearly complete – only two of the class have been scrapped to date: 754.017/038. The locomotives continue to work most diesel-hauled passenger trains in both the Czech Republic and Slovakia.

At the time of writing passenger turns for the class included the following (* shared with Class 750/7): Praha–Jílové u Prahy–Čerčany and Praha–Tanvald (both weekends only), Plzeň–Domažlice (now mostly replaced by Class 844), Klatovy–Železná Ruda-Alžbětín, České Budějovice–Nové Udolí (summer-dated trains), Hradec Králové–Trutnov portions of Praha–Trutnov trains (*), Olomouc–Uničov–Šumperk (*), Zábřeh na Moravě–Jesenik (*), Brno–Jihlava portions of Brno–Plzeň trains and local trains on the same route (*), Luhačovice–Staré Město u Uherského Hradiště portions of Luhačovice–Praha trains (*) and Ostrava–Frenštát pod Radhoštěm. The last is one of the busiest routes for diesel loco-hauled passenger trains, with five diagrams daily for Bohumín-based Class 754s.

At one time the passenger Class 750s and 754s were a very colourful class, particularly in southern Moravia, with more than 40 different liveries. However many have now been removed in favour of the new ČD blue livery. Standard livery is light grey and green unless stated.

Built: 1979–80.
Former ČSD Class: T478.4.
Builder: ČKD.
Engine: ČKD 12V230DR; v 12VZ230T.
Power: 1472 kW (1975 hp).
Transmission: Electric.
Maximum Tractive Effort: 185 kN.

Total No. Built: 86†.
Wheel Diameter: 1000 mm.
Train Heating Equipment: Electric 400 kW.
Weight: 74.4 tonnes.
Length over Buffers: 16.50 m.
Maximum Speed: 100 km/h.
EVN: 92 54 2 754 0xx-c.

Non-Standard Liveries: 754.013/019/020/024/027/029/051/057/059/060: Blue & white (some with yellow stripe).
754.012: Red, white & yellow.
754.044/049/062/078: Red & yellow.
754.050: Orange & grey.
754.061: Maroon & cream.
754.066: Maroon.

k   754.025/026/028/037/046 have been modified to operate in Poland and are on hire to PKP (Polish Railways), working trains from Białystok depot. However they remain based at Bohumín depot and return there for maintenance.

v   Re-engined with updated version of 12V230 engine.

754.006-5	B		PLK	754.029-7	0		PLZ	754.059-4	0	CTC
754.007-3	B		PRG	754.030-5			CTT	754.060-2	0	CTH
754.008-1	B		PRG	754.031-3			PRG	754.061-0	0	PRD
754.009-9	B		PLK	754.037-0	B	k	OLB	754.062-8	0	BRM
754.012-3	0		BRM	754.039-6			PLB	754.063-6		PLZ
754.013-1	0	v	BRV	754.040-4			OLB	754.064-4		PLZ
754.015-6	B		PLK	754.041-2	B		PLK	754.065-1		OLB
754.016-4			BRM	754.042-0			PRG	754.066-9	0	PLZ
754.018-0			BRM	754.043-8			BRO	754.067-7	B	BRM
754.019-8	0		BRM	754.044-6	0		PRG	754.068-5	B	OLB
754.020-6	0		PLZ (S)	754.045-3			PLZ	754.074-3		PLK
754.021-4	B		OLB	754.046-1	B	k	OLB	754.075-0	B	BRM
754.022-2			PLB	754.047-9			OLB	754.076-8	B	OLB
754.023-0			BRM	754.048-7			CTL	754.077-6		OLB
754.024-8	0		PLT	754.049-5	0		OLB	754.078-4	0	PLZ (S)
754.025-5	B	k	OLB	754.050-3	0		CTT	754.079-2	B	OLO
754.026-3	B	k	OLB	754.051-1	0		PRD	754.080-0		OLO
754.027-1	0		PLZ	754.057-8	0		PLZ	754.081-8		OLB
754.028-9	B	k	OLB	754.058-6	B		PLZ	754.086-7	B	v	OLB

CLASS 755   Bo-Bo

It was at one time anticipated that 20 locomotives would be converted from Classes 750 or 753 to Class 755 with Caterpillar engines, similar to those in the rebuilt Class 753.7 locomotives for private operators and fitted with 1710 kW electric dynamic braking. However the programme was changed and the ČD Cargo 753.7s emerged instead. The two Class 755s that were converted are now based at Ústí nad Labem and can often be found on freights around Kralupy nad Vltavou.

Livery is a unique mid blue with red cabs.

Built: Rebuilt 2005 from Class 753.
Former ČSD Class: Not applicable.
Builder: ČMKS.
Engine: Caterpillar 3512B.
Power: 1500 kW (2010 hp).
Transmission: Electric.
Maximum Tractive Effort: 185 kN.

Total No. Built: 2.
Wheel Diameter: 1000 mm.
Train Heating Equipment: None.
Weight: 72 tonnes.
Length over Buffers: 16.66 m.
Maximum Speed: 100 km/h.
EVN: 92 54 2 755 00x-c.

755.001-5	(753.305)	*F*	FSU		755.002-3	(753.345)	*F*	FSU

CLASS 771   Co-Co

Collectively Classes 770/771 were one of the world's most numerous types, totalling well over 8000 examples. They were known as "Cmelak", meaning "bumble bee" because of their distinctive engine noise when on full power. Built for heavy shunting and trip work, the type was exported to the Soviet Union, Poland, Albania, India, Syria and Iraq. Originally a Soviet specification, the Praha factory was so overwhelmed by ChME3 production that most domestic ČSD Class T669.0s (later Class 770) were built by SMZ Dubnica. Class 771 is a slightly modified version of Class 770, with improved suspension and adhesion. All were devised and built by SMZ.

Just Česká Třebová's "pet" locomotive 771.172 remains in ČD stock, and still has occasional outings, even being noted working passenger trains in 2015 when there were overhead line problems. A handful of Class 771s are still operated by ČD Cargo, mainly on heavy coal trains in the Ostrava area. Larger numbers of this class are still active in Slovakia or with private operators.

Livery is green with a broad cream stripe, unless stated.

Built: 1968–72.
Former ČSD Class: T669.1.
Builder: SMZ.
Engine: ČKD K6S310DR.
Power: 993 kW (1330 hp).
Transmission: Electric.
Maximum Tractive Effort: 240 kN.

Total No. Built: 207†.
Wheel Diameter: 1050 mm.
Train Heating Equipment: None.
Weight: 116 tonnes.
Length over Buffers: 17.24 m.
Maximum Speed: 90 km/h.
EVN: 92 54 2 771 xxx-c.

771.046-0	*F*	FSC (S)	771.110-4	*F*	FSO	771.172-4		+	CTC
771.099-9	*F*	FSO	771.137-7	*F*	FSC	771.182-3	**B** *F*		FSO
771.103-9	*F*	FSO (S)							

CLASS 799   Bo

Class 799 is a dual-power battery/diesel shunting tractor locomotive for use within depots, often to move electric locomotives on and off turntables. They were built on the underframes of Classes 700–703, although little else remains of the original machines.

As these locomotives rarely move between depots, the actual location for each is shown in this list. 799.011/015/022/037 are now owned by DPOV and can be found under the Private Operators section of this book.

Livery is a rusty orange colour unless stated.

Built: 1992–2000.
Former ČSD Class: Not applicable.
Builder: JLS Jihlava.
Engine: Zetor Z5801.
Power: 37 kW (50 hp) (19.5 kW (26 hp) on battery).
Transmission: Electric.
Maximum Tractive Effort: 32 kN.
Non-Standard Livery: 799.001: Yellow.

Total No. Built: 41.
Wheel Diameter: 1000 mm.
Train Heating Equipment: None.
Weight: 22 tonnes.
Length over Buffers: 7.24 m.
Maximum Speed: 10 km/h (5 km/h on battery).
EVN: 98 54 4 799 0xx-c.

* fitted with remote control equipment.

799.001-3	(702.044)	**0** *F*	Olomouc	
799.002-1	(702.068)		Česká Třebová	
799.003-9	(700.116)		Liberec	
799.004-7	(702.067)		Trutnov	
799.005-4	(702.045)		Děčín	
799.006-2	(702.061)		Hradec Králové	
799.007-0	(702.036)		Česká Třebová	
799.008-8	(701.046)	*F*	Ostrava	
799.009-6	(701.054)		Louny	
799.010-4	(701.053)	*F*	Most	
799.012-0	(701.052)		Opava	
799.013-8	(703.039)	*F*	Ústí nad Labem	
799.014-6	(702.063)	*F*	Ústí nad Labem	
799.016-1	(702.040)		Veselí nad Moravou	
799.017-9	(702.065)		Kolín	
799.018-7	(702.066)	*F*	Břeclav	
799.019-5	(702.050)		Znojmo	
799.020-3	(702.022)		Česká Lípa	
799.021-1	(702.043)		Bohumín	
799.023-7	(702.033)		Brno Maloměřice	

799.024-5	(702.038)		Plzeň	
799.025-2	(702.041)	*F*	Ostrava	
799.026-0	(702.077)		Brno Maloměřice	
799.027-8	(701.063)		Rakovník	
799.028-6	(701.064)		Cheb	
799.029-4	(702.070)		Šumperk	
799.030-2	(702.054)		Brno Maloměřice	
799.031-0	(702.064)		Pardubice	
799.032-8	(702.048)		Děčín	
799.033-6	(702.026)		České Budějovice	
799.034-4	(702.027)		Tábor	
799.035-1	(702.032)		Olomouc	
799.036-9	(702.047)		Bohumín	
799.038-5	(702.058)	*F*	Ostrava	
799.039-3	(701.062)		Klatovy	
799.040-1	(702.052)	*	Brno Maloměřice	
799.041-9	(702.053)		Cheb	

▲ 799.006 stands at the fuelling point at Hradec Králové depot on 11 May 2015. **Robert Pritchard**

1.4. ČD DIESEL MULTIPLE UNITS

Czech Railways have a long history of DMU working on rural branch lines, and in more recent years regional DMUs have arrived and have replaced some locomotive-hauled trains.

All DMUs are numbered in the Class 8xx series, with DMU Driving Trailers numbered in the 9xx series, and intermediate vehicles for the 3-car Class 814 units numbered in the 014.xxx series.

All DMUs are in fixed formations unless stated. A notable feature of Czech DMUs is that all can couple together; this can result in some interesting combinations at busy times, with even the new Class 840/841 types being able to run with the older 4-wheel Class 810s.

CLASSES 809, 810 & 811   MOTOR COACHES

These four-wheel railbuses with their original low-back, barely padded 3+2 bench seats were the essence of Czech and Slovak branch lines for many years. They descended from a heritage of four-wheel railbuses in the region dating from the 1920s. In total 680 were built as passenger cars and a further 115 for overhead catenary maintenance (Class 892, now MVTV2). Prototype 810.001 was rebuilt for departmental use as track test car MD1-01 whilst 810.002 has now been preserved by ČD at NTM Lužná u Rakovníka (see Preserved DMUs). Similar Czech-built cars are found in Hungary as MAV-START Class 117 (formerly Type Bzmot).

Between 2005 and 2012 a large number of Class 810s were withdrawn for rebuilding into Class 814. Despite this there are still more than 250 Class 809s and 810s in traffic at the time of writing, although they are nowhere near as widespread as they once were, when they could be found on virtually any branch line across the entire country. Most of the remaining units have been fitted with more comfortable high-back seats and refurbishments and repaints into the new blue livery are continuing to take place at DPOV Veselí nad Moravou.

Today most depots still have an allocation of Classes 809 or 810 and they usually tend to work on more lightly-used branches. Trutnov now has the largest allocation of Class 810 (25), to operate a number of branch lines in North Bohemia. Classes 809/810 need to run round their trailers (see ČD Non-Powered Trailers section) as the latter are without driving cabs. Typical trains are formed of one Class 810 either on its own or with one or two trailers, although longer formations such as 810+010+010+810 can be found at busy times.

Class 809s were converted in 1994–96 for driver only operation and generally operate on their own. Most are fitted with self-service ticket machines (some of the tip-up seats were removed) and kept the last three digits of their serial number (being renumbered by reducing the 810.xxx number by 1000). More recently some Class 810s have also been fitted with ticket machines.

Livery is red & cream unless stated.

Built: 1973–84.
Builder: MSV Studénka.
Engine: Liaz ML634 of 155 kW (210 hp).
Transmission: Mechanical.
Former ČSD Class: M152.0.
Wheel Arrangement: A-1.
Formation: DMSO.

Total No. Built: 680†.
Accommodation: –/50(+5).
Weight: 20 tonnes.
Length over Buffers: 13.97 m.
Maximum Speed: 80 km/h.
EVN: 95 54 5 809 xxx-c or
     95 54 5 810 xxx-c or
     95 54 5 811 xxx-c.

Non-Standard Liveries: 809.281, 809.534, 810.271: Red & yellow.
                  810.191: Original cream & red.

h   fitted with high-back seats.
*   Fitted with a newer type of high back seat to a modified layout. –/45(+4).

Class 809. Modified for driver-only operation and fitted with ticket machines.

809.057-3	**B**	h	BRV	809.209-0	**B**	h	OLP	809.307-2	**B**	h	OLP
809.080-5		h	PLL	809.232-2	**B**	h	BRV	809.336-1	**B**	h	BRV
809.140-7	**B**	h	PLL	809.239-7	**B**	h*	BRV	809.342-9	**B**	h	PLL
809.163-9	**B**	h*	PLL	809.249-6	**B**	h	PLL	809.345-2	**B**	h	PLL
809.179-5		h	BRV	809.281-9	**0**	h	PLL	809.350-2	**B**	h*	PLL
809.208-2		h	PLL	809.282-7	**B**	h*	OLP	809.358-5	**B**	h	BRV

Part			Code
809.398-1		h	OLP
809.434-4	B	h*	PLL
809.495-5	B	h	PLL
809.502-8	B	h	PLL
809.534-1	0		PLL
809.596-0		h	OLP
809.657-0	B	h	PLL
809.677-8	B	h	PLL

Class 810. Original version with ML634 engine.

Part			Code
810.007-5		h	PRC
810.009-1		h	OLB
810.015-8	B	h	OLV
810.026-5		h	OLS
810.032-3			PLK
810.034-9			PLZ
810.036-4			CTC (S)
810.039-8	B	h*	CTT
810.041-4		h	PLC
810.043-0		h	PLK
810.044-8			CTC (S)
810.046-3			PLK
810.049-7		h	OLS
810.050-5			PLR
810.052-1			OLB
810.054-7			PLR
810.055-4		h	OLP
810.056-2			CTC
810.058-8			CTC
810.059-6			CTP
810.060-4			CTT
810.070-3			OLP
810.071-1			OLS
810.073-7			PLR
810.077-8		h	PLV
810.094-3			OLS
810.097-6			BRO
810.098-4			PRK
810.100-8		+	CTT
810.106-5		h	OLP
810.110-7			CTC (S)
810.111-5		h	PLK
810.113-1	B	h*	PRK
810.114-9			PLZ (S)
810.123-0		h	BRO
810.124-8		h	CTT
810.150-3			PLL
810.152-9			PLV
810.157-8		h	BRV
810.162-8			CTC (S)
810.165-1		h	PRD
810.173-5			OLV
810.174-3		h	PLT
810.176-8	B	h	PLT
810.177-6		h	PLV
810.180-0			OLB
810.181-8			OLV
810.182-6		h	PLK
810.183-4			PRK
810.184-2		h	PRC
810.191-7	0		OLV
810.192-5			OLB (S)
810.193-3		h	PLV
810.194-1		h	PLT
810.195-8		h	PLT
810.199-0	B	h	OLP
810.201-4		h	PLC
810.210-5			PLT
810.212-1	B	h*	BRO

Part			Code
810.213-9			PLL
810.216-2		h	PRK
810.217-0		h	PRC
810.220-4		h	PRK
810.222-0		h	BRO
810.223-8		h	BRV
810.224-6	B	h*	PRG
810.226-1			PLC
810.228-7			CTT
810.229-5		h	PRK
810.231-1			PLZ (S)
810.233-7			CTT
810.234-5	B	h	OLP
810.236-0	B	h*	PRG
810.240-2		h	PRK
810.245-1		h	CTC
810.250-1		h	PLK
810.262-6		h	OLS
810.263-4		h	BRV
810.265-9			PLK
810.271-7	0		OLV
810.287-3			CTC (S)
810.288-1			CTC (S)
810.289-9			CTP
810.290-7		h	BRV
810.291-5		h	OLB
810.292-3	B	h*	OLS
810.296-4	B	h	CTP
810.297-2			CTP
810.298-0			CTP
810.304-6			PLR
810.306-1		h	PRG
810.310-3			PLL
810.312-9			CTT
810.313-7	B	h	PLR
810.318-6		h	PLK
810.319-4			PLR
810.320-2		h	PLR
810.325-1		h	CTC
810.326-9			PRC
810.327-7			PRC
810.329-3	B	h*	PLA
810.333-5		h	PLV
810.334-3		h	PRG
810.337-6			PLR
810.339-2			OLP
810.340-0		h	PRC
810.341-8	B	h	PLC
810.343-4	B	h*	CTT
810.349-1	B	h	PRC
810.351-7		h	CTP
810.353-3	B	h*	CTT
810.359-0		h	PLK
810.362-4			PRK (S)
810.368-1	B	h	PLZ
810.369-9		h	PLK
810.371-5			OLB
810.373-1	B	h*	OLV
810.375-6			PLB

Part			Code
810.382-2		h	PLK
810.383-0		h	PLK
810.385-5			CTC (S)
810.394-7	B	h	OLV
810.399-6			OLP
810.406-9		h	PLK
810.408-5		h	BRV
810.411-9			PLR
810.416-8		h	PLV (S)
810.417-6			PLC
810.418-4	B	h	PLZ
810.419-2		h	PLK
810.424-2	B	h*	PLZ
810.425-9	B	h	PLC
810.430-9		h	PLK
810.431-7		h	OLS
810.433-3	B	h	BRV
810.436-6			PRC
810.444-0			OLO
810.446-5		h	PRC
810.448-1	B	h	CTT
810.449-9		h	BRO
810.455-6		h	BRV
810.458-0			CTC
810.459-8			PLR
810.468-9		h	OLS
810.469-7		h	BRV
810.472-1	B	h	PRC
810.476-2			OLB
810.479-6	B	h	OLB
810.482-0			PLR
810.486-1		h	BRV
810.487-9	B	h	PRC
810.493-7	B	h	CTT
810.500-9		h	PRC
810.501-7			PRC
810.506-6	B	h	OLV
810.507-4			OLV
810.508-2	B	h	OLS
810.510-8		h	PLK
810.511-6		h	PRC
810.512-4			PRK
810.515-7			CTT
810.519-9	B	h	OLV
810.520-7			OLV
810.524-9			OLB
810.528-0			PLL
810.529-8			CTC (S)
810.533-0	B	h	OLP
810.537-1		h	BRV
810.538-9			PLR
810.539-7			CTT
810.540-5		h	CTP
810.541-3			CTT
810.545-4			CTT
810.546-2		h	OLO
810.548-8		h	PLC
810.549-6			CTT
810.550-4	B	h	CTT

810.551-2			CTT	810.597-5		h	CTP	810.642-9			PRK
810.559-5			PLL	810.599-1	**B**	h*	PLA	810.644-5		h	PLB
810.560-3			PLL	810.600-7			PRD	810.645-2		h	PLT
810.561-1	**B**	h	PLR	810.601-5		h	PLV	810.646-0	**B**	h*	OLO
810.563-7	**B**	h	CTT (S)	810.608-0	**B**	h	PRC	810.651-0	**B**	h	BRV
810.564-5		h	CTT	810.616-3		h	PRK	810.652-8	**B**	h*	CTT
810.565-2	**B**	h	CTT	810.617-1	**B**	h	CTC	810.654-4		h	PRK
810.566-0			PLC	810.618-9		h	CTC	810.655-1			CTT
810.569-4		h	BRZ	810.620-5			PLA	810.663-5		h	BRV
810.570-2	**B**	h	PLA	810.621-3	**B**	h	PRC	810.664-3			OLS (S)
810.571-0		h	PLA	810.622-1	**B**	h	PLA	810.665-0			CTT
810.572-8		h	PLA	810.627-0		h	BRV	810.666-8			PLC
810.573-6	**B**	h	PLB	810.628-8		h	BRV	810.667-6			BRO
810.575-1	**B**	h*	PLA	810.629-6		h	CTC	810.668-4			PRD
810.578-5	**B**	h	CTC	810.630-4		h	CTC	810.669-2			PLC
810.583-5		h	OLO	810.631-2			PRK	810.670-0	**B**	h	PLZ
810.585-0	**B**	h	PLR	810.632-0	**B**	h*	PRK	810.673-4		h	CTT
810.587-6			PRC	810.633-8		h	PLA	810.674-2	**B**	h*	BRO
810.589-2		h	PRG	810.635-3	**B**	h	PLK	810.675-9		h	OLS
810.590-0		h	PRK	810.639-5			OLB	810.676-7		h	PLZ
810.594-2		h	PLR	810.640-3		h	BRO	810.678-3			OLB
810.595-9		h	PLB	810.641-1	**B**	h*	PLA				

Class 811. Rebuilt Pars nova Šumperk 1997 from 810.082 with new ML636 engine.

811.082-7	h	PLR

▲ Refurbished 810.575 stands at Blatná after arrival with train Os27912, the 16.37 from Nepomuk on 11 May 2014. **Robert Pritchard**

CLASS 812   ESMERALDA   3-CAR UNITS

Class 812 is a unique rebuild of a Class 810 motor (810.613) and Class 010 trailer coaches into a unit known as "Esmeralda". Unlike Class 810s, this unit has a driving trailer of Class 912, formerly 010.171. Fitted with new seats to a 2+2 layout. Now based at Praha Libeň and used for special workings, such as weekend bicycle or children's trains.

Livery is a unique green & white.

Built: Rebuilt 2001–02 from Class 810 and 010. **Total No. Built:** 1 x 3-car set.
Builder: Pars Nova Šumperk. **Accommodation:** –/38 + –/60 + –/36.
Engine: Liaz ML640 of 242 kW (325 hp). **Weight:** 22 + 14 + 14 tonnes.
Transmission: Mechanical, Voith. **Length over Buffers:** 14.47 m per car.
Wheel Arrangement: A-1 + 2-2 + 2-2. **Maximum Speed:** 80 km/h.
Formation: DMSO–TSO–DTSO.
EVN: 95 54 5 812 613-8 + 50 54 24-29 801-4 + 50 54 80-29 101-0.

812.613-8   011.434-8   912.001-5   PRL

CLASS 814   REGIONOVA   2- OR 3-CAR UNITS

Class 814s can be seen on branch lines and also on some regional services across the Czech Republic, having replaced Class 810+trailer formations on many duties. In fact more than 30% of all trains in the country are now worked by Class 814s. They are based at 21 different depots, the largest allocation being at Rakovník: these units are a regular sight working into Praha Masarykovo.

Heavy rebuilds of Classes 810 and 010 (or 012/013), Class 814 were ordered in several different batches, creating a final fleet of 210 2-cars and 26 3-cars. 2-car units have a Class 814 motor and a Class 914 driving trailer. 3-car units have a Class 814 motor either side of a Class 014 trailer, thereby giving a better power-to-weight ratio for use on lines with steep gradients, such as Praha–Vrané nad Vltavou–Dobříš/Čerčany, Olomouc–Uničov–Šumperk and Tišnov–Žďár nad Sázavou. The centre sections of 014 and 914 cars are dropped for low height platform access with wheelchair lifts. Misformed 3-car sets are not unknown.

The 3+2 seating layout of Class 810 has been replaced by more comfortable 2+2 seating arranged mainly in bays of four. Original Liaz engines and mechanical transmission have been replaced by more environmentally friendly engines and new Voith hydraulic drives. Tedom is the former Liaz company.

Sets 814.080 onwards incorporate a number of modifications compared to the first batch, mainly to the interiors and to provide better noise insulation: there had been many comments that although more comfortable, Class 814s are actually much noisier than Class 810s. Units from 814.138 onwards (including all the 3-cars) are fitted with a modified Tedom engine.

Livery as outshopped was a class specific yellow and green except two units which were outshopped in revised ČD blue livery and 814.166 and 814.177 which have been given advertising vinyls on their yellow and green livery. In 2015 units started to receive the standard ČD corporate livery as part of overhauls at DPOV Veselí nad Moravou, with 814.007 the first to be repainted.

Built: Rebuilt 2005–12 from Class 810 and 010/012/013.
Total No. Built: 210 x 2-car sets & 26 x 3-car sets.
Builder: Pars nova Šumperk.
Accommodation: 2-cars: –/48 + –/28(+8) 1TD 2W.
                3-cars: –/48 + –/31(+8) 1TD 2W + –/48.
Engine: Tedom ML640SE of 242 kW (325 hp) (814.001–137);
           Tedom RHTA25s of 242 kW (325 hp) (814.138–199/201–252/300–310).
Weight: 814 car 22 tonnes, 914 and 014 cars 17 tonnes (combined weight 2-car 39 tonnes, 3-car 61 tonnes).
Transmission: Hydraulic: Voith Diwa 864.3E (814.001–137/201–252);
                     Voith Diwa 884.5 (814.138–199/300–310).
Length over Buffers: 14.22 m + 13.97 m or 14.22 m + 13.97 m + 14.22 m.
Wheel Arrangement: A-1 + 1-1 or A-1 + 1-1 + 1-A.
Maximum Speed: 80 km/h.
Formation: DMSO–DTSO or DMSO–TSO–DMSO.
EVN: 95 54 5 814 xxx-c + 95 54 5 914 xxx-c or
      95 54 5 814 xxx-c + 95 54 5 014 0xx-c + 95 54 5 814 xxx-c.

Class 814.0. 2-car units.

814.001-4	(810.225)	914.001-3	(010.522)		PLR
814.002-2	(810.284)	914.002-1	(010.479)		OLV
814.003-0	(810.051)	914.003-9	(010.071)		OLV
814.004-8	(810.615)	914.004-7	(010.011)		PLC
814.005-5	(810.259)	914.005-4	(010.599)		PLC
814.006-3	(810.409)	914.006-2	(010.261)	B	CTH
814.007-1	(810.227)	914.007-0	(013.101)	B	CTH
814.008-9	(810.062)	914.008-8	(010.500)		OLO
814.009-7	(810.025)	914.009-6	(010.450)		OLO
814.010-5	(810.164)	914.010-4	(010.217)		BRO
814.011-3	(810.108)	914.011-2	(010.074)		PLT
814.012-1	(810.008)	914.012-0	(010.220)		PLT
814.013-9	(810.037)	914.013-8	(010.225)		PLT
814.014-7	(810.361)	914.014-6	(010.215)		PLK
814.015-4	(810.153)	914.015-3	(010.436)		PLK
814.016-2	(810.279)	914.016-1	(010.170)		PRD
814.017-0	(810.301)	914.017-9	(010.358)		PRD
814.018-8	(810.132)	914.018-7	(010.219)		CTP
814.019-6	(810.189)	914.019-5	(010.134)		CTP
814.020-4	(810.048)	914.020-3	(010.252)		OLP
814.021-2	(810.276)	914.021-1	(010.150)		OLP
814.022-0	(810.478)	914.022-9	(010.395)		PLR
814.023-8	(810.147)	914.023-7	(010.353)		PLR
814.024-6	(810.112)	914.024-5	(013.075)		CTH
814.025-3	(810.260)	914.025-2	(010.116)		CTH
814.026-1	(810.532)	914.026-0	(010.123)		PLT
814.027-9	(810.120)	914.027-8	(010.370)		PLT
814.028-7	(810.167)	914.028-6	(010.229)		OLV
814.029-5	(810.454)	914.029-4	(010.560)		OLV
814.030-3	(810.190)	914.030-2	(010.574)		CTC
814.031-1	(810.102)	914.031-0	(010.393)		CTC
814.032-9	(810.258)	914.032-8	(010.336)		PLR
814.033-7	(810.156)	914.033-6	(010.420)		PLR
814.034-5	(810.115)	914.034-4	(010.399)		PLC
814.035-2	(810.331)	914.035-1	(010.455)		PLC
814.036-0	(810.107)	914.036-9	(010.203)		OLP
814.037-8	(810.091)	914.037-7	(010.238)		OLP
814.038-6	(810.144)	914.038-5	(010.104)		CTH
814.039-4	(810.247)	914.039-3	(010.365)		PLK
814.040-2	(810.658)	914.040-1	(010.208)		PLK
814.041-0	(810.072)	914.041-9	(010.318)		CTP
814.042-8	(810.442)	914.042-7	(010.109)		BRO
814.043-6	(810.308)	914.043-5	(010.312)		BRO
814.044-4	(810.038)	914.044-3	(010.233)		PLR
814.045-1	(810.283)	914.045-0	(010.199)		PLR
814.046-9	(810.185)	914.046-8	(010.255)		PLR
814.047-7	(810.338)	914.047-6	(010.556)		PLR
814.048-5	(810.096)	914.048-4	(010.152)		CTP
814.049-3	(810.423)	914.049-2	(010.541)		CTP
814.050-1	(810.317)	914.050-0	(010.538)		CTP
814.051-9	(810.261)	914.051-8	(010.128)		PLT
814.052-7	(810.235)	914.052-6	(010.079)		OLV
814.053-5	(810.011)	914.053-4	(010.118)		CTH
814.054-3	(810.330)	914.054-2	(010.531)		CTH
814.055-0	(810.242)	914.055-9	(010.181)		CTH
814.056-8	(810.151)	914.056-7	(010.494)		PLR
814.057-6	(810.126)	914.057-5	(010.433)		PLR
814.058-4	(810.522)	914.058-3	(010.322)		PLZ
814.059-2	(810.257)	914.059-1	(010.108)		PLR
814.060-0	(810.149)	914.060-9	(010.357)		PLT
814.061-8	(810.441)	914.061-7	(010.041)		PLR
814.062-6	(810.248)	914.062-5	(010.256)		OLV

814.063-4	(810.010)	914.063-3	(010.014)	OLV
814.064-2	(810.461)	914.064-1	(010.230)	PLR
814.065-9	(810.088)	914.065-8	(010.445)	PLT
814.066-7	(810.090)	914.066-6	(010.137)	PLR
814.067-5	(810.047)	914.067-4	(010.517)	BRO
814.068-3	(810.246)	914.068-2	(010.378)	BRO
814.069-1	(810.619)	914.069-0	(010.458)	BRO
814.070-9	(810.346)	914.070-8	(010.429)	PLR
814.071-7	(810.171)	914.071-6	(010.548)	PLR
814.072-5	(810.396)	914.072-4	(010.235)	PLV
814.073-3	(810.028)	914.073-2	(010.031)	PLT
814.074-1	(810.045)	914.074-0	(010.546)	CTP
814.075-8	(810.273)	914.075-7	(010.466)	CTC
814.076-6	(810.016)	914.076-5	(010.049)	OLV
814.077-4	(810.202)	914.077-3	(010.187)	OLV
814.078-2	(810.142)	914.078-1	(010.295)	PRK
814.079-0	(810.172)	914.079-9	(010.484)	PRK
814.080-8	(810.395)	914.080-7	(010.472)	PRK
814.081-6	(810.314)	914.081-5	(010.099)	PLC
814.082-4	(810.053)	914.082-3	(010.216)	PLT
814.083-2	(810.270)	914.083-1	(010.080)	PLT
814.084-0	(810.267)	914.084-9	(010.601)	CTC
814.085-7	(810.206)	914.085-6	(010.575)	CTC
814.086-5	(810.521)	914.086-4	(010.274)	PRD
814.087-3	(810.101)	914.087-2	(010.527)	PRD
814.088-1	(810.218)	914.088-0	(010.038)	PLZ
814.089-9	(810.187)	914.089-8	(010.127)	PLZ
814.090-7	(810.316)	914.090-6	(010.227)	PLR
814.091-5	(810.204)	914.091-4	(010.162)	OLV
814.092-3	(810.457)	914.092-2	(010.262)	OLV
814.093-1	(810.105)	914.093-0	(010.243)	OLV
814.094-9	(810.421)	914.094-8	(010.008)	OLO
814.095-6	(810.328)	914.095-5	(010.583)	OLO
814.096-4	(810.410)	914.096-3	(010.341)	PRD
814.097-2	(810.127)	914.097-1	(010.491)	PRD
814.098-0	(810.440)	914.098-9	(010.493)	PRK
814.099-8	(810.274)	914.099-7	(010.086)	PLR
814.100-4	(810.302)	914.100-3	(010.081)	PLR
814.101-2	(810.089)	914.101-1	(010.039)	PLR
814.102-0	(810.130)	914.102-9	(010.597)	PLR
814.103-8	(810.401)	914.103-7	(010.234)	BRV
814.104-6	(810.178)	914.104-5	(010.381)	BRV
814.105-3	(810.024)	914.105-2	(010.047)	PRK
814.106-1	(810.122)	914.106-0	(010.237)	PRK
814.107-9	(810.188)	914.107-8	(010.290)	CTH
814.108-7	(810.196)	914.108-6	(010.155)	PRD
814.109-5	(810.480)	914.109-4	(010.383)	PRD
814.110-3	(810.031)	914.110-2	(010.580)	PRK
814.111-1	(810.079)	914.111-0	(010.459)	PLR
814.112-9	(810.363)	914.112-8	(010.025)	PLK
814.113-7	(810.305)	914.113-6	(010.451)	PLV
814.114-5	(810.332)	914.114-4	(010.469)	PLV
814.115-2	(810.087)	914.115-1	(010.589)	PRK
814.116-0	(810.116)	914.116-9	(010.177)	PRD
814.117-8	(810.075)	914.117-7	(010.286)	PRD
814.118-6	(810.166)	914.118-5	(010.149)	OLV
814.119-4	(810.244)	914.119-3	(010.144)	OLP
814.120-2	(810.269)	914.120-1	(010.323)	OLP
814.121-0	(810.148)	914.121-9	(010.570)	OLP
814.122-8	(810.237)	914.122-7	(010.435)	PLR
814.123-6	(810.300)	914.123-5	(010.183)	PLR
814.124-4	(810.145)	914.124-3	(010.228)	PLK
814.125-1	(810.470)	914.125-0	(010.317)	PLR
814.126-9	(810.155)	914.126-8	(010.508)	PRD

814.127-7	(810.412)	914.127-6	(010.369)		PRD
814.128-5	(810.295)	914.128-4	(010.278)		PRK
814.129-3	(810.256)	914.129-2	(010.179)		PRK
814.130-1	(810.027)	914.130-0	(010.213)		PRK
814.131-9	(810.400)	914.131-8	(010.368)		PLV
814.132-7	(810.214)	914.132-6	(010.389)		BRV
814.133-5	(810.092)	914.133-4	(010.221)		BRV
814.134-3	(810.143)	914.134-2	(010.536)		PLV
814.135-0	(810.074)	914.135-9	(010.533)		PLV
814.136-8	(810.278)	914.136-7	(010.191)		CTP
814.137-6	(810.303)	914.137-5	(010.188)		CTP
814.138-4	(810.139)	914.138-3	(010.106)		PLR
814.139-2	(810.005)	914.139-1	(012.503)		PLR
814.140-0	(810.462)	914.140-9	(010.163)		PRK
814.141-8	(810.475)	914.141-7	(010.424)		PRK
814.142-6	(810.207)	914.142-5	(010.195)		PLR
814.143-4	(810.593)	914.143-3	(010.537)		PLR
814.144-2	(810.315)	914.144-1	(010.168)		PLR
814.145-9	(810.017)	914.145-8	(010.558)		PLR
814.146-7	(810.146)	914.146-6	(010.130)		PLT
814.147-5	(810.335)	914.147-4	(010.544)		PLT
814.148-3	(810.197)	914.148-2	(010.528)		PLT
814.149-1	(810.321)	914.149-0	(010.470)		CTH
814.150-9	(810.200)	914.150-8	(010.513)		CTH
814.151-7	(810.035)	914.151-6	(010.534)		CTH
814.152-5	(810.294)	914.152-4	(010.521)		PLR
814.153-3	(810.168)	914.153-2	(010.121)		PLR
814.154-1	(810.460)	914.154-0	(010.606)		PLR
814.155-8	(810.557)	914.155-7	(010.604)		PLR
814.156-6	(810.109)	914.156-5	(010.065)		PLR
814.157-4	(810.251)	914.157-3	(010.391)		PLR
814.158-2	(810.393)	914.158-1	(010.410)		PLR
814.159-0	(810.198)	914.159-9	(010.224)		PLR
814.160-8	(810.012)	914.160-7	(010.407)		PLT
814.161-6	(810.634)	914.161-5	(010.030)		CTL
814.162-4	(810.099)	914.162-3	(010.077)		CTL
814.163-2	(810.103)	914.163-1	(010.083)		CTL
814.164-0	(810.643)	914.164-9	(010.236)		CTL
814.165-7	(810.523)	914.165-6	(010.026)		CTL
814.166-5	(810.086)	914.166-4	(010.564)		CTP
814.167-3	(810.293)	914.167-2	(010.063)		OLV
814.168-1	(810.420)	914.168-0	(010.084)		PRK
814.169-9	(810.129)	914.169-8	(010.078)		PLT
814.170-7	(810.264)	914.170-6	(010.082)		PLR
814.171-5	(810.473)	914.171-4	(010.018)		PLR
814.172-3	(810.121)	914.172-2	(010.618)		PLR
814.173-1	(810.653)	914.173-0	(010.614)		PLR
814.174-9	(810.509)	914.174-8	(010.308)		PLR
814.175-6	(810.466)	914.175-5	(010.446)		PLR
814.176-4	(810.078)	914.176-3	(010.267)		PLR
814.177-2	(810.014)	914.177-1	(010.253)		CTC
814.178-0	(810.588)	914.178-9	(010.004)		PLA
814.179-8	(810.255)	914.179-7	(010.147)		PLT
814.180-6	(810.372)	914.180-5	(010.205)		CTH
814.181-4	(810.347)	914.181-3	(010.452)		CTH
814.182-2	(810.386)	914.182-1	(010.271)		PRK
814.183-0	(810.598)	914.183-9	(010.291)		PRK
814.184-8	(810.311)	914.184-7	(010.307)		PRK
814.185-5	(810.133)	914.185-4	(010.270)		PRK
814.186-3	(810.577)	914.186-2	(010.464)		PRK
814.187-1	(810.033)	914.187-0	(010.136)		OLV
814.188-9	(810.083)	914.188-8	(010.122)		OLV
814.189-7	(810.040)	914.189-6	(010.132)		OLV
814.190-5	(810.215)	914.190-4	(010.254)	B	OLV

814.191-3	(810.513)	914.191-2	(010.299)	**B**	OLV
814.192-1	(810.558)	914.192-0	(010.028)		CTL
814.193-9	(810.322)	914.193-8	(010.015)		CTL
814.194-7	(810.498)	914.194-6	(010.300)		PLR
814.195-4	(810.586)	914.195-3	(010.304)		PLZ
814.196-2	(810.576)	914.196-1	(010.207)		PLZ
814.197-0	(810.029)	914.197-9	(010.242)		BRM
814.198-8	(811.494)	914.198-7	(010.245)		BRM
814.199-6	(810.018)	914.199-5	(010.384)		BRM

Class 814.2. 3-car units.

814.201-0	(810.286)	014.001-2	(010.462)	814.202-8	(810.131)	PRL
814.203-6	(810.230)	014.002-0	(010.315)	814.204-4	(810.134)	PRL
814.205-1	(810.095)	014.003-8	(010.516)	814.206-9	(810.591)	BRV
814.207-7	(810.397)	014.004-6	(010.218)	814.208-5	(810.488)	BRV
814.209-3	(810.614)	014.005-3	(010.497)	814.210-1	(809.552)	BRV
814.211-9	(810.253)	014.006-1	(010.259)	814.212-7	(810.484)	PRL
814.213-5	(810.277)	014.007-9	(010.535)	814.214-3	(810.299)	PRL
814.215-0	(810.219)	014.008-7	(010.496)	814.216-8	(810.093)	PRL
814.217-6	(810.456)	014.009-5	(010.142)	814.218-4	(810.013)	BRM
814.219-2	(810.023)	014.010-3	(010.492)	814.220-0	(810.238)	BRM
814.221-8	(810.285)	014.011-1	(010.476)	814.222-6	(810.081)	PRL
814.223-4	(810.084)	014.012-9	(010.244)	814.224-2	(810.483)	PRL
814.225-9	(810.117)	014.013-7	(010.593)	814.226-7	(810.553)	PRL
814.227-5	(810.128)	014.014-5	(010.337)	814.228-3	(810.169)	BRM
814.229-1	(810.377)	014.015-2	(010.405)	814.230-9	(810.030)	BRM
814.231-7	(810.068)	014.016-0	(010.068)	814.232-5	(810.211)	OLO
814.233-3	(810.170)	014.017-8	(010.486)	814.234-1	(810.252)	OLO
814.235-8	(810.344)	014.018-6	(010.340)	814.236-6	(810.443)	PRL
814.237-4	(810.374)	014.019-4	(010.005)	814.238-2	(810.085)	BRM
814.239-0	(810.388)	014.020-2	(010.447)	814.240-8	(810.069)	BRM
814.241-6	(810.243)	014.021-0	(010.454)	814.242-4	(810.161)	OLO
814.243-2	(810.592)	014.022-8	(010.223)	814.244-0	(810.324)	OLO
814.245-7	(810.268)	014.023-6	(010.360)	814.246-5	(810.042)	OLO
814.247-3	(810.606)	014.024-4	(010.431)	814.248-1	(810.241)	OLO
814.249-9	(810.309)	014.025-1	(010.356)	814.250-7	(810.582)	OLO
814.251-5	(810.407)	014.026-9	(010.379)	814.252-3	(810.491)	OLO

Class 814.0. 2-car units (continued).

814.300-0	(810.471)	914.300-9	(010.406)	OLO
814.301-8	(810.348)	914.301-7	(010.408)	PLZ
814.302-6	(810.467)	914.302-5	(010.594)	PLZ
814.303-4	(810.275)	914.303-3	(010.140)	PLZ
814.304-2	(810.254)	914.304-1	(010.139)	PLZ
814.305-9	(810.266)	914.305-8	(010.160)	PLA
814.306-7	(810.445)	914.306-6	(010.554)	PLA
814.307-5	(810.384)	914.307-4	(010.392)	PLA
814.308-3	(810.205)	914.308-2	(010.416)	PLA
814.309-1	(810.323)	914.309-0	(010.373)	PLT
814.310-9	(810.076)	914.310-8	(010.419)	PLT

▲ The Regionova Class 814s have been a successful rebuild of 4-wheel Class 810s and trailers and can be seen across the whole country. On 9 July 2013 814.167 is seen at Veřovice in east Moravia with train Os3169, the 09.17 Valašské Meziříčí–Frenštát pod Radhoštěm. **Robert Pritchard**

▼ Stadler-built Class 840s work many local services around Liberec. On 6 July 2013 840.015+ 840.010 arrive at Tanvald with train Os16222, the 11.10 Harrachov–Liberec. **Robert Pritchard**

CLASS 840 REGIO-SHUTTLE RS1 SINGLE-CARS

These single-car Stadler DMUs are based on the DB Class 650, which has also been built in large numbers for German private operators (originally it was an Adtranz design). Classes 840/841 are very similar, the differences being the brakes and maximum speed. Both classes have been branded "RegioSpiders" by ČD. The 840s are used on routes radiating north and east of Liberec – to Černousy, Jindřichovice pod Smrkem, Bílý Potok pod Smrkem, Tanvald and Harrachov/Szklarska Poręba Górna (Poland). At busy times as many as four units may operate together. They are fitted with two magnetic track brakes for the steep gradients on the (previously rack-operated) Harrachov branch.

Built: 2011–12.
Builder: Stadler Pankow.
Engine: 2 x Iveco Cursor8 of 265 kW (355 hp).
Transmission: Hydrodynamic, Voith DIWA D864.5/D864.3E.
Length over Buffers: 25.50 m.
Wheel Arrangement: B-B.
Formation: DMSO.

Total No. Built: 16.
Accommodation: –/51(+20) 1TD 2W.
Weight: 46 tonnes.
Maximum Speed: 100 km/h.
EVN: 95 54 5 840 0xx-c.

840.001-2	B	CTL	840.007-9	B	CTL	840.012-9	B	CTL
840.002-0	B	CTL	840.008-7	B	CTL	840.013-7	B	CTL
840.003-8	B	CTL	840.009-5	B	CTL	840.014-5	B	CTL
840.004-6	B	CTL	840.010-3	B	CTL	840.015-2	B	CTL
840.005-3	B	CTL	840.011-1	B	CTL	840.016-0	B	CTL
840.006-1	B	CTL						

CLASS 841 REGIO-SHUTTLE RS1 SINGLE-CARS

The new-build ČD Class 841 is mainly used in the Vysočina region around Havlíčkův Brod and Jihlava, including the Humpolec branch, Havlíčkův Brod–Světlá nad Sázavou–Ledeč nad Sázavou, Kostelec–Telč–Slavonice, Havlíčkův Brod–Křižanov and Křižanov–Studenec. The Česká Třebová-based units are used on the Lanškroun branch and Česká Třebová–Žďár nad Sázavou stopping services.

Most of the Havlíčkův Brod units carry vinyls displaying local attractions on the ČD blue livery.

In addition to 841.001–017, in spring 2015 ČD leased a further four units from Vogtlandbahn for use in the Hradec Králové area, including the Hradec Králové–Týniště nad Orlicí–Doudleby nad Orlici, Týniště–Náchod and Častolovice–Rychnov nad Kněžnou lines. These are former ODEG (Ostdeutsche Eisenbahn)-operated units and are on a 6-year lease to ČD. Units have received numbers in the ČD 841.xxx series, using the last two numbers of their Class 650 serial number. Livery is ODEG yellow, white & green.

Built: 2011–13.
Builder: Stadler Pankow.
Engine: 2 x Iveco Cursor8 of 265 kW (355 hp).
Transmission: Hydrodynamic, Voith DIWA D864.5/D864.3E.
Length over Buffers: 25.50 m.
Wheel Arrangement: B-B.
Formation: DMSO.

Total No. Built (for ČD): 17.
Accommodation: –/51(+20) 1TD 2W.
Weight: 46 tonnes.
Maximum Speed: 120 km/h.
EVN: 95 54 5 841 0xx-c.

Class 841. New build units for ČD.

841.001-1	B	BRO	841.007-8	B	CTC	841.013-6	B	BRO
841.002-9	B	BRO	841.008-6	B	BRO	841.014-4	B	BRO
841.003-7	B	BRO	841.009-4	B	BRO	841.015-1	B	CTC
841.004-5	B	BRO	841.010-2	B	BRO	841.016-9	B	CTC
841.005-2	B	BRO	841.011-0	B	BRO	841.017-7	B	CTC
841.006-0	B	BRO	841.012-8	B	BRO			

Class 841. Former ODEG units on lease to ČD to 2021. Details as above except:

Built: 2004.
Engine: 2 x MAN D2866 LH21 of 265 kW (355 hp).
Accommodation: –/72 1TD 2W.
Weight: 42 tonnes.

841.065-6	(650.065/VT650.65)	CTH	841.073-0	(650.073/VT650.73)	CTH
841.072-2	(650.072/VT650.72)	CTH	841.074-8	(650.074/VT650.74)	CTH

CLASS 842   MOTOR COACHES

Class 842 was ordered by ČSD and is very much in the line of traditional double-cabbed tractor units that can run on their own or hauling a number of trailers. The first two units (842.001/002) were built as prototypes a few years ahead of the batch of 35 production units. They were going to be given the ČSD Classification M273.2, but in the end this designation was not used. There were no matching trailers built at the same time, although four coaches were rebuilt as Class 042 in 1989, but these are now used as locomotive-hauled stock. Classes 842 and 843 can normally haul up to four Class 021 or two Class 043, 050 or 053 trailers. They can also operate with the former Class 954 driving trailers.

Between 2010 and 2013 the 842s were modernised by Pars nova Šumperk with more powerful Tedom 242 kW engines to replace their original Liaz 212 kW engines.

The main routes for the Brno based units include Brno–Jihlava, Brno–Oslavany/Hrušovany nad Jevišovkou, Břeclav–Znojmo, Šakvice–Hustopeče u Brna, Brno–Uherské Hradiště, Staré Město u Uherského Hradiště–Bylnice and also as far as Přerov and Prostějov on Lines 300/301. Valašské Meziříčí units are mainly used on Line 323 between Valašské Meziříčí and Ostrava. Plzeň units work the semi-fast services from Plzeň to Most via Line 160, and also some local services at the Plzeň end of this line. Finally, the České Budějovice units are used between České Budějovice and Volary/Nové Údolí.

Built: *1988–89; 1993–94.
Builder: MSV Studénka.
Engine: 2 x Tedom TD242RH TA25 of 242 kW (325 hp).
Transmission: Hydraulic.
Wheel Arrangement: 1-A-A-1.
Formation: DMBSO.

Total No. Built: 37.
Accommodation: –/64(+2) 1T.
Weight: 47 tonnes.
Length over Buffers: * 24.70 m; 25.20 m.
Maximum Speed: 100 km/h.
EVN: 95 54 5 842 0xx-c.

842.001-0	B	*	BRH	842.014-3	B	BRH	842.026-7	B	BRH
842.002-8	B	*	BRH	842.015-0	B	BRH	842.027-5	B	BRH
842.003-6	B		PLZ	842.016-8	B	BRH	842.028-3	B	BRH
842.004-4	B		BRH	842.017-6	B	BRH	842.029-1	B	PLZ
842.005-1	B		OLV	842.018-4	B	BRH	842.030-9	B	PLZ
842.006-9	B		PLB	842.019-2	B	BRH	842.031-7	B	BRH
842.007-7	B		PLB	842.020-0	B	PLB	842.032-5	B	BRH
842.008-5	B		PLZ	842.021-8	B	OLV	842.033-3	B	BRH
842.009-3	B		BRH	842.022-6	B	BRH	842.034-1	B	PLZ
842.010-1	B		OLV	842.023-4	B	PLZ	842.035-8	B	OLV
842.011-9	B		OLV	842.024-2	B	PLZ	842.036-6	B	PLZ
842.012-7	B		PLB	842.025-9	B	OLV	842.037-4	B	BRH
842.013-5	B		PLB					

CLASS 843   MOTOR COACHES

Almost certainly the last of the single-car tractor units, Class 843s are diesel-electric compared with the previous hydraulic transmission of Class 842. At the same time as the 843s were built, so were 32 matching Class 043 (now Btn753) intermediate trailers and 11 Class 943 (now Bftn791) driving trailers (see Non-Powered Trailers section).

Today Class 843s are based at two depots: Liberec and Olomouc. The Liberec based units work Liberec–Česká Lípa–Děčín–Ústí nad Labem plus some Liberec–Děčín stopping trains and Liberec–Turnov–Hradec Králové–Pardubice. The Olomouc units work Olomouc–Krnov–Opava–Ostrava Svinov and some services on the Olomouc–Jeseník–Krnov and Olomouc–Uničov–Šumperk routes.

At the time of writing most of Class 843 had received the new ČD blue livery, but a number are still in the original red & cream livery.

Built: 1995–97.
Builder: MSV Studénka.
Engine: 2 x Liaz ML640D of 300 kW (400 hp).
Transmission: Electric.
Wheel Arrangement: Bo-Bo.
Formation: DMBSO.

Total No. Built: 31.
Accommodation: –/54(+6) 1T.
Weight: 56 tonnes.
Length over Buffers: 25.20 m.
Maximum Speed: 110 km/h.
EVN: 95 54 5 843 0xx-c.

▲ Valašské Meziříčí-based Class 842s work some trains on Line 325. On 6 July 2014 842.005 with two trailers – Bdtn757 20-29 224 and Bdtn756 21-29 359 leave Ostrava Kunčice with train Os3156, the 14.22 Ostrava hl.n–Frýdlant nad Ostravicí. ZSSK Cargo 131.081/082 is alongside. **Robert Pritchard**

▼ Olomouc-based 843.023, with Btn753 trailers 29-29 019+29-29 015, leaves Jindřichov na Moravě with train Sp1702, the 10.54 Jeseník–Zábřeh na Moravě on 7 July 2014. **Robert Pritchard**

843.001-9	B	OLO	843.012-6	B	CTL	843.022-5		OLO
843.002-7		OLO	843.013-4	B	CTL	843.023-3	B	OLO
843.003-5	B	OLO	843.014-2	B	CTL	843.024-1	B	OLO
843.004-3	B	CTL	843.015-9		CTL	843.025-8	B	CTL
843.005-0		CTL	843.016-7	B	CTL	843.026-6	B	OLO
843.006-8	B	CTL	843.017-5		CTL	843.027-4		OLO
843.007-6	B	CTL	843.018-3	B	CTL	843.028-2	B	OLO
843.008-4		CTL	843.019-1	B	OLO	843.029-0	B	OLO
843.009-2	B	CTL	843.020-9		OLO	843.030-8	B	CTL
843.010-0		CTL	843.021-7	B	OLO	843.031-6		OLO
843.011-8		CTL						

CLASS 844   REGIOSHARK   2-SECTION ARTICULATED UNITS

These articulated 2-car units, built by PESA in Poland and also called "PESA Link II", are the latest DMUs to enter traffic in the Czech Republic. The comfortable saloons include low floor sections, air conditioning, a small First Class area, wi-fi and power sockets at some seats. Since the ČD order was placed PESA has won further orders for the type from Germany and Poland.

Plzeň-based Class 844s can be found on the Plzeň–Domažlice route and some trains on Line 160 to Žihle and Plzeň–Stříbro. Cheb units work Mariánské Lázně–Cheb–Karlovy Vary–Klášterec nad Ohří (despite this line being electrified) and some local lines around Cheb, including to Aš/Hranice v Čechách (Line 148), Luby u Chebu (Line 146) and Johanngeorgenstadt (Line 142). Valašské Meziříčí units work Valašské Meziříčí–Hulín–Kojetín, Valašské Meziříčí–Rožnov pod Radhoštěm, Otrokovice–Vizovice and Hulín–Otrokovice–Staré Město u Uherského Hradiště. Děčín based units operate stopping services from Děčín to Liberec and also Děčín–Jedlova–Rumburk–Dolní Poustevna. The two Pardubice units work on Line 238 from Pardubice to Havlíčkův Brod.

As these units are articulated just the one running number is allocated for each full set, the two sections being called "A" and "B".

Built: 2012–13.
Builder: PESA Bydgoszcz, Poland.
Engine: 2 x MTU 6H 1800 R85L of 390 kW (525 hp).
Transmission: Mechanical – ZF EcoLife Rail.
Wheel Arrangement: B-2-B.
Formation: DMSO–DMCO.

Total No. Built: 31.
Accommodation: A: –/64(+2) + B: 9/32(+14) 1TD 2W.
Weight: 86 tonnes.
Length over Buffers: 43.73 m.
Maximum Speed: 120 km/h.
EVN: 95 54 5 844 0xx-c.

844.001-8	B	PLC	844.012-5	B	PLZ	844.022-4	B	OLV
844.002-6	B	PLZ	844.013-3	B	OLV	844.023-2	B	PLC
844.003-4	B	OLV	844.014-1	B	OLV	844.024-0	B	PLC
844.004-2	B	PLC	844.015-8	B	PLZ	844.025-7	B	PRD
844.005-9	B	PLC	844.016-6	B	PLC	844.026-5	B	PRD
844.006-7	B	PLZ	844.017-4	B	PLC	844.027-3	B	PRD
844.007-5	B	PLZ	844.018-2	B	PLC	844.028-1	B	PRD
844.008-3	B	PLZ	844.019-0	B	PLC	844.029-9	B	PRD
844.009-1	B	PLZ	844.020-8	B	OLV	844.030-7	B	CTP
844.010-9	B	PLZ	844.021-6	B	OLV	844.031-5	B	CTP
844.011-7	B	PLZ						

CLASS 850   MOTOR COACHES

Classes 850 and 851, nicknamed "Crocodiles", were once the mainstay of many Czech and Slovak longer distance branch line and regional services. They are twin-cab tractor units that could operate singly or with the similarly styled Class 050 trailers. The last unit in traffic with ČD, 851.028, was withdrawn in 2014 and all remaining units listed are stored or awaiting disposal.

Built: 1962–67.
Builder: MSV Studénka.
Engine: CKD K12V170DR of 515 kW (690 hp).
Transmission: Hydrodynamic.
Former ČSD Class: M286.0.
Wheel Arrangement: B-2.
Formation: DMBSO.

Total No. Built: 52.
Accommodation: –/48 1T.
Weight: 50.2 tonnes.
Length over Buffers: 24.79 m.
Maximum Speed: 110 km/h.

EVN: 95 54 5 850 0xx-c.

850.015-9		CTC (S)	850.028-2		CTC (S)	850.029-0		CTC (S)

▲ RegioShark DMU 844.029 arrives at Česká Lípa with train Os6609, the 12.41 Děčín hl.n–Liberec stopping service on 11 March 2015. **Robert Pritchard**

▼ Still in the old red & cream livery, at the time of this photograph, 854.010 and Bdtn757 trailer 20-29 201 leave Praha hl.n with train R1240, the 17.45 to České Budějovice via Příbram on 14 July 2014. **Robert Pritchard**

CLASS 851 MOTOR COACHES

Class 851 is fitted with a more powerful engine compared to Class 850. A number of these popular units (both Classes 850/851) have been preserved or are in use as test units (see separate sections).

Built: 1967–68.
Builder: MSV Studénka.
Engine: CKD KS12V170DR of 588 kW (790 hp).
Transmission: Hydrodynamic.
Former ČSD Class: M286.1.
Wheel Arrangement: B-2.
Formation: DMBSO.

Total No. Built: 37.
Accommodation: –/48 1T.
Weight: 50.2 tonnes.
Length over Buffers: 24.79 m.
Maximum Speed: 110 km/h.

EVN: 95 54 5 851 0xx-c.

851.006-7	CTC (S)	851.012-5	CTC (S)	851.027-3	CTC (S)

CLASS 854 MOTOR COACHES

These diesel tractor units were constructed from bodyshells similar to contemporary loco-hauled stock. Built 1968–71 as 60 Class M296.2/M296.1 (later Classes 852/853). They were rebuilt 1997–2006, internally refurbished, and fitted with new Caterpillar engines. 146 trailer cars (later Classes 053/054/056) were also built. As well as running with up to four trailers, Class 854 also now operate with Class 954 Driving Trailers (see Non-Powered Trailers section).

Based at Praha Vršovice, Trutnov or Brno, Class 854s are mainly used on medium-long distance services on the following routes. Praha units: Praha–Příbram–České Budějovice and Praha–Mladá Boleslav–Tanvald. Trutnov units: Trutnov–Hradec Králové, Trutnov–Stará Paka–Chlumec nad Cidlinou–Kolín and Rumburk–Česká Lípa–Mladá Boleslav–Kolín. Brno units: Brno–Hrušovany nad Jevišovkou, Znojmo–Břeclav and Brno–Veselí nad Moravou–Uherské Hradiště–Bylnice.

Most units are still in ČD red livery, but repaints into the new blue livery are taking place.

Built: 1968–71; rebuilt as Class 854 1997–2006.
Builder: Pars nova Šumperk.
Engine: Caterpillar 3412 E DI-TA of 596 kW (800 hp).
Transmission: Hydrodynamic.
Former ČSD Class: M296.1 or M296.2.
Wheel Arrangement: B-2.
Formation: DMBSO.

Total No. Built: 50.
Accommodation: –/48 1T.
Weight: 50.2 tonnes.
Length over Buffers: 24.79 m.
Maximum Speed: 120 km/h.
EVN: 95 54 5 854 xxx-c.

Non-Standard Livery: 854.021/027: Original red & cream. Carry original numbers M296.1021/1027.

Class 854.0. Rebuilt from Class 853.

854.001-5		PRG	854.014-8	B	CTT	854.026-2			BRH
854.002-3	B	PRG	854.015-5		CTT	854.027-0	0	+	PRG
854.004-9	B	PRG	854.016-3		CTT	854.028-8	B		BRH
854.005-6		CTT	854.017-1		CTT	854.029-6	B		PRG
854.006-4	B	PRG	854.019-7	B	CTT	854.030-4	B		BRH
854.007-2	B	PRG	854.020-5		CTT	854.031-2			PRG
854.008-0		CTT	854.021-3	0	+ PRG	854.032-0			PRG
854.009-8		PRG	854.022-1	B	CTT	854.033-8			PRG
854.010-6	B	PRG	854.023-9	B	CTT	854.034-6			PRG
854.012-2		BRH	854.024-7		BRH	854.035-3	B		PRG
854.013-0		BRH	854.025-4	B	BRH				

Class 854.2. Rebuilt from Class 852.

854.201-1	B	BRH	854.207-8	B	BRH	854.216-9		BRH
854.202-9		CTT	854.209-4		BRH	854.217-7		BRH
854.203-7	B	BRH	854.210-2		CTT	854.218-5		BRH
854.204-5	B	CTT	854.212-8		BRH	854.222-7	B	BRH
854.205-2		CTT	854.213-6		CTT	854.223-5		BRH
854.206-0	B	BRH	854.215-1		BRH	854.225-0		CTT

1.5. ČD NON-POWERED TRAILERS

Except where noted, multiple units are made up of driving motor and unpowered trailer coaches in no fixed formation. During 2009–10 the 000 number series for diesel trailers was abandoned with numbering reverting to the 12-digit EVN carriage stock series. Note that trailers are listed in order of their former class number, not in strict EVN number order, as this would have led to a mixed list of four-wheel and bogie trailers.

Where known and confirmed, the former number is shown alongside the existing number. In the old number series 9xx.xxx were driving trailers and 0xx.xxx intermediate trailers. ČD trailers that have been reserved for NTM Lužná u Rakovníka are shown.

The livery of trailers is original ČD red & cream unless shown otherwise.

1.5.1. DRIVING TRAILERS

FORMER CLASS 943   DRIVING TRAILERS

These loose driving trailers were built new for use with Class 843 DMUs, and have a similar cab end, although they use shorter bodyshells. They are used with Class 843s based at Olomouc or Liberec.

Type Bftn791. Formerly numbered 943.001–011.

Built: 1996–97.
Builder: MSV Studénka.   **Weight:** 28 tonnes.
Accommodation: –/64 1T.   **Length over Buffers:** 19.70 m.
Maximum Speed: 120 km/h.

50 54 80-29 001-2	(943.001)	B	OLO		50 54 80-29 007-9	(943.007)	B	CTL
50 54 80-29 002-0	(943.002)	B	OLO		50 54 80-29 008-7	(943.008)	B	OLO
50 54 80-29 003-8	(943.003)	B	OLO		50 54 80-29 009-5	(943.009)	B	OLO
50 54 80-29 004-6	(943.004)	B	OLO		50 54 80-29 010-3	(943.010)	B	CTL
50 54 80-29 005-3	(943.005)	B	OLO		50 54 80-29 011-1	(943.011)	B	OLO
50 54 80-29 006-1	(943.006)	B	OLO					

FORMER CLASS 954   DRIVING TRAILERS

These vehicles were converted from locomotive-hauled postal coaches (Postw cars in the 90 40 200–270 series built by MSV) for operation with tractor units. Interestingly the new driving cabs replicate the 35-year old non-gangwayed ends of Class 854 DMUs. These driving trailers not only operate with Class 842 or 854 tractor units but also with locomotive-hauled trains. The former Class 954.2 vehicles have an area of First Class seating whilst the former Class 954.0 vehicles are Second Class only.

Type ABfbrdtn795. Formerly numbered 954.201–226.

Built: Original vehicles built: 1984–85; rebuilt 2006–09.
Builder: Pars nova Šumperk.   **Weight:** 41 tonnes.
Accommodation: 15/38(+8) 1TD 2W + bike spaces.   **Length over Buffers:** 24.50 m.
Maximum Speed: 120 km/h.

50 54 80-29 201-8	(954.201)		BRH		50 54 80-29 214-1	(954.214)		CTT
50 54 80-29 202-6	(954.202)		BRH		50 54 80-29 215-8	(954.215)		CTT
50 54 80-29 203-4	(954.203)		BRH		50 54 80-29 216-6	(954.216)		BRH
50 54 80-29 204-2	(954.204)		CTT		50 54 80-29 217-4	(954.217)	B	PLZ
50 54 80-29 205-9	(954.205)		CTT		50 54 80-29 218-2	(954.218)		PLZ
50 54 80-29 206-7	(954.206)		CTT		50 54 80-29 219-0	(954.219)		PLZ
50 54 80-29 207-5	(954.207)		CTT		50 54 80-29 220-8	(954.220)		PLR
50 54 80-29 208-3	(954.208)		CTT		50 54 80-29 221-6	(954.221)	B	PLR
50 54 80-29 209-1	(954.209)		CTT		50 54 80-29 222-4	(954.222)	B	PLR
50 54 80-29 210-9	(954.210)	B	CTT		50 54 80-29 223-2	(954.223)	B	BRH
50 54 80-29 211-7	(954.211)	B	CTT		50 54 80-29 224-0	(954.224)		BRH
50 54 80-29 212-5	(954.212)		CTT		50 54 80-29 225-7	(954.225)		PLZ
50 54 80-29 213-3	(954.213)		CTT		50 54 80-29 226-5	(954.226)		PLZ

▲ Type Bftn791 Driving Trailer 80-29 007 and 843.004 are seen stabled at Liberec on 6 July 2013.
Robert Pritchard

▼ Type ABfbrdtn795 Driving Trailer 80-29 223 arrives at the attractive station of Uherské Hradiště with train Os4121, the 16.14 Brno hl.n–Staré Město u Uherského Hradiště on 8 July 2013. Also in the formation are Bdtn756 trailer 21-29 305 and DMU motor coach 854.013. **Robert Pritchard**

Type Bfbrdtn794. Formerly numbered 954.001–008.

Built: Original vehicles built: 1984; rebuilt 2006–07.
Builder: Pars nova Šumperk.
Accommodation: –/63(+8) 1TD + bike spaces.   **Weight:** 41 tonnes.
Length over Buffers: 24.50 m.
Maximum Speed: 120 km/h.

50 54 80-29 301-6	(954.001)	BRH		50 54 80-29 305-7	(954.005)	BRH
50 54 80-29 302-4	(954.002)	BRH		50 54 80-29 306-5	(954.006)	BRH
50 54 80-29 303-2	(954.003)	BRH		50 54 80-29 307-3	(954.007)	BRH
50 54 80-29 304-0	(954.004)	BRH		50 54 80-29 308-1	(954.008)	BRH

1.5.2. INTERMEDIATE FOUR-WHEELED TRAILERS

FORMER CLASSES 010–016   FOUR-WHEELED TRAILERS

912 four-wheel trailer cars were built for use with similar Class 810 motor coaches, but were also used with other tractor units and some diesel and electric locomotives. The basic original type was Class 010 (Class 011 is now the equivalent in Slovakia) while other ČD versions classified 011–016 carry seating layout modifications or cycle or parcels accommodation. Vehicles have low back 3+2 seating unless shown (some have now been fitted with high-back seating).

Originally numbered in the 70 54 25 09 xxx carriage number series and then in the 010–016.xxx series. From 2009 all four-wheeled trailers were renumbered in the 12 digit carriage number series. Most also still carry their 010–016.xxx number in small type on the vehicle ends or wheelsets.

A large number of four-wheeled trailers have been withdrawn and scrapped or converted into Class 914/014 DMUs in recent years. The remaining serviceable vehicles are used on a number of routes across the country, mainly hauled by Class 810 DMUs or Class 714 locomotives.

Built: 1973–83.   **Weight:** 15 tonnes.
Builder: MSV Studénka.   **Length over Buffers:** 13.97 m.
Former ČSD Class: Baafx.   **Maximum Speed:** 80 km/h.

h   fitted with new high-back seats.

Type Btax780. Formerly numbered Class 010. The Class 010s were renumbered in the series 50 54 24-29 001–419. **Accommodation:** –/62 1T.

50 54 24-29 004-5	(010.349)		CTC (S)		50 54 24-29 212-4	(010.475)		OLP
50 54 24-29 019-3	(010.457)	B	OLP		50 54 24-29 226-4	(010.567)		OLP
50 54 24-29 046-6	(010.363)		PRK (S)		50 54 24-29 228-0	(010.568)	h	OLP
50 54 24-29 057-3	(010.001)		BRO		50 54 24-29 229-8	(010.201)	h	PRG (S)
50 54 24-29 058-1	(010.002)	h	PRG (S)		50 54 24-29 230-6	(010.067)		PLT
50 54 24-29 075-5	(010.044)		PLZ (S)		50 54 24-29 231-4	(010.110)	h	PRG
50 54 24-29 076-3	(010.045)	h	BRV		50 54 24-29 258-7	(010.185)		PLL
50 54 24-29 099-5	(010.151)	h	BRM		50 54 24-29 261-1	(010.578)		CTC (S)
50 54 24-29 104-3	(010.413)		BRZ		50 54 24-29 263-7	(010.581)		PRG (S)
50 54 24-29 106-8	(010.009)		BRM		50 54 24-29 270-2	(010.327)		PLL
50 54 24-29 107-6	(010.525)	h	OLP		50 54 24-29 274-4	(010.020)		BRV
50 54 24-29 110-0	(010.010)		BRV		50 54 24-29 275-1	(010.021)	h	BRV
50 54 24-29 112-6	(010.276)	h	OLP		50 54 24-29 280-1	(010.288)		OLV (S)
50 54 24-29 126-6	(010.376)		BRM		50 54 24-29 297-5	(010.302)		OLP
50 54 24-29 133-2	(010.326)		BRV		50 54 24-29 300-7	(010.112)		PLC (S)
50 54 24-29 135-7	(010.540)		CTC (S)		50 54 24-29 301-5	(010.113)		PLC
50 54 24-29 145-6	(010.385)		PLL		50 54 24-29 302-3	(010.206)		PLK
50 54 24-29 151-4	(010.427)	B h	PRG		50 54 24-29 314-8	(010.328)		PLL
50 54 24-29 157-1	(010.388)	h	BRV		50 54 24-29 317-1	(010.330)		PLL
50 54 24-29 168-8	(010.060)		BRM		50 54 24-29 320-5	(010.190)	h	PRG
50 54 24-29 177-9	(010.439)	h	OLP		50 54 24-29 326-2	(010.488)		OLP
50 54 24-29 178-7	(010.440)		OLP		50 54 24-29 328-8	(010.333)		PLL
50 54 24-29 180-3	(010.442)		BRV		50 54 24-29 329-6	(010.334)		PLL
50 54 24-29 183-7	(010.550)		BRO		50 54 24-29 336-1	(010.596)		CTH
50 54 24-29 184-5	(010.551)		BRO		50 54 24-29 355-1	(010.607)		PLL
50 54 24-29 196-9	(010.222)		PLL		50 54 24-29 358-5	(010.194)		BRV

50 54 24-29 362-7	(010.412)	h	PRG
50 54 24-29 366-8	(010.090)		CTC
50 54 24-29 369-2	(010.095)		PLB
50 54 24-29 371-8	(010.348)		PLL
50 54 24-29 379-1	(010.239)		PLL
50 54 24-29 381-7	(010.096)		PLT
50 54 24-29 382-5	(010.097)		PLK
50 54 24-29 389-0	(010.247)		PLL
50 54 24-29 390-8	(010.248)		PLZ (S)
50 54 24-29 400-5	(010.611)		OLP
50 54 24-29 401-3	(010.612)		BRV
50 54 24-29 404-7	(010.615)		BRV
50 54 24-29 408-8	(010.617)		BRV

Type Btax781. Formerly numbered Class 011. Converted from Class 010 in 1997. New high-back seats. **Accommodation:** –/62 1T.

Similar vehicle 50 54 24 29 801 (ex-011.434) is used with the Class 812 DMU (see DMU section).

50 54 24-29 802-2   (011.843)   h   PRL

Type BDtax782. Formerly numbered Class 012. Converted from Class 010 in 1995–2010. Modified with a small area for transporting bikes. Class 012s were originally renumbered in the series 50 54 93-29 001–117, with vehicles 50 54 93-29 118/125/237 converted from Class 010 in 2014. **Accommodation:** –/52 1T.

50 54 93-29 118 was previously numbered 50 54 24-24 219, 50 54 93-29 125 was previously numbered 50 54 24-24 361 and 50 54 93-29 237 was previously numbered 50 54 93-29 117.

50 54 93-29 002-5	(012.064)		BRV
50 54 93-29 003-3	(012.075)		PLR
50 54 93-29 004-1	(012.092)		CTC
50 54 93-29 005-8	(012.094)		CTT
50 54 93-29 006-6	(012.099)		CTC
50 54 93-29 007-4	(012.106)		PLR
50 54 93-29 008-2	(012.113)		BRV
50 54 93-29 009-0	(012.114)		BRO
50 54 93-29 010-8	(012.117)		OLB (S)
50 54 93-29 011-6	(012.229)		PRK
50 54 93-29 012-4	(012.579)		BRV
50 54 93-29 013-2	(012.126)		PLC
50 54 93-29 014-0	(012.)		
50 54 93-29 015-7	(012.148)		BRZ (S)
50 54 93-29 017-3	(012.169)		PLK
50 54 93-29 018-1	(012.170)		PLA
50 54 93-29 019-9	(012.172)		PLT
50 54 93-29 020-7	(012.173)		PLT
50 54 93-29 021-5	(012.180)		PRK
50 54 93-29 022-3	(012.184)		PLA
50 54 93-29 023-1	(012.186)		BRV
50 54 93-29 024-9	(012.190)		PLL
50 54 93-29 025-6	(012.198)		OLS
50 54 93-29 026-4	(012.216)		PLT
50 54 93-29 027-2	(012.217)		PLL
50 54 93-29 028-0	(012.236)		OLB
50 54 93-29 029-8	(012.253)		OLB
50 54 93-29 030-6	(012.244)		OLP
50 54 93-29 031-4	(012.250)		OLV
50 54 93-29 032-2	(012.251)		OLV
50 54 93-29 033-0	(012.259)	B	CTT
50 54 93-29 034-8	(012.263)		OLP
50 54 93-29 035-5	(012.279)		OLV
50 54 93-29 036-3	(012.282)		CTC
50 54 93-29 038-9	(012.298)		CTH
50 54 93-29 039-7	(012.214)		CTH
50 54 93-29 041-3	(012.313)		PRC
50 54 93-29 043-9	(012.353)		PRK
50 54 93-29 044-7	(012.355)		OLP
50 54 93-29 045-4	(012.364)		PRC
50 54 93-29 046-2	(012.366)		PRG (S)
50 54 93-29 047-0	(012.370)	B h	PRC
50 54 93-29 048-8	(012.016)	B h	OLB
50 54 93-29 049-6	(012.374)		PLZ
50 54 93-29 050-4	(012.376)	h	OLV
50 54 93-29 051-2	(012.391)		PLC (S)
50 54 93-29 052-0	(012.392)		OLS
50 54 93-29 053-8	(012.393)	h	OLV
50 54 93-29 054-6	(012.394)	h	OLV
50 54 93-29 055-3	(012.396)		PRC
50 54 93-29 056-1	(012.397)		PLB
50 54 93-29 057-9	(012.411)		OLV
50 54 93-29 058-7	(012.439)		PRG (S)
50 54 93-29 060-3	(012.264)	B	PRG (S)
50 54 93-29 063-7	(012.565)		CTT
50 54 93-29 064-5	(012.488)		OLB
50 54 93-29 067-8	(012.500)		OLP
50 54 93-29 069-4	(012.138)		PRG (S)
50 54 93-29 070-2	(012.517)		PLV
50 54 93-29 071-0	(012.520)		PRG
50 54 93-29 072-8	(012.521)		PLC (S)
50 54 93-29 073-6	(012.535)		CTH
50 54 93-29 074-4	(012.541)	B	PRK (S)
50 54 93-29 075-1	(012.550)		OLB
50 54 93-29 077-7	(012.555)		PLR
50 54 93-29 078-5	(012.)		OLB
50 54 93-29 079-3	(012.567)		PRG
50 54 93-29 080-1	(012.248)		PRC
50 54 93-29 081-9	(012.588)		OLV
50 54 93-29 082-7	(012.589)		PLL
50 54 93-29 084-3	(012.595)		OLV
50 54 93-29 085-0	(012.604)		OLB
50 54 93-29 086-8	(012.605)		BRM
50 54 93-29 087-6	(012.606)		PLK
50 54 93-29 088-4	(012.607)		PLK
50 54 93-29 089-2	(012.609)		OLB
50 54 93-29 090-0	(012.680)	h	PLC
50 54 93-29 091-8	(012.)		CTC
50 54 93-29 092-6	(012.687)		BRO
50 54 93-29 093-4	(012.692)	B	PLK
50 54 93-29 094-2	(012.694)		PRC
50 54 93-29 095-9	(012.704)		PRK (S)
50 54 93-29 096-7	(012.712)		OLP
50 54 93-29 097-5	(012.716)		PLK
50 54 93-29 098-3	(012.)		CTT
50 54 93-29 099-1	(012.751)		CTH
50 54 93-29 100-7	(012.772)		PLV
50 54 93-29 101-5	(012.774)		PLL

50 54 93-29 103-1	(012.778)		OLS
50 54 93-29 105-6	(012.785)	h	PLC
50 54 93-29 106-4	(012.786)		OLS
50 54 93-29 107-2	(012.800)		PRC
50 54 93-29 108-0	(012.802)		PLA
50 54 93-29 109-8	(012.827)	B	PRC
50 54 93-29 110-6	(012.840)		OLV
50 54 93-29 111-4	(012.237)	h	BRV

50 54 93-29 112-2	(012.852)		CTC
50 54 93-29 113-0	(012.853)	h	BRM
50 54 93-29 114-8	(012.855)		OLV
50 54 93-29 115-5	(012.816)		PLL
50 54 93-29 116-3	(012.)	B	PLL
50 54 93-29 118-9	(010.559)		CTH
50 54 93-29 125-4	(010.411)		PLC
50 54 93-29 237-7	(010.111)		PLC

Type Bdtax785. Formerly numbered Class 015. Converted from Class 010 in 2001–05 as bicycle carrying vehicles – one side of the vehicle has had the seats removed and bike racks fitted in their place. Class 015s were renumbered in the series 50 54 24-29 501–545.
Accommodation: –/26 1T + bike racks.

50 54 24-29 549 was previously numbered 50 54 24-29 545.

50 54 24-29 503-6	(015.069)		OLV
50 54 24-29 504-4	(015.087)		PRD
50 54 24-29 505-1	(015.103)		PRD (S)
50 54 24-29 506-9	(015.165)		PLT
50 54 24-29 507-7	(015.174)		PLB
50 54 24-29 508-5	(015.175)		BRZ
50 54 24-29 509-3	(015.187)		PLV
50 54 24-29 510-1	(015.194)		OLB
50 54 24-29 513-5	(015.323)	B	BRV
50 54 24-29 514-3	(015.326)		OLO
50 54 24-29 517-6	(015.320)		PRK
50 54 24-29 518-4	(015.324)		PRG
50 54 24-29 519-2	(015.332)		BRM
50 54 24-29 522-6	(015.333)		CTH
50 54 24-29 523-4	(015.339)		OLB
50 54 24-29 524-2	(015.367)		BRO
50 54 24-29 525-9	(015.368)	B	PLB
50 54 24-29 526-7	(015.373)		PLV

50 54 24-29 527-5	(015.431)	OLP
50 54 24-29 529-1	(015.492)	PLB
50 54 24-29 530-9	(015.494)	PLT
50 54 24-29 531-7	(015.501)	PLT
50 54 24-29 532-5	(015.539)	BRZ
50 54 24-29 533-3	(015.573)	PLL
50 54 24-29 534-1	(015.705)	PRG (S)
50 54 24-29 535-8	(015.718)	BRO
50 54 24-29 537-4	(015.757)	OLV
50 54 24-29 538-2	(015.761)	PLL
50 54 24-29 539-0	(015.766)	BRV
50 54 24-29 540-8	(015.803)	PLB
50 54 24-29 541-6	(015.814)	PLL
50 54 24-29 542-4	(015.826)	BRV
50 54 24-29 543-2	(015.527)	PLC
50 54 24-29 544-0	(015.796)	PLC
50 54 24-29 549-9	(015.071)	CTH

Type BDtax783. Formerly numbered Class 014 and then Class 016 (renumbered to avoid confusion with Class 814 DMUs). Converted from Class 010 (010.306) in 1997. Modified with a small area for transporting bikes. **Accommodation:** –/52 1T.

50 54 93-29 601-4   (016.824)   h PLL

1.5.3. INTERMEDIATE BOGIE TRAILERS

FORMER CLASS 021   TRAILERS

Type Bix bogie trailers, with their distinctive rounded glazed observation ends, offer basic accommodation for local trains, although they are vastly superior to the Baafx four-wheel vehicles that superseded them. 711 were built, originally designated Type Balm. The bodyshell is similar to that of Class 820 motor coaches (all now withdrawn from normal service).

Type Btx761 cars (formerly numbered Class 020 and later 50 54 29-29 301–367) and BDdtx 764 (formerly Class 022 and later 50 54 82-29 001–003) have all now been withdrawn from normal service – a number have been preserved at Lužná u Rakovníka, Tanvald, Brno or Chomutov.

The remaining vehicles with ČD are former Class 021s. They were modernised from Class 020 by MSV and ŽOS Nymburk Works with new plastic seating. The remaining vehicles are normally hauled by Class 714s (with a control cable linking cars for door operation) but can also be hauled by Classes 842/843 or Class 113 locomotives (Tábor–Bechyně) or Class 210 (Rybník–Lipno nad Vltavou). Other services include commuter trains from Praha Masarykovo and Břeclav–Znojmo local trains.

Built: 1958–69.
Builder: MSV Studénka.
Former ČSD Class: Bix.

Weight: 24.5 tonnes.
Length over Buffers: 18.50 m.
Maximum Speed: 80 km/h.

Type Btx763. Refurbished 1995–97 from Class 020. Formerly numbered Class 021.
Accommodation: –/64(+2) 1T.

50 54 28-29 001-7	(021.060)	BRZ		50 54 28-29 032-2	(021.005)	PLR (S)
50 54 28-29 002-5	(021.061)	CTC (S)		50 54 28-29 033-0	(021.045)	BRZ
50 54 28-29 003-3	(021.042)	PLT		50 54 28-29 034-8	(021.038)	PLR
50 54 28-29 004-1	(021.064)	PLZ (S)		50 54 28-29 035-5	(021.023)	(S)
50 54 28-29 005-8	(021.056)	BRZ		50 54 28-29 036-3	(021.034)	PLL (S)
50 54 28-29 006-6	(021.047)	BRZ		50 54 28-29 038-9	(021.010)	PLR (S)
50 54 28-29 007-4	(021.054)	BRZ		50 54 28-29 039-7	(021.046)	CTC (S)
50 54 28-29 008-2	(021.039)	PLT		50 54 28-29 040-5	(021.007)	PLL (S)
50 54 28-29 009-0	(021.068)	CTC (S)		50 54 28-29 041-3	(021.013)	CTC (S)
50 54 28-29 010-8	(021.050)	PLR		50 54 28-29 042-1	(021.053)	PLR
50 54 28-29 011-6	(021.049)	BRZ		50 54 28-29 043-9	(021.008)	BRM (S)
50 54 28-29 012-4	(021.041)	PLT		50 54 28-29 044-7	(021.004)	PLT (S)
50 54 28-29 013-2	(021.051)	PLR		50 54 28-29 045-4	(021.015)	BRZ
50 54 28-29 014-0	(021.052)	BRZ (S)		50 54 28-29 046-2	(021.016)	PLR (S)
50 54 28-29 015-7	(021.031)	PLB (S)		50 54 28-29 047-0	(021.012)	BRZ (S)
50 54 28-29 016-5	(021.032)	PLZ (S)		50 54 28-29 048-8	(021.024)	PLR
50 54 28-29 017-3	(021.065)	PLL (S)		50 54 28-29 049-6	(021.035)	PLT
50 54 28-29 018-1	(021.059)	CTC (S)		50 54 28-29 050-4	(021.067)	PLR
50 54 28-29 019-9	(021.044)	CTC (S)		50 54 28-29 051-2	(021.028)	PLR
50 54 28-29 020-7	(021.048)	CTC (S)		50 54 28-29 052-0	(021.036)	PLT
50 54 28-29 021-5	(021.057)	BRZ		50 54 28-29 053-8	(021.029)	BRZ
50 54 28-29 022-3	(021.063)	BRZ		50 54 28-29 054-6	(021.006)	PLR
50 54 28-29 023-1	(021.011)	PLR		50 54 28-29 055-3	(021.030)	PLR
50 54 28-29 024-9	(021.009)	PLT (S)		50 54 28-29 056-1	(021.017)	PLR
50 54 28-29 025-6	(021.040)	PLR		50 54 28-29 057-9	(021.062)	BRZ
50 54 28-29 026-4	(021.020)	BRZ		50 54 28-29 058-7	(021.018)	PLB (S)
50 54 28-29 027-2	(021.043)	PLB (S)		50 54 28-29 059-5	(021.037)	PLR
50 54 28-29 028-0	(021.025)	PLR		50 54 28-29 060-3	(021.001)	PLB (S)
50 54 28-29 029-8	(021.026)	CTC (S)		50 54 28-29 062-9	(021.003)	PLR (S)
50 54 28-29 031-4	(021.014)	PLR				

Type Bdtx766. Modified 2007–11 by ŽOS Krnov from Class 021 with the provision of dedicated bicycle spaces. **Accommodation:** –/44(+10) 1T.

50 54 84-29 001-8	(021.022)	BRZ		50 54 84-29 005-9	(021.055)	BRZ
50 54 84-29 002-6	(021.058)	BRZ		50 54 84-29 006-7	(021.033)	PLB
50 54 84-29 003-4	(021.027)	BRZ		50 54 84-29 007-5	(021.019)	PLB
50 54 84-29 004-2	(021.066)	BRZ				

FORMER CLASS 042   TRAILERS

Loose trailer cars rebuilt for use with Class 842. These vehicles were rebuilt from locomotive-hauled Bmnp carriages 20 09 228/241/242/284 by ŽOS Krnov in 1989 and were renumbered 20 09 496–499, before being reclassified as Class 042. They are now used as hauled stock on a weekday return trip from Louny to Praha Masarykovo (hauled by a Class 714).

Built: 1969–70; rebuilt 1989.
Builder: MSV Studénka.   **Weight:** 34.5 tonnes.
Former ČSD Class: Bmnp.   **Length over Buffers:** 24.50 m.
Accommodation: –/88 2T.   **Maximum Speed:** 120 km/h.

Type Btn752. Formerly numbered Class 042.

50 54 21-29 201-0	(042.002)	PLL		50 54 21-29 203-6	(042.004)	PLL
50 54 21-29 202-8	(042.003)	PLL		50 54 21-29 204-4	(042.001)	PL

FORMER CLASS 043   TRAILERS

These vehicles were built new as Type Bhfn intermediate trailers for use with Class 842 or 843 tractor units and Class 943 driving trailers. They can also work with Class 742 locomotives equipped with door operation controls. The doors are laid out to a one-third/two-thirds design – with three sections of 24 seats each.

They are used on services from Liberec and Olomouc including Liberec–Turnov–Hradec Králové–Pardubice, Liberec–Děčín, Olomouc–Krnov–Ostrava and Olomouc–Jeseník–Krnov.

Built: 1995 (043.001/002); 1997 (043.003–032).
Builder: MSV Studénka.
Former ČSD Class: Not applicable.
Accommodation: –/72 1T.
Weight: 31 tonnes.
Length over Buffers: 19.70 m.
Maximum Speed: 120 km/h.

Type Btn753. Formerly numbered Class 043 (renumbered into the new EVN series in sequence).

50 54 29-29 001-6	(043.001)	B	OLO		50 54 29-29 017-2	(043.017)	B	OLO
50 54 29-29 002-4	(043.002)	B	OLO		50 54 29-29 018-0	(043.018)	B	OLO
50 54 29-29 003-2	(043.003)	B	CTL		50 54 29-29 019-8	(043.019)	B	OLO
50 54 29-29 004-0	(043.004)		CTL		50 54 29-29 020-6	(043.020)	B	OLO
50 54 29-29 005-7	(043.005)	B	CTL		50 54 29-29 021-4	(043.021)	B	OLO
50 54 29-29 006-5	(043.006)	B	CTL		50 54 29-29 022-2	(043.022)	B	OLO
50 54 29-29 007-3	(043.007)	B	CTL		50 54 29-29 023-0	(043.023)		OLO
50 54 29-29 008-1	(043.008)	B	CTL		50 54 29-29 024-8	(043.024)		CTL
50 54 29-29 009-9	(043.009)	B	CTL		50 54 29-29 025-5	(043.025)	B	CTL
50 54 29-29 010-7	(043.010)	B	OLO		50 54 29-29 026-3	(043.026)		CTL
50 54 29-29 011-5	(043.011)	B	OLO		50 54 29-29 027-1	(043.027)	B	CTL
50 54 29-29 012-3	(043.012)		OLO		50 54 29-29 028-9	(043.028)	B	CTL
50 54 29-29 013-1	(043.013)		OLO		50 54 29-29 029-7	(043.029)	B	CTL
50 54 29-29 014-9	(043.014)	B	OLO		50 54 29-29 030-5	(043.030)		CTL
50 54 29-29 015-6	(043.015)	B	OLO		50 54 29-29 031-3	(043.031)	B	CTL
50 54 29-29 016-4	(043.016)	B	CTL		50 54 29-29 032-1	(043.032)		CTL

FORMER CLASS 050   TRAILERS

Trailer cars of similar body style to Class 850 and Class 851 tractor units with rounded ends. 182 were built, with the original carriage number series being the 70 20 09 000–181 range. Most of the remaining serviceable vehicles are used with Classes 842 and 854 on services around Brno.

Built: 1962 (prototype); 1966–68 (production batch).
Builder: MSV Studénka.
Former ČSD Class: Balm.
Accommodation: –/72(+8) 2T.
Weight: 32 tonnes.
Length over Buffers: 24.79 m.
Maximum Speed: 120 km/h.

Type Bmx765. Formerly numbered Class 050.

Vehicles shown at DPOV Veselí nad Moravou are assigned to NTM Lužná u Rakovníka and sometimes used on steam specials. 50 54 20-29 102 is also assigned to NTM Lužná.

50 54 20-29 101-3	(050.013)	DPVE		50 54 20-29 120-3	(050.023)	BRH
50 54 20-29 102-1	(050.001)	OLO		50 54 20-29 122-9	(050.132)	BRH
50 54 20-29 104-7	(050.025)	DPVE		50 54 20-29 124-5	(050.006)	BRH
50 54 20-29 107-0	(050.014)	DPVE		50 54 20-29 126-0	(050.009)	BRH
50 54 20-29 109-6	(050.002)	BRH		50 54 20-29 128-6	(050.012)	BRH
50 54 20-29 110-4	(050.)	OLO		50 54 20-29 129-4	(050.034)	DPVE
50 54 20-29 112-0	(050.028)	OLO (S)		50 54 20-29 133-6	(050.038)	OLO (S)
50 54 20-29 113-8	(050.029)	OLO		50 54 20-29 134-4	(050.039)	BRH
50 54 20-29 114-6	(050.030)	BRH		50 54 20-29 136-9	(050.040)	BRH
50 54 20-29 115-3	(050.077)	BRH		50 54 20-29 137-7	(050.018)	BRH
50 54 20-29 118-7	(050.033)	CTC (S)		50 54 20-29 138-5	(050.041)	DPVE

FORMER CLASSES 053–056   TRAILERS

Built new with Class 852 and 853 tractor units. Class 053s were originally numbered 20 09 200–319 (Type Baim) for use on regional services. 26 further cars; First Class 19 09 900–909, Standard Class 20 09 950–954 and restaurant cars 85 09 000–010, were for express work as 6-car trains composed of four trailers between two motor coaches.

97 Class 053 vehicles were rebuilt by ŽOS Krnov 2004–13 as Bdtn756 or Bdtn757 and renumbered (some of them have carried at least two EVN numbers).

These are now mainly used with Class 854 or 842/843 on a number of routes, including Praha–Příbram–České Budějovice, Praha–Mladá Boleslav–Tanvald, Liberec–Ústí nad Labem, Brno–Veselí–Bylnice, Liberec–Turnov–Hradec Králové–Pardubice, Trutnov–Hradec Kralové, Trutnov–Stará Paka–Kolín, Ostrava–Frýdlant–Valašské Meziříčí and České Budejovice–Nové Údolí. Rakovník-based vehicles are used on locomotive-hauled services between Praha Masarykovo and Rakovník.

Built: Original vehicles built: 1969–70; rebuilt 2004–13.
Builder: MSV Studénka.   **Weight:** 37 tonnes.
Former ČSD Class: Bmnp.   **Length over Buffers:** 24.50 m.
Maximum Speed: 120 km/h.

Type Bdtn756. Formerly numbered as Class 053. Rebuilt 2004–11 from Btn053 or Bnp vehicles from Slovakia (50 54 21-29 317–330). **Accommodation:** –/88 2T.

50 54 21-29 301-8	(053.072)	BRH		50 54 21-29 333-1	(053.005)		PLR
50 54 21-29 302-6	(053.017)	BRH		50 54 21-29 334-9	(053.058)		PLR
50 54 21-29 303-4	(053.077)	BRH		50 54 21-29 335-6	(053.033)		PLR
50 54 21-29 304-2	(053.021)	BRH		50 54 21-29 336-4	(053.014)		PLR
50 54 21-29 305-9	(053.019)	BRH		50 54 21-29 337-2	(053.070)		PLR
50 54 21-29 306-7	(053.040)	BRH		50 54 21-29 338-0	(053.041)		PLR
50 54 21-29 307-5	(053.026)	BRH		50 54 21-29 339-8	(053.076)	B	PLR
50 54 21-29 308-3	(053.069)	BRH		50 54 21-29 340-6	(053.045)	B	PLR
50 54 21-29 309-1	(053.056)	BRH		50 54 21-29 341-4	(053.052)	B	PLR
50 54 21-29 310-9	(053.012)	BRH		50 54 21-29 342-2	(053.024)		CTL
50 54 21-29 311-7	(053.036)	BRH		50 54 21-29 343-0	(053.028)		PLR
50 54 21-29 312-5	(053.004)	BRH		50 54 21-29 344-8	(053.037)		CTL
50 54 21-29 313-3	(053.074)	BRH		50 54 21-29 345-5	(053.079)		CTL
50 54 21-29 314-1	(053.043)	BRH		50 54 21-29 346-3	(053.025)		CTL
50 54 21-29 315-8	(053.073)	BRH		50 54 21-29 347-1	(053.003)		CTL
50 54 21-29 316-6	(053.082)	BRH		50 54 21-29 348-9	(053.051)		BRH
50 54 21-29 317-4	(053.274)	BRH		50 54 21-29 349-7	(053.048)		CTT
50 54 21-29 318-2	(053.283)	BRH		50 54 21-29 350-5	(053.020)		CTT
50 54 21-29 319-0	(053.214)	BRH		50 54 21-29 351-3	(053.054)		CTT
50 54 21-29 320-8	(053.277)	BRH		50 54 21-29 352-1	(053.053)		CTT
50 54 21-29 321-6	(053.316)	BRH		50 54 21-29 353-9	(053.035)		PRG
50 54 21-29 322-4	(053.313)	PRG		50 54 21-29 354-7	(053.080)		BRH
50 54 21-29 323-2	(053.213)	PRG		50 54 21-29 355-4	(053.062)		OLV
50 54 21-29 324-0	(053.278)	PRG		50 54 21-29 356-2	(053.078)		OLV
50 54 21-29 325-7	(053.317)	PRG		50 54 21-29 357-0	(053.039)		OLV
50 54 21-29 326-5	(053.318)	PRG		50 54 21-29 358-8	(053.081)		OLV
50 54 21-29 327-3	(053.276)	PRG		50 54 21-29 359-6	(053.022)		OLV
50 54 21-29 328-1	(053.273)	PRG		50 54 21-29 360-4	(053.049)		OLV
50 54 21-29 329-9	(053.285)	PRG		50 54 21-29 361-2	(053.068)		BRH
50 54 21-29 330-7	(053.315)	PRG		50 54 21-29 362-0	(053.071)		BRH
50 54 21-29 331-5	(053.050)	PRG		50 54 21-29 363-8	(053.042)		PLZ
50 54 21-29 332-3	(053.057)	PLR		50 54 21-29 364-6	(053.013)		PLZ

Type Bdtn757. Formerly numbered as Class 053. Rebuilt 2004–13 from Btn053 vehicles with additional space for bicycles. **Accommodation:** –/80(+4) 2T.
Non-standard Livery: Original red & cream.

50 54 20-29 201-1	(053.032)	PRG		50 54 20-29 221-9	(053.044)		OLV
50 54 20-29 202-9	(053.027)	PRG		50 54 20-29 222-7	(053.063)		OLV
50 54 20-29 203-7	(053.038)	PRG		50 54 20-29 223-5	(053.011)		OLV
50 54 20-29 204-5	(053.015)	PRG		50 54 20-29 224-3	(053.030)		OLV
50 54 20-29 208-6	(053.055)	PRG		50 54 20-29 225-0	(053.018)		BRZ
50 54 20-29 209-4	(053.031)	PRG		50 54 20-29 226-8	(053.059)		BRZ
50 54 20-29 210-2	(053.034)	CTL		50 54 20-29 227-6	(053.083)		CTT
50 54 20-29 211-0	(053.061)	CTL		50 54 20-29 228-4	(053.009)		PLB
50 54 20-29 212-8	(053.060)	CTL		50 54 20-29 229-2	(053.023)		PLB
50 54 20-29 213-6	(053.067)	CTL		50 54 20-29 230-0	(053.047)		PLB
50 54 20-29 214-4	(053.065)	CTT		50 54 20-29 231-8	(053.002)		PLB
50 54 20-29 215-1	(053.066)	CTT		50 54 20-29 232-6	(053.007)		PLB
50 54 20-29 216-9	(053.010)	CTT		50 54 20-29 233-4	(053.016)		PLB
50 54 20-29 217-7	(053.084)	CTT		50 54 20-29 234-2	(053.075)		PLB
50 54 20-29 218-5	(053.029)	CTT		50 54 20-29 235-9	(053.008)	0	PRG
50 54 20-29 219-3	(053.064)	CTT		50 54 20-29 236-7	(053.006)	0	PRG
50 54 20-29 220-1	(053.001)	OLV					

Type Bdt754. Formerly numbered as Class 056. Unrefurbished and stored out of use for a number of years. **Accommodation:** –/84 2T.

50 54 20-29 001-5	(056.001)	DPNY (S)		50 54 20-29 002-3	(056.002)	DPNY (S)

1.6. ČD NARROW GAUGE STOCK

760 mm gauge locomotives are used on two surviving systems. One is privately operated by JHMD (see Private Passenger Operators section) whilst ČD retains the Třemešná ve Slezsku–Osoblaha line in northern Moravia (Line 298). The main depot is at the far end of the 20 km line at Osoblaha, very close to the Polish border, whilst a second small depot at Třemešná houses one of the steam locomotives (see Preserved Locomotives section). The normal service of five return trips needs only one train to work everything: normally with just one trailer.

CLASS 705.9   Bo-Bo

Built: 1958.
Former ČSD Class: TU47.0.
Builder: ČKD, model T47.0.
Engine: ČKD 12V170DR.
Power: 258 kW (345 hp).
Transmission: Electric.
Maximum tractive effort: 88 kN.

Total No. Built: 21.
Wheel Diameter: 760 mm.
Train Heating Equipment: None.
Weight: 32 tonnes.
Length over Buffers: 12.69 m.
Maximum Speed: 50 km/h.
EVN: 92 54 2 705 91x-c.

*   Refurbished with Tedom M1.2C 640 S engine at 242 kW (325 hp).

705.913-2	*	OLH	705.914-0	OLH	705.917-3	OLH (S)

CLASS 005.9   TRAILERS

Built: 1966.
Builder: ČKD Tatra.
Former ČSD Class: Balm/ú.
Accommodation: –/46 1T.

Total No. Built: 30.
Weight: 13.2 tonnes.
Length over Couplers: 14.80 m.
Maximum Speed: 50 km/h.

55 54 28-29 901-3	OLH	55 54 28-29 905-4	OLH
55 54 28-29 902-1	OLH (S)	55 54 28-29 907-0	OLH
55 54 28-29 904-7	OLH		

▲ Refurbished 705.913 normally works services on ČD's only narrow gauge line. On 12 June 2012 it stands at the northern terminus at Osoblaha awaiting departure with train Os20610, the 17.50 to Třemešná ve Slezsku, hauling Class 005.9 trailer 55 54 28-29 901. **Robert Pritchard**

2. SLOVAK RAILWAYS

ZSSK and ZSSK Cargo operate passenger and freight as wholly separate businesses. The state system ŽSR was created on 1 January 1993 at the same time as the independent Slovakia. In 2001 ŽSR split into the first form of ZSSK, with three main divisions; passenger, freight and rolling stock, leaving ŽSR for the infrastructure. In 2004, after Slovakia joined the European Union, operations split into passenger Železničná Spoločnosť Slovensko (ZSSK), and freight Železničná Spoločnosť Cargo Slovakia (ŽSCS, commonly now branded as ZSSK Cargo). Dopravný Úrad (DÚ) is the regulatory body (it was ÚRZD, Úrad pre Reguláciu Železničnej Dopravy, until the end of 2013).

ZSSK

The national passenger operator is Železničná Spoločnosť Slovensko (ZSSK) that came into being on 1 January 2005. Before this took place, financial difficulties resulted in several lines closing in February 2003, some re-opening in June that year through regional support.

The public timetable "Cestovný poriadok vlakov" is issued by ŽSR, and runs annually from December to December. The book also contains those lines worked by private operators. Timetable pages are also freely available from the official website www.zsr.sk as pdf files. The crossed hammers timetable symbol used by Slovak Railways means Mondays–Fridays not Mondays–Saturdays.

ZSSK carried 57.3 million passengers in 2015, a rise of more than 20% compared to 2014 and the highest number since 1989. The high figure for 2015 is attributed to the introduction of free travel for pensioners and students in late 2014. The total Slovak railway network stretches to more than 3600 km of track.

ZSSK CARGO

Freight business Železničná Spoločnosť Cargo Slovakia (ŽSCS or ZSSK Cargo) is a lucrative concern due to a high proportion of trainload transit traffic. Negotiations for a complete sale were advanced in the mid 2000s but then postponed, then following elections the new Government halted the sale completely. ZSSK Cargo is the main operator on the 1520 mm gauge SRT line between Haniska pri Košiciach, south of Košice, to Maťovce, and the Ukraine border from Uzhorod. There are no booked passenger duties for any ZSSK Cargo locomotives, but they do appear during emergencies, especially Class 240 electric locomotives.

ZSSK Cargo locomotives are indicated by the letter *F* in class listings.

DEPOTS – ZSSK

ZSSK has four main motive power areas – Bratislava, Košice, Žilina and Zvolen. In 2008 Prešov depot closed with locomotives mainly reassigned to Humenné and this was followed by the closure of Margecany, with multiple units transferred to Košice. Allocation codes used in this book for ZSSK locomotives and railcars are as follows:

BLH	Bratislava hlavná		NZK	Nové Zámky*
BRZ	Brezno		POP	Poprad-Tatry
CAD	Čadca		PVZ	Prievidza*
FIL	Fiľakovo		STR	Štrba
HUM	Humenné*		TTP	Trenčianska Teplá*
KRA	Kraľovany		ZIL	Žilina*
KOS	Košice*		ZVO	Zvolen*

* shared with ZSSK Cargo.

DEPOTS – ZSSK CARGO

ZSSK Cargo has six main motive power areas; Bratislava Východ, Košice, Nové Zámky, Spišská Nová Ves, Žilina and Zvolen. Lucenec has now closed, with most locomotives transferred to Plesivec, while Leopoldov depot is being run down and now has very few locomotives allocated there. Allocation codes used in this book for ZSSK Cargo locomotives are as follows:

BLV	Bratislava Východ	PLV	Plesivec
CNT	Čierna nad Tisou	PVZ	Prievidza
HAN	Haniska pri Košiciach	SNV	Spišská Nová Ves
HUM	Humenné	TTP	Trenčianska Teplá
KOS	Košice	ZIL	Žilina
LEO	Leopoldov	ZVO	Zvolen
NZK	Nové Zámky		

MAIN WORKS

There are three main works in Slovakia, all prefixed with ŽOS (Železničné Opravovne a Strojárne or "Railway Repair & Engineering works") but not directly related.

ŽOS Zvolen (code ŽOSZ) mainly carries out diesel locomotive overhauls and rebuilts, both for the home market and for export. It also specialises in overhauling preserved locomotives and railcars.

ŽOS Vrutky (code ŽOSV) mainly carries out electric locomotive overhauls and rebuilds, as well as constructing new DMUs (most recently Class 861 for ZSSK) and overhauling ZSSK coaches.

ŽOS Trnava specialises in wagon maintenance and overhauls, as well as carriage refurbishment and new build wagons and coaches.

Depots also carry out their own heavy repairs, especially Zvolen on diesels, Nové Zámky on AC electrics, and Žilina and Spišská Nová Ves on DC electrics.

LIVERIES

Since 2006 passenger operator ZSSK has used a bright red scheme for all traction – this is mostly red, with white and grey bands on the lower bodyside on locomotives, coaching stock and multiple units. Some DMUs are still in the older red & white style. ZSSK Cargo has no corporate livery, instead retaining the traditional 1990s style locomotive liveries.

Whilst most ZSSK locomotives are now in the new red livery, the following still applies to ZSSK Cargo locomotives. Electric locomotives had been following the green, red and blue base colours for DC, AC and AC/DC machines. Most are relieved by some kind of yellow or cream or silver band or stripes or two-tone shades of the same basic colour.

Under ČSD, standard diesel locomotive livery was maroon with very little relief. Yellow bands or cab surrounds or other markings were then commonly applied. Diesels later reverted to early or ex-factory colours. Class 721s are dark blue & cream, Class 731/742 are red with a yellow stripe, Classes 751/752 are largely grey with respectively red and light blue upper side panels, Classes 750/754 dark green & grey and Classes 770/771 green & cream.

Rebuilt locomotives carry unique colours: light blue and white on Class 736s and dark blue & white on Classes 746, 756 and 773.

The livery of each class is as indicated in the class headings unless shown as one of the following codes:

A   Advertising Livery (see class heading for details).
0   Non-standard livery (see class heading for details).
R   New ZSSK red locomotive or railcar livery.

▲ ŽOS Zvolen is one of three major railway workshops in Slovakia, and specialises in rebuilding diesel locomotives. Recent work has included the rebuild of 25 Class 750 to Class 757 for ZSSK. On 4 June 2014 work is nearing completion on 757.015, with the new Caterpillar 3512C engine to be installed seen alongside.   **Robert Pritchard**

▼ A line up of three different classes of electric locomotive outside Bratislava hlavná depot on hot and sunny 12 May 2015 – 350.008, 263.011 plus rebuilt 361.103.   **Robert Pritchard**

2.1. ZSSK & ZSSK CARGO ELECTRIC LOCOMOTIVES

CLASS 110   Bo-Bo

These centre-cab locomotives were built for trip and yard shunting and station pilot duties. All ZSSK Cargo and most ZSSK machines have been stored, leaving just two serviceable at Košice.

Livery is dark green & yellow.

System: 3000 V DC.   **Total No. Built:** 52†.
Built: 1971–73.   **Wheel Diameter:** 1050 mm.
Former ČSD Class: E458.0.   **Weight:** 72 tonnes.
Builder: Škoda, model 33E.   **Length over Buffers:** 14.40 m.
Continuous Rating: 800 kW (1070 hp).   **Maximum Speed:** 80 km/h.
Maximum Tractive Effort: 160 kN.   **EVN:** 97 56 8 110 0xx-c.

110.002-3	F	SNV (S)		110.015-5	F	TTP (S)		110.033-8	F	SNV (S)
110.008-0	F	SNV (S)		110.021-3	F	ZIL (S)		110.034-6		KOS
110.010-6		KOS		110.023-9	F	SNV (S)		110.041-1	F	TTP (S)
110.011-4	F	SNV (S)		110.026-2	F	SNV (S)		110.049-4	F	ZIL (S)
110.014-8	F	TTP (S)		110.031-2	F	ZIL (S)		110.050-2	F	TTP (S)

CLASS 125   Bo-Bo + Bo-Bo

Class 125 are single cab locomotives operating in back-to-back pairs coupled in consecutive number and used on the Širokorozchodná trať (SRT) in eastern Slovakia. This Russian gauge (1520 mm), 95 km route (87 km of which is in Slovakia) connects with Ukraine Railways (UZ) at Užgorod, through Maťovce, Veľké Kapušany and Trebišov to Haniska pri Košiciach, south of Košice, where the Class 125s are based. Major overhauls are sometimes undertaken at Žilina depot.

Constructed from 1963 to feed the then new VSZ (Eastern Slovakian Steelworks) south of Košice (principally with iron ore), the SRT opened in 1966 with diesel motive power. Electric working began in 1978. The SRT is also built to Soviet loading gauge but Class 125 are of normal ČSD loading gauge, so their pantographs sit on raised platforms. Fitted with SA3 centre couplers. Technical details apply to single Class 125s; normal operation is always in pairs, which are limited to 350 kN tractive effort. The maximum weight for a loaded train of iron ore is 4200 tonnes.

Traffic on the SRT in recent years has required just seven pairs, including locomotives providing banking between Trebišov and Slančík. Photography on the single track SRT line, which parallels the ZSSK Košice–Trebišov line and also the (now closed to passenger services) Line 195 for much of the route, requires patience as there can be long gaps between trains.

Livery is the 3000 V DC green with a yellow stripe.

See Diesel Locomotive Classes 721.8, 770.8, 771.8 and 773.8 for other 1520 mm traction.

System: 3000 V DC.   **Total No. Built:** 22 (double locomotives).
Built: 1975–76.   **Wheel Diameter:** 1250 mm.
Former ČSD Class: E469.5.   **Weight:** 85 tonnes.
Builder: Škoda, model 67E.   **Length over Buffers:** 17.19 m.
Continuous Rating: 2040 kW (2735 hp).   **Maximum Speed:** 90 km/h.
Maximum Tractive Effort: 224 kN.   **EVN:** 91 56 6 125 8xx-c.
Gauge: 1520 mm.

125.801-1 + 125.802-9	F	HAN		125.825-0 + 125.826-8	F	HAN
125.803-7 + 125.804-5	F	HAN		125.827-6 + 125.828-4	F	HAN
125.805-2 + 125.806-0	F	HAN (S)		125.829-2 + 125.830-0	F	HAN
125.807-8 + 125.808-6	F	HAN (S)		125.831-8 + 125.832-6	F	HAN
125.811-0 + 125.812-8	F	HAN		125.833-4 + 125.834-2	F	HAN (S)
125.813-6 + 125.814-4	F	HAN		125.835-9 + 125.836-7	F	HAN
125.815-1 + 125.816-9	F	HAN		125.837-5 + 125.838-3	F	HAN
125.817-7 + 125.818-5	F	HAN		125.839-1 + 125.840-9	F	HAN
125.819-3 + 125.820-1	F	HAN		125.841-7 + 125.842-5	F	HAN
125.821-9 + 125.822-7	F	HAN		125.843-3 + 125.844-1	F	HAN
125.823-5 + 125.824-3	F	HAN				

▲ 110.034 shunts coaches at Košice station on 9 June 2012. **Robert Pritchard**

▼ Broad gauge 125.844/843+125.837/838 haul a train of iron ore empties away from US Steel, Košice on the SRT line, past their home depot at Haniska on 5 June 2014. Note how the pantographs sit on raised platforms. **Robert Pritchard**

CLASS 131   Bo-Bo + Bo-Bo

Class 131s are single cab locomotives operating in back-to-back pairs with consecutive numbers. They were developed from Class 130 but use similar bodyshells to Classes 163/263/363. Apart from being single-cabbed, Class 131 can be distinguished by additional cantrail ventilation grilles and heavy deformation zone buffer beams. Class 131s may haul 3300 tonnes unassisted in flatlands but on their principal duties on the Čierna nad Tisou–Košice–Žilina corridor they are limited to 1600 tonnes unassisted over the 1.5% ruling grades to Štrba summit. Between Spišská Nová Ves and Liptovský Mikuláš, Class 131s are normally banked by Class 183s, or occasionally Class 363s. Traffic can include anything from heavy coal or iron ore trains to timber or mixed freights.

As well as the main line, other routes include Košice–Plaveč, which includes the equally severely graded Pusté Pole summit, from Žilina to Čadca and Zwardoń (Poland) and also to Ostrava in the Czech Republic. There is also some work into Poland.

Recent developments are enhanced electric dynamic braking and electronic traction control. Technical data refers to single sections. A pair of Class 131s is limited by coupling strain to 350 kN tractive effort.

Livery is the 3000 V DC green with a yellow stripe.

System: 3000 V DC.
Built: 1980–82.
Former ČSD Class: E479.1.
Builder: Škoda, model 58E.
Continuous Rating: 2240 kW (3000 hp).
Maximum Tractive Effort: 230 kN.

Total No. Built: 50 (double locomotives).
Wheel Diameter: 1250 mm.
Weight: 84.5 tonnes.
Length over Buffers: 17.21 m.
Maximum Speed: 100 km/h.
EVN: 91 56 6 131 xxx-c.

e   Fitted with 5000 kW dynamic braking.
t   Fitted with electronic traction control.

131.001-0 + 131.002-8	F		SNV	131.051-5 + 131.052-3	F	e	SNV
131.003-6 + 131.004-4	F		SNV	131.053-1 + 131.054-9	F		SNV
131.005-1 + 131.006-9	F	e	SNV	131.055-6 + 131.056-4	F		SNV
131.007-7 + 131.008-5	F		SNV	131.057-2 + 131.058-0	F		SNV
131.009-3 + 131.010-1	F	e	SNV	131.059-8 + 131.060-6	F	e	SNV
131.011-9 + 131.012-7	F		SNV	131.061-4 + 131.062-2	F		SNV
131.013-5 + 131.014-3	F		SNV	131.063-0 + 131.064-8	F	e	SNV
131.015-0 + 131.016-8	F		SNV	131.065-5 + 131.066-3	F	e	SNV
131.017-6 + 131.018-4	F		SNV	131.067-1 + 131.068-9	F		SNV
131.019-2 + 131.020-0	F	e	SNV	131.069-7 + 131.070-5	F		SNV
131.021-8 + 131.022-6	F		SNV	131.071-3 + 131.072-1	F		SNV
131.023-4 + 131.024-2	F	et	SNV	131.073-9 + 131.074-7	F		SNV
131.025-9 + 131.026-7	F	et	SNV	131.075-4 + 131.076-2	F	e	SNV
131.027-5 + 131.028-3	F		SNV	131.077-0 + 131.078-8	F		SNV
131.029-1 + 131.030-9	F		SNV	131.079-6 + 131.080-4	F		SNV
131.031-7 + 131.032-5	F		SNV	131.081-2 + 131.082-0	F		SNV
131.033-3 + 131.034-1	F	t	SNV	131.083-8 + 131.084-6	F		SNV
131.035-8 + 131.036-6	F	et	SNV	131.085-3 + 131.086-1	F		SNV
131.037-4 + 131.038-2	F	e	SNV	131.087-9 + 131.088-7	F		SNV
131.039-0 + 131.040-8	F		SNV	131.089-5 + 131.090-3	F		SNV
131.041-6 + 131.042-4	F		SNV	131.091-1 + 131.092-9	F	e	SNV
131.043-2 + 131.044-0	F	e	SNV	131.093-7 + 131.094-5	F		SNV
131.045-7 + 131.046-5	F	e	SNV	131.095-2 + 131.096-0	F		SNV
131.047-3 + 131.048-1	F		SNV	131.097-8 + 131.098-6	F	e	SNV
131.049-9 + 131.050-7	F		SNV	131.099-4 + 131.100-0	F		SNV

▲ One of the best places in Slovakia for photography, or to simply sit and watch the trains go by, is in the Štrba area, beneath the High Tatra mountain range. Here a procession of passenger and freight trains, many of the latter often banked, passes. On 7 June 2014 131.055+056 head downgrade just beyond Štrba station with an eastbound train of iron ore empties. **Robert Pritchard**

CLASS 162 {.Bo-Bo}

CLASS 162   **Bo-Bo**

Class 162 is an updated 140 km/h version of Class 163. Like ČD, ŽSR exchanged bogies between Classes 162 and 363 to create more Class 163 and 362 (see Classes 163/362 for details).

ZSSK's few remaining Class 162s are based at Žilina and mainly used on stopping and semi-fast trains from Žilina east as far as both Poprad-Tatry and Košice. They are also used on trains between Žilina and Čadca/Zwardoń (Poland).

Most Class 162s and 163s are now in ZSSK red livery, otherwise they are in green with a yellow stripe.

System: 3000 V DC.
Built: 1991.
Former ČSD Class: Not applicable.
Builder: Škoda, model 98E.
Continuous Rating: 3480 kW (4665 hp).
Maximum Tractive Effort: 258 kN.

Total No. Built: 60†.
Wheel Diameter: 1250 mm.
Weight: 85 tonnes.
Length over Buffers: 16.80 m.
Maximum Speed: 140 km/h.
EVN: 91 56 6 162 0xx-c.

162.001-2	**R**	ZIL	162.004-6	**R**	ZIL	162.007-9	**R**	ZIL
162.002-0	**R**	ZIL	162.005-3	**R**	ZIL	162.008-7	**R**	ZIL
162.003-8	**R**	ZIL	162.006-1		ZIL			

CLASS 163   Bo-Bo

CLASS 163   **Bo-Bo**

Class 163 was built in two batches of 60 with a five year gap between production – see ČD section for details. The original 163.112–120 never entered service with Czech or Slovak Railways, and were sold to FNM in Italy before later being sold to Regiojet (and renumbered 162.112–120). However bogie swaps between Classes 162 and 363 have created more Class 163s, now operated by ZSSK, that were numbered 163.112–125 (some of which have since been rebuilt again as Class 361s!).

Since 2010 ZSSK has been steadily reducing its Class 163 fleet as 15 have been converted to dual-voltage Class 361 by ŽOS Vrútky. In 2015 it was announced that a further 11, starting with 163.122 and 163.119, would be rebuilt as Class 361.1.

The remaining locomotives are based at Košice or Žilina and have diagrams the whole length of the DC main line between Žilina, Poprad-Tatry, Košice and Čierna nad Tisou. One of the Košice locomotives is also allocated to work the twice-daily cross-border train between Čierna nad Tisou and Chop in Ukraine, which runs with just one or two coaches. Another duty comprises some Košice–Trebišov portions of loco-hauled Košice–Humenné trains.

System: 3000 V DC.
Built: 1984–86 and 1991–92.
Former ČSD Class: E499.3.
Builder: Škoda, model 71E or 99E.
Continuous Rating: 3480 kW (4665 hp).
Maximum Tractive Effort: 250 kN.

Total No. Built: 120†.
Wheel Diameter: 1250 mm.
Weight: 85 tonnes.
Length over Buffers: 16.80 m.
Maximum Speed: 120 km/h.
EVN: 91 56 6 163 xxx-c.

Class 163. Original build, Škoda model 71E (163.001–060), lower continuous tractive effort of 176.1 kN at 66.5 km/h.

163.054-0	**R**	KOS	163.057-3	**R**	KOS	

Class 163. Second build, Škoda model 99E (163.061–120), higher continuous tractive effort of 186 kN at 66 km/h.

163.101-9	**R**	KOS	163.106-8	**R**	ZIL	163.109-2		ZIL
163.104-3		KOS	163.107-6		KOS	163.110-0	**R**	KOS
163.105-0	**R**	KOS	163.108-4	**R**	KOS	163.111-8	**R**	KOS

Class 163. Converted from Class 162. To be converted to Class 361 in 2016–17.

163.112-6	(162.029)	**R**	KOS	163.121-7	(162.032)	**R**	KOS
163.113-4	(162.028)	**R**	ZIL	163.124-1	(162.026)	**R**	ZIL
163.114-2	(162.024)	**R**	ZIL				

CLASS 183 Co-Co

These Co-Co electrics were a development of Classes 181/182 (none still in regular use with ZSSK Cargo), and were the last six-axle locomotives to be delivered by ČSD. Originally some were delivered to Olomouc in the Czech Republic, but soon the whole class was concentrated in Slovakia. In common with the earlier Classes 181/182, due to the nature of their sustained slow speed work on steep gradients, Class 183 has a 51 notch control system and three traction motor groupings; all series, two groups of three, and three groups of two.

Their main duties today are banking heavy freight trains on the main line through Štrba – this can account for more than 30 trains in a busy 24-hour period. On the eastern ascent all banking is from Spišská Nová Ves to Štrba (45 km). On the west side banking is from Liptovská Teplá (57 km), Liptovský Mikuláš (39 km) or Liptovský Hrádok (28 km). Banking locomotives do not necessarily detach at Štrba but may remain on the rear of the train for the descent to reposition. The 1.5% grades between Spišská Nová Ves and Východná limit loads of Classes 163/363 to 800 tonnes, Class 183 to 1180 tonnes and double Class 131 locomotives to 1600 tonnes compared to around double these weights in flatlands.

Some locomotives are also still used on general freight duties, including long distance freight from Čierna nad Tisou to Ostrava. In more recent years a number of the class have been placed on long-term lease to operators in Poland, or sold to private operators.

Livery is an attractive retro-style two-tone green and grey.

System: 3000 V DC.
Built: 1971.
Former ČSD Class: E669.3.
Builder: Škoda, model 61E.
Continuous Rating: 2790 kW (3740 hp).
Maximum Tractive Effort: 345 kN.
Total No. Built: 74.
Wheel Diameter: 1250 mm.
Weight: 120 tonnes.
Length over Buffers: 18.94 m.
Maximum Speed: 90 km/h.
EVN: 91 56 6 183 0xx-c.

183.001-7	F	SNV	183.013-2	F	ZIL	183.030-6	F	ZIL
183.004-1	F	SNV	183.017-3	F	ZIL	183.034-8	F	CNT
183.005-8	F	SNV	183.019-9	F	ZIL	183.037-1	F	SNV
183.006-6	F	SNV	183.021-5	F	CNT	183.038-9	F	ZIL
183.008-2	F	KOS	183.022-3	F	CNT	183.041-3	F	CNT
183.011-6	F	ZIL	183.025-6	F	CNT	183.042-1	F	CNT
183.012-4	F	CNT	183.026-4	F	ZIL	183.043-9	F	SNV

CLASS 199 Bo

Class 199 is not an electric locomotive but a battery tractor used for shunting within depots – the equivalent of ČD Class 799 but without a diesel engine. They are heavy rebuilds on frames of Class 701/702 diesel locomotives, equipped with a 45 kWh capacity battery. The gearbox is driven by one DC Type 022 tram motor (recovered from Tatra T3 trams).

Originally 199.401–416 were all built for the Cargo operation, but six locomotives were sold to ZSSK in 2012. 199.401 retained its Class 701 style cab, but subsequent locomotives were rebuilt with a new cab and front end sections. 199.411–416 are equipped for remote control operation.

199.951 is 1000 mm gauge; see ZSSK Narrow Gauge Stock section. Livery is all over yellow.

System: Battery.
Built: 1992–2004.
Former ČSD Class: Not applicable.
Builder: ŽSR/ZSSK/ŽOS Vrútky.
Continuous Rating: 37.5 kW (50 hp).
Maximum Tractive Effort: 40 kN.
Total No. Built: 17 (inc narrow gauge 199.951).
Wheel Diameter: 1000 mm.
Weight: 22 tonnes (* 19.5 tonnes).
Length over Buffers: 7.24 m.
Maximum Speed: 10 km/h.
EVN: 97 56 8 199 4xx-c.

199.401-1	(701.541)	*	F	TTP	199.409-4			F	ZIL
199.402-9	(701.953)			BLH	199.410-2				HUM
199.403-7	(702.549)			NZK	199.411-0	(701.011)			KOS
199.404-5	(701.707)		F	ZVO (S)	199.412-8	(701.024)		F	BLV
199.405-2	(701.937)		F	PLV	199.413-6	(701.002)		F	ZVO
199.406-0	(701.021)			PVZ	199.414-4			F	BLV
199.407-8	(701.029)		F	ZVO	199.415-1				BLH
199.408-6	(701.009)		F	LEO	199.416-9			F	ZIL

▲ A typical duty for a Class 183, as 183.006 banks a westbound freight (hauled by 131.055+056 and mostly consisting of timber) on the approach to the summit at Štrba on 7 June 2014. **Robert Pritchard**

▼ Ex-works in the new ZSSK red & white livery, 240.092 leaves Levice with train Os5701, the 15.46 Nové Zámky–Zvolen on 13 June 2014. **Robert Pritchard**

CLASS 210   Bo-Bo

The majority of the ZSSK Class 210s were with ZSSK Cargo and have been stored. The remaining serviceable locomotives are used for light or trip freight work or station pilot, shunting and empty coaching stock duties.

Livery is light blue or red.

System: 25 kV AC 50 Hz.
Built: 1972–73 and 1979–83.
Former ČSD Class: S458.0.
Builder: Škoda, model 51E.
Continuous Rating: 880 kW (1180 hp).
Maximum Tractive Effort: 164 kN.

Total No. Built: 74†.
Wheel Diameter: 1050 mm.
Weight: 72 tonnes.
Length over Buffers: 14.40 m.
Maximum Speed: 80 km/h.
EVN: 97 56 8 210 0xx-c.

x   Fitted with jumper cables for operating with Class 010 battery vans.

210.004-8	F	LEO (S)	210.022-0		BLH	210.051-9	F	LEO (S)
210.006-3	F x	ZVO	210.033-7	F	BLV	210.060-0		BLH
210.007-1	F	ZVO	210.034-5	F	ZVO (S)	210.061-8	F	LEO (S)
210.009-7	F	ZVO (S)	210.035-2	F	LEO (S)	210.062-6	F	LEO (S)
210.010-5	F	ZVO (S)	210.040-2		NZK	210.063-4	F	LEO (S)
210.011-3		ZVO	210.041-0		BLH	210.064-2		BLH
210.012-1	F	ZVO (S)	210.042-8	F	LEO (S)	210.065-9	F x	BLV
210.013-9	F	ZVO (S)	210.044-4	F	LEO (S)	210.068-3	F	LEO (S)
210.017-0	F x	ZVO	210.048-5	F	LEO (S)	210.069-1	F	BLV (S)
210.018-8	F	ZVO (S)	210.049-3	F	LEO (S)	210.070-9	F	BLV
210.019-6	F x	ZVO (S)	210.050-1	F	LEO (S)	210.071-7	F	BLV

CLASS 240   Bo-Bo

These mixed traffic locomotives form an important part of both ZSSK and ZSSK Cargo's fleets, mainly operating in the west of the country. Originally 27 locomotives of this class were designated Class S499.1 (to be Class 241) for 140 km/h operation, but these were later redesignated Class 240. Most survivors of this batch are now in ZSSK/ZSSK Cargo service.

Based at Bratislava and Nové Zámky, Class 240s are used on freight on all AC routes radiating from Bratislava to the Austria, Czech Republic and Hungary borders, and to the AC/DC change point towards Žilina at Púchov. ZSSK Cargo locomotives are sometimes hired to ZSSK for use on passenger trains.

With ZSSK they are extensively used on slow and fast passenger trains radiating from Bratislava across the whole of south-west Slovakia, reaching as far east as Banská Bystrica. There are 13 diagrams from Nové Zámky depot and 12 from Bratislava. Class 263 or Class 381 and push-pull sets are used on some trains around Bratislava, but Class 240 can substitute if required, using the push-pull sets as conventional coaching stock.

System: 25 kV AC 50 Hz.
Built: 1968–70.
Former ČSD Class: S499.0 or S499.1.
Builder: Škoda, model 47E.
Continuous Rating: 3080 kW (4130 hp).
Maximum Tractive Effort: 255 kN.

Total No. Built: 145†.
Wheel Diameter: 1250 mm.
Weight: 85 tonnes.
Length over Buffers: 16.44 m.
Maximum Speed: 120 km/h.
EVN: 91 56 6 240 xxx-c.

240.001-8	F	NZK	240.020-8	F	NZK	240.036-4	R	NZK
240.002-6	F	BLV	240.022-4		NZK	240.037-2		NZK
240.003-4	F	BLV	240.024-0	F	BLV	240.038-0	F	NZK
240.004-2	F	NZK	240.027-3		NZK (S)	240.040-6	F	NZK
240.005-9	R	NZK	240.028-1	R	NZK	240.041-4	F	BLV (S)
240.009-1	F	BLV (S)	240.029-9	F	BLV	240.042-2	F	BLV
240.013-3	R	BLH	240.030-7		BLH	240.043-0	R	NZK
240.015-8	F	BLV	240.031-5	F	BLV	240.046-3	R	NZK
240.017-4	F	NZK	240.032-3	F	NZK	240.051-3	R	NZK
240.018-2	F	BLV (S)	240.033-1	F	LEO (S)	240.054-7		NZK
240.019-0	F	NZK	240.034-9	F	NZK	240.059-6	R	NZK

240.061-2	F	BLV	240.093-5	F	BLV	240.122-2	R		BLH
240.067-9	F	NZK	240.095-0	F	BLV	240.123-0	R		BLH
240.068-7		BLH	240.096-8		NZK (S)	240.124-8		F	BLV (S)
240.070-3	F	NZK	240.097-6	R	BLH	240.125-5		F	BLV
240.072-9	R	NZK	240.098-4	R	NZK	240.126-3		F	NZK
240.073-7	R	NZK	240.099-2	F	BLV	240.127-1	R		BLH
240.074-5	F	BLV (S)	240.100-8	R	BLH	240.128-9		F	BLV
240.075-2	R	NZK	240.102-4	F	BLV	240.129-7	R		BLH
240.076-0		BLH	240.103-2		NZK	240.130-5			NZK (S)
240.078-6	R	NZK	240.104-0	F	BLV	240.131-3		F	BLV (S)
240.079-4	F	NZK	240.105-7	F	BLV (S)	240.132-1	R		BLH
240.080-2		NZK	240.111-5	R	BLH	240.133-9			BLH
240.081-0	R	NZK	240.112-3	F	NZK	240.134-7	R		BLH
240.082-8	F	BLV (S)	240.113-1	R	NZK (S)	240.135-4		F	BLV (S)
240.083-6	F	NZK	240.114-9	R	NZK	240.136-2	R		BLH
240.084-4	R	BLH	240.115-6	R	BLH	240.137-0		F	BLV (S)
240.087-7	R	NZK	240.116-4	F	LEO (S)	240.140-4		F	BLV
240.088-5	F	BLV	240.118-0	F	NZK	240.141-2		F	BLV (S)
240.089-3		BLH	240.119-8	R	BLH	240.142-0			BLH
240.090-1	F	NZK	240.120-6	F	NZK	240.144-6		F	BLV (S)
240.092-7	R	NZK	240.121-4		NZK	240.145-3			BLH

▲ Superbly restored into original livery, 263.005 awaits departure from Bratislava hlavná stanica with train Os3011, the 09.00 to Leopoldov on 12 June 2014. Rolling stock is the usual 3-coach push-pull set for this route. On the right Regiojet DMU 642.35 awaits departure with the 09.05 to Komarno.

Robert Pritchard

CLASS 263 Bo-Bo

ZSSK Class 263 is slightly more powerful than the two 1984-built ČD pre-series locomotives (263.001/002).

The class is now exclusively used with double-deck push-pull sets, with six diagrams operating from Bratislava to Nové Zámky, Malacky/Kúty/Holíč nad Moravou and Leopoldov, some trains operating as cross-Bratislava services (often with around 20 minutes standing time at Bratislava hlavná stanica). Class 263s also regularly provide cover for the two Class 381 diagrams.

System: 25 kV AC 50 Hz.
Built: 1988.
Former ČSD Class: S499.2.
Builder: Škoda, model 70E.
Continuous Rating: 3200 kW (4290 hp).
Maximum Tractive Effort: 300 kN.
Non-Standard Livery: 263.005 – Orange & yellow. Carries original number S499.2005.

Total No. Built: 12†.
Wheel Diameter: 1250 mm.
Weight: 84.2 tonnes.
Length over Buffers: 16.80 m.
Maximum Speed: 120 km/h.
EVN: 91 56 6 263 0xx-c.

263.003-6	R	NZK	263.007-7	R	NZK	263.010-1	R	NZK
263.004-4	R	NZK	263.008-5	R	NZK	263.011-9	R	NZK
263.005-1	0	NZK	263.009-3	R	NZK	263.012-7	R	NZK
263.006-9	R	NZK						

CLASS 350 Bo-Bo

ZSSK Class 350 is a dual-voltage version of ČD Classes 150/151, built before Class 150 for high speed, long distance passenger duties. When built they were ČSD's first dual-voltage locomotives, and were initially used on Praha–Bratislava trains. In 2016 there are ten diagrams for the class, which include use on some "R" services between Bratislava, Žilina and Košice and "EC" trains between Praha, Brno, Bratislava and Budapest (work now shared with Class 380).

Missing locomotives 350.009 and 350.010 were written off in accidents – 350.009 in 1989 at Praha and 350.010 in 1977 at Bratislava.

Livery for those locomotives not in the new red ZSSK livery is blue & white. Recently 350.001 and 350.004 have been repainted into "retro" liveries.

System: 25 kV AC 50 Hz and 3000 V DC.
Built: 1973–75.
Former ČSD Class: ES499.0.
Builder: Škoda, model 55E.
Continuous Rating: 4000 kW (5360 hp).
Maximum Tractive Effort: 210 kN.
Non-Standard Liveries: 350.001 – Grey & white. Carries original number ES499.0001.
350.004 – Blue & cream.

Total No. Built: 20.
Wheel Diameter: 1250 mm.
Weight: 89.6 tonnes.
Length over Buffers: 16.74 m.
Maximum Speed: 160 km/h.
EVN: 91 56 6 350 0xx-c.

e   Equipped with improved electric dynamic braking.

350.001-4	0	e	BLH	350.007-1	R		BLH	350.015-4	R	e	BLH
350.002-2	R	e	BLH	350.008-9	R		BLH	350.016-2	R		BLH
350.003-0	R		BLH	350.011-3	R		BLH	350.017-0	R		BLH
350.004-8	0		BLH	350.012-1	R	e	BLH	350.018-8	R		BLH
350.005-5			BLH	350.013-9	R		BLH	350.019-6	R		BLH
350.006-3	R		BLH	350.014-7			BLH	350.020-4	R	e	BLH

CLASS 361 Bo-Bo

In 2011 ZSSK awarded ŽOS Vrútky a contract to rebuild 15 Class 163s as dual voltage Class 361s, in conjunction with the planned conversion to 25 kV AC 50 Hz of the Púchov–Žilina line. The rebuild programme is similar to the conversion of Class 163 to Class 363.5 for ČD Cargo in the Czech Republic. The first five locomotives were geared for a 140 km/h top speed and designated Class 361.0, whilst the next ten (and all subsequent rebuilds) are geared for 160 km/h running, and numbered in the Class 361.1 series.

In summer 2015, as the tenth Class 361.1 was being delivered, ZSSK announced it was ordering a further 11 locomotives (to be numbered 361.111–114/120–130), for delivery by early 2017.

Work includes the installation of 25 kV AC equipment and new transformers and IGBT control system supplied by EVPÚ Nová Dubnica. The complete modernisation of these locomotives should give them a further 25 years service, according to ZSSK.

Class 361 now forms a key part of ZSSK's long distance fleet, and has taken over from Class 350 (or ČD Classes 150/151) on some through services to Praha. They are based at both Bratislava and Košice. At Bratislava there are ten diagrams which include most of the "R" semi-fast trains between Bratislava, Žilina and Košice (these are heavy trains which load up to 13 or 14 coaches) and also some of the Žilina–Praha "EC" trains.

At the time of writing there were seven diagrams for Košice based Class 361s, mainly working trains between Košice and Poprad Tatry or Čierna nad Tisou as well as the two daily trains between Košice and Budapest, worked by a Class 361 as far as Hidasnémeti.

System: 3000 V DC and 25 kV AC 50 Hz.
Built: 1984–86 and 1991–92; rebuilt 2011–17.
Former ČSD Class: Not applicable.
Builder: Škoda, rebuilt by ŽOS Vrútky.
Continuous Rating: DC 3600 kW (4830 hp); AC 3200 kW (4290 hp).
Maximum Speed: 361.0: 140 km/h; 361.1: 160 km/h.
Maximum Tractive Effort: 361.0: 258 kN; 361.1: 220 kN.
EVN: 91 56 6 361 xxx-c.

Total No. Built: 19 (+7 on order).
Wheel Diameter: 1250 mm.
Weight: 361.0: 85 tonnes; 361.1: 86 tonnes.
Length over Buffers: 16.80 m.

▲ The first rebuilt Class 361.1, 361.101, leaves Bratislava Vinohrady with train R634, the 15.02 Zvolen–Bratislava (actually booked for a Class 362) on 14 June 2014. **Robert Pritchard**

Class 361.0. Rebuilt from Class 163 2011–12. 140 km/h.

361.001-1	(163.053)	R	KOS		361.004-5	(162.025, 163.120)	R	KOS
361.002-9	(163.060)	R	KOS		361.005-2	(163.056)	R	KOS
361.003-7	(163.103)	R	KOS					

Class 361.1. Rebuilt from Class 163 2012–15. 160 km/h.

361.101-9	(163.102)	R	BLH		361.106-8	(163.059)	R	BLH
361.102-7	(162.009, 163.125)	R	BLH		361.107-6	(163.050)	R	BLH
361.103-5	(163.058)	R	BLH		361.108-4	(163.055)	R	BLH
361.104-3	(163.051)	R	BLH		361.109-2	(163.052)	R	BLH
361.105-0	(163.049)	R	BLH		361.110-0	(162.023, 163.117)	R	BLH

Class 361.1. Rebuilt from Class 163 2015–17. 160 km/h. Various software modifications compared to earlier Class 361.1. 361.124–130 under conversion/on order.

361.120-9	(162.022, 163.122)	R	KOS		361.126-6
361.121-7	(162.010, 163.118)	R	KOS		361.127-4
361.122-5	(162.027, 163.123)	R	KOS		361.128-2
361.123-3	(162.021, 163.116)	R	KOS		361.129-0
361.124-1	(162.030, 163.115)				361.130-8
361.125-8	(162.031, 163.119)				

CLASS 362   Bo-Bo

362.001 was a one-off 1990-built 140 km/h prototype, and unlike other Class 362s was not converted from a Class 363. Confusingly both ČD and ZSSK now have a 362.001, ČD's locomotive having been renumbered from 363.001! All other ZSSK Class 362s are former Class 363s modified by exchanging original 120 km/h bogies with Class 162s. ZSR converted batches 362.121–124/164–168 in 1993–94 and 362.060/112/118–120 in 2000–01.

ZSSK uses its Class 362s and 363s on fast trains between Bratislava and Zvolen (some trains continue to Košice via Fiľakovo behind Class 757s), Bratislava–Zilina–Kosice (those trains that aren't Classes 350 or 361) and Bratislava–Trenčín/Žilina, plus some stopping trains on the main line, such as between Žilina and Púchov/Nové Mesto nad Váhom.

362.008/009/011 are in the original two-tone blue & white livery, whilst others are in ZSSK red or advertising liveries.

System: 3000 V DC and 25 kV AC 50 Hz.
Built: 1990.
Former ČSD Class: ES499.1.
Builder: Škoda, model 69E.
Continuous Rating: DC 3480 kW (4665 hp); AC 3060 kW (4100 hp).
Maximum Speed: 140 km/h.
Maximum Tractive Effort: 285 or 258 kN.
Total No. Built: 1+15 converted from Class 363†.
Wheel Diameter: 1250 mm.
Weight: 87 tonnes.
Length over Buffers: 16.80 m.

EVN: 91 56 6 362 0xx-c.
Advertising Liveries: 362.002: Všeobecná zdravotná poisťovňa (white & blue).
362.012: www.okay.sk (blue).

Class 362. Original version built for 140 km/h.

362.001-0   R   BLH

Class 362. Converted from Class 363; maximum tractive effort 258 kN.

362.002-8	(363.148)	A	BLH		362.010-1	(363.157)	R	BLH
362.003-6	(363.149)	R	BLH		362.011-9	(363.176)		BLH
362.004-4	(363.150)	R	BLH		362.012-7	(363.177)	A	BLH
362.005-1	(363.151)	R	BLH		362.013-5	(363.178)	R	BLH
362.006-9	(363.152)	R	BLH		362.014-3	(363.179)	R	BLH
362.007-7	(363.154)	R	BLH		362.015-0	(363.180)	R	BLH
362.008-5	(363.155)		BLH		362.016-8	(363.181)	R	BLH
362.009-3	(363.156)		BLH					

CLASS 363 Bo-Bo

This batch of Class 363, mostly operated by ZSSK Cargo on main line freight, was built for 120 km/h. Locomotives in the 363.148–157/176–181 series have been rebuilt as Class 362. Missing 363.153 is the only locomotive of this design to have been scrapped: it was badly damaged after a head-on collision with 240.143 (also scrapped) at Svätý Jur, near Bratislava, in 1995.

A recent development has been the modification of four locomotives to operate in semi-permanently coupled pairs on heavy freight trains on the AC/DC network. Modifications include multiple control, an upgraded electrodynamic brake, new electronics and upgraded cab.

All of the ZSSK Class 363s are in red livery, apart from 363.136 which carries blue livery with a yellow stripe. Livery for the freight locomotives is blue & white.

System: 3000 V DC and 25 kV AC 50 Hz.
Built: 1988.
Former ČSD Class: ES499.1.
Builder: Škoda, model 69E.
Continuous Rating: DC 3480 kW (4665 hp); AC 3060 kW (4100 hp).
Maximum Speed: 120 km/h.
Maximum Tractive Effort: 285 kN.

Total No. Built: 181†.
Wheel Diameter: 1250 mm.
Weight: 87 tonnes.
Length over Buffers: 16.80 m.

EVN: 91 56 6 363 xxx-c.

m   modified for multiple operation (as 363.103+104 & 363.138+142).

363.088-6	F	BLV	363.100-9	F	BLV	363.137-1	R	BLH
363.089-4	F	BLV	363.101-7	R	BLH	363.138-9	F m	BLV
363.090-2	F	BLV	363.102-5	F m	BLV	363.139-7	F	BLV
363.091-0	F	BLV	363.103-3	F	BLV	363.140-5	F	BLV
363.092-8	F	BLV	363.104-1	F m	BLV	363.141-3	F	BLV
363.093-6	F	BLV	363.105-8	F	BLV	363.142-1	F m	BLV
363.094-4	F	BLV	363.106-6	F	BLV	363.143-9	R	BLH
363.095-1	F	BLV	363.107-4	R	BLH	363.144-7	R	BLH
363.096-9	F	BLV	363.133-0	R	BLH	363.145-4	R	BLH
363.097-7	F	BLV	363.134-8	R	BLH	363.146-2	R	BLH
363.098-5	F	BLV	363.135-5	R	BLH	363.147-0	R	BLH
363.099-3	F	BLV	363.136-3		BLH			

CLASS 381 Bo-Bo

Following ČD's order for 20 Class 380s, ZSSK followed with an order for two locomotives. However unlike the Class 380s, the 381s are not used on long-distance trains but with push-pull stock on shorter distance workings from Bratislava, and as a result are geared for a maximum speed of 160 km/h rather than 200 km/h. They work alongside Class 263, mainly on the Bratislava–Leopoldov and Bratislava–Kúty routes.

System: 3000 V DC, 15 kV AC 16.7 Hz and 25 kV AC 50 Hz.
Built: 2011–12.
Former ČSD Class: Not applicable.
Builder: Škoda, model 109E2.
Continuous Rating: 6400 kW (8580 hp).
Maximum Tractive Effort: 274 kN.

Total No. Built: 2.
Wheel Diameter: 1250 mm.
Weight: 86 tonnes.
Length over Buffers: 18.00 m.
Maximum Speed: 160 km/h.
EVN: 91 56 6 381 00x-c.

381.001-7	R	BLH	381.002-5	R	BLH

2.2. ZSSK ELECTRIC MULTIPLE UNITS & TRAILERS

Until the delivery of Class 671, ZSSK had just Classes 460 and 560 EMUs for working suburban and regional services, in recent years mainly around Košice and Nové Zámky. All of Class 560 have now been withdrawn from traffic.

Numbering and formations follow the ČD examples. Class 460 operate as separate motor coaches and trailers; unlike the ČD units they do not operate in semi-permanent formations, and formations change frequently, so are not listed here. Class 671s are fixed formation.

CLASS 460   MOTOR COACHES

Motor coaches for 4- or 5-car EMUs operating with Class 063 trailers. All units are based at Košice depot and used on commuter or regional services on the following routes: Košice–Čierna nad Tisou, Košice–Prešov–Lipany and Trebišov–Michaľany. The introduction of Class 671 around Košice means that some services are now shared with these units.

Livery is the old ZSSK EMU colours of green & cream, apart from a few units repainted into the new ZSSK red livery, shown as **R**.

System: 3000 V DC.
Built: 1974–78.
Builder – Mechanical Parts: MSV Studénka.
Builder – Electrical Parts: Škoda.
Traction Motors: 4 x 250 kW (335 hp) DC.
Former ČSD Class: EM488.0.
Wheel Arrangement: Bo-Bo.
Formation: DMBSO.

Total No. Built: 86 motor cars†.

Accommodation: –/48 1T.
Weight: 64 tonnes.
Length over Couplers: 24.50 m.
Maximum Speed: 110 km/h.
EVN: 94 56 0 460 0xx-c.

460.029-2		KOS	460.039-1	**R**	KOS	460.046-6		KOS
460.030-0		KOS	460.040-9	**R**	KOS	460.051-6		KOS
460.031-8	**R**	KOS	460.041-7		KOS	460.052-4		KOS
460.032-6	**R**	KOS	460.042-5		KOS	460.053-2		KOS
460.033-4		KOS	460.043-3	**R**	KOS	460.054-0		KOS
460.034-2		KOS	460.044-1	**R**	KOS	460.057-3	**R**	KOS
460.037-5		KOS	460.045-8		KOS	460.058-1	**R**	KOS
460.038-3		KOS						

CLASS 063   INTERMEDIATE TRAILERS

Intermediate trailers used with Class 460 EMU motor coaches (see above) in 4- or 5-car sets.

Built: 1974–78.
Builder: MSV Studénka.
Former ČSD Class: N488.03.
Accommodation: –/80 2T.

Weight: 55.3 tonnes.
Length over Buffers: 24.50 m.
Maximum Speed: 110 km/h.
EVN: 94 56 0 063 xxx-c.

063.333-9		KOS	063.361-0		KOS	063.379-2		KOS
063.344-6		KOS	063.363-6		KOS	063.380-0		KOS
063.345-3		KOS	063.364-4		KOS	063.381-8		KOS
063.346-1	**R**	KOS	063.366-9		KOS	063.382-6		KOS
063.347-9	**R**	KOS	063.367-7		KOS	063.383-4		KOS
063.348-7	**R**	KOS	063.368-5		KOS	063.384-2		KOS
063.350-3		KOS	063.369-3		KOS	063.385-9	**R**	KOS
063.351-1		KOS	063.376-8		KOS	063.386-7		KOS
063.356-0	**R**	KOS	063.377-6		KOS (S)	063.387-5	**R**	KOS
063.357-8		KOS	063.378-4		KOS (S)			

CLASS 560   MOTOR COACHES

By spring 2015 all of the ZSSK Class 560s had been withdrawn, having finished in service in a deplorable state, both externally and internally. The units taken out of traffic have been stored at Nové Zámky, their duties having been taken over by new Class 671s.

System: 25 kV AC 50 Hz.
Built: 1970–71.
Builder – Mechanical Parts: MSV Studénka.
Builder – Electrical Parts: Škoda.
Traction Motors: 4 x 210 kW (280 hp) DC.
Former ČSD Class: SM488.0.
Wheel Arrangement: Bo-Bo.
Formation: DMBSO.

Total No. Built: 34 motor cars†.

Accommodation: –/48 1T.
Weight: 64 tonnes.
Length over Couplers: 24.50 m.
Maximum Speed: 110 km/h.
EVN: 94 56 0 560 0xx-c.

560.011-9	**R**	NZK (S)	560.016-8		ŽOSV (S)	560.031-7	**R**	NZK (S)
560.012-7	**R**	NZK (S)	560.020-0		ŽOSV (S)	560.032-5	**R**	NZK (S)
560.013-5	**R**	NZK (S)	560.029-1	**R**	NZK (S)	560.033-3	**R**	NZK (S)
560.014-3	**R**	NZK (S)	560.030-9	**R**	NZK (S)	560.034-1	**R**	NZK (S)

CLASS 060   INTERMEDIATE TRAILERS

Intermediate trailers used with Class 560 EMU motor coaches but all currently stored.

Built: 1970–71.
Builder: MSV Studénka.
Former ČSD Class: N488.0.
Accommodation: –/80 2T.

Weight: 55.3 tonnes.
Length over Buffers: 24.50 m.
Maximum Speed: 110 km/h.
EVN: 94 56 0 060 xxx-c.

060.020-5	**R**	NZK (S)	060.031-2	**R**	NZK (S)	060.049-4	**R**	NZK (S)
060.026-2	**R**	NZK (S)	060.044-5	**R**	NZK (S)	060.050-2	**R**	NZK (S)
060.028-8	**R**	NZK (S)	060.045-2	**R**	NZK (S)	060.051-0	**R**	NZK (S)

▲ In the new ZSSK red livery 460.057/063.356/063.387/063.385/460.058 arrives at Čierna nad Tisou zastávka with train Os8810, the 12.12 Čierna nad Tisou–Košice on 6 June 2014.   **Robert Pritchard**

CLASS 671+071+971   3-CAR UNITS

These are 3-car, IGBT asynchronous motored, double-deck multiple units similar to ČD Class 471 "CityElefants" but equipped for dual-voltage operation and geared for a higher top speed of 160 km/h to reflect their operation on some main line semi-fast services. The units were delivered in two batches, the first ten units in 2010–12 and then a further nine in 2014–15. There are some interior differences compared to the ČD units, in particular the ZSSK sets are Second Class only. The 071.xxx and 971.xxx numbers duplicate those on ČD Class 471.

Those units based at Žilina are used on stopping services on the main line from Žilina, mainly between Žilina, Trenčín and Nové Mesto nad Váhom plus some services running further east to Poprad-Tatry. They are also used on some trains between Žilina, Čadca and Skalité/Zwardoň (Poland). Some units are also outbased at Košice for regional services in eastern Slovakia, including some trains on the Čierna nad Tisou and Prešov routes.

The second batch of units are based at Nové Zámky to replace Class 560. They are used on the Nové Zámky–Štúrovo and Galanta–Trnava routes, as well as working some trains on the Nové Zámky–Bratislava corridor, mainly in the hands of double-deck push-pull stock built to the same design as Class 671 (see Non-Powered Trailers section).

System: 3000 V DC and 25 kV AC 50 Hz.
Built: 2010–15.   **Total No. Built:** 19 x 3-car sets.
Builders – Mechanical Parts: MSV/Škoda.
Builders – Electrical Parts: Škoda Ostrava.
Accommodation: –/61(+6) 1TD 1T + –/134 2T + –/94(+12) 1T.
Traction Motors: 4 x 500 kW (670 hp) AC.   **Weight:** 72 + 48 + 50 tonnes.
Wheel Arrangement: Bo-Bo + 2-2 + 2-2.   **Maximum Speed:** 160 km/h.
Formation: DMSO–TSO–DTSO.   **Length over Couplers:** 26.40 m per car.
EVN: 94 56 0 671 0xx-c + 94 56 0 071 0xx-c + 96 56 4 971 0xx-c.

671.001-6	071.001-2	971.001-3	**R**	ZIL	671.011-5	071.011-1	971.011-2	**R**	NZK
671.002-4	071.002-0	971.002-1	**R**	ZIL	671.012-3	071.012-9	971.012-0	**R**	NZK
671.003-2	071.003-8	971.003-9	**R**	ZIL	671.013-1	071.013-7	971.013-8	**R**	NZK
671.004-0	071.004-6	971.004-7	**R**	ZIL	671.014-9	071.014-5	971.014-6	**R**	NZK
671.005-7	071.005-3	971.005-4	**R**	ZIL	671.015-6	071.015-2	971.015-3	**R**	NZK
671.006-5	071.006-1	971.006-2	**R**	ZIL	671.016-4	071.016-0	971.016-1	**R**	NZK
671.007-3	071.007-9	971.007-0	**R**	ZIL	671.017-2	071.017-8	971.017-9	**R**	NZK
671.008-1	071.008-7	971.008-8	**R**	ZIL	671.018-0	071.018-6	971.018-7	**R**	NZK
671.009-9	071.009-5	971.009-6	**R**	ZIL	671.019-8	071.019-4	971.019-5	**R**	NZK
671.010-7	071.010-3	971.010-4	**R**	ZIL					

2.3. ZSSK & ZSSK CARGO DIESEL LOCOMOTIVES

CLASS 710   C

This successful class of centre cab light shunting locomotives was mainly built for industrial use, or for export – to Germany, Romania, Hungary and India. A small number are still used by ZSSK for depot or yard pilot duties but most are now stored. A number of others are in departmental or industrial use in the Czech Republic or Slovakia.

Built: 1961–73.
Former ČSD Class: T334.0.
Builder: ČKD, SMZ or TSM.
Engine: ČKD 12V170DR.
Power: 301 kW (405 hp).
Transmission: Hydraulic.
Maximum Tractive Effort: 100 kN.

Total No. Built: 475 (inc some for export).
Wheel Diameter: 1000 mm.
Train Heating Equipment: None.
Weight: 40.5 tonnes.
Length over Buffers: 9.44 m.
Maximum Speed: 60 km/h.
EVN: 98 56 3 710 0xx-c.

710.001-9		BLH	710.005-0	F	ZIL (S)	710.030-8		BLH
710.002-7	F	ZIL (S)	710.016-7	F	TTP (S)	710.075-3	F	SNV (S)

CLASS 721   Bo-Bo

Class 721 was derived from the 1958–61 built Class 720, but is heavier and slightly longer. Class 721 has the same six cylinder power unit as Class 751 but without turbochargers. They were used for many years for yard shunting, station pilot and short-medium trip freight work throughout Slovakia.

Today, ZSSK Cargo has withdrawn all its Class 721s, apart from two 721.8s built to run on broad gauge access tracks at Čierna nad Tisou or Košice. These have SA3 centre couplers as well as side buffers. ZSSK still uses a number of the class for station pilot duties at major stations, and some locomotives have received the new red livery. However ŽOS Zvolen Class 712 rebuilds have now taken over some Class 721 duties. Many other Class 721.5s and 721.6s are used by private operators or industrial users throughout the Czech Republic and Slovakia.

Livery is dark blue with a cream stripe and red solebar unless stated.

Built: 1962–68.
Former ČSD Class: T458.1.
Builder: ČKD, model T458.1.
Engine: ČKD 6S310DR.
Power: 551 kW (740 hp).
Transmission: Electric.
Maximum Tractive Effort: 186 kW.

Total No. Built: 283 (inc some for export).
Wheel Diameter: 1050 mm.
Train Heating Equipment: None.
Weight: 74 tonnes.
Length over Buffers: 13.28 m.
Maximum Speed: 80 km/h.
EVN: 92 56 1 721 xxx-c.

Class 721.0. 1435 mm gauge.

721.004-0		ZVO	721.073-5		HUM	721.120-4	F	Maťovce (S)
721.012-3		ZIL	721.075-0	F	TTP (S)	721.123-8	F	Maťovce (S)
721.022-2		ZIL	721.079-2	F	PVZ (S)	721.124-6	F	TTP (S)
721.027-1		PVZ	721.093-3	F	CNT (S)	721.126-1	F	TTP (S)
721.028-9	F	PLV (S)	721.096-6		ZIL	721.128-7	R	NZK
721.030-5	R	KOS	721.098-2	R	HUM	721.131-1	R	BLH
721.043-8	F	KOS (S)	721.099-0	F	CNT (S)	721.134-5	F	CNT (S)
721.046-1	R	NZK	721.102-2		KOS	721.140-2		HUM
721.051-1	F	CNT (S)	721.105-5	F	CNT (S)	721.189-9	F	CNT (S)
721.058-6	R	ZIL	721.106-3	F	HAN (S)	721.220-2	F	TTP (S)
721.060-2		KOS	721.110-5	R	KOS	721.227-7	F	CNT (S)
721.062-8	F	KOS (S)	721.116-2		ZIL	721.228-5	F	Maťovce (S)
721.063-6	F	KOS (S)	721.117-0		ZVO	721.230-1	F	TTP (S)
721.065-1		HUM	721.119-6	F	TTP (S)	721.231-9	F	CNT (S)
721.071-9	F	CNT (S)						

Class 721.8. 1520 mm gauge and SA3 couplers.

721.802-7	F	Maťovce (S)	721.803-5	F	CNT (S)

▲ Newly painted in ZSSK red & white passenger livery, 721.046 shunts coaching stock in the yard at Nové Zámky on 12 June 2014. **Robert Pritchard**

▼ ZSSK Cargo locos 731.033, 752.052 and 742.400 are seen stabled at the former depot at Prešov (now closed as a maintenance facility) on 8 June 2014. **Robert Pritchard**

CLASS 731 Bo-Bo

The small fleet of ZSSK Cargo Class 731s are all allocated to Spišská Nová Ves and outbased at Poprad Tatry, Margecany and Prešov for working freights over non-electrified routes in these areas.

Livery is red with a broad yellow stripe.

Built: 1988–92.
Former ČSD Class: T457.1.
Builder: ČKD, model T457.1.
Engine: ČKD K6S230DR.
Power: 600 kW (805 hp).
Transmission: Electric.
Maximum Tractive Effort: 205 kN.

Total No. Built: 62†.
Wheel Diameter: 1000 mm.
Train Heating Equipment: None.
Weight: 68 tonnes.
Length over Buffers: 15.28 m.
Maximum Speed: 80 km/h.
EVN: 92 56 1 731 0xx-c.

731.033-7	F	SNV	731.037-8	F	SNV	731.053-5	F	SNV
731.034-5	F	SNV	731.038-6	F	SNV	731.054-3	F	SNV
731.035-2	F	SNV	731.051-9	F	SNV	731.055-0	F	SNV
731.036-0	F	SNV	731.052-7	F	SNV			

CLASS 736 Bo-Bo

Class 736 is a heavy rebuild of Class 735, replacing everything above the main underframe. Like Classes 746 and 773, high bonnets are replaced by low hoods and the ČKD engine and generator replaced by a Caterpillar engine and Siemens alternator. They look very much like contemporary new German machines, except for the exhaust pipe sprouting from the bonnet rather than being integrated into the cab housing. The first 18 locomotives (736.001–018) are equipped with 1020 kW dynamic braking, a 124 kW Caterpillar 3056 auxiliary diesel engine and electric train heating as they were intended for passenger work before ZSCS and ZSSK separated.

On freight duties, operating ability is approximately the same as Classes 751/752 and they share work over the same scenic steeply-graded lines radiating from Zvolen, often operating in pairs. Two routes north from Zvolen to Vrútky each have freights which are shared between pairs of Classes 736, 746 or 751/752. The section via Kremnica from Hronská Dúbrava to Kremnické Bane (775 m above sea level) is very steeply graded, and trains require banking as well as double-heading. The line from Banská Bystrica to Čremošné is slightly less graded, with fewer trains requiring banking.

ZSSK also ordered five of the class for passenger duties, and today these are based at Nové Zámky and Bratislava. In Bratislava the class are generally used for depot shunting or station pilot duties, whilst the Nové Zámky machines have two daily diagrams operating between Nové Zámky, Nitra and Prievidza on Line 140.

Livery for the ZSSK Cargo locomotives is a light blue and white not carried by other locomotives, whilst ZSSK locomotives carry the standard red & white livery.

Built: Rebuilt 1998–2009 from Class 735.
Former ČSD Class: Not applicable.
Builder: ŽOS Zvolen.
Engine: Caterpillar 3512 DI-TA.
Power: 1080 (1450 hp) (* 990 kW (1325 hp)).
Transmission: Electric.
Maximum Tractive Effort: 168 kN.

Total No. Built: 29.
Wheel Diameter: 1000 mm.
Train Heating Equipment: Electric 120 kVA.
Weight: 64 tonnes.
Length over Buffers: 14.34 m.
Maximum Speed: 100 km/h.
EVN: 92 56 1 736 xxx-c.

Class 736.0. Conversions for ZSSK Cargo. 736.001–002 rebuilt 1998/2001 as prototypes. 736.003–024 rebuilt 2002–09 with more powerful engines.

736.001-9	(735.016)	F *	ZVO	736.008-4	(735.078)	F	ZVO
736.002-7	(735.079)	F *	ZVO	736.009-2	(735.052)	F	ZVO
736.003-5	(735.051)	F	ZVO	736.010-0	(735.061)	F	ZVO
736.004-3	(735.121)	F	ZVO	736.011-8	(735.183)	F	ZVO
736.005-0	(735.252)	F	ZVO	736.012-6	(735.120)	F	ZVO
736.006-8	(735.182)	F	ZVO	736.013-4	(735.094)	F	ZVO
736.007-6	(735.060)	F	ZVO	736.014-2	(735.111)	F	ZVO

736.015-9	(735.076)	F	ZVO		736.020-9	(735.110)	F	ZVO
736.016-7	(735.119)	F	ZVO		736.021-7	(735.256)	F	ZVO
736.017-5	(735.112)	F	ZVO		736.022-5	(735.043)	F	ZVO
736.018-3	(735.255)	F	ZVO		736.023-3	(735.050)	F	ZVO
736.019-1	(735.109)	F	ZVO		736.024-1	(735.053)		

Class 736.1. Conversions for ZSSK. Rebuilt 2008–09.

736.101-7	(735.080)	R	NZK		736.104-1	(735.093) R	NZK
736.102-5	(735.091)	R	BLH		736.105-8	(735.113) R	NZK
736.103-3	(735.092)	R	BLH				

CLASS 742   Bo-Bo

Slovak Class 742s are all operated by the Cargo business except 742.398 at Poprad-Tatry. Unlike ČD locomotives the class are not commonly used in pairs, instead being used on lighter trip working or yard shunting duties. The class is spread fairly evenly across the country.

Notable locomotives include 742.037, which was the 10 000th locomotive built by ČKD, and 742.611/618/629/634, which are ex-Slovak industry.

Livery is red with a broad yellow stripe unless stated.

Built: 1977–86.
Former ČSD Class: T466.2.
Builder: ČKD, model T466.2.
Engine: ČKD K6S230DR.
Power: 883 kW (1185 hp).
Transmission: Electric.
Maximum Tractive Effort: 193 kN.
Non-Standard Livery: 742.611/618/629/634: Blue & white.

Total No. Built: 453 (plus 41 for industry)†.
Wheel Diameter: 1000 mm.
Train Heating Equipment: None.
Weight: 64 tonnes.
Length over Buffers: 13.60 m.
Maximum Speed: 90 km/h.
EVN: 92 56 1 742 xxx-c.

742.001-1	F	HUM		742.181-1	F	BLV		742.313-0	F	BLV
742.002-9	F	PVZ		742.182-9	F	HAN		742.324-7	F	BLV
742.003-7	F	BLV		742.183-7	F	HAN		742.325-4	F	ZIL
742.004-5	F	BLV		742.222-3	F	HUM		742.326-2	F	ZVO
742.005-2	F	BLV		742.223-1	F	NZK		742.327-0	F	BLV
742.006-0	F	TTP (S)		742.227-2	F	CNT		742.337-9	F	ZIL
742.019-3	F	LEO		742.228-0	F	TTP (S)		742.338-7	F	TTP
742.020-1	F	PVZ		742.232-2	F	PLV (S)		742.339-5	F	TTP
742.021-9	F	PLV		742.234-8	F	ZVO (S)		742.340-3	F	TTP
742.022-7	F	LEO		742.235-5	F	NZK		742.351-0	F	BLV
742.023-5	F	NZK		742.244-7	F	ZVO		742.352-8	F	BLV
742.024-3	F	BLV		742.245-4	F	NZK		742.363-5	F	BLV
742.037-5	F	ZIL		742.246-2	F	LEO		742.364-3	F	BLV
742.038-3	F	ZIL		742.255-3	F	NZK		742.368-4	F	ZIL
742.039-1	F	CNT		742.256-1	F	TTP (S)		742.373-4	F	BLV
742.040-9	F	CNT		742.266-0	F	ZIL		742.374-2	F	BLV
742.041-7	F	LEO		742.267-8	F	CNT		742.375-9	F	ZVO
742.042-5	F	ZIL (S)		742.268-6	F	TTP		742.376-7	F	HAN
742.051-6	F	BLV		742.277-7	F	HUM		742.386-6	F	ZIL
742.052-4	F	TTP (S)		742.278-5	F	HAN		742.387-4	F	TTP
742.053-2	F	BLV		742.286-8	F	ZIL		742.388-2	F	TTP
742.054-0	F	NZK		742.287-6	F	LEO		742.389-0	F	TTP
742.055-7	F	NZK		742.296-7	F	CNT		742.398-1		POP
742.056-5	F	HAN		742.297-5	F	BLV		742.400-5	F	HUM
742.121-7	F	CNT		742.298-3	F	BLV		742.401-3	F	TTP
742.122-5	F	NZK		742.299-1	F	ZIL		742.611-7	0 F	CNT
742.123-3	F	PLV		742.310-6	F	ZIL		742.618-2	0 F	CNT
742.124-1	F	LEO		742.311-4	F	CNT		742.629-9	0 F	HAN
742.125-8	F	LEO		742.312-2	F	HUM		742.634-9	0 F	LEO

▲ One of the five ZSSK Class 736 rebuilds, 736.105, stands at Nitra between duties on 12 June 2014. **Robert Pritchard**

▼ 751.204 stands at Prievidza with a loaded timber train on 14 May 2015. **Robert Pritchard**

CLASS 746   Bo-Bo

These locomotives are heavy rebuilds of Class 742 with new Caterpillar engines and Siemens alternators. Like Class 736 they were rebuilt by ŽOS Zvolen, and are a similar rebuild to Class 742.7 rebuilt by CZ LOKO for ČD Cargo and private operators. Externally they look similar to Class 736, but have slightly less powerful 8-cylinder engines.

All were rebuilt using Class 742s acquired from ČD, except 746.017, which is ex-ZSSK Cargo 742.233. Like Class 736s they can usually be found operating in pairs, the Zvolen locomotives often working heavy freights on Line 160 towards Plešivec. The last four machines are based at Haniska pri Košiciach for freight traffic on non-electrified lines in the area.

The livery is different again, being dark blue with white stripes.

Built: 2009–11.
Former ČSD Class: Not applicable.
Builder: ŽOS Zvolen.
Engine: Caterpillar 3508B.
Power: 970 kW (1300 hp).
Transmission: Electric.
Maximum Tractive Effort: 204 kN.

Total No. Built: 17.
Wheel Diameter: 1000 mm.
Train Heating Equipment: None.
Weight: 66.5 tonnes.
Length over Buffers: 13.82 m.
Maximum Speed: 90 km/h.
EVN: 92 56 1 746 0xx-c.

746.001-7	(742.120)	F	ZVO		746.010-8	(742.258)	F	ZVO
746.002-5	(742.012)	F	ZVO		746.011-6	(742.356)	F	ZVO
746.003-3	(742.060)	F	SNV		746.012-4	(742.423)	F	ZVO
746.004-1	(742.444)	F	SNV		746.013-2	(742.071)	F	ZVO
746.005-8	(742.448)	F	ZVO		746.014-0	(742.237)	F	HAN
746.006-6	(742.259)	F	ZVO		746.015-7	(742.145)	F	HAN
746.007-4	(742.342)	F	ZVO		746.016-5	(742.078)	F	HAN
746.008-2	(742.168)	F	ZVO		746.017-3	(742.233)	F	HAN
746.009-0	(742.097)	F	ZVO					

CLASS 750   Bo-Bo

In 1989, pilot conversions of 753.181 (Zvolen) and 753.242 (Brno) from steam to electric heat produced 750.181 and 750.242. ČSD started, and ŽSR continued, to convert 46 locomotives for use in Slovakia by 1995.

By 2015 most had been rebuilt again, as Class 757. The handful of remaining serviceable machines usually act as standby power for Class 754 and Class 757.

Built: Rebuilt 1991–95 from Class 753.
Former ČSD Class: Not applicable.
Builder: ČKD.
Engine: ČKD 12V230DR.
Power: 1325 kW (1775 hp).
Transmission: Electric.
Maximum Tractive Effort: 185 kN.
Non-Standard Liveries: 750.037: Light blue & grey.
750.164: Light red & two-tone grey.
750.183: Light grey, blue & yellow.
750.300: Original ČSD maroon & yellow.

Total No. Built: 163†.
Wheel Diameter: 1000 mm.
Train Heating Equipment: Electric.
Weight: 74 tonnes.
Length over Buffers: 16.50 m.
Maximum Speed: 100 km/h.
EVN: 92 56 1 750 xxx-c.

750.037-4	(753.037)	**O**	F	ZVO (S)		750.182-8	(753.182)	**R**	NZK
750.131-5	(753.131)	**R**		NZK		750.183-6	(753.183)	**O**	NZK
750.164-6	(753.164)	**O**		KOS		750.300-6	(753.300)	**O**	POP

CLASSES 751 & 752 Bo-Bo

The Slovak Class 751/752s have had no booked passenger work since 2004 – and there is no ETH Class 749 equivalent in Slovakia. However the two Classes are still in regular use with ZSSK Cargo, operating from a number of depots. They are often used on heavy long distance trains in pairs (such as on the non-electrified east–west Line 160) and on local trip freights singly. Both classes are still receiving major overhauls at ŽOS Zvolen so should continue in service for a number of years yet.

Locomotives known to be fitted with a silencer are shown *, however silencers are being removed as locomotives are overhauled at ŽOS Zvolen.

Livery is red and two-tone grey for the Class 751s, and blue and two-tone grey for the Class 752s.

Built: 1964–71.
Former ČSD Class: T478.1 or T478.2.
Builder: ČKD.
Engine: ČKD K6S310DR.
Power: 1103 kW (1480 hp).
Transmission: Electric.
Maximum Tractive Effort: 185 kN.

Total No. Built: Class 751: 230†; Class 752: 82.
Wheel Diameter: 1000 mm.
Train Heating Equipment: Steam/none.
Weight: 75 tonnes.
Length over Buffers: 16.50 m.
Maximum Speed: 100 km/h.
EVN: 92 56 1 751 xxx-c or
92 56 1 752 xxx-c.

Class 751. Built with steam heating boilers (it is understood all boilers have now been isolated or removed).

751.023-3	F		PLV (S)	751.074-6	F		HUM	751.132-2	F		TTP (S)

751.023-3	F	PLV (S)	751.074-6	F	HUM	751.132-2	F	TTP (S)
751.024-1	F *	HAN	751.075-3	F	PVZ	751.171-0	F	PLV
751.025-8	F	ZVO (S)	751.076-1	F *	PLV	751.173-6	F	PLV
751.026-6	F	PLV	751.077-9	F	PLV	751.174-4	F	PVZ
751.027-4	F	NZK	751.078-7	F	ZVO (S)	751.175-1	F *	TTP (S)
751.032-4	F	NZK	751.082-9	F	BLV	751.188-4	F	ŽOSZ (S)
751.033-2	F	PVZ	751.083-7	F *	NZK	751.191-8	F	ZIL
751.034-0	F	PLV (S)	751.084-5	F	PVZ	751.192-6	F *	PVZ
751.035-7	F	PVZ	751.085-2	F *	CNT (S)	751.193-4	F *	CNT (S)
751.036-5	F	PLV	751.109-0	F	TTP	751.195-9	F *	BLV
751.037-3	F	ZIL	751.112-4	F	ZIL	751.196-7	F	PVZ
751.043-1	F	ZVO (S)	751.113-2	F	HAN	751.197-5	F *	TTP (S)
751.046-4	F *	PVZ	751.114-0	F	PLV (S)	751.198-3	F *	ŽOSZ (S)
751.047-2	F	PVZ	751.116-5	F *	PLV (S)	751.199-1	F *	PLV
751.055-5	F	BLV	751.118-1	F	PLV	751.200-7	F *	ZVO (S)
751.056-3	F	HUM	751.123-1	F	PLV	751.202-3	F	ZIL (S)
751.057-1	F	PLV	751.124-9	F	PVZ	751.203-1	F *	BLV
751.058-9	F *	TTP (S)	751.125-6	F	PLV	751.204-9	F	PVZ
751.059-7	F	PLV	751.126-4	F	PLV	751.205-6	F *	ŽOSZ (S)
751.062-1	F	BLV	751.127-2	F	BLV	751.206-4	F	PLV
751.072-0	F	HUM	751.128-0	F	PVZ	751.207-2	F *	TTP (S)
751.073-8	F	HUM	751.129-8	F	PLV	751.208-0	F *	BLV

Class 752. Built as a no-train-heat version.

752.018-2	F	HUM	752.027-3	F	PLV (S)	752.046-3	F	HUM
752.020-8	F	ZVO	752.028-1	F	CNT (S)	752.047-1	F	ZVO
752.021-6	F	HUM	752.030-7	F	HUM	752.048-9	F	HUM
752.022-4	F	PLV (S)	752.040-6	F	HUM	752.049-7	F	PLV (S)
752.023-2	F	HUM	752.041-4	F	ZVO	752.051-3	F	HAN
752.024-0	F	PLV (S)	752.043-0	F	HAN	752.052-1	F	HUM
752.025-7	F	PLV (S)	752.045-5	F *	HAN	752.070-3	F *	ZVO
752.026-5	F	HUM						

CLASS 754 Bo-Bo

ZSSK Class 754s are used on passenger trains based at three depots – Zvolen, Prievidza and Humenné. Zvolen depot has 13 diagrams for Class 754s over some highly scenic routes. They operate to Vrútky and Žilina – via Hronská Dúbrava to Kremnické Bane and Horna Stubna and via Banská Bystrica to Čremošné and Diviaky (diagrams on these routes are shared with Class 757). They also work some local trains between Zvolen and Lučenec/Fiľakovo and between Zvolen/Banská Bystrica and Brezno. The Zvolen allocation also covers for unavailable Class 757s, and conversely 757s can also be used on 754 diagrams.

Locomotives based at Humenné and Prievidza are standbys for unavailable Class 757s.

Most locomotives are now in the new red livery, otherwise the livery is the light red & two-tone grey scheme.

Built: 1978–80.
Former ČSD Class: T478.4.
Builder: ČKD.
Engine: ČKD 12V230DR.
Power: 1472 kW (1975 hp).
Transmission: Electric.
Maximum Tractive Effort: 185 kN.
Non-Standard Liveries: 754.036: Red & yellow.
754.054: Original ČSD maroon & yellow.

Total No. Built: 86†.
Wheel Diameter: 1000 mm.
Train Heating Equipment: Electric 400 kW.
Weight: 74.4 tonnes.
Length over Buffers: 16.50 m.
Maximum Speed: 100 km/h.
EVN: 92 56 1 754 0xx-c.

754.003-2		ZVO	754.035-4	R	ZVO (S)	754.070-1	R	ZVO
754.004-0	R	ZVO	754.036-2	O	ZVO	754.071-9	R	ZVO
754.005-7	R	ZVO	754.052-9	R	ZVO	754.072-7		PVZ
754.010-7	R	ZVO	754.053-7	R	ZVO	754.073-5	R	KOS
754.011-5	R	ZVO	754.054-5	O	ZVO	754.082-6	R	ZVO
754.014-9	R	ZVO	754.055-2		ZVO	754.083-4	R	HUM
754.032-1	R	HUM	754.056-0	R	ZVO	754.084-2		ZVO
754.033-9	R	ZVO	754.069-3	R	PVZ	754.085-9	R	HUM
754.034-7	R	ZVO						

CLASS 756 Bo-Bo

This small batch of ten Class 756 "Goggle" rebuilds for ZSSK Cargo use the same Caterpillar engines and Siemens alternators as fitted to ČD Cargo Class 753.7 which were rebuilt by CZ LOKO Česká Třebová. Most of this class were rebuilt from ZSSK Cargo Class 753s, except 756.001/003 which were rebuilt from ZSSK Class 750s.

All based at Zvolen, Class 756s are used on freights on the non-electrified lines in central Slovakia, and also between Zvolen and Bratislava.

Livery is the same dark blue & white carried by Classes 746/773.

Built: Rebuilt 2008–10 from Classes 750/753.
Former ČSD Class: Not applicable.
Builder: ŽOS Zvolen.
Engine: Caterpillar 3512B.
Power: 1455 kW (1950 hp).
Transmission: Electric.
Maximum Tractive Effort: 185 kN.

Total No. Built: 10.
Wheel Diameter: 1000 mm.
Train Heating Equipment: None.
Weight: 74 tonnes.
Length over Buffers: 16.60 m.
Maximum Speed: 100 km/h.
EVN: 92 56 1 756 0xx-c.

756.001-4	(750.219)	F	ZVO	756.006-3	(753.220)	F	ZVO
756.002-2	(753.053)	F	ZVO	756.007-1	(753.256)	F	ZVO
756.003-0	(750.149)	F	ZVO	756.008-9	(753.299)	F	ZVO
756.004-8	(753.147)	F	ZVO	756.009-7	(753.165)	F	ZVO
756.005-5	(753.255)	F	ZVO	756.010-5	(753.237)	F	ZVO

CLASS 757   Bo-Bo

Just as ZSSK Cargo Class 756 is a similar rebuild to ČD Cargo Class 753.7, ZSSK Class 757 is similar to ČD Class 750.7 rebuilds. In 2010 ŽOS Zvolen embarked on a major programme to rebuild 20 Class 750s for ZSSK for top-link passenger work on long distance services. The first 20 locomotives, completed by the end of 2014, were a success and a further order for five more followed – the last of these, 757.025, was completed in late 2015.

Whilst the same engines and Siemens alternators are used, Class 757 rebuilds are even more comprehensive than the ČD Class 750.7s. Only the main frame and bogies are left. All of the bodyside panels are replaced, meaning Class 757s lose the distinctive round upper bodyside windows so can be easily differentiated from a Class 750 or 754. New cabs still feature the distinctive "Goggle" windows though. The engine room is adapted to fit the new Caterpillar engine, and at the same time there is greater sound proofing and silencing – Class 757 is one of the quietest diesels in Europe, even when operating with heavy trains on routes with steep gradients. The cabs have also been rebuilt for driver comfort, featuring air-conditioning and even a wash basin, fridge and microwave oven!

Initially ZSSK used these impressive machines on top-link work purely from Zvolen depot, but in 2014 some of the class migrated east to Humenné. At the time of writing there are nine diagrams for the class based at Zvolen. They are used on the express trains between Zvolen and Košice via Line 160 and also on the few trains between Zvolen and Margecany via Brezno (Line 172/173). This highly scenic line climbs in a spiral above Telgart to an altitude of 930 m above sea level at Vernár (the highest point on the Slovakia standard gauge network). In addition, Class 757 shares diagrams with Class 754 between Zvolen and Vrútky/Žilina.

The Humenné-based locomotives have eight diagrams, mainly working Humenné–Trebišov portions of Humenné–Košice trains, and also certain trains (normally Fridays/Sundays) on the mostly multiple-unit operated Humenné–Prešov line.

There are four diagrams for Prievidza-based locomotives, working on Line 140/141 to Topol'cany and Leopoldov and on Line 145/170 to Horná Štubňa and Vrútky.

Built: Rebuilt 2010–15 from Class 750.
Former ČSD Class: Not applicable.
Builder: ŽOS Zvolen.
Engine: Caterpillar 3512C.
Power: 1550 kW (2080 hp).
Transmission: Electric.
Maximum Tractive Effort: 202 kN.

Total No. Built: 25.
Wheel Diameter: 1000 mm.
Train Heating Equipment: Electric.
Weight: 75.4 tonnes.
Length over Buffers: 16.50 m.
Maximum Speed: 100 km/h.
EVN: 92 56 1 757 0xx-c.

757.001-3	(750.092)	R	ZVO	757.014-6	(750.238)	R	ZVO
757.002-1	(750.150)	R	HUM	757.015-3	(750.058)	R	PVZ
757.003-9	(750.271)	R	HUM	757.016-1	(750.151)	R	PVZ
757.004-7	(750.272)	R	HUM	757.017-9	(750.198)	R	PVZ
757.005-4	(750.148)	R	ZVO	757.018-7	(750.032)	R	ZVO
757.006-2	(750.366)	R	ZVO	757.019-5	(750.094)	R	PVZ
757.007-0	(750.129)	R	ZVO	757.020-3	(750.221)	R	PVZ
757.008-8	(750.203)	R	ZVO	757.021-1	(750.181)	R	HUM
757.009-6	(750.185)	R	ZVO	757.022-9	(750.110)	R	HUM
757.010-4	(750.184)	R	ZVO	757.023-7	(750.201)	R	HUM
757.011-2	(750.093)	R	HUM	757.024-5	(750.031)	R	HUM
757.012-0	(750.166)	R	ZVO	757.025-2	(750.365)	R	HUM
757.013-8	(750.273)	R	ZVO				

▲ 757.002, when photographed here based at Zvolen but now at Humenné, stands at Banská Bystrica having taken over train R811, the 06.37 Bratislava–Košice via Brezno on 7 June 2012. Through trains on this route (just two pairs per day) now only run between Zvolen and Margecany. **Robert Pritchard**

▼ Broad gauge 771.812 and 771.809 are seen at Čierna nad Tisou depot on a very hot 6 June 2014. Note the lack of buffers and SA3 couplers. **Robert Pritchard**

CLASS 770   Co-Co

Rationalisation in the late 2000s left very few of this class active, except for a handful spread across the country for trip freight (such as Žilina–Rajec) or heavy shunting duties – also acting as reserve machines for Classes 771/773. Sub-class 770.8 are Russian 1520 mm gauge and have centre couplers without side buffers for exchange traffic between Čierna nad Tisou and Ukraine Railways (UZ) at Chop. UZ Class ChME3s (equivalent to Class 770) and Class M62s running on both 1435 mm and 1520 mm gauge may also be seen on similar transfer duties here.

Livery for both Classes 770 and 771 is green with a broad cream stripe.

Built: 1963–69.	**Total No. Built:** 108.
Former ČSD Class: T669.0 or T669.05.	**Wheel Diameter:** 1000 mm.
Builder: SMZ or ČKD.	**Train Heating Equipment:** None.
Engine: ČKD K6S310DR.	**Weight:** 114.6 tonnes.
Power: 993 kW (1330 hp).	**Length over Buffers:** 17.24 m.
Transmission: Electric.	**Maximum Speed:** 90 km/h.
Maximum Tractive Effort: 195 kN.	**EVN:** 92 56 1 770 xxx-c.

Class 770.0. 1435 mm gauge, all built by SMZ (as T669.0).

770.005-7	F	CNT (S)	770.057-8	F	CNT	770.080-0	F	ZIL (S)
770.019-8	F	CNT (S)	770.058-6	F	ZIL	770.092-5	F	CNT
770.021-4	F	BLV	770.059-4	F	ZIL (S)	770.094-1	F	HAN
770.027-1	F	CNT	770.071-9	F	BLV (S)	770.095-8	F	CNT
770.055-2	F	CNT	770.073-5	F	BLV (S)	770.106-3	F	HAN (S)

Class 770.8. 1520 mm gauge and SA3 couplers; all built by ČKD (as T669.05).

770.801-9	F	CNT	770.806-8	F	CNT	770.808-4	F	CNT (S)
770.802-7	F	CNT	770.807-6	F	CNT	770.811-8	F	CNT
770.803-5	F	CNT						

CLASS 771   Co-Co

The remaining serviceable Class 771s are used on heavy trip freights or shunting duties. Most are now concentrated in the east of the country, at Čierna nad Tisou or Haniska pri Košiciach. Like the other sub-classes in the xxx.800 series (721.8xx, 770.8xx and 773.8xx), the 771.8s are 1520 mm gauge.

Built: 1968–72.	**Total No. Built:** 207†.
Former ČSD Class: T669.1 or T669.15.	**Wheel Diameter:** 1000 mm.
Builder: SMZ.	**Train Heating Equipment:** None.
Engine: ČKD K6S310DR.	**Weight:** 116 tonnes.
Power: 993 kW (1330 hp).	**Length over Buffers:** 17.24 m.
Transmission: Electric.	**Maximum Speed:** 90 km/h.
Maximum Tractive Effort: 240 kN.	**EVN:** 92 56 1 771 xxx-c.

Class 771.0. 1435 mm gauge.

771.001-5	F	BLH	771.058-5	F	CNT (S)	771.141-9	F	ŽOSV (S)
771.017-1	F	ZIL (S)	771.059-3	F	CNT	771.155-9	F	ŽOSZ (S)
771.020-5	F	ZIL (S)	771.072-6	F	ZIL	771.157-5	F	CNT
771.021-3	F	HAN	771.075-9	F	BLV	771.158-3	F	CNT
771.022-1	F	ŽOSZ (S)	771.077-5	F	CNT (S)	771.174-0	F	ŽOSV (S)
771.052-8	F	CNT (S)	771.093-2	F	ZIL	771.194-8	F	ŽOSV (S)
771.054-4	F	ZIL	771.094-0	F	ZIL (S)	771.195-5	F	CNT
771.056-9	F	ZIL						

Class 771. Converted from 1520 mm to 1435 mm gauge.

771.196-3   (771.803)   F   ŽOSZ (S)

Class 771.8. 1520 mm gauge and SA3 couplers.

771.801-8	F	CNT (S)	771.806-7	F	CNT	771.811-7	F	CNT
771.802-6	F	CNT	771.808-3	F	CNT	771.812-5	F	CNT
771.804-2	F	CNT	771.809-1	F	CNT			

CLASS 773

Co-Co

These locomotives are major rebuilds of Class 771, with new Caterpillar engines and Siemens alternators. Originally standard gauge and based at Zvolen, reliability problems led to a further overhaul at ŽOS Zvolen in 2009–10. The locomotives were regauged with 1520 mm wheelsets, fitted with SA3 couplers and had their front buffers removed. Upon completion of this work they were renumbered in the Class 773.8 series and transferred east to Čierna nad Tisou where they have replaced some Class 770.8/771.8 on exchange traffic between Čierna and Chop (Ukraine). Some are also outbased at Haniska pri Košiciach for tripping broad gauge wagons for repair at Trebišov, plus maintenance work on the 1520 mm SRT line.

773.001–005 (now 773.806–810) had Caterpillar 3512 DI-TA/2 engines and later build 773.006–010 (now 773.801–805) Caterpillar 3512B engines. Notably 773.804 has carried four identities, as it was also previously 1520 mm gauge 771.807.

Livery is the same dark blue and white carried by Classes 746/756.

Built: Rebuilt 1998–2001 from Class 771.
Former ČSD Class: Not applicable.
Builder: ZTS Dubnica.
Engine: Caterpillar 3512B or Caterpillar 3512 DI-TA/2.
Power: 1300 kW (1745 hp).
Transmission: Electric.
Maximum Tractive Effort: 340 kN.
Gauge: 1520 mm.

Total No. Built: 10.
Wheel Diameter: 1000 mm.
Train Heating Equipment: None.
Weight: 112 tonnes.
Length over Buffers: 17.36 m.
Maximum Speed: 100 km/h.
EVN: 92 56 1 773 8xx-c.

773.801-6	(771.176, 773.006)	F	CNT
773.802-4	(771.073, 773.008)	F	CNT
773.803-2	(771.125, 773.007)	F	CNT
773.804-0	(771.199, 771.807, 773.009)	F	CNT
773.805-7	(771.055, 773.010)	F	CNT
773.806-5	(771.095, 773.001)	F	CNT
773.807-3	(771.140, 773.002)	F	CNT
773.808-1	(771.013, 773.003)	F	CNT
773.809-9	(771.177, 773.004)	F	CNT
773.810-7	(771.144, 773.005)	F	CNT

▲ 1520 mm gauge 773.809 receives attention at Haniska depot on 5 June 2014. **Robert Pritchard**

2.4. ZSSK DIESEL MULTIPLE UNITS

Like Czech Railways, Slovakia has a long history of using DMUs on rural branches. ZSSK rebuilt most of its Class 810s in the 1990s and 2010s as Classes 811/812/813. In more recent years Class 840 arrived, followed by the successful Class 861, built locally by ŽOS Vrútky.

All DMUs are numbered in the Class 8xx series, and DMU driving trailers in the 9xx series. All run in fixed formations. Livery is the older style red and white colours unless stated (most DMUs are now in the newer ZSSK red & white livery, shown **R**).

CLASS 810   MOTOR COACHES

Very few ZSSK Class 810s are left in service, and most of those that are act as reserve power for Classes 811–813. Several ZSSK Class 810s have been sold to private companies in the Czech Republic such as Railway Capital or GW Train Regio. 810.674 (ex-810.802) belongs to ZSSK Cargo and is 1520 mm gauge for staff transport on the broad gauge lines from Čierna nad Tisou.

Built: 1973–84.
Builder: MSV Studénka.
Engine: Liaz ML634 of 155 kW (210 hp).
Transmission: Mechanical.
Wheel Arrangement: A-1.
Formation: DMSO.

Total No. Built: 680†.
Accommodation: –/50(+5).
Weight: 20 tonnes.
Length over Buffers: 13.97 m.
Maximum Speed: 80 km/h.
EVN: 95 56 7 810 xxx-c.

810.004 has been restored to original condition and carries original number M152.0004.

810.004-6		HUM (S)	810.450-1		KOS	
810.138-2	**R**	BLH	810.474-1		HUM	
810.159-8	**R**	BLH	810.489-9	**R**	PVZ (S)	
810.160-6	**R**	TTP (S)	810.624-1	**R**	PVZ (S)	
810.404-8	**R**	HUM (S)				

810.625-8	**R**		TTP
810.636-5			HUM
810.661-3	**R**		TTP (S)
810.674-2		*F*	CNT

▲ Trenčianska Teplá has the largest allocation of Class 811s. On 10 June 2014 811.007+011.084 are seen near Trenčín predmestie with train Os5406, the 15.36 Trenčín–Chynorany.   **Robert Pritchard**

CLASS 811   MOTOR COACHES

Class 811 was rebuilt as diesel-electric with both axles powered and new cab ends, making them look rather different to Class 810. They were converted from a mixture of Classes 810/011, with 811.003–012 using newly built bodyshells constructed by MSV. The more powerful engines fitted to Classes 811/812 allow haulage of up to three Class 011/012 trailers rather than two for Class 810. Fitted with high-back seating.

Accident or fire damage has written off two Class 811s (811.024/026) which have been scrapped, whilst 811.003 was also damaged in an accident in 2014 and is now stored at Poprad-Tatry.

Mainly based in the west of the country, Class 811s work these routes (some shared with other classes): Trenčín–Chynorany/Topoľčany, Nové Mesto nad Váhom–Vrbovce, Trenčianska Teplá–Horné Srnie/Vlárský průsmyk, Kraľovany–Trstená, Čadca–Makov and Cadca–Mosty u Jablunkova (CZ).

Original livery was all over orange, at the time of writing only still carried by 811.008/009.

Built: 1995–98 (most rebuilt from Class 011/810).   **Total No. Built:** 27.
Builder: ŽOS Zvolen and ŽOS Vrutky.   **Accommodation:** –/50(+3).
Engine: Liaz ML640F of 238 kW (320 hp).   **Weight:** 23.6 tonnes.
Transmission: Electric.   **Length over Buffers:** 13.97 m.
Wheel Arrangement: A-A.   **Maximum Speed:** 80 km/h.
Formation: DMSO.   **EVN:** 95 56 7 811 0xx-c.

811.001-1	(011.017)	R	TTP	811.014-4	(011.004)	R	CAD
811.002-9	(011.662)	R	TTP	811.015-1	(011.037)	R	TTP
811.003-7	–	R	POP (S)	811.016-9	(011.171)	R	CAD
811.004-5	–	R	KRA	811.017-7	(011.177)	R	CAD
811.005-2	–	R	KRA	811.018-5	(011.399)	R	KRA
811.006-0	–	R	TTP	811.019-3	(011.628)	R	TTP
811.007-8	–	R	TTP	811.020-1	(011.655)	R	TTP
811.008-6	–		TTP	811.021-9	(011.866)	R	TTP
811.009-4	–		TTP	811.022-7	(011.877)	R	CAD
811.010-2	–	R	TTP	811.023-5	(011.901)	R	ZIL
811.011-0	–	R	TTP	811.025-0	(810.019)	R	CAD
811.012-8	–	R	TTP	811.027-6	(810.064)	R	KRA
811.013-6	(011.003)	R	KRA				

CLASS 812   MOTOR COACHES

Class 812 is again rebuilt from trailers or Class 810 with new MAN engines to meet exhaust emissions requirements, but to a simpler specification than Class 811. They retain the hydraulic transmission and the original single powered axle. Unlike Class 811 they were not fitted with new driving cabs, retaining the old Class 810 style front ends. The first ten units were converted from Class 011 trailers and the remaining units from Class 810.

Vehicles numbered 812.xx8 were rebuilt out of sequence. The original plan was for these to be "Lux" versions with air conditioning and 2+2 seating for InterCity feeder shuttles. However only 812.008 was done and the other 812.xx8 numbers were later filled with standard conversions. One other notable unit is 812.043, which was rebuilt from former 1520 mm gauge set 810.801.

Class 812s can be found on branch line and also regional services throughout much of central and eastern Slovakia, hauling Class 011/012 trailers on busier trains. They work the following lines, some shared with Class 813 or in the case of Humenné units Class 861: Zvolen/Banská Bystrica–Brezno, Brezno–Červená Skala, Brezno–Tisovec, Fiľakovo–Jesenské–Tisovec, Lučenec–Utekáč, Štúrovo–Čata–Levice, Čata–Šahy, local services around Humenné, Prešov–Bardejov and local services into Košice from Line 160 and into Margecany from Line 173.

The original livery for 812.001–050 was all over red with a white stripe, which is still carried by most units, although the class is slowly being repainted into the standard ZSSK red livery.

Built: 2001–08 (Rebuilt from Class 810/011).   **Total No. Built:** 64.
Builder: ŽOS Zvolen.   **Accommodation:** –/50(+3), * –/38.
Engine: MAN D2866 LUH21 of 257 kW (345 hp).   **Weight:** 20 tonnes.
Transmission: Hydraulic: Voith Diwa 863.3.   **Length over Buffers:** 13.97 mm.
Wheel Arrangement: A-1.   **Maximum Speed:** 90 km/h.
Formation: DMSO.   **EVN:** 95 56 7 812 0xx-c.
Non-Standard Livery: 812.035: "camouflage".

812.001-0	(011.325)			BRZ	812.033-3	(810.119)		ZVO
812.002-8	(011.651)			BRZ	812.034-1	(810.006)	R	ZVO
812.003-6	(011.400)			BRZ	812.035-8	(810.556)	0	ZVO
812.004-4	(011.904)			BRZ	812.036-6	(810.439)		HUM
812.005-1	(011.658)			BRZ	812.037-4	(810.464)		FIL
812.006-9	(011.341)			BRZ	812.038-2	(810.437)		HUM
812.007-7	(011.623)			BRZ	812.039-0	(810.438)		HUM
812.008-5	(011.659)	R	*	NZK	812.040-8	(810.672)		NZK
812.009-3	(011.587)	R		NZK	812.041-6	(810.451)		NZK
812.010-1	(011.097)			BRZ	812.042-4	(810.637)		KOS
812.011-9	(810.422)			BRZ	812.043-2	(810.801)	R	NZK
812.012-7	(810.647)			HUM	812.044-0	(810.605)		KOS
812.013-5	(810.367)	R		HUM	812.045-7	(810.497)	R	NZK
812.014-3	(810.135)			HUM	812.046-5	(810.376)		HUM
812.015-0	(810.429)	R		HUM	812.047-3	(810.463)		NZK
812.016-8	(810.609)			BRZ	812.048-1	(810.355)		BRZ
812.017-6	(810.021)	R		HUM	812.049-9	(810.496)		NZK
812.018-4	(810.067)			NZK	812.050-7	(810.389)		NZK
812.019-2	(810.370)			HUM	812.051-5	(810.020)	R	HUM
812.020-0	(810.610)	R		HUM	812.052-3	(810.562)	R	FIL
812.021-8	(810.580)			HUM	812.053-1	(810.352)	R	FIL
812.022-6	(810.415)			KOS	812.054-9	(810.379)	R	FIL
812.023-4	(810.568)			KOS	812.055-6	(810.136)	R	FIL
812.024-2	(810.650)	R		HUM	812.056-4	(810.402)	R	HUM
812.025-9	(810.137)			KOS	812.057-2	(810.530)	R	ZVO
812.026-7	(810.118)			NZK	812.058-0	(810.662)	R	ZVO
812.027-5	(810.356)			BRZ	812.059-8	(810.354)	R	ZVO
812.028-3	(810.648)			NZK	812.060-6	(810.503)	R	HUM
812.029-1	(810.547)			FIL	812.061-4	(810.490)	R	ZVO
812.030-9	(810.660)			NZK	812.062-2	(810.366)	R	HUM
812.031-7	(810.531)			POP	812.063-0	(810.403)	R	FIL
812.032-5	(810.392)			BRZ	812.064-8	(810.357)	R	FIL

▲ A busy scene at Čata on 13 June 2014 as 812.041 (old livery)+011.865/011.639+812.050 arrive with train Os5910, the 15.10 Levice–Štúrovo. To the right 812.030 waits to leave for Šahy.

Robert Pritchard

CLASS 813
2-CAR UNITS

ZSSK Class 813/913 sets are the Slovak equivalent of ČD Class 814/914; a similar permanently coupled motor+trailer pair with slightly more power than Class 810. ŽOS Zvolen completed a prototype rebuild in 2006 (813.001+913.001) and this entered regular service from Prievidza in spring 2007. Production of a further 43 units followed between 2007 and 2010.

The Slovak units differ to ČD Class 814 in a number of ways. Most have been rebuilt from trailers, and the Class 813s are fitted with MAN engines compared to the Czech Tedom power units, although both use the same Voith hydraulic transmission. Another difference is that the Class 913 trailers retain the original floor level and do not feature the low level centre section. Neither do they feature the controlled emission toilet fitted to ČD units, but do have air-conditioning and small folding windows, rather than the drop-down windows of the ČD Class 814. The ZSSK units are noticeably quieter than their ČD counterparts. They are fitted with 2+2 seating throughout, compared to the 3+2 seating in Classes 810–812.

Class 813s are spread across Slovakia, operating from nine different depots. Many routes are shared with other DMU classes. Routes include: Prievidza–Topoľčany, Prievidza–Horná Štubňa–Vrútky, Čadca–Makov, Lučenec–Utekáč, Kraľovany–Trstená, Žilina–Rajec, Margecany–Nálepkovo/Dobšinská ľadová jaskyňa (Košice-based units), Nové Zámky–Trnava, Nové Zámky–Zlaté Moravce plus Zohor–Záhorská Ves and Kuty–Skalica na Slovensku (using Bratislava units).

A 2013 ŽOS Zvolen rebuild numbered 813.110+913.110 has also been used by ZSSK Zvolen depot on a trial basis, see ŽOS Zvolen under Private Operators for details.

Built: 2006–10 (rebuilt from Class 011/810).
Builder: ŽOS Zvolen.
Engine: MAN D 2876 LUE 21 of 257 kW (345 hp).
Transmission: Hydraulic: Voith Diwa 864.3E.
Wheel Arrangement: 1-A+1-1.
Formation: DMSO–DTSO.

Total No. Built: 44.
Accommodation: –/30(+5) 1T + –/48.
Weight: 22 + 17 tonnes.
Length over Buffers: 28.82 m.
Maximum Speed: 90 km/h.
EVN: 95 56 7 813 0xx-c + 96 56 4 913 0xx-c.

813.001-9	(011.030)	913.001-4	(011.861)	R	FIL
813.002-7	(011.358)	913.002-2	(011.663)	R	FIL
813.003-5	(011.007)	913.003-0	(011.642)	R	TTP
813.004-3	(011.578)	913.004-8	(011.010)	R	CAD
813.005-0	(011.012)	913.005-5	(011.645)	R	ZVO
813.006-8	(011.637)	913.006-3	(011.082)	R	FIL
813.007-6	(011.656)	913.007-1	(011.668)	R	PVZ
813.008-4	(011.154)	913.008-9	(011.647)	R	PVZ
813.009-2	(011.671)	913.009-7	(011.033)	R	PVZ
813.010-0	(011.667)	913.010-5	(011.666)	R	KRA
813.011-8	(011.670)	913.011-3	(011.673)	R	TTP
813.012-6	(810.518)	913.012-1	(011.875)	R	ZVO
813.013-4	(011.258)	913.013-9	(011.898)	R	KRA
813.014-2	(011.575)	913.014-7	(011.028)	R	KRA
813.015-9	(810.603)	913.015-4	(011.032)	R	KRA
813.016-7	(810.390)	913.016-2	(011.025)	R	ZIL
813.017-5	(011.905)	913.017-0	(011.035)	R	ZIL
813.018-3	(810.544)	913.018-8	(011.277)	R	ZIL
813.019-1	(810.567)	913.019-6	(011.179)	R	KRA
813.020-9	(810.505)	913.020-4	(011.900)	R	ZVO
813.021-7	(810.158)	913.021-2	(011.315)	R	CAD
813.022-5	(810.579)	913.022-0	(011.648)	R	CAD
813.023-3	(810.612)	913.023-8	(011.672)	R	CAD
813.024-1	(810.525)	913.024-6	(011.402)	R	ZVO
813.025-8	(810.574)	913.025-3	(011.027)	R	TTP
813.026-6	(810.555)	913.026-1	(011.885)	R	FIL
813.027-4	(810.584)	913.027-9	(011.303)	R	KOS
813.028-2	(810.065)	913.028-7	(011.888)	R	KOS
813.029-0	(810.504)	913.029-5	(011.669)	R	PVZ
813.030-8	(810.414)	913.030-3	(011.586)	R	KOS
813.031-6	(810.638)	913.031-1	(011.657)	R	ZIL
813.032-4	(810.022)	913.032-9	(011.874)	R	ZIL
813.033-2	(810.364)	913.033-7	(011.160)	R	KRA
813.034-0	(810.485)	913.034-5	(011.584)	R	PVZ

▲ 813.039+913.039 await departure from Zlaté Moravce with train Os5808, the 15.40 to Úľany nad Žitavou on 12 June 2014. This branch line has been threatened with closure (to passenger services) in recent years. **Robert Pritchard**

▼ A pair of Class 861s, led by 861.019, are seen at Strážske with train REx912, the 15.28 Humenné–Košice on 7 June 2015. **Jörg Flecks**

813.035-7	(810.542)	913.035-2	(011.638)	R	PVZ
813.036-5	(810.516)	913.036-0	(011.641)	R	PVZ
813.037-3	(810.428)	913.037-8	(011.038)	R	CAD
813.038-1	(810.481)	913.038-6	(011.329)	R	BLH
813.039-9	(810.066)	913.039-4	(011.001)	R	KOS
813.040-7	(810.426)	913.040-2	(011.859)	R	BLH
813.041-5	(810.671)	913.041-0	(011.034)	R	BLH
813.042-3	(810.465)	913.042-8	(011.398)	R	BLH
813.043-1	(810.432)	913.043-6	(011.895)	R	KOS
813.044-9	(810.452)	913.044-4	(011.650)	R	KOS

CLASS 840   2-SECTION ARTICULATED UNITS

This small class is based on the articulated Stadler GTW 2/6 design and was constructed by a consortium of ŽOS Vrútky, Bombardier and Stadler. Originally used in the Zvolen area, they are now based at Poprad-Tatry and used on Line 185 to Studený potok, Tatranská Lomnica and Plaveč. The units are mostly low floor, and feature an engine, or "power pack" in the middle. As both Classes 840 and 861 are articulated only one number is carried.

Livery is a non-standard dark blue and light grey.

Built: 2003.
Builder: ŽOS Vrútky/Bombardier/Stadler.
Engine: MTU 12V 183 TD13 of 550 kW (740 hp).
Transmission: Electric.
Wheel Arrangement: 2-Bo-2.
Formation: DMSO–DMSO.

Total No. Built: 6.
Accommodation: –/94(+16) 1T.
Weight: 58.7 tonnes.
Length over Buffers: 38.47 m.
Maximum Speed: 115 km/h.
EVN: 95 56 7 840 00x-c.

| 840.001-6 | POP | 840.003-2 | POP | 840.005-7 | POP |
| 840.002-4 | POP | 840.004-0 | POP | 840.006-5 | POP |

CLASS 861   3-SECTION ARTICULATED UNITS

These articulated units for regional services are a design developed by ŽOS Vrútky Works following experience with Class 840. Called "Regiomover", the units have a mix of high and low floor sections with two motor cars either side of an intermediate trailer. Bogies were supplied by Siemens. The units are air-conditioned and have wi-fi. They can operate in pairs on busier trains.

The fleet was ordered and delivered in two batches. The first batch of 12 units (861.001–012) arrived in 2011–13. These proved successful and a larger order worth €78 million for a further 20 units followed in 2013, these being delivered in 2014–15. The second batch has some minor detail differences to meet the latest crashworthiness standards. All units are based at either Humenné or Nové Zámky depots. Routes include Humenné–Prešov, Humenné–Stakčín, Humenné–Medzilaorce mesto and Humenné–Košice and various routes around Nové Zámky, including to Nitra/Leopoldov, Prievidza and Trnava.

Built: 2010–15.
Builder: ŽOS Vrútky.
Accommodation: –/60(+4) + –/44(+5) 1TD 1T + –/60(+4).
Engine: 2 x MAN D2842 LE 622 of 588 kW (790 hp).
Transmission: Hydraulic: Voith.
Wheel Arrangement: B-2-2-B.
Formation: DMSO–TSO–DMSO.

Total No. Built: 32.
Weight: 120 tonnes.
Length over Buffers: 57.95 m.
Maximum Speed: 140 km/h.
EVN: 95 56 7 861 0xx-c.

861.001-0	R	HUM	861.012-7	R	NZK	861.023-4	R	NZK
861.002-8	R	HUM	861.013-5	R	HUM	861.024-2	R	NZK
861.003-6	R	HUM	861.014-3	R	HUM	861.025-9	R	NZK
861.004-4	R	HUM	861.015-0	R	HUM	861.026-7	R	NZK
861.005-1	R	HUM	861.016-8	R	HUM	861.027-5	R	NZK
861.006-9	R	HUM	861.017-6	R	HUM	861.028-3	R	NZK
861.007-7	R	NZK	861.018-4	R	HUM	861.029-1	R	NZK
861.008-5	R	NZK	861.019-2	R	HUM	861.030-9	R	NZK
861.009-3	R	NZK	861.020-0	R	HUM	861.031-7	R	NZK
861.010-1	R	NZK	861.021-8	R	HUM	861.032-5	R	NZK
861.011-9	R	NZK	861.022-6	R	HUM			

2.5. ZSSK NON-POWERED TRAILERS

Except where noted, multiple units are made up of driving motor and unpowered trailer coaches in no fixed formation. In Slovakia 9xx.xxx are driving trailers, and 0xx.xxx intermediate trailers. Unlike in the Czech Republic, the intermediate trailers have not been renumbered in the coaching stock series.

Livery is the older version of ZSSK red with a white stripe unless shown as **R** – the new ZSSK red & white livery.

2.5.1. DRIVING TRAILERS

CLASS 912   DRIVING TRAILER

This is a one-off pilot conversion of a Class 011 to work with Classes 811/812, using the same new cab section and interior layout as Class 811. 912.001 is used on the Čadca–Makov branch. It was rebuilt from Baafx car 70 56 24 29 005 (later 011.005).

Built: 1996 (rebuilt from Class 011).
Builder: ŽOS Vrútky.   **Weight:** 16 tonnes.
Accommodation: –/50(+3) 1T.   **Length over Buffers:** 13.97 m.
Maximum Speed: 80 km/h.   **EVN:** 96 56 4 912 001-c.

912.001-5 **R**   CAD

CLASS 951   DOUBLE-DECK DRIVING TRAILERS

These ten double-deck push-pull driving trailers are based on the Škoda/MSV Class 971 EMU trailer vehicles used with ČD Class 471 and ZSSK Class 671. They are used on regional services radiating from Bratislava (to Galanta, Nové Zámky, Leopoldov and Kúty) in ten 3-coach sets operated by modified Class 263 locomotives or Class 381s formed 263/381+051+051+951. They can also be used with Class 240s as conventional hauled stock.

Built: 2010–12.
Builder: MSV/Škoda.   **Weight:** 51 tonnes.
Accommodation: –/90(+12) 1T.   **Length over Buffers:** 26.4 m.
Maximum Speed: 160 km/h.   **EVN:** 96 56 4 951 0xx-c.

951.001-7	**R**	NZK	951.005-8	**R**	NZK	951.008-2	**R**	NZK
951.002-5	**R**	NZK	951.006-6	**R**	NZK	951.009-0	**R**	NZK
951.003-3	**R**	NZK	951.007-4	**R**	NZK	951.010-8	**R**	NZK
951.004-1	**R**	NZK					

2.5.2. INTERMEDIATE FOUR-WHEELED TRAILERS

CLASS 010   BATTERY VAN

Slovak Class 010s are not passenger trailers but 900 kWh battery vans ("batériový vozeň") for powering Class 210 electric locomotives away from overhead wires. They were easily identified by their matching red and yellow locomotive livery, although many mistake them for wagons. All are now stored out of use.

Built: 1991–93.   **Weight:** 18.4 tonnes.
Builder: Rebuilt by ŽOS Trnava from wagons.   **Length over Buffers:** 10.58 m.
Maximum Speed: 80 km/h.   **EVN:** 60 56 0 010 0xx-c.

010.001-6	*F*	ZVO (S)	010.004-0	*F*	ZVO (S)	010.007-3	*F*	BLV (S)
010.002-4	*F*	BLV (S)	010.005-7	*F*	ZVO (S)	010.008-1	*F*	BLV (S)
010.003-2	*F*	ZVO (S)	010.006-5	*F*	BLV (S)	010.009-9	*F*	ZVO (S)

CLASS 011 TRAILERS

Four-wheel trailer cars of similar design to Class 810 DMUs. ZSSK Class 011 is the equivalent of ČD Class 010, being from the same original series. Used with Class 810–812 DMUs.

Built: 1973–83.
Builder: MSV Studénka.
Former ČSD Class: Baafx.
Accommodation: –/59 1T.

Weight: 15 tonnes.
Length over Buffers: 13.97 m.
Maximum Speed: 80 km/h.
EVN: 96 56 4 011 xxx-c.

011.000-7		ŽOSZ (S)	011.627-7	R	POP	011.849-7	R	BRZ
011.002-3		HUM (S)	011.629-3		ZVO	011.850-5		HUM
011.006-4		HUM (S)	011.630-1		NZK	011.858-8	R	PVZ
011.009-8	R	TTP	011.631-9		ZVO (S)	011.865-3		FIL
011.026-2	R	HUM	011.633-5	R	HUM	011.867-9	R	TTP
011.029-6		HUM	011.635-0	R	NZK	011.868-7	R	FIL
011.036-1	R	ZVO	011.639-2	R	FIL	011.871-1		ZVO
011.084-1	R	TTP	011.640-0	R	POP	011.872-9		ZIL (S)
011.210-3		ŽOSZ(S)	011.643-4	R	KRA	011.873-7		ZVO
011.238-3	R	BRZ	011.644-2		TTP	011.876-0	R	KRA
011.260-7	R	TTP (S)	011.649-1	R	FIL	011.878-6	R	KRA
011.281-3		CAD (S)	011.652-5	R	NZK	011.881-0	R	HUM (S)
011.340-7		KOS	011.653-3		FIL (S)	011.882-8		BRZ
011.345-6	R	KRA	011.654-1	R	HUM (S)	011.884-4	R	HUM
011.348-0	R	TTP	011.660-8	R	TTP	011.886-9		FIL
011.407-4		PVZ (S)	011.661-6		BRZ	011.887-7	R	BRZ
011.426-4	R	PVZ	011.664-0		HUM	011.889-3		BRZ
011.455-3		TTP	011.665-7		NZK	011.891-9		BRZ
011.577-4		FIL (S)	011.674-9		BRZ	011.893-5	R	ZIL
011.585-7	R	FIL	011.679-8	R	BRZ	011.894-3		BRZ
011.613-7	R	FIL	011.825-7		TTP	011.899-2		TTP
011.624-4		HUM (S)	011.847-1	R	CAD	011.902-4		TTP
011.625-1		NZK	011.848-9		TTP	011.903-2		TTP
011.626-9		HUM						

CLASS 012 TRAILERS

These are rebuilds from Class 011 with new high-back seating for use on longer distance services.

Rebuilt: 2009–10 (rebuilt from Class 011).
Builder: ŽOS Zvolen.
Former ČSD Class: Baafx.
Accommodation: –/32(+6) 1T.

Weight: 16 tonnes.
Length over Buffers: 13.97 m.
Maximum Speed: 80 km/h.
EVN: 96 56 4 012 0xx-c.

012.001-4	R	ZVO	012.008-9	R	NZK	012.015-4	R	HUM
012.002-2	R	BRZ	012.009-7	R	NZK	012.016-2	R	HUM
012.003-0	R	BRZ	012.010-5	R	NZK	012.017-0	R	HUM
012.004-8	R	BRZ	012.011-3	R	NZK	012.018-8	R	HUM
012.005-5	R	BRZ	012.012-1	R	NZK	012.019-6	R	HUM
012.006-3	R	BRZ	012.013-9	R	NZK	012.020-4	R	HUM
012.007-1	R	NZK	012.014-7	R	NZK			

2.5.3. BOGIE TRAILERS

CLASS 051   DOUBLE-DECK INTERMEDIATE TRAILERS

These 20 double-deck push-pull intermediate trailers are based on Class 071 EMU trailer vehicles like those used with ČD Class 471 and ZSSK Class 671. They are used on regional services from Bratislava with Class 263 or Class 381 locomotives, formed 263/381+051+051+951. They operate as ten semi-permanently coupled, consecutively numbered sets, ie Locomotive+051.001+051.002+951.001. They can also be used as conventional hauled stock with Class 240 (none of which have been modified for push-pull operation), on occasions when there are shortages of Classes 263/381.

Built: 2010–12.
Builder: MSV/Škoda.
Accommodation: –/130 2T.
Maximum Speed: 160 km/h.

Weight: 48 tonnes.
Length over Buffers: 26.40 m.
EVN: 94 56 0 051 0xx-c.

051.001-6	**R**	NZK	051.008-1	**R**	NZK	051.015-6	**R**	NZK
051.002-4	**R**	NZK	051.009-9	**R**	NZK	051.016-4	**R**	NZK
051.003-2	**R**	NZK	051.010-7	**R**	NZK	051.017-2	**R**	NZK
051.004-0	**R**	NZK	051.011-5	**R**	NZK	051.018-0	**R**	NZK
051.005-7	**R**	NZK	051.012-3	**R**	NZK	051.019-8	**R**	NZK
051.006-5	**R**	NZK	051.013-1	**R**	NZK	051.020-6	**R**	NZK
051.007-3	**R**	NZK	051.014-9	**R**	NZK			

▲ Class 951 push-pull double-deck driving trailer 951.003 leads intermediate trailers 051.005 and 051.006, with 263.007 providing power as the train arrives at Bratislava Lamač on 11 June 2014 with train Os3024, the 15.56 Leopoldov–Bratislava–Malacky. Another set, with 951.007 nearest the camera, can be seen to the right on its way into Bratislava.   **Robert Pritchard**

2.6. ZSSK NARROW GAUGE STOCK

ZSSK operates the two main transport systems in the High Tatras in northern Slovakia under the brands "Ozubnicovej Železnice" (OŽ) or "Cog Railway" (Line 182 in the timetable) and "Tatranských Elektrických Železníc" (TEŽ) or "Tatra Electric Railways" (Lines 183/184). Both are metre gauge. In the High Tatra range there are 17 peaks over 2500 metres, the highest of which is Gerlachovský štít at 2655 m (8711 ft). The range extends into neighbouring Poland. ČSD also used to operate all of the cable cars in the Tatras, but these are now run by private operators.

The rack railway opened with steam traction in 1896 but was closed in 1932 and the tracks lifted during World War II. It was rebuilt in the late 1960s and reopened in 1970, in time for the 1970 World Skiing Championships being held in the High Tatras. The service is roughly hourly, connecting with trains on the main line at Štrba. Journey time for the stunning 4.8 km journey is 15–18 minutes, climbing 444 m with a maximum gradient of 15%.

Plans were drawn up to build the TEŽ electric railway on the southern side of the High Tatra mountains in the 1900s, with the first section from Poprad-Tatry (altitude 670 m above sea level) to Starý Smokovec (13.6 km) opening in December 1908. Extensions to Tatranská Lomnica (5.9 km) and Štrbské Pleso (15.5 km and 1325 m above sea level) followed by 1911, the latter connecting with the rack railway. This made the whole "T-shaped" TEŽ network 35 km.

The operating pattern is generally hourly through trains from Poprad-Tatry to Štrbské Pleso, a journey time of 1h13 for the 29 km and often using pairs of units. Trains used to depart from outside Poprad-Tatry station with street running crossing the main line by the depot. Since 1991 they have left from a new elevated platform alongside the main station. A single-unit shuttle operates from Starý Smokovec to Tatranská Lomnica, with standard gauge DMUs (Class 840) operating from Poprad-Tatry to Tatranská Lomnica via Studený potok.

A useful Soviet era TEŽ and rack railway map at Štrbské Pleso.

CLASSES 405.95 & 905.95 — RACK UNITS

This design was imported from Switzerland for the Štrba–Štrbské Pleso rack railway. Trains are normally formed of a identical serial numbered motor coach + trailer, just one unit being required for the service. Maximum speeds during rack working are 15 km/h ascending and 10 km/h descending. The vehicles are serviced at the small depot at Štrba (alongside the station). Doors are on one side of the vehicles only. Livery is red & cream.

System: 1500 V DC.
Built: 1969–70.
Builder – Mechanical Parts: SLM, Winterthur, Switzerland.
Builder – Electrical Parts: Brown Boveri.
Traction Motors: 2 x 168 kW (225 hp); * none.
Former ČSD Class: EMU29.0; * R29.0.
Wheel Arrangement: 2z2z; * 2-2.
Gauge: 1000 mm.

Total No. Built: 3 motor & 3 trailer cars.

Accommodation: –/60 + * –/66.
Weight: 25.3 tonnes; * 12.8 tonnes.
Length over Couplers: 16.60 m.
Maximum Speed: 30 km/h.
EVN: 94 56 0 405 95x-c.

Class 405. Motor coach.

405.951-5		STR	405.952-3		STR	405.953-1		STR

Class 905. Trailer coach.

905.951-0	*	STR	905.952-8	*	STR	905.953-6	*	STR

CLASS 420.95   3-SECTION ARTICULATED UNITS

These 3-section articulated enlarged street tramcars were derived from the classic ČKD Tatra T2/T3 trams, and even painted in the standard Eastern Bloc red & cream tram livery. Class 420 worked all TEŽ services before Class 425 arrived in the early 2000s. The remaining two units had been kept as reserve units but have now been withdrawn, 420.959 being stored in a compound close to the main Poprad-Tatry station.

System: 1500 V DC.
Built: 1965–69.
Builder – Mechanical Parts: ČKD Tatra.
Builder – Electrical Parts: ČKD.
Traction Motors: 8 x 40 kW (53 hp).
Former ČSD Class: EMU89.0.
Wheel Arrangement: Bo-Bo-Bo-Bo.
Gauge: 1000 mm.

Total No. Built: 18.

Accommodation: –/32(+7) + –/48 + –/40(+7).
Weight: 47.4 tonnes.
Length over Couplers: 37.53 m.
Maximum Speed: 50 km/h.

420.953-2	POP (S)		420.959-9	POP (S)

CLASS 425.95   3-SECTION ARTICULATED UNITS

New rolling stock for TEŽ arrived in the early 2000s in the form of these Stadler Type GTW 2/6 units built by a consortium of ŽOS Vrútky Works, Adtranz and Stadler. Providing level access with their low floor sections, the units now work all TEŽ services, running in pairs on the core route. Large windows were designed to provide optimum views of the mountain scenery.

A spare central power unit was supplied with the initial order, and in 2006 Stadler supplied two further driving trailers so these were married up as the 15th unit, 425.965.

Livery is all over red with grey bands at the top and bottom.

System: 1500 V DC.
Built: 2000–02; * 2006.
Builders – Mechanical Parts: ŽOS Vrútky/Stadler.
Builder – Electrical Parts: Adtranz.
Traction Motors: 2 x 300 kW (400 hp) AC.
Former ČSD Class: Not applicable.
Wheel Arrangement: 2-Bo-2.
Gauge: 1000 mm.

Total No. Built: 15.

Accommodation: –/44(+10) + –/44(+10).
Weight: 42 tonnes.
Length over Couplers: 32.98 m.
Maximum Speed: 80 km/h.
EVN: 94 56 0 425 9xx-c.

425.951-1	POP	425.956-0	POP	425.961-0		POP
425.952-9	POP	425.957-8	POP	425.962-8		POP
425.953-7	POP	425.958-6	POP	425.963-6		POP
425.954-5	POP	425.959-4	POP	425.964-4		POP
425.955-2	POP	425.960-2	POP	425.965-1	*	POP

DEPARTMENTAL NARROW GAUGE LOCOMOTIVES

The following 1000 mm gauge locomotives are based at Poprad-Tatry for use on engineers' or maintenance trains on the TEŽ network. The battery Class 199 will only normally be used for movements within the depot, with the more powerful Russian-built Class 706.9s suitable for powering heavier permanent way trains and also operate with snowploughs.

A number of other 1000 mm historical items are also based at Poprad-Tatry, for details see the Preserved Locomotives section.

Number	Builder	Built	Type	kW	Details	Comments
199.951-5	ŽOS Vrútky	2001	rT211.0	38	Bo BE	Rebuilt ex-T211.035
702.951-1	ČKD	1968	TU29.1	147	B DM	Ex-T29.1001
706.951-1	Kaluga	1985	TU46.0	294	BB DH	Ex-TU46.001
706.952-9	Kaluga	1985	TU46.0	294	BB DH	Ex-TU46.002

▲ Swiss-built Rack unit 405.952+905.952 (nearest camera) arrives at the Štrba terminus of the rack railway with train Os8023, the 15.44 from Štrbské Pleso on 7 June 2014. **Robert Pritchard**

▼ Articulated TEŽ 1000 mm gauge EMU 425.965 (the extra unit which was delivered in 2006) is seen on the non-passenger line that loops down to Poprad-Tatry depot on 7 June 2014. On the right 425.956 can be seen in the elevated TEŽ platform of Poprad-Tatry station. **Robert Pritchard**

3. INTERNATIONAL LOCOMOTIVES & RAILCARS

Because of their location in Central Europe, the Czech Republic and Slovakia see a number of "foreign" locomotives, especially at border stations, but also passing through on freights. Details of German and Austrian locomotives and railcars can be found in the Platform 5 "German Railways" and "Austrian Railways" handbooks. A summary of locomotives and railcars that can be seen in the Czech Republic and Slovakia at the time of writing is given here.

LOCOMOTIVES & RAILCARS FROM AUSTRIA

Siemens ÖBB Class 1116 "Taurus" electric locomotives operate cross-border services from Linz to České Budějovice (via Horní Dvořiště), with some continuing to Praha (behind ČD locomotives), from Wien to České Velenice (via Gmünd) and from Wien to Znojmo (via Šatov). Class 1144 also appear on the Znojmo route. MÁV-START Class 470s are also hired to work services on the České Velenice route. ÖBB Class 1116 1116 041–049 are cleared for operation in Slovakia on freights.

Siemens ÖBB Class 1216.2 "Taurus" electric locomotives work the ČD/ÖBB jointly-operated two-hourly Praha–Brno–Břeclav–Wien–Graz service using 7-coach fixed-formation Railjet sets. There are eight diagrams daily using the seven ČD Railjet sets delivered in 2014, plus ÖBB RJ sets RJ29–RJ31. Some 1216.2s have been painted into ČD blue livery and are preferred for these trains, being leased to ČD. The following 1216.2s are cleared for operation in the Czech Republic, C indicates ÖBB Cargo locomotives, although these can also find use on the Railjet trains during locomotive shortages. **RJ** is ÖBB Railjet livery and **B** is ČD blue livery.

1216 210-5	C	1216 230-3	RJ	1216 235-2	B	1216 239-4	C
1216 226-1	C	1216 231-1	RJ	1216 236-0	B	1216 240-2	C
1216 227-9	C	1216 233-7	B	1216 237-8	B	1216 249-3	B
1216 228-7	C	1216 234-5	B	1216 238-6	C	1216 250-1	B
1216 229-5	RJ						

Siemens ÖBB Class 2016 "Hercules" diesel locomotives operate the hourly cross-border services from Wien to Bratislava hlavná (via Marchegg) using push-pull stock.

ÖBB Class 4124 "Talent" EMUs operate most of the hourly (on weekdays) cross-border services from Deutschkreutz/Wien to Bratislava-Petržalka (via Kittsee) with some trains in the hands of Class 1116 with push-pull stock.

Other Austrian private operators' locomotives can also be seen, especially at border points such as Břeclav and Bratislava.

LOCOMOTIVES & RAILCARS FROM GERMANY

German locomotives and railcars can be seen on many routes in both countries, particularly the Czech Republic. The following list gives locomotives and railcars that work in on scheduled passenger services in the Czech Republic, working clockwise from west of Plzeň.

Siemens Eurorunner Class 223 diesels, operated by Die Länderbahn (DLB) subsidiary Alex, work trains from München to Plzeň (Class 223s work from Regensburg) via Furth im Wald and Domažlice. Coaches are attached to some ČD Plzeň–Praha trains to form through München–Praha services. The Class 223s are listed below:

223 061-3	223 064-7	223 067-0	223 070-4
223 062-1	223 065-4	223 068-8	223 071-2
223 063-9	223 066-2	223 069-6	223 072-0

ČD/DB jointly operate five return trains from Cheb to Nürnberg via Marktredwitz and Line 179, using DB Class 612 DMUs. A DLB-operated local service also operates from Hof to Cheb (Line 148, reopened December 2015), then on to Marktredwitz using DLB Class 642/650 DMUs.

GW Train Regio and DLB subsidiary Vogtlandbahn jointly operate Line 145 using Vogtlandbahn Class 650/654 and GWTR Class 810 between Sokolov and Kraslice and Vogtlandbahn Class 650/654 on the cross-border trains to Mehltheuer/Zwickau.

DB operates one return trip from Vejprty to Chemnitz on summer weekends using a Class 642 DMU. DB Class 642s are also used on the newly-introduced cross-border service from Děčín to Bad Schandau, Dolní Poustevna and Rumburk.

The main Czech–Germany cross-border route between Děčín and Dresden is used by international services and freight traffic.

Finally, Line 089 linking Rybniště with Liberec via Zittau is operated by Vogtlandbahn using its Class 642 DMUs. After Zittau this line crosses briefly into Poland before crossing back into the Czech Republic. Some trains also run Liberec–Zittau–Dresden.

DB Cargo operates freight trains through the Czech Republic using Class 189 electric locomotives, principally between Děčín and Břeclav via Pardubice and Brno, using the license of Czech subsidiary Arriva vlaky. Class 189 can also be seen on other routes. Other German private operators' locomotives can also be seen, especially at border stations such as Děčín and Cheb. Details of these can be found in the Platform 5 "German Railways" European handbooks.

LOCOMOTIVES & RAILCARS FROM POLAND

PKP locomotives work deep into the Czech Republic on passenger trains. There are two diagrams which take a Class EP09 Bo-Bo electric to from Warszawa to Praha (trains EC112/113 and EN404/405) and several other diagrams that see them reach Bohumín and Ostrava from Warszawa. 47 Class EP09 were produced, numbered EP09-01–47.

There is one diagram which takes a PKP Class 370 electric locomotive (ten built, 370.001–010) into Bohumín from Warszawa and also one which takes a Class EU07 electric locomotive (more than 540 exist, some converted from ET41) into Bohumín from Krakow (overnight).

Kolej Dolny Śląsk Class EN57 suburban/regional EMUs can be seen at Ústí nad Orlicí, operating services on Line 024 from Kłodzko/Wrocław via Letohrad.

PKP Cargo locomotives can be seen in both the Czech Republic and Slovakia, particularly since the takeover of AWT by PKP Cargo. The most common types seen on freights are Classes ET22 and ET41 (double-locomotives).

LOCOMOTIVES FROM HUNGARY

ÖBB uses MÁV-START Siemens Class 470 electric locomotives (470.001–010) on some of the services between Wien and České Velenice. This class can also be seen on freights at Břeclav. MÁV-START Class 431 electric locomotives worked into Slovakia on passenger trains up to 2015 but at the time of writing have no booked workings. Other MÁV or Hungarian private locomotives may be seen at Slovak border stations and yards such as at Komárno and Štúrovo.

▲ ÖBB 1216 237, leased to ČD and painted in its blue livery to match the seven ČD Railjet sets, passes Nová Ves u Kolína on 13 January 2015 with train railjet73, the 08.42 Praha–Graz. **Quintus Vosman**

4. SŽDC & ŽSR DEPARTMENTAL RAILCARS

This section mainly contains the 4-wheel MVTV2 overhead catenary maintenance cars (M153.0, later Class 892) which were constructed by MSV Studénka to the same design as Class 810 (M152.0) passenger railcars. They have roof-mounted inspection platforms and single or dual-voltage pantographs for repairing or testing overhead equipment and also staff facilities such as a toilet and seating area. Designed to replace older departmental railcars, following a 1981 prototype (892.001), 103 were built in 1983 (892.002–101 plus broad gauge 892.801–803) and then ten further for ČSD in 1992 (892.102–111) plus one for DNT (892.112, later sold to Viamont DSP, now Strabag see Private Freight Operators section), making a total of 115.

When ČSD split into ČD and ZSR in 1993 the split of MVTV was 77 to ČD (and then SŽDC from 2008) and 37 to Slovakia. The Czech and Slovak MVTVs have duplicated serial numbers.

There are also older MVTV3s (M250.0, later Class 893) which are based on Class 820 DMUs. 30 were built (893.001–030) in 1972. A few of these linger on in service with SŽDC, the last of this class having been withdrawn in Slovakia in the mid 1990s.

When not out and about, MVTVs can be hard to track down, as they are usually not based at ČD or ZSSK depots, but rather at smaller engineering facilities. However some also stable in stations, Pardubice being a good example. Livery was originally plain ČSD maroon, but in more recent years there have been various shades of red and blue, and more recently SŽDC yellow.

4.1. CZECH DEPARTMENTAL RAILCARS

The Czech infrastructure management company SŽDC doesn't own any locomotives of its own but operates the departmental railcars shown below. Most are MVTV2s, plus some rebuilt former ČD Class 850/851s. The MVTVs are maintained by SŽDC at Letohrad (a former ČD depot). Missing 892.008 has been scrapped.

MVTV2   DEPARTMENTAL MOTOR COACHES

Built: 1983–92.
Builder: MSV Studénka.
Engine: Liaz ML634 of 155 kW (210 hp).
Transmission: Mechanical (* Hydraulic).
Former ČSD Class: M153.0 & M153.5.

Total No. Built: 115†.
Weight: 23.5 tonnes.
Length over Buffers: 13.97 m.
Maximum Speed: 80 km/h (* 90 km/h).
Wheel Arrangement: A-1.

*   MVTV2.1 Rebuilt by Pars nova Šumperk 2007 with a Tedom RHTA25s engine of 242 kW.

Number	EVN	Former No.	Built	Operating base
MVTV2-007	99 54 9439 065-2	892.007	1983	Bohumín
MVTV2-009	99 54 9439 067-8	892.009	1983	Bohumín
MVTV2-010	99 54 9439 086-8	892.010	1983	Zábřeh na Moravě
MVTV2-012	99 54 9439 075-1	892.012	1983	Česká Třebová
MVTV2-013	99 54 9439 002-5	892.013	1983	Hradec Králové
MVTV2-014	99 54 9439 015-7	892.014	1983	Choceň
MVTV2-016	99 54 9439 048-8	892.016	1983	Ústí nad Labem
MVTV2-017	99 54 9439 063-7	892.017	1983	Karlovy Vary
MVTV2-018	99 54 9439 057-9	892.018	1983	Cheb
MVTV2-019	99 54 9439 058-7	892.019	1983	Planá u Mariánské Lázně
MVTV2-025	99 54 9439 016-5	892.025	1983	Bohumín
MVTV2-026	99 54 9439 087-6	892.026	1983	Vestín
MVTV2-027	99 54 9439 005-8	892.027	1983	Brno Modřice
MVTV2-028	99 54 9439 088-4	892.028	1983	Lipník nad Bečvou
MVTV2.1-029 *	99 54 9439 006-6	892.029	1983	Horní Cerekev
MVTV2-030	99 54 9439 038-9	892.030	1983	Česká Třebová
MVTV2-031	99 54 9439 024-9	892.031	1983	Olbramovice
MVTV2-032	99 54 9439 025-6	892.032	1983	Karlštejn
MVTV2-033	99 54 9439 031-4	892.033	1983	Kolín
MVTV2-034	99 54 9439 077-7	892.034	1983	Ražice
MVTV2-035	99 54 9439 078-5	892.035	1983	Horní Dvořiště

MVTV2-036	99 54 9439 079-3	892.036	1983	České Budějovice
MVTV2-043	99 54 9439 021-5	892.043	1983	Zábřeh na Moravě
MVTV2-044	99 54 9439 003-3	892.044	1983	Břeclav
MVTV2-045	99 54 9439 073-6	892.045	1983	Bzenec-Přívoz
MVTV2-046	99 54 9439 050-4	892.046	1983	Most
MVTV2-047	99 54 9439 049-6	892.047	1983	Děčín
MVTV2-048	99 54 9439 051-2	892.048	1983	Litoměřice
MVTV2-049	99 54 9439 007-4	892.049	1983	Havlíčkův Brod
MVTV2-050	99 54 9439 039-7	892.050	1983	Lysá nad Labem
MVTV2-051	99 54 9439 080-1	892.051	1983	Veselí nad Lužnicí
MVTV2-052	99 54 9439 081-9	892.052	1983	Veselí nad Lužnicí
MVTV2-053	99 54 9439 082-7	892.053	1983	Ražice
MVTV2-059	99 54 9439 068-6	892.059	1983	Bohumín
MVTV2-060	99 54 9439 069-4	892.060	1983	Bohumín
MVTV2-061	99 54 9439 022-3	892.061	1983	Hulín
MVTV2-062	99 54 9439 023-1	892.062	1983	Grygov
MVTV2-063	99 54 9439 026-4	892.063	1983	Poříčany
MVTV2-064	99 54 9439 027-2	892.064	1983	Praha Horní Počernice
MVTV2-065	99 54 9439 028-0	892.065	1983	Praha Vršovice
MVTV2-067	99 54 9439 004-1	892.067	1983	Oldřchov u Duchcova
MVTV2-068	99 54 9439 059-5	892.068	1983	Nepomuk
MVTV2-076	99 54 9439 090-0	892.076	1983	Grygov
MVTV2-077	99 54 9439 012-4	892.077	1983	Křenovice u Slavkova
MVTV2-079	99 54 9439 009-0	892.079	1983	Žďár nad Sázavou
MVTV2-081	99 54 9439 001-7	892.081	1983	Nymburk
MVTV2-082	99 54 9439 041-3	892.082	1983	Pardubice hl.n.
MVTV2-083	99 54 9439 029-8	892.083	1983	Praha Vršovice
MVTV2-084	99 54 9439 033-0	892.084	1983	Praha Vršovice
MVTV2-085	99 54 9439 084-3	892.085	1983	Nepomuk
MVTV2-086	99 54 9439 061-1	892.086	1983	Plzeň
MVTV2-087	99 54 9439 062-9	892.087	1983	Zdice
MVTV2-093	99 54 9439 091-8	892.093	1983	Přerov
MVTV2-095	99 54 9439 042-1	892.095	1983	Pardubice hl.n.
MVTV2-096	99 54 9439 030-6	892.096	1983	Strancice
MVTV2-097	99 54 9439 053-8	892.097	1983	Lovosice
MVTV2-098	99 54 9439 054-6	892.098	1983	Usti nad Labem

▲ Rebuilt SŽDC MVTV2.2-006 heads east at Zábřeh na Moravě on 7 July 2014.   **Robert Pritchard**

MVTV2-099	99 54 9439 055-3	892.099	1983	Oldřchov u Duchcova
MVTV2-100	99 54 9439 017-3	892.100	1983	Český Těšín
MVTV2-101	99 54 9439 070-2	892.101	1983	Studénka
MVTV2-106	99 54 9439 071-0	892.106	1992	Studénka
MVTV2-107	99 54 9439 020-7	892.107	1992	Tišnov
MVTV2-108	99 54 9439 010-8	892.108	1992	Blansko
MVTV2-109	99 54 9439 056-1	892.109	1992	Chomutov
MVTV2-110	99 54 9439 034-8	892.110	1992	Praha hl.n.
MVTV2-111	99 54 9439 074-4	892.111	1992	Hradec Králové

MVTV2.2   REBUILT DEPARTMENTAL MOTOR COACHES

Ten MVTV2s have been modernised and rebuilt by CZ LOKO. They have new Tedom engines, electric transmission and both axles are now powered. A new independent diesel generator has been installed instead of the toilet. The prototype MVTV2 (892.001) was one of those converted.

Built: 1981 (892.001)/1983; rebuilt by CZ LOKO, Česká Třebová/Jihlava 2011–15.
Builder: MSV Studénka/CZ LOKO.   **Weight:** 27.6 tonnes.
Engine: Tedom TD265 RHTA26 of 266 kW (355 hp).   **Length over Buffers:** 13.97 m.
Transmission: Electric.   **Maximum Speed:** 90 km/h.
Former ČSD Class: M153.0 & M153.5.   **Wheel Arrangement:** A-A.

Number	EVN	Former MVTV No	Former set No.	Operating base
MVTV2.2-001	99 54 9439 089-2	MVTV2-042	892.042	Hulín
MVTV2.2-002	99 54 9439 064-5	MVTV2-001	892.001	Bohumín
MVTV2.2-003	99 54 9439 060-3	MVTV2-070	892.070	Havlíčkův Brod
MVTV2.2-004	99 54 9439 092-6	MVTV2-094	892.094	České Budějovice
MVTV2.2-005	99 54 9439 032-2	MVTV2-015	892.015	Ústí nad Labem
MVTV2.2-006	99 54 9439 008-2	MVTV2-078	892.078	Zábřeh na Moravě
MVTV2.2-007	99 54 9439 040-5	MVTV2-080	892.080	Plzeň
MVTV2.2-008	99 54 9439 093-4	MVTV2-011	892.011	Hradec Králové
MVTV2.2-009	99 54 9439 052-2	MVTV2-066	892.066	Brno Modřice
MVTV2.2-010	99 54 9439 083-5	MVTV2-069	892.069	Kralupy nad Vltavou

MVTV3   DEPARTMENTAL MOTOR COACHES

Built: 1972.   **Total No. Built:** 30.
Builder: MSV Studénka.   **Weight:** 34.3 tonnes.
Engine: Tatra T930-4 of 206 kW (275 hp).   **Length over Buffers:** 20.80 m.
Transmission: Hydraulic.   **Maximum Speed:** 80 km/h.
Former ČSD Class: M250.0.   **Wheel Arrangement:** B-2.

Number	EVN	Former No.	Built	Operating base
MVTV3-004	99 54 9439 011-6	893.004	1972	Břeclav
MVTV3-005	99 54 9439 035-5	893.005	1972	Kolín (S)
MVTV3-015	99 54 9439 019-9	893.015	1972	Blansko
MVTV3-017	99 54 9439 072-8	893.017	1972	Horní Cerekev
MVTV3-021	99 54 9439 046-2	893.021	1972	Poříčany (S)
MVTV3-025	99 54 9439 013-2	893.025	1972	Bzenec-Přívoz
MVTV3-029	99 54 9439 036-3	893.029	1972	Kolín (S)

MISCELLANEOUS SŽDC DEPARTMENTAL VEHICLES

MD1-01 is former Class 810 prototype 810.001. This normally operates with engineering measuring car MD1. The former Class 851 DMUs were rebuilt by DPOV Nymburk 2013–14 as a diagnostics measuring vehicle or ETCS test car. They have been fitted with new CAT C27 550 kW engines.

Identity	EVN	Former No/Nos.	Built	Notes
MD1	99 54 9462 001-7	-		Measuring car. Based at Praha
MD1-01	60 54 8929 017-7	810.001/892.601	1973	Measuring car. Based at Praha
FS3	99 54 9464 001-5	810.272	1978	Measuring car. Based at Ústí nad Labem
FŠT-4	99 54 9162 001-0	851.013	1968	Diagnostics measuring car
TÚDC	99 54 9165 002-5	851.014	1968	ETCS test unit
-	-	850.021	1967	Being rebuilt as SŽDC test car

4.2. SLOVAK DEPARTMENTAL RAILCARS

Apart from purpose-built catenary maintenance car MVTV-01, the ŽSR departmental fleet consists entirely of as-built MVTV2s. The ŽSR renumbering of MVTV2 started from 01, duplicating the ČD series. Missing MVTV02-01 (ex-892.037) and MVTV03-01 (ex-892.801) have been scrapped.

MVTV1   CATENARY MAINTENANCE CAR

Purpose-built prototype. Equipped with batteries for operating in tunnels.

Built: 1991.
Builder: MTH Praha, Hranice na Moravě.
Engine: 400 kW (535 hp).
Transmission: Electric.
Wheel Arrangement: 1-A-A-1.

Total No. Built: 1.
Weight: 74.5 tonnes.
Length over Buffers: 22.40 m.
Maximum Speed: 100 km/h.

Number	EVN	Operating base
MVTV-01	99 56 9184 100-2	Nové Zámky

MVTV02/03   DEPARTMENTAL MOTOR COACH

For details see Section 4.1. Note that MVTV02-34 has no roof-mounted inspection platform or pantograph. MVTV03s are broad gauge for use on the 1520 mm SRT line in east Slovakia.

Number	EVN	Former No.	Built	Operating base
MVTV02-02	99 56 9484 202-3	892.039	1983	Nové Zámky
MVTV02-03	99 56 9484 203-1	892.054	1983	Trnava
MVTV02-04	99 56 9484 204-9	892.055	1983	Trnava
MVTV02-05	99 56 9484 205-6	892.056	1983	Nové Mesto nad Váhom
MVTV02-06	99 56 9484 206-4	892.071	1983	Bratislava
MVTV02-07	99 56 9484 207-2	892.072	1983	Trnava
MVTV02-08	99 56 9484 208-0	892.073	1983	Bratislava
MVTV02-09	99 56 9484 209-8	892.074	1983	Bratislava
MVTV02-10	99 56 9484 210-6	892.075	1983	Bratislava
MVTV02-11	99 56 9484 211-4	892.089	1983	Nové Mesto nad Váhom
MVTV02-12	99 56 9484 212-2	892.104	1992	Zvolen
MVTV02-13	99 56 9484 213-0	892.002	1983	Košice
MVTV02-14	99 56 9484 214-8	892.003	1983	Žilina
MVTV02-15	99 56 9484 215-5	892.004	1983	Čierna nad Tisou
MVTV02-16	99 56 9484 216-3	892.006	1983	Čierna nad Tisou
MVTV02-17	99 56 9484 217-1	892.021	1983	Košice
MVTV02-18	99 56 9484 218-9	892.022	1983	Košice
MVTV02-19	99 56 9484 219-7	892.023	1983	Žilina
MVTV02-20	99 56 9484 220-5	892.090	1983	Poprad-Tatry
MVTV02-21	99 56 9484 221-3	892.102	1992	Košice
MVTV02-22	99 56 9484 222-1	892.088	1983	Zvolen
MVTV02-23	99 56 9484 223-9	892.105	1992	Zvolen
MVTV02-24	99 56 9484 224-7	892.005	1983	Košice
MVTV02-25	99 56 9484 225-4	892.020	1983	Žilina
MVTV02-26	99 56 9484 226-2	892.024	1983	Košice
MVTV02-27	99 56 9484 227-0	892.038	1983	Trenčianska Teplá
MVTV02-28	99 56 9484 228-8	892.040	1983	Poprad-Tatry
MVTV02-29	99 56 9484 229-6	892.057	1983	Púchov
MVTV02-30	99 56 9484 230-4	892.058	1983	Čadca
MVTV02-31	99 56 9484 231-2	892.091	1983	Liptovský Mikuláš
MVTV02-32	99 56 9484 232-0	892.092	1983	Štrba
MVTV02-33	99 56 9484 233-8	892.103	1992	Poprad-Tatry
MVTV02-34	99 56 9484 239-5	892.041	1983	Košice

Broad gauge (1520 mm):

Number	EVN	Former No.	Built	Operating base
MVTV03-02		892.802	1983	Košice
MVTV03-03		892.803	1983	Košice

5. CZECH & SLOVAK PRIVATE OPERATORS

5.1. PRIVATE PASSENGER OPERATORS

There are a small number of Private Passenger Operators in the Czech Republic, although ČD operates the vast majority of passenger services. There are two types of Private Passenger operators – open access operators such as Regiojet and Leo Express which compete with ČD on core routes and other operators such as GW Train Regio which are contracted to operate services over mainly rural routes.

As this book closed for press in 2016 the trend was actually starting to swing back to ČD, with the state operator now operating Line 036 instead of GWTR and being due to take back Line 293 from Arriva Morava in the summer.

In Slovakia just one line is currently operated by a private operator – RegioJet.

5.1.1. ARRIVA MORAVA: "ŽELEZNICE DESNÁ"   CZ

www.arriva-morava.cz/dopravni-sluzby/zeleznice-desna   VKM: CXM

Železnice Desná (ŽD) took over the Šumperk–Kouty nad Desnou line plus the short Sobotín branch (table 293 in the timetable) in 1998–99. The two routes (total 22 km) had been devastated by flooding in the north Moravia region in July 1997, with ČD attempting to use the cost of rebuilding as an excuse to force closure. After rebuilding the lines were reopened, with ŽD initially operated by a federation of River Desna valley municipalities (Stavby a Rekonstrukce (SART), not SŽDC, owns the infrastructure). The operation was subsequently privatised and Connex Morava (later Veolia) took over from 2002. In 2013 DB bought Veolia's Czech transport business and integrated the operation into its Arriva passenger subsidiary, although the Železnice Desná brand and distinctive blue, green & white livery is still used.

The fleet consists of three former ČD Class 810s plus two trailers along with a 2-car Class 814/914 set which is like the ČD 814 rebuilds. The fleet is tightly diagrammed, with three sets normally required daily. The Class 814 unit is usually used on the Kouty route. The operational headquarters is at Petrov nad Desnou and maintenance of the fleet is carried out by ČD at Šumperk.

In 2013 electrification of the Kouty line was announced with the aim of reducing journey times and attracting more tourists into the Jeseníky mountains. The work, which also included upgrading the track and stations, was completed in late 2015, involving the extension of 3000 V DC electrification northwards from Šumperk (the 3.4 km Sobotín branch was not included).

ČD has been awarded a 10-year contract to operate trains to Kouty from June 2016. The current Nezamyslice–Olomouc–Šumperk service, mainly worked by Class 640 RegioPanter EMUs, will be extended to Kouty, leaving Arriva Morava with just the Petrov nad Desnou–Sobotín branch.

Number	Builder	Built	Type	kW	Details	Comments
810.141-2	MSV	1976	M152.0	155	A1 DM	Ex-ČD
810.221-2	MSV	1978	M152.0	155	A1 DM	Ex-ČD
810.435-8	MSV	1981	M152.0	155	A1 DM	Ex-ČD
814.501-3	Pars Nova	2007	814	242	A1 DH	Rebuilt ex-ČD 810.607
914.501-2	Pars Nova	2007	914	-	2	Rebuilt ex-ČD 010.609
010.432-3	MSV	1979	010	-	2	Ex-ČD. EVN 50 54 24-29 418-7
010.549-4	MSV	1982	010	-	2	Ex-ČD. EVN 50 54 24-29 419-5

5.1.2. ARRIVA VLAKY   CZ/SK

Arriva Vlaky has run various experimental open access services using a former DB Class 628 DMU, now refurbished and carrying Arriva blue livery. From late February 2016 the company used it on seven daily suburban trains between Praha hl.n and Benešov u Prahy on weekdays and then at weekends on a Praha–Trenčín (Slovakia) service (out Saturday, return Sunday).

Number	Builder	Built	Type	kW	Details	Comments
845.001-7+945.001-6	Duewag	1988	628.2	410	2-B + 2-2	Ex-DB 628 246/928 246

5.1.3. GW TRAIN REGIO — CZ

www.gwtr.cz — VKM: GWTR

GW Train Regio is an Ústí nad Labem based passenger operator that runs trains over five lines in the Czech Republic, two of them cross-border routes:

*   Line 043 Trutnov–Lubawka (Poland);
*   Line 045 Trutnov–Svoboda nad Úpou;
*   Line 145 Sokolov–Klingenthal–Zwickau (Germany);
*   Line 149 Karlovy Vary–Mariánské Lázně;
*   Line 313 Milotice nad Opavou–Vrbno pod Pradědem.

GW Train Regio was until 2011 Viamont Regio, the passenger side of the Viamont business, but the freight part of this business was sold to OKD (later AWT). In 2014 GWTR was acquired by bus company ČSAD Jihotrans, but the GWTR brand was retained. Until December 2015 the company also operated Line 036 from Harrachov to Szklarska Poręba Górna (Poland), but this is now operated by ČD, with through trains from Liberec.

GWTR uses a mix of DMUs, but has slowly been upgrading to more modern rolling stock in recent years, some of it second hand stock from Germany. Former ZSSK Class 810s are used on Lines 045 and 313 and on some services on Line 145. The longer Line 149 now mainly uses three former Rurtalbahn RegioSpinter Class 654 DMUs and a single RegioShuttle unit, these having replaced the two Class 813s that were rebuilt by ŽOS Zvolen (to a similar specification to ZSSK Class 813 rebuilds). A small depot at Bečov nad Teplou maintains the Line 149 units, whilst others tend to be maintained by ČD, such as at Trutnov.

RegioSprinter units hired from German company Vogtlandbahn are mainly used on Line 145 (for details of these see German Railway Part 2: Private Operators). Finally, a Pesa Class SA134 DMU is hired from Polish operator Kolej Dolnislask for use on the limited services on Line 043 (three train pairs on summer weekends only). These trains continue to Jelenia Góra.

In 2015 GWTR won a 15-year contract to operate regional services on Lines 194, 197 and 198 (České Budějovice and Volary areas) in South Bohemia, currently operated by ČD. GWTR is due to take over these lines in December 2016, although ČD has lodged an appeal. At 229 km this was the largest contract ever awarded for the operation of regional lines in the Czech Republic.

Livery is yellow and black, apart from some units which are still in ZSSK red & cream.

Number	Builder	Built	Type	kW	Details	Comments
650.064-8	Stadler	2004	RegioShuttle	530	B-B DH	Ex-ODEG, Germany (VT650.64)
654.015-6	Duewag	1995	RegioSprinter	396	A-2-A DM	Ex-Rurtalbahn, Germany
654.016-4	Duewag	1995	RegioSprinter	396	A-2-A DM	Ex-Rurtalbahn, Germany
654.017-2	Duewag	1995	RegioSprinter	396	A-2-A DM	Ex-Rurtalbahn, Germany
810.543-9	MSV	1982	M152.0	155	A1 DM	Ex-ZSSK
810.602-3	MSV	1983	M152.0	155	A1 DM	Ex-ZSSK
810.659-3	MSV	1984	M152.0	155	A1 DM	Ex-ZSSK
50 54 24-29 420-3	MSV		Baafx	-	2	Ex-ZSSK 011.406
50 54 24-29 421-1	MSV		Baafx	-	2	Ex-ZSSK 011.896
50 54 24-29 422-9	MSV		Baafx	-	2	Ex-ZSSK 011.
50 54 24-29 423-7	MSV		Baafx	-	2	Ex-ZSSK 011.
50 54 24 29 424-5	MSV		Baafx	-	2	Ex-ZSSK 011.

In addition the following units and trailers have been purchased from ZSSK by holding company ČSAD Jihotrans and are stored at Týn nad Vltavou:

Number	Builder	Built	Type	kW	Details	Comments
810.365-1	MSV	1981	M152.0	155	A1 DM	Ex-ZSSK. (S) Týn nad Vltavou
810.387-5	MSV	1981	M152.0	155	A1 DM	Ex-ZSSK. (S) Týn nad Vltavou
810.492-3	MSV	1982	M152.0	155	A1 DM	Ex-ZSSK. (S) Týn nad Vltavou
810.554-0	MSV	1982	M152.0	155	A1 DM	Ex-ZSSK. (S) Týn nad Vltavou
810.649-4	MSV	1984	M152.0	155	A1 DM	Ex-ZSSK. (S) Týn nad Vltavou
011.245-8	MSV		Baafx	-	2	Ex-ZSSK. (S) Týn nad Vltavou
011.678-0	MSV		Baafx	-	2	Ex-ZSSK. (S) Týn nad Vltavou
011.870-3	MSV		Baafx	-	2	Ex-ZSSK. (S) Týn nad Vltavou

5.1.4. JINDŘICHOHRADECKÉ MÍSTNÍ DRÁHY (JHMD)   CZ

www.jhmd.cz   760 mm

Despite its outward image, JHMD is not a museum or tourist line. The company runs an essential service through a sparsely populated but highly scenic area over the southern Bohemia 760 mm gauge lines that were offered for sale by ČD. JHMD was established in 1994, completing the takeover from ČD in 1998 for a token one Crown.

The two JHMD lines are the southern line – Jindřichův Hradec–Nová Bystřice (33 km, opened 1897) and the northern line – Jindřichův Hradec–Obrataň (46 km, opened 1906) – Tables 228/229 in the timetable. Both diverge from dual gauge 760/1435 mm track just east of Jindřichův Hradec.

JHMD has eight Type T47.0 (now Class 705.9) diesel locomotives acquired from ČD. Four of these (T47.018/19/20/21) were originally built for the Ružomberok narrow gauge network. Another three are in service with ČD on its Třemešná ve Slezsku–Osoblaha line in Silesia (see ČD Narrow Gauge Stock section for full technical details of these locomotives). Following the introduction of DMUs some locomotives were stored. T47.020 was plinthed at Nová Bystřice and T47.021 exported to Russia. Locomotives marked * have been re-engined with a Tedom M1.2C 640 S engine (242 kW) between 2002 and 2009. The locomotives are very colourful, with several different liveries. They normally haul either one or two Balm/ú trailers and there are even occasional mixed trains also conveying freight traffic.

T29.014 (normally based at Kamenice) was acquired from Sokolov coal mines and rebuilt from 900 mm gauge. TU48.001 is a Romanian Lxd2 acquired from a sugar beet plant at Tuczno, Poland, with Mercedes MB836 engine and Voith transmission. Steam locomotives are used on special seasonal services on both routes, and these are listed in the Preserved Locomotives section.

In 2013–14 four Romanian-built MBxd2 diesel railbuses were refurbished for JHMD. They had been acquired 2005–06 and one was previously used in unrefurbished condition. The railcars were originally from a class of 32 built in 1984–86 for narrow gauge lines in Poland. The refurbishment of these units, carried out by 4RAIL of České Budějovice, was unconventional and not uncontroversial. The windows are circular, earning the vehicles the nickname "submarines", whilst many of the 38 seats (reconditioned from trolleybuses) are arranged in a longitudinal layout. The units are air-conditioned and feature one toilet. They were fitted with Tedom TD 242 R6H TA26 engines. The railcars are now used on most services on the Obrataň line, with trains to Nová Bystřice still in the hands of T47s in the summer. The November–April service on this line can be operated by either T47s or railcars, but it is a very sparse one train per day (two at weekends).

The main depot is at Jindřichův Hradec, with a further depot and steam locomotive workshop at Kamenice, a storage shed at Lovětín and a small shed for stabling at Nová Bystřice.

Number	Builder		Built	Type	kW	Details	Comments
M27.001	Faur		1986	MBxd2	242	B-B DH	Ex-MBxd2-213. EVN 90 54 3 805 901-6
M27.002	Faur		1985	MBxd2	242	B-B DH	Ex-MBxd2-303. EVN 90 54 3 805 902-4
M27.003	Faur		1985	MBxd2	242	B-B DH	Ex-MBxd2-305. EVN 90 54 3 805 903-2
M27.004	Faur		1986	MBxd2	242	B-B DH	Ex-MBxd2-223. EVN 90 54 3 805 904-0
T29.014	TSM		1967	T29.0	147	B DM	Ex-702.901; HDBS 14
T47.005	ČKD	*	1954	T47.0	242	Bo-Bo DE	Ex-705.905; green livery.
T47.006	ČKD		1954	T47.0	258	Bo-Bo DE	Ex-705.906; red livery.
T47.007	ČKD		1958	T47.0	258	Bo-Bo DE	Ex-705.907; blue livery. (S) Lovětín
T47.011	ČKD		1958	T47.0	258	Bo-Bo DE	Ex-705.911; red livery.
T47.015	ČKD	*	1958	T47.0	242	Bo-Bo DE	Ex-705.915; blue livery.
T47.018	ČKD	*	1958	T47.0	242	Bo-Bo DE	Ex-705.918; red livery.
T47.019	ČKD	*	1958	T47.0	242	Bo-Bo DE	Ex-705.919; lilac livery.
T47.020	ČKD		1958	T47.0	258	Bo-Bo DE	Ex-705.920; red livery. Plinth Nová Bystřice
TU48.001	Faur		1980	Lxd2	330	B-B DH	Ex-706.901; Lxd2-331 (Poland)
630	ČKD		1966	Balm/ú	-	2-2	Ex-005.901
632	ČKD		1966	Balm/ú	-	2-2	Ex-005.903
633	ČKD		1966	Balm/ú	-	2-2	Ex-005.904
635	ČKD		1966	Balm/ú	-	2-2	Ex-005.906
637	ČKD		1966	Balm/ú	-	2-2	Ex-005.908
638	ČKD		1966	Balm/ú	-	2-2	Ex-005.909
639	ČKD		1966	Balm/ú	-	2-2	Ex-005.910
660	ČKD		1966	Balm/ú	-	2-2	Ex-005.916
662	ČKD		1966	Balm/ú	-	2-2	Rebuilt to works car ex-Pom46560
665	ČKD		1966	Balm/ú	-	2-2	Ex-005.920

5.1.5. KŽC DOPRAVA CZ

www.kzc.cz VKM: KZC

KŽC Doprava is the main line operating arm of historical club and tourist train operator KŽC (Klub Železničních Cestovatelů, meaning "The Railway Travellers Club" in English). Established in 1985 the main depot is at Lysá nad Labem. The company has amassed a fantastic collection of locomotives and particularly DMUs, which for the purposes of this publication are classed as preserved and are listed in the Preserved Locomotives & Railcars section.

Listed in this section are four Class 810s plus two four-wheel trailers acquired in 2015 which are used on the subsidised passenger service between Praha Masarykovo and Praha Čakovice (19 km), which started in 2013 (two sets are required daily). This is a 10-year contract and was let by Praha urban transport authority Ropid. It requires the use of partly low-floor vehicles from 2019. 810.517/535 and the trailers have been repainted in the original old style red & cream livery and also carry their original numbers. Trialled on the route in 2015 were the ŽOS Zvolen Class 813 rebuilds.

KŽC also operates an extensive programme of heritage services; the company's website (Czech language only) provides details of these, and many are also listed at the rear of the main ČD timetable book.

Number	Builder	Built	Type	kW	Details	Comments
810.381-4	MSV	1981	M152.0	155	A1 DM	Ex-ZSSK
810.517-3	MSV	1982	M152.0	155	A1 DM	Ex-ZSSK
810.535-5	MSV	1982	M152.0	155	A1 DM	Ex-ZSSK
810.656-9	MSV	1984	M152.0	155	A1 DM	Ex-ZSSK
50 54 24-29 185-2	MSV		Baafx	-	2	Ex-010.420/ČD 010.552
50 54 24-29 235-5	MSV		Baafx	-	2	Ex-010.509/ČD 010.072

▲ Leo Express's distinctive black & gold-liveried Class 480s are now a regular sight on the main Praha–Ostrava line. On 6 July 2014 480.001 leaves Ostrava hl.n with train LE1361, the 16.06 Praha hl.n–Karviná hl.n. **Robert Pritchard**

5.1.6. LEO EXPRESS   CZ/SK

www.le.cz   VKM: LE

Praha-based Leo Express commenced operating between Praha and Ostrava in November 2012, setting up to compete directly with ČD and RegioJet on this route. The company was established in 2010 (originally called Rapid Express), using backing from Aakon Capital.

Unlike RegioJet which chose to use refurbished locomotives and carriages on its services, Leo Express ordered five new 5-car articulated 190 km/h FLIRT EMUs from Swiss firm Stadler (although infrastructure restrictions means the useable maximum speed is 160 km/h). They were assembled at Stadler's plant at Siedlce, Poland. The units offer high quality interiors, with three classes: there are six luxurious Premium Class seats, 19 First Class seats and 212 Second Class seats in each set. The units are maintained by Stadler at Bohumín.

By 2016 Leo had expanded from a basic 2-hourly Praha–Bohumín timetable to serve a number of other destinations. There are nine departures from Praha daily. Instead of just running to Bohumín most trains now extend to Karviná and two trains divert to Přerov and Staré Město u Uherského Hradiště. There are also two daily trains to Košice in Slovakia (some trips running overnight) . A number of different stations are also now served on the main line, such as Kolín and Suchdol nad Odrou. All trains operate as compulsory reservation. Livery is black and gold.

Number	Builder	Built	Type	kW	Details	Comments
480.001-7	Stadler	2011	FLIRT EMU	2600	Bo-2-2-2-2-Bo	
480.002-5	Stadler	2011	FLIRT EMU	2600	Bo-2-2-2-2-Bo	
480.003-3	Stadler	2011	FLIRT EMU	2600	Bo-2-2-2-2-Bo	
480.004-1	Stadler	2011	FLIRT EMU	2600	Bo-2-2-2-2-Bo	
480.005-8	Stadler	2011	FLIRT EMU	2600	Bo-2-2-2-2-Bo	

5.1.7. RAILWAY CAPITAL   CZ

www.railwaycapital.cz   VKM: RCAS

Praha-based private operator Railway Capital was established in 2011 to operate low-cost branch line services where subsidies from local authorities were available. It was set up by Jan Šatava, formerly the founder of JHMD. The company acquired four Class 810s from ZSSK and also owns two Class 720s and a Class 748 which are hired to infrastructure operators.

Railway Capital launched its first service in summer 2014 on Line 314 to Jakartovice (extended the following year to Svobodné Heřmanice), a line closed by ČD in April 2014. Three trains a day run at weekends.

At the time of writing the company provides seasonal (mainly July–August/September) weekend tourist services on the following lines (Line 113 is normally a Hanzalík Class 831, see Preserved section for details). Readers are advised to check the RC website for up to date timetables:

• Line 113 Litoměřice–Lovosice–Čížkovice–Obrnice–Most
• Line 164 Kadaň-Prunéřov–Kaštice–Podbořany/Line 165 Vilémov u Kadaň–Radonice u Kadaně
• Line 243 Moravské Budějovice–Jemnice
• Line 314 Opava východ–Jakartovice–Svobodné Heřmanice

Number	Builder	Built	Type	kW	Details	Comments
710.682-6	ČKD	1966	T334.0	301	C DH	Ex-T334.0682
720.039-7	ČKD	1959	T435.0	551	Bo-Bo DE	
720.097-5	ČKD	1961	T435.0	551	Bo-Bo DE	
748.536-0	Faur	1982	LDH125	920	B-B DH	
810.391-3	MSV	1981	M152.0	155	A1 DM	Ex-ZSSK (S)
810.405-1	MSV	1981	M152.0	155	A1 DM	Ex-ZSSK
810.492-3	MSV	1982	M152.0	155	A1 DM	Ex-ZSSK (S)
810.499-4	MSV	1982	M152.0	155	A1 DM	Ex-ZSSK
810.526-4	MSV	1982	M152.0	155	A1 DM	Ex-ZSSK. "Scenic" livery
810.536-3	MSV	1982	M152.0	155	A1 DM	Ex-ZSSK
810.623-9	MSV	1984	M152.0	155	A1 DM	Ex-ZSSK
011.636-8	MSV		Baafx	-	2	Ex-ZSSK
50 54 24-29.701-2	MSV		Baafx	-	2	Ex-010. "Scenic" livery

5.1.8. REGIOJET

CZ/SK

www.regiojet.cz

VKM: RJ/RJSK

RegioJet was the first open access passenger operator which set up to compete with ČD on the lucrative Praha–Ostrava/Bohumín corridor. The company is a subsidiary of long-distance Central European transportation group Student Agency, owned by Czech entrepreneur Radim Jančura. The firm's headquarters is in Brno. For 2015 the company reported profits of CZK 40 million, with an increase in passengers of 26% year-on-year. It has now secured more than 40% of the lucrative Praha–Ostrava/Bohumín market.

RegioJet started operating InterCity trains on the main east–west route in autumn 2011, using nine former Škoda-built Class 162s (ex-Class 163s), which had been used in Italy by Ferrovie Nord Milano (FNM) since 1995. Initially trains ran with just four or five coaches, rolling stock being sourced mainly from Austria, Switzerland or Belgium. Slowly patronage built up, helped by highly competitive fares and special deals available on the internet, as well as offering quality rolling stock and a high level of customer service (including complimentary refreshments).

In late 2014 RegioJet leased three Siemens Class 193 Vectron locomotives (193.205/206/214) from European Locomotive Leasing (ELL) of Austria for its new Bratislava–Žilina–Košice service (three trains a day, rising to five or six a day from 2016). A Class 193 is also normally used on the Praha–Košice trains, with Class 162s continuing to be used on the Praha–Ostrava–Havířov/Návsí route (roughly a two-hourly service). Trains have now been extended to between eight and ten coaches, and new services continue to be added – including an overnight train from Praha to Košice in summer 2015 and a Praha–Staré Město u Uherského Hradiště service. Also from December 2015 a Praha–Zvolen train was launched, using a diesel locomotive hired from KDS (normally 750.096) between Martin and Zvolen.

RegioJet acquired a fourth Vectron in December 2015, and plans to take more in December 2016, with the number of coaches the company operates also rising to around 200. At times of high demand other Vectrons may be leased on short-term deals from Siemens. The company has plans to introduce new InterCity routes across the Czech Republic and it has also bid to operate tendered services in the country.

Locomotives and rolling stock are serviced in the former Siemens production facility at Praha Zličín, and also use the sidings opposite Praha-Smíchov station for stabling. A Class 703 and 721 are based here to assist with shunting operations. The Class 162s have also been seen undergoing overhauls at ČMŽO Přerov, whilst maintenance of the Vectron fleet has taken place at the Dyko repair shops at Kolín. A depot for locomotive and DMU maintenance is planned to be built in Bratislava in 2016.

Whilst most will associate RegioJet with its bright yellow InterCity trains linking major cities in the Czech Republic and Slovakia, the company also operates a regional service between Bratislava and Komarno (a distance of 100 km) in Slovakia. RegioJet won the tender to operate this route (Line 131 in the ZSR timetable) in 2011, breaking ZSSK's monopoly of passenger services in the country.

The service started in 2012, with the contract running for 9 years. Since 2012 RegioJet has used various Class 642 Desiro or Class 643 Talent articulated DMUs that previously operated in Germany (for full technical details see the Platform 5 German Railways handbooks). Originally nine 3-car Class 643s were leased from AlphaTrains, but in 2014 five of these were returned and instead six 2-car Class 642s were leased. This allowed peak-hour trains to be formed of four cars and also 2-car sets to be used on their own on the quieter Dunajská Streda–Komárno section. In 2015 two further Class 643s were leased, giving an overall fleet of six Class 642s and six Class 643s – leased from AlphaTrains or PEG. Routine maintenance is carried out at Bratislava Východ depot by ZSSK Cargo, with units having been noted at Lokotrans Slovakia's facility at Šurany for more major attention.

All RegioJet InterCity trains are compulsory reservation, although if seats are available you are welcome to board and pay on the train, as long as you ask one of the stewards before boarding.

RegioJet livery is all over yellow, with grey window surrounds on the coaches.

Number	Builder	Built	Type	kW	Details	Comments
162.112-7	Škoda	1992	99E	3480	Bo-Bo E DC	Ex-163.112/FNM E630.01
162.113-5	Škoda	1992	99E	3480	Bo-Bo E DC	Ex-163.113/FNM E630.02
162.114-3	Škoda	1992	99E	3480	Bo-Bo E DC	Ex-163.114/FNM E630.03
162.115-0	Škoda	1992	99E	3480	Bo-Bo E DC	Ex-163.115/FNM E630.04

162.116-8	Škoda	1992	99E	3480	Bo-Bo E DC	Ex-163.116/FNM E630.05
162.117-6	Škoda	1992	99E	3480	Bo-Bo E DC	Ex-163.117/FNM E630.06
162.118-4	Škoda	1992	99E	3480	Bo-Bo E DC	Ex-163.118/FNM E630.07
162.119-2	Škoda	1992	99E	3480	Bo-Bo E DC	Ex-163.119/FNM E630.08
162.120-0	Škoda	1992	99E	3480	Bo-Bo E DC	Ex-163.120/FNM E630.09
193.205-2	Siemens	2014	Vectron MS	6400	Bo-Bo E AC/DC	Leased from ELL
193.206-0	Siemens	2014	Vectron MS	6400	Bo-Bo E AC/DC	Leased from ELL
193.214-4	Siemens	2014	Vectron MS	6400	Bo-Bo E AC/DC	Leased from ELL
193.226-8	Siemens	2015	Vectron MS	6400	Bo-Bo E AC/DC	Leased from ELL
703.602-3	TSM	1977	T212.1	169	B DH	Carries original No. T212.1602
721.151-9	ČKD	1965	T458.1	551	Bo-Bo DE	

Unit No.	Formation	Builder	Built	Type
VT642.35	642.335-3+642.835-2	Siemens	2001	Desiro Classic
VT642.36	642.336-1+642.836-0	Siemens	2001	Desiro Classic
VT642.37	642.337-9+642.837-8	Siemens	2001	Desiro Classic
VT642.38	642.338-7+642.838-6	Siemens	2001	Desiro Classic
VT642.44	642.344-5+642.844-4	Siemens	2002	Desiro Classic
VT642.47	642.347-8+642.847-7	Siemens	2002	Desiro Classic
VT643.05	643.362-6+943.362-9+643.862-1	Bombardier	2003	Talent
VT643.06	643.363-4+943.363-1+643.863-3	Bombardier	2003	Talent
VT643.09	643.365-9+943.365-6+643.865-8	Bombardier	2004	Talent
VT643.10	643.366-7+943.366-4+643.866-6	Bombardier	2004	Talent
VT643.11	643.367-5+943.367-2+643.867-4	Bombardier	2004	Talent
VT643.14	643.370-9+943.370-6+643.870-8	Bombardier	2004	Talent

▲ New RegioJet Vectron 193.206, leased from ELL, leaves the tunnels beyond Praha hlavní nádraží and takes the Smíchov line, for the stabling sidings at Smíchov (having just worked train IC1004 05.52 Třinec–Praha hl.n in place of the more usual Class 162) on 7 May 2015. **Robert Pritchard**

5.2. PRIVATE FREIGHT OPERATORS

The number of private freight operators in both the Czech Republic and Slovakia has increased substantially in recent years – from the "big players" such as AWT to smaller companies with just a few locomotives, there are now more than 40 different companies operating trains on the national networks. Many operate open access freights in competition with the state operators ČD Cargo and ZSSK Cargo, whilst others are infrastructure companies supplying locomotives and other machinery for major infrastructure projects.

This first edition of Czech & Slovak Railways lists the fleets of many known industrial railway systems, but compiling a complete list of all industrial locomotives is inevitably a very difficult task and one that will take many years to complete! Whilst we are confident that all locomotives that can operate on main lines are contained in this list, readers are invited to send any observations, additions or changes relating to this section, in particular relating to small shunting locomotives, to the address given in the Introduction of this book.

Technical details of most locomotives listed in this section may be found under the relevant class number in the main ČD and ZSSK sections. Note that the number range T669.0501–0518 (770.501–518) was duplicated at construction by the two builders SMZ (built 1967–69) and ČKD (built 1979–81). ČKD T669.0501–0518 were mostly later renumbered in the 770.6xx series.

Note that for modern electric locomotives, such as Vectrons and TRAXX, MS stands for "multi-system".

5.2.1. ADVANCED WORLD TRANSPORT (AWT)   CZ/SK

www.awt.eu   VKM: AWT

AWT, member of the PKP CARGO Group, is one of the largest providers of rail services in Europe, and the second largest freight operator in the Czech Republic after ČD Cargo. The company operates around 12% of all freight in the Czech Republic and also operates trains across much of Central and Eastern Europe.

80% of AWT shares were sold to Polish state rail freight operator PKP CARGO in 2015. The remaining 20% of shares remain in the hands of Czech company Minezit SE, with the well-established AWT brand retained. AWT already often hired electric locomotives (of Classes ET22, ET41 and Class 189) from PKP CARGO.

Originating in 1952 as Ostrava & Karviná coalfields transport, the company was privatised in 1994 and renamed OKD Doprava. It had set up at other locations by 1999. OKD's core motive power was around 60 Class 740s, mainly inherited from the original concern. OKD was still involved with coal movement between Ostrava coal mines and coking, heating and power plants, dominated by its Class 770/771 Co-Cos. OKD acquired Viamont Cargo in 2008, and in 2010 the company was renamed Advanced World Transport.

AWT has a presence across the Czech Republic. One of the main operating bases is Ostrava, with depots at Paskov (alongside the container terminal owned by AWT), Darkov and Šverma. The company owns and operates over some 400 km of lines in the Ostrava-Karviná and Kladno coal basins and provides rail services at around 60 industrial sidings, mostly coal and power plants. Long distance freight includes coal, steel, oil, fuel, chemical products, automotive and intermodal.

As well as the aforementioned Class 740 and 770 the company operates a large fleet of refurbished Class 753 "Goggles" (with CAT 3512 engines), which often operate in pairs on heavy freight trains. Some are cleared for operation in Hungary. The four Class 752s were rebuilt in 2004 and have less powerful ČKD 310 engines. 740.301–323 have Caterpillar 3406 DITA engines that are significantly less powerful than the original ČKD engines for heavy shunting operations at much lower operating costs. The Class 741s are rebuilt Class 740s with lowered cab hoods. The Class 704.7s were rebuilt by CZ LOKO with CAT C13 engines. A small fleet of modern electric locomotives are used on longer distance flows on electrified routes.

AWT livery is a distinctive orange and grey, with some locomotives still in the old OKD, Doprava livery of yellow & dark blue.

▲ AWT uses a small number of modern electric locomotives. On 18 February 2016 Siemens Taurus 183.719 is seen between Praha Dolní Počernice and Praha Běchovice with an automotive train from Leipzig, Germany to Devínska Nová Ves, Bratislava. **Quintus Vosman**

▼ Coal Services (Most) electric mining locomotive 127.707 is seen at the head of a coal train near the Coal Services depot at Komořany on 10 May 2013. **Robert Pritchard**

Number	Builder	Built	Type	kW	Details	Notes
121.038-4	Škoda	1960	E469.1	2032	Bo-Bo E DC	
130.049-0	Škoda	1977	E479.0	2040	Bo-Bo E DC	
181.024-1	Škoda	1961	E669.1	2790	Co-Co E DC	
181.040-7	Škoda	1961	E669.1	2790	Co-Co E DC	
182.053-9	Škoda	1964	E669.2	2790	Co-Co E DC	Leased from ZOS Zvolen
183.714-5	Siemens	2011	ES 64 U4	6400	Bo-Bo E MS	Taurus
183.718-6	Siemens	2011	ES 64 U4	6400	Bo-Bo E MS	Taurus
183.719-4	Siemens	2011	ES 64 U4	6400	Bo-Bo E MS	Taurus
189.151-4	Siemens	2009	ES 64 F4	6400	Bo-Bo E MS	EuroSprinter. Leased from MRCE
223.008-4	Siemens	2004	ER 20	2000	Bo-Bo DE	"ER 20-008". Leased from MRCE
701.652-0	ČKD	1959	T211.1	169	B DM	Hexion Specialty Chemicals, Sokolov
701.691-8	ČKD	1958	T211.1	169	B DM	Setuza, Ústí nad Labem
703.521-5	TSM	1973	T212.2	169	B DH	Plzeň Doudlevce steelworks
704.505-7	ČKD	1991	T238.0	250	Bo DE	Spolchemie, Ústí nad Labem
704.519-8	ČKD	1992	T238.0	250	Bo DE	
704.701-2	ČKD	1988	T237.0	328	Bo DE	Rebuilt ex-T237.0001/704.401
704.704-6	ČKD	1993	T238.0	328	Bo DE	Rebuilt ex-T238.0044/704.544
704.705-3	ČKD	1992	T238.0	328	Bo DE	Rebuilt ex-T238.0020/704.520
709.513.6	ČKD	1993	T239.1	327	Bo DE	
709.529-2	ČKD	1996	T239.1	327	Bo DE	
709.532-6	ČKD	1996	T239.1	327	Bo DE	
710.415-1	ČKD	1970	T334.1	301	C DH	
720.502-4	ČKD	1958	T435.0	551	Bo-Bo DE	
720.593-3	ČKD	1961	T435.0	551	Bo-Bo DE	
720.595-8	ČKD	1962	T435.0	551	Bo-Bo DE	
720.604-8	ČKD	1962	T435.0	551	Bo-Bo DE	
724.713-3	CZ LOKO	r2008	ex-T448.0	627	Bo-Bo DE	Rebuilt ex-740.439
730.612-9	ČKD	1988	T457.0	600	Bo-Bo DE	
740.301-7	ČKD	1983	T448.0	369	Bo-Bo DE	Ex-740.768. CAT 3406 engine
740.302-5	ČKD	1978	T448.0	369	Bo-Bo DE	Ex-740.624. CAT 3406 engine
740.303-3	ČKD	1976	T448.0	369	Bo-Bo DE	Ex-740.568. CAT 3406 engine
740.304-1	ČKD	1987	T448.0	369	Bo-Bo DE	Ex-740.423. CAT 3406 engine
740.305-8	ČKD	1974	T448.0	369	Bo-Bo DE	Ex-740.520. CAT 3406 engine
740.306-6	ČKD	1978	T448.0	369	Bo-Bo DE	Ex-740.623. CAT 3406 engine
740.307-4	ČKD	1976	T448.0	369	Bo-Bo DE	Ex-740.587. CAT 3406 engine
740.311-6	ČKD	1978	T448.0	369	Bo-Bo DE	Ex-740.623. CAT 3406 engine
740.312-4	ČKD	1976	T448.0	369	Bo-Bo DE	Ex-740.577. CAT 3406 engine
740.313-2	ČKD	1983	T448.0	369	Bo-Bo DE	Ex-740.767. CAT 3406 engine
740.314-0	ČKD	1976	T448.0	369	Bo-Bo DE	Ex-740.596. CAT 3406 engine
740.318-1	ČKD	1975	T448.0	392	Bo-Bo DE	Ex-740.531. CAT 3406 engine
740.319-9	ČKD	1976	T448.0	392	Bo-Bo DE	Ex-740.580. CAT 3406 engine
740.320-7	ČKD	1976	T448.0	392	Bo-Bo DE	Ex-740.589. CAT 3406 engine
740.321-5	ČKD	1982	T448.0	392	Bo-Bo DE	Ex-740.706. CAT 3406 engine
740.322-3	ČKD	1976	T448.0	392	Bo-Bo DE	Ex-740.566. CAT 3406 engine
740.323-1	ČKD	1976	T448.0	392	Bo-Bo DE	Ex-740.537. CAT 3406 engine
740.401-5	ČKD	1986	T448.0	883	Bo-Bo DE	
740.404-9	ČKD	1986	T448.0	883	Bo-Bo DE	
740.407-2	ČKD	1986	T448.0	883	Bo-Bo DE	
740.414-8	ČKD	1987	T448.0	883	Bo-Bo DE	
740.422-1	ČKD	1987	T448.0	880	Bo-Bo DE	Rebuilt. CAT 3512 engine
740.424-7	ČKD	1987	T448.0	880	Bo-Bo DE	Rebuilt. CAT 3512 engine
740.425-4	ČKD	1987	T448.0	883	Bo-Bo DE	
740.426-2	ČKD	1987	T448.0	883	Bo-Bo DE	
740.437-9	ČKD	1987	T448.0	883	Bo-Bo DE	
740.443-7	ČKD	1988	T448.0	883	Bo-Bo DE	
740.450-2	ČKD	1988	T448.0	883	Bo-Bo DE	
740.456-9	ČKD	1989	T448.0	883	Bo-Bo DE	
740.457-7	ČKD	1989	T448.0	883	Bo-Bo DE	
740.458-5	ČKD	1989	T448.0	883	Bo-Bo DE	
740.460-1	ČKD	1988	T448.0	883	Bo-Bo DE	Ex-Polish industry T448.P141
740.517-8	ČKD	1974	T448.0	883	Bo-Bo DE	
740.534-3	ČKD	1975	T448.0	883	Bo-Bo DE	
740.551-7	ČKD	1976	T448.0	883	Bo-Bo DE	

740.552-5	ČKD	1976	T448.0	883	Bo-Bo DE	
740.604-4	ČKD	1977	T448.0	883	Bo-Bo DE	
740.618-4	ČKD	1978	T448.0	883	Bo-Bo DE	
740.622-6	ČKD	1978	T448.0	883	Bo-Bo DE	
740.638-2	ČKD	1978	T448.0	883	Bo-Bo DE	
740.639-0	ČKD	1978	T448.0	883	Bo-Bo DE	
740.650-7	ČKD	1978	T448.0	883	Bo-Bo DE	
740.664-8	ČKD	1979	T448.0	883	Bo-Bo DE	
740.673-9	ČKD	1979	T448.0	883	Bo-Bo DE	
740.674-7	ČKD	1979	T448.0	883	Bo-Bo DE	
740.681-2	ČKD	1980	T448.0	883	Bo-Bo DE	
740.682-0	ČKD	1980	T448.0	883	Bo-Bo DE	
740.685-3	ČKD	1980	T448.0	883	Bo-Bo DE	
740.686-1	ČKD	1980	T448.0	883	Bo-Bo DE	
740.701-8	ČKD	1981	T448.0	883	Bo-Bo DE	
740.707-5	ČKD	1982	T448.0	883	Bo-Bo DE	
740.734-9	ČKD	1982	T448.0	883	Bo-Bo DE	
740.736-4	ČKD	1982	T448.0	883	Bo-Bo DE	
740.738-0	ČKD	1982	T448.0	883	Bo-Bo DE	
740.745-5	ČKD	1982	T448.0	883	Bo-Bo DE	
740.746-3	ČKD	1982	T448.0	883	Bo-Bo DE	
740.762-0	ČKD	1983	T448.0	883	Bo-Bo DE	
740.766-1	ČKD	1983	T448.0	883	Bo-Bo DE	
740.769-5	ČKD	1983	T448.0	883	Bo-Bo DE	
740.772-9	ČKD	1983	T448.0	883	Bo-Bo DE	
740.797-6	ČKD	1983	T448.0	883	Bo-Bo DE	
740.801-6	ČKD	1984	T448.0	883	Bo-Bo DE	
740.818-0	ČKD	1984	T448.0	883	Bo-Bo DE	
740.819-8	ČKD	1984	T448.0	883	Bo-Bo DE	
740.828-9	ČKD	1984	T448.0	883	Bo-Bo DE	
740.837-0	ČKD	1984	T448.0	883	Bo-Bo DE	
740.842-0	ČKD	1984	T448.0	883	Bo-Bo DE	
740.844-6	ČKD	1985	T448.0	883	Bo-Bo DE	
740.845-3	ČKD	1985	T448.0	883	Bo-Bo DE	
740.868-5	ČKD	1985	T448.0	883	Bo-Bo DE	
740.887-5	ČKD	1986	T448.0	883	Bo-Bo DE	
741.501-1	ČKD	1983	T448.0	883	Bo-Bo DE	Rebuilt ex-740.793
741.502-9	ČKD	1986	T448.0	883	Bo-Bo DE	Rebuilt ex-740.896
741.503-7	ČKD	1984	T448.0	883	Bo-Bo DE	Rebuilt ex-740.809
741.504-5	ČKD	1979	T448.0	883	Bo-Bo DE	Rebuilt ex-740.665
741.505-2	ČKD	1979	T448.0	883	Bo-Bo DE	Rebuilt ex-740.669
741.506-0	ČKD	1984	T448.0	883	Bo-Bo DE	Rebuilt ex-740.835
741.507-8	ČKD	1976	T448.0	883	Bo-Bo DE	Rebuilt ex-740.550
741.508-6	ČKD	1986	T448.0	883	Bo-Bo DE	Rebuilt ex-740.878
741.509-4	ČKD	1976	T448.0	883	Bo-Bo DE	Rebuilt ex-740.598
742.361-9	ČKD	1983	T466.2	883	Bo-Bo DE	Rebuilt ex-742.603
742.507-7	ČKD	1983	T466.2	883	Bo-Bo DE	Rebuilt ex-742.614
742.520-0	ČKD	1983	T466.2	883	Bo-Bo DE	Rebuilt ex-742.624
750.059-8	ČKD	1972	T478.3	1325	Bo-Bo DE	Ex-ZSSK
750.199-2	ČKD	1974	T478.3	1325	Bo-Bo DE	Ex-ZSSK
752.601-5	ČKD	1974	T478.3	990	Bo-Bo DE	Rebuilt ex-753.205/753.355
752.602-3	ČKD	1975	T478.3	990	Bo-Bo DE	Rebuilt ex-753.296
752.603-1	ČKD	1974	T478.3	990	Bo-Bo DE	Rebuilt ex-753.154/753.304
752.604-9	ČKD	1977	T478.3	990	Bo-Bo DE	Rebuilt ex-753.382
753.306-0	ČKD	1975	T478.3	1325	Bo-Bo DE	(S) Steti
753.703-8	ČKD	1974	T478.3	1500	Bo-Bo DE	Rebuilt ex-750.134
753.704-6	ČKD	1975	T478.3	1500	Bo-Bo DE	Rebuilt ex-750.284
753.705-3	ČKD	1975	T478.3	1500	Bo-Bo DE	Rebuilt ex-753.297
753.706-1	ČKD	1972	T478.3	1500	Bo-Bo DE	Rebuilt ex-753.072
753.707-9	ČKD	1972	T478.3	1500	Bo-Bo DE	Rebuilt ex-753.045
753.708-7	ČKD	1973	T478.3	1500	Bo-Bo DE	Rebuilt ex-753.084
753.709-5	ČKD	1976	T478.3	1500	Bo-Bo DE	Rebuilt ex-753.350
753.710-3	ČKD	1976	T478.3	1500	Bo-Bo DE	Rebuilt ex-753.351
753.711-1	ČKD	1976	T478.3	1500	Bo-Bo DE	Rebuilt ex-753.319

753.712-9	ČKD	1976	T478.3	1500	Bo-Bo DE	Rebuilt ex-753.332
753.713-7	ČKD	1976	T478.3	1500	Bo-Bo DE	Rebuilt ex-753.317
753.714-5	ČKD	1976	T478.3	1500	Bo-Bo DE	Rebuilt ex-753.353
753.723-6	ČKD	1972	T478.3	1500	Bo-Bo DE	Rebuilt ex-753.052
753.724-4	ČKD	1974	T478.3	1500	Bo-Bo DE	Rebuilt ex-753.168
753.725-1	ČKD	1975	T478.3	1500	Bo-Bo DE	Rebuilt ex-753.248
753.726-9	ČKD	1973	T478.3	1500	Bo-Bo DE	Rebuilt ex-753.086
753.727-7	ČKD	1976	T478.3	1500	Bo-Bo DE	Rebuilt ex-753.354
753.728-5	ČKD	1974	T478.3	1500	Bo-Bo DE	Rebuilt ex-750.210
753.729-3	ČKD	1975	T478.3	1500	Bo-Bo DE	Rebuilt ex-750.250
753.730-1	ČKD	1974	T478.3	1500	Bo-Bo DE	Rebuilt ex-753.155/752.001
753.731-9	ČKD	1977	T478.3	1500	Bo-Bo DE	Rebuilt ex-750.363
753.732-7	ČKD	1974	T478.3	1500	Bo-Bo DE	Rebuilt ex-750.180
753.733-5	ČKD	1977	T478.3	1500	Bo-Bo DE	Rebuilt ex-750.397
753.734-3	ČKD	1975	T478.3	1500	Bo-Bo DE	Rebuilt ex-750.234
753.735-0	ČKD	1975	T478.3	1500	Bo-Bo DE	Rebuilt ex-750.225
753.736-8	ČKD	1972	T478.3	1500	Bo-Bo DE	Rebuilt ex-753.060
753.737-6	ČKD	1977	T478.3	1500	Bo-Bo DE	Rebuilt ex-750.400
753.738-4	ČKD	1977	T478.3	1500	Bo-Bo DE	Rebuilt ex-750.408
753.739-2	ČKD	1974	T478.3	1500	Bo-Bo DE	Rebuilt ex-750.217
770.506-4	ČKD	1979	T669.0	993	Co-Co DE	
770.507-2	ČKD	1979	T669.0	993	Co-Co DE	
770.508-0	ČKD	1979	T669.0	993	Co-Co DE	
770.514-8	ČKD	1980	T669.0	993	Co-Co DE	
770.518-9	ČKD	1981	T669.0	993	Co-Co DE	
770.520-5	ČKD	1981	T669.0	993	Co-Co DE	
770.525-4	ČKD	1984	T669.0	993	Co-Co DE	
770.532-0	ČKD	1986	T669.0	993	Co-Co DE	
770.533-8	ČKD	1986	T669.0	993	Co-Co DE	
770.534-6	ČKD	1986	T669.0	993	Co-Co DE	
770.606-2	SMZ	1968	T669.0	993	Co-Co DE	
770.614-6	SMZ	1969	T669.0	993	Co-Co DE	
771.036-1	SMZ	1969	T669.1	993	Co-Co DE	
771.515-4	SMZ	1971	T669.1	993	Co-Co DE	
771.701-0	SMZ	1970	T669.2	993	Co-Co DE	Ex-T669.2501/T669.2001

5.2.2. ARCELORMITTAL OSTRAVA   CZ

www.arcelormittal.cz   VKM: AMO

Established in 1951 as Nová Huť Klementa Gottwalda (NHKG), this large Ostrava steelworks east of Ostrava Kunčice station was renamed simply Nová Huť in 1992 before privatisation and acquisition as Mittal Steel Ostrava, becoming ArcelorMittal Ostrava in 2007. Today the company is the largest steel manufacturer in the Czech Republic and has an annual production capacity of 3 million tonnes of steel. Located in a veritable maze of lines east of Ostrava, ArcelorMittal locomotives access main line tracks at several locations. Locomotives haul internal traffic including regular trains of molten iron torpedo wagons usually worked by Class 729.5 or Class 729.6 locomotives (ballasted industrial versions of ČD Class 731s). The internal railway network stretches to almost 200 km.

In 2015 CZ LOKO won a contract to operate the ArcelorMittal complex. The contract involves servicing the locomotive fleet, and the leasing of a batch of 20 rebuilt Class 741.7 locomotives (741.711–730) that will replace most of the existing ArcelorMittal fleet. Class 741.7 are fitted with CAT 3508C engines. The first emerged in late 2015 and carries CZ LOKO livery. All remaining locomotives are due to be delivered in 2016. At the time of writing 740.417/463/466/467/725/831 have been withdrawn from the ArcelorMittal fleet for rebuilding as Class 741.7 but the order in which these are to be rebuilt is not yet known.

Number	Builder	Built	Type	kW	Details	Notes
704.521-4	ČKD	1992	T238.0	250	Bo DE	
704.522-2	ČKD	1992	T238.0	250	Bo DE	
704.523-0	ČKD	1992	T238.0	250	Bo DE	
709.506-0	ČKD	1993	T239.1	327	Bo DE	
709.508-6	ČKD	1993	T239.1	327	Bo DE	
709.509-4	ČKD	1993	T239.1	327	Bo DE	
709.514-4	ČKD	1993	T239.1	327	Bo DE	
711.589-2	ŽOS Zvo	1996	ex-T334.1	210	C DE	
729.501-7	ČKD	1983	T419.0	600	Bo-Bo DE	
729.505-8	ČKD	1986	T419.0	600	Bo-Bo DE	
729.506-6	ČKD	1986	T419.0	600	Bo-Bo DE	
729.511-6	ČKD	1986	T419.0	600	Bo-Bo DE	
729.602-3	ČKD	1989	T419.1	600	Bo-Bo DE	
729.603-1	ČKD	1989	T419.1	600	Bo-Bo DE	
729.608-0	ČKD	1989	T419.1	600	Bo-Bo DE	
729.611-4	ČKD	1991	T419.1	600	Bo-Bo DE	
740.405-6	ČKD	1986	T448.0	883	Bo-Bo DE	
740.462-7	ČKD	1980	T448.0	883	Bo-Bo DE	Ex-Polish industry T448.P106
740.464-3	ČKD	1979	T448.0	883	Bo-Bo DE	Ex-Polish industry T448.P055
740.527-7	ČKD	1975	T448.0	883	Bo-Bo DE	
740.600-2	ČKD	1976	T448.0	883	Bo-Bo DE	
740.689-5	ČKD	1980	T448.0	883	Bo-Bo DE	
740.813-1	ČKD	1984	T448.0	883	Bo-Bo DE	
740.847-9	ČKD	1985	T448.0	883	Bo-Bo DE	
741.711-6	CZ LOKO	r2015	ex-T448.0	1000	Bo-Bo DE	Rebuilt ex-740.
741.712-4	CZ LOKO	r2016	ex-T448.0	1000	Bo-Bo DE	Rebuilt ex-740.
741.713-2	CZ LOKO	r2016	ex-T448.0	1000	Bo-Bo DE	Rebuilt ex-740.
741.714-0	CZ LOKO	r2016	ex-T448.0	1000	Bo-Bo DE	Rebuilt ex-740.417
741.715-7	CZ LOKO	r2016	ex-T448.0	1000	Bo-Bo DE	Rebuilt ex-740.
741.716-5	CZ LOKO	r	ex-T448.0	1000	Bo-Bo DE	Rebuilt ex-740.
741.717-3	CZ LOKO	r	ex-T448.0	1000	Bo-Bo DE	Rebuilt ex-740.
741.718-1	CZ LOKO	r	ex-T448.0	1000	Bo-Bo DE	Rebuilt ex-740.
741.719-9	CZ LOKO	r	ex-T448.0	1000	Bo-Bo DE	Rebuilt ex-740.
741.720-7	CZ LOKO	r	ex-T448.0	1000	Bo-Bo DE	Rebuilt ex-740.
741.721-5	CZ LOKO	r	ex-T448.0	1000	Bo-Bo DE	Rebuilt ex-740.
741.722-3	CZ LOKO	r	ex-T448.0	1000	Bo-Bo DE	Rebuilt ex-740.
741.723-1	CZ LOKO	r	ex-T448.0	1000	Bo-Bo DE	Rebuilt ex-740.
741.724-9	CZ LOKO	r	ex-T448.0	1000	Bo-Bo DE	Rebuilt ex-740.
741.725-6	CZ LOKO	r	ex-T448.0	1000	Bo-Bo DE	Rebuilt ex-740.
741.726-4	CZ LOKO	r	ex-T448.0	1000	Bo-Bo DE	Rebuilt ex-740.
741.727-2	CZ LOKO	r	ex-T448.0	1000	Bo-Bo DE	Rebuilt ex-740.
741.728-0	CZ LOKO	r	ex-T448.0	1000	Bo-Bo DE	Rebuilt ex-740.
741.729-8	CZ LOKO	r	ex-T448.0	1000	Bo-Bo DE	Rebuilt ex-740.
741.730-6	CZ LOKO	r	ex-T448.0	1000	Bo-Bo DE	Rebuilt ex-740.

5.2.3. AUTODOPRAVA HANZALÍK   CZ

www.hanzalik.cz   VKM: AHD

Hanzalík is an automotive company that launched rail operations in 2012. It operates trains of Mattoni bottled mineral water from the Kyselka bottling plant (accessed via the reopened 9 km branch from Vojkovice nad Ohří) to Chomutov. The trains, dubbed "Mattoni Express", are then hauled to Prostějov by ČD Cargo. A second Hanzalík locomotive then takes over to the distribution centre at Mostkovice. Locomotives may be hired from KPKV for use on these trains.

Hanzalík's two Class 749 diesels (749.262 is unsilenced) are painted in an attractive two-tone blue livery. Hanzalík also owns two Class 831 heritage DMUs (see Preserved DMUs section).

Number	Builder	Built	Type	kW	Details	Notes
749.262-2	ČKD	1970	T478.1	1103	Bo-Bo DE	Ex-752.066
749.263-0	ČKD	1970	T478.1	1103	Bo-Bo DE	Ex-752.056

5.2.4. AŽD PRAHA   CZ

www.azd.cz

Automatizace Železniční Dopravy (AŽD) Praha is a large Praha-based company which develops and manufactures railway and road signalling, safety and telecommunication equipment for the global market. 749.039 (which has been in AŽD Praha advertising livery for a number of years) was purchased from ČD in 2014.

DMU 851.026 was converted by CZ LOKO Česká Třebová in 2013 as an ETCS test car for touring the network. Along with an ex-ČD Class 050 bogie trailer, both have been renumbered in the 12-digit EVN series and are normally based in part of the ČD depot at Kolín. The Class 851 was fitted with a new CAT C27 engine and the interior has been fitted out with sleeping accommodation and a new toilet. A second trailer was purchased in 2015.

AŽD Praha produces an excellent monthly video magazine "Pozor Vlak", which is available (with English subtitles) via YouTube – see www.youtube.com/user/azdpraha1. Livery is dark blue & yellow.

Number	Builder	Built	Type	kW	Details	Notes
749.039-4	ČKD	1967	T478.1	1103	Bo-Bo DE	Ex-751.039
50 54 20-29 103-9	ČKD	1966	Bmx765	-	2-2	Ex-ČD 050.024 (S)
60 54 89-29 001-1	ČKD	1967	Bmx765	-	2-2	Ex-ČD 050.004/50 54 20-29 111
99 54 91-65 001-7	ČKD	1968	M286.1	630	B-2	Ex-ČD 851.026

5.2.5. BF LOGISTICS   CZ/SK

www.bfl.cz   VKM: BFL

This Praha based company was established in 2005. It operates freight and infrastructure services, mainly using pairs of Classes 740/741/742 in the Czech Republic and also Slovakia, as well as some cross-border services into Hungary and Germany (from Děčín), in partnership with other operators. The company also operates 27 railway sidings in the Czech Republic.

BF Logistics livery is orange & grey. Locomotives have been noted visiting the ČD depot at Valašské Meziříčí for maintenance.

Number	Builder	Built	Type	kW	Details	Notes
701.535-7	ČKD	1962	T211.1	169	B DM	Ex-T211.0917
703.005-9	TSM	1977	T212.1	169	B DH	
703.007-5	TSM	1977	T212.1	169	B DH	
703.008-3	TSM	1977	T212.1	169	B DH	UNEX, Uničov
703.022-4	TSM	1978	T212.1	169	B DH	
703.599-1	TSM	1977	T212.1	169	B DH	
703.632-0	TSM	1978	T212.1	169	B DH	
704.529-7	ČKD	1992	T238.0	250	Bo DE	
704.533-9	ČKD	1992	T238.0	250	Bo DE	
704.545-3	ČKD	1993	T238.0	250	Bo DE	
710.597-6	ČKD	1965	T334.0	301	C DH	
740.445-2	ČKD	1988	T448.0	883	Bo-Bo DE	Leased from Česká Lokomotivka
740.621-8	ČKD	1978	T448.0	883	Bo-Bo DE	
740.634-1	ČKD	1978	T448.0	883	Bo-Bo DE	
740.705-9	ČKD	1982	T448.0	883	Bo-Bo DE	
740.709-1	ČKD	1982	T448.0	883	Bo-Bo DE	
740.770-3	ČKD	1983	T448.0	883	Bo-Bo DE	
740.861-0	ČKD	1985	T448.0	883	Bo-Bo DE	
740.899-0	ČKD	1986	T448.0	883	Bo-Bo DE	
741.517-7	ČKD	1976	T448.0	883	Bo-Bo DE	Rebuilt ex-740.560
741.518-5	ČKD	1986	T448.0	883	Bo-Bo DE	Rebuilt ex-740.893
742.506-9	ČKD	1983	T466.2	883	Bo-Bo DE	Ex-742.613
742.615-8	ČKD	1984	T466.2	883	Bo-Bo DE	Ex-742.014
742.627-3	ČKD	1985	T466.2	883	Bo-Bo DE	Ex-742.524
744.502-6	ČKD	1970	T475.1	920	Bo-Bo DE	
770.536-1	ČKD	1987	T669.0	993	Co-Co DE	

5.2.6. COAL SERVICES (MOST)   CZ

www.coalservices.cz   VKM: Coal

Coal Services is part of the Czech Coal Group which controls the largest coal reserves in the Czech Republic. It was established in 2005 with assets that included the Mostecká Uhelná Spolecnost (MUS) mining company. The company has an extensive private network around Most and owns a large fleet of more than 30 Bo-Bo-Bo 1500 V DC "Crocodile" mining locomotives. 90 of these Škoda-built machines were constructed in the 127.2xx, 127.6xx and 127.7xx series' in the 1980s; some are also operated by Sokolovská Uhelná (SU). Although most were built as recently as 1989 the decline in coal mining in recent years has seen a number of this class scrapped already. Ex-Coal Services 127.673 is now operated by SU as 127.503. Casual travellers through the area may be lucky and catch a passing glimpse of one of these mining locomotives, often as the main line crosses over one of the Coal Services lines, but there are also a number of locations available to view them at work for those who wish to explore the area.

The Class 127s haul coal from the large opencast sites around Třebusice, west of Most, to the coal processing plant at Čepirohy, just south of the town. Many trains are then forwarded (or propelled) in shorter trains to Počerady power station along a non-electrified freight only line by Class 709 or 740 diesels.

Coal Services' depot is at Komořany, near Třebusice. Livery for the diesel locomotives is green, offset with yellow and red stripes. Internal numbers are carried by the diesels. Recently repainted Class 127s are in all over green, whilst others still operate in the original all-over red.

Number	Builder	Built	Type	kW	Details	Notes
127.670-8	Škoda	1984	27 E	2190	Bo-Bo-Bo E DC	
127.676-5	Škoda	1985	27 E	2190	Bo-Bo-Bo E DC	
127.679-9	Škoda	1985	27 E	2190	Bo-Bo-Bo E DC	
127.681-5	Škoda	1985	27 E	2190	Bo-Bo-Bo E DC	
127.682-3	Škoda	1985	27 E	2190	Bo-Bo-Bo E DC	
127.683-1	Škoda	1985	27 E	2190	Bo-Bo-Bo E DC	
127.684-9	Škoda	1985	27 E	2190	Bo-Bo-Bo E DC	
127.685-6	Škoda	1985	27 E	2190	Bo-Bo-Bo E DC	
127.687-2	Škoda	1985	27 E	2190	Bo-Bo-Bo E DC	
127.690-6	Škoda	1985	27 E	2190	Bo-Bo-Bo E DC	
127.696-3	Škoda	1985	27 E	2190	Bo-Bo-Bo E DC	
127.698-9	Škoda	1985	27 E	2190	Bo-Bo-Bo E DC	
127.699-7	Škoda	1989	27 E	2190	Bo-Bo-Bo E DC	
127.700-3	Škoda	1989	27 E	2190	Bo-Bo-Bo E DC	
127.701-1	Škoda	1989	27 E	2190	Bo-Bo-Bo E DC	
127.702-9	Škoda	1989	27 E	2190	Bo-Bo-Bo E DC	
127.703-7	Škoda	1989	27 E	2190	Bo-Bo-Bo E DC	
127.704-5	Škoda	1989	27 E	2190	Bo-Bo-Bo E DC	
127.705-2	Škoda	1989	27 E	2190	Bo-Bo-Bo E DC	
127.706-0	Škoda	1989	27 E	2190	Bo-Bo-Bo E DC	
127.707-8	Škoda	1989	27 E	2190	Bo-Bo-Bo E DC	
127.708-6	Škoda	1989	27 E	2190	Bo-Bo-Bo E DC	
127.712-8	Škoda	1989	27 E	2190	Bo-Bo-Bo E DC	
127.714-4	Škoda	1989	27 E	2190	Bo-Bo-Bo E DC	
127.715-1	Škoda	1989	27 E	2190	Bo-Bo-Bo E DC	
127.716-9	Škoda	1989	27 E	2190	Bo-Bo-Bo E DC	
127.717-7	Škoda	1989	27 E	2190	Bo-Bo-Bo E DC	
127.718-5	Škoda	1989	27 E	2190	Bo-Bo-Bo E DC	
127.719-3	Škoda	1989	27 E	2190	Bo-Bo-Bo E DC	
127.720-1	Škoda	1989	27 E	2190	Bo-Bo-Bo E DC	
127.721-9	Škoda	1989	27 E	2190	Bo-Bo-Bo E DC	
127.723-5	Škoda	1989	27 E	2190	Bo-Bo-Bo E DC	
709.502-9	ČKD	1993	T239.1	327	Bo DE	Internal 304
709.503-7	ČKD	1993	T239.1	327	Bo DE	Internal 301
709.504-5	ČKD	1993	T239.1	327	Bo DE	Internal 302
709.505-2	ČKD	1993	T239.1	327	Bo DE	Internal 303
709.517-7	ČKD	1994	T239.1	327	Bo DE	Internal 305
709.524-3	ČKD	1995	T239.1	327	Bo DE	Internal 306
709.525-2	ČKD	1995	T239.1	327	Bo DE	Internal 307

709.534-2	ČKD	1996	T239.1	327	Bo DE		Internal 308
709.702-5	CZ LOKO	2006	709.7	403	Bo DE		Internal 309
709.703-3	CZ LOKO	2007	709.7	403	Bo DE		Internal 310
709.704-1	CZ LOKO	2007	709.7	403	Bo DE		Internal 311
721.556-9	ČKD	1971	T458.1	551	Bo-Bo DE		Internal 209
740.585-5	ČKD	1976	T448.0	883	Bo-Bo DE		Internal 230
740.888-3	ČKD	1986	T448.0	883	Bo-Bo DE		Internal 266
740.889-1	ČKD	1986	T448.0	883	Bo-Bo DE		Internal 267
740.890-9	ČKD	1986	T448.0	883	Bo-Co DE		Internal 268
770.516-3	ČKD	1980	T669.0	993	Co-Co DE		Internal 239

5.2.7. CENTRAL RAILWAYS (CRW) SK

www.crw.sk   VKM: CRW

This Košice-based Slovak open access freight operator, part of Constantin Group, specialises in the movement of oil and chemicals using its mixed diesel/electric fleet. It can also be seen hauling coal trains in the Bratislava area. The electric fleet includes five former Romanian Class 43 AC electrics, renumbered as Class 241. A Bo-Bo-Bo Class 362 has also been sourced from Slovenia, but to date has remained stored at ŽOS Zvolen. Livery is deep orange & black.

Number	Builder	Built	Type	kW	Details	Notes
182.115-6	Škoda	1965	E669.2	2790	Co-Co E DC	
189.153-0	Siemens	2009	ES 64 F4	6400	Bo-Bo E MS	Leased from MRCE
241.001-7	Končar	1973	CFR 43	3400	Bo-Bo E AC	Ex-CFR 43.0065
241.002-5	Končar	1973	CFR 43	3400	Bo-Bo E AC	Ex-CFR 43.0018
241.003-3	Končar	1973	CFR 43	3400	Bo-Bo E AC	Ex-CFR 43.0009
241.004-1	Končar	1973	CFR 43	3400	Bo-Bo E AC	Ex-CFR 43.0017
241.005-8	Končar	1973	CFR 43	3400	Bo-Bo E AC	Ex-CFR 43.0120
362.034-5	Ansaldo SG	1963	SŽ 362	2790	Bo-Bo-Bo E DC	Ex-SŽ(Slovenia). (S) ŽOS Zvolen
740.044-3	ČKD	1978	T448.0	883	Bo-Bo DE	Ex-Polish industry T448.P044
740.049-2	ČKD	1978	T448.0	883	Bo-Bo DE	Ex-Polish industry T448.P049
740.595-4	ČKD	1976	T448.0	883	Bo-Bo DE	
740.722-4	ČKD	1982	T448.0	883	Bo-Bo DE	
742.193-6	ČKD	1980	T466.2	883	Bo-Bo DE	Ex-ČD
742.275-1	ČKD	1982	T466.2	883	Bo-Bo DE	Ex-ČD

5.2.8. CZ LOKO CZ

www.czloko.cz   VKM: CZL

Probably the largest works in the Czech Republic is the CZ LOKO workshops at Česká Třebová (called ČMKS until 2006). CZ LOKO has in recent years specialised in diesel locomotive overhauls and rebuilds using new CAT engines, from straightforward overhauls to more radical full rebuilds, for both the home market and for export. The most successful rebuilds have been of the Class 740/742 and 750/753 types, although the company overhauls a wide range of rolling stock, also including electric locomotives and SŽDC departmental railcars.

In 2015 the company secured an order for 20 Class 741.7s from ArcelorMittal of Ostrava (see section 5.2.2). The history of the first ten Class 741.7 is complex. 741.701/707 both initially operated in the Czech Republic but have now been exported to DP of Italy while 741.708/709 were built for Turkish State Railways. 741.702–705 form part of Strabag's fleet and 741.706 is operated by SD-KD. 741.710 forms part of CZ LOKO's own locomotive hire fleet, which also includes four Class 742.7. These can often be found operating trains on the main line for Unipetrol Doprava.

There are four former ČD Class 750/753 that are owned by CZ LOKO but still stored in the ČD Česká Třebová depot yard.

As well as the Česká Třebová site, CZ LOKO has a second site at Jihlava (the former JLS workshops). CZ LOKO livery is red & grey.

Number	Builder	Built	Type	kW	Details	Notes
704.201-3	ČKD	1992	A219.0	192	Bo BE	CZ LOKO, Jihlava (A219.0001)
704.703-8	CZ LOKO	r2012	ex-T238.0	328	Bo DE	Rebuilt ex-704.508

709.401-4	ČMKS	2004	709.4	392	Bo DE		
709.601-9	ČMKS	r1999	ex-T239.2	390	Bo DE	Ex-T239.2001/DB 353 001	
719.701-5	CZ LOKO	2008	719.7	403	Bo DE	CZ LOKO, Jihlava	
741.710-8	CZ LOKO	r2015	ex-T448.0	1000	Bo-Bo DE	Rebuilt ex-740.	
742.702-4	CZ LOKO	r2010	ex-T466.2	1000	Bo-Bo DE	Internal 018. Rebuilt ex-742.257	
742.703-2	CZ LOKO	r2010	ex-T466.2	1000	Bo-Bo DE	Internal 019. Rebuilt ex-742.011	
742.704-0	CZ LOKO	r2010	ex-T466.2	1000	Bo-Bo DE	Internal 023. Rebuilt ex-742.288	
742.705-7	CZ LOKO	r2010	ex-T466.2	1000	Bo-Bo DE	Internal 024. Rebuilt ex-742.177	
744.001-9	CZ LOKO	2012	744.0	1000	Bo-Bo DE		
750.063-0	ČKD	1972	T478.3	1325	Bo-Bo DE	Ex-753.063. (S) ČD Česká Třebová	
750.116-6	ČKD	1973	T478.3	1325	Bo-Bo DE	Ex-753.116. (S) ČD Česká Třebová	
750.380-8	ČKD	1977	T478.3	1325	Bo-Bo DE	Ex-753.380. (S) ČD Česká Třebová	
753.265-8	ČKD	1975	T478.3	1325	Bo-Bo DE	(S) ČD Česká Třebová	
753.605-5	CZ LOKO	r2016	ex-T478.3	1550	Bo-Bo DE	Rebuilt ex-750.288	
794.001-8	CZ LOKO	2014	794.0	328	B DE	On lease to ČD Praha	

5.2.9. DPOV   CZ

www.dpov.cz

DPOV (Dílny Pro Opravy Vozidel) is part of the Czech Railways Group, principally servicing rolling stock for its parent company (ČD) and mainly operating out of former ČD depots. The main workshops are at Přerov, which mainly undertakes electric locomotive overhauls and Nymburk, which deals with diesels and other types such as departmental vehicles. At Veselí nad Moravou DPOV shares depot space with ČD and a new shed has been constructed to maintain and overhaul ČD's large Class 814 Regionova DMU fleet. There are further DPOV outposts at Olomouc, Valašské Meziříčí and Břeclav. The Class 799s are ex-ČD. Livery is light blue & white.

Number	Builder	Built	Type	kW	Details	Notes
141.023-2	Škoda	1959	E499.1	2032	Bo-Bo E DC	(S) Přerov station
141.055-4	Škoda	1960	E499.1	2032	Bo-Bo E DC	(S) Přerov station
703.717-9	JLS		ex-T212.0	170	B DH	Nymburk. Frame ex-702.
740.603-6	ČKD	1977	T448.0	883	Bo-Bo DE	Nymburk (stripped)
742.197-7	ČKD	1980	T466.2	883	Bo-Bo DE	Nymburk (stripped)
742.218-1	ČKD	1980	T466.2	883	Bo-Bo DE	Nymburk (stripped)
799.011-2	JLS		ex-T212.0	37	Bo BE/DE	Přerov. Frame ex-702.023.
799.015-3	JLS		ex-T212.0	37	Bo BE/DE	Veselí nad Mor. Frame ex-702.042.
799.022-9	JLS		ex-T211	37	Bo BE/DE	Přerov. Frame ex-701.058.
799.037-7	JLS		ex-T212-0	37	Bo BE/DE	Nymburk. Frame ex-702.025.

5.2.10. ELEKTRIZACE ŽELEZNICE PRAHA (EŽ)   CZ/SK

www.elzel.cz   VKM: ELZEL

EŽ, established in 1954, is a Praha-based maintenance and construction company specialising in overhead electrification work and is active in both countries. The company owns a fleet of mainly small diesel locomotives, as well as some Class 740. The odd-looking MV97s were constructed on the frames of former Class 721 locomotives for both catenary maintenance and works train haulage with an overhead line inspection platform. They have been fitted with CAT 3406 DTTA engines. EŽ livery is light blue & silver.

Number	Builder	Built	Type	kW	Details	Notes
703.702-1	JLS	1998	ex-T212.1	170	B DH	Frame ex-
703.712-0	JLS	2011	ex-T212.1	170	B DH	Frame ex-703.006
703.713-8	JLS		ex-T212.1	170	B DH	Frame ex-703.004
703.714-6	JLS		ex-T212.1	170	B DH	Frame ex-
703.715-3	JLS		ex-T212.1	170	B DH	Frame ex-
703.716-1	JLS		ex-T212.1	170	B DH	Frame ex-703.015
720.508-1	ČKD	1958	T435.0	551	Bo-Bo DE	
720.539-6	ČKD	1960	T435.0	551	Bo-Bo DE	Ex-720.601
720.541-2	ČKD	1960	T435.0	551	Bo-Bo DE	
730.632-7	ČKD	1989	T457.0	600	Bo-Bo DE	

▲ EŽ uses a number of rebuilt Class 703/797 4-wheel shunting locomotives. On 10 May 2014 797.706 stands at Veselí nad Lužnicí during the rebuilding of the station. **Robert Pritchard**

▼ METRANS operates several daily intermodal trains between Germany and its Czech terminals at Praha Uhříněves and Česká Třebová. On 10 March 2015 386.013 passes Roztoky u Prahy with train Nex42313 from Hamburg to Praha Uhříněves. **Robert Pritchard**

740.559-0	ČKD	1976	T448.0	883	Bo-Bo DE	
740.609-3	ČKD	1977	T448.0	883	Bo-Bo DE	
740.655-6	ČKD	1979	T448.0	883	Bo-Bo DE	
740.676-2	ČKD	1979	T448.0	883	Bo-Bo DE	
740.843-8	ČKD	1984	T448.0	883	Bo-Bo DE	
797.701-0	ČMKS	2002	ex-T212.0	187	B DE	Frame ex-702.
797.702-8	ČMKS	2002	ex-T212.0	187	B DE	Frame ex-702.
797.703-6	ČMKS	2002	ex-T212.0	187	B DE	Frame ex-702.
797.704-4	ČMKS	2003	ex-T212.0	187	B DE	Frame ex-702.
797.705-1	ČMKS	2003	ex-T212.0	187	B DE	Frame ex-702.
797.706-9	ČMKS	2003	ex-T212.0	187	B DE	Frame ex-702.
797.707-7	ČMKS	2006	ex-T212.0	187	B DE	Frame ex-702.
MV97.001	JLS	1997	ex-T458.1	285	Bo-Bo DE	Frame ex-721.201
MV97.002	JLS	2000	ex-T458.1	285	Bo-Bo DE	Frame ex-721.507
MV97.003	JLS	2001	ex-T458.1	285	Bo-Bo DE	Frame ex-721.137

5.2.11. EXPRESS GROUP SK

www.express-rail.sk
VKM: EXSK

Express Group (previously Express Rail Slovakia until 2014) is a Bratislava based open-access freight operator owned by Optifin Invest, mainly using leased locomotives on a variety of freight flows in Slovakia.

Number	Builder	Built	Type	kW	Details	Notes
242.556-9	Škoda	1975	S499.02	3080	Bo-Bo E AC	Ex-ČD 242.202. Leased from ZOS Zvolen
390.001-6	Siemens	2011	ES 64 F4	6400	Bo-Bo E MS	Ex-189.845
740.628-3	ČKD	1978	T448.0	883	Bo-Bo DE	Leased from ZOS Zvolen
740.790-1	ČKD	1983	T448.0	883	Bo-Bo DE	Leased from ZOS Zvolen
740.947-7	ČKD	1988	T448.0	883	Bo-Bo DE	Leased from ZOS Zvolen
742.610-0	ČKD	1983	T466.2	883	Bo-Bo DE	Ex-ČD 742.164. Leased from ZOS Zvolen
761.101-5	Siemens	2005	ER 20	2000	Bo-Bo DE	Ex-Dispolok ER 20-009[II]

5.2.12. GJW PRAHA CZ

www.gjw-praha.cz
VKM: GJW

This Praha-based infrastructure company supplies locomotives to haul infrastructure and overhead wiring trains country-wide. All six locomotives in the fleet can sometimes be seen engaged in one particular project, such as a station reconstruction. Livery is yellow, white & blue.

Number	Builder	Built	Type	kW	Details	Notes
702.087-3	TSM	1971	T212.0	147	B DH	
721.526-2	ČKD	1968	T458.1	551	Bo-Bo DE	
721.540-3	ČKD	1968	T458.1	551	Bo-Bo DE	
740.561-6	ČKD	1976	T448.0	883	Bo-Bo DE	
740.619-2	ČKD	1978	T448.0	883	Bo-Bo DE	
740.865-1	ČKD	1985	T448.0	883	Bo-Bo DE	

5.2.13. HORNONITRIANSKE BANE PRIEVIDZA (HBP) SK

www.hbp.sk
VKM: HBP

The majority of Slovakia's modest coal production is in the Prievidza area, although most of the coal mined from the three HBP-operated brown coal miles at Nováky, Handlová and Cigeľ – all south of Prievidza in the Upper Nitra brown coal basin – is consumed locally at the large Nováky power station. The Nováky plant (operated by Slovenské Elektrárne) is the largest generator of electricity in Slovakia.

HBP operates its own coal trains, mainly using Class 770 and 771 Co-Co locomotives which carry a deep green livery. The locomotive depot is at Cigeľ. Visitors to the depot in 2015 also found two former DB Schenker Poland ČKD Co-Cos stored, to provide spares for the operational fleet.

Number	Builder	Built	Type	kW	Details	Notes
620.010-1	ČKD	1988	S200	993	Co-Co DE	(S) Ex-DBS Poland S200-2108
620.037-3	ČKD	1986	S200	993	Co-Co DE	(S) Ex-DBS Poland S200-297
721.555-1	ČKD	1971	T458.1	551	Bo-Bo DE	Ex-Coal Services Most
740.602-8	ČKD	1976	T448.0	883	Bo-Bo DE	Carries original No. T448.0602
740.606-9	ČKD	1977	T448.0	883	Bo-Bo DE	Carries original No. T448.0606
770.026-3	SMZ	1967	T669.0	993	Co-Co DE	Ex-ZSSK Cargo
770.522-1	ČKD	1981	T669.0	993	Co-Co DE	Carries original No. T669.0522
770.613-8	SMZ	1969	T669.0	993	Co-Co DE	Ex-Coal Services Most
771.501-4	SMZ	1969	T669.1	993	Co-Co DE	Carries original No. T669.1501
771.509-7	SMZ	1970	T669.1	993	Co-Co DE	Carries original No. T669.1509
771.514-7	SMZ	1971	T669.1	993	Co-Co DE	Carries original No. T669.1514

5.2.14. IDS CARGO   CZ/SK

www.ids-cargo.cz

VKM: IDSC

Inženýrské a Dopravní Stavby, or IDS Cargo, is an Olomouc-based operator supplying traction for infrastructure projects and also for its own freight trains. The company was established in 2007 as a subsidiary of construction company IDS. It has achieved success as an open access freight operator, using ex-ČD and ZSSK locomotives (some Class 121 were acquired from CTL in Poland, and indeed are still registered in Poland). It also operates some cross-border freight into both Germany and Poland and operates a number of industrial sidings in the Czech Republic.

Newer locomotives have also been acquired, in the form of Voith diesel locomotive 783.001 and also a TRAXX Class 186 electric. Diesel locomotives are maintained at the Správa Ústecké Dráhy (SUD) depot at Teplice and can often be found stabled at Ústí nad Labem Střekov station.

Livery is deep orange & cream.

Number	Builder	Built	Type	kW	Details	Notes
121.041-8	Škoda	1960	E469.1	2032	Bo-Bo E DC	
121.065-7	Škoda	1960	E469.1	2032	Bo-Bo E DC	
121.077-2	Škoda	1960	E469.1	2032	Bo-Bo E DC	Registered in Poland as 150.751
121.084-8	Škoda	1961	E469.1	2032	Bo-Bo E DC	Registered in Poland as 150.754
140.094-4	Škoda	1958	E499.0	2032	Bo-Bo E DC	
182.041-4	Škoda	1964	E669.2	2790	Co-Co E DC	Leased from ZOS Zvolen
186.435-4	Bombardier	2015	TRAXX	5600	Bo-Bo E MS	Leased from RAILPOOL
242.288-9	Škoda	1971	S499.02	3080	Bo-Bo E AC	Ex-BDŽ 43.523
700.687-7	ČKD	1960	T211.0	121	B DM	
700.700-8	ČKD	1960	T211.0	121	B DM	
701.478-0	ČKD	1962	T211.1	147	B DM	Ex-700.686
701.738-7	ČKD	1959	T211.1	147	B DM	ADM, Olomouc
701.739-5	ČKD	1958	T211.1	147	B DM	
702.531-5	TSM	1967	T212.0	147	B DM	Dalkia, Kolín
702.673-5	TSM		T212.0	147	B DM	
703.503-3	TSM	1972	T212.1	169	B DH	Kovošrot, Praha Hostivař
703.591-8	TSM	1976	T212.1	169	B DH	Dalkia, Kolín
704.513-1	ČKD	1992	T238.0	250	Bo DE	
710.455-7	TSM	1972	T334.0	301	C DH	
710.666-9	ČKD	1965	T334.0	301	C DH	
710.779-0	SMZ	1967	T334.0	301	C DH	
710.833-5	SMZ	1968	T334.0	301	C DH	
711.703-9	JLS	r1998	ex-T334.0	365	C DE	
721.179-0	ČKD	1965	T458.1	551	Bo-Bo DE	
721.203-8	ČKD	1965	T458.1	551	Bo-Bo DE	ADM, Olomouc
730.634-3	ČKD	1989	T457.0	600	Bo-Bo DE	
730.635-0	ČKD	1989	T457.0	600	Bo-Bo DE	
740.459-3	ČKD	1989	T448.0	883	Bo-Bo DE	Ex-T448.0959
740.518-6	ČKD	1974	T448.0	883	Bo-Bo DE	
740.721-6	ČKD	1982	T448.0	883	Bo-Bo DE	C&T Litoměřice livery
740.758-8	ČKD	1983	T448.0	883	Bo-Bo DE	
740.763-8	ČKD	1983	T448.0	883	Bo-Bo DE	
740.860-2	ČKD	1985	T448.0	883	Bo-Bo DE	C&T Litoměřice livery

742.260-3	ČKD	1982	T466.2	883	Bo-Bo DE	
742.516-8	ČKD	1984	T466.2	883	Bo-Bo DE	
742.522-6	ČKD	1985	T466.2	883	Bo-Bo DE	
742.529-1	ČKD	1985	T466.2	883	Bo-Bo DE	
749.162-4	ČKD	1969	T478.1	1103	Bo-Bo DE	Ex-751.162
749.181-4	ČKD	1970	T478.1	1103	Bo-Bo DE	Ex-751.181
783.001-1	Voith	2009	Maxima 30cc	2750	Co-Co DH	Built as 263 003 for Germany

5.2.15. JUNIOR MARKET CZ

www.juniormarket.cz VKM: JUMA

This Uhlířské Janovice-based company has a diverse portfolio ranging from a grocery store and kitchenware shop to a rail transportation company! Its rail transport business started in 2006, using a fleet of mainly former ČD or ZSSK locomotives. The company hires these locomotives to main line operators or for spot-hire and also offers private or corporate special trains. Junior Market locomotives can often be found stabled at Kolín station. The company also owns a number of heritage DMUs (see Preserved DMUs section for details).

Number	Builder	Built	Type	kW	Details	Notes
141.018-2	Škoda	1959	E499.1	2032	Bo-Bo E DC	
710.433-4	TSM	1971	T334.0	301	C DH	Ex-T334.0933
710.466-4	TSM	1973	T334.0	301	C DH	Ex-T334.0966
710.781-6	SMZ	1967	T334.0	301	C DH	Ex-T334.0781
710.797-2	SMZ	1967	T334.0	301	C DH	Ex-T334.0797
720.099-1	ČKD	1961	T435.0	551	Bo-Bo DE	Carries original No. T435.0099
721.081-8	ČKD	1964	T458.1	551	Bo-Bo DE	Ex-ZSSK
721.113-9	ČKD	1964	T458.1	551	Bo-Bo DE	Ex-ZSSK
721.122-0	ČKD	1964	T458.1	551	Bo-Bo DE	Ex-ZSSK
721.130-3	ČKD	1964	T458.1	551	Bo-Bo DE	Ex-ZSSK
721.549-4	ČKD	1971	T458.1	551	Bo-Bo DE	Carries original No. T458.1549
726.562-2	TSM	1966	T444.15	515	B-B DH	Ex-T444.1562
752.069-5	ČKD	1970	T478.2	1103	Bo-Bo DE	

5.2.16. JUSO SK/CZ

www.juso.sk VKM: JUSO

Juso is a Zvolen based locomotive hire company. Locomotives are often hired to infrastructure operators to support engineering works etc, mainly in Slovakia.

Number	Builder	Built	Type	kW	Details	Notes
703.554-6	TSM	1974	T212.1	169	B DH	
703.555-3	TSM	1974	T212.1	169	B DH	
703.556-1	TSM	1974	T212.1	169	B DH	
704.009-0	ČKD	1991	T238.0	250	Bo DE	Ex-T238.0009
704.032-2	ČKD	1992	T238.0	250	Bo DE	Ex-704.532/T238.0032
704.038-9	ČKD	1992	T238.0	250	Bo DE	Ex-704.538/T238.0038
704.510-7	ČKD	1991	T238.0	250	Bo DE	Ex-T238.0010
720.594-1	ČKD	1962	T435.0	551	Bo-Bo DE	Carries original No. T435.0594
740.794-3	ČKD	1983	T448.0	883	Bo-Bo DE	
740.804-0	ČKD	1984	T448.0	883	Bo-Bo DE	
740.821-4	ČKD	1984	T448.0	883	Bo-Bo DE	

5.2.17. PROVOZ A OPRAVY LOKOMOTIV (KK) CZ/SK

VKM: KK

KK is a Býškovice-based locomotive hire company, also specialising in locomotive repairs. The company usually hires its locomotives to infrastructure companies such as EŽ and they can be seen in either the Czech Republic or Slovakia.

Number	Builder	Built	Type	kW	Details	Notes
701.599-3	ČKD	1958	T211.1	147	B DM	
702.652-9	TSM	1969	T212.0	147	B DM	EZ Velký Osek
702.653-7	TSM	1969	T212.0	147	B DM	(S) Brno Dolní
703.549-6	TSM	1973	T212.1	169	B DH	Veselí nad Lužnicí
703.558-7	TSM	1974	T212.1	169	B DH	EZ Velký Osek
703.630-4	TSM	1978	T212.1	169	B DH	EZ Velký Osek
720.091-8	ČKD	1961	T435.0	551	Bo-Bo DE	Carries original No. T435.0091
740.575-6	ČKD	1976	T448.0	883	Bo-Bo DE	DPOV Přerov
740.732-3	ČKD	1982	T448.0	883	Bo-Bo DE	

5.2.18. KLADENSKÁ DOPRAVNÍ A STROJNÍ (KDS) CZ/SK

www.kdskladno.cz   VKM: KDS

KDS is a locomotive repair company based in Kladno, the name translating in English as "Kladno Transport & Machinery Ltd". The company (previously named "Radek Sauer" after its Director) also owns a mixed fleet of locomotives which are hired to various companies, including IDS Cargo, Unipetrol, AWT and METRANS. It also owns a small fleet of coaches and operates occasional railtours, usually using one of the Class 750 or 753 "Goggles" locomotives. One of these is also hired to RegioJet for use on the Martin–Zvolen leg of RJ's Praha–Zvolen train.

The workshops at Kladno undertake repairs and overhauls on a wide variety of locomotive types, including electric locomotives.

Number	Builder	Built	Type	kW	Details	Notes
703.021-6	TSM	1978	T212.1	169	B DH	Metal Trade Comax, Velvary
704.518-0	ČKD	1993	T238.0	250	Bo DE	
721.517-1	ČKD	1965	T458.1	551	Bo-Bo DE	
730.613-7	ČKD	1988	T457.0	600	Bo-Bo DE	
730.625-1	ČKD	1989	T457.0	600	Bo-Bo DE	
740.419-7	ČKD	1987	T448.0	883	Bo-Bo-DE	
740.895-8	ČKD	1986	T448.0	883	Bo-Bo DE	
740.898-2	ČKD	1986	T448.0	883	Bo-Bo DE	
750.096-0	ČKD	1976	T478.3	1325	Bo-Bo DE	Ex-ČD 750.312 (frame swap)
751.115-7	ČKD	1968	T478.1	1103	Bo-Bo DE	Ex-ZSSK Cargo
753.197-3	ČKD	1974	T478.3	1325	Bo-Bo DE	
770.529-6	ČKD	1984	T669.0	993	Co-Co DE	
770.541-1	ČKD	1989	T669.0	993	Co-Co DE	Ex-Polish Industry S2134

5.2.19. LOGISTIK A TRANSPORT SLOVAKIA (LTE) SK/CZ

www.lte.sk   VKM: LTE

LTE Slovakia is a subsidiary of the large Austrian open access freight operator LTE (a subsidiary of Graz Köflacher Bahn). The company operates bulk long distance freights between Slovakia, the Czech Republic, Germany and Austria, mainly using its fleet of leased modern diesel and electric locomotives. Only LTE locomotives that are expected to appear in Slovakia and the Czech Republic are listed here. Livery is blue & silver.

Number	Builder	Built	Type	kW	Details	Notes
185.621-0	Bombardier	2008	TRAXX	5600	Bo-Bo E MS	Leased from RAILPOOL
186.237-4	Bombardier	2009	TRAXX	5600	Bo-Bo E MS	
186.238-2	Bombardier	2009	TRAXX	5600	Bo-Bo E MS	
186.426-3	Bombardier	2015	TRAXX	5600	Bo-Bo E MS	Leased from RAILPOOL
189.155-5	Siemens	2009	ES 64 F4	6400	Bo-Bo E MS	Leased from MRCE
189.156-3	Siemens	2009	ES 64 F4	6400	Bo-Bo E MS	Leased from MRCE
189.158-9	Siemens	2010	ES 64 F4	6400	Bo-Bo E MS	Leased from MRCE
193.203-7	Siemens	2014	Vectron AC	6400	Bo-Bo E AC	Leased from ELL
193.207-8	Siemens	2014	Vectron MS	6400	Bo-Bo E MS	Leased from ELL
193.215-1	Siemens	2014	Vectron MS	6400	Bo-Bo E MS	Leased from ELL
193.216-9	Siemens	2014	Vectron MS	6400	Bo-Bo E MS	Leased from ELL
703.034-9	TSM	1979	T212.1	169	B DH	Ex-ČD

740.413-0	ČKD	1987	T448.0	883	Bo-Bo DE	
740.541-8	ČKD	1976	T448.0	883	Bo-Bo DE	
740.711-7	ČKD	1982	T448.0	883	Bo-Bo DE	
740.883-4	ČKD	1985	T448.0	883	Bo-Bo DE	
1216.910-0	Siemens	2008	ES 64 U4	6400	Bo-Bo E	
1216.920-9	Siemens	2008	ES 64 U4	6400	Bo-Bo E	
2016.903-4	Siemens	2004	ER 20	2000	Bo-Bo DE	Ex-Dispolok ER 20-009[1]
2016.904-1	Siemens	2007	ER 20	2000	Bo-Bo DE	Ex-DE2000-05
2016.909-1	Siemens	2007	ER 20	2000	Bo-Bo DE	
2016.920-8	Siemens	2011	ER 20	2000	Bo-Bo DE	Owned by Adria Transport
2016.921-6	Siemens	2011	ER 20	2000	Bo-Bo DE	Owned by Adria Transport
2016.922-4	Siemens	2004	ER 20	2000	Bo-Bo DE	

5.2.20. LOKORAIL   SK

www.lokorail.eu   VKM: LRL

Bratislava-based Lokorail was established in 2004 and started main line open access freight operations in 2006, winning further contracts since then using its second-hand fleet of former ČD and ZSSK locomotives. Livery is red, white & blue.

Number	Builder	Built	Type	kW	Details	Notes
182.072-9	Škoda	1964	E669.2	2790	Co-Co E DC	
230.045-7	Škoda	1966	S489.0	3080	Bo-Bo E AC	On long-term lease from ČD
242.555-1	Škoda	1971	S499.02	3080	Bo-Bo E AC	Ex-BDŽ 43.555
730.630-1	ČKD	1989	T457.0	600	Bo-Bo DE	
740.016-1	ČKD	1977	T448.0	883	Bo-Bo DE	Ex-Polish industry T448.P016
740.684-6	ČKD	1980	T448.0	883	Bo-Bo-DE	Carries T448.0684
740.787-7	ČKD	1983	T448.0	883	Bo-Bo-DE	
770.519-7	SMZ	1969	T669.1	993	Co-Co DE	Ex-771.012
770.604-7	SMZ	1967	T669.0	993	Co-Co-DE	Ex-770.504[i]

5.2.21. LOKOTRAIN   CZ/SK

www.lokotrain.eu   VKM: LTEU

Česká Třebová-based LokoTrain is principally a lessor of rolling stock and also provides training and education facilities for training new drivers etc. EP Cargo, a subsidiary of power and industrial holding EPH, bought a 65% stake in the company in 2015. The remaining 35% is held by LokoTrain founder Evžen Nečas.

LokoTrain leases three Class 193 Vectron locomotives from ELL, which are available to hire to freight operators, and also owns ex-Bulgarian State Railways 242.558, which has received a two-tone grey & white livery. In addition EP Cargo itself purchased Vectron 193.823 in 2016.

Number	Builder	Built	Type	kW	Details	Notes
193.220-1	Siemens	2014	Vectron MS	6400	Bo-Bo E MS	Leased from ELL
193.221-9	Siemens	2015	Vectron MS	6400	Bo-Bo E MS	Leased from ELL
193.222-7	Siemens	2015	Vectron MS	6400	Bo-Bo E MS	Leased from ELL
193.823-2	Siemens	2013	Vectron MS	6400	Bo-Bo E MS	Owned by EP Cargo
242.558-5	Škoda	1982	S499.02	3080	Bo-Bo E AC	Ex-BDŽ 45.154

5.2.22. LOKOTRANS/LOKOTRANS SERVIS   CZ/SK

www.lokotrans.cz   VKM: LTB

Lokotrans is a Brno-based locomotive overhaul and hire company. It has workshops at Brno Dolní, Brno Slatina and Střelice. As well as the locomotive fleet, the company also leases and overhauls a large wagon fleet. One of the company's jobs in recent years has been overhauling locomotives (mainly Class 740) for export. The company has four Class 242 on lease to PSŽ.

Number	Builder	Built	Type	kW	Details	Notes
703.020-8	TSM	1972	T212.1	169	B DH	Ex-703.617
703.594-2	TSM	1977	T212.1	169	B DH	
704.504-0	ČKD	1991	T238.0	250	Bo DE	
721.553-6	ČKD	1971	T458.1	551	Bo-Bo DE	Carries original No. T458.1553
740.712-5	ČKD	1982	T448.0	883	Bo-Bo DE	
740.800-8	ČKD	1984	T448.0	883	Bo-Bo DE	
740.848-7	ČKD	1985	T448.0	883	Bo-Bo-DE	Ex-KDS
742.616-6	ČKD	1984	T466.2	883	Bo-Bo DE	Ex-742.509

5.2.23. LOKOTRANS SLOVAKIA SK/CZ

www.lokotransslovakia.sk

VKM: LTS

Lokotrans Slovakia is a locomotive overhaul and hire company with workshops at Šurany, restoring locomotives for the Slovak, Czech and Polish markets. Established in 1997 the company also owns its own fleet of mainly Class 740/742 locomotives that are hired to main line operators. Livery is red & white.

Number	Builder	Built	Type	kW	Details	Notes
703.598-3	TSM	1977	T212.1	169	B DH	Bratislava
703.622-1	TSM	1978	T212.1	169	B DH	Střelice
703.624-7	TSM	1978	T212.1	169	B DH	Střelice
704.403-5	ČKD	1992	T238.0	250	Bo DE	Šurany
710.622-2	ČKD	1965	T334.0	301	C DH	
710.762-6	SMZ	1967	T334.0	301	C DH	Continental Matador Rubber, Púchov
710.838-4	SMZ	1968	T334.0	301	C DH	Ex-710.659
740.549-1	ČKD	1976	T448.0	883	Bo-Bo DE	
740.591-3	ČKD	1989	T448.0	883	Bo-Bo DE	Ex-Polish T448.P157
740.657-2	ČKD	1979	T448.0	883	Bo-Bo DE	
742.112-6	ČKD	1984	T466.2	883	Bo-Bo DE	Ex-742.615
742.119-1	ČKD	1978	T466.2	883	Bo-Bo DE	Ex-ČD
742.164-7	ČKD	1983	T466.2	883	Bo-Bo DE	Ex-742.502/742.610I
742.276-9	ČKD	1982	T466.2	883	Bo-Bo DE	Ex-ČD
742.348-6	ČKD	1983	T466.2	883	Bo-Bo DE	Ex-ČD
742.512-7	ČKD	1984	T466.2	883	Bo-Bo DE	Ex-742.619
770.527-0	ČKD	1984	T669.0	993	Co-Co DE	

5.2.24. METRANS CZ/SK

www.metrans.eu

VKM: MT

METRANS is a subsidiary of Hamburger Hafen und Logistik (HHLA). The company operates container trains from ports in northern Germany (such as Hamburg) and the Netherlands (such as Rotterdam) to its terminals in the Czech Republic at Praha Uhříněves and Česká Třebová. Trains also operate from Bratislava to Haniska, near Kosice in eastern Slovakia, to Budapest in Hungary, as well as to Austria and Slovenia. There is also a train from Česká Třebová to Brest (Poland). A full list of routes operated can be found on the METRANS website.

Freight operations are carried out by daughter companies METRANS Rail (in the Czech Republic & Slovakia), METRANS Danubia (Slovakia & Hungary), METRANS Rail Deutschland (Germany) and METRANS Railprofi Austria (Austria). Only locomotives that are registered for operation in the Czech Republic and Slovakia are shown in this listing (additional electric locomotives are used for internal German trains or, for example, Austria-Hungary trains).

The company mainly used hired-in electric locomotives until 2014 when 20 new Class 386 TRAXX locomotives arrived. The Class 386 are all owned outright by METRANS. Initially all 20 locomotives can operate in the Czech Republic, Germany and Austria but will also be approved for other countries in the future. In late 2015 386.001–005 were approved for operation into Hungary. A further ten Class 386s are on order (386.021–030) which will also be passed for operation in Poland, Slovakia and Hungary, as well as the Netherlands (386.028–030), reducing the requirement to hire Class 186s from RAILPOOL.

Due to growing traffic METRANS has been leasing additional locomotives in 2015–16. 186.455 had been leased as a temporary replacement for 186.182 which is undergoing modifications.

Siemens Class 761 Eurorunners, including 223.002, are used on trains between Slovakia, Austria, Hungary and Slovenia. These locomotives are owned by METRANS Dunubia, 223.002 being purchased from MRCE Dispolok. Classes 740 and 745 are principally used for shunting at terminals, such as the one at Praha Uhříněves.

METRANS livery is plain silver for the electrics, and white & blue for the diesels.

Number	Builder	Built	Type	kW	Details	Notes
186.182-2	Bombardier	2008	TRAXX	5600	Bo-Bo E MS	Leased from RAILPOOL
186.187-1	Bombardier	2011	TRAXX	5600	Bo-Bo E MS	Leased from RAILPOOL
186.289-4	Bombardier	2011	TRAXX	5600	Bo-Bo E MS	Leased from RAILPOOL
186.291-1	Bombardier	2012	TRAXX	5600	Bo-Bo E MS	Leased from RAILPOOL
186.433-9	Bombardier	2015	TRAXX	5600	Bo-Bo E MS	Leased from RAILPOOL
186.437-0	Bombardier	2015	TRAXX	5600	Bo-Bo E MS	Leased from RAILPOOL
186.455-2	Bombardier	2015	TRAXX	5600	Bo-Bo E MS	Leased from RAILPOOL
223.002-7	Siemens	2003	ER 20	2000	Bo-Bo DE	"ER 20-002"
386.001-2	Bombardier	2014	TRAXX	5600	Bo-Bo E MS	
386.002-0	Bombardier	2014	TRAXX	5600	Bo-Bo E MS	
386.003-8	Bombardier	2014	TRAXX	5600	Bo-Bo E MS	
386.004-6	Bombardier	2014	TRAXX	5600	Bo-Bo E MS	
386.005-3	Bombardier	2014	TRAXX	5600	Bo-Bo E MS	
386.006-1	Bombardier	2014	TRAXX	5600	Bo-Bo E MS	
386.007-9	Bombardier	2014	TRAXX	5600	Bo-Bo E MS	
386.008-7	Bombardier	2014	TRAXX	5600	Bo-Bo E MS	
386.009-5	Bombardier	2014	TRAXX	5600	Bo-Bo E MS	
386.010-3	Bombardier	2014	TRAXX	5600	Bo-Bo E MS	
386.011-1	Bombardier	2014	TRAXX	5600	Bo-Bo E MS	
386.012-9	Bombardier	2014	TRAXX	5600	Bo-Bo E MS	
386.013-7	Bombardier	2015	TRAXX	5600	Bo-Bo E MS	
386.014-5	Bombardier	2015	TRAXX	5600	Bo-Bo E MS	
386.015-2	Bombardier	2015	TRAXX	5600	Bo-Bo E MS	
386.016-0	Bombardier	2015	TRAXX	5600	Bo-Bo E MS	
386.017-8	Bombardier	2015	TRAXX	5600	Bo-Bo E MS	
386.018-6	Bombardier	2015	TRAXX	5600	Bo-Bo E MS	
386.019-4	Bombardier	2015	TRAXX	5600	Bo-Bo E MS	
386.020-2	Bombardier	2015	TRAXX	5600	Bo-Bo E MS	
386.021-0	Bombardier		TRAXX	5600	Bo-Bo E MS	
386.022-8	Bombardier		TRAXX	5600	Bo-Bo E MS	
386.023-6	Bombardier		TRAXX	5600	Bo-Bo E MS	
386.024-4	Bombardier		TRAXX	5600	Bo-Bo E MS	
386.025-1	Bombardier		TRAXX	5600	Bo-Bo E MS	
386.026-9	Bombardier		TRAXX	5600	Bo-Bo E MS	
386.027-7	Bombardier		TRAXX	5600	Bo-Bo E MS	
386.028-5	Bombardier		TRAXX	5600	Bo-Bo E MS	
386.029-3	Bombardier		TRAXX	5600	Bo-Bo E MS	
386.030-1	Bombardier		TRAXX	5600	Bo-Bo E MS	
716.505-3	LEW	1981	V60	478	D DH	Ex-V60-17422
740.444-5	ČKD	1988	T448.0	883	Bo-Bo DE	
740.513-7	ČKD	1974	T448.0	883	Bo-Bo DE	
740.651-5	ČKD	1978	T448.0	883	Bo-Bo DE	
740.749-7	ČKD	1982	T448.0	883	Bo-Bo DE	
740.830-5	ČKD	1984	T448.0	883	Bo-Bo DE	
745.701-3	LEW	1970	V100.1	736	B-B DH	Ex-DB 202.260
745.702-1	LEW	1974	V100.1	736	B-B DH	Ex-DB 202.661
761.001-7	Siemens	2010	ER 20	2000	Bo-Bo DE	
761.002-5	Siemens	2010	ER 20	2000	Bo-Bo DE	
761.003-3	Siemens	2010	ER 20	2000	Bo-Bo DE	
761.004-1	Siemens	2011	ER 20	2000	Bo-Bo DE	
761.005-8	Siemens	2012	ER 20	2000	Bo-Bo DE	
761.006-6	Siemens	2012	ER 20	2000	Bo-Bo DE	
761.007-4	Siemens	2012	ER 20	2000	Bo-Bo DE	

5.2.25. MONDI SCP, RUŽOMBEROK   SK

www.mondigroup.com/scp

Mondi SCP in Ružomberok is the largest paper and pulp mill in Slovakia. There has been paper making in Ružomberok for more than 300 years with the current Severoslovenské Celulózky a Papierne (SCP) plant being established in 1958. Mondi SCP says that 94% of its energy comes from renewable resources. Timber arrives by train from Slovak forests. The four Class 740s shunt trains within the complex and also into the exchange sidings for onward movement.

Number	Builder	Built	Type	kW	Details	Notes
740.403-1	ČKD	1986	T448.0	883	Bo-Bo DE	Carries original No. T448.0903
740.452-8	ČKD	1988	T448.0	883	Bo-Bo DE	Carries original No. T448.0952
740.617-6	ČKD	1978	T448.0	883	Bo-Bo DE	Carries original No. T448.0617
740.737-2	ČKD	1982	T448.0	883	Bo-Bo DE	Carries original No. T448.0737

5.2.26. ODOS   CZ/SK

www.odos.cz   VKM: ODOS

Ostravská Dopravní Společnost (ODOS) is an Ostrava-based open access freight operator that began operations in 2006 as a subsidiary company of NH-Trans. ČD Cargo holds a 20% stake. As well as operating a mixture of freight traffic, both in the Czech Republic and in Slovakia, locomotives are also hired to other operators. Locomotives can also sometimes be found on engineering work, especially in Moravia. Many locomotives have been acquired from Slovakia and most of the Class 742 are ex-industrial. Livery is two tone blue (plus white for electrics). At the time of writing 182.080/099 are leased from ČD Cargo.

Number	Builder	Built	Type	kW	Details	Notes
140.062-1	Škoda	1957	E499.0	2032	Bo-Bo E DC	
140.087-8	Škoda	1958	E499.0	2032	Bo-Bo E DC	
181.064-7	Škoda	1964	E669.1	2790	Co-Co E DC	
182.166-9	Škoda	1965	E669.2	2790	Co-Co E DC	
701.483-0	ČKD	1962	T211.1	169	B DM	Ex-700.691/701.683
730.614-5	ČKD	1988	T457.0	600	Bo-Bo DE	
742.131-6	ČKD	1982	T466.2	883	Bo-Bo DE	Ex-ČD 742.257
742.501-0	ČKD	1983	T466.2	883	Bo-Bo DE	Ex-742.609
742.503-6	ČKD	1984	T466.2	883	Bo-Bo DE	Ex-ČD 742.370 (frame swap)
742.505-1	ČKD	1983	T466.2	883	Bo-Bo DE	Ex-742.612
742.510-1	ČKD	1984	T466.2	883	Bo-Bo DE	Ex-742.617
742.513-5	ČKD	1984	T466.2	883	Bo-Bo DE	Ex-742.620
742.514-3	ČKD	1984	T466.2	883	Bo-Bo DE	Ex-742.621
742.523-4	ČKD	1985	T466.2	883	Bo-Bo DE	Ex-742.626
742.525-9	ČKD	1985	T466.2	883	Bo-Bo DE	Ex-742.628
742.538-2	ČKD	1986	T466.2	883	Bo-Bo DE	Ex-742.633
742.540-8	ČKD	1986	T466.2	883	Bo-Bo DE	Ex-742.635
742.541-6	ČKD	1986	T466.2	883	Bo-Bo DE	Ex-742.636
750.111-7	ČKD	1973	T478.3	1325	Bo-Bo DE	Ex-753.111
750.132-3	ČKD	1973	T478.3	1325	Bo-Bo DE	Ex-753.132
750.202-4	ČKD	1974	T478.3	1325	Bo-Bo DE	Ex-753.202
750.204-0	ČKD	1974	T478.3	1325	Bo-Bo DE	Ex-753.204
771.170-8	SMZ	1971	T669.1	993	Co-Co DE	

5.2.27. PRVÁ SLOVENSKÁ ŽELEZNIČNÁ (PSŽ)   SK/CZ

www.psz.sk   VKM: PSŽ

PSŽ, or "The First Slovak Railway Company" is a Bratislava-based open-access freight operator, hauling a wide range of commodities, mainly in south Slovakia. Principal motive power is refurbished ex-ČD or ZSSK Class 240/242 electrics, along with Classes 740/742. PSŽ purchased Vectron 193.820 from Siemens in late 2015, making it the first Slovak freight operator to take the class. The locomotive is cleared for operation in Slovakia, the Czech Republic and Hungary. PSŽ also now leases two Co-Co electrics from DB Cargo Romania.

PSŽ livery is bright green & yellow.

Number	Builder	Built	Type	kW	Details	Notes
140.067-0	Škoda	1957	E499.0	2032	Bo-Bo E DC	
193.820-8	Siemens	2013	Vectron MS	6400	Bo-Bo E MS	
240.039-8	Škoda	1968	S499.0	3080	Bo-Bo E AC	Ex-ZSSK
242.206-1	Škoda	1975	S499.02	3080	Bo-Bo E AC	Ex-ČD. Leased from Lokotrans
242.262-4	Škoda	1981	S499.02	3080	Bo-Bo E AC	Ex-ČD. Leased from Lokotrans
242.282-2	Škoda	1981	S499.02	3080	Bo-Bo E AC	Ex-ČD. Leased from Lokotrans
242.287-1	Škoda	1971	S499.02	3080	Bo-Bo E AC	Ex-BDŽ 43.554. Leased from Lokotrans
468.002-4	ČKD	1974	T478.3	1325	Bo-Bo DE	Ex-753.167. Registered in Hungary
480.005-4	Softronic	2013	480.0	6000	Co-Co E AC	Leased from DB Cargo Romania
480.012-4	Softronic	2014	480.0	6000	Co-Co E AC	Leased from DB Cargo Romania
710.776-6	SMZ	1967	T334.1	301	C DH	
711.619-7	ŽOS Zvo		ex-T334.1	210	C DE	Ex-T334.0619
740.148-2	ČKD	1989	T448.0	883	Bo-Bo DE	Ex-Polish industry T448.P148
740.826-3	ČKD	1984	T448.0	883	Bo-Bo DE	
740.855-2	ČKD	1985	T448.0	883	Bo-Bo DE	
742.213-2	ČKD	1980	T466.2	883	Bo-Bo DE	Ex-ČD
742.384-1	ČKD	1984	T466.2	883	Bo-Bo DE	Ex-ČD
770.538-7	ČKD	1989	T669.0	993	Co-Co DE	Ex-Polish industry S2140
770.602-1	SMZ	1969	T669.0	993	Co-Co DE	Ex-770.517ᴵ

5.2.28. RM LINES/SPEDICA GROUP   CZ

www.spedica.cz   VKM: RML

Sokolov-based Czech open access freight operator RM Lines was acquired by the Spedica Group in 2012, the company's diesel locomotives now appearing in grey & green Spedica livery, but with RM Lines logos. The electrics have recently appeared in RM Lines all-over red livery. The company's locomotives can often be found in the Děčín area, also operating into Germany.

Number	Builder	Built	Type	kW	Details	Notes
121.007-9	Škoda	1960	E469.1	2032	Bo-Bo E DC	Registered in Poland as 150.756
140.045-6	Škoda	1957	E499.0	2032	Bo-Bo E DC	
140.074-6	Škoda	1958	E499.0	2032	Bo-Bo E DC	
740.545-9	ČKD	1976	T448.0	883	Bo-Bo DE	
740.723-2	ČKD	1982	T448.0	883	Bo-Bo DE	
742.205-8	ČKD	1980	T466.2	883	Bo-Bo DE	
742.515-0	ČKD	1984	T466.2	883	Bo-Bo DE	

5.2.29. SD-KD   CZ

www.sd-kd.cz   VKM: SDKD

Severočeské doly-Kolejová doprava (SD-KD) was established in 2001 out of the Bohemian mines transport utility Doly Nastup Tušimice (DNT). Since 2005 it has been majority owned by energy giant ČEZ Group. SD-KD operates a 23 km 3000 V DC electrified industrial line between coal mines and Prunéřov and Tušimice power stations, with connections with the ČD network at Kadaň and Březno u Chomutova.

SD-KD's fleet is very varied. It operates 11 of the 14 Škoda-built 79Es that were identical to ČD Class 130s, numbered in the same original series (as E479.0041–0054). ČD later acquired 130.042, SD-KD sold 130.049 (now with AWT) and 130.043 was scrapped. Class 130 work some longer distance coal trains to power stations across the Czech Republic, including Počerady, Mělník and also Ledvice in Moravia. Class 114.5 were updated AC motor versions of Class 110/111, although 114.503/504 were stored in 2009 and used for spares. In 2015–16 114.501/502 were rebuilt as diesel-electric remote control-fitted locomotives by CZ LOKO Jihlava, numbered 114.001/002. They have been fitted with CAT C15 engines.

The four Class 184s possess a phenomenal 575 kN starting tractive effort. These 123-tonne beasts were intended for Praha–Košice corridor freight services but as neither ČD nor ŽSR had the money for this the two prototypes, 93 E0 01 and 02, passed to DNT; two more were also built. Class 184 are usually used on shorter haul coal trains in north Bohemia.

▲ Carrying the colourful PSŽ livery, ex-ZSSK 240.039 passes Bratislava Lamač with a train of grain hoppers on 11 June 2014. **Robert Pritchard**

▼ Rebuilt SD-KD Class 753.6s 753.602 and 753.603 haul the regular limestone train from Nučice to Kadaň, seen just west of Hostivice on the afternoon of 12 July 2013. **Robert Pritchard**

As well as a number of shunting locomotives, of which 704.526/550/554 have been fitted with CAT 3406 engines, the SD-KD diesel fleet consists of a few unrebuilt Class 740s and a number of different locomotives rebuilt by CZ LOKO. Class 724.6 have CAT C15 engines, Class 724.7 a CAT 3412 engine, Class 741.7 and Class 744.7 CAT 3508C engines and Class 774.7 a CAT 3512B engine. In 2012 SD-KD ordered three rebuilt Class 753s, with CAT 3512CHB engines. Unlike previous reconstructions the cab is also replaced with a new single window pane replacing the distinctive protruding "Goggle" windows, earning these locomotives the nickname "Bison". A pair of these locomotives is normally used on a limestone train from near Beroun to Kadaň (via Hostivice and Kladno). Former CZ LOKO demonstrator 753.604 was acquired later.

SD-KD's principal locomotive depot is at Tušimice, near Kadaň, alongside the power station. Livery is dark green with black and white stripes.

Number	Builder	Built	Type	kW	Details	Notes
114.001-0	Škoda	1996	90E	403	Bo-Bo DE	Ex-Škoda 90 E0 01/114.501
114.002-8	Škoda	1996	90E	403	Bo-Bo DE	Ex-Škoda 90 E0 02/114.502
114.503-6	Škoda	1999	90E	1600	Bo-Bo E DC	Ex-Škoda 90 E0 03 (S)
114.504-4	Škoda	2000	90E	1600	Bo-Bo E DC	Ex-Škoda 90 E0 04 (S)
121.023-6	Škoda	1960	E469.1	2032	Bo-Bo E DC	Ex-121.025/CTL (PL) ET05-R010
130.041-7	Škoda	1977	E479.0	2040	Bo-Bo E DC	
130.044-1	Škoda	1977	E479.0	2040	Bo-Bo E DC	
130.045-8	Škoda	1977	E479.0	2040	Bo-Bo E DC	
130.046-6	Škoda	1977	E479.0	2040	Bo-Bo E DC	
130.047-4	Škoda	1977	E479.0	2040	Bo-Bo E DC	
130.048-2	Škoda	1977	E479.0	2040	Bo-Bo E DC	
130.050-8	Škoda	1977	E479.0	2040	Bo-Bo E DC	
130.051-6	Škoda	1977	E479.0	2040	Bo-Bo E DC	
130.052-4	Škoda	1977	E479.0	2040	Bo-Bo E DC	
130.053-2	Škoda	1977	E479.0	2040	Bo-Bo E DC	
130.054-0	Škoda	1977	E479.0	2040	Bo-Bo E DC	
184.501-5	Škoda	1994	93E	5220	Bo-Bo-Bo E DC	Ex-Škoda 93 E0 01
184.502-3	Škoda	1995	93E	5220	Bo-Bo-Bo E DC	Ex-Škoda 93 E0 02
184.503-1	Škoda	1998	93E	5220	Bo-Bo-Bo E DC	Ex-Škoda 93 E0 11
184.504-9	Škoda	1999	93E	5220	Bo-Bo-Bo E DC	Ex-Škoda 93 E0 12
701.302-2	ČKD	1959	T211.0	169	B DM	Ex-T211.0609
702.683-6	TSM	1970	T212.0	147	B DM	Carries original No. T212.0683
702.684-4	TSM	1970	T212.0	147	B DM	
704.526-3	ČKD	1992	T238.0	299	Bo DE	Ex-T238.0026
704.534-7	ČKD	1992	T238.0	220	Bo DE	Ex-T238.0034
704.550-3	ČKD	1994	T238.0	299	Bo DE	Ex-T238.0050
704.554-5	ČKD	1994	T238.0	299	Bo DE	Ex-T238.0054
711.004-2	ŽOS Nyb	r1996	ex-T334.0	224	C DE	Rebuilt ex-710.674
721.524-7	ČKD	1968	T458.1	551	Bo-Bo DE	Ex-T458.1524
724.605-1	CZ LOKO	r2010	ex-T448.0	392	Bo-Bo DE	Rebuilt ex-740.554
724.606-9	CZ LOKO	r2010	ex-T448.0	392	Bo-Bo DE	Rebuilt ex-740.812
724.706-7	ČMKS	r2003	ex-T448.0	627	Bo-Bo DE	Rebuilt ex-740.570
740.590-5	ČKD	1976	T448.0	883	Bo-Bo DE	
740.599-6	ČKD	1976	T448.0	883	Bo-Bo DE	
740.642-4	ČKD	1978	T448.0	883	Bo-Bo DE	
740.744-8	ČKD	1982	T448.0	883	Bo-Bo DE	
741.706-6	CZ LOKO	r2010	ex-T448.0	1000	Bo-Bo DE	Rebuilt ex-740.
744.702-2	ČMKS	r2002	ex-T448.0	970	Bo-Bo DE	Rebuilt ex-740.643
744.703-0	CZ LOKO	r2008	ex-T448.0	970	Bo-Bo DE	Rebuilt ex-740.451
753.601-4	CZ LOKO	r2012	ex-T478.3	1550	Bo-Bo DE	Rebuilt ex-753.314
753.602-2	CZ LOKO	r2012	ex-T478.3	1550	Bo-Bo DE	Rebuilt ex-750.159
753.603-0	CZ LOKO	r2012	ex-T478.3	1550	Bo-Bo DE	Rebuilt ex-750.398
753.604-8	CZ LOKO	r2013	ex-T478.3	1550	Bo-Bo DE	Rebuilt ex-750.088
770.505-6	ČKD	1979	T669.0	993	Co-Co DE	
774.704-1	CZ LOKO	r2008	ex-T669.1	1455	Co-Co DE	Rebuilt ex 770.501[II]

5.2.30. SKANSKA CZ/SK

www.skanska.cz

VKM: SKANS

Skanska is a Swedish-based multi-national construction company. A small part of the company's portfolio is its involvement with many railway rebuilding jobs in both the Czech Republic and Slovakia, using the locomotive fleet listed here.

Number	Builder	Built	Type	kW	Details	Notes
702.618-0	TSM	1968	T212.0	147	B DM	
703.017-4	TSM	1978	T212.1	169	B DH	
703.018-2	TSM	1978	T212.1	169	B DH	
730.601-2	ČKD	1988	T457.0	600	Bo-Bo DE	
730.624-4	ČKD	1989	T457.0	600	Bo-Bo DE	
740.536-8	ČKD	1976	T448.0	883	Bo-Bo DE	
740.557-4	ČKD	1976	T448.0	883	Bo-Bo DE	
740.704-2	ČKD	1981	T448.0	883	Bo-Bo DE	
740.874-3	ČKD	1985	T448.0	883	Bo-Bo DE	

5.2.31. SLEZSKOMORAVSKÁ DRÁHA (SMD) CZ

www.slezskomoravskadraha.cz

VKM: SMD

This Ostrava based open access freight company can mainly be found operating trains in the east of the Czech Republic, especially in the Ostrava area. The Class 710 is based at Eurovia, Jakubčovice nad Odrou for shunting – this is one of the largest quarries in the Czech Republic. SMD's livery is blue & silver.

Number	Builder	Built	Type	kW	Details	Notes
710.079-5	ČKD	1972	T334.1	301	C DH	Eurovia, Jakubčovice nad Odrou
721.518-9	ČKD	1965	T458.1	551	Bo-Bo DE	
740.503-8	ČKD	1973	T448.0	883	Bo-Bo DE	
740.597-0	ČKD	1976	T448.0	883	Bo-Bo DE	
740.645-7	ČKD	1978	T448.0	883	Bo-Bo DE	
740.720-8	ČKD	1982	T448.0	883	Bo-Bo DE	
770.016-4	SMZ	1967	T669.0	993	Co-Co DE	

5.2.32. SLOVNAFT BRATISLAVA SK

www.slovnaft.sk/en

VKM: SLOVN

Slovak petrochemical company Slovnaft operates a large oil refinery to the south-east of Bratislava, refining almost 6 million tonnes of crude oil per year. With a large internal railway network the company owns a fleet of diesel locomotives for internal shunting. Five of the fleet are rebuilt Class 744.7, fitted with CAT 3508B engines and Siemens alternators. The company also operates some original Class 740s and a British-built Hunslet 0-6-0 shunter. Slovnaft also operates a number of other sites, locomotives at these are listed under "Other Operators". Livery is yellow & black.

Number	Builder	Built	Type	kW	Details	Notes
717.601-9	Hunslet	1969	717.6	230	C DE	
740.614-3	ČKD	1978	T448.0	883	Bo-Bo DE	Carries T448.0614
740.743-0	ČKD	1982	T448.0	883	Bo-Bo DE	Carries T448.0743
740.829-7	ČKD	1984	T448.0	883	Bo-Bo DE	
744.704-8	ŽOS Zvolen	r2005	ex-T448.0	970	Bo-Bo DE	Rebuilt ex-740.728/744.728
744.705-5	ŽOS Zvolen	r2005	ex-T448.0	970	Bo-Bo DE	Rebuilt ex-740.953/744.953
744.706-3	ŽOS Zvolen	r2007	ex-T448.0	970	Bo-Bo DE	Rebuilt ex-740.886/744.886
744.707-1	ŽOS Zvolen	r2008	ex-T448.0	970	Bo-Bo DE	Rebuilt ex-740.827/744.827
744.708-9	ŽOS Zvolen	r2015	ex-T448.0	970	Bo-Bo DE	Rebuilt ex-740.731/744.731

▲ SU-operated coal trains can be seen on the main line in the Karlovy Vary area. On 3 September 2012 Class 774.7 Co-Co CZ LOKO rebuild 774.702 hauls a train of empties west round the curve near Vojkovice nad Ohří. **Robert Pritchard**

▼ The ubiquitous Class 740 can be seen at industrial sites across both countries. However many Class 740 have been rebuilt with new engines etc. One machine in original condition, and even carrying its original number is T448.0859 (740.859), operated by Železiarne Podbrezová ironworks, central Slovakia, where it is seen shunting on 16 May 2015. **Robert Pritchard**

5.2.33. SOKOLOVSKÁ UHELNÁ (SU)

CZ

www.suas.cz

VKM: SUAS

SU is a Sokolov-based lignite mining company operating its own trains conveying brown coal from the opencast coal mines around Sokolov. The company is also one of the largest independent producers of electricity in the country. Class 774.7 is similar to Slovakian Class 744.5 with CAT 3512 engines but retains the full-height long engine hood. SU also operates internal locomotives on mining systems, including three section Bo+Bo+Bo electric "crocodile" locomotives in the 127.2xx/127.5xx number ranges. These 165-tonne beasts haul the coal right out of the mine itself, as can be seen from the viewing area above the vast Družba opencast site – well worth a visit! 2 million tonnes of brown coal is extracted from this site alone every year.

The Class 127s in the 127.2xx series carry only their last three numbers. 127.501–511 were rebuilt 2009–10. The Class 703.7s were rebuilt by JLS 1997–2011 with CAT engines.

Number	Builder	Built	Type	kW	Details	Notes
(127).226	Škoda	1972	26 Em	2190	Bo-Bo-Bo E DC	(S)
(127).235	Škoda	1989	27 E	2190	Bo-Bo-Bo E DC	
(127).236	Škoda	1989	27 E	2190	Bo-Bo-Bo E DC	
(127).237	Škoda	1989	27 E	2190	Bo-Bo-Bo E DC	
(127).238	Škoda	1989	27 E	2190	Bo-Bo-Bo E DC	
(127).239	Škoda	1989	27 E	2190	Bo-Bo-Bo E DC	
(127).245	Škoda	1989	27 E	2190	Bo-Bo-Bo E DC	
(127).246	Škoda	1989	27 E	2190	Bo-Bo-Bo E DC	
(127).247	Škoda	1989	27 E	2190	Bo-Bo-Bo E DC	
(127).248	Škoda	1989	27 E	2190	Bo-Bo-Bo E DC	
(127).249	Škoda	1989	27 E	2190	Bo-Bo-Bo E DC	
(127).251	Škoda	1989	27 E	2190	Bo-Bo-Bo E DC	
(127).254	Škoda	1989	27 E	2190	Bo-Bo-Bo E DC	
(127).256	Škoda	1989	27 E	2190	Bo-Bo-Bo E DC	
(127).259	Škoda	1989	27 E	2190	Bo-Bo-Bo E DC	
127.501-5	Škoda	1989	27 E	2190	Bo-Bo-Bo E DC	Rebuilt ex-127.258
127.502-3	Škoda	1989	27 E	2190	Bo-Bo-Bo E DC	Rebuilt ex-127.257
127.503-1	Škoda	1984	27 E	2190	Bo-Bo-Bo E DC	Rebuilt ex-127.253 (ex-MUS 127.673)
127.504-8	Škoda	1989	27 E	2190	Bo-Bo-Bo E DC	Rebuilt ex-127.255
127.505-6	Škoda	1989	27 E	2190	Bo-Bo-Bo E DC	Rebuilt ex-127.242
127.506-4	Škoda	1989	27 E	2190	Bo-Bo-Bo E DC	Rebuilt ex-127.240
127.507-2	Škoda	1989	27 E	2190	Bo-Bo-Bo E DC	Rebuilt ex-127.243
127.508-0	Škoda	1989	27 E	2190	Bo-Bo-Bo E DC	Rebuilt ex-127.250
127.509-8	Škoda	1989	27 E	2190	Bo-Bo-Bo E DC	Rebuilt ex-127.241
127.510-6	Škoda	1989	27 E	2190	Bo-Bo-Bo E DC	Rebuilt ex-127.244
127.511-4	Škoda	1989	27 E	2190	Bo-Bo-Bo E DC	Rebuilt ex-127.252
703.701-3	JLS	r1997	ex-T211.1	170	B DH	Internal 421. Rebuilt ex-701.511
703.703-9	JLS	r1998	ex-	170	B DH	Internal 415.
703.704-7	JLS	r	ex-	170	B DH	Internal 414.
703.705-4	JLS	r	ex-T212.1	170	B DH	Internal 418. Rebuilt ex-703.615
703.706-2	JLS	r2000	ex-T212.0	170	B DH	Internal 413. Rebuilt ex-702.805
703.708-8	JLS	r	ex-	170	B DH	Internal 420.
703.709-6	JLS	r2001	ex-	170	B DH	Internal 419.
703.710-4	JLS	r2002	ex-	170	B DH	Internal 417.
703.711-2	JLS	r2003	ex-	170	B DH	Internal 416.
724.703-4	ČMKS	r2001	ex-T448.0	627	Bo-Bo DE	Internal 407. Rebuilt ex-740.661
724.704-2	ČMKS	r2002	ex-T448.0	627	Bo-Bo DE	Internal 434. Rebuilt ex-740.696
724.705-9	ČMKS	r2003	ex-T448.0	627	Bo-Bo DE	Internal 432. Rebuilt ex-740.798
724.707-5	ČMKS	r2004	ex-T448.0	627	Bo-Bo DE	Internal 437. Rebuilt ex-740.652
724.708-3	ČMKS	r2004	ex-T448.0	627	Bo-Bo DE	Internal 406. Rebuilt ex-740.885
724.709-1	ČMKS	r2004	ex-T448.0	627	Bo-Bo DE	Internal 436. Rebuilt ex-740.717
724.710-9	ČMKS	r2004	ex-T448.0	627	Bo-Bo DE	Internal 438. Rebuilt ex-740.507
740.716-6	ČKD	1982	T448.0	883	Bo-Bo DE	Internal 435.
740.808-1	ČKD	1984	T448.0	883	Bo-Bo DE	Internal 431.
774.701-7	ČMKS	r2005	ex-T669.1	1455	Co-Co DE	Internal 429. Rebuilt ex-770.512[II]
774.702-5	CZ LOKO	r2007	ex-T669.1	1455	Co-Co DE	Internal 428. Rebuilt ex-770.513[II]
774.703-3	CZ LOKO	r2008	ex-T669.1	1455	Co-Co DE	Internal 430. Rebuilt ex-770.530

5.2.34. STRABAG RAIL   CZ

www.strabag.cz   VKM: VDSP

The large European construction company Strabag took over Viamont DSP in 2010, although the Strabag Rail logos weren't applied to locomotives until more recently. Viamont sold its Viamont Cargo business to OKD, Doprava (later AWT) in 2008 and passenger services were hived off to a new subsidiary, Viamont Regio (later GW Train Regio, see Private Passenger Operators). The small fleet can be seen on infrastructure duties across the country. The Class 741s have been rebuilt with CAT 3508C engines. Livery is still the Viamont inspired yellow & black.

Number	Builder	Built	Type	kW	Details	Notes
704.511-5	ČKD	1992	T238.0	250	Bo DE	
720.567-7	ČKD	1961	T435.0	551	Bo-Bo DE	
740.469-2	ČKD	1979	T448.0	883	Bo-Bo DE	Ex-Polish industry T448.P054
740.658-0	ČKD	1979	T448.0	883	Bo-Bo DE	Leased from Česká Lokomotivka
740.678-8	ČKD	1980	T448.0	883	Bo-Bo DE	Leased from Česká Lokomotivka
741.702-5	ČKD	r2010	ex-T448.0	1000	Bo-Bo DE	Rebuilt ex-740.667
741.703-3	ČKD	r2010	ex-T448.0	1000	Bo-Bo DE	Rebuilt ex-740.702
741.704-1	ČKD	r2010	ex-T448.0	1000	Bo-Bo DE	Rebuilt ex-Polish T448.P043
741.705-8	ČKD	r2010	ex-T448.0	1000	Bo-Bo DE	Rebuilt ex-740.442
MV97.004	CZ LOKO	r2006	ex-T458.1	360	Bo-Bo DE	Frame ex-721.508
MV97.005	CZ LOKO	r2009	ex-T458.1	384	Bo-Bo DE	Frame ex-721.187
MVTV02-112	MSV	1992	M153.0	155	A1 DM	Ex-892.112

5.2.35. SŽDS   SK/CZ

www.szds.sk   VKM: SZDS

Established in 2003, Slovenská Železničná Dopravná Spoločnosť (SŽDS) translates as the "Slovak Railway Transport Company" (not to be confused with SŽDC, the Czech infrastructure operator!). SŽDS is a Bratislava-based open access freight operator mainly active in Slovakia but also cleared for operation into the Czech Republic and Hungary. The company uses a small fleet of vintage electrics and Class 740/742/770 diesels. The two Class 770s are 1520mm gauge with SA3 couplers for use on the SRT line in eastern Slovakia.

Number	Builder	Built	Type	kW	Details	Notes
121.004-6	Škoda	1960	E459.1	2032	Bo-Bo E DC	
121.068-1	Škoda	1960	E459.1	2032	Bo-Bo E DC	Leased from ZOS Zvolen
140.076-1	Škoda	1957	E499.0	2032	Bo-Bo E DC	
242.559-3	Škoda	1981	S499.02	3080	Bo-Bo E AC	Ex-ČD 242.280
740.641-6	ČKD	1978	T448.0	883	Bo-Bo DE	
740.873-5	ČKD	1985	T448.0	883	Bo-Bo DE	
742.622-4	ČKD	1984	T466.2	883	Bo-Bo DE	Ex-742.518
770.817-5	ČKD	1984	T669.0	883	Co-Co DE	Also carries T669.5502. 1520 mm
770.818-3	SMZ	1968	T669.0	883	Co-Co DE	Ex-ZSSK Cargo 770.074. 1520 mm

5.2.36. TRAMO RAIL   CZ

www.tramo-rail.cz   VKM: TRAMO

This Olomouc-based overhead line maintenance company, established in 1997, uses its two Class 721s to power its overhead electrification train, which can mainly be seen in Moravia. Livery is blue with an orange stripe.

Number	Builder	Built	Type	kW	Details	Notes
703.657-7	TSM	1978	T212.1	169	B DH	
721.544-5	ČKD	1968	T458.1	551	Bo-Bo DE	Also carries original No.T458.1544
721.545-2	ČKD	1968	T458.1	551	Bo-Bo DE	Also carries original No.T458.1545

5.2.37. TSS CARGO

www.tsscargo.cz

VKM: TSSC

Trat'ová strojní spolecnost (TSS Cargo) is an Ostrava-based freight company, specialising in infrastructure trains, as well as general freight such as coal and intermodal. The company has depots at Hulín and Starý Plzenec. TSS translates to "Trackside Machinery Company" in English. The company was founded in 1952 and part-privatised in 2005 as part of the restructuring process for Czech Railways (CD still retained a 51% stake). This stake was sold in 2010.

In 2014–15 the company acquired 16 of the 20 former DB Class 180, although at the time of writing most are still stored and awaiting overhaul at Přerov. Those Class 180s not with TSS Cargo are 180.001 (with CD as 371.201), 180.004/005 (scrapped) and 180.014, which is preserved in Germany. Active Class 180s are used on freights across the country, including container trains between Ostrava and Mělník. The rest of the fleet mainly consists of ex-ČKD Classes 730, 740 and 742. The four Class 753 "Goggles" have been hired to ČD Cargo in the past. The company also has a large fleet of On-Track Machines to support line rebuilding projects.

TSS Cargo livery is blue & yellow.

Number	Builder	Built	Type	kW	Details	Notes
180.002-8	Škoda	1991	80E	3080	Bo-Bo E AC/DC	
180.003-6	Škoda	1991	80E	3080	Bo-Bo E AC/DC	
180.006-9	Škoda	1991	80E	3080	Bo-Bo E AC/DC	
180.007-7	Škoda	1991	80E	3080	Bo-Bo E AC/DC	
180.008-5	Škoda	1991	80E	3080	Bo-Bo E AC/DC	
180.009-3	Škoda	1991	80E	3080	Bo-Bo E AC/DC	
180.010-1	Škoda	1991	80E	3080	Bo-Bo E AC/DC	
180.011-9	Škoda	1991	80E	3080	Bo-Bo E AC/DC	
180.012-7	Škoda	1991	80E	3080	Bo-Bo E AC/DC	
180.013-5	Škoda	1991	80E	3080	Bo-Bo E AC/DC	
180.015-0	Škoda	1991	80E	3080	Bo-Bo E AC/DC	
180.016-8	Škoda	1991	80E	3080	Bo-Bo E AC/DC	
180.017-6	Škoda	1991	80E	3080	Bo-Bo E AC/DC	
180.018-4	Škoda	1991	80E	3080	Bo-Bo E AC/DC	
180.019-2	Škoda	1991	80E	3080	Bo-Bo E AC/DC	
180.020-0	Škoda	1991	80E	3080	Bo-Bo E AC/DC	
711.002-6	ŽOS Nym	r1995	ex-T334.1	242	C DE	Borohrádek. Ex-710.669.
721.111-3	ČKD	1964	T458.1	551	Bo-Bo DE	
721.546-0	ČKD	1971	T458.1	551	Bo-Bo DE	
730.602-0	ČKD	1988	T457.0	600	Bo-Bo DE	
730.604-6	ČKD	1988	T457.0	600	Bo-Bo DE	
730.606-1	ČKD	1988	T457.0	600	Bo-Bo DE	
730.622-8	ČKD	1988	T457.0	600	Bo-Bo DE	(S) Hulín
730.623-6	ČKD	1988	T457.0	600	Bo-Bo DE	(S) Hulín
730.626-9	ČKD	1989	T457.0	600	Bo-Bo DE	
730.627-7	ČKD	1989	T457.0	600	Bo-Bo DE	
730.628-5	ČKD	1989	T457.0	600	Bo-Bo DE	
740.429-6	ČKD	1987	T448.0	883	Bo-Bo DE	
740.588-9	ČKD	1976	T448.0	883	Bo-Bo DE	
740.608-5	ČKD	1977	T448.0	883	Bo-Bo DE	
740.750-5	ČKD	1982	T448.0	883	Bo-Bo DE	
740.751-3	ČKD	1982	T448.0	883	Bo-Bo DE	
742.360-1	ČKD	1983	T466.2	883	Bo-Bo DE	Ex-742.602
742.408-8	ČKD	1984	T466.2	883	Bo-Bo DE	Ex-742.641
742.410-4	ČKD	1984	T466.2	883	Bo-Bo DE	Ex-742.608
742.411-2	ČKD	1985	T466.2	883	Bo-Bo DE	Ex-742.630
742.412-0	ČKD	1985	T466.2	883	Bo-Bo DE	Ex-742.631
742.521-8	ČKD	1984	T466.2	883	Bo-Bo DE	Ex-742.625
742.532-5	ČKD	1985	T466.2	883	Bo-Bo DE	Ex-742.642
742.533-3	ČKD	1985	T466.2	883	Bo-Bo DE	Ex-742.637
742.534-1	ČKD	1985	T466.2	883	Bo-Bo DE	Ex-742.638
742.535-8	ČKD	1985	T466.2	883	Bo-Bo DE	Ex-742.639
742.536-6	ČKD	1985	T466.2	883	Bo-Bo DE	Ex-742.640
742.537-4	ČKD	1985	T466.2	883	Bo-Bo DE	Ex-742.606

742.623-2	ČKD	1984	T466.2	883	Bo-Bo DE	Ex-742.519
753.781-4	ČKD	1974	T478.3	1500	Bo-Bo DE	Ex-750.139
753.782-2	ČKD	1973	T478.3	1500	Bo-Bo DE	Ex-750.077
753.783-0	ČKD	1974	T478.3	1500	Bo-Bo DE	Ex-750.214
753.784-8	ČKD	1974	T478.3	1500	Bo-Bo DE	Ex-750.175

5.2.38. TSS GRADE — SK/CZ

www.tss.sk — VKM: TSS TT

This Bratislava-based company provides locomotives and trains for infrastructure projects, mainly in Slovakia. Note that 740.604 is a different locomotive to AWT-operated 740.604 registered in the Czech Republic. Livery is red & grey.

Number	Builder	Built	Type	kW	Details	Notes
730.618-6	ČKD	1988	T457.0	600	Bo-Bo DE	
740.604-4	ČKD	1982	T448.0	883	Bo-Bo DE	Ex-740.752
742.605-9	ČKD	1984	T466.2	883	Bo-Bo DE	Ex-742.407
742.644-8	ČKD	1985	T466.2	883	Bo-Bo DE	Ex-742.415
742.645-5	ČKD	1985	T466.2	883	Bo-Bo DE	Ex-742.416

5.2.39. TŘINECKÉ ŽELEZÁRNY — CZ

www.trz.cz — VKM: TŽ

The vast iron and steelworks at Třinec dates back to 1839. Today the company produces around a third of all steel produced in the Czech Republic, exporting finished products worldwide and employing more than 5000 staff. It specialises in rails, steel rods, bars and tubes.

The locomotive fleet is used exclusively on internal workings. Classes 724/729.7 have been rebuilt with new CAT engines. 723.701 is a new CZ LOKO prototype delivered to Třinecké Železárny in 2015 for trial operation.

Number	Builder	Built	Type	kW	Details	Notes
702.532-3	JLS	r1996	ex-T212.0			
709.515-1	ČKD	1994	T239.1	327	Bo DE	
709.516-9	ČKD	1994	T239.1	327	Bo DE	
721.542-9	ČKD	1968	T458.1	551	Bo-Bo DE	
723.701-9	CZ LOKO	2015	ex-T448.0	522	Bo-Bo DE	
724.701-8	ČMKS	r1999	ex-T448.0	627	Bo-Bo DE	Rebuilt ex-740.594
724.702-6	ČMKS	r2000	ex-T448.0	627	Bo-Bo DE	Rebuilt ex-740.574
724.801-6	ČMKS	r2004	ex-T448.0	709	Bo-Bo DE	Rebuilt ex-740.626
724.802-4	ČMKS	r2005	ex-T448.0	709	Bo-Bo DE	Rebuilt ex-740.532
724.803-2	CZ LOKO	r2007	ex-T448.0	709	Bo-Bo DE	Rebuilt ex-Polish T448.P086
724.804-0	CZ LOKO	r2007	ex-T448.0	709	Bo-Bo DE	Rebuilt ex-Polish T448.P075
724.805-7	CZ LOKO	r2008	ex-T448.0	709	Bo-Bo DE	Rebuilt ex-Polish T448.P079
724.806-5	CZ LOKO	r2008	ex-T448.0	709	Bo-Bo DE	Rebuilt ex-740.563
724.807-3	CZ LOKO	r2009	ex-T448.0	709	Bo-Bo DE	Rebuilt ex-740.702
729.607-2	ČKD	1989	T419.1	600	Bo-Bo DE	
729.618-9	ČKD	1992	T419.1	600	Bo-Bo DE	
729.619-7	ČKD	1992	T419.1	600	Bo-Bo DE	
729.701-3	CZ LOKO	r2007	ex-T419.0	709	Bo-Bo DE	Rebuilt ex-729.503
729.702-1	CZ LOKO	r2007	ex-T419.0	709	Bo-Bo DE	Rebuilt ex-729.512
740.418-9	ČKD	1987	T448.0	883	Bo-Bo DE	
740.565-7	ČKD	1976	T448.0	883	Bo-Bo DE	
740.680-4	ČKD	1980	T448.0	883	Bo-Bo DE	
740.729-9	ČKD	1982	T448.0	883	Bo-Bo DE	
740.755-4	ČKD	1983	T448.0	883	Bo-Bo DE	
740.756-2	ČKD	1983	T448.0	883	Bo-Bo DE	
740.783-6	ČKD	1983	T448.0	883	Bo-Bo DE	
740.807-3	ČKD	1984	T448.0	883	Bo-Bo DE	
740.834-7	ČKD	1984	T448.0	883	Bo-Bo DE	
740.867-7	ČKD	1985	T448.0	883	Bo-Bo DE	

5.2.40. UNIPETROL DOPRAVA   CZ

www.unipetroldoprava.cz   VKM: UNIDO

Unipetrol Doprava is part of the Polish Orlen Group and is based in the former petrochemical works, Chemopetrol, at Litvínov. In 2004 the company commenced main line operations with one pair of refurbished "Goggles" diesel locomotives and a handful of Class 740s, and since then has grown to become the third largest freight carrier in the Czech Republic, specialising in the transport of dangerous goods such as chemicals, fuel oil and fertilizers. Unipetrol trains can be seen across the country, although much of its traffic is in the industrial north-west – around Most and Litvínov to locations including Neratovice, Kralupy nad Vltavou and Rumburk. Unipetrol locomotives can be found at chemical factories in the Neratovice, Pardubice and Kolín areas. There is also some cross-border traffic to Poland and Slovakia. The main depot is located alongside the Litvínov chemical works, close to Most-Minerva station.

The company uses two ex-ČD Class 121 electrics for main line flows. In addition, in 2015 the company leased TRAXX electric locomotive 186.432 from RAILPOOL. Initially it is being used between Litvínov and Kralupy nad Vltavou, but will later be used between Děčín and Břeclav.

Some of the Class 724 and 740 diesels and also the small diesels may be restricted to operating within plant sites. The Class 724s were rebuilt by ČMKS/CZ LOKO Jihlava in the mid 2000s with new but lower powered CAT engines designed for short distance main line work or heavy shunting duties. The six Class 741 were rebuilt by ČMKS in the early 2000s from Class 740 to a similar design as the rebuilt ČD Cargo Class 742, with a reduced height front at the cab end to give better visibility. On main line work Classes 740/741 and 753 are often used in pairs on heavier trains. The former ČD Class 753s have been fitted with CAT 3512 engines. 753.740/741 were originally outshopped for AWT before being transferred to Unipetrol in 2011.

The Class 820 DMU is based at Litvínov depot and is used for transferring staff between local industrial locations. It may also sometimes be used for other charter work.

Unipetrol livery is deep blue and green.

Number	Builder	Built	Type	kW	Details	Notes
121.056-6	Škoda	1960	E469.1	2032	Bo-Bo E DC	Internal 143
121.073-1	Škoda	1960	E469.1	2032	Bo-Bo E DC	Internal 144
186.432-1	Bombardier	2015	TRAXX	5600	Bo-Bo E MS	Leased from RAILPOOL
709.518-5	ČKD	1995	T239.1	327	Bo DE	Internal 111
709.519-3	ČKD	1995	T239.1	327	Bo DE	Internal 112
711.081-0	ŽOS Zvolen	r1996	ex-T334.0	210	C DE	Internal 134. Rebuilt ex-710.081
711.501-7	JLS	r2000	ex-T334.0	242	C DE	Internal 133. Rebuilt ex-710.749
724.601-0	ČMKS	r2005	ex-T448.0	392	Bo-Bo DE	Internal 101. Rebuilt ex-740.504
724.602-8	CZ LOKO	r2006	ex-T448.0	392	Bo-Bo DE	Internal 122. Rebuilt ex-740.633
724.603-6	CZ LOKO	r2006	ex-T448.0	392	Bo-Bo DE	Internal 103. Rebuilt ex-740.546
724.604-4	CZ LOKO	r2006	ex-T448.0	392	Bo-Bo DE	Internal 128. Rebuilt ex-740.558
724.711-7	CZ LOKO	r2007	ex-T448.0	627	Bo-Bo DE	Internal 120. Rebuilt ex-740.727
724.712-5	CZ LOKO	r2008	ex-T448.0	627	Bo-Bo DE	Internal 129. Rebuilt ex-740.598
729.610-6	ČKD	1991	T419.15	600	Bo-Bo DE	Internal 105
740.410-6	ČKD	1984	T448.0	883	Bo-Bo DE	Internal 131
740.514-5	ČKD	1974	T448.0	883	Bo-Bo DE	Internal 121
740.719-0	ČKD	1982	T448.0	883	Bo-Bo DE	Internal 115
740.735-6	ČKD	1982	T448.0	883	Bo-Bo DE	Internal 104
740.774-5	ČKD	1983	T448.0	883	Bo-Bo DE	Internal 109
740.784-4	ČKD	1983	T448.0	883	Bo-Bo DE	Internal 123
740.802-4	ČKD	1984	T448.0	883	Bo-Bo DE	Internal 108
740.803-2	ČKD	1984	T448.0	883	Bo-Bo DE	Internal 107
740.824-8	ČKD	1984	T448.0	883	Bo-Bo DE	Internal 116
740.839-6	ČKD	1984	T448.0	883	Bo-Bo DE	Internal 132
741.510-2	ČKD	1985	T448.0	883	Bo-Bo DE	Internal 124. Rebuilt ex-740.879
741.511-0	ČKD	1980	T448.0	883	Bo-Bo DE	Internal 130. Rebuilt ex-740.677
741.512-8	ČKD	1974	T448.0	883	Bo-Bo DE	Internal 102. Rebuilt ex-740.510
741.513-6	ČKD	1982	T448.0	883	Bo-Bo DE	Internal 110. Rebuilt ex-740.726
741.514-4	ČKD	1977	T448.0	883	Bo-Bo DE	Internal 117. Rebuilt ex-740.607
741.515-1	ČKD	1980	T448.0	883	Bo-Bo DE	Internal 119. Rebuilt ex-740.690
744.701-4	ČMKS	r1998	ex-T448.1	970	Bo-Bo DE	Internal 118. Rebuilt ex-740.635
753.715-2	ČKD	1975	T478.3	1500	Bo-Bo DE	Internal 135. ex-753.260

753.716-0	ČKD	1973	T478.3	1500	Bo-Bo DE	Internal 136. ex-753.082
753.717-8	ČKD	1977	T478.3	1500	Bo-Bo DE	Internal 137. ex-753.384
753.718-6	ČKD	1977	T478.3	1500	Bo-Bo DE	Internal 138. ex-753.392
753.719-4	ČKD	1976	T478.3	1500	Bo-Bo DE	Internal 139. ex-753.331
753.720-2	ČKD	1977	T478.3	1500	Bo-Bo DE	Internal 140. ex-753.370
753.721-0	ČKD	1977	T478.3	1500	Bo-Bo DE	Internal 141. ex-753.406
753.722-8	ČKD	1973	T478.3	1500	Bo-Bo DE	Internal 142. ex-753.075
753.740-0	ČKD	1975	T478.3	1500	Bo-Bo DE	Internal 145. ex-750.257
753.741-8	ČKD	1972	T478.3	1500	Bo-Bo DE	Internal 146. ex-750.038
820.528-8	ČKD	1963	M240	206	B2 DH	Ex-820.028

5.2.41. U.S. STEEL KOŠICE   SK

www.usske.sk   VKM: USSK

Steel production at the Východoslovenské Železiarne (VSŽ, the East Slovakian Iron Works) started in 1965. The massive plant is located a few miles south of Košice and is the largest employer in the area. The 1520 mm-gauge SRT line was built to feed VSŽ with iron ore from Ukraine and opened in 1966. In 2000 the steelworks was bought by US Steel, by which time VSŽ was already running its own freight trains over ŽSR tracks, including limestone trains between Turňa nad Bodvou and Haniska pri Košiciach (now worked by Class 774.7 rebuilds).

US Steel's own fleet of locomotives can be observed in the huge yards and exchange sidings close to the ZSSK Cargo depot at Haniska pri Košiciach, whilst the smaller locomotives are normally used for internal shunting within the vast site. The Class 774.5 Co-Co rebuilds are similar to Czech Class 774.7 with CAT 3512 engines. The rebuilt Class 724 kept the serial numbers of the Class 740 from which each locomotive was rebuilt. These have CAT 3412 engines. The rebuild work on Classes 724/774 was undertaken by ŽOS Zvolen under licence to ČMKS/CZ LOKO. Livery is all over yellow with a red stripe.

Number	Builder	Built	Type	kW	Details	Notes
709.520-1	ČKD	1995	T239.1	327	Bo DE	Carries original No. T239.1020
709.521-9	ČKD	1995	T239.1	327	Bo DE	Carries original No. T239.1021
709.522-7	ČKD	1995	T239.1	327	Bo DE	Carries original No. T239.1022
709.523-5	ČKD	1995	T239.1	327	Bo DE	Carries original No. T239.1023
709.530-0	ČKD	1996	T239.1	327	Bo DE	Carries original No. T239.1030
709.531-8	ČKD	1996	T239.1	327	Bo DE	Carries original No. T239.1031
724.516-0	ŽOS Zvolen	r2004	ex-T448.0	627	Bo-Bo DE	Rebuilt ex-740.516
724.538-4	ŽOS Zvolen	r2003	ex-T448.0	627	Bo-Bo DE	Rebuilt ex-740.538
724.540-0	ŽOS Zvolen	r2007	ex-T448.0	627	Bo-Bo DE	Rebuilt ex-740.540
724.571-5	ŽOS Zvolen	r2005	ex-T448.0	627	Bo-Bo DE	Rebuilt ex-740.571
724.576-4	ŽOS Zvolen	r2006	ex-T448.0	627	Bo-Bo DE	Rebuilt ex-740.576
724.654-9	ŽOS Zvolen	r2004	ex-T448.0	627	Bo-Bo DE	Rebuilt ex-740.654
724.700-0	ŽOS Zvolen	r2005	ex-T448.0	627	Bo-Bo DE	Rebuilt ex-740.700
724.710-9	ŽOS Zvolen	r2008	ex-T448.0	627	Bo-Bo DE	Rebuilt ex-740.710
724.875-0	ŽOS Zvolen	r2009	ex-T448.0	627	Bo-Bo DE	Rebuilt ex-740.875
724.932-9	ŽOS Zvolen	r2008	ex-T448.0	627	Bo-Bo DE	Rebuilt ex-740.932
724.935-2	ŽOS Zvolen	r2003	ex-T448.0	627	Bo-Bo DE	Rebuilt ex-740.935
729.507-4	ČKD	1986	T419.0	600	Bo-Bo DE	Carries original No. T419.0507
729.508-2	ČKD	1986	T419.0	600	Bo-Bo DE	Carries original No. T419.0508
729.509-0	ČKD	1986	T419.0	600	Bo-Bo DE	Carries original No. T419.0509
729.606-4	ČKD	1989	T419.1	600	Bo-Bo DE	Carries original No. T419.1506
729.612-2	ČKD	1991	T419.1	600	Bo-Bo DE	Carries original No. T419.1512
729.613-0	ČKD	1991	T419.1	600	Bo-Bo DE	Carries original No. T419.1513
729.615-5	ČKD	1992	T419.1	600	Bo-Bo DE	Carries original No. T419.1515
740.431-2	ČKD	1987	T448.0	883	Bo-Bo DE	Carries original No. T448.0931
740.522-8	ČKD	1974	T448.0	883	Bo-Bo DE	Carries original No. T448.0522
740.605-1	ČKD	r1997	ex-T448.0	654	Bo-Bo DE	Rebuilt with 2 x MTU 8V183 engines Carries original No. T448.0605
740.805-7	ČKD	1984	T448.0	883	Bo-Bo DE	Carries original No. T448.0805
740.941-0	ČKD	1987	T448.0	883	Bo-Bo DE	Carries original No. T448.0941
770.511-4	SMZ	1968	T669.0	993	Co-Co DE	1520 mm gauge. Ex-T669.0511i
770.516-3	SMZ	1969	T669.0	993	Co-Co DE	1520 mm gauge. Ex-T669.0516i
770.523-9	ČKD	1982	T669.0	993	Co-Co DE	1520 mm gauge

770.535-3	ČKD	1986	T669.0	993	Co-Co DE	
774.501-1	ŽOS Zvolen	r2009	ex-T669.1	1455	Co-Co DE	Rebuilt ex-770.501ᴵ
774.502-9	ŽOS Zvolen	r2003	ex-T669.1	1455	Co-Co DE	Rebuilt ex-770.502ᴵ
774.503-7	ŽOS Zvolen	r2004	ex-T669.1	1455	Co-Co DE	Rebuilt ex-770.503ᴵ
774.507-8	ŽOS Zvolen	r	ex-T669.1	1455	Co-Co DE	Rebuilt ex-770.507ᴵ

5.2.42. VÍTKOVICE DOPRAVA   CZ

www.vitkovice.cz   VKM: VD

A somewhat older concern than the nearby ArcelorMittal Ostrava steelworks, the Vítkovice iron works was established in 1828. Privatised in 1998, the subsidiary transport service company Vítkovice Doprava was set up in 2004, initially to work its own traffic over main line tracks. Although mainly limited to operating within its own internal complex, Vítkovice Doprava does have country-wide access, although its locomotives are normally limited to relatively short-distance trips from Ostrava, such as to Štramberk. The company also has some narrow gauge DH200 locomotives. 714.811 has been converted to operate on natural gas, with a CAT3412G engine. Shunter 703.821 has also been converted to operate on natural gas.

Former Type 81-71 Praha Metro cars 2395 and 2501 are also on site and used to convey visitors around the site during open days etc. Livery is blue & orange.

Number	Builder	Built	Type	kW	Details	Notes
701.774-2	ČKD	1962	T211.1	147	B DM	(S) Ex-T211.0894
702.629-6	TSM	1971	T212.0	147	B DM	(S) Ex-T212.0088/702.088
703.501-7	TSM	1969	T212.1	169	B DH	
703.821-9	TSM	1978	T212.1	159	B DH	Ex-703.023/703.610
709.507-8	ČKD	1993	T239.1	327	Bo DE	
709.510-2	ČKD	1993	T239.1	327	Bo DE	
709.511-0	ČKD	1993	T239.1	327	Bo DE	
709.533-4	ČKD	1996	T239.1	327	Bo DE	
710.698-2	ČKD	1966	T334.0	301	C DH	(S)
714.811-7	ČKD	1993	714.8	600	Bo-Bo	Rebuilt ex-735.170/714.002
729.504-1	ČKD	1986	T419.0	600	Bo-Bo DE	
729.604-9	ČKD	1989	T419.1	600	Bo-Bo DE	
729.605-6	ČKD	1989	T419.1	600	Bo-Bo DE	
729.616-3	ČKD	1992	T419.1	600	Bo-Bo DE	
729.617-1	ČKD	1992	T419.1	600	Bo-Bo DE	
740.309-0	ČKD	1976	T448.0	392	Bo-Bo DE	Ex-740.544
740.315-7	ČKD	1976	T448.0	392	Bo-Bo DE	Ex-740.530
740.317-3	ČKD	1976	T448.0	392	Bo-Bo DE	Ex-740.526
740.631-7	ČKD	1978	T448.0	883	Bo-Bo DE	
740.660-6	ČKD	1979	T448.0	883	Bo-Bo DE	Leased from Česká Lokomotivka
740.785-1	ČKD	1983	T448.0	883	Bo-Bo DE	
740.880-0	ČKD	1985	T448.0	883	Bo-Bo DE	
741.519-3	ČKD	1978	T448.0	883	Bo-Bo DE	Rebuilt ex-740.632
742.118-3	ČKD	1978	T466.2	883	Bo-Bo DE	(S) Ex-ČD

5.2.43. VUZ VELIM   CZ

www.cdvuz.cz   VKM: VUZ

"VUZ" stands for Výzkumný Ústav Železniční or "Railway Research Institute" in English. The company, part of the Czech Railways Group, is responsible for operating one of the most advanced train testing centres in Europe, located around 50 km east of Praha, and accessed via a short (non-electrified) connecting line from the main Praha–Kolín line at Velim station. The test centre was built in the early 1960s.

The test centre has two circuits, a 13 km large ring, where trains can be tested at up to 210 km/h (230 km/h for tilting trains) and a 4 km small ring. It is visited by new trains from all over Europe (including from the UK), and even those built by Siemens, which has its own testing facilities but cannot match Velim for its tight radius curves etc. Velim is also extensively used for signalling and ETCS testing.

VUZ has its own small fleet of locomotives. 124.601 was originally built as E469.3030 (which would have been 123.030, the last-built of the Class 121–123 design locomotives). It has a 200 km/h maximum speed, and when on test shortly after being built in 1972 it reached 219 km/h on the Velim test track – a new speed record for Czechoslovak railway vehicles. Today it is used to haul coaching stock at the test centre. The Class 740 or Class 751 are used to haul trains from the main line connection into the site. 751.010 is a locomotive designated for the NTM, in the care of VUZ Velim.

T499 "Kyklop" prototype 759.002 is one of two prototypes built in 1974. These were the most powerful diesel locomotives produced in Czechoslovakia, intended for express passenger trains at 140 km/h. On test at Velim 759.001 (which was scrapped in 1989 after fire damage), reached 176 km/h. However in the end further electrification was decided upon, rather than an order for T499.0s. 759.002 received an extensive overhaul at DPOV Nymburk in 2014–15, and now tours the country visiting open days and working special trains etc.

"MV1" is one of the former Class 560 driving trailers, converted to a measuring vehicle in 1973.

Number	Builder	Built	Type	kW	Details	Notes
124.601-6	Škoda	1971	E469.3	2472	Bo-Bo E DC	Ex-E469.3030
740.420-5	ČKD	1987	T448.0	883	Bo-Bo DE	
751.010-0	ČKD	1967	T478.1	1103	Bo-Bo DE	Carries original No. T478.1010
759.002-9	ČKD	1974	T499.0	1765	Bo-Bo DE	Former prototype T499.0002
MV1	ČKD	1966	SM488.0	–	Bo-Bo E	Former Class 560 driving trailer EVN: 99 54 9 360 001-0

5.2.44. XTR LOGISTICS   CZ

www.xtrlogistic.cz

As this book closed for press in spring 2016, all 12 members of Belgian SNCB Class 12 were in the Czech Republic, 1203 having arrived in 2014 for testing and the remainder following in 2016. They have been acquired by Czech leasing company XTR Logistics and will be overhauled by CZ LOKO for hire to Czech freight operators. Class 12 were built in 1986 and operated passenger and freight trains between Belgium and France before being stored in 2013. Their 3000 V DC and 25 kV AC capabilities correspond with the two voltages in the Czech Republic, plus neighbouring Hungary (25 kV AC) and Poland (3000 V DC). If successful then members of SNCB Class 11 (12 locos, 1500/3000 V DC) and Class 21 (60 locomotives in total, 3000 V DC only) could follow.

In this listing the locomotives' SNCB numbers are shown. Czech numbers are not yet known.

Number	Builder	Built	Type	kW	Details	Notes
1201	BN/ACEC	1986	SNCB 12	3310	Bo-Bo E MS	
1202	BN/ACEC	1986	SNCB 12	3310	Bo-Bo E MS	
1203	BN/ACEC	1986	SNCB 12	3310	Bo-Bo E MS	
1204	BN/ACEC	1986	SNCB 12	3310	Bo-Bo E MS	
1205	BN/ACEC	1986	SNCB 12	3310	Bo-Bo E MS	
1206	BN/ACEC	1986	SNCB 12	3310	Bo-Bo E MS	
1207	BN/ACEC	1986	SNCB 12	3310	Bo-Bo E MS	
1208	BN/ACEC	1986	SNCB 12	3310	Bo-Bo E MS	
1209	BN/ACEC	1986	SNCB 12	3310	Bo-Bo E MS	
1210	BN/ACEC	1986	SNCB 12	3310	Bo-Bo E MS	
1211	BN/ACEC	1986	SNCB 12	3310	Bo-Bo E MS	
1212	BN/ACEC	1986	SNCB 12	3310	Bo-Bo E MS	

5.2.45. ŽELEZIARNE PODBREZOVÁ   SK

www.zelpo.eu   VKM: ZELPO

Železiarne Podbrezová ironworks, in Central Slovakia, was established in 1840 and today is one of the leading producers of steel tube and pipes in Europe, employing more than 3000 staff. Around 160 000 tonnes of products are produced every year, much of it from scrap metal – generating inbound and outbound freight at Podbrezová.

The ŽP fleet of six locomotives is involved in internal shunting within the vast site – visible from the Zvolen–Brezno line, and also moving wagons into and out of the adjacent exchange yard for onward movement by ZSSK Cargo.

Number	Builder	Built	Type	kW	Details	Notes
729.601-5	ČKD	1989	T419.1	600	Bo-Bo DE	Carries original No. T419.1501
729.620-0	ČKD	1989	T419.1	600	Bo-Bo DE	
740.547-5	ČKD	1976	T448.0	883	Bo-Bo DE	Carries original No. T448.0547
740.695-2	ČKD	1981	T448.0	883	Bo-Bo DE	Carries original No. T448.0695
740.781-0	ČKD	1983	T448.0	883	Bo-Bo DE	Carries original No. T448.0781
740.859-4	ČKD	1985	T448.0	883	Bo-Bo DE	Carries original No. T448.0859

5.2.46. ŽELEZNIČNÉ STAVBY KOŠICE (ŽS KOŠICE) SK

www.zeleznicnestavby.sk   VKM: ZSKE

This Košice-based infrastructure operator was established in 1996 from a former departmental organisation (TSS Košice). It operates four Class 740/742 locomotives which can mainly be seen in the east of Slovakia. The company also operates a number of On-Track Machines which are used on infrastructure duties. Livery is green & yellow.

Number	Builder	Built	Type	kW	Details	Notes
740.687-9	ČKD	1980	T448.0	883	Bo-Bo DE	
740.742-2	ČKD	1976	T448.0	883	Bo-Bo DE	Ex-740.584
740.810-7	ČKD	1984	T448.0	883	Bo-Bo DE	
742.601-8	ČKD	1983	T466.2	883	Bo-Bo DE	Ex-742.359

5.2.47. ŽOS VRÚTKY SK

www.zos-vrutky.sk   VKM: ŽOS Vr

While ŽOS Zvolen Works (see below) specialises in diesel locomotives, ŽOS Vrútky, on the Žilina–Košice main line, specialises in electrics. The vast works, dating from 1874, has also built new DMUs (Class 861 for ZSSK) and also recently EMUs (1000 mm gauge Class 425.95 units for the High Tatra Electric Railway). The company also undertakes carriage overhauls for ZSSK and main component overhauls, particularly traction motor overhauls. It also specialises in accident damage repairs. One of the major projects ongoing at the time of writing is the rebuilding of ZSSK Class 163 as dual-voltage Class 361.

As well as locomotives for internal shunting, ŽOS Vrútky has a locomotive hire fleet, including some Classes 770/771, of which two are 1520 mm gauge and can usually be found around Haniska pri Košiciach. Livery is blue & white.

Number	Builder	Built	Type	kW	Details	Notes
181.065-4	Škoda	1961	E669.1	2790	Co-Co E DC	(S) Ex-LOTOS (PL) 150.711
181.066-2	Škoda	1961	E669.1	2790	Co-Co E DC	(S) Ex-LOTOS (PL) 150.700
181.089-4	Škoda	1962	E669.1	2790	Co-Co E DC	(S) Ex-LOTOS (PL) 150.702
701.635-5	ČKD	1960	T211.1	147	B DM	
702.609-9	TSM	1968	T212.0	147	B DM	
720.013-2	ČKD	1959	T435.0	551	Bo-Bo DE	Ex-720.602
740.649-9	ČKD	1978	T448.0	883	Bo-Bo DE	
740.816-4	ČKD	1984	T448.0	883	Bo-Bo DE	
740.853-7	ČKD	1985	T448.0	883	Bo-Bo DE	
770.610-4	SMZ	1968	T669.0	993	Co-Co DE	Ex-770.510[I]
770.812-6	SMZ	1969	T669.0	993	Co-Co DE	Ex-770.102. 1520 mm gauge
770.814-2	ČKD	1980	T669.0	993	Co-Co DE	Ex-770.515[II]. 1520 mm gauge
771.507-1	SMZ	1970	T669.1	993	Co-Co DE	
771.513-9	SMZ	1971	T669.1	993	Co-Co DE	

5.2.48. ŽOS ZVOLEN

SK

www.zoszv.sk

VKM: ŽOSZV

ŽOS Zvolen works is one of the principal railway works establishments in Slovakia, overhauling not only complete locomotives but also components. A works on the site was established in 1872 and today it employs more than 600 staff. The company specialises in rebuilding diesel locomotives, recent successes including the 25 Class 757 rebuilds for ZSSK top-link passenger work. It has also rebuilt a large number of DMUs for ZSSK. 813.101/102 were leased to GW Train Regio until 2015. 813.110 is an even more radical rebuild of Class 810 which has seen use with ZSSK on a trial basis.

The company also owns its own fleet of hire locomotives for use on the main line. This includes 740.044/049 leased to CRW and 140.067 to PSŽ. Class 712 (heavy rebuild of Class 710) is now in use with a number of companies, and ZSSK has used them to replace ageing Class 721 shunters at some locations.

Originally part of the state railway until 1994, the company was then privatised, and in 2008 became part of the ŽOS Trnava group. It should not be confused with the almost identically named ZOS Zvolen (a locomotive hire company) or ZOS Loko, also based in Zvolen!

Number	Builder	Built	Type	kW	Details	Notes
140.058-9	Škoda	1957	E499.0	2032	Bo-Bo E DC	
181.121-5	Škoda	1965	E669.1	2790	Co-Co E DC	(S)
712.407-6	ŽOS Zvolen	r	ex-T334.0	328	C DE	Ex-710.907. ZSSK Zvolen
712.416-7	ŽOS Zvolen	r2011	ex-T334.0	328	C DE (008)	Ex-710.916. ŽOS Zvolen Works
712.422-5	ŽOS Zvolen	r	ex-T334.0	328	C DE	Ex-710.922. ZSSK Zvolen
712.440-7	ŽOS Zvolen	r2009	ex-T334.0	328	C DE (005)	Ex-710.940. ZSSKC Spišská Nová Ves
712.523-0	ŽOS Zvolen	r2007	ex-T334.0	328	C DE (004)	Ex-T334.0523. ELTRA, Košice
712.752-5	ŽOS Zvolen	r2012	ex-T334.0	328	C DE (009)	Ex-710.752. ZSSK Nove Zamky depot
712.765-7	ŽOS Zvolen	r	ex-T334.0	328	C DE	Ex-710.765. ZSSKC Bratislava Východ
721.512-2	ČKD	1965	T458.1	551	Bo-Bo DE	
742.321-3	ČKD	1983	T466.2	883	Bo-Bo DE	Ex-ČD
813.101-3	ŽOS Zvolen	r2012	813	310	A1 DH	Ex-810.413.
913.101-2	ŽOS Zvolen	r2012	913	-	2	Ex-011.404.
813.102-1	ŽOS Zvolen	r2012	813	310	A1 DH	Ex-810.581.
913.102-0	ŽOS Zvolen	r2012	913	-	2	Ex-011.008.
813.110-8	ŽOS Zvolen	r2013	813.1	310	A1 DH	Ex 810.380
913.110-3	ŽOS Zvolen	r2013	913.1	-	2	Ex 810.447

5.2.49. ŽELEZNICE SLOVENSKEJ REPUBLIKY (ŽSR)   SK

VKM: ŽSR

www.zsr.sk

ŽSR is the state-owned railway infrastructure company in Slovakia, which, unlike SŽDC in the Czech Republic also has a fleet of its own locomotives which are used for infrastructure work across the network. Normally the shunting locomotives are outbased at sites for some time, and locations known at the time of going to press are shown below.

Number	Builder	Built	Type	kW	Details	Notes
701.020-0	ČKD	1962	T211.1	169	B DM	Bratislava
701.612-4	ČKD	1959	T211.1	169	B DM	Ex-T211.1031. Levice
701.615-7	ČKD	1958	T211.1	169	B DM	Bratislava
701.790-8	ČKD	1961	T211.1	169	B DM	Vrútky
702.523-2	ČKD	1967	T212.0	147	B DM	Bratislava
702.603-2	TSM	1968	T212.0	147	B DM	Zvolen
702.619-8	TSM	1968	T212.0	147	B DM	Žilina
702.622-2	TSM	1971	T212.0	147	B DM	Ex-T212.0081. Poprad-Tatry
702.627-1	TSM	1971	T212.0	147	B DM	Ex-T212.0086. Bratislava
703.719-5	CZ LOKO	r2014	ex-T212.0	205	B DH	Ex-703.026. Vrútky
710.429-2	TSM	1971	T334.1	301	C DH	Zvolen

710.606-5	TSM	1972	T334.1	301	C DH	Bratislava
721.602-1	ČKD	1971	T458.1	551	Bo-Bo DE	Ex-721.547. Košice
725.070-7	TSM	1964	T444.0	515	B-B DH	Levice
730.605-3	ČKD	1988	T457.0	600	Bo-Bo DE	Košice
730.617-8	ČKD	1988	T457.0	600	Bo-Bo DE	Žilina
730.619-4	ČKD	1988	T457.0	600	Bo-Bo DE	Košice
730.621-0	ČKD	1988	T457.0	600	Bo-Bo DE	Zvolen
730.629-3	ČKD	1989	T457.0	600	Bo-Bo DE	Spišská Nová Ves
742.418-7	ČKD	1985	T466.2	883	Bo-Bo DE	Ex-742.647
742.643-0	ČKD	1985	T466.2	883	Bo-Bo DE	Ex-742.414. Bratislava
742.646-3	ČKD	1985	T466.2	883	Bo-Bo DE	Ex-742.417. Spišská Nová Ves
745.608-0	LEW	1983	V100.1	736	B-B DH	ex-DR 110 969-3. Fiľakovo
850.018-7	MSV	1967	M286.0	515	B-2	Converted to test unit

5.3. OTHER PRIVATE LOCOMOTIVES

Other operator's locomotives are shown in the lists below. The author would be pleased to receive any additions or location changes, particularly to Classes 700–711, that readers may observe.

Class 199 JLS; 37.5 kW; Bo BE.

199.001-9 1993 ŽĎAS, Žďár nad Sázavou

Class 242 Škoda S499.02; 3080 kW; Bo-Bo E AC.

242.219-4 1975 CER Cargo Slovakia. Ex-ČD
242.543-7 1973 Railtrans International, Slovakia. Ex-BDŽ 43.543
242.557-7 1975 Railtrans International, Slovakia. Ex-ČD 242.203

Class 700 ČKD T211.0; 121 kW; B DM.

700.009-4	1958	MJM, Litovel předměstí		700.618-2	1959	MTC, Velvary
700.060-7	1960	Puš, Dvůr Králové nad Labem		700.634-9	1958	Cemex, Brno Komárov
700.164-7	1962	Cerea, Chotěboř		700.704-0	1960	Kotouč, Štramberk
700.435-1	1962	Kolín scrapyard		700.831-1	1961	Brno Dolní depot (S)

Class 701 ČKD T211.1; 169 kW; B DM.

701.016-8		ACHP Sadová		701.653-8		Vendys & V, Česká Lípa
701.060-6		Šrot Gebeshuber, Sokolnice		701.666-0	1959	NCH, Měšice u Prahy
701.067-1	1961	Eurovia, Řevnice		701.667-8		ATECO, Praha-Bubny
701.301-4	1961	ACHP Sadová		701.681-9		ZZN Velké Meziříčí
701.420-2	1961	Českomoravský Cem,		701.687-6	1962	MTH, Hradec Králové
		Mokrá-Horákov		701.688-4		SMZ, Jelšava
701.430-1		ŽS Brno, Brno Královo Pole		701.709-8	1959	PASO, Brno Modřice
701.432-7	1961	Trojek, Ostrava Přívoz		701.712-2	1961	TOS, Čelákovice
701.439-2	1962	TRAKCE, Ostrava		701.715-5		Kovošrot Ostrava Přívoz
701.441-8		Excalibur Army, Přelouc		701.721-3	1961	Chart Ferox, Děčín
701.450-9	1961	Legios, Louny		701.735-3	1960	Třebíč, Šlapanice
701.549-8	1958	Drahspol, Libuň		701.746-0		Kovosteel, Staré Město u Uh
701.557-1		Dopraspol, Břeclav				Hradiště
701.596-9	1961	Brno Dolní depot (S)		701.750-2	1958	Koop Agro, Přerov
701.608-2	1961	Lafarge Cement, Čížkovice		701.751-0		Unex, Uničov
701.616-5		DOBET, Ústí nad Labem		701.773-4	1961	Trojek, Ostrava Přívoz
701.623-1	1959	Kámen Zbraslav, Středokluky		701.775-9	1962	Olšanské Papírny, Lukavice
701.634-8	1962	BEZ Transformátory,		701.779-1		Kolín
		Bratislava Rača		701.783-3		Tonaso, Neštěmice
701.643-9	1960	Sigma Doprava, Lutín		701.784-1		ZZN, Ivančice
701.650-4	1958	Onivon, Chrudim		701.828-6		ŽĎAS, Žďár nad Sázavou

188

Class 702 TSM T212.0; 147 kW; B DM.

702.001-9		DYKO, Kolín. Ex-702.601
702.009-2		Pars nova, Šumperk Works
702.014-2	1968	Vitana, Roudnice nad Labem
702.024-1		LYCOS, Trnava
702.099-3		PSP, Přerov
702.511-7		ZZN, Pečky
702.513-3	1967	ZZN, Kolín
702.521-6	1967	BRKS, Nymburk
702.526-5	1967	AGRO, Žamberk
702.528-1	1967	Klima, Prachatice
702.529-9	1967	Zempo, Bečváry
702.538-0	1967	SEP, Chrlice
702.545-5	1967	P-d Refractories, Velké Opatovice
702.546-3	1967	Quelle, Březhrad
702.548-9	1967	Rockwool, Bohumín
702.554-7	1967	Alstom, Brno
702.564-6	1967	Kovohute, Mníšek pod Brdy
702.574-5	1968	Mondi Bupak, České Budějovice
702.582-8	1968	ŽPSV, Čerčany
702.585-1	1968	TON, Holešov
702.594-3	1968	SUD, Teplice
702.597-6	1968	Raven, Hradec Králové
702.610-7	1968	Cerera, Nový Bydžov
702.613-1	1968	Brno Královopolská
702.615-6	1968	Geomonta, Banská Bystrica
702.618-0	1968	Unex, Uničov
702.620-6	1968	ŽDB, Bohumín
702.621-4	1968	Buzuluk, Komárov
702.631-3		Chemické Závody, Žilina
702.641-2		Technoplast, Chropyně
702.643-8	1969	Slévárna, Liberec
702.645-3	1969	ZZN, Rakovník
702.661-0		TON, Bystřice pod Hostýnem
702.663-6		Magnezitke, Košice
702.669-3		Šrot Gebeshuber, Sokolnice
702.679-2	1970	Kovošrot, Česká Lípa
702.688-3	1970	AgroZZN, Kojetice na Moravě

Class 703 TSM T212.1; 169 kW; B DH. * Rebuilt by CZ LOKO.

703.002-6	1977	Pars nova, Šumperk Works
703.012-5	1978	COMAX, Bratislava
703.024-0		BEZ MOTORY, Hradec Králové
703.302-2		DZ Steel, Soběslav (ex-703.542)
703.510-8	r	Škoda, Plzeň Works*
703.511-6	1972	Kovošrot, Děčín
703.512-4	1972	Ethanol Energy, Vrdy
703.514-0	1972	Kovošrot, Kolín
703.517-3	1972	CEREA, Smiřice
703.518-1		GeLiMa, Liptovský Mikuláš
703.520-7		Kovošrot, Česká Lípa
703.522-3		ŽPSV, Uherský Ostroh
703.524-9		Ferona, Chomutov
703.526-4	1973	Vitana, Byšice
703.535-5		Calmit, Margecany (S)
703.539-7	1973	Břeclav station
703.540-5	1973	Raven, Ostrava Svinov
703.546-2	1974	Carmeuse Slovakia, Gombasek
703.548-8	1974	Kovošrot, Staré Město u Uh Hradiště
703.550-4	1974	Cukrovar, Vrbátky
703.553-3	1974	MOVO, Plzeň
703.557-9	1974	Agru, Streda nad Bodrogom
703.559-5	1974	Carmeuse Slovakia, Gombasek
703.562-9	1974	ZZN, Strakonice
703.564-5	1974	Fosfa, Břeclav
703.569-4	1974	Enaspol, Velvěty
703.573-6	1974	ZZN, Batelov
703.574-4	1974	RYKO, Děčín
703.577-7	1974	ACHP, Slavkov u Brna
703.579-3	1974	ALAS Morava, Mohelnice
703.580-1	1974	Tereos TTD, Dobrovice
703.581-9	1974	CHEMIS, Slavkov u Brna
703.586-8		Ferona, Brno Modřice
703.601-5		MTH Vrútky (T212.1001)
703.606-4	1977	Havelka, Křinec
703.610-6	1977	ČLZ, Nové Strašecí
703.616-3	1978	Českomoravská Inv, Humpolec
703.621-3		OMV, Komárno (ex-T212.1052)
703.629-6	1978	ZSNP, Žiar nad Hronom
703.631-3	1978	Česká Lokomotivka, Kolín
703.635-3	1978	AFEED, Šakvice
703.637-9	1978	DIAMO, Rožná
703.638-7	1978	Kovošrot, Chomutov
703.647-8	1978	Doagra, Domažlice
703.648-6	1978	BPS Market, Nemšová
703.656-9	1978	Lias, Vintířov
703.659-3	1978	ADW AGRO, Kojetice na Moravě
703.660-0	1978	Tento, Žilina
703.663-5	1979	SEP, Brno-Chrlice
703.667-6	1979	Česká Lokomotivka, Kolín
703.669-8	1979	Calmit, Margecany
703.670-0	1978	Čepro, Včelná (ex-703.016)
703.671-8	1979	Ferona, Brno Modřice
703.718-7	r2012	Budějovický Budvar, České Budějovice Ex-703.603*

Class 704 ČKD T238.0; 250–328 kW; Bo DE.

704.402-7	r	Vápenka Čertovy schody, Tmaň (ex-704.021)
704.501-6	1991	Lovochemie, Městec Králové
704.506-5	1991	Fatra, Napajedla
704.514-9	1992	Kovošrot, Brno
704.515-6	1992	Sigma Doprava, Lutín
704.516-4	1992	Slovnaft, Prešov
704.517-2	1992	Baňa Handlová HBP?
704.527-1	1992	OFZ Široká, Medzibrodie nad Oravou
704.528-9	1992	OFZ Široká, Medzibrodie nad Oravou
704.530-5	1992	Českomoravský Cem, Mokrá-Horákov
704.531-3	1992	Českomoravský Cem, Mokrá-Horákov
704.535-4	1992	Sladovny, Nymburk
704.537-0	1992	Unex, Uničov
704.540-4	1992	ŽDB Drátovna, Bohumín
704.541-2	1992	Tatramat, Matejovce pri Poprade
704.542-0	1993	Fosfa, Břeclav
704.543-8	1993	Kovohutě, Krompachy
704.546-1	1993	Technoplast, Chropyně
704.547-9	1993	PSP, Přerov
704.553-7	1994	Doagra, Domažlice
704.702-2	1994	OOS, Ostrava (ex-704.551)

Class 709 ČKD T239.1; 327–403 kW; Bo DE. * Rebuilt by CZ LOKO.

709.501-1	1993	ČEPRO, Cerekvice nad Bystřicí		709.535-9	1996	Teplárna, České Budějovice
709.512-8	1993	Lafarge Cement, Čížkovice		709.536-7	1996	ČEPRO, Třemošná
709.528-3	1996	ČEPRO, Loukov		709.705-8	2009	OOS, Ostrava*

Class 710 ČKD/TSM/SMZ T334.0; 301 kW; C DH.

710.634-2	1967	ŽPSV Přerov		710.693-3	1966	ŽPSV, Uherský Ostroh
710.644-6	1967	Haniska pri Košiciach (S)		710.739-4	1966	Teplárna, České Budějovice
710.645-3	1967	Haniska pri Košiciach (S)		710.790-7		TRAKCE, Ostrava
710.837-6	1968	Saz, Sázava u Žďáru		710.852-5		Draslovka, Kolín
710.649-5	1967	Vápenka Vitošov		710.877-2	1969	ido EET, Levice
710.655-2	1965	Alfa Plastik, Kutná Hora		710.886-3		TatraVagonka, Trebišov (S)
710.680-0		Železničné Stavebníctvo Bratislava				

Class 711 ČKD/TSM/SMZ rebuilt by ŽOS Nymburk/ŽOS Zvolen/JLS ex-T334.0; 210 kW; C DE.

711.001-8	r1995	Holcim, Rohožník	711.701-3	r1997	ČCB, Beroun. Ex-710.628
711.003-4	r1996	ŽDB, Ostrava Vítkovice	711.702-1	r1997	ŽDB, Ostrava Vítkovice
711.008-3	r1997	Puš, Pardubice. Ex-T334.0900			

Class 720 ČKD T435.0; 551 kW; Bo-Bo DE.

720.524-8	1960	Teplárna, Otrokovice	720.607-1	1963	Draslovka, Kolín
720.597-4	1962	AgroZZN, Černovice u Chomutova			

Class 721 ČKD T458.1; 551 kW; Bo-Bo DE.

721.222-8	1971	TSR, Plzeň Jateční	721.520-5	1965	SWS, Vojany
721.519-7	1965	SUD, Teplice	721.525-4	1968	Škoda, Mladá Boleslav

Class 724 CZ LOKO ex-T448.0; 627 kW; Bo-Bo DE.

724.714-1 r2012 Tereos TTD, Dobrovice. Ex-740.454

Class 726 TSM ex-T444.1; 515 kW; B-B DH.

726.609-1	1967	Teplárna, Otrokovice	726.701-6	1965	Elektrárna Mělník

Class 730 ČKD ex-T457.0; 600 kW; Bo-Bo DE. VVÚ is responsible for the state military transport fleet.

730.501-4	1982	AGRO CS, České Skalice	730.633-5	1989	Vetropack Moravia Glass, Kyjov
730.608-7	1988	UC, Kostelec u Heřmanova Městce	730.636-8	1989	Legios, Louny
730.609-5	1988	VVÚ, Týniště nad Orlicí	730.637-6	1989	VVÚ, Čáslav
730.610-3	1988	VVÚ, Zemianske Kostoľany	730.638.4	1989	VVÚ, Čáslav
730.611-1	1988	VVÚ, Nováky	730.639-2	1989	VVÚ, Nováky
730.615-2	1988	VVÚ, Trenčín	730.640-0	1989	VVÚ, Nováky
730.616-0	1988	VVÚ, Trenčín	730.641-8	1989	VVÚ, Halenkov
730.631-9	1989	Energaspol, Trmice			

Class 740 ČKD T448.0; 392–883 kW; Bo-Bo DE.

740.103-7*	1980	ZSNP, Žiar nad hronom Ex-Polish T448.P103	740.446-0*	1988	Ferona, Žilina-Bytčica
			740.508-7	1974	SGJW, Hradec Králové
740.308-2	1973	Vápenka Čertovy schody, Tmaň. Ex-740.502	740.509-5	1974	Vápenka Vitošov, Zábřeh na Moravě
			740.512-9*	1974	DUSLO, Šaľa
740.310-8	1983	DEZA, Valašské Meziříčí. Ex-740.767	740.519-4	1974	Slov-vagon, Strážske
			740.523-6*	1974	DUSLO, Šaľa
740.316-5	1976	Českomoravský Cem, Mokrá-Horákov Ex-740.578	740.524-4	1974	Progress Trading, Trebišov
			740.525-1	1975	KD Trans, Králův Dvůr
740.324-9	1985	DEZA, Jihlava. Ex-740.871	740.528-5*	1975	CLL, Lietavská Lúčka
740.325-6	1976	Cepro, Hněvice. Ex-740.562	740.529-3	1975	Teplárna, Příbram
740.326-4	1986	Cepro, Šlapanov. Ex-740.411	740.535-0*	1975	DUSLO, Bratislava
740.402-3*	1986	Ferona, Žilina-Bytčica.	740.548-3	1976	Tereos TTD, Dobrovice
740.406-4	1986	KD Trans, Beroun	740.553-3	1976	Slovenské Elektrárne, Nováky
740.408-0†	1986	Českomoravský Cem, Mokrá-Horákov	740.556-6	1976	DIAMO, Stráži pod Ralskem
740.412-2*	1986	Novácke Chemické Závody, Novaky	740.564-0	1976	Škoda, Mladá Boleslav
740.416-3*	1987	Novácke Chemické Závody, Novaky	740.567-3	1976	ZOS LOKO, Zvolen
740.430-4*	1987	Forest Trade, Pezinok	740.572-1*	1976	Novácke Chemické Závody, Novaky
740.433-8*	1987	Smurfit Kappa Obaly, Štúrovo	740.573-1	1976	ŽDB, Brno
740.434-6	1987	Českomoravský Cem, Mokrá-Horákov	740.582-2	1976	Lovochemie, Lovosice

740.583-0*	1976	Drôtovňa, Hlohovec
740.593-9	1976	ŽDB, Bohumín
740.611-9	1977	Vápenka Vitošov, Kunčice n Labem
740.613-5	1978	Holcim, Prachovice
740.625-9	1978	Holcim, Prachovice
740.653-1	1979	EP Cargo, Opatovice nad Labem
740.659-8*	1979	Novácke Chemické Závody, Novaky
740.663-0	1979	Slovenské Elektrárne, Nováky
740.666-3*	1979	SMZ, Jelšava
740.668-9	1979	Lomy Mořina, Mořina, Beroun
740.675-4†	1979	Kronospan, Jihlava
740.679-6	1980	Gypstrend, Kobeřice
740.683-8	1980	Continental Barum, Otrokovice
740.688-7*	1980	Drôtovňa, Hlohovec
740.691-1	1980	ZSNP, Žiar nad Hronom
740.693-7*	1980	Jaderná Elektrárna, Dukovany
740.697-8*	1981	VSH Trans, Turňa nad Bodvou
740.699-4	1981	ZOS LOKO, Zvolen
740.708-3	1982	DIAMO, Stráž pod Ralskem
740.713-3	1982	Kronospan, Jihlava
740.718-2	1982	Slov-vagon, Strážske
740.730-7	1982	CH, Hranice na Morave
740.733-1*	1982	Interport, Veľká Ida
740.739-8	1982	CER Cargo Slovakia
740.741-4	1982	Železárny, Veselí nad Moravou
740.747-1*	1982	Považská Cementáreň, Ladce
740.748-9*	1982	DUSLO, Šaľa
740.754-7*	1982	Jaderná Elektrárna, Dukovany
740.757-0*	1983	JAVYS, Velké Kostolany
740.759-6	1983	Kotouč, Štramberk
740.773-7	1983	AGC Glass, Teplice
740.775-2	1983	Metalšrot, Tlumačov
740.776-0	1983	TOMA, Otrokovice
740.778-6	1983	ZVVZ, Milevsko
740.780-2*	1983	Holcim, Rohožník
740.782-8	1983	Vápenka Čertovy schody, Tmaň
740.786-9*	1983	SMZ, Jelšava
740.788-5	1983	AGC Processing, Teplice
740.789-3	1983	Slovnaft, Stožok
740.795-0	1983	Alpiq, Zlín Střed
740.799-2*	1984	Slovnaft, Horný Hričov
740.806-5	1984	Gypstrend, Kobeřice
740.814-9	1984	Teplárna, Plzeň
740.820-6	1984	DEZA, Valašské Meziříčí
740.823-0	1984	DIAMO, Stráži pod Ralskem
740.825-5*	1984	Izomat, Nová Baňa
740.832-1	1984	Vápenka Čertovy Schody, Tmaň
740.833-9	1984	Vápenka Čertovy Schody, Tmaň
740.840-4*	1984	Slovnaft, Kľačany pri Hlohovci
740.841-2*	1984	Novácke Chemické Závody, Novaky
740.846-1*	1985	Elektrárna, Mochovce
740.850-3†	1985	Českomoravský Cem, Mokrá-Horákov
740.851-1	1985	EP Cargo, Opatovice nad Labem
740.852-9	1985	Volkswagen, Devínska nová Ves
740.854-5	1985	Slovenské Elektrárne, Nováky
740.858-6*	1985	Slovnaft, Kľačany pri Hlohovci
740.863-6	1985	Lomy Mořina, Mořina, Beroun
740.866-9	1985	Kotouč, Štramberk
740.869-3	1985	ZOS LOKO, Zvolen
740.870-1	1985	Petrolsped, Bratislava
740.872-7*	1985	Trans Plus, Turňa nad Bodvou
740.876-8	1985	TransportServis, Králův Dvůr
740.877.6	1985	Metalšrot, Tlumačov
740.881-8	1985	Lovochemie, Lovosice
740.882-6*	1985	CLL, Lietavská Lúčka
740.891-7	1986	Čepro, Mstětice
740.892-5	1986	ŽDAS, Žďár nad Sázavou
740.897-4	1986	Teplárna, Písek

* Carries original T448.0xxx number. Note 740.103 carries T448.0103, 740.402 carries T448.0902, 740.412 carries T448.0912, 740.416 carries T448.0916, 740.430 carries T448.0930, 740.433 carries T448.0933 and 740.446 carries T448.0946. † rebuilt with CAT engine

Class 741 ČKD T448.0; 883 kW; Bo-Bo DE.

741.516-9	1978	ČMŽO Přerov Works. Ex-740.615.

Class 742 ČKD T466.2; 883 kW; Bo-Bo DE.

742.057-3	1978	TJ Cementárna, Mokrá-Horákov	742.527-5	1985	UC, Kostelec u Heřmanova Městce
742.517-6	1984	VVÚ, Týniště nad Orlicí	742.530-9	1985	VVÚ, Bechyně

Class 744 ČKD T475.1; 845 kW; Bo-Bo DE.

744.501-8	1970	Škoda, Mladá Boleslav

Class 770/771 ČKD/SMZ T669.0/T669.1; 993 kW; Co-Co DE.

770.056-0	1968	Bulk Transshipment Slovakia	770.804-3		Interport, Velká Ida. 1520 mm
770.105-5	1969	Bulk Transshipment Slovakia	770.805-0		Interport, Velká Ida. 1520 mm
770.412-5	1970	Retrolok. Ex-771.512	770.813-4	1979	TatraVagonka, Trebišov. Ex-770.510"
T669.5501	1974	Interport, Velká Ida. 1520 mm	771.511-3	1971	EP Cargo, Opatovice nad Labem

Class 796 MTH; 35 kW; B BE.

796.502-3	1997	Cemix, Studénka

Class 797 ČKD/TSM rebuilt by ŽOS Vrútky, JLS or CZ LOKO ex-T211.0/T212.0; 187–205 kW; B DE.

797.501-4	r	Kovošrot, Hradec Králové	797.506-3	r	Kovohutě, Příbram
797.502-2	r1995	SES Tlmače	797.507-1	r	Ferona, Praha Malešice
797.503-0	r1995	AM Gnol, Předměřice n. Labem	797.508-9	r	Ferona, Brno Slatina
797.504-8	r	Teplárna, Strakovice	797.708-5	r2009	Havelka, Křinec. Ex-702.565
797.505-5	r	Agroslužby, Cheb	797.709-3	r2011	Pars nova, Šumperk. Ex-702.631

5.4 PRIVATE LOCOMOTIVES SIMPLIFIER TABLE

This list shows all standard gauge locomotives owned by private passenger and freight operators in the Czech Republic and Slovakia. For more details of each locomotive see the relevant section for each operator. If a locomotive listed in this book is not shown in this list, it can be found under the "Other Private Locomotives" section.

No.	Operator	No.	Operator	No.	Operator	No.	Operator	No.	Operator
114.001	SD-KD	127.712	Coal Serv	181.089	ŽOS Vrut	386.001	Metrans	702.629	Vitkovice
114.002	SD-KD	127.714	Coal Serv	181.121	ŽOS Zvo	386.002	Metrans	702.652	KK
114.503	SD-KD	127.715	Coal Serv	182.041	IDS	386.003	Metrans	702.653	KK
114.504	SD-KD	127.716	Coal Serv	182.053	AWT	386.004	Metrans	702.673	IDS
121.004	SŽDS	127.717	Coal Serv	182.072	Lokorail	386.005	Metrans	702.683	SD-KD
121.007	RM Lines	127.718	Coal Serv	182.115	CRW	386.006	Metrans	702.684	SD-KD
121.023	SD-KD	127.719	Coal Serv	182.166	ODOS	386.007	Metrans	703.005	BF Log
121.038	AWT	127.720	Coal Serv	183.714	AWT	386.008	Metrans	703.007	BF Log
121.041	IDS	127.721	Coal Serv	183.718	AWT	386.009	Metrans	703.008	BF Log
121.056	Unipetrol	127.723	Coal Serv	183.719	AWT	386.010	Metrans	703.017	Skanska
121.065	IDS	130.041	SD-KD	184.501	SD-KD	386.011	Metrans	703.018	Skanska
121.068	SŽDS	130.044	SD-KD	184.502	SD-KD	386.012	Metrans	703.020	Lokotrans
121.073	Unipetrol	130.045	SD-KD	184.503	SD-KD	386.013	Metrans	703.021	KDS
121.077	IDS	130.046	SD-KD	184.504	SD-KD	386.014	Metrans	703.022	BF Log
121.084	IDS	130.047	SD-KD	185.621	LTE	386.015	Metrans	703.034	LTE
124.601	VUZ	130.048	SD-KD	186.182	Metrans	386.016	Metrans	703.501	Vitkovice
127.226	SU	130.049	AWT	186.187	Metrans	386.017	Metrans	703.503	IDS
127.235	SU	130.050	SD-KD	186.237	LTE	386.018	Metrans	703.521	AWT
127.236	SU	130.051	SD-KD	186.238	LTE	386.019	Metrans	703.549	KK
127.237	SU	130.052	SD-KD	186.289	Metrans	386.020	Metrans	703.554	JUSO
127.238	SU	130.053	SD-KD	186.291	Metrans	386.021	Metrans	703.555	JUSO
127.239	SU	130.054	SD-KD	186.426	LTE	386.022	Metrans	703.556	JUSO
127.245	SU	140.045	RM Lines	186.432	Unipetrol	386.023	Metrans	703.558	KK
127.246	SU	140.058	ŽOS Zvo	186.433	Metrans	386.024	Metrans	703.591	IDS
127.247	SU	140.062	ODOS	186.435	IDS	386.025	Metrans	703.594	Lokotrans
127.248	SU	140.067	PSŽ	186.437	Metrans	386.026	Metrans	703.598	Lokot Slv
127.249	SU	140.074	RM Lines	186.455	Metrans	386.027	Metrans	703.599	BF Log
127.251	SU	140.076	SŽDS	189.151	AWT	386.028	Metrans	703.602	Regiojet
127.254	SU	140.087	ODOS	189.153	CRW	386.029	Metrans	703.622	Lokot Slv
127.256	SU	140.094	IDS	189.155	LTE	386.030	Metrans	703.624	Lokot Slv
127.259	SU	141.018	Jnr Mkt	189.156	LTE	390.001	Express	703.630	KK
127.501	SU	141.023	DPOV	189.158	LTE	468.002	PSŽ	703.632	BF Log
127.502	SU	141.055	DPOV	193.203	LTE	480.005	PSŽ	703.657	Tramo
127.503	SU	162.112	Regiojet	193.205	Regiojet	480.012	PSŽ	703.701	SU
127.504	SU	162.113	Regiojet	193.206	Regiojet	620.010	HBP	703.702	SU
127.505	SU	162.114	Regiojet	193.214	Regiojet	620.037	HBP	703.703	SU
127.506	SU	162.115	Regiojet	193.226	Regiojet	700.687	IDS	703.704	SU
127.507	SU	162.116	Regiojet	193.207	LTE	700.700	IDS	703.705	SU
127.508	SU	162.117	Regiojet	193.215	LTE	701.020	ŽSR	703.706	SU
127.509	SU	162.118	Regiojet	193.216	LTE	701.302	SD-KD	703.708	SU
127.510	SU	162.119	Regiojet	193.220	LokoTrain	701.478	IDS	703.709	SU
127.511	SU	162.120	Regiojet	193.221	LokoTrain	701.483	ODOS	703.710	SU
127.670	Coal Serv	180.002	TSS	193.222	LokoTrain	701.507	SU	703.711	SU
127.676	Coal Serv	180.003	TSS	193.802	PSŽ	701.535	BF Log	703.712	EŽ
127.679	Coal Serv	180.006	TSS	193.823	LokoTrain	701.599	KK	703.713	EŽ
127.681	Coal Serv	180.007	TSS	223.002	Metrans	701.612	ŽSR	703.714	EŽ
127.682	Coal Serv	180.008	TSS	230.045	Lokorail	701.615	ŽSR	703.715	EŽ
127.683	Coal Serv	180.009	TSS	240.039	PSŽ	701.635	ŽOS Vrut	703.716	EŽ
127.684	Coal Serv	180.010	TSS	241.001	CRW	701.652	AWT	703.717	DPOV
127.685	Coal Serv	180.011	TSS	241.002	CRW	701.691	AWT	703.719	ŽSR
127.687	Coal Serv	180.012	TSS	241.003	CRW	701.738	IDS	703.821	Vitkovice
127.690	Coal Serv	180.013	TSS	241.004	CRW	701.739	IDS	704.009	JUSO
127.696	Coal Serv	180.015	TSS	241.005	CRW	701.774	Vitkovice	704.032	JUSO
127.698	Coal Serv	180.016	TSS	242.206	PSŽ	701.790	ŽSR	704.038	JUSO
127.699	Coal Serv	180.017	TSS	242.262	PSŽ	702.087	GJW	704.201	CZ LOKO
127.700	Coal Serv	180.018	TSS	242.282	PSŽ	702.531	IDS	704.403	Lokot Slv
127.701	Coal Serv	180.019	TSS	242.287	PSŽ	702.532	Trinecké	704.504	Lokotrans
127.702	Coal Serv	180.020	TSS	242.288	IDS	702.603	ŽSR	704.505	AWT
127.703	Coal Serv	181.024	AWT	242.555	Lokorail	702.609	ŽOS Vrut	704.510	JUSO
127.704	Coal Serv	181.040	AWT	242.556	Express	702.618	Skanska	704.511	Strabag
127.706	Coal Serv	181.064	ODOS	242.558	LokoTrain	702.619	ŽSR	704.513	IDS
127.707	Coal Serv	181.065	ŽOS Vrut	242.559	SŽDS	702.622	ŽSR	704.518	KDS
127.708	Coal Serv	181.066	ŽOS Vrut	362.034	CRW	702.627	ŽSR	704.519	AWT

Number	Operator	Number	Operator	Number	Operator	Number	Operator	Number	Operator
704.521	Arc Mittal	711.589	Arc Mittal	724.708	SU	740.044	CRW	740.565	Třinecké
704.522	Arc Mittal	711.619	PSŽ	724.709	SU	740.049	CRW	740.575	KK
704.523	Arc Mittal	711.703	IDS	724.710[1]	SU	740.148	PSŽ	740.585	Coal Serv
704.526	SD-KD	712.407	ŽOS Zvo	724.710[2]	US Steel	740.301	AWT	740.588	TSS
704.529	BF Log	712.416	ŽOS Zvo	724.711	Unipetrol	740.302	AWT	740.590	SD-KD
704.533	BF Log	712.422	ŽOS Zvo	724.712	Unipetrol	740.303	AWT	740.591	Lokot Slv
704.534	SD-KD	712.440	ŽOS Zvo	724.713	AWT	740.304	AWT	740.595	CRW
704.545	BF Log	712.523	ŽOS Zvo	724.801	Třinecké	740.305	AWT	740.597	SMD
704.550	SD-KD	712.752	ŽOS Zvo	724.802	Třinecké	740.306	AWT	740.599	SD-KD
704.554	SD-KD	712.765	ŽOS Zvo	724.803	Třinecké	740.307	AWT	740.600	Arc Mittal
704.701	AWT	714.811	Vitkovice	724.804	Třinecké	740.309	Vitkovice	740.602	HBP
704.703	CZ LOKO	716.505	Metrans	724.805	Třinecké	740.311	AWT	740.603	DPOV
704.704	AWT	717.601	Slovnaft	724.806	Třinecké	740.312	AWT	740.604[1]	AWT
704.705	AWT	719.701	CZ LOKO	724.807	Třinecké	740.313	AWT	740.604[2]	TSS Gde
709.401	CZ LOKO	720.013	ŽOS Vrut	724.875	US Steel	740.314	AWT	740.605	US Steel
709.502	Coal Serv	720.039	Rly Cap	724.932	US Steel	740.315	Vitkovice	740.606	HBP
709.503	Coal Serv	720.091	KK	724.935	US Steel	740.317	Vitkovice	740.608	TSS
709.504	Coal Serv	720.097	Rly Cap	725.070	ŽSR	740.318	AWT	740.609	EŽ
709.505	Coal Serv	720.099	Jnr Mkt	726.562	Jnr Mkt	740.319	AWT	740.614	Slovnaft
709.506	Arc Mittal	720.502	AWT	729.501	Arc Mittal	740.320	AWT	740.617	Mon SCP
709.507	Vitkovice	720.508	EŽ	729.504	Vitkovice	740.321	AWT	740.618	AWT
709.508	Arc Mittal	720.539	EŽ	729.505	Arc Mittal	740.322	AWT	740.619	GJW
709.509	Arc Mittal	720.541	EŽ	729.506	Arc Mittal	740.323	AWT	740.621	BF Log
709.510	Vitkovice	720.567	Strabag	729.507	US Steel	740.401	AWT	740.622	AWT
709.511	Vitkovice	720.593	AWT	729.508	US Steel	740.403	Mon SCP	740.628	Express
709.513	AWT	720.594	JUSO	729.509	US Steel	740.404	AWT	740.631	Vitkovice
709.514	Arc Mittal	720.595	AWT	729.511	Arc Mittal	740.405	Arc Mittal	740.634	BF Log
709.515	Třinecké	720.604	AWT	729.601	Ž Podbrez	740.407	AWT	740.638	AWT
709.516	Třinecké	721.081	Jnr Mkt	729.602	Arc Mittal	740.410	Unipetrol	740.639	AWT
709.517	Coal Serv	721.111	TSS	729.603	Arc Mittal	740.413	LTE	740.641	SŽDS
709.518	Unipetrol	721.113	Jnr Mkt	729.604	Vitkovice	740.414	AWT	740.642	SD-KD
709.519	Unipetrol	721.122	Jnr Mkt	729.605	Vitkovice	740.418	Třinecké	740.645	SMD
709.520	US Steel	721.130	Jnr Mkt	729.606	US Steel	740.419	KDS	740.649	ŽOS Vrut
709.521	US Steel	721.151	Regiojet	729.607	Třinecké	740.420	VUZ	740.650	AWT
709.522	US Steel	721.179	IDS	729.608	Arc Mittal	740.422	AWT	740.651	Metrans
709.523	US Steel	721.203	IDS	729.610	Unipetrol	740.424	AWT	740.655	EŽ
709.524	Coal Serv	721.512	ŽOS Zvo	729.611	Arc Mittal	740.425	AWT	740.657	Lokot Slv
709.525	Coal Serv	721.517	KDS	729.612	US Steel	740.426	AWT	740.658	Strabag
709.529	AWT	721.518	SMD	729.613	US Steel	740.429	TSS	740.660	Vitkovice
709.530	US Steel	721.524	SD-KD	729.615	US Steel	740.431	US Steel	740.664	AWT
709.531	US Steel	721.526	GJW	729.616	Vitkovice	740.437	AWT	740.673	AWT
709.532	AWT	721.540	GJW	729.617	Vitkovice	740.443	AWT	740.674	AWT
709.533	Vitkovice	721.542	Třinecké	729.618	Třinecké	740.444	Metrans	740.676	EŽ
709.534	Coal Serv	721.544	Tramo	729.619	Třinecké	740.445	BF Log	740.678	Strabag
709.601	CZ LOKO	721.545	Tramo	729.620	Ž Podbrez	740.450	AWT	740.680	Třinecké
709.702	Coal Serv	721.546	TSS	729.701	Třinecké	740.452	Mon SCP	740.681	AWT
709.703	Coal Serv	721.549	Jnr Mkt	729.702	Třinecké	740.456	AWT	740.682	AWT
709.704	Coal Serv	721.551	Lokotrans	730.601	Skanska	740.457	AWT	740.684	Lokorail
710.079	SMD	721.555	HBP	730.602	TSS	740.458	AWT	740.685	AWT
710.415	AWT	721.556	Coal Serv	730.604	TSS	740.459	IDS	740.686	AWT
710.429	ŽSR	721.602	ŽSR	730.605	ŽSR	740.460	AWT	740.687	ŽS Kosice
710.433	Jnr Mkt	723.701	Třinecké	730.606	TSS	740.462	Arc Mittal	740.689	Arc Mittal
710.455	IDS	724.516	US Steel	730.612	AWT	740.464	Arc Mittal	740.695	Ž Podbrez
710.466	Jnr Mkt	724.538	US Steel	730.613	KDS	740.469	Strabag	740.701	AWT
710.597	BF Log	724.540	US Steel	730.614	ODOS	740.503	SMD	740.704	Skanska
710.606	ŽSR	724.571	US Steel	730.617	ŽSR	740.513	Metrans	740.705	BF Log
710.622	Lokot Slv	724.576	US Steel	730.618	TSS Gde	740.514	Unipetrol	740.707	AWT
710.666	IDS	724.601	Unipetrol	730.619	ŽSR	740.517	AWT	740.709	BF Log
710.682	Rly Cap	724.602	Unipetrol	730.621	ŽSR	740.518	IDS	740.711	LTE
710.698	Vitkovice	724.603	Unipetrol	730.622	TSS	740.522	US Steel	740.712	Lokotrans
710.762	Lokot Slv	724.604	Unipetrol	730.623	TSS	740.527	Arc Mittal	740.716	SU
710.776	PSŽ	724.605	SD-KD	730.624	Skanska	740.534	AWT	740.719	Unipetrol
710.779	IDS	724.606	SD-KD	730.625	KDS	740.536	Skanska	740.720	SMD
710.781	Jnr Mkt	724.654	US Steel	730.626	TSS	740.541	LTE	740.721	IDS
710.797	Jnr Mkt	724.700	US Steel	730.627	TSS	740.545	RM Lines	740.722	CRW
710.833	IDS	724.701	Třinecké	730.628	TSS	740.547	Ž Podbrez	740.723	RM Lines
710.838	Lokot Slv	724.702	Třinecké	730.629	ŽSR	740.549	Lokot Slv	740.729	Třinecké
710.866	Jnr Mkt	724.703	SU	730.630	Lokorail	740.551	AWT	740.732	KK
711.002	TSS	724.704	SU	730.632	EŽ	740.552	AWT	740.734	AWT
711.004	SD-KD	724.705	SU	730.634	IDS	740.557	Skanska	740.735	Unipetrol
711.081	Unipetrol	724.706	SD-KD	730.635	IDS	740.559	EŽ	740.736	AWT
711.501	Unipetrol	724.707	SU	740.016	Lokorail	740.561	GJW	740.737	Mon SCP

Number	Operator	Number	Operator	Number	Operator	Number	Operator	Number	Operator
740.738	AWT	740.898	KDS	742.503	ODOS	752.069	Jnr Mkt	770.514	AWT
740.742	ŽS Kosice	740.899	BF Log	742.505	ODOS	752.601	AWT	770.516[1]	Coal Serv
740.743	Slovnaft	740.941	US Steel	742.506	BF Log	752.602	AWT	770.516[2]	US Steel
740.744	SD-KD	740.947	Express	742.507	AWT	752.603	AWT	770.518	AWT
740.745	AWT	741.501	AWT	742.510	ODOS	752.604	AWT	770.519	Lokorail
740.746	AWT	741.502	AWT	742.512	Lokot Slv	753.197	KDS	770.520	AWT
740.749	Metrans	741.503	AWT	742.513	ODOS	753.306	AWT	770.522	HBP
740.750	TSS	741.504	AWT	742.514	ODOS	753.265	CZ LOKO	770.523	US Steel
740.751	TSS	741.505	AWT	742.515	RM Lines	753.601	SD-KD	770.525	AWT
740.755	Třinecké	741.506	AWT	742.516	IDS	753.602	SD-KD	770.527	Lokot Slv
740.756	Třinecké	741.507	AWT	742.520	AWT	753.603	SD-KD	770.529	KDS
740.758	IDS	741.508	AWT	742.521	TSS	753.604	SD-KD	770.532	AWT
740.762	AWT	741.509	AWT	742.522	IDS	753.605	CZ LOKO	770.533	AWT
740.763	IDS	741.510	Unipetrol	742.523	ODOS	753.703	AWT	770.534	AWT
740.766	AWT	741.511	Unipetrol	742.525	ODOS	753.704	AWT	770.535	US Steel
740.769	AWT	741.512	Unipetrol	742.529	IDS	753.705	AWT	770.536	BF Log
740.770	BF Log	741.513	Unipetrol	742.532	TSS	753.706	AWT	770.538	PSŽ
740.772	AWT	741.514	Unipetrol	742.533	TSS	753.707	AWT	770.541	KDS
740.774	Unipetrol	741.515	Unipetrol	742.534	TSS	753.708	AWT	770.602	PSŽ
740.781	Ž Podbrez	741.517	BF Log	742.535	TSS	753.709	AWT	770.604	Lokorail
740.783	Třinecké	741.518	BF Log	742.536	TSS	753.710	AWT	770.606	AWT
740.784	Unipetrol	741.519	Vitkovice	742.537	TSS	753.711	AWT	770.610	ŽOS Vrut
740.785	Vitkovice	741.702	Strabag	742.538	ODOS	753.712	AWT	770.613	HBP
740.787	Lokorail	741.703	Strabag	742.540	ODOS	753.713	AWT	770.614	AWT
740.790	Express	741.704	Strabag	742.541	ODOS	753.714	AWT	770.812	ŽOS Vrut
740.797	AWT	741.705	Strabag	742.601	ŽS Kosice	753.715	Unipetrol	770.814	ŽOS Vrut
740.800	Lokotrans	741.706	SD-KD	742.605	TSS Gde	753.716	Unipetrol	770.817	SŽDS
740.801	AWT	741.710	CZ LOKO	742.610	Express	753.717	Unipetrol	770.818	SŽDS
740.802	Unipetrol	741.711	Arc Mittal	742.615	BF Log	753.718	Unipetrol	771.036	AWT
740.803	Unipetrol	741.712	Arc Mittal	742.616	Lokotrans	753.719	Unipetrol	771.170	ODOS
740.804	JUSO	741.713	Arc Mittal	742.622	SŽDS	753.720	Unipetrol	771.501	HBP
740.805	US Steel	741.714	Arc Mittal	742.623	TSS	753.721	Unipetrol	771.507	ŽOS Vrut
740.807	Třinecké	741.715	Arc Mittal	742.627	BF Log	753.722	Unipetrol	771.509	HBP
740.808	SU	741.716	Arc Mittal	742.643	ŽSR	753.723	AWT	771.513	ŽOS Vrut
740.810	ŽS Kosice	741.717	Arc Mittal	742.644	TSS Gde	753.724	AWT	771.514	HBP
740.813	Arc Mittal	741.718	Arc Mittal	742.645	TSS Gde	753.725	AWT	771.515	AWT
740.816	ŽOS Vrut	741.719	Arc Mittal	742.646	ŽSR	753.726	AWT	771.701	AWT
740.818	AWT	741.720	Arc Mittal	742.702	CZ LOKO	753.727	AWT	774.501	US Steel
740.819	AWT	741.721	Arc Mittal	742.703	CZ LOKO	753.728	AWT	774.502	US Steel
740.821	JUSO	741.722	Arc Mittal	742.704	CZ LOKO	753.729	AWT	774.503	US Steel
740.824	Unipetrol	741.723	Arc Mittal	742.705	CZ LOKO	753.730	AWT	774.507	US Steel
740.826	PSŽ	741.724	Arc Mittal	744.001	CZ LOKO	753.731	AWT	774.701	SU
740.828	AWT	741.725	Arc Mittal	744.502	BF Log	753.732	AWT	774.702	SU
740.829	Slovnaft	741.726	Arc Mittal	744.701	Unipetrol	753.733	AWT	774.703	SU
740.830	Metrans	741.727	Arc Mittal	744.702	SD-KD	753.734	AWT	774.704	SD-KD
740.834	Třinecké	741.728	Arc Mittal	744.703	SD-KD	753.735	AWT	783.001	IDS
740.837	AWT	741.729	Arc Mittal	744.704	Slovnaft	753.736	AWT	794.001	CZ LOKO
740.839	Unipetrol	741.730	Arc Mittal	744.705	Slovnaft	753.737	AWT	797.701	EZ
740.842	AWT	742.112	Lokot Slv	744.706	Slovnaft	753.738	AWT	797.702	EZ
740.843	EZ	742.118	Vitkovice	744.707	Slovnaft	753.739	AWT	797.703	EZ
740.844	AWT	742.119	Lokot Slv	744.708	Slovnaft	753.781	TSS	797.704	EZ
740.845	AWT	742.131	ODOS	745.608	ŽSR	753.782	TSS	797.705	EZ
740.847	Arc Mittal	742.164	Lokot Slv	745.701	Metrans	753.783	TSS	797.706	EZ
740.848	Lokotrans	742.193	CRW	745.702	Metrans	753.784	TSS	797.707	EZ
740.853	ŽOS Vrut	742.197	DPOV	748.536	Rly Cap	753.740	Unipetrol	799.011	DPOV
740.855	PSŽ	742.205	RM Lines	749.039	AŽD	753.741	Unipetrol	799.015	DPOV
740.859	Ž Podbrez	742.213	PSŽ	749.162	IDS	759.002	VUZ	799.022	DPOV
740.860	IDS	742.218	DPOV	749.181	IDS	761.001	Metrans	799.037	DPOV
740.861	BF Log	742.260	IDS	749.262	Hanzalík	761.002	Metrans		
740.865	GJW	742.275	CRW	749.263	Hanzalík	761.003	Metrans	1216.910	LTE
740.867	Třinecké	742.276	Lokot Slv	750.059	AWT	761.004	Metrans	1216.920	LTE
740.868	AWT	742.321	ŽOS Zvo	750.063	CZ LOKO	761.005	Metrans	2016.903	LTE
740.873	SŽDS	742.348	Lokot Slv	750.096	KDS	761.006	Metrans	2016.904	LTE
740.874	Skanska	742.360	TSS	750.111	ODOS	761.007	Metrans	2016.909	LTE
740.880	Vitkovice	742.361	AWT	750.116	CZ LOKO	761.101	Express	2016.920	LTE
740.883	LTE	742.384	PSŽ	750.132	ODOS	770.016	SMD	2016.921	LTE
740.887	AWT	742.408	TSS	750.199	AWT	770.026	HBP	2016.922	LTE
740.888	Coal Serv	742.410	TSS	750.202	ODOS	770.505	SD-KD		
740.889	Coal Serv	742.411	TSS	750.204	ODOS	770.506	AWT	MV97.001	EZ
740.890	Coal Serv	742.412	TSS	750.380	CZ LOKO	770.507	AWT	MV97.002	EZ
740.895	KDS	742.418	ŽSR	751.010	VUZ	770.508	AWT	MV97.003	EZ
		742.501	ODOS	751.115	KDS	770.511	US Steel	MV97.004	Strabag
								MV97.005	Strabag

6. PRESERVED LOCOMOTIVES & RAILCARS

Preserved items from both the Czech Republic and Slovakia are listed together in this section, denoted respectively by "CZ" and "SK" in the listings.

The current status of locomotives and railcars is indicated as follows:

A   Locomotive or railcar that is Active at the time of writing. Location may vary, especially during summer (operating) or winter months.
M   Locomotive or railcar located in a Museum or in museum status.
P   Locomotive or railcar that is Plinthed.
R   Locomotive or railcar under long-term Restoration.
S   Locomotive or railcar that is Stored or has been retained for spares only.

Both countries have their own national preservation centres. In the Czech Republic the main centre is the ČD preservation depot at Lužná u Rakovníka, which also houses some NTM (National Technical Museum) locomotives. As well as the main NTM museum in Praha there are NTM depositories at Chomutov and Čelákovice. Chomutov has occasional open days. There are long-term plans to turn the former depot alongside Praha Masarykovo station into another annex of the NTM. ČD museum items are also kept at operational depots such as Česká Lípa, Olomouc, Louny, Valašské Meziříčí, Bohumín and Česká Třebová.

In Slovakia the MDC (Múzejno Dokumentačné Centrum) museum is adjacent to Bratislava main station, with Bratislava Východ (I) depot being the maintenance and operating base. This is open to the public on summer Wednesdays and Saturdays. There is a further museum and store at Vrútky.

6.1. OPERATING MAIN LINE LOCOMOTIVES

Space constraints mean that it is not possible to give full technical listings for all steam locomotive types, but the following entries are the main classes of locomotive used on main lines in Czechoslovakia, and are classes with at least one locomotive still active on the main line. See the main listing table (Section 6.2.1) for individual locomotives.

6.1.1. STEAM LOCOMOTIVES

CLASS 464.0   4-8-4T

Class 464.0 was a 14 tonne axle-load tank locomotive with wide route availability, nicknamed "Ušatá". They were built in three series': 464.001–003, 464.004–020 and 464.021–076, of slightly different weights and details. Class 464.0 was the mainstay of passenger train operation on many secondary routes across the whole network, working until 1981 around Česká Lípa, Nymburk, Olomouc, Ostrava, Valašské Meziříčí and Jihlava.

Built: 1933–38.
Builder: ČKD.
Wheel Diameter: 1574 mm.
Length over Buffers: 15.33 m.
Maximum Speed: 90 km/h.

Total No. Built: 76.
Boiler Pressure: 13 bar.
Weight: 113.3 tonnes.
Power: 1170 kW (1570 hp).
Cylinders: 2.

CLASS 464.1   4-8-4T

Two impressive prototypes of this class were built in 1940, and worked until 1978. They had the same 14 tonne axle-load but with a much higher boiler pressure than Class 464.0. 464.101 was the 2000th locomotive produced by ČKD in Praha. 464.102 survives today.

Built: 1940.
Builder: ČKD.
Wheel Diameter: 1625 mm.
Length over Buffers: 15.33 m.
Maximum Speed: 90 km/h.

Total No. Built: 2.
Boiler Pressure: 18 bar.
Weight: 113.3 tonnes.
Power: 1250 kW (1675 hp).
Cylinders: 2.

CLASS 464.2   4-8-4T

Class 464.2, nicknamed "Rosnička", were two further prototypes built in 1956, lasting in service until 1975. Based in Brno they worked to Česká Třebová, Havlíčkův Brod and Přerov. They earned their place in world history, hauling Soviet premiere Khrushchev from Bratislava for the 1961 Wien Summit where his (paraphrased) words "Force will be met by force" were answered by US President Kennedy "It will be a cold winter". The Berlin Wall went up two months later. They were constructed by Škoda at the same time that the company was well into the production of Class E499.0 (later Class 140) electric locomotives. This was the final new steam design for ČSD keeping the axle load to just 14 tonnes despite managing to look much larger than Class 464.1.

Built: 1956.
Builder: Škoda.
Wheel Diameter: 1625 mm.
Length over Buffers: 16.57 m.
Maximum Speed: 90 km/h.

Total No. Built: 2.
Boiler Pressure: 18 bar.
Weight: 112 tonnes.
Power: 1250 kW (1675 hp).
Cylinders: 2.

CLASS 475.1   4-8-2

Class 475 was one of the main Czechoslovak passenger locomotives for medium-to-heavy trains over steeply-graded routes. The type entered ČSD traffic from most depots from 1947, with the last withdrawn from normal operation in 1980. They were nicknamed "Šľachtičná" ("noble-lady"). The class was one of the first ČSD types with post-war standard steel fireboxes, long combustion chamber, thermic syphon, Kylchap double blast pipes, Friedman exhaust steam injector, mechanical stoker, rocking grate and air-operated cut-off adjustment, and Trofimoff valves. 147 locomotives (475.101–1147) were built in four batches between 1947 and 1950. A further 25 locomotives (numbered 475.1148–1172) were then built for export to Korea. Seven have been preserved, four of which are currently operational.

Built: 1947–50.
Builder: Škoda.
Wheel Diameter: 1750 mm.
Length over Buffers: 15.25 m.
Maximum Speed: 100 km/h.

Total No. Built: 147 for ČSD; 25 for export.
Boiler Pressure: 16 bar.
Weight: 99.3–102.7 tonnes.
Power: 1430 kW (1920 hp).
Cylinders: 2.

▲ Class 475.1 4-8-2 475.196, normally based at MDC Vrútky Museum, stands at Vrútky station with a special for Oravský Podzámok on 1 June 2014.   **Robert Pritchard**

CLASS 477.0 4-8-4T

Class 477.0, or "Papoušek", was basically a tank version of Class 498.1. Built 1950–55, the last was withdrawn from traffic in 1981. They feature a mechanical stoker, three cylinders, thermic siphon, two arch tubes, and double Kylchap exhaust. They were based around Zvolen, Nové Zámky, Leopoldov, Břeclav, Brno, Ostrava, Krnov, Olomouc, Česká Lípa, Nymburk, Kralupy nad Vltavou and Praha, principally for suburban transport. The first batch of 38 were built 1950–51 and had two small side water tanks added after stability problems with full back tanks, increasing axle load to 17 tonnes from 16 tonnes (hence the original Class 476.0 designation). The second batch of 22 built in 1955 appear to have full side tanks, but these are false valances covering small tanks. All were in an attractive and distinctive mid blue livery. Three of this type have been preserved, two of which are operational.

Built: 1950–55.
Builder: ČKD.
Wheel Diameter: 1625 mm.
Length over Buffers: 17.30 m.
Maximum Speed: 100 km/h.

Total No. Built: 60.
Boiler Pressure: 16 bar.
Weight: 128.7 tonnes.
Power: 1540 kW (2065 hp).
Cylinders: 3; 450 mm x 680 mm.

CLASS 486.0 4-8-2

In 1932 ČSD ordered two 3-cylinder four-coupled prototypes, one each from Škoda and ČKD. Evaluation was at Spišská Nová Ves depot. The ČKD 2-8-4 Class 486.1 was not taken further, but eight Škoda 4-8-2 Class 486.0s were built up to 1938. They were the last pre-war ČSD passenger design, and significantly more powerful than the various 4-6-2 types they were intended to replace. The post-war Class 498.0 was developed from this design.

Built: 1933–38.
Builder: Škoda.
Wheel Diameter: 1830 mm.
Length over Buffers: 15.56 m.
Maximum Speed: 110 km/h.

Total No. Built: 9.
Boiler Pressure: 13 bar.
Weight: 102.3 tonnes.
Power: 1690 kW (2265 hp).
Cylinders: 3; 550 mm x 680 mm.

▲ Class 477.0 4-8-4T 477.013 leaves Bratislava Rača station with a special train back to Bratislava Východ during the annual "Bratislava Rendez" festival on 14 June 2014. **Robert Pritchard**

CLASS 498.0   4-8-2

40 Class 486.0s were ordered in October 1945 for urgent post-war recovery, but many construction changes were forced by material shortages. A new all-welded boiler design, cylinders reduced from 550 to 500 mm bore (680 mm stroke unchanged), axle load increased from 16 to 17.5 tonnes, and maximum speed increased from 110 to 120 km/h, all led to a new classification of Class 498.0. All were ordered from Škoda but the last 11 were built by ČKD. Mechanical stokers, Kylchap double blastpipes and rocking grates were introduced from 1951, raising their power output by about 20%. The locomotives were delivered in the blue livery and nicknamed "Albatros". They were used on express passenger services between Praha and Bohumín, Přerov and Bratislava, between Košice and Žilina, and between Praha and Plzeň until electrification displaced them to České Budějovice, Tábor and Děčín. The last locomotive was withdrawn in 1976. Five of the type have been preserved, of which two are currently operational.

Built: 1946–49.
Builder: Škoda and ČKD.
Wheel Diameter: 1830 mm.
Length over Buffers: 15.56 m.
Maximum Speed: 120 km/h.

Total No. Built: 40.
Boiler Pressure: 16 bar.
Weight: 106.1 tonnes.
Power: 1600 kW (2145 hp).
Cylinders: 3; 500 mm x 680 mm.

CLASS 498.1   4-8-2

Also known as "Albatros", Class 498.1 was the final express passenger type to be built for ČSD. 15 were built in 1954–55, numbered 498.101–115. Every modern feature was fitted; long combustion chamber, thermic syphon, two arch tubes, Kylchap exhausts, exhaust steam injector, mechanical stoker, main connecting and coupling rod roller bearings, air servo reverser, and light steel alloy reciprocating parts. Significantly more powerful than Class 498.0, the Class 498.1s could haul 600 tonnes at 116 km/h on level track. 496.106 reached a top speed of 162 km/h at the Velim test circuit in 1964, a Czech speed record for a steam locomotive. Delivered in a deeper plum-blue livery, the class was shared between Žilina and Praha for Praha–Spišská Nová Ves work, and later with Přerov and Bratislava. All migrated to Bratislava by 1960 where they worked between Česká Třebová and Štúrovo. As electrification spread they drifted to Plzeň, Brno and Nové Zámky. Three of the type are still in existence in the Czech Republic and Slovakia.

Built: 1954–55.
Builder: Škoda.
Wheel Diameter: 1830 mm.
Length over Buffers: 15.82 m.
Maximum Speed: 120 km/h.

Total No. Built: 15.
Boiler Pressure: 16 bar.
Weight: 113.5 tonnes
Power: 1840 kW (2470 hp).
Cylinders: 3; 500 mm x 680 mm.

CLASS 556.0   2-10-0

These heavy freight locomotives were nicknamed "Štokr". 510 were built between 1952 and 1958 for increasing freight traffic after World War II. The boiler is the same as Class 475.1 but with pressure raised from 16 to 18 bar. They were used on ever increasingly heavy loads: 4000 tonnes was routine. An absolute record was claimed in December 1958 when a Kojetín–Ostrava coal train weighing 8272 tonnes (121 bogie wagons) was headed by 556.0338, with 556.020 pushing and additional banker 556.0155 from Přerov to Hranice na Moravě. The type was used throughout the entire ČSD network on local passenger as well as heavy freight until the early 1980s. Seven are preserved, including last-built 556.0510 (the last new ČSD steam locomotive).

Built: 1952–58.
Builder: Škoda.
Wheel Diameter: 1400 mm.
Length over Buffers: 14.66 m.
Maximum Speed: 80 km/h.

Total No. Built: 510.
Boiler Pressure: 18 bar.
Weight: 99 tonnes.
Power: 1472 kW (1975 hp).
Cylinders: 2; 550 mm x 680 mm.

6.1.2. ELECTRIC LOCOMOTIVES

Details of electric locomotive classes not already shown in the main ČD or ZSSK sections are shown below. See the main listing table (Section 6.2.2) for individual locomotives.

CLASS 100   Bo-Bo

Two ČSD-owned rural electric railways, Tábor–Bechyně and Rybník–Lipno nad Vltavou, were converted to 1500 V DC in the 1930s. The Tábor line was the first Czech railway to be electrified, in 1903 at 1400 V DC using a 700 V system, and is similar to a tramway in nature. Class 100s were built in the mid-1950s specifically for these light traffic lines, and have small baggage compartments in the bodies. Today three remain, one of which sees occasional use on special trains between Tábor and Bechyně.

System: 1500 V DC.
Built: 1956–57.
Former ČSD Class: E422.0.
Builder: Škoda, model 15E.
Continuous Rating: 360 kW (480 hp).
Maximum Tractive Effort: 140 kN.

Total No. Built: 4.
Wheel Diameter: 1050 mm.
Weight: 48 tonnes.
Length over Buffers: 12.94 m.
Maximum Speed: 50 km/h.

CLASS 102   Bo-Bo

One of two locomotives dating from 1927, E423.001 is a survivor of the 1500 V DC "Praha Junctions" system, and was intended for shunting. The class was transferred to the Rybník–Lipno line when Praha switched to 3000 V DC. 102.001 is now part of the NTM Praha collection, and currently located at Chomutov. The Class 102 number is administrative, as like Class 103, it was never carried in traffic.

System: 1500 V DC.
Built: 1927.
Former ČSD Class: E423.0.
Builder: Adamov.
Continuous Rating: 540 kW (725 hp).
Maximum Tractive Effort:

Total No. Built: 2.
Wheel Diameter: 996 mm.
Weight: 50.6 tonnes.
Length over Buffers: 11.40 m.
Maximum Speed: 50 km/h.

CLASS 103   Bo-Bo

E436.004 is another NTM Praha museum locomotive that can now be found at Chomutov. Another survivor from the "Praha Junctions" system, the four Class E436.0s were designed for local freight.

System: 1500 V DC.
Built: 1927.
Former ČSD Class: E436.0.
Builder: ČKD.
Continuous Rating: 875 kW (1175 hp).
Maximum Tractive Effort:

Total No. Built: 4.
Wheel Diameter: 1100 mm.
Weight: 65.6 tonnes.
Length over Buffers: 12.09 m.
Maximum Speed: 60 km/h.

CLASS 140   Bo-Bo

Class 140 was the first main line electric locomotive for post-war electrification. Originally designated Class E499.0 they were greatly influenced by the Swiss BLS Ae 4/4 (although 3000 V DC). SLM and Secheron licenced the locomotive design and traction motors to Škoda for a period of ten years from 1949.

Class 140 set the body style for future Czechoslovak DC locomotives, but are easily distinguishable from all later types by their circular porthole bodyside windows. As electrification was completed along the whole of the Praha–Bohumín–Žilina–Košice corridor Class 140s spread to all depots along the route. Žilina–Spišská Nová Ves was the first Czechoslovak main line section to be electrified, completed between 1955 and 1957, and the first Class 140, E499.001, appeared in 1953. The class are affectionately nicknamed "Bobina".

System: 3000 V DC.
Built: 1953–58.
Former ČSD Class: E499.0.
Builder: Škoda, model 12E.
Continuous Rating: 2032 kW (2725 hp).
Maximum Tractive Effort: 212 kN.

Total No. Built: 100.
Wheel Diameter: 1250 mm.
Weight: 82 tonnes.
Length over Buffers: 15.60–15.80 m.
Maximum Speed: 120 km/h.

CLASS 180 Co-Co

The two Class 180 six-axle prototypes were originally numbered E698.001 and E698.002, then E669.001 and E669.002, before being swapped during renumbering to 180.002/001. When new they were additionally equipped for 1500 V DC operation. ČSD Co-Co Classes 181, 182 and 183 were developed based on experience gained with the two Class 180s.

System: 3000 V DC.
Built: 1958.
Former ČSD Class: E698.0/E669.0.
Builder: Škoda, model 23E.
Continuous Rating: E669.001 2610 kW (3500 hp); E669.002 3048 kW (4085 hp).
Maximum Tractive Effort: 345 kN.

Total No. Built: 2.
Wheel Diameter: 1250 mm.
Weight: 119 tonnes.
Length over Buffers: 18.80 m.
Maximum Speed: 90 km/h.

6.1.3. DIESEL LOCOMOTIVES

Details of main line diesel locomotive classes not already shown in the main ČD or ZSSK sections are shown below. See the main listing table (Section 6.2.3) for individual locomotives.

CLASS 715 RACK LOCOMOTIVES Dzz

Four Class 715s were built as rack locomotives for passenger and freight traffic on the steeply graded and rack-operated Tanvald–Kořenov and Polhora–Tisovec lines. Originally T426.001/003 were allocated to Tisovec and T426.002/004 to Tanvald, but they proved unreliable and were replaced by Class 820 DMUs and new Class 743s from 1988. Two are still maintained by VTS at Tanvald museum and see regular use on special services on the rack railway to Kořenov.

Built: 1961.
Former ČSD Class: T426.0.
Builder: SGP Wien.
Engine: Simmering T12b.
Power: 809 kW (1085 hp).
Transmission: Hydraulic.
Maximum Tractive Effort: 257 kN/rack 147 kN.

Total No. Built: 4.
Wheel Diameter: 1100 mm.
Train Heating Equipment:
Weight: 62.8 tonnes.
Length over Buffers: 12.14 m.
Maximum Speed: 50 km/h or 20 km/h (rack).

CLASS 720 Bo-Bo

Class 720, nicknamed, "malý Hektor" ("little Hector"), was the first domestic main line diesel locomotive in Czechoslovakia. Eight Class T434.0/T436.0 prototypes, built in 1953, had short and long bonnets either side of a cab set towards one end. All production Class T435.0 (Class 720) have a full width cab at one end and hoods extending to cab height. Up to 720.086, they have Pennsylvania drop equalisation beam bogies and are limited to 60 km/h. Later locomotives were 80 km/h with the characteristic ČKD H-frame bogies as used on all subsequent types. As late as the 1990s, Class 720s were used on branch line mixed trains using passenger coaches heated by coal-fired stoves.

The pioneer locomotive of this type, T435.001 (720.001), is part of the NTM collection. Many of this type were built for industry, and are still used by a number of different private companies on the main line. ZSSK also still uses several of the similar 1962–68-built Class 721s in Slovakia.

Built: 1958–62.
Former ČSD Class: T435.0.
Builder: ČKD, model T435.0.
Engine: ČKD 6S310DR.
Power: 551 kW (740 hp).
Transmission: Electric.
Maximum Tractive Effort: 160 kN.

Total No. Built: 150 for ČSD; 83 for industry/export.
Wheel Diameter: 1000 mm.
Train Heating Equipment: None.
Weight: 61 tonnes.
Length over Buffers: 12.44 m.
Maximum Speed: 60 or 80 km/h.

CLASS 725   B-B

Following two ČKD-built 1959 prototypes (T444.001/002, both now scrapped) was a production run of 172 of these centre-cab locomotives built by TSM in 1963–65. 111 were constructed for ČSD (T444.003–0113) and 61 for industry (T444.0501–0561). Class 725 was designed with light axle loading for use on light and medium-distance freight trip workings on branch lines.

Following construction of the passenger Class T444.1 (Class 726, see below) further locomotives using this slightly longer bodyshell were built without steam heating boilers for both ČSD and industry, designated T444.02 (T444.0201–0290 for ČSD) and T444.15 (T444.1501–1628 for industry).

The locomotives were mostly replaced in the 1980s by new Class 742s and the remainder in the 1990s by Class 731s. Some of the ČSD examples were then sold for industrial use.

Built: 1959 (prototypes); 1963–67.
Former ČSD Class: T444.0/* T444.02/* T444.15.
Builder: TSM.
Engine: ČKD K12V170DR.
Power: 515 kW (690 hp).
Transmission: Hydraulic.
Maximum Tractive Effort: 158 kN.

Total No. Built: 203 for ČSD; 189 for industry.
Wheel Diameter: 1000 mm.
Train Heating Equipment: None.
Weight: 56 tonnes.
Length over Buffers: 12.64 m (* 13.34 m).
Maximum Speed: 70 km/h.

CLASS 726   B-B

Class 726 was a passenger version of Class 725 designed for branch line passenger trains. They were fitted with a steam heating boiler and a modified, slightly longer, bodyshell. Following a 1963 prototype (T444.101), 100 further locomotives were built for ČSD (T444.102–T444.1101), 11 T444.0 were converted to T444.1 in 1973–74 (as T444.0291–0301).

Class 726 was withdrawn during the 1980s and 1990s as they were replaced by new DMUs.

Built: 1963–65.
Former ČSD Class: T444.1.
Builder: TSM.
Engine: ČKD K12V170DR.
Power: 515 kW (690 hp).
Transmission: Hydraulic.
Maximum Tractive Effort: 158 kN.

Total No. Built: 101.
Wheel Diameter: 1000 mm.
Train Heating Equipment: Steam.
Weight: 57 tonnes.
Length over Buffers: 13.34 m.
Maximum Speed: 70 km/h.

CLASS 735   Bo-Bo

Mixed-traffic Class 735 was also built by TSM in Slovakia, but became an increasingly unreliable machine with its licence-built Pielstick engine. The locomotives were designed for light passenger and freight trains, plus heavy shunting. They were mostly phased out during the late 1980s and early 1990s, but a handful of examples lingered on. Many remained on the books as donors for major rebuilds to ČD Class 714 or ZSCS/ZSSK Class 736.

Built: 1971–79.
Former ČSD Class: T466.0.
Builder: TSM.
Engine: Pielstick 12PA4-185.
Power: 926 kW (1240 hp).
Transmission: Electric.
Maximum Tractive Effort: 133 kN.

Total No. Built: 299 for ČSD; 5 for industry.
Wheel Diameter: 1000 mm.
Train Heating Equipment: Steam.
Weight: 64 tonnes.
Length over Buffers: 14.18 m.
Maximum Speed: 90 km/h.

CLASS 740   Bo-Bo

The hugely successful Class 740 is still used in large numbers by industrial operators and private freight companies across both the Czech Republic and Slovakia and also in Poland and several other countries worldwide. Only one locomotive has been "preserved" to date, 740.692 owned by KŽC, and this is frequently hired to main line companies. The last ČD examples were withdrawn in the 2000s.

Collectively Class 740s and similar Class 742s are the most numerous main line diesels (953 were built for the home market) and are commonly known as "kocur" meaning (purring) "cat" because of their equipment noise. They were developed for local freight and industrial use.

Generic prototypes T475.1501/1502 of 1970 survive today, albeit as heavily rebuilt industrial 744.701/702. A large number were built for export to Poland and in more recent years locomotives of this type have been exported to other countries, such as North Korea and Italy.

The main difference between Class 740 and Class 742 is that the 740 is heavier, ballasted, lower-geared and with a higher tractive effort. Class 742 is 8 tonnes lighter and 20 km/h quicker than Class 740, with a continuous tractive effort of 121 kN at 19.6 km/h compared to 131 kN at 18 km/h.

Original numbers were T448.0501–0959, with T448.0901–0959 later amended to T448.0401–0459. Renumbering was a: 740.501–740.899, and 740.401–459. They were built in 12 batches with detailed differences: Series I 740.501–524, Series II 740.525–584, Series III 740.585–612, Series IV 740.613–651, Series V 740.652–676, Series VI 740.677–694, Series VII 740.695–754, Series VIII 740.755–807, Series IX 740.808–863, Series X 740.864–899 and 740.401–413, Series XI 740.414–454 and Series XII 740.455–459. Similar T448.P001–P161 were built for Polish Industry. Several of these are now back in the Czech Republic/Slovakia, and have either been renumbered in the 740.460–469 series or in the 740.001–161 series (ie T448.P049 is now 740.049).

Built: 1973–89.
Former ČSD Class: T448.0.
Builder: ČKD, model T448.0.
Engine: ČKD K6S230DR.
Power: 883 kW (1185 hp).
Transmission: Electric.
Maximum Tractive Effort: 216 kN.

Total No. Built: 459 for ČSD/industry; 161 for export.
Wheel Diameter: 1000 mm.
Train Heating Equipment: None.
Weight: 72 tonnes.
Length over Buffers: 13.60 m.
Maximum Speed: 70 km/h.

CLASSES 775 & 776   Co-Co

Known as "Pomeranče" (orange) or "cenula" (carrot) owing to their bright orange livery, 44 six-axle Class T678.0 (Class 775 no heat) and Class T679.0 (Class 776 steam heat) were built in the 1960s. They were the first, and only, large domestic diesels, arising from three slightly different prototypes. The diesel engine used is an 8-cylinder version of that used in the Class 751/749 family. 20 near-identical machines went to Iraq as Class DEM2000 and were used on the Baghdad–Basra line until 1975. Further building was prevented by the Soviets, who forced ČSD to take Class M62 (Class 781), see below.

Classes 775/776/781 are good examples of the Kryspin numbering (see Introduction) where two alike types, T678.0 and T679.0, have what might seem to be different class digits, while two very different types, T679.0 and T679.1, appear from numbers to be only different sub-Classes. Classes 775/776 were displaced in ČSD times by electrification. All had moved to southern and eastern Slovakia by the 1990s where they latterly worked heavy freights.

Built: 1961–65.
Former ČSD Class: T678.0; * T679.0.
Builder: ČKD.
Engine: ČKD K8S310DR.
Power: 1470 kW (1970 hp); * 1325 kW (1775 hp).
Transmission: Electric.
Maximum Tractive Effort: 244 kN.

Total No. Built: T678.0: 17; T679.0: 27.
Wheel Diameter: 1000 mm.
Train Heating Equipment: None; * Steam.
Weight: 111 tonnes; * 114 tonnes.
Length over Buffers: 18.00 m.
Maximum Speed: 100 km/h.

CLASS 781   Co-Co

Class 781 is a Soviet-built Type M62, as built for Hungary (M62), Poland (ST44), DDR (DR 120, later DB 220) and still at work in Russia and Ukraine. Several thousand were built at Lugansk, today part of Ukraine. 599 were built for ČSD plus two more for industry. In the Czech Republic and Slovakia the type is more commonly known as "Sergej". The last examples were withdrawn from normal service in the early-mid 2000s.

Slovak MDC locomotive 781.168 has been restored to as-built unsilenced condition that inspired the German name "taiga trommel" ("Drums of Taiga").

Built: 1966–79.
Former ČSD Class: T679.1.
Builder: Luhansk, model M62.
Engine: Kharkov 14D40.
Power: 1470 kW (1970 hp).
Transmission: Electric.
Maximum Tractive Effort: 260 kN.

Total No. Built: 599 for ČSD; 2 for industry.
Wheel Diameter: 1050 mm.
Train Heating Equipment: None.
Weight: 116 tonnes.
Length over Buffers: 17.55 m.
Maximum Speed: 100 km/h.

6.2. LISTS OF PRESERVED LOCOMOTIVES

Locomotives shown with "+" after the number form part of the national museum collections of either the Czech Republic (ČD/NTM collection) or Slovakia (MDC collection). Many steam locomotives listed here are serviceable and can be seen on specials on the main line or participating in open days. For steam locomotive builder abbreviations, see the list in the Introduction of this book.

6.2.1. STEAM LOCOMOTIVES

Standard gauge (1435 mm) locomotives:

Pre-1988 No.	Works No.	Type	Built	Builder	Stat.	Location	
3	3037	0-4-0T	1894	KrLi	M	Brno Líšeň Technical Museum (tram engine)	CZ
6+	611	0-6-0T	1876	KrMu	M	ČD Lužná u Rakovníka museum	CZ
6 "GARTENAU"	1879	0-4-0T	1887	KrLi	S	ČD Chomutov museum store	CZ
9	3611	0-6-0T	1957	ČKD	P	Podbrezová station	SK
10	2165	0-6-0T	1889	KrLi	A	Brno Líšeň Technical Museum (tram engine)	CZ
29+	2438	0-6-0T	1950	Škoda	M	ČD Lužná u Rakovníka museum	CZ
103+"KLADNO"	295	0-6-0	1855	KrMu	M	ČD Praha Technical Museum	CZ
92-57	3633	0-6-0T	1957	ČKD	P	Dobrovice Sugar Museum	CZ
10390	10390	0-6-0T	1923	O&K	M	Zlonice museum	CZ
33-032	27938	2-10-0	1944	Hens	S	KPKV Brno Dolní depot	CZ
200.001	3625	0-4-0T	1897	KrMu	P	Former Litoměřice Dolní station (café)	CZ
200.003	6084	0-4-0T	1908	KrMu	R	ČD Turnov depot	CZ
"200.003"+	3581	0-4-0T	1955	ČKD	S	ČD Lužná u Rakovníka museum	CZ
200.1172	1172	0-4-0T	1921	KrLi	S	Zlonice museum	CZ
210.001	3201	0-4-0T	1905	ŠtEG	S	NTM Chomutov museum store (dismantled)	CZ
210.901	3842	0-4-0T	1956	ČKD	P	ČD Meziměstí depot (replica ex-BN60)	CZ
213.901	3579	0-4-0T	1954	ČKD	A	KPKV Koryčany	CZ
213.902	2207	0-4-0T	1947	ČKD	A	Praha Zlíchov museum	CZ
252.008+	2586	4-4-0T	1881	WNL	M	NTM Praha Technical Museum	CZ
300.619+	1633	0-6-0T	1905	WLF	M	ČD Lužná u Rakovníka museum	CZ
303.202+	1594	0-6-0F	1931	ČKD	S	NTM Čelákovice store	CZ
310.001+	2782	0-6-0T	1883	WNL	P	ČD Olomouc depot entrance	CZ
310.006+	2371	0-6-0T	1879	WNL	M	Jaroměř museum	CZ
310.037	2528	0-6-0T	1896	ŠtEG	M	KHKD Kněževes museum	CZ
310.072+	4093	0-6-0T	1899	KrLi	A	ČD Plzeň depot	CZ
310.076+	1295	0-6-0T	1899	WLF	M	ČD Lužná u Rakovníka museum	CZ
310.093+	63	0-6-0T	1901	BMM	A	ČD České Budějovice depot	CZ
310.097+	67	0-6-0T	1901	BMM	A	MDC Bratislava Východ depot	SK
310.0102+	74	0-6-0T	1902	BMM	P	Přerov station	CZ
310.0107+	4776	0-6-0T	1902	KrLi	M	MDC Bratislava museum	SK
310.0118+	108	0-6-0T	1903	BMM	S	NTM Chomutov museum store	CZ
310.0123+	5128	0-6-0T	1904	KrLi	R	ZSSK Nové Zámky depot	SK
310.0134+	482	0-6-0T	1913	BMM	A	ČD Turnov depot	CZ
310.127+	4096	0-6-0T	1898	WNL	P	Prostějov hl.n station	CZ
310.134	4326	0-6-0T	1900	WNL	M	Brno Líšeň Technical Museum	CZ
310.433+	957	0-6-0T	1896	MÁV	M	MDC Bratislava Východ depot (MÁV 377.313)	SK
310.442	1165	0-6-0T	1897	MÁV	P	Tvrdošovce village (MÁV 377.374)	SK
310.443	30	0-6-0T	1898	MÁV	P	Čierna nad Tisou station (MÁV 377.380)	SK
310.507+	1347	0-6-0T	1899	MÁV	P	MDC Bratislava Východ depot entrance	SK
310.513	497	0-6-0T	1893	ČSD	P	ŽOS Vrútky Works (entrance)	SK
310.901	362	0-6-0T	1926	Škoda	S	ČD Turnov depot	CZ
310.922+	580	0-6-0T	1930	Škoda	A	ČD Česká Třebová depot	CZ
312.3629	3629	0-6-0T	1957	ČKD	S	ČD Turnov depot	CZ
"312.801"	2911	0-6-0T	1908	O&K	P	Trnava station	SK
313.432+	128	0-6-0T	1904	BMM	A	ČD Lužná u Rakovníka museum	CZ
313.901	3623	0-6-0T	1957	ČKD	S	Praha Zlíchov museum	CZ
313.902	2642	0-6-0T	1949	ČKD	S	Muzeum Výtopna Zdice	CZ
314.303+	2695	0-6-0T	1898	ŠtEG	A	ČD Olomouc depot (museum)	CZ
"317.001"	3208	0-6-0T	1952	ČKD	S	Zlonice museum	CZ
317.015	2466	0-6-0T	1950	Škoda	P	ArcelorMittal Steelworks, Ostrava	CZ

▲ KPKV's 0-4-0T 213.901 at Telč with a special train for Slavonice on 5 July 2014. **Keith Fender**

▼ Both countries have a tradition of having plinthed steam locomotives at some railway stations and depots. Some of these are now in a rather tired condition, but others have been recently restored – such as 0-6-0T 310.0102 outside Přerov station, seen here on 8 July 2013. Note that this, and some other plinthed station locomotives, are not easily visible from trains passing through the station. **Robert Pritchard**

317.053	2453	0-6-0T	1950	Škoda	P	near Lupěné (roadside, on old trackbed)	CZ
317.123	2458	0-6-0T	1950	Škoda	P	Hornické Museum, Landek Park, Ostrava	CZ
317.903	2475	0-6-0T	1950	Škoda	S	Praha Zlíchov museum	CZ
322.302+	424	0-6-0	1870	Hart	S	NTM Chomutov museum store	CZ
324.391+	3527	0-6-0	1908	StEG	M	ČD Lužná u Rakovníka museum	CZ
327.006	3673	0-6-0T	1956	ČKD	P	ZSSK Zvolen depot (carries "323.006")	SK
327.203+	3244	0-6-0T	1953	ČKD	S	NTM Čelákovice store	CZ
327.904	3676	0-6-0T	1956	ČKD	S	Praha Zlíchov museum	CZ
328.011+	3704	0-6-0T	1956	ČKD	A	Rokytnice v Orlických Horách museum	CZ
331.019	3732	2-6-2T	1915	MÁV	S	MDC Bratislava Východ depot	SK
331.037+	5984	2-6-2T	1949	MÁV	A	MDC Bratislava Východ depot (MÁV 375.666)	SK
354.195+	1055	4-6-2T	1925	BMM	A	ČD Lužná u Rakovníka museum	CZ
354.1178+	680	4-6-2T	1931	Škoda	R	ZSSK Zvolen depot	SK
354.1217+	958	4-6-2T	1938	Škoda	M	Techmania Science Centre, Plzeň	CZ
354.7152+	657	2-6-2	1917	BMM	A	ČD Lužná u Rakovníka museum	CZ
365.020+	914	2-6-2	1921	BMM	S	NTM Chomutov museum store	CZ
365.024	968	2-6-2	1923	BMM	R	Jaroměř museum	CZ
375.007+	390	2-6-4	1911	BMM	M	NTM Praha Technical Museum	CZ
387.017+	760	4-6-2	1932	Škoda	S	MDC Bratislava Východ depot	SK
387.019+	762	4-6-2	1932	Škoda	S	MDC Bratislava Východ depot	SK
387.043+	847	4-6-2	1937	Škoda	M	ČD Lužná u Rakovníka museum	CZ
399.005+	1000	4-6-2	1939	Škoda	R	MDC Bratislava Východ depot	SK
400.901	3161	0-8-0T	1905	StEG	M	Brno Líšeň Technical Museum	CZ
403.303	1619	0-8-0	1880	StEG	S	Jaroměř museum	CZ
404.003+	1472	0-8-2RT	1901	WLF	S	NTM Chomutov museum store	CZ
411.019	1740	0-8-0	1873	WLF	R	Jaroměř museum	CZ
414.096	3282	0-8-0	1906	StEG	S	ČD Lužná u Rakovníka museum (dism)	CZ
414.404+	2416	0-8-0	1894	StEG	S	NTM Chomutov museum store	CZ
414.407	2531	0-8-0	1896	StEG	M	Křimov museum	CZ
422.002+	4430	0-8-0T	1900	KrLi	M	ČD Lužná u Rakovníka museum	CZ
422.012	1502	0-8-0T	1902	WLF	P	ŽOS Zvolen Works	SK
422.025+	203	0-8-0T	1907	BMM	S	NTM Chomutov museum store	CZ
422.062+	6619	0-8-0T	1911	KrLi	S	ČD Lužná u Rakovníka museum	CZ
422.098+	7140	0-8-0T	1916	KrLi	M	KHKD Kněževes museum	CZ
422.0108+	346	0-8-0T	1909	BMM	A	ZSSK Zvolen depot	SK
423.001+	915	2-8-2T	1921	BMM	S	NTM Chomutov museum store	CZ
423.009+	923	2-8-2T	1922	BMM	A	ČD Česká Třebová depot	CZ
423.041+	1011	2-8-2T	1924	BMM	A	ČD Brno Maloměřice depot	CZ
423.094+	1428	2-8-2T	1928	BMM	A	ČD Lužná u Rakovníka museum	CZ
423.0145	1719	2-8-2T	1937	ČKD	A	MBŽS Račice nad Trotinou	CZ
431.014+	16084	2-8-2T	1944	WLF	S	MDC Bratislava Východ depot	SK
433.001+	2398	2-8-2T	1948	ČKD	A	ČD Lužná u Rakovníka museum	CZ
433.002+	2399	2-8-2T	1948	ČKD	A	ČD Valašské Meziříčí depot	CZ
433.008	2405	2-8-2T	1948	ČKD	P	Zvolen Castle grounds ("armoured train")	SK
433.014	2411	2-8-2T	1948	ČKD	S	ČD Turnov depot	CZ
433.015	2412	2-8-2T	1948	ČKD	S	ZMŽ Lovosice depot	CZ
433.023+	2420	2-8-2T	1948	ČKD	A	MDC Vrútky museum	SK
433.025	2422	2-8-2T	1948	ČKD	S	ČD Plzeň depot	CZ
433.049+	2446	2-8-2T	1948	ČKD	M	ČD Lužná u Rakovníka museum	CZ
434.128+	808	2-8-0	1920	BMM	M	MDC Bratislava museum	SK
434.0170+	5496	2-8-0	1918	WNL	S	NTM Chomutov museum store	CZ
434.1100+	1	2-8-0	1920	Škoda	A	ČD Lužná u Rakovníka museum	CZ
434.2186+	95	2-8-0	1917	BrDa	A	ČD Praha Vršovice depot	CZ
434.2218+	3921	2-8-0	1913	StEG	R	ČD Lužná u Rakovníka museum	CZ
434.2298+	5199	2-8-0	1914	WLF	S	NTM Chomutov museum store	CZ
434.2315+	519	2-8-0	1914	BMM	S	ČD Lužná u Rakovníka museum	CZ
434.2338[1]+	646	2-8-0	1917	WLF	R	ZSSK Cargo Haniska pri Košiciach depot	SK
464.001+	1618	4-8-4T	1933	ČKD	A	ZSSK Prievidza depot	SK
464.008+	1667	4-8-4T	1935	ČKD	A	ČD Hradec Králové depot	CZ
464.044	1716	4-8-4T	1937	ČKD	S	ČD Hradec Králové depot	CZ
464.053+	1764	4-8-4T	1938	ČKD	S	NTM Chomutov museum store	CZ
464.102	2001	4-8-4T	1940	ČKD	A	ČD Praha Libeň depot	CZ
464.202+	3378	4-8-4T	1955	Škoda	A	ČD Olomouc depot (museum)	CZ
475.101+	1823	4-8-2	1947	Škoda	A	ČD Brno Maloměřice depot	CZ

475.111	1833	4-8-2	1947	Škoda	A	ČD Plzeň depot	CZ
475.179+	1901	4-8-2	1949	Škoda	A	ČD Česká Lípa depot	CZ
475.194	2617	4-8-2	1950	Škoda	S	Brno Teplárna (industrial site)	CZ
475.196+	2619	4-8-2	1950	Škoda	A	MDC Vrútky museum	SK
475.1130	2653	4-8-2	1950	Škoda	S	MDC Vrútky museum	SK
475.1142+	2665	4-8-2	1950	Škoda	S	NTM Chomutov museum store	CZ
477.013+	3012	4-8-4T	1950	ČKD	A	ZSSK Podrad-Tatry depot	SK
477.043+	3042	4-8-4T	1954	ČKD	A	ČD Lužná u Rakovníka museum	CZ
477.060+	3059	4-8-4T	1955	ČKD	S	NTM Chomutov museum store	CZ
486.007+	815	4-8-2	1936	Škoda	M	MDC Vrútky museum	SK
486.008+	568	4-8-2	1938	Škoda	S	MDC Bratislava Východ depot	SK
498.014+	1719	4-8-2	1947	Škoda	S	NTM Čelákovice store	CZ
498.022+	1727	4-8-2	1947	Škoda	A	ČD Praha Libeň depot	CZ
498.104+	3055	4-8-2	1954	Škoda	A	ZSSK Bratislava hlavná depot	SK
498.106+	3057	4-8-2	1955	Škoda	S	NTM Chomutov museum store	CZ
498.112+	3063	4-8-2	1955	Škoda	S	ČD Louny depot	CZ
524.159+	1461	2-10-2T	1929	ČKD	M	ČD Lužná u Rakovníka museum	CZ
524.184+	1498	2-10-2T	1930	ČKD	S	NTM Chomutov museum store	CZ
524.1110+	1569	2-10-2T	1931	ČKD	A	ČD Česká Lípa depot	CZ
524.1117+	733	2-10-2T	1931	Škoda	S	MDC Vrútky museum	SK
534.027+	267	2-10-0	1923	Škoda	S	NTM Chomutov museum store	CZ
534.0301+	1626	2-10-0	1945	Škoda	S	NTM Chomutov museum store	CZ
534.0323+	1648	2-10-0	1946	Škoda	A	ČD Lužná u Rakovníka museum	CZ
534.0432+	2335	2-10-0	1947	ČKD	A	ČD Olomouc depot (museum)	CZ
534.0471+	1778	2-10-0	1948	Škoda	M	MDC Bratislava museum	SK
555.0153[2]	16968	2-10-0	1944	WLF	A	ČD Lužná u Rakovníka museum	CZ
555.0301[3]+	17221	2-10-0	1943	WLF	A	KHKD Kněževes museum	CZ
555.3008[4]	1523	2-10-0	1943	Škoda	A	MDC Bratislava Východ depot	SK
555.3221[5]+	16500	2-10-0	1943	WLF	S	Muzeum Výtopna Zdice	CZ
555.3254[6]+	16913	2-10-0	1944	WLF	S	MDC Bratislava Východ depot	SK
556.036+	2803	2-10-0	1952	Škoda	A	MDC Vrútky museum	SK
556.039	2806	2-10-0	1952	Škoda	S	ZSSK Zvolen depot	SK
556.0210	2977	2-10-0	1953	Škoda	R	MOVO Plzeň Carriage Works	CZ
556.0271+	3165	2-10-0	1955	Škoda	S	ČD Lužná u Rakovníka museum	CZ
556.0298+	3192	2-10-0	1955	Škoda	R	ČD Lužná u Rakovníka museum	CZ
556.0304	3198	2-10-0	1955	Škoda	S	ČD Lužná u Rakovníka museum (dism)	CZ
556.0506+	3531	2-10-0	1957	Škoda	A	ČD České Budějovice depot	CZ
556.0510+	3535	2-10-0	1958	Škoda	S	NTM Chomutov museum store	CZ
998.200-0	03200	0-6-0F	1988	Mein	S	AWT Kladno depot	CZ
998.201-8	03201	0-6-0F	1988	Mein	S	KPKV Brno Dolní depot	CZ
A-03	3541	0-6-0F	1955	ČKD	M	ČD Telč depot	CZ
A912	3647	0-6-0F	1955	ČKD	S	České Velenice works	CZ
A918	3539	0-6-0F	1955	ČKD	S	KPKV Brno Dolní depot	CZ
A920	11873	0-4-0F	1929	O&K	S	ZMŽ Zubrnice	CZ
CS-400 3614+	3614	0-6-0T	1957	ČKD	P	MDC Vrútky museum entrance	SK
CP-600 3243	3243	0-6-0T	1953	ČKD	S	Ostrava Vítkovice Doprava steelworks	CZ
CP-600 3679+	3679	0-6-0T	1956	ČKD	M	MDC Bratislava museum	SK
CFR 40.003+	1784	2-8-2T	1908	WLF	S	MDC Vrútky museum	SK
CFR 40.006+	1787	2-8-2T	1908	WLF	A	Tisovec depot (carries MÁV 4296)	SK
CN-350	2641	0-6-0T	1949	ČKD	P	Vsetín station	CZ
CN-40 2483+	2483	0-6-0F	1947	ČKD	M	MDC Bratislava Museum	SK
CS-400 312.05	3615	0-6-0T	1957	ČKD	S	Sázava u Žďáru	CZ
EP-1000 32	3591	0-10-0T	1956	ČKD	R	ČD Veselí nad Moravou depot	CZ
KM 15591	15591	0-4-0T	1936	KrMu	S	Muzeum Starých Strojů, Žamberk	CZ
"ADOLF"	1004	0-6-0T	1882	KrMu	P	ČD Liberec depot	CZ
"DZURKO"	1082	0-4-0T	1882	KrMu	P	Veľký Šariš station	SK
"LUDVÍK"	9764	0-4-0T	1922	O&K	S	Zlonice museum	CZ
"PJ MOST"	3609	0-6-0T	1957	ČKD	P	ČD Cargo Most depot	CZ
"PRINC ERICH"	2339	0-6-0T	1890	KrLi	A	Sázava u Žďáru	CZ
– +	3624	0-6-0T	1957	ČKD	M	ČD Lužná u Rakovníka museum	CZ
–	3627	0-6-0T	1957	ČKD	P	Pilsner Urquell Brewery, Plzeň	CZ

1000 mm gauge locomotives:

U36.003	174	0-6-0T	1884	Hags	A	Košice Children's Railway ("Katka")	SK

900 mm gauge locomotives:

373	4023	0-4-0T	1958	ČKD	P	Muzeum Starých Strojů, Žamberk	CZ
381	4037	0-4-0T	1958	ČKD	P	Hornické mining museum, Krásno	CZ
853	3708	0-4-0T	1957	ČKD	P	Podkrušnohorské technické muzeum, Most	CZ
881+	3929	0-4-0T	1957	ČKD	S	NTM Chomutov museum store	CZ

800 mm gauge locomotives:

4+	1576	0-4-0WT	1884	KrMu	M	NTM Praha Technical Museum	CZ
7	11792	0-4-0T	1928	O&K	P	Třinec steelworks museum	CZ
7+	1724	0-4-0WT	1937	ČKD	M	ČD Lužná u Rakovníka museum	CZ
9	1999	0-4-0T	1940	ČKD	S	Praha Zlíchov museum	CZ
21+	6682	0-4-0WT	1912	KrLi	A	ČD Lužná u Rakovníka museum	CZ

760 mm gauge locomotives:

U17.543	2607	0-6-0T	1948	ČKD	P	Vígľaš village (carries "U175.48")	SK
U25.001	2985	0-4-0T	1951	ČKD	A	SPM, Nitra	SK
U34.901	2282	0-6-0T	1909	MÁV	A	HLÚŽ, Vychylovka	SK
U35.901	7493	0-6-0T	1918	KrLi	A	SPM, Nitra "Križko"	SK
U36.001	2495	0-6-0T	1949	ČKD	A	SPM, Nitra	SK
U37.002[7]	3814	0-6-2T	1898	KrLi	A	JHMD Jindřichův Hradec	CZ
"U37.002"	2210	0-6-0T	1948	ČKD	S	Muzeum Starých Strojů, Žamberk	CZ
U37.006	285	0-6-2T	1908	BMM	P	Ružomberok station	SK
U46.001	1458	0-8-0T	1958	Res	A	JHMD Jindřichův Hradec	CZ
U46.002	1186	0-8-0T	1951	Res	A	ČD Osoblaha depot	CZ
U46.101	3073	0-8-0	1953	Chrz	A	JHMD Jindřichův Hradec (ex-Px48-1916)	CZ
U46.902	5278	0-8-0T	1905	KrLi	S	Muzeum Starých Strojů, Žamberk ("OTTO")	CZ
U47.001	7930	0-4-4-0T	1907	Hens	A	JHMD Kamenice nad Lipou	CZ
U47.002	2788	0-4-4-0T	1911	Hohe	P	Prešov depot	SK
U57.001	1932	0-10-0	1949	Škoda	A	ČD Tremešná ve Slezsku depot	CZ
1	2609	0-6-0T	1948	ČKD	S	ČHŽ Hronec	SK
2 / U45.903	4280	0-8-0T	1916	MÁV	A	ČHŽ Čierny Balog (ex-PLDU 45.903)	SK
2 / U34.904	1879	0-6-0T	1906	MÁV	A	ČHŽ Čierny Balog "Joy"	SK
3	2209	0-6-0T	1948	ČKD	S	ČHŽ Hronec	SK
3 (RIIIc)	625	0-6-0T	1918	Smo	A	ČHŽ Čierny Balog	SK
5	2971	0-4-0T	1951	ČKD	S	Muzeum Průmyslových Železnic, Zbýšov	CZ
5 / U35.902	2611	0-6-0T	1948	ČKD	S	ČHŽ Hronec	SK
5 / U46.903	604	0-8-0T	1985	Reg	A	ČHŽ Čierny Balog (ex-CFF 764.407)	SK
7 / U35.903	2610	0-6-0T	1948	ČKD	P	ČHŽ Vydrovo	SK
222	20036	0-8-0T	1923	Hens	P	Osloboditeľov, Kamenica nad Cirochou	SK
100.15	17611	0-4-0T	1947	WLF	A	Tankodrom Military Park, Milovice	CZ

640/650 mm gauge locomotives:

1	3195	0-4-0T	1951	ČKD	R	Mladějov Industrial Museum	CZ
14	2140	0-4-0T	1944	ČKD	P	SPM, Nitra	SK
15	3200	0-4-0WT	1951	ČKD	M	Jaroměř museum	CZ
16	2958	0-4-0T	1951	ČKD	M	Muzeum Průmyslových Železnic, Zbýšov	CZ
32+	3190	0-4-0	1951	ČKD	M	ČD Lužná u Rakovníka museum	CZ

600 mm gauge locomotives:

1	7485	0-6-2T	1920	KrLi	A	Mladějov Industrial Museum	CZ
3	165	0-6-0T	1919	BrDa	S	Muzeum Průmyslových Železnic, Zbýšov	CZ
4	2992	0-4-0WT	1951	ČKD	S	Muzeum Starých Strojů, Žamberk	CZ
5	1518	0-6-2T	1929	KrLi	A	Mladějov Industrial Museum	CZ
10	2984	0-4-0WT	1951	ČKD	A	Kolín Sugar Beet Railway	CZ
40 HP	1	0-6-0WT	2014	Kolín	A	Kolín Sugar Beet Railway (new replica)	CZ
–	12311	0-4-0T	1913	Hens	S	Muzeum Průmyslových Železnic, Zbýšov	CZ

Notes:

[1] Originally 434.0226.
[2] Ex-DR 52-7620.
[3] Ex-SZD TE-3644/DR 52-3644.
[4] Ex-DR 52-7447.
[5] Ex-DR 52-7047.
[6] Ex-DR 52-7565.
[7] A heavy rebuild using parts from both U37.002 and U37.008.

6.2.2. ELECTRIC LOCOMOTIVES

Pre-1988 No.	1988 No.	Type	Built	Builder	Stat.	Location	
2	103.002-2	Bo DC	1916	Ring	M	Jaroměř museum	CZ
E212.001+	103.001-4	Bo DC	1958	Škoda	M	ČD Lužná u Rakovníka museum	CZ
E225.001+	101.001-6	Bo DC	1905	Křiž	S	NTM Chomutov museum store	CZ
E406.0501+	106.501-0	Bo-Bo BE	1959	Škoda	S	NTM Chomutov museum store	CZ
E422.001+	100.001-7	Bo-Bo DC	1956	Škoda	A	ČD Tábor depot	CZ
E422.002+	100.002-5	Bo-Bo DC	1957	Škoda	S	NTM Chomutov museum store	CZ
E422.003+	100.003-3	Bo-Bo DC	1957	Škoda	S	ČD Tábor depot	CZ
E423.001+	102.001-5	Bo-Bo DC	1927	Adam	S	NTM Chomutov museum store	CZ
E424.001	–	D DC	1928	Škoda	M	Techmania Science Centre, Plzeň	CZ
E436.004+	103.004-8	Bo-Bo DC	1927	BMM	S	NTM Chomutov museum store	CZ
E469.117+	121.017-8	Bo-Bo DC	1960	Škoda	S	NTM Chomutov museum store	CZ
E469.159+	121.059-0	Bo-Bo DC	1960	Škoda	P	ČDC Ústí nad Labem depot ("E469.110")	CZ
E499.001	140.001-9	Bo-Bo DC	1953	Škoda	S	ZSSK Žilina depot	SK
E499.004+	140.004-3	Bo-Bo DC	1953	Škoda	A	ČD Bohumín depot	CZ
E499.005+	140.005-0	Bo-Bo DC	1953	Škoda	P	ZSSK Cargo Spišská Nová Ves depot	SK
E499.047+	140.047-2	Bo-Bo DC	1957	Škoda	A	MDC Vrútky museum	SK
E499.085+	140.085-2	Bo-Bo DC	1958	Škoda	A	ČD Olomouc depot (museum)	CZ
E499.089+	140.089-4	Bo-Bo DC	1958	Škoda	S	NTM Chomutov museum store	CZ
E499.092	140.092-8	Bo-Bo DC	1958	Škoda	P	ČMŽO Přerov Works ("E499.072")	CZ
E499.1001+	141.001-8	Bo-Bo DC	1957	Škoda	S	ČD Česká Třebová depot (store)	CZ
E499.5001	169.001-5	Bo-Bo DC	1986	Škoda	S	Škoda, Plzeň Works	CZ
E698.001+	180.002-8	Co-Co DC	1958	Škoda	S	NTM Chomutov museum store	CZ
E698.001+	180.001-0	Co-Co DC	1958	Škoda	A	ČD Česká Třebová depot	CZ
E669.1001	181.001-9	Co-Co DC	1961	Škoda	S	ČD Česká Třebová depot	CZ
E669.1030+	181.030-8	Co-Co DC	1961	Škoda	S	NTM Chomutov museum store	CZ
E669.2133+	182.133-9	Co-Co DC	1965	Škoda	A	MDC Vrútky museum	SK
S489.0022+	230.022-6	Bo-Bo AC	1966	Škoda	S	NTM Chomutov museum store	CZ
S489.0050+	230.050-7	Bo-Bo AC	1966	Škoda	S	NTM Chomutov museum store	CZ
S699.001	280.001-9	Co-Co AC	1962	Škoda	M	Techmania Science Centre, Plzeň	CZ

▲ E499.004 (140.004) inside ČD Bohumín depot on 14 March 2015.　　**Robert Pritchard**

6.2.3. DIESEL LOCOMOTIVES

A large number of diesel locomotives have been preserved in both the Czech Republic and Slovakia, with many forming part of the National Collection of each country and a number also active on the main line. It should be noted that some locomotives, such as those owned by preservation group Posázavský Pacifik, can also be hired to main line freight or infrastructure companies and be seen on the main line on such duties.

In the case of Classes 749 and 751, some have carried three or four numbers, and the number shown in the main listing is that currently carried, with other numbers listed at the end.

Only serviceable narrow gauge diesel locomotives are listed.

Pre-1988 No.	1988 No.	Type	Built	Builder	Stat.	Location	
T200.002+	–	B DM	1931	ČKD	S	NTM Chomutov museum store	CZ
T201.9001	796.401-8	B DM	1916	MTH	S	ZMŽ Zubrnice	CZ
T211.0066	700.066-4	B DM	1959	ČKD	A	ČD Turnov depot	CZ
T211.0091	700.091-2	B DM	1960	ČKD	A	ČD Sumperk depot	CZ
T211.0101+	700.101-9	B DM	1960	ČKD	A	ČD Cheb depot	CZ
T211.0162	700.162-1	B DM	1962	ČKD	S	Benešov u Prahy museum (Pos. Pacifik)	CZ
T211.0926	700.426-7	B DM	1962	ČKD	M	KHKD Kněževes museum	CZ
T211.0533	700.533-3	B DM	1958	ČKD	R	KŽC Česká Kamenice	CZ
T211.0536	700.536-6	B DM	1958	ČKD	A	Ostrava Martinov tram depot ("8101")	CZ
T211.0548+	700.548-6	B DM	1958	ČKD	M	NTM Chomutov museum store	CZ
T211.0551	700.551-5	B DM	1958	ČKD	M	Vojenské Technické Muzeum, Lešany	CZ
T211.0586	700.586-1	B DM	1959	ČKD	M	KHKD Kněževes museum	CZ
T211.0128	700.648-9	B DM	1961	ČKD	R	Muzeum Výtopna, Zdice	CZ
T211.0689	700.689-3	B DM	1960	ČKD	A	Brno Dolní depot	CZ
T211.0741	700.741-2	B DM	1960	ČKD	A	Praha Zlíchov museum	CZ
T211.05347	700.770-1	B DM	1961	ČKD	A	Praha Zlíchov museum	CZ
T211.0777	700.777-6	B DM	1961	ČKD	A	KPKV Brno Dolní depot	CZ
T211.0790	700.790-9	B DM	1961	ČKD	S	Brno Dolní depot	CZ
T211.0814	700.814-7	B DM	1961	ČKD	A	ČD Bezdružice depot	CZ
T211.0823+	700.823-9	B DM	1961	ČKD	M	MDC Bratislava vychod depot	SK
T211.0838	700.838-6	B DM	1961	ČKD	A	LŽK, Letohrad depot	CZ
T211.004	701.004-4	B DM	1959	ČKD	M	MDC Vrútky museum	SK
T211.0055	701.055-6	B DM	1959	ČKD	A	MOVO Plzeň Carriage Works	CZ
T211.0069	701.069-7	B DM	1960	ČKD	R	Benešov u Prahy museum (Pos. Pacifik)	CZ
T211.2005	701.305-5	B DM	1958	ČKD	A	KŽC Lysá nad Labem depot (ex-T211.0018)	CZ
T211.2009	701.309-7	B DM	1962	ČKD	A	ČD Turnov depot	CZ
T211.2010	701.310-5	B DM	1959	ČKD	A	ZMŽ Velké Březno	CZ
T211.0037	701.460-8	B DM	1959	ČKD	A	Tanvald museum	CZ
T211.0042	701.463-2	B DM	1959	ČKD	A	ČD Plzeň depot (IMC) (ex-700.620)	CZ
T211.0522	701.484-8	B DM	1958	ČKD	A	ČD Česká Třebová depot (ex-700.690)	CZ
T211.0063	701.485-5	B DM	1959	ČKD	S	ČD Olomouc depot (ex-700.063)	CZ
T211.1532	701.532-4	B DM	1960	ČKD	S	Jaroměř museum (ex-T211.0672)	CZ
T211.1611	701.611-6	B DM	1960	ČKD	S	Tanvald museum (ex-T211.0725)	CZ
T211.0624	701.656-1	B DM	1958	ČKD	S	Sázava u Žďáru	CZ
T211.0930	701.674-4	B DM	1962	ČKD	S	Praha Zlíchov museum	CZ
T211.0952	701.678-5	B DM	1962	ČKD	R	Praha Zlíchov museum	CZ
T211.0608	701.680-1	B DM	1959	ČKD	A	Křimov museum	CZ
T211.0052	701.700-7	B DM	1959	ČKD	S	Praha Zlíchov museum	CZ
T211.1721	701.721-3	B DM	1961	ČKD	A	Praha Zlíchov museum	CZ
T211.1722	701.722-1	B DM	1959	ČKD	M	Podkrušnohorské technické muzeum, Most	CZ
T211.1728	–	B DM	1959	ČKD	A	ZMŽ Zubrnice	CZ
T211.1742	–	B DM	1960	ČKD	S	Brno Dolní depot	CZ
T211.0167	701.745-2	B DM	1962	ČKD	S	Kutná Hora Město station	CZ
T211.1754	701.754-4	B DM	1960	ČKD	A	ČD Valašské Meziříčí depot	CZ
T211.0104+	701.776-7	B DM	1960	ČKD	M	ČD Lužná u Rakovníka museum	CZ
T211.0727	701.777-5	B DM	1960	ČKD	S	Brno Dolní depot	CZ
T29.043	–	B DE	1968	ČKD	P	Hornické mining museum, Krásno ("310")	CZ
T212.0005	702.005-0	B DM	1967	TSM	A	ČD Valašské Meziříčí depot (ex-702.604)	CZ
T212.0015	702.015-9	B DM	1968	TSM	A	Praha Zlíchov museum	CZ
T212.0026	702.026-6	B DM	1968	TSM	R	ČD Turnov depot	CZ

T212.0062+	702.062-1	B DM	1969	TSM	A	ČD Olomouc depot (museum)	CZ
T212.0069+	702.069-6	B DM	1969	TSM	M	ČD Lužná u Rakovníka museum	CZ
T212.0091	702.091-0	B DM	1971	TSM	S	ČD Česká Třebová depot	CZ
T212.0515+	702.515-8	B DM	1967	TSM	S	NTM Chomutov museum store	CZ
T212.0520+	702.520-8	B DM	1967	TSM	S	NTM Chomutov museum store	CZ
T212.0581	702.581-0	B DM	1968	TSM	A	Muzeum Výtopna, Zdice	CZ
T212.0094	702.635-4	B DM	1971	TSM	A	ZMŽ Velke Brezno (ex-702.094)	CZ
T212.0657	702.657-8	B DM	1969	TSM	S	NTM Čelákovice store	CZ
T212.0667	702.667-7	B DM	1970	TSM	M	Signal Mont museum, Hradec Králové	CZ
T212.0680	702.680-0	B DM	1970	TSM	S	Retrolok, Horažďovice Předměstí depot	CZ
T212.1044	703.044-8	B DH	1979	TSM	A	ČD Turnov depot	CZ
T212.1050+	703.050-5	B DH	1979	TSM	A	ČD Valašské Meziříčí depot	CZ
T212.1051	703.051-3	B DH	1979	TSM	M	ČD Kolín depot	CZ
T212.1507	703.507-4	B DH	1972	TSM	M	KHKD Kněževes museum	CZ
T212.1575	703.575-1	B DH	1974	TSM	A	Benešov u Prahy museum (Pos. Pacifik)	CZ
T212.1614	703.614-8	B DH	1968	TSM	M	Praha Střešovice tramway museum	CZ
Ls150-7110	706.401-7	B DM	1965	Zas	S	ČD Česká Třebová depot	CZ
–	706.453-8	B DH	1976	Zas	A	SVD-JZM, Moravské Budějovice	CZ
T203.0531	706.531-1	B DH	1979	Kal	A	Praha Zlíchov museum	CZ
T203.0544	706.544-4	B DH	1986	Kal	S	KPKV Brno Dolní depot	CZ
BN60.3564	706.601-2	B DM	1955	ČKD	A	Benešov u Prahy museum (Pos. Pacifik)	CZ
BN60.3566	–	B DM	1955	ČKD	A	ČD Česká Třebová depot	CZ
BN60.3571+	706.604-6	B DM	1955	ČKD	M	ČD Lužná u Rakovníka museum	CZ
BN60.3857	706.605-3	B DM	1956	ČKD	S	Bohušovice nad Ohří	CZ
BN60.3870+	706.606-1	B DM	1955	ČKD	M	ČD Olomouc depot (museum)	CZ
BN60.3848+	706.607-9	B DM	1956	ČKD	S	NTM Chomutov museum store	CZ
BN60.3854	–	B DM	1956	ČKD	A	ČD Brno Maloměřice depot	CZ
BN60.3859	–	B DM	1957	ČKD	M	Jaroměř museum	CZ
BN60.3876	–	B DM	1957	ČKD	M	Muzeum Výtopna, Zdice	CZ
T334.004+	710.004-3	C DH	1943	ČKD	M	ČD Lužná u Rakovníka museum	CZ
T334.019+	710.019-1	C DH	1962	ČKD	P	Kladno station	CZ
T334.069+	710.069-6	C DH	1965	ČKD	M	ZSSK Nové Zámky depot	SK
T334.085+	710.085-2	C DH	1966	ČKD	A	ČD Bohumín depot	CZ
T334.090+	710.090-2	C DH	1966	ČKD	A	ČD Valašské Meziříčí depot	CZ
T334.0525	710.525-7	C DH	1962	ČKD	A	Praha Zlíchov museum	CZ
T334.0627	710.627-9	C DH	1965	ČKD	R	Muzeum Výtopna, Zdice	CZ
T334.0647	710.647-9	C DH	1965	ČKD	A	Praha Zlíchov museum	CZ
T334.0722	710.722-0	C DH	1966	ČKD	A	KŽC Lysá nad Labem depot	CZ
T334.0778	710.778-2	C DH	1966	SMZ	S	ČD Česká Třebová depot	CZ
T334.0866	710.866-5	C DH	1969	TSM	R	ČD Turnov depot	CZ
T334.0869+	710.869-9	C DH	1969	TSM	M	ČD Lužná u Rakovníka museum	CZ
T334.0894	710.894-7	C DH	1970	TSM	M	Křimov museum	CZ
T334.0944	710.444-1	C DH	1971	TSM	S	Praha Zlíchov museum	CZ
T334.0969	710.469-8	C DH	1973	TSM	S	KPKV Brno Dolní depot	CZ
T466.0117+	714.001-5	Bo-Bo DE	r1992	ČKD	S	ČD Česká Třebová depot (ex-735.117)	CZ
T426.001+	715.001-4	Dzz DH	1961	SGP	A	Tanvald museum	CZ
T426.003	715.003-0	Dzz DH	1961	SGP	A	Tanvald museum	CZ
V60.16761	–	D DH	1982	LEW	S	ZSSK Zvolen depot	SK
V60.16994	–	D DH	1981	LEW	S	KPKV Brno Dolní depot	CZ
V60.16995	716.517-8	D DH	1981	LEW	M	Jaroměř museum	CZ
T435.001+	720.001-7	Bo-Bo DE	1958	ČKD	S	NTM Chomutov museum store	CZ
T435.003	720.003-3	Bo-Bo DE	1959	ČKD	A	Benešov u Prahy museum (Pos. Pacifik)	CZ
T435.016+	720.016-5	Bo-Bo DE	1959	ČKD	S	ČD Česká Třebová depot (store)	CZ
T435.040+	720.040-5	Bo-Bo DE	1959	ČKD	A	ČD Hradec Králové depot	CZ
T435.058+	720.058-7	Bo-Bo DE	1960	ČKD	A	ČD Lužná u Rakovníka museum	CZ
T435.087+	720.087-6	Bo-Bo DE	1960	ČKD	S	NTM Chomutov museum store	CZ
T435.093+	720.093-4	Bo-Bo DE	1961	ČKD	M	MDC Vrútky museum	SK
T435.0108	720.108-0	Bo-Bo DE	1961	ČKD	A	Benešov u Prahy museum (Pos. Pacifik)	CZ
T435.0111+	720.111-4	Bo-Bo DE	1961	ČKD	A	Tanvald museum	CZ
T435.0113	720.113-0	Bo-Bo DE	1961	ČKD	A	KPKV, Brno Dolní depot	CZ
T435.0114	720.114-8	Bo-Bo DE	1961	ČKD	A	Benešov u Prahy museum (Pos. Pacifik)	CZ
T435.0139+	720.139-5	Bo-Bo DE	1962	ČKD	S	NTM Chomutov museum store	CZ
T435.0145+	720.145-2	Bo-Bo DE	1963	ČKD	A	ČD Plzeň depot	CZ
T435.0509	720.509-9	Bo-Bo DE	1958	ČKD	A	Benešov u Prahy museum (Pos. Pacifik)	CZ

T458.1035	721.035-4	Bo-Bo DE	1963	ČKD	A	Retrolok, Praha Zlíchov	CZ
T458.1091	721.091-7	Bo-Bo DE	1964	ČKD	S	ČD Česká Třebová depot	CZ
T458.1141	721.141-0	Bo-Bo DE	1965	ČKD	A	MDC Bratislava Východ depot	SK
T458.1152	721.152-7	Bo-Bo DE	1965	ČKD	S	Nymburk	CZ
T458.1190+	721.190-7	Bo-Bo DE	1965	ČKD	A	ČD Lužná u Rakovníka museum	CZ
T458.1222	721.222-8	Bo-Bo DE	1970	ČKD	A	ČD Plzeň depot	CZ
T458.1511	721.511-4	Bo-Bo DE	1965	ČKD	A	MDC Vrútky museum	SK
T458.1532	721.532-0	Bo-Bo DE	1971	ČKD	A	KŽC Lysá nad Labem depot	CZ
T444.0030+	725.030-1	B-B DH	1963	TSM	A	ČD Lužná u Rakovníka museum	CZ
T444.0037	725.037-6	B-B DH	1963	TSM	R	Retrolok, Horažďovice Předměstí depot	CZ
T444.0055+	725.055-8	B-B DH	1963	TSM	A	MDC Bratislava museum	SK
T444.0060+	725.060-8	B-B DH	1963	TSM	M	MDC Bratislava Východ depot	SK
T444.0078	725.078-0	B-B DH	1964	TSM	A	Praha Zlíchov museum	CZ
T444.0080	725.080-6	B-B DH	1964	TSM	S	Muzeum Výtopna, Zdice	CZ
T444.0101+	725.101-0	B-B DH	1964	TSM	S	NTM Chomutov museum store	CZ
T444.0225	725.225-7	B-B DH	1966	TSM	S	Muzeum Výtopna Zdice	CZ
T444.0247+	725.247-1	B-B DH	1966	TSM	S	ČD Valašské Meziříčí depot	CZ
T444.0255	725.255-4	B-B DH	1966	TSM	M	ZMŽ Zubrnice	CZ
T444.0551	725.551-6	B-B DH	1965	TSM	S	Brno Dolní depot	CZ
T444.162+	726.062-3	B-B DH	1965	TSM	A	ČD Praha Vršovice depot	CZ
T444.1082+	726.082-1	B-B DH	1965	TSM	A	Tisovec depot	SK
T444.1508	726.508-5	B-B DH	1965	TSM	M	Křimov museum	CZ
T444.1516	726.516-8	B-B DH	1965	TSM	A	Tovačov	CZ
T444.1532	726.532-5	B-B DH	1965	TSM	A	Brno	CZ
T448.0692	740.692-9	Bo-Bo DE	1980	ČKD	A	KŽC Lysá nad Labem depot	CZ
T466.0006	735.006-9	Bo-Bo DE	1973	TSM	S	KPKV Brno	CZ
T466.0007+	735.007-7	Bo-Bo DE	1973	TSM	A	ČD Olomouc depot (museum)	CZ
T466.0057+	735.057-2	Bo-Bo DE	1975	TSM	S	NTM Chomutov museum store	CZ
T466.0175+	735.175-2	Bo-Bo DE	1977	TSM	S	ČD Louny depot	CZ
T466.0253+	735.253-7	Bo-Bo DE	1979	TSM	A	ZSSK Zvolen depot	SK
T466.0254+	735.254-5	Bo-Bo DE	1979	TSM	A	ZSSK Poprad-Tatry depot	SK
T466.0286+	735.286-7	Bo-Bo DE	1979	TSM	A	ČD Lužná u Rakovníka museum	CZ
T466.0502	735.502-7	Bo-Bo DE	1978	TSM	A	Vladimír Kríž Kladno depot	CZ
T466.2103+	742.103-5	Bo-Bo-DE	1978	ČKD	A	ČD Valašské Meziříčí depot	CZ
LDH45-001	748.451-2	B-B DH	1973	Faur	S	Brno Dolní depot (carries No. "748.471")	CZ
LDH45-006	748.457-9	B-B DH	1974	Faur	S	Brno Dolní depot	CZ
LDH70-414	748.471-0	B-B DH	1976	Faur	S	Brno Dolní depot	CZ
LDH125.037	748.537-8	B-B DH	1982	Faur	A	KPKV Koryčany	CZ
LDH125.038	748.538-6	B-B DH	1982	Faur	A	KPKV Koryčany	CZ
T478.1001+	751.001-9	Bo-Bo DE	1964	ČKD	A	ČD Brno Maloměřice depot	CZ
T478.1002+	751.002-7	Bo-Bo DE	1964	ČKD	A	ČD Veselí nad Moravou depot	CZ
T478.1004+	751.004-3	Bo-Bo DE	1966	ČKD	A	ČD Lužná u Rakovníka museum	CZ
T478.1007	751.007-6	Bo-Bo DE	1966	ČKD	R	Retrolok, Horažďovice Předměstí depot	CZ
T478.1008+	749.008-9[1]	Bo-Bo DE	1967	ČKD	A	ČD Praha Vršovice depot	CZ
T478.1131	751.131-4	Bo-Bo DE	1968	ČKD	A	ZSSK Prievidza depot	SK
T478.1146	749.146-7	Bo-Bo DE	1969	ČKD	A	Retrolok, Praha Zlíchov	CZ
T478.1148	751.148-8	Bo-Bo DE	1969	ČKD	A	ČD Louny depot	CZ
T478.1201+	751.201-5	Bo-Bo DE	1970	ČKD	A	ZSSK Cargo Bratislava Východ depot	SK
T478.1215	749.253-1[2]	Bo-Bo DE	1971	ČKD	A	KŽC Lysá nad Labem depot	CZ
T478.2011	749.246-5[3]	Bo-Bo DE	1968	ČKD	A	MDC Vrútky museum	SK
T478.2012	749.248-1[4]	Bo-Bo DE	1968	ČKD	A	MDC Vrútky museum	SK
T478.2036	749.250-7[5]	Bo-Bo DE	1969	ČKD	A	ČD Olomouc depot (museum)	CZ
T478.2065	749.259-8[6]	Bo-Bo DE	1970	ČKD	A	KŽC Lysá nad Labem depot	CZ
T478.2078	749.240-8[7]	Bo-Bo DE	1970	ČKD	A	Vladimír Kríž Kladno depot	CZ
T478.3001+	753.001-7	Bo-Bo DE	1968	ČKD	A	ČD Česká Lípa depot	CZ
T478.3016+	753.016-5	Bo-Bo DE	1971	ČKD	S	NTM Chomutov museum store	CZ
T478.3101+	753.101-5	Bo-Bo DE	1973	ČKD	A	ČD Lužná u Rakovníka museum	CZ
T478.3109	753.109-8	Bo-Bo DE	1973	ČKD	A	ZSSK Zvolen depot	SK
T478.3127	753.127-0	Bo-Bo DE	1973	ČKD	A	Vladimír Kríž Kladno depot	CZ
T478.3308	750.308-9[8]	Bo-Bo DE	1975	ČKD	A	ČD Turnov depot	CZ
− +	755.001-5	Bo-Bo DE	r1994	ŽSR	M	MDC Vrútky museum (ex-753.055)	SK
T669.0001+	770.001-6	Co-Co DE	1963	ČKD	A	ČD Lužná u Rakovníka museum	CZ
T669.0069+	770.069-3	Co-Co DE	1968	SMZ	S	NTM Chomutov museum store	CZ
T669.0085+	770.085-9	Co-Co DE	1968	SMZ	S	DPOV Nymburk Works	CZ

T669.1069+	771.069-2	Co-Co DE	1970	SMZ	S	NTM Chomutov museum store	CZ
T669.1130	771.130-2	Co-Co DE	1971	SMZ	A	Vladimír Kríž Kladno depot	CZ
–	772.001-4	Co-Co DE	r1998	ŽSR	S	TatraVagonka, Trebišov (ex-771.057)	SK
T678.012+	775.012-8	Co-Co DE	1963	ČKD	A	ZSSK Zvolen depot	SK
T678.016+	775.016-9	Co-Co DE	1964	ČKD	S	MDC Bratislava Východ depot	SK
T679.019+	776.019-2	Co-Co DE	1965	ČKD	A	MDC Bratislava Východ depot	SK
T679.1168+	781.168-0	Co-Co DE	1968	Luhan	A	MDC Vrútky museum	SK
T679.1312+	781.312-4	Co-Co DE	1971	Luhan	S	MDC Bratislava Východ depot	SK
T679.1529+	781.529-3	Co-Co DE	1973	Luhan	A	ČD Česká Třebová depot	CZ
T679.1578	781.578-0	Co-Co DE	1979	Luhan	A	Vladimír Kríž Kladno depot	CZ
T679.1592+	781.592-1	Co-Co DE	1979	Luhan	S	NTM Chomutov museum store	CZ
T679.1600+	781.600-2	Co-Co DE	1979	Luhan	A	ČD Lužná u Rakovníka museum	CZ

1000 mm gauge locomotives:

TU29.2002	701.952-4	B DM	1959	ČKD	A	Košice Children's Railway ("Janka")	SK
TU29.2003	701.953-2	B DM	1960	ČKD	A	Košice Children's Railway ("Danka")	SK

760 mm gauge locomotives:

TU24.901	–		1968		A	ČHŽ Čierny Balog	SK
TU38.001	Lyd2-01	C DH	1977		A	ČD Tremešná ve Slezsku depot	CZ
TU45.001	–	B-B DE	1961		A	ČHŽ Čierny Balog	SK
TU47.016+	705.916-5	Bo-Bo DE	1958	ČKD	M	ČD Lužná u Rakovníka museum	CZ
TU48.001	–	Bo-Bo DE	1972		A	ČHŽ Čierny Balog (ex-Lxd 2-302)	SK

Renumbering notes:

[1] Also numbered 751.008-4.
[2] Also numbered 751.215-5 and 752.083-6.
[3] Also numbered 752.011-7.
[4] Also numbered 752.012-5.

[5] Also numbered 752.036-4.
[6] Also numbered 752.065-3.
[7] Also numbered 752.078-6.
[8] Also numbered 753.308-6.

▲ The first built Class 751, T478.1001 (751.001) is preserved by ČD at Brno Maloměřice. On 7 February 2016 it is seen at Bruntál with a british enthusiast "Not-For-Profit" railtour from Jeseník to Brno. **Robert Pritchard**

6.2.4. DIESEL MULTIPLE UNITS

The first diesel railcars were introduced in Czechoslovakia for operation on rural lines in the 1920s and 1930s. ČSD placed a large order for Class M131 railcars in 1946: 549 were built 1948–56 by Tatra Kopřivnice and Vagónka Studénka. The M131s were mainly replaced by Class 810 during the late 1970s and early 1980s (although the last two survived into the early 1990s). 85 were rebuilt as M131.2s in 1967–80 as overhead engineers cars. Large numbers of M131s have been preserved, many of which are serviceable and can be seen on the main line.

In terms of other major ČSD DMU classes, 120 Class 820 (M240.0) were built by Vagónka Studénka 1963–65 (plus two prototypes). The first bogie railcars were the 238 Class 831s (M262.0) built by a consortium of Královopolská (Brno), Tatra and ČKD 1949–60: the last were withdrawn from normal service in 2003 in Slovakia and 2007 in the Czech Republic. 41 Class 830 were rebuilt as Class 831 (M262.1) in the 1980s, the last of these being withdrawn in 2011. Finally, 52 Class 850 (M286.0) and 37 Class 851 (M286.1) were built by Studénka 1962–68, the last being withdrawn in 2013. Preserved DMU and EMU trailer vehicles are not listed.

Pre-1988 No.	1988 No.	Type	Built	Origin	Stat.	Location	
M120.206	–	A1 DM	1928	ČSD	R	Pardubice Rosice station	CZ
M120.417	806.417-2	A1 DM	1931	ČSD	S	ČD Šumperk depot (ex-M120.437)	CZ
M120.485	806.485-9	A1 DM	1932	ČSD	R	Křimov museum	CZ
M131.101+	801.001-9	A1 DM	1948	ČSD	A	ČD Šumperk depot	CZ
M131.105+	801.005-0	A1 DM	1948	ČSD	S	ČD Louny depot	CZ
M131.109	801.009-2	A1 DM	1948	ČSD	A	ZMŽ Zubrnice	CZ
M131.1012	801.012-6	A1 DM	1948	ČSD	S	ZMŽ Velke Brezno	CZ
M131.1013	801.013-4	A1 DM	1948	ČSD	S	ZMŽ Velke Brezno	CZ
M131.1029	801.029-0	A1 DM	1948	ČSD	S	KPKV Brno Dolní depot	CZ
M131.1053+	801.053-0	A1 DM	1948	ČSD	A	ZSSK Zvolen depot	SK
M131.1081	801.081-1	A1 DM	1949	ČSD	A	MBŽS Skalsko depot	CZ
M131.1100	801.100-9	A1 DM	1956	ČSD	S	MDC Vrutky museum (ex-M131.1527)	SK
M131.1116	801.116-5	A1 DM	1949	ČSD	P	Pardubice Rosice station (PSHŽD)	CZ
M131.1125+	801.125-6	A1 DM	1949	ČSD	A	ZSSK Košice depot	SK
M131.1130+	801.130-6	A1 DM	1954	ČSD	A	ČD Česká Lípa depot (ex-M131.1357)	CZ
M131.1133+	801.133-0	A1 DM	1949	ČSD	A	ČD Pardubice depot (PSHŽD)	CZ
M131.1145	801.145-4	A1 DM	1949	ČSD	S	Krnov depot (ZMŽ)	CZ
M131.1163	801.163-7	A1 DM	1949	ČSD	A	Jaroměř museum	CZ
M131.1179	801.179-3	A1 DM	1949	ČSD	R	Kadaň Prunéřov wagon works	CZ
M131.1184+	801.184-3	A1 DM	1949	ČSD	R	ČD Cheb depot	CZ
M131.1186	801.186-8	A1 DM	1949	ČSD	P	Pars nova Šumperk Works	CZ
M131.1198	801.198-3	A1 DM	1950	ČSD	S	ZSSK Poprad-Tatry depot	SK
M131.1228+	801.228-8	A1 DM	1956	ČSD	A	ČD Pardubice depot (PSHŽD) (ex-M131.1532)	CZ
M131.1238	801.238-7	A1 DM	1950	ČSD	A	KHKD Kněževes museum	CZ
M131.1243	801.243-7	A1 DM	1950	ČSD	S	ZMŽ Velke Brezno	CZ
M131.1266	801.266-8	A1 DM	1950	ČSD	A	Vladimír Kríž Kladno depot	CZ
M131.1280	801.280-9	A1 DM	1951	ČSD	A	ZMŽ Zubrnice	CZ
M131.1286	801.286-6	A1 DM	1951	ČSD	S	Muzeum Výtopna Zdice	CZ
M131.1302	801.302-1	A1 DM	1951	ČSD	A	KŽC Česká Kamenice	CZ
M131.1313	801.313-8	A1 DM	1951	ČSD	S	Domašín (PVTKZ)	CZ
M131.1365	801.365-8	A1 DM	1954	ČSD	S	ČD Plzeň depot	CZ
M131.1386	801.386-4	A1 DM	1954	ČSD	P	Bezdružice station	CZ
M131.1405+	801.405-2	A1 DM	1955	ČSD	S	NTM Chomutov museum store	CZ
M131.1413+	801.413-6	A1 DM	1955	ČSD	R	ČD Cheb depot	CZ
M131.1441	801.441-7	A1 DM	1955	ČSD	A	Jaroměř museum	CZ
M131.1443+	801.443-3	A1 DM	1955	ČSD	A	ZSSK Žilina depot	SK
M131.1448+	801.448-2	A1 DM	1955	ČSD	A	ČD Brno Maloměřice (carries 801.615-6)	CZ
M131.1453	801.453-2	A1 DM	1955	ČSD	S	Krnov depot	CZ
M131.1454	801.454-0	A1 DM	1955	ČSD	A	ČD Kroměříž depot	CZ
M131.1463+	801.463-1	A1 DM	1955	ČSD	A	ČD Břeclav depot	CZ
M131.1470	801.470-6	A1 DM	1955	ČSD	S	Slaný depot	CZ
M131.1473	801.473-0	A1 DM	1955	ČSD	S	KHKD Kněževes museum	CZ
M131.1478	801.478-9	A1 DM	1955	ČSD	R	ZMŽ Lovosice depot	CZ
M131.1487+	801.487-0	A1 DM	1955	ČSD	A	ČD Bezdružice depot	CZ
M131.1513	801.513-3	A1 DM	1956	ČSD	A	Křimov museum	CZ
M131.1515+	801.515-8	A1 DM	1956	ČSD	A	ČD Kolín depot	CZ

M131.1538	801.538-0	A1 DM	1956	ČSD	A	ZSSK Košice depot	SK
M131.1541	801.541-4	A1 DM	1956	ČSD	S	Dvůr Králové nad Labem	CZ
M131.1546+	801.546-3	A1 DM	1956	ČSD	R	MDC Vrútky museum	SK
M131.1549	801.549-7	A1 DM	1956	ČSD	A	Junior Market, Kolín	CZ
M131.2053	801.342-7	A1 DM	1954	ČSD	A	Pardubice Rosice station (ex-M131.1342)	CZ
M131.2069	801.261-9	A1 DM	1950	ČSD	S	KHKD Kněževes museum (ex-M131.1261)	CZ
M133.005	–	A1 DM	1943	ČSD	S	CD Plzeň depot	CZ
M140.101+	–	A1 DM	1928	ČSD	M	MDC Bratislava museum	SK
M144.0004	891.004-4	A1 DM	1957	ČSD	S	ČD Turnov depot	CZ
M144.0006	891.006-9	A1 DM	1957	ČSD	S	ČD Česká Třebová depot	CZ
M144.0007	891.007-7	A1 DM	1959	ČSD	S	ČD Louny depot (ex-991.0277)	CZ
M144.0008	891.008-5	A1 DM	1959	ČSD	S	Brno Dolní depot	CZ
M144.0016+	891.016-8	A1 DM	1961	ČSD	S	ČD Česká Třebová depot	CZ
M152.0002+	810.002-6	A1 DM	1973	ČSD	A	ČD Lužná u Rakovníka museum	CZ
M152.0453	810.453-5	A1 DM	1981	ČSD	A	Tanvald museum	CZ
M152.0477	810.477-0	A1 DM	1982	ČSD	A	Vladimír Kríž Kladno depot	CZ
M152.0604	810.604-9	A1 DM	1983	ČSD	A	ČD Turnov depot	CZ
M152.0626	810.626-6	A1 DM	1984	ČSD	A	ZSSK Košice depot	SK
M21.004	–	A1 DM	1939	ČSD	A	ČHŽ Čierny Balog (760 mm)	SK
M222.006+		B2 DM	1932	ČSD	S	NTM Čelákovice museum store	CZ
M234.001	–	B2 DM	1932	ČSD	S	Kutná Hora Město station	CZ
M240.0033	820.033-9	B2 DH	1963	ČSD	R	Kadaň Prunéřov wagon works	CZ
M240.0039+	820.039-6	B2 DH	1963	ČSD	A	Tisovec depot	SK
M240.0042+	820.042-0	B2 DH	1963	ČSD	S	MDC Bratislava Východ depot	SK
M240.0046+	820.046-1	B2 DH	1964	ČSD	S	NTM Chomutov museum store	CZ
M240.0056	820.056-0	B2 DH	1964	ČSD	A	Tanvald museum	CZ
M240.0057	820.057-0	B2 DH	1964	ČSD	A	Tanvald museum	CZ
M240.0086	820.086-7	B2 DH	1964	ČSD	R	ZSSK Zvolen depot	SK
M240.0089+	820.089-1	B2 DH	1964	ČSD	S	ČD Valašské Meziříčí depot	CZ
M240.0100+	820.100-6	B2 DH	1964	ČSD	A	ČD Lužná u Rakovníka museum	CZ
M240.0113	820.113-9	B2 DH	1964	ČSD	A	KPKV Brno Dolní depot	CZ
M240.0114+	820.114-7	B2 DH	1964	ČSD	S	ČD Turnov depot	CZ
M260.001+	825.001-1	1A-A1 DM	1938	ČSD	A	VUZ Velim	CZ
M262.0004	830.004-8	Bo2 DE	1949	ČSD	A	MDC Bratislava Východ depot (vlaky.net)	SK
M262.0005	830.005-5	Bo2 DE	1949	ČSD	R	Junior Market, Kolín	CZ
M262.0007+	830.007-1	Bo2 DE	1949	ČSD	A	MDC Bratislava Východ depot	SK
M262.0012+	830.012-1	Bo2 DE	1949	ČSD	S	NTM Chomutov museum store	CZ
M262.0018+	830.018-8	Bo2 DE	1949	ČSD	A	ČD Brno Maloměřice depot	CZ
M262.0045	830.045-1	Bo2 DE	1950	ČSD	S	Benešov u Prahy museum (Pos. Pacifik)	CZ
M262.0056	830.056-8	Bo2 DE	1952	ČSD	A	KŽC Lysá nad Labem depot	CZ
M262.0075+	830.075-8	Bo2 DE	1953	ČSD	S	NTM Chomutov museum store	CZ
M262.0076+	830.076-6	Bo2 DE	1953	ČSD	A	ČD Lužná u Rakovníka museum	CZ
M262.0084	830.084-0	Bo2 DE	1953	ČSD	S	KPKV Brno Dolní depot	CZ
M262.0090+	830.090-7	Bo2 DE	1953	ČSD	S	ČD Louny depot	CZ
M262.0098	830.098-0	Bo2 DE	1958	ČSD	S	EŽ Česká Třebová depot	CZ
M262.0124	830.124-4	Bo2 DE	1958	ČSD	A	KŽC Lysá nad Labem depot	CZ
M262.0154+	830.154-1	Bo2 DE	1959	ČSD	A	ČD Česká Lípa depot	CZ
M262.0159+	830.159-0	Bo2 DE	1959	ČSD	A	ČD Česká Lípa depot	CZ
M262.0180	830.180-6	Bo2 DE	1959	ČSD	A	KŽC Lysá nad Labem depot	CZ
M262.0193	830.193-9	Bo2 DE	1959	ČSD	S	Retrolok, Horažďovice Předměstí depot	CZ
M262.0206	830.206-9	Bo2 DE	1960	ČSD	A	JHMD Jindřichův Hradec depot	CZ
M262.0209	830.209-3	Bo2 DE	1959	ČSD	A	Junior Market, Kolín	CZ
M262.1002	831.113-6	Bo2 DE	1958	ČSD	A	Junior Market, Kolín	CZ
M262.1043+	831.043-5	Bo2 DE	1950	ČSD	A	ČD Louny depot	CZ
M262.1105	831.105-2	Bo2 DE	1958	ČSD	A	ZMŽ Lovosice depot (Hanzalík)	CZ
M262.1110	831.110-2	Bo2 DE	1958	ČSD	A	ZMŽ Lovosice depot (Hanzalík)	CZ
M262.1117	831.117-1	Bo2 DE	1958	ČSD	A	KŽC Lysa nad Labem depot	CZ
M262.1167	831.167-2	Bo2 DE	1958	ČSD	A	JHMD Jindřichův Hradec depot	CZ
M262.1168	831.168-0	Bo2 DE	1959	ČSD	A	KŽC Lysá nad Labem depot	CZ
M262.1183	831.183-9	Bo2 DE	1959	ČSD	A	KŽC Lysá nad Labem depot	CZ
M262.1187+	831.187-0	Bo2 DE	1959	ČSD	S	NTM Chomutov museum store	CZ
M262.1212	831.212-6	Bo2 DE	1959	ČSD	A	KŽC Lysá nad Labem depot	CZ
M263.0017+	894.017-3	1A-A1 DM	1964	ČSD	S	ČD Česká Třebová depot	CZ
M274.003	–	Bo2 DE	1934	ČSD	S	Kutná Hora Město station	CZ

▲ 549 of the two-axle M131 (later given the 1988 number series Class 801) railcars were built between 1948 and 1956, and many still survive in preservation. M131.1125 and M131.1053, along with two trailers, stand at Bratislava hlavná station on 14 June 2014 with a special shuttle service to the annual "Rendez" event being held at Bratislava Východ museum. **Robert Pritchard**

▼ M286.0044 (850.044) runs onto the turntable at Praha Vršovice depot on 13 May 2014 after arriving with the annual "STARS" enthusiast tour – the "Central Czech-Out". **Robert Pritchard**

M274.004+	–	Bo2 DE	1934	ČSD	A	MDC Vrútky museum	SK
M286.0001+	850.001-9	B2 DH	1962	ČSD	A	ČD Olomouc depot (museum)	CZ
M286.0002	850.002-7	B2 DH	1962	ČSD	S	ŽOS Vrútky Works	SK
M286.0008+	850.008-4	B2 DH	1966	ČSD	S	NTM Chomutov museum store	CZ
M286.0011	850.011-8	B2 DH	1966	ČSD	S	ŽOS Vrútky Works	SK
M286.0013	850.013-4	B2 DH	1967	ČSD	S	ŽOS Vrútky Works	SK
M286.0022	850.022-5	B2 DH	1967	ČSD	S	KPKV Brno Dolní depot	CZ
M286.0039	850.039-9	B2 DH	1967	ČSD	S	ŽOS Vrútky Works	SK
M286.0043	850.043-1	B2 DH	1967	ČSD	S	ŽOS Vrútky Works	SK
M286.0044	850.044-9	B2 DH	1967	ČSD	A	KPKV Brno Dolní depot	CZ
M286.0045	850.045-6	B2 DH	1967	ČSD	S	ŽOS Vrútky Works	SK
M286.1002	851.002-6	B2 DH	1968	ČSD	S	ŽOS Vrútky Works	SK
M286.1005+	851.005-9	B2 DH	1968	ČSD	S	ČD Česká Třebová depot (store)	CZ
M286.1008	851.008-3	B2 DH	1968	ČSD	A	KŽC Lysá nad Labem depot	CZ
M286.1022	851.022-4	B2 DH	1968	ČSD	S	ŽOS Vrútky Works	SK
M286.1029	851.029-9	B2 DH	1968	ČSD	S	ŽOS Vrútky Works	SK
M286.1032	851.032-3	B2 DH	1968	ČSD	A	Brno Dolní depot	CZ
M290.001	–	1A-A1 DM	1936	ČSD	P	Tatra museum, Kopřivnice	CZ
M475.0001+	860.001-7	Bo-Bo DE	1974	ČSD	S	NTM Chomutov museum store	CZ

6.2.5. STEAM MOTOR UNIT

Pre-1988 No.	Works No.	Type	Built	Builder	Status	Location	
M124.001+	65168	A1 0-2-2	1903	Ring	A	ČD Lužná u Rakovníka museum	CZ

6.2.6. ELECTRIC MULTIPLE UNITS

Vintage EMU 400.001 is used on occasional specials from Tábor to Bechyně (Line 202), the line for which it was built to operate in 1903. Pars nova at Šumperk has preserved a 4-car former ČD Class 451, and this can sometimes be seen out on the main line. 451.045/046 operate with two trailers 051.045+051.049.

Pre-1988 No.	1988 No.	Type	Built	Builder	Status	Location	
EM400.001+	400.001-4	Bo-Bo DC	1903	ČSD	A	ČD Tábor depot	CZ
EM475.1045	451.045-9	Bo-Bo DC	1966	ČSD	A	Pars nova Šumperk Works	CZ
EM475.1046	451.046-7	Bo-Bo DC	1966	ČSD	A	Pars nova Šumperk Works	CZ

6.2.7. NARROW GAUGE EMUS

The 1000 mm gauge lines in the north of Slovakia are detailed in the ZSSK Narrow Gauge Stock section. In addition there are the heritage cars listed here, which are used on special services on the TEŽ network.

The Trenčianska Elektrická Železnica (TREŽ) electric railway in the west of Slovakia was previously operated by ZSSK until it closed in 2011. The 5.4 km, 760 mm line runs as an interurban tramway linking Trenčianska Teplá station with the spa town of Trenčianske Teplice. It is now run as a heritage operation, using the three Tatra motor cars (the trailer vehicles have now been withdrawn) which were heavily modernised in the 1980s. It usually operates around once a month and at weekends in July and August, for dates of operation and timetables see the website: www.trezka.sk.

Pre-1988 No.	1988 No.	Type	Built	Builder	Status	Location	
22 (EMU 26.001)+	–	Bo DC	1913	TEŽ	A	ZSSK Poprad-Tatry depot	SK
EMU 49.001+	–	Bo-Bo DC	1931	TEŽ	A	ZSSK Poprad-Tatry depot	SK
EMU 49.005+	495.955-7	Bo-Bo DC	1956	TEŽ	S	ZSSK Poprad-Tatry depot	SK
M46.003	411.901-2	Bo-Bo DC	1951	ČSD	A	TREŽ, Trenčianska Teplá	SK
M46.002	411.902-0	Bo-Bo DC	1951	ČSD	A	TREŽ, Trenčianska Teplá	SK
M46.001	411.903-8	Bo-Bo DC	1951	ČSD	A	TREŽ, Trenčianska Teplá	SK

7. MUSEUMS & HERITAGE LINES

This listing provides a brief guide to the main museums and heritage lines in the Czech Republic and Slovakia. Since the 1990s preservation has flourished, with many new lines opening. Railtours on the main lines also operate, both steam and diesel hauled, and details of some of these can be found in the back of the ČD and ZSSK timetable books. For details of individual locomotives preserved see Section 6. Note that traditionally most museums close on Mondays.

7.1. CZECH MUSEUMS & HERITAGE LINES

Národní Technické Muzeum (National Technical Museum, NTM), Praha 7
www.ntm.cz
This Praha museum embraces all technical matters. Only three steam locomotives from the vast NTM railway collection of around 130 vehicles are on display here. Many items are stored or loaned out to other locations. A further NTM museum is planned in the former depot at Masarykovo station in Praha and it is expected that many of the items currently stored at Chomutov will then be based here. The NTM is closed on Mondays. Note that as with some other Czech museums there is an additional charge for taking photographs.

Muzeum MHD Praha (Praha Public Transport Museum), Praha 6
www.dpp.cz/en/urban-mass-transit-museum/
The former tram depot at Střešovice houses the official collection of Praha city transport trams and buses. Metro car 1009 from the 1974 ECS type stock is located here. Open late March–mid November, weekends and public holidays. Operational preserved trams work tram route 91 between Střešovice and the city centre on the same dates.

ČD Železniční Muzeum (Czech Railways Museum), Lužná u Rakovníka
www.cdmuzeum.cz/en
The main ČD museum is located at Lužná u Rakovníka depot, west of Praha on ČD timetable Table 120. It is the official home to the ČD operational main line steam and diesel locomotives and also houses NTM and KHKD locomotives. Some locomotives may not always be on public view, or may be undergoing renovation. Open late April to late October and daily (except Mondays) in June, July and August.

ČD Chomutov depository
A museum depository located in a former running depot. The large site is normally open for visits just two or three days a year, normally including the last weekend in August. Details are published on the ČD website.

ČD Olomouc museum
Part of Olomouc depot is reserved for ČD preserved items and is open to the public around eight weekends every year. See the cdmuzeum.cz website for opening dates.

Železniční muzeum výtopna Jaroměř (Jaroměř Railway Museum), Jaroměř
www.vytopnajaromer.cz
Established in 1987 as a private museum in a former locomotive depot (roundhouse) with a fine collection of steam and diesel locomotives. Operates regular main line steam excursions between Jaroměř and a number of destinations, including Náchod and Stará Paka. Open May to October weekends and all week in July and August.

ZMZ – Zubrnická muzeální železnice (Zubrnice Railway Museum), Zubrnice
www.zmz.cz
A short museum operation running Class 801 DMUs and some locomotive-hauled trains between Velké Březno, Zubrnice and also onto Ústí nad Labem Střekov at weekends.

KHKD Hercules club ("History of Rail Transport Club")
www.khkd.cz
The club was founded in 1981 to collect and renovate rail vehicles. KHKD operates steam-hauled trains on Saturdays in July and August from Lužná u Rakovníka to Kolešovice, via Kněževes where the main workshops are located.

Klub Železničních Cestovatelů (KŽC, "The Railway Travellers Club")
www.kzc.cz
This Lysá nad Labem club operates an extensive programme of heritage services over various routes, mainly using DMUs. Details are on the KZC website or in the ČD timetable.

Iron Monument Club, Plzeň
www.imcplzen.cz
Owners of four steam locomotives, mostly based at CD's Plzeň depot. Operates main line steam trips.

JHMD – Jindřichohradecké Místní Dráhy, Jindřichův Hradec
JHMD is the private operator running scheduled service trains between Jindřichův Hradec and Obrataň/Nová Bystřice (see Private Passenger Operators section). It also operates a regular programme of steam-hauled trains in the summer months. These are shown in Tables 228/229.

Osoblažská Úzkokolejka (Osoblaha Narrow Gauge Railway)
www.osoblazsko.com
CD operates the 20 km 760 mm line from Třemešná to Osoblaha (see ČD Narrow Gauge Stock section), whilst a local group (SZD) operates steam trains on summer weekends and selected other dates (see the website for details). The impressive 0-10-0 U57.001 is normally used.

Kolínská Řepařská Drážka (Kolín Sugar Beet Railway)
www.zeleznicka.bloudil.cz
This line originally formed part of a 130 km long, 600 mm system of railways in the region used to transport sugar beet into Kolín. The current running line runs for around 6 km from Sendražice, on the outskirts of Kolín, to Býchory. It often uses a new build 0-6-0WT steam locomotive built locally. Operates weekends and holidays May to September.

Železniční Muzeum Zlonice (Zlonice Railway Museum)
www.zmzlonice.sweb.cz
Located near Zlonice station, north-west of Praha on Tables 095/110. A small collection of steam, diesel and industrial locomotives with a short demonstration running line. Open weekends May to October and daily (except Mondays) in July and August.

Technické muzeum v Brně (Brno Technical Museum), Brno Líšeň
www.technicalmuseum.cz
The Brno Líšeň depository is an annex of the Brno Technical Museum, mostly housing trams from across the Czech Republic and Slovakia. It is only normally open for pre-arranged visits.

Techmania Science Centre, Plzeň
www.techmania.cz
This new science centre opened in 2013 and is principally aimed at children and school groups etc. It is located within the Škoda works site near Plzeň Jižní předměstí station. Worth a visit to see the two electric locomotives here, plus the one steam locomotive. Open daily.

Muzeum Průmyslových Železnic ve Zbýšově (Museum of Industrial Railways in Zbýšov)
www.mpz.cz
This was a standard gauge coal mining line until 2005 when it was regauged to 600 mm after mining ceased. The railway operates steam and diesel heritage services on summer weekends.

PSHŽD Pardubice Rosice station museum
www.pshzd.cz/museum-rosice.html
A small museum at Pardubice Rosice station. Open Saturdays May to October.

Muzeum Výtopna Zdice (Zdice museum)
www.saxi.cz
A museum collection established in the former locomotive depot (closed 2002) at Zdice, on the Praha–Plzeň main line. Open the first weekend of every month, April to October. SAXI also operates main line excursions, often using one of their diesel shunting locomotives.

Průmyslové Muzeum Mladějov na Moravě (Industrial Museum Mladějov)
www.mpz.cz
600 mm gauge former industrial line now running for 11 km from Mladějov na Moravě (Line 017) to Hřebeč doly as a heritage operation with steam locomotives. The line was originally built to convey shale, clay and coal from mines to local furnaces. Operates on summer weekends.

Technické muzeum Tatra (Tatra Technical Museum), Kopřivnice
www.tatramuseum.cz
Mainly road transport items built under the famous Tatra name, but this museum also houses the M290.0 Intercity Slovenská strela railcar of 1936. Open daily except Mondays.

Horská Ozubnicová Dráha (Horska rack railway), Tanvald
www.zubacka.cz
This preservation group is based at Tanvald, and is also restoring the former depot at Kořenov as a new headquarters. It operates regular trains over the one of the few standard gauge rack-

operated lines in Europe from Tanvald to Kořenov, normally using a Class 715. ČD operates normal service trains over the same route with DMUs.

Výtopna Zlíchov (Zlíchov roundhouse), Praha 5
www.masinka.cz
A small museum just south of Praha Smichov station, established in 1999 with the aim of preserving steam and diesel locomotives. Operates charter trains, usually using steam locomotive 313.901.

Loko-motiv Křimov (Křimov museum)
www.loko-motiv.cz
Museum established in the former Křimov depot, on Line 137 and open on selected dates.

7.2. SLOVAK MUSEUMS & HERITAGE LINES

MDC Múzejno Dokumentačné Centrum (National Museum Collection), Bratislava Východ Depot
www.mdc.sk
The official national railway collection is housed at Bratislava and Vrútky with some items also outbased at ZSSK depots such as Previdza and Poprad-Tatry. Bratislava Vychod depot is in two parts – the operational ZSSK Cargo depot and the MDC museum depository and workshops. The Východ depot site, to the north-east of the city close to Bratislava Rača station, is open between April and October on Wednesdays and Saturdays. In mid June every year the large "Rendez" festival is held at the site with visiting locomotives and special charter trains.

Slovenské technické múzeum, Bratislava
www.muzeumdopravy.com
This museum, alongside Bratislava hlavná station, houses a number of preserved steam and diesel locomotives, managed by the MDC, as well as a collection of road transport. Open all week except Mondays.

MDC Múzejno Dokumentačné Centrum (National Museum Collection), Vrútky Depot
www.vyhrevna-vrutky.sk
Home to a number of the MDC fleet in this former running depot, now also used to restore steam locomotives. Normally open for special events including an annual "childrens weekend" in early June.

Detská Železnica Košice (Košice Pioneer Railway), Čermel, Košice
www.detskazeleznica.sk
This delightful 4.2 km, 1000 mm gauge line was opened 1956 as an education line for children, hence its name. One steam locomotive, U36.003 "Katka" (built 1884), is based here along with two Class 702 shunters. Operates weekends May–October and also Tues–Fri in July and August.

Čiernohronská Železnica (ČHŽ – Čierny Balog Railway), Čierny Balog
www.chz.sk
Čierny Hron forestry railway was constructed from 1908 and extended into a 133 km maze of 760 mm gauge lines. ČHŽ carried passengers until 1962 and closed completely in 1982. In 1993 museum operation over the main Čierny Balog–Hronec section started and since then there have been several extensions so the current network is around 20 km. ČHŽ uses a number of steam locomotives. The 2016 timetable shows operation in July and August only (daily).

Historická Lesná Úvraťová Železnica (HLÚŽ – Historic Logging Switchback Railway), nr Čadca
www.kysuckemuzeum.sk
HLÚŽ operates over 8 km of the former 107 km Kysuca–Orava 760 mm gauge forestry network, located about 20 km east of Čadca within the Kysucké museum area. Operates May–October with steam or diesel. A further 3 km section of this former system is operated by Oravská lesná Železnica (the Oravská Forest Railway).

Slovenské Poľnohospodárske Múzeum (Slovak Agricultural Museum), Nitra
www.spmnitra.sk
This 760 mm railway, opened in 1985, is part of the open air Slovak Agricultural Museum and located on the east side of the town. It is based on a 1.7 km loop and adjoining 1 km branch with steam operation.

Múzeum Liptovskej Dediny Pribylina (Museum of Liptov village in Pribylina)
www.plz.sk
Exhibition of rolling stock from the former Považská forest railway.

8. PRAHA METRO

Praha's efficient Metro is operated by Dopravní Podnik hlavního města Prahy (DPP), the city public transport authority that also operates the trams and buses. A simple three line network intersects in a star pattern in the city centre. The system is 1435 mm gauge, using 750 V DC third rail. Line C was constructed in 1974, Line A in 1978 and Line B in 1985. Almost all of the Metro is underground, with much of the city centre sections being relatively deep, having been designed for use as shelter in case of nuclear attack.

All three main line railway stations; Hlavní Nádraží, Holešovice and Masarykovo, have Metro stations (Náměstí Republiky is the one which serves Masarykovo).

The Metro operates from between 04.00–05.00 and midnight, and to a very high frequency at peak times (for example Line C operates with a train every 2 minutes in the morning peak).

There have been a number of extensions to the original lines, the most recent being Dejvická–Nemocnice Motol, a 6 km extension to Line A which opened in April 2015. Line A now runs from Nemocnice Motol to Depo Hostivař and is 17.1 km with 17 stations, Line B runs from Zličín to Černý Most and is 25.6 km with 24 stations and Line C runs from Háje to Letňany and is 22.4 km with 20 stations. This gives a network of around 65.2 km, with 61 stations.

It had at one time been proposed to continue Line A to Praha Airport, but these plans have been dropped in favour of connecting the Airport via a new heavy rail branch from Praha-Ruzyně station. However there are plans for a Metro "Line D", which will use driverless trains and connect the southern suburbs with the city centre, running from Náměstí Míru via Pankrac and Nádraží Krč to Depo Písnice. Total length will be 10.6 km with completion scheduled for 2022–23.

METRO TRAIN SETS

All of the current metro trains are 5-car sets with all axles powered on all cars. Maximum speed is 80 km/h. There have been three generations of metro stock, but original Type Ečs cars from 1974 are no longer in normal service, one set being kept as a Historic Train (plus cars 1009 and 2374 which are at the Střešovice city transport museum).

Type 81-71 cars entered service in 1978–90, slowly being refurbished as Type 81-71M from 2000 onwards. One set has been kept in its original condition as a Historic Train. The latest M1 type dates from the 2000s and is used only on Line C.

There are three depots, one for each line, at Hostivař (Line A), Zličín (Line B), and Kačerov (Line C).

TYPE Ečs   HISTORIC TRAIN

This remaining train of original stock is kept for special operations. The 3-car Historic Train gives rides once a month in the summer, for details of dates of operation see www.dpp.cz/historicka-souprava-metra. It can operate on any of the three lines but is normally based at Zličín depot.

Built: 1976–77.
Builder: Mytiščinský Strojírenský Závod, Soviet Union.
Seats: 42 + 42 + 42.
Weight: 32.5 + 32.5 + 32.5 tonnes.
Length over Buffers: 19.21 + 19.21 + 19.21 m.
Continuous Power: 864 kW (1160 hp) (one 72 kW traction motor per axle).

1083   1085   1084

TYPE 81-71   HISTORIC TRAIN

Original unrebuilt train of this type kept as an operational Historic Train. Based at Zličín depot.

Built: 1978–90.
Builder: Mytiščinský Strojírenský Závod, Soviet Union.
Seats: 42 + 44 + 44 + 44 + 42.
Weight: 33.5 + 33.0 + 33.0 + 33.0 + 33.5 tonnes.
Length over Buffers: 19.21 + 19.21 + 19.21 + 19.21 + 19.21 m.
Continuous Power: 2200 kW (2950 hp) (one 110 kW traction motor per axle).

2159   2213   2429   2637   2504

TYPE 81-71M   LINE A (GREEN)

Driving cars are Type 81-714M and intermediate cars Type 81-717M. These sets were rebuilt from Types 81-714 and 81-717 and at the same time were renumbered by adding 1000 to the number (apart from five centre cars converted to driving cars which were given completely new numbers in the 39xx series: 3900 ex-2667, 3901 ex-2657, 3902 ex-2619, 3903 ex-2656 and 3904 ex-2684).

The 41 trains used on Line A are based at Hostivař depot, which is at the eastern terminus of the line. This fleet was also sufficient to cover the Nemocnice Motol extension, which opened in 2015.

Built: Originally built 1978–90; Rebuilt by Škoda 2001–11.
Builder: Mytiščinský Strojírenský Závod, Soviet Union.
Seats: 38 + 48 + 48 + 48 + 38.
Weight: 32 + 31 + 31 + 31 + 32 tonnes.
Length over Buffers: 19.40 + 19.21 + 19.21 + 19.21 + 19.40 m.
Continuous Power: 2340 kW (3135 hp) (one 117 kW traction motor per axle).

3101	3273	3208	3201	3106	3147	3449	3244	3205	3180	3371	3671	3672	3673	3375
3103	3219	3223	3226	3141	3149	3243	3288	3274	3163	3376	3663	3664	3665	3377
3104	3238	3434	3446	3300	3151	3240	3410	3414	3152	3378	3694	3695	3696	3389
3108	3246	3286	3252	3109	3158	3271	3435	3436	3160	3383	3660	3661	3662	3384
3113	3254	3270	3218	3301	3175	3402	3279	3248	3165	3385	3677	3678	3679	3386
3115	3287	3265	3220	3130	3185	3450	3451	3452	3186	3391	3685	3686	3687	3392
3119	3266	3298	3404	3139	3190	3235	3259	3267	3199	3393	3697	3698	3699	3394
3120	3251	3253	3255	3146	3192	3275	3276	3443	3195	3397	3690	3689	3688	3396
3125	3228	3264	3210	3124	3310	3415	3444	3418	3317	3398	3691	3692	3693	3399
3126	3245	3256	3433	3144	3329	3442	3484	3493	3340	3500	3674	3675	3676	3900
3127	3232	3257	3224	3140	3330	3603	3626	3649	3355	3502	3800	3801	3802	3503
3135	3222	3272	3234	3123	3335	3494	3608	3613	3339	3901	3803	3668	3638	3902
3142	3249	3430	3440	3162	3343	3604	3666	3670	3356	3903	3680	3681	3683	3904
3143	3242	3241	3206	3161	3362	3633	3628	3639	3367					

TYPE 81-71M   LINE B (YELLOW)

For technical details see above. These cars were rebuilt by Škoda 2000–09.

The 52 trains used on Line B are based at Zličín depot, at the western terminus of the line.

3111	3225	3231	3230	3122	3191	3473	3475	3479	3194	3338	3617	3627	3632	3336
3112	3204	3215	3233	3116	3196	3280	3281	3289	3197	3341	3606	3607	3609	3349
3117	3202	3258	3229	3136	3302	3438	3441	3454	3322	3342	3293	3299	3401	3354
3121	3610	3611	3612	3131	3303	3426	3427	3480	3345	3344	3641	3642	3644	3346
3132	3239	3237	3217	3118	3304	3411	3412	3413	3177	3347	3431	3497	3462	3348
3134	3214	3212	3207	3110	3305	3471	3453	3437	3307	3350	3615	3624	3630	3353
3138	3268	3211	3250	3150	3311	3602	3605	3406	3369	3351	3423	3489	3476	3352
3153	3203	3209	3216	3154	3312	3400	3420	3421	3326	3357	3646	3648	3652	3358
3155	3227	3260	3261	3156	3313	3470	3472	3474	3316	3359	3469	3487	3495	3361
3157	3634	3635	3636	3169	3314	3488	3439	3432	3308	3363	3659	3669	3682	3364
3171	3290	3296	3297	3172	3315	3465	3478	3481	3327	3366	3466	3467	3486	3368
3173	3455	3448	3447	3174	3318	3463	3464	3491	3319	3370	3650	3651	3425	3365
3170	3403	3416	3417	3176	3320	3614	3616	3618	3321	3372	3640	3643	3647	3373
3178	3498	3600	3601	3179	3323	3262	3284	3285	3324	3379	3653	3654	3655	3380
3181	3456	3457	3459	3306	3328	3620	3621	3622	3333	3381	3263	3269	3483	3382
3182	3405	3419	3458	3193	3331	3468	3496	3499	3332	3387	3631	3645	3658	3388
3183	3460	3477	3492	3184	3334	3461	3482	3485	3337	3390	3623	3625	3629	3360
3188	3422	3424	3428	3189										

▲ A view inside the Line B Zličín depot on 9 May 2015 sees Type 81-71M set 3344/3641/3642/3644/3346 stabled alongside Historic Type 81-71 set 2159/2213/2429/2637/2504 and Historic Ečs set 1084/1085/1083.   **Robert Pritchard**

▼ Line A Type 81-71M unit 3124/3210/3264/3228/3125 stands at the new Nemocnice Motol terminus of Line A with a service to Depo Hostivař on 6 May 2015.   **Robert Pritchard**

TYPE M1 LINE C (RED)

These trains were delivered in the 2000s and are formed as follows: M1.1+M1.2+M1.3+M1.2+M1.1. Deliveries were as follows: 4101–4143 2000–01, 4145–4183 2002–04, 4185–95 2005–07 and 4197–4305 2010. Sets are generally kept in their as-delivered formations, and misformed sets are unusual, although not unknown.

The 53 trains used on Line C are based at Kačerov depot, in the south of the city.

Built: 1998–2005 (4101–4195) and 2009–10 (4197–4305).
Builder: Siemens/ČKD Praha/Adtranz.
Seats: 40 + 48 + 48 + 48 + 40.
Weight: 27.9 + 25.9 + 25.6 + 25.9 + 27.9 tonnes.
Length over Buffers: 19.52 + 19.21 + 19.21 + 19.21 + 19.52 m.
Continuous Power: 3200 kW (4290 hp) (one 160 kW traction motor per axle).
Advertising Livery: 4123/24 Equabank (white).

4101	4201	4202	4203	4102	4137	4255	4256	4257	4138	4173	4409	4410	4411	4174
4103	4204	4205	4206	4104	4139	4258	4259	4260	4140	4175	4412	4413	4414	4176
4105	4207	4208	4209	4106	4141	4261	4262	4263	4142	4177	4415	4416	4417	4178
4107	4210	4211	4212	4108	4143	4264	4265	4266	4144	4179	4418	4419	4420	4180
4109	4213	4214	4215	4110	4145	4267	4268	4269	4146	4181	4421	4422	4423	4182
4111	4216	4217	4218	4112	4147	4270	4271	4272	4148	4183	4424	4425	4426	4184
4113	4219	4220	4221	4114	4149	4273	4274	4275	4150	4185	4427	4428	4429	4186
4115	4222	4223	4224	4116	4151	4276	4277	4278	4152	4187	4430	4431	4432	4188
4117	4225	4226	4227	4118	4153	4279	4280	4281	4154	4189	4433	4434	4435	4190
4119	4228	4229	4230	4120	4155	4282	4283	4284	4156	4191	4436	4437	4438	4192
4121	4231	4232	4233	4122	4157	4285	4286	4287	4158	4193	4439	4440	4441	4194
4123	4234	4235	4236	4124	4159	4288	4289	4290	4160	4195	4442	4443	4444	4196
4125	4237	4238	4239	4126	4161	4291	4292	4293	4162	4197	4445	4446	4447	4198
4127	4240	4241	4242	4128	4163	4294	4295	4296	4164	4199	4448	4449	4450	4300
4129	4243	4244	4245	4130	4165	4297	4298	4299	4166	4301	4451	4452	4453	4302
4131	4246	4247	4248	4132	4167	4400	4401	4402	4168	4303	4454	4455	4456	4304
4133	4249	4250	4251	4134	4169	4403	4404	4405	4170	4305	4457	4458	4459	4306
4135	4252	4253	4254	4136	4171	4406	4407	4408	4172					

CLASS 797.8 PRAHA METRO WORKS LOCOMOTIVES

The Praha Metro shunting locomotive fleet consists of these four-wheel diesel-hydraulic shunters extensively rebuilt by JLS/ČMKS from Classes 700–702 to diesel-electric. The missing locomotive 797.803/T13 was sold to the Budapest metro system.

Built: 1996–2002; * 2005.
Former ČSD Class: T211.0/T211.1/T212.0.
Builder: JLS/ČMKS Jihlava.
Engine: Liaz M640SE; * Caterpillar 3406.
Power: 242 kW (* 250 kW).
Transmission: Electric.
Maximum Tractive Effort: 77 kN.
Wheel Arrangement: Bo.

Total No. Built: 18.
Wheel Diameter: 1000 mm.
Train Heating Equipment: None.
Weight: 26 tonnes.
Length over Buffers: 7.24 m.
Maximum Speed: 40 km/h.
EVN: 92 54 2 797 8xx-c.

797.801-8	T11	Zličín	797.808-3	T8	Hostivař	797.814-1		T4	Kačerov
797.802-6	T12	Hostivař	797.809-1	T9	Kačerov	797.815-8		T15	Hostivař
797.804-2	T14	Zličín	797.810-9	T10	Zličín	797.816-6		T16	Hostivař
797.805-9	T6	Hostivař	797.811-7	T5	Kačerov	797.817-4		T17	Kačerov
797.806-7	T1	Zličín	797.812-5	T2	Kačerov	797.818-2	*	T18	Kačerov
797.807-5	T7	Kačerov	797.813-3	T3	Kačerov				

▲ Line C set 4101/4201/4202/4203/4102 arrives at Vyšehrad with a service for Letňany on 14 May 2014. This station is elevated, just before the Vyšehrad Viaduct, and is one of the few where there is daylight. It is also the only place in the city where the metro, trams and trains can all be seen! (the last two can be viewed some way below the Metro station). **Robert Pritchard**

▼ Works locomotive 797.818 (T18) stands outside Kačerov depot on 13 May 2014. **Robert Pritchard**

9. CZECH & SLOVAK TRAM SYSTEMS

There are seven tram systems in the Czech Republic and two in Slovakia. Most are urban systems, but within these there are also a number of inter-urban/semi-rural routes. All nine are electrified at 600 V DC. All are standard 1435 mm gauge except Bratislava which is 1000 mm and Liberec which is mixed 1435/1000 mm. Most trams are single-ended, with one cab and doors on one side only. Because of this almost all routes are laid out with turning circles at the ends.

Tramcars of standard types are found on every system. As with railway vehicles, post-war Czechoslovakia built trams in huge numbers for the entire Eastern Bloc. ČKD Tatra, formerly Ringhoffer, took out a PCC licence resulting in over 1000 Type T1 and T2 from 1951 (only Liberec still has T2s still in normal traffic). In 1960 Type T3 appeared – this became the standard Eastern Bloc car with no less than 13 991 built in various versions to 1989 (large numbers were exported to Russia). Praha alone took more than 1100 T3s.

In 1966 the K2 appeared, a two-section articulated tram using similar traction systems to T3 – 567 were built (although none for Praha). From 1976, export T3 Soviet Union version SU was introduced for domestic use, directly as SU or as SUCS (the Soviet model with modifications for the Czech market). T3Ms were the first T3s to be modernised with TV1 thyristor control equipment, replacing the mechanical system. By the 1990s operators were upgrading their T3 fleets with new equipment. Some new T3 bodies were also supplied. The T3R.P became the standard modernised model for Praha and a number of other systems. These were fitted with Progress thyristor control equipment (hence the "R" for reconstructed and "P" for Progress). T3R.PVs and T3R.PLFs used new bodies built by Pragoimex based on classic T3 design.

The next 2-axle tram to be developed for the Czech market was the T6 – 296 were built in the 1990s for Praha (150), Brno (20), Ostrava (38), Bratislava (58) and Košice (30). The KT8D5 used the similar, more angular, design and was developed as a bi-directional three-section articulated four bogie all-motor-axle tram. 207 of these were built for the home market and export before ČKD Tatra ceased trading in 1999. KT8D5s were delivered to Praha (48), Brno (38), Plzeň (12), Ostrava (16), Most (8, now sold to Miskolc, Hungary) and Košice (40, most now elsewhere). Despite privatisation by the new Czech Government ČKD was unable to survive in a free market economy following the collapse of communism and its assets were sold, with Siemens taking on the Praha factory. However this closed in 2009 and part of it is now a shopping centre.

In more recent years Škoda and Inekon have built trams for the Czech and Slovak systems, but in smaller numbers. The Skoda 03T (also sometimes called the "Astra" or LTM10.08) became the standard early low-floor tram and examples can be seen in Brno, Ostrava, Most, Olomouc and Plzeň. The design was later taken forward as the similar "Trio" by Inekon, who had originally been in partnership with Škoda. Inekon assembled these cars in the Martinov workshops of the Ostrava tramway, but few orders were forthcoming from the home market (although some were built for export). Inekon Trios can be seen in Ostrava and Olomouc.

In the last ten years Škoda has won significant orders, first with the 13Ts and 14Ts for Brno and Praha and later with large orders for 250 15Ts for Praha and 60 29T and 30Ts for Bratislava.

The newest manufacturer is Pragoimex/Alliance TW Team (TWT). TWT is formed of an alliance of Pragoimex of Praha, Krnovske opravny a strojírny of Krnov and VKV Praha. The company markets itself as "continuing the ČKD tradition" – although it has no legal connection to ČKD it took on some of the redundant technical experts when the company was sold. Pragoimex sees a continued demand for 2-axle vehicles, which are not now offered by the larger manufacturers. Initially the company specialised in providing like-for-like replacements for T3 cars, before a new "stretched" partially low-floor bodyshell, christened "Vario", was developed in 2004. There are now various types of Vario car. Vario LF are completely new vehicles, while Vario LF.Rs use components, such as bogies, from withdrawn T3 or K2 trams. The letters in the tram name also refer to the traction equipment used – the standard T3 replacement model Vario LFR.E uses Cegelec traction equipment whilst the similar Vario LFR.S use Škoda equipment.

An illustration of the success of the Pragoimex models is that some of the company's trams are now operating on all nine systems listed here. Pragoimex's latest development is its "EVO1" demonstrator, now on trial in Praha. This is a 15 m, 100% low-floor car.

It is impossible to give full technical details for every type of tram here, but the manufacturers' standard types produced since 1950 are listed below. Some have been rebuilt with low-floor sections. Each type is often configured differently for each system – details of seating numbers are given in the relevant headings. Maximum speed for tramcars listed is generally 65–70 km/h.

Builder	Type	Built	Wheel Arr.	Length	Width	Motors	Seats	Low floor
ČKD Tatra	T1	1951–58	Bo-Bo	14.50	2.40	4 x 40	26	No
ČKD Tatra	T2	1955–62	Bo-Bo	15.20	2.50	4 x 40	25	No
ČKD Tatra	T3	1960–99	Bo-Bo	14.00	2.50	4 x 40	23	No*
ČKD Tatra	K2	1966–83	Bo-2-Bo	21.60	2.50	4 x 40	49	No
ČKD Tatra	T6A5	1991–97	Bo-Bo	14.70	2.50	4 x 45	30	No
ČKD Tatra	KT8D5	1986–99	Bo-Bo-Bo-Bo	30.30	2.48	8 x 45	54	No*
Škoda	03T	1997–06	Bo-Bo	20.10	2.46	4 x 90	41	Yes: 50%
Škoda	13T/14T	2005–16	Bo-Bo-Bo	31.80	2.48	6 x 90	68/69	Yes: 48%
Škoda	15T	2009–18	Bo-Bo-Bo-Bo	31.40	2.46	16 x 45	60	Yes: 100%
Škoda	29T	2014–16	Bo-2-Bo-Bo	32.50	2.48	6 x 100	69	Yes: 88%
Škoda	30T	2014–16	Bo-2-Bo-Bo	32.50	2.48	6 x 100	52	Yes: 92%
Inekon	Trio	2004–06	Bo-Bo	20.10	2.46	4 x 90	41	Yes: 50%
Pragoimex	Vario LF+	2010–13	Bo-Bo	15.10	2.48	4 x 80	35	Yes: 36%
Pragoimex	Vario LF.E	2006	Bo-Bo	15.10	2.48	4 x 90	26	Yes: 36%
Pragoimex	Vario LF.S	2012–14	Bo-Bo	15.10	2.48	4 x 90	33	Yes: 36%
Pragoimex	Vario LFR.E	2004–16	Bo-Bo	15.10	2.48	4 x 90	26–32	Yes: 36%
Pragoimex	Vario LFR.S	2010–14	Bo-Bo	15.10	2.48	4 x 80	22–31	Yes: 36%
Pragoimex	Vario LF2R.E	2008–16	Bo-Bo-Bo	22.60	2.48	6 x 90	46	Yes: 43%
Pragoimex	Vario LF2+	2007–15	Bo-Bo-Bo	22.60	2.48	6 x 80	44–52	Yes: 43%
Pragoimex	Vario LF3+	2006–11	Bo-Bo-Bo-Bo	30.10	2.48	8 x 80	54	Yes: 50%
Pragoimex	Vario LF+/o	2013	Bo-Bo	15.10	2.48	4 x 90	26	Yes: 36%
Pragoimex	Vario LF2/2 IN	2013–14	Bo-Bo-Bo	23.70	2.48	6 x 80	44	Yes: 43%

* Many have now been rebuilt, some with new bodies incorporating a low-floor section.

All systems also have at least one museum car that is used on special trips, often on Bank Holidays (and more extensively in Praha), but do not form part of the normal fleet. These are listed separately under the Heritage/Museum Trams section. Preserved trailer cars are not listed. Status codes used are:

A: Active/serviceable.   M: Tramcar in a museum   R: Under restoration.   S: Stored.

(S) in the main listings also denotes a vehicle in store.

The standard livery for each system is given. Most also have some cars in advertising liveries.

The "Tramway Established" date refers to the operation of the first electric tramways in that city.

All nine tram systems are municipally operated, the transport company also operating local buses (and sometimes trolleybuses). Travelling on the various tram systems can be very enjoyable and also a good way to see different parts of the various cities. The system websites usually have an English section, and maps and timetables can be downloaded prior to a visit. Ticket machines are provided at stops on most systems, the exceptions being Plzeň (machines have been removed but tickets can be purchased from the tram driver or from newsagents and hotels etc) and Most-Litvínov (tickets need to be purchased from machines on the tram or from the driver). Tickets **must be validated** by using one of the machines on the tram (or at the entrance to the Metro stations if using the Praha Metro). 24 hour tourist type tickets can be purchased for all systems except Most-Litvínov.

It should be noted that none of the tramways use tram conductors, instead they use the "honesty system" that requires tickets to be purchased and validated in advance. Tickets may be checked at any time by plain clothed staff who will identify themselves to you by showing you an official badge, usually with the phrase "jízdenka prosím" ("tickets please"). Whilst experience has shown that such inspections are few and far between, there are hefty fines imposed for those caught travelling without a validated ticket.

Praha and Ostrava are the only systems that operate night trams, although most others start operating in the very early hours of the morning.

A final point to note is that the tram systems often use the quieter months of July and August for maintenance and track replacement works, with temporary line closures in place. In cities with extensive systems such as Praha and Brno this often just results in a route taking a diversion, but it can also mean bus replacements.

As well as the nine tramways of the Czech Republic and Slovakia there are also 18 towns and cities that have trolleybus systems (five have both trams and trolleybuses). In the Czech Republic Brno, České Budějovice, Chomutov/Jirkov, Hradec Králové, Jihlava, Mariánské Lázně, Opava, Ostrava, Pardubice, Plzeň, Teplice, Ústí nad Labem and Zlín/Otrokovice have trolleybuses, as do Banská Bystrica, Bratislava, Košice, Prešov and Žilina in Slovakia.

9.1. CZECH TRAM SYSTEMS

9.1.1. BRNO

www.dpmb.cz   **Network:** 70 km.   **Lines:** 13.   **Depots:** 2.
Standard livery: Red, cream & grey.   **Tramway established:** 1900.
Depot codes: Pl   Pisárky   ME   Medlánky

Brno is the second biggest city in the Czech Republic and capital of the South Moravian region, with a population of 380 000. It also boasts the second biggest tram network after Praha. Today's tramway includes a mixture of on-street running in the centre (including Lines 4/9 which run through the main square and pedestrianised streets) and segregated running: a number of lines are classed as express tramways. The most impressive is Line 1 which serves the large housing estate at Bystrc. The Line 8 terminus at Mifkova is unusual as it doesn't have a turning circle – so must be served by the bi-directional KT8D5 trams (this 2004 extension had originally been planned to extend further). The most recent extension was to Technology Park, opened in 2008.

The tram fleet is diverse, with an amazing 24 different types of tram making it the most varied of all the Czech systems. A large fleet of K2 and T3 trams are supplemented by more modern T6 and Škoda 03Ts. There are also 38 KT8D5s, all now with low-floor sections, whilst the newest vehicles are 29 Škoda 13Ts, similar to the 14Ts delivered to Praha. Another 20 13Ts are on order for delivery in 2016; these will replace most of the remaining unmodernised K2s. There are also a small number of non-standard (early low-floor) vehicles and four unpowered trailers. Pragoimex Vario LF2R.Es and Vario LFR.Es are currently being delivered. These new trams use a number of components from withdrawn K2 and T3 cars and each are given the same fleet number as the K2 or T3 tram that provides parts – essentially being classed as "book rebuilds". A number of K2 and T3 trams had previously been rebuilt with new bodies by Pars nova Šumperk.

The system is operated by Dopravní podnik města Brna (DPMB), which also operates the city's extensive trolleybus network, which is the country's biggest and features some inter-urban lines. Note that the last two stops of the Modřice route (Line 2) fall outside the city zones 100 and 101 and even if a 24 hour day ticket is held, then a separate ticket is needed for this section.

TATRA K2

Original vehicles built 1967–83, some rebuilt with new bodies 1996–2002.

p   K2P. 47 seats.   r   K2R. Rebuilt 1996–98.   y   K2YU. 49 seats.
q   K2R.03. Rebuilt 1998–2002. t   K2T.   *   Rebuilt as a "party tram".

1018	r*	Pl	1037	q	Pl	1051	p	ME	1080	p	ME	1120	y	Pl
1023	p	ME	1038	t	Pl	1052	p	ME	1081	q	Pl	1121	y	Pl
1024	p	ME	1039	r	Pl	1053	r	Pl	1085	p	ME	1122	y	Pl
1026	p	ME	1040	q	Pl	1054	t	Pl	1086	p	ME	1124	y	Pl
1027	q	Pl	1041	p	ME	1059	q	Pl	1090		Pl	1125	y	Pl
1028	r	Pl	1042	p	ME	1060	q	Pl	1097	p	ME	1126	y	Pl
1029	q	Pl	1044	t	Pl	1062	p	ME	1107	p	ME	1128	y	Pl
1030	q	Pl	1046	p	ME	1064	r	Pl	1110		Pl	1129	y	Pl
1031	p	ME	1047	p	ME	1066	r	Pl	1116	p	ME	1130	y	Pl
1032	p	ME	1048	p	ME	1077	p	ME	1118	p	ME	1131	y	Pl
1033	t	Pl	1049	q	Pl	1079	q	Pl	1119	p	ME	1132	y	Pl
1036	p	ME												

PRAGOIMEX VARIO LF2R.E

Built 2008–present. New trams which use some components from withdrawn K2s. 46 seats.

1069	Pl	1084	Pl	1096	Pl	1102	Pl	1112	Pl
1072	Pl	1088	Pl	1098	Pl	1103	Pl	1114	Pl
1078	Pl	1092	Pl	1099	Pl	1106	Pl	1117	Pl
1082	Pl	1093	Pl	1100	Pl	1108	Pl	1127	Pl
1083	Pl	1094	Pl	1101	Pl	1109	Pl		

TATRA T6A5

Built 1995.

1201	ME	1205	ME	1209	ME	1213	ME	1217	ME
1202	ME	1206	ME	1210	ME	1214	ME	1218	ME
1203	ME	1207	ME	1211	ME	1215	ME	1219	ME
1204	ME	1208	ME	1212	ME	1216	ME	1220	ME

PRAGOIMEX VV60LF

Built 2003–06. 26 seats. Unpowered trailer cars, used behind a T3 or between two trams.

1301	ME (S)	1302	ME	1303	ME (S)	1304	ME

TATRA T3/T3 DESIGN

Original vehicles built 1966–89, some rebuilt with new bodies 1995–2006.

e	T3R.EV. Rebuilt 2002–03.	m	T3M.	r	T3R. Rebuilt 1995–97 (except 1615).
f	T3RF. Rebuilt 1999.	o	T3M.03.	v	T3R.PV. Rebuilt 2003–06.
g	T3G.	p	T3P	w	works/staff training car.

1517	v	PI	1595	p	PI	1620	p	PI	1637	g	PI	1654	v	PI
1531	e	ME	1603	v	PI	1621	g	PI	1638	g	PI	1655	v	PI
1532	mw	ME	1604	g	PI	1622	p	PI	1639	g	PI	1656	v	PI
1543	p	ME	1605	g	PI	1623	p	PI	1640	g	PI	1657	v	ME
1544	m	ME	1606	g	PI	1624	g	PI	1641	g	PI	1658	v	ME
1555	m	ME	1607	g	PI	1625	g	PI	1642	g	PI	1659	r	PI
1558	v	ME	1608	g	PI	1626	g	PI	1643	g	PI	1660	r	PI
1560	e	ME	1609	g	PI	1627	o	PI	1644	g	PI	1661	r	PI
1561	v	PI	1610	g	PI	1628	p	PI	1645	g	PI	1662	r	PI
1562	e	ME	1611	g	PI	1629	p	PI	1646	g	PI	1663	r	PI
1564	p	PI	1612	g	PI	1630	o	PI	1647	g	PI	1664	r	PI
1569	e	ME	1613	g	PI	1631	g	PI	1648	g	PI	1665	r	PI
1576	p	ME	1614	g	PI	1632	p	PI	1649	g	PI	1666	r	PI
1583	p	ME	1615	r	ME	1633	p	PI	1650	g	PI	1667	r	PI
1587	p	ME	1616	g	PI	1634	p	PI	1651	g	PI	1668	r	PI
1589	p	ME	1617	g	PI	1635	g	PI	1652	g	PI	1669	f	PI
1593	mw	PI	1619	g	PI	1636	g	PI	1653	v	PI	1670	f	PI

PRAGOIMEX VARIO LFR.E

Built 2006–present. New trams which use some components from withdrawn T3s. 32 seats.

1497	PI	1551	PI	1567	PI	1582	PI	1596	PI
1523	PI	1553	PI	1573	PI	1584	PI	1597	PI
1530	PI	1554	PI	1574	PI	1586	PI	1598	PI
1539	PI	1556	PI	1575	PI	1590	PI	1599	PI
1541	PI	1557	PI	1580	PI	1592	PI	1601	PI

TATRA KT8D5

Built 1986–99. KT8D5R.N2 rebuilt 2002–14 with new low-floor centre section. 1736–1738 ex-Košice.

n	KT8D5N. Built 1998–99 with low-floor centre section as new. 50 seats.
r	KT8D5R.N2. Built 1986–93 as KT8D5. Later rebuilt with low-floor centre section. 58 seats.

1701	r	ME	1709	r	ME	1717	r	ME	1725	r	ME	1732	n	ME
1702	r	ME	1710	r	ME	1718	r	ME	1726	r	ME	1733	n	ME
1703	r	ME	1711	r	ME	1719	r	ME	1727	r	ME	1734	n	ME
1704	r	ME	1712	r	ME	1720	r	ME	1728	r	ME	1735	n	ME
1705	r	ME	1713	r	ME	1721	r	ME	1729	n	ME	1736	r	ME
1706	r	ME	1714	r	ME	1722	r	ME	1730	n	ME	1737	r	ME
1707	r	ME	1715	r	ME	1723	r	ME	1731	n	ME	1738	r	ME
1708	r	ME	1716	r	ME	1724	r	ME						

TATRA K3R-N

Originally built as K2s 1974–77, rebuilt as K3R-N 2002–06 with new low-floor centre section.

1751	ME (S)	1752	ME	1753	ME (S)	1754	ME

TATRA RT6N1

Built 1996. An early design of articulated low-floor tram. Ten are also used in Poznań, Poland (four of which are ex-Praha), and Brno car 1804 was sold to Poznań in 2015. 46 seats.

1801	ME (S)	1802	ME	1803	ME (S)

ŠKODA 03T

Built 2002–05. 39 seats.

1805	PI	1809	PI	1813	PI	1816	PI	1819	PI
1806	PI	1810	PI	1814	PI	1817	PI	1820	PI
1807	PI	1811	PI	1815	PI	1818	PI	1821	PI
1808	PI	1812	PI						

ŠKODA 13T

Built 2007–11. These low-floor cars are similar to Praha 14Ts, but with a number of modifications, for example the front driver's door is a passenger door on the Brno 13Ts. The seating layout for 1920–1929 was revised – with more facing seats. 68 seats.

1901	ME	1907	ME	1913	ME	1919	ME	1925	ME
1902	ME	1908	ME	1914	ME	1920	ME	1926	ME
1903	ME	1909	ME	1915	ME	1921	ME	1927	ME
1904	ME	1910	ME	1916	ME	1922	ME	1928	ME
1905	ME	1911	ME	1917	ME	1923	ME	1929	ME
1906	ME	1912	ME	1918	ME	1924	ME		

A second batch of 20 13Ts is on order for delivery between July 2016 and late 2016. Number series is provisional.

1930	1934	1938	1942	1946
1931	1935	1939	1943	1947
1932	1936	1940	1944	1948
1933	1937	1941	1945	1949

HERITAGE/MUSEUM FLEET

The Heritage fleet in Brno consists mostly of vehicles at the Brno Líšeň depository – an annex of Brno Technical Museum located at the former railway station at Líšeň. The site is only open for pre-arranged visits, see www.sabdigital.cz/expozicemhd. In addition to the trams the museum also houses locomotives of the former Brno Líšeň railway (see Preserved Locomotives section).

Most trams here are cars that used to run in Brno, but there are also examples from systems across the country. As well as the Líšeň museum cars, there are also a few cars based at the DPMB depots and used for special trips etc.

No.	Type	Built	St	Notes
–	2-axle works car	1925	M	Rail Cleaner
1	Lederer & Porges MV2 2-axle motor car	1903	M	Wooden-bodied tram. Ex-500
3	Vitkovice 2-axle motor car	1934	M	Wooden-bodied tram. Ex-Ostrava 85
AC3	Trenčianská Teplá 2-axle motor car	1909	M	Wooden-bodied tram. 760 mm
5	SZD 4-axle motor car	1912	M	Wooden-bodied tram. Ex-Ostrava, 760 mm
6	Lederer & Porges MV3 2-axle motor car	1904	M	Wooden-bodied tram.
7	SZD 4-axle motor car	1920	M	Wooden-bodied tram. Ex-Ostrava, 760 mm
10	Graz MV1 2-axle motor car	1899	M	Wooden-bodied tram. Ex-503/803/4030
16	Studénka 2-axle motor car	1914	M	Wooden-bodied tram. Owned by DPMO Olomouc
26	Ostrava 2-axle motor car	1923	M	Wooden-bodied tram.

31	SZD Tatra 4-axle motor car	1954 M	Ex-Ostrava, 760 mm
33	Ostrava 2-axle motor car	1927 M	Wooden-bodied tram. Ex-8033
52	Graz MV4 2-axle motor car	1911 M	Wooden-bodied tram. Ex 13/817
56	Ostrava 2-axle motor car	1951 M	Wooden-bodied tram.
57	Vagónka CMg 2-axle motor car	1913 M	Wooden-bodied tram. Ex-Wien 1603/Brno 15/815
72	Graz MV5 2-axle motor car	1919 M	Wooden-bodied tram. Ex-72/32/802/4002
81	Královopolská 2-axle motor car	1926 M	Wooden-bodied tram
99	Královopolská 2-axle motor car	1941 A	Wooden-bodied tram. Ex-140. Medlánky depot.
103	Královopolská 2-axle motor car	1929 M	Wooden-bodied tram. Ex-Ostrava
107	Královopolská 2-axle motor car	1954 A	Wooden-bodied tram. Medlánky depot
126	Královopolská 4MT1 2-axle motor car	1950 M	
203	Studénka 2-axle motor car	1930 M	Wooden-bodied tram. Ex-Bratislava, 1000 mm
205	Ringhoffer 2-axle motor car	1923 M	Wooden-bodied tram. Ex-Olomouc/Praha 430
405	Královopolská 2-axle motor car	1946 M	Wooden-bodied tram. Ex-116
473	Tatra T2	1961 M	Ex-1473/4110
685	Tatra T2	1961 R	Ex-Ostrava works car 8205. Medlánky depot.
1095	Tatra K2	1977 M	
1123	Tatra K2	1983 R	Pisárky depot
1521	Tatra T3	1966 M	Ex-521
1525	Tatra T3	1967 A	Medlánky depot
1594	Tatra T3M	1972 A	Medlánky depot
2051	Ringhoffer 2-axle motor car	1927 M	Wooden-bodied tram. Ex-Praha
3005	Ringhoffer/Tatra 2-axle motor car	1935 M	Wooden-bodied tram. Ex-Praha
4033	Schörling grinding motor car	1969 M	Rail grinder
4058	SBEPD 4MT4 2-axle motor car	1954 A	Pisárky depot
4101	Tatra T3	1963 M	Ex-driving training car 501/1501
5064	Tatra T1	1955 M	Ex-Praha

▲ Škoda 13T 1909 passes beneath Petrov Cathedral on the short 4-track section heading southwards from hlavní nádraží with a Line 1 service to Výstaviště on 10 September 2012. **Robert Pritchard**

9.1.2. LIBEREC

<www.dpmlj.cz> **Network:** 21 km. **Lines:** 4. **Depots:** 1 (Rybníček).

Standard livery: Green & white. **Gauge:** 1000/1435 mm. **Tramway established:** 1897.

Liberec is the fifth largest city in the Czech Republic with a population of around 100 000. Lying close to both the Polish and German borders the city is the biggest in the Czech Republic without an electrified railway, but does have an electric tramway. Links to the capital by rail are poor and direct buses tend to pick up much of this market. By rail one has either to travel via Děčín and then across on Line 081/086 or on a convoluted route via Mladá Boleslav and Turnov, requiring at least one change.

A highly scenic 12 km metre gauge tramway links Liberec with the towns of Vratislavice nad Nisou and Jablonec nad Nisou to the north. This line was constructed in the early 1950s and runs through the deeply wooded Nisa Valley – it is a superb example of inter-urban/rural segregated operation. It runs as Line 11 from Liberec Viadukt, via the city centre and Fügnerova interchange, the combined tram and bus station. Frequency during the day is every 15 minutes as the line is mainly single track with crossing loops and a number of request stops. Over recent years this line has been slowly upgraded. As far as U Lomu it has been rebuilt as dual (standard/metre) gauge. For 15 months in 2014–15 the rest of the route to Jablonec was closed for upgrading, still as metre gauge but with some longer double track sections. Plans are also at an early stage to extend the tramway a short distance into Jablonec town centre. As well as Line 11, short Line 5 runs from Viadukt to Vratislavice výhybna.

There is also the "city line" from Lidové Sady, via Liberec town centre, to Horní Hanychov, near the terminal for the cable car to Ještěd television tower, from where superb views of the city and surrounding countryside can be had. The cable car is run by ČD and is shown as Line 900 in the ČD timetable. Lidové Sady–Viadukt is dual metre/standard gauge and Viadukt–Horní Hanychov is standard gauge. Line 3 runs the full length of this route from Lidové Sady to Horní Hanychov and Line 2 runs Lidové Sady–Dolní Hanychov only. Much of the route involves street running.

▲ Liberec still has three T2s in its fleet. Standard gauge No. 17 is classed as a museum car, whilst metre gauge 18 and 19 are part of the normal fleet. On 6 September 2012 19 arrives at the upgraded U Lomu stop (now dual gauge) with a Vratislavice výhybna–Rybníček Line 5 service. **Robert Pritchard**

The fleet is almost solely composed of T3s or T3 rebuilds. The designs with new bodies are T3R.PV, T3R.PLF and T3R.SLF. All look outwardly similar to the T3 and the last two models, supplied by Pragoimex, feature low-floor centre sections. Like Brno a new tram takes the number of the vehicle that has provided parts, and the old T3 body is then scrapped. The T3s run in pairs during the day and singly off-peak.

Liberec is believed to be the last town anywhere to be operating T2 trams in normal service (a type introduced in 1955!). It has two metre gauge T2Rs (ex-Ostrava) used on Line 5 or Line 11.

In 2012 Liberec took delivery of a prototype Pragoimex "EVO2" tram. There was an option for eight such vehicles, but a proposed extension to the suburb of Rochlice has been shelved for the time being due to financial constraints and this order is on hold. In the meantime the articulated six-axle EVO2 tram, No. 84, is used on Line 2 or 3. Every September an open day is held at the tram depot at Rybníček and on Bank Holidays vintage trams are used on historic Line 1 from Viadukt to Lidové Sady and also sometimes to Jablonec, these being operated by local enthusiasts club Boveraclub, in association with DPMLJ.

The system is operated by Dopravní podnik měst Liberce a Jablonce nad Nisou (DPMLJ). 24-hour tickets are available for both Liberec (Zone 1) and to Jablonec (Zones 1–2) as well as the usual time based tickets. Allow around 30 minutes to reach Jablonec from Liberec city centre. From a lay-by off the road leading down into the city from the station an excellent elevated view can be had of Rybníček depot, with its separate metre gauge and standard gauge sheds. Whilst the standard livery is green & white, the T3s also carry a number of colourful advertising liveries.

†   1000 mm gauge (all others standard 1435 mm gauge).

T2R

Built 1958/1962. 25 seats.

18	†		19	†

TATRA T3/T3 DESIGN

Built 1963–87 (f, s & v rebuilt 2003–15). 23–29 seats.

f   T3R.PLF (low-floor centre section). Rebuilt 2005–08.   m   T3M.
s   T3R.SLF (low-floor centre section). Rebuilt 2011–15.   o   T3M.04.
v   T3R.PV. Rebuilt 2003–08.

20	† v	31	† m	42	† f	53	o	64	o	74	† m
21	† v	32	m	43	† s	54	† f	65	s	75	† m
22	† f	33	v	44	† s	55	† m	66	s	76	o
23	† f	34	† v	45	f	56	o	67	o	77	o
24	v	35	† f	46	f	57	† m	68	o	78	v
25	v	36	† m	47	f	58	† m	69	s	79	o
26	† v	37	f	48	f	59	o	70	o	80	o
27	† v	38	s	49	† m	60	o	71	o	81	o
28	† f	39	† v	50	o	61	† m	72	† m	82	s
29	† f	40	† v	51	o	62	† m	73	† m	83	o
30	o	41	v	52	† m	63	o				

PRAGOIMEX EVO2

Built 2012. 47 seats.

84

HERITAGE/MUSEUM FLEET

Cars 78 and 117 are maintained by local enthusiasts group Boveraclub – www.boveraclub.drat.eu.

No.	Type	Built	Status	Notes
17	Tatra T2R	1961	A	Ex-Ostrava 640
78	Ringhoffer 2-axle motor car	1929	A	Ex-Ústí nad Labem, 1000 mm
117	Tatra Česká Lípa 6MT	1952	A	Ex-Jablonec nad Nisou, 1000 mm
8106	Tatra T3M	1973	A	Ex-Praha

9.1.3. MOST-LITVÍNOV

www.dpmost.cz **Network:** 19 km. **Lines:** 4. **Depots:** 2.

Standard livery: Yellow & red. **Tramway established:** 1901.

Depot codes: MO Most LI Litvínov

The town of Most (population 70 000) in north Bohemia is a new town constructed in the late 1960s and 1970s, following the demolition of Most old town so that the large reserves of brown coal lying beneath it could be mined out. Being almost completely devoid of historic buildings, Most is well off the tourist trail, however the town is laid out with wide streets and parks. The 16th century church, which was fortunately preserved and incredibly moved on rails for more than half a mile to a new location in 1975, is well worth a visit. The tramway, which had been metre gauge until rebuilding as standard gauge in the late 1950s, was rerouted away from the old town with the new route opened in 1978. Today it is an excellent example of inter-urban operation. Operating from two termini in Most (one outside the station and the other to the south at Most Interspar) the lines join together at a triangular junction at Zimní Stadion and then head north to the smaller town of Litvínov (also linked to Most by railway Line 135). The tramway is almost all on reserved track apart from a short section of street running in Litvínov. It runs through a heavily industrialised area, serving a chemical works and oil refinery.

The fleet is dominated by T3s, as it has been for the last 30 years. Some run in semi-permanently coupled pairs. The T3s are supplemented by two Škoda 03T low-floor trams and two new Pragoimex Vario trams used on Line 2, linking the station and Most Interspar (the most recent extension, dating from 1981). The other regular route is Line 4 from Most Dopravní podnik to Litvínov Citadela. Lines 1 (Most Interspar–Litvínov) and Line 3 (Most station– Litvínov) operate in connection with shift changes at the chemical works, typically early morning and mid-afternoon. There are two depots, one at Most Dopravní podnik and the other near the Litvínov station stop.

The system is operated by DOPRAVNÍ PODNIK měst Mostu a Litvínova (DP Most). It should be noted that no day tickets are available, and there are no ticket machines at stops. Tickets must be purchased from ticket machines on the trams, or from the driver. 30/60/90 minute tickets are offered, the last is long enough for a return trip to Litvínov. Note that a zonal system also applies, so if travelling from Most to Litvínov a 60 minute ticket is required.

ŠKODA 03T

Built 2001–02. 41 seats.

201	MO		202	MO

TATRA T3

Built 1982–87. 22–36 seats. c T3SUCS. m T3M. w works/driver training vehicles.

204	m	MO	241	m	LI	252	cw	LI	277	c	MO	304	m	MO
205	m	MO	242	m	MO	253	c	LI	278	c	LI	305	m	MO
222	m	LI	243	m	LI	254	m	LI	279	c	MO	306	m	MO
227	c	MO	244	m	MO	257	m	MO	282	m	LI	307	m	MO
229	c	MO	245	m	MO	260	m	LI	283	m	LI	308	m	LI
233	c	LI	246	m	LI	263	cw	MO	284	c	LI	309	m	LI
234	c	MO	247	m	LI	264	c	MO	300	m	MO	310	m	LI
236	m	LI	248	m	MO	266	c	MO	301	m	MO	311	m	LI
237	m	LI	249	c	LI	269	c	LI	302	m	MO	312	m	LI
240	m	MO	250	c	MO	275	m	MO	303	m	MO	313	m	LI

PRAGOIMEX VARIO LF.S

Built 2012/14. 33 seats.

314	MO		315	MO

HERITAGE/MUSEUM FLEET

273	Tatra T5B6		1976	A	One of two T5B6 prototypes

▲ On the section of street running in Litvínov, T3Ms 282+247 are seen between the Litvínov obchodní dům and Litvínov Poliklinika stops with a Line 4 service from Most to Litvínov Citadela on 31 May 2012. The journey time from end to end on this route is 35 minutes.　　**Robert Pritchard**

▼ On 31 August 2015 one of the two new Pragoimex Vario LF.S cars, 315, leaves Zimní Stadion with a Line 2 service to Most Interspar. The famous "Moving Church of Most" can be seen to the right.
　　Quintus Vosman

9.1.4. OLOMOUC

www.dpmo.cz   **Network:** 16 km.   **Lines:** 7.   **Depots:** 1 (Koželužska).

Standard livery: White, red, blue & grey.   **Tramway established:** 1899.

This important Moravian town, located on the main line between Praha and Ostrava, has the smallest tramway system of the nine in the Czech Republic/Slovakia, but it is also the only one in the Czech Republic that is currently being extended. Olomouc is the sixth biggest city in the country with a population of around 100 000. Designated a UNESCO World Heritage Site, its main squares rival Praha, but without the hordes of tourists.

All tram routes converge at the main railway station and adjacent Fibichova interchange, to the west of the city centre. One route runs along cobbled streets to the north of the city centre, and another, opened in 1997, follows a main road to the south. An extension from this latter route (near the Trznice stop) to Nove Sady, in the south-east of the city, is currently being built. This will open in three stages, and during this time no turning loops will be built at the temporary termini. The first section of this extension from Trznice to Trnkova opened in late 2013: Phase 2 is Trnkova–Druzebni (due to open 2018) and Phase 3 Druzebni–Jizni (to be completed by 2020). Trams operate over the new extension as Line 3 (every 15 minutes on weekdays turning left at the junction near Trznice) and Line 5 (every 30 minutes and turning right at that junction).

Unusually for a small system there is a "grand union" junction in the city centre, from where a separate line diverges to the tram depot at Koželužska. Adjacent to the depot there is a separate yard for stabling trams. Another interesting feature of the system is the flat crossing of railway lines – on the Neředín Krematorium and Nová Ulice lines.

As a result of the Trnkova extension a fleet of 14 new Pragoimex trams to a new design have been supplied. Like traditional Czech trams these still have a cab at just one end but have doors on both sides and are designed to always operate in coupled pairs, back-to-back, to enable them to reverse at a terminus without a turning circle. Helped by the introduction of these new vehicles, more than half the Olomouc fleet is now low-floor, recent years having seen T3s withdrawn in favour of a small number of Škoda/Inekon trams introduced between 1998 and 2006 and subsequent deliveries of Pragoimex vehicles. In fact at off-peak times a complete low-floor service may often be seen in operation. The LFR.E and LF.E trams are the same apart from the fact that LF.Es are completely new cars, whilst LFR.Es use some components from withdrawn T3s.

The tramway is operated by Dopravní podnik města Olomouce (DPMO). Most routes operate at 15 minute frequencies and 24 hr tickets as well as the usual time based tickets are available.

PRAGOIMEX VARIO LF+/o

Built 2013. New single-ended trams that always operate in pairs, back-to-back. 26 seats.

101	104	107	109	111	113
102	105	108	110	112	114
103	106				

TATRA T3

Built 1970–87. 23 seats.

c   T3SUCS.   r   T3R.P.   w   works/staff training car.

136	w	153	r	162	r	168	r	173	r	180	r
138		154	r	163	r	169	r	175	c	181	r
141		155	r	164	r	170	r	176	c	182	r
143	w	156	r	165	r	171	r	178	r	183	r
147	r	158	r	166	c	172	c	179	r	184	r
148	r	159	r								

ŠKODA 03T

Built 1998–99. 41 seats.

201	202	203	204

INEKON TRIO(01)

Built 2005–06. 41 seats.

| 205 | 206 | 207 |

PRAGOIMEX VARIO LFR.E

Built 2007–11. 26 seats.

| 231 | 233 | 234 | 235 | 236 | 237 |
| 232 | | | | | |

PRAGOIMEX VARIO LFR.S

Built 2012–13. 26 seats. 244/245 on order.

| 238 | 240 | 242 | 243 | 244 | 245 |
| 239 | 241 | | | | |

PRAGOIMEX VARIO LF.E

Built 2006. 26 seats.

| 251 | 252 | 253 |

HERITAGE/MUSEUM FLEET

Car 223 normally operates with two-axle trailer car No. 99.

No.	Type	Built	Status	Notes
223	Ringhoffer 2-axle motor car	1930	A	Wooden-bodied tram. Ex-Praha 2238

▲ Olomouc has a fleet consisting of mainly modern low-floor trams. On 9 July 2014 two of the new bi-directional Pragoimex Vario LF+/o cars, 108+107, head away from the camera at Fibichova with a Line 3 service to Trnkova via the city centre as Inekon TRIO(01) 205 approaches. **Robert Pritchard**

9.1.5. OSTRAVA

www.dpo.cz   **Network:** 65.7 km.   **Lines:** 17.   **Depots:** 2 + works.

Standard livery: Blue, white & yellow.   **Tramway established:** 1894.

Depot codes: MO   Moravská Ostrava   PO   Poruba

The industrial city of Ostrava, part of the Moravian-Silesian region, has a population of around 305 000 and the third largest tramway in the country. The city lies just 10 km from the Polish border. The tramway has a complex history, with different tramways being brought together under one company in the 1950s, when the city had a tram network of some 174 km – the largest in the country. However many lines were narrow gauge and were replaced by buses or trolleybuses with operator DPO concentrating on the standard gauge network. An interesting history of the Ostrava tramway is available on the English version of the operator's website at www.dpo.cz/history.

Today's tram system is largely on reserved track, apart from some street running in the city centre. In total there are nine different termini around the city, the tramway having few lines to the east of the city centre, this area being mainly served by the trolleybus network. The tramway highlight is inter-urban Line 5 to Zátiší, which is single track with crossing loops and traditional railway style signals. The service frequency on this route is normally half-hourly. Frequent services operate on the other routes except Lines 17–19, which are the night lines. Trams serve both the main stations of hlavní nádraží and Svinov. In the Vítkovice district Line 2 runs through part of the massive steelworks complex, and a number of the routes also cross the internal railway lines of Vítkovice Doprava and ArcelorMittal.

In recent years Ostrava has been replacing its Tatra fleet with new vehicles, mainly from Pragoimex, although there were also some Škoda 03T and Inekon TRIO vehicles. The standard T3 replacement has come in the form of the Vario LFR.E or LFR.S, whilst there are also smaller numbers of longer articulated cars supplied by Pragoimex. Some of the Vario cars have been assembled in the Martinov tram workshops. This facility, which also overhauls cars for other countries, is in addition to the two large tram depots at Moravská Ostrava and Poruba, the latter having been built in the 1960s to maintain tram cars in this growing district to the west of the city. There are still plenty of T3s in the fleet, along with some T6s, KT8D5.RN1s with low-floor centre section and a small number of articulated K2s.

The operator is Dopravní Podnik Ostrava (DPO). 24-hour tourist type tickets are available. In 2016 these offered excellent value at 80czk (just over £2). Standard time-based tickets are also available.

PRAGOIMEX VV60LF

Built 2004–06. Unpowered trailer cars. 26 seats.

301	PO		302	PO

TATRA K2P/K2G

Built 1965–68.

g   K2G.   p   K2P.

802	p	PO		805	g	PO		806	g	PO		807	g	PO		811	g	PO
803	p	PO												

TATRA T3

Original vehicles built 1982–87, T3G (1028–47) rebuilt with new bodies 1995–97. 30–31 seats.

c	T3SUCS.			r	T3R.P.		w	works/staff training cars.
g	T3G (rebuilt with new bodies).			s	T3SU.			

901	s	PO		905	s	PO		911	c	PO		914	c	PO		917	c	PO
902	s	PO		908	c	PO		912	c	PO		915	c	PO		918	s	MO
904	s	PO		909	c	PO		913	c	PO		916	c	PO		919	r	PO

924	c	PO	953	c	MO	975	r	PO	1002	r	PO	1028	g	MO
926	c	PO	954	c	PO	976	r	PO	1003	r	PO	1029	g	MO
929	c	MO	955	c	PO	977	r	PO	1004	r	PO	1031	g	MO
931	g	MO	956	r	PO	978	g	MO	1006	c	PO	1033	g	MO
933	c	PO	957	c	MO	979	r	PO	1007	r	PO	1035	g	MO
936	c	PO	958	c	PO	983	r	PO	1008	r	PO	1036	g	MO
937	r	PO	959	c	PO	984	g	MO	1010	r	PO	1037	g	MO
938	r	PO	960	r	PO	986	c	MO	1011	r	PO	1038	g	MO
939	g	MO	961	c	PO	987	c	PO	1014	g	MO	1039	g	MO
940	c	MO	962	r	PO	988	g	MO	1015	r	PO	1040	g	MO
941	c	MO	963	c	PO	990	c	MO	1016	r	PO	1041	g	MO
942	c	PO	964	r	PO	991	r	PO	1017	g	MO	1042	g	MO
943	g	MO	965	c	MO	992	g	MO	1019	r	PO	1043	g	MO
944	r	PO	966	c	MO	994	r	PO	1020	r	PO	1044	g	MO
946	c	PO	967	r	PO	995	r	PO	1021	r	PO	1045	g	MO
947	r	PO	968	r	PO	996	r	PO	1023	r	PO	1046	g	MO
948	r	PO	970	r	PO	998	r	PO	1024	r	PO	1047	g	MO
949	r	PO	972	r	PO	999	c	PO	1025	r	PO	8201	w	PO
950	c	PO	973	r	PO	1000	r	PO	1026	r	PO	8204	w	Martinov
951	c	PO	974	r	PO	1001	g	MO	1027	r	PO	8208	w	Martinov
952	r	PO												

TATRA T6A5

Built 1994–97. 31 seats.

1101	PO	1109	PO	1117	PO	1125	PO	1132	PO
1102	PO	1110	PO	1118	PO	1126	PO	1133	PO
1103	PO	1111	PO	1119	PO	1127	PO	1134	PO
1104	PO	1112	PO	1120	PO	1128	PO	1135	PO
1105	PO	1113	PO	1121	PO	1129	PO	1136	PO
1106	PO	1114	PO	1122	PO	1130	PO	1137	PO
1107	PO	1115	PO	1123	PO	1131	PO	1138	PO
1108	PO	1116	PO	1124	PO				

ŠKODA 03T

Built 1998–2001. 42 seats.

1201	MO	1204	MO	1207	MO	1210	MO	1213	MO
1202	MO	1205	MO	1208	MO	1211	MO	1214	MO
1203	MO	1206	MO	1209	MO	1212	MO		

INEKON TRIO(01)

Built 2002–04. 41 seats.

1251	PO	1253	PO	1255	PO	1257	PO	1259	PO
1252	PO	1254	PO	1256	PO	1258	PO		

PRAGOIMEX VARIO T3R.EV

Built 2004 (prototype).

1301	PO

PRAGOIMEX VARIO LFR.E

Built 2004–12. 31–32 seats.

1311	PO	1314	PO	1317	PO	1320	PO	1323	PO
1312	PO	1315	PO	1318	PO	1321	PO	1324	PO
1313	PO	1316	PO	1319	PO	1322	PO	1325	PO

▲ Three-section articulated Inekon TRIO(01) 1256 is seen at Pohraniční with a Line 3 service to Dubina Interspar on 14 May 2013. **Robert Pritchard**

▼ Ostrava has been rapidly standardising its fleet on Pragoimex trams. On 14 May 2013 Vario LFR.Es 1353+1324 have just left hlavní nádraží with a Line 8 service for Vřesinská. **Robert Pritchard**

1326	PO	1333	MO	1340	MO	1346	MO	1352	PO
1327	MO	1334	MO	1341	MO	1347	MO	1353	PO
1328	MO	1335	MO	1342	MO	1348	MO	1354	PO
1329	MO	1336	MO	1343	MO	1349	MO	1355	PO
1330	MO	1337	MO	1344	MO	1350	MO	1356	PO
1331	MO	1338	MO	1345	MO	1351	PO	1357	PO
1332	MO	1339	MO						

PRAGOIMEX VARIO LFR.S

Built 2013–14. 31 seats.

1358	PO	1362	PO	1365	PO	1368	PO	1371	PO
1359	PO	1363	PO	1366	PO	1369	PO	1372	PO
1360	PO	1364	PO	1367	PO	1370	PO	1373	PO
1361	PO								

PRAGOIMEX VARIO LF2/LF2.RS

Built 2007 (prototype 1401) / 2013. 45 seats.

1401	PO	1402	PO	1403	PO

PRAGOIMEX VARIO LF2+

Built 2009 (prototype). 52 seats.

1411	MO

TATRA KT8D5.RN1

Built 1984 (1500) / 1989. Rebuilt from KT8D5 with low-floor centre section 2003–11. 65 seats.

1500	MO	1504	MO	1507	MO	1510	MO	1513	MO
1501	MO	1505	MO	1508	MO	1511	MO	1514	MO
1502	MO	1506	MO	1509	MO	1512	MO	1515	MO
1503	MO								

PRAGOIMEX VARIO LF3

Built 2006–07.

1601	PO	1602	PO

PRAGOIMEX VARIO LF3/2

Built 2008–11. 54 seats.

1651	MO	1652	MO	1653	MO

HERITAGE/MUSEUM FLEET

The Museum Fleet is based at the Martinov workshops.

No.	Type	Built	Status	Notes
21	Ringhoffer 2-axle motor car	1922	A	Wooden-bodied tram "Barborka"
24	Ringhoffer 2-axle works car	1919	A	Wooden-bodied tram with service platform
25	Ringhoffer 2-axle motor car	1919	A	Wooden-bodied tram
31	Ringhoffer 2-axle motor car	1927	S	Wooden-bodied tram
35	Ringhoffer 2-axle motor car	1932	A	Wooden-bodied tram. Ex-works car 8035
50	Ringhoffer 2-axle motor car	1948	A	
94	Ringhoffer 2-axle motor car	1949	A	
106	Ringhoffer 2-axle works car	1951	A	Wooden-bodied works car
528	Tatra T1	1957	A	
681	Tatra T2	1961	A	
752	Tatra T3	1970	A	

9.1.6. PLZEŇ (PILSEN)

www.pmdp.cz   **Network:** 26 km.   **Lines:** 3.   **Depots:** 1 (Slovany).

Standard livery: Yellow & grey.   **Tramway established:** 1899.

This industrial city in west Bohemia, 113 km from Praha by rail, is the fourth largest in the Czech Republic, with a population of around 170 000. The city is famous both for its cars and trains produced by the Škoda works and for Pilsner beer. It has an attractive main square, dominated by St Bartholomew's Cathedral, which has the tallest tower (335 ft) in the country – well worth a climb for the views over the city.

The tramway has three routes (Lines 1, 2 & 4), all crossing from one side of the city to the other and taking around 25–30 minutes end-to-end: Line 1 Slovany–Bolevec, Line 2 Světovar–Skvrňany and Line 4 Bory– Košutka. The Bolevec extension is the most recent, opening in 1990. Most of the lines operate on reserved track. The routes that run via the main square (Lines 1 and 2) operate to a one way system, as narrow streets mean there is only room for single track on either side of the square. Lines 1 and 2 also both serve the main station (hlavní nádraží). The depot at Slovany lies between the southern termini of Lines 1 and 2, and there is a connecting line between the two, but it has no scheduled services. In recent years, and particularly ahead of 2015 – Plzeň's European Capital of Culture year – the tram operator invested heavily in upgrading the track, and also its fleet.

Plzeň is proud to now have a largely low-floor fleet of trams – by the end of 2015 only nine formations of high-floor trams (pairs of T3s) were left in operation. There are other high-floor T3R.Ps in operation – but they are usually coupled behind T3R.PLF rebuilds which have a low-floor centre section. The last T3Ms were exported to Mykolaiv, Ukraine in 2015. The varied Plzeň fleet also includes a dozen KT8D5.RN2Ps – like Brno, Praha and some of the Košice trams of this type these have been fitted with low-floor centre sections. There are also Škoda 03Ts delivered in the late 1990s. In recent years Pragoimex trams have dominated. There have been standard Vario LFR.S type as well as four of a new design called LF2/2 IN. This is a six-axle, double ended, 100% low-floor car.

The tramway is operated by Plzeňské Městské Dopravní Podniky (PMDP), which also operates the city's trolleybus network of nine lines. Day tickets and the normal time-based tickets are available, but recently ticket machines have been removed from stops, although tickets can be purchased from tram drivers and are on sale in some shops and also from hotels.

TATRA T3

Original vehicles built 1971–87, 196/198 rebuilt with new bodies. 23 seats.

r   T3R.P.
v   T3R.PV. Rebuilt with new bodies 2002.
w   works car.

175	r w	234	r	248	r	256	r	264	r	280	r
196	v	235	r	249	r	257	r	265	r	281	r
198	v	236	r	252	r	260	r	268	r	282	r
208	r	243	r	253	r	261	r	269	r	283	r
217	r	244	r	254	r	262	r	276	r	286	r
218	r	245	r	255	r	263	r	277	r	287	r
233	r										

TATRA KT8D5.RN2P

Built 1989. Rebuilt from KT8D5 with low-floor centre section 2007–09. 50 seats.

288	290	292	294	296	298
289	291	293	295	297	299

▲ Tatra KT8D5.RN2P 291 approaches the Mikulášské náměstí stop with a Sunday morning Line 1 service to Slovany on 13 July 2014. **Robert Pritchard**

▼ With part of the steelworks complex visible behind, Pragoimex Vario LFR.S 358 has just left Škoda III. brána stop with an evening Line 2 service to Skvrňany on 12 July 2014. **Robert Pritchard**

ŠKODA 03T

Built 1998–2000. Original prototype 300 was scrapped in 2008 after collision damage. 41 seats.

301	303	305	307	309	310
302	304	306	308		

TATRA K3R.NT

Built 2006–07. These trams are effectively two T3 trams coupled together with a low-floor centre section fitted in-between (rebuilt by Pars nova, Šumperk). 54 seats.

311	312	313	314

PRAGOIMEX T3R.PLF

Built 2008–10. New trams with a low-floor centre section, built to the classic T3 design. 24 seats.

315	318	321	324	327	330
316	319	322	325	328	331
317	320	323	326	329	332

PRAGOIMEX VARIO LFR.S/LF+

Built 2010–14. 333–335/338–353/356–360/364–365 are Type Vario LFR.S (31 seats) and 336/337 and 354/355 are Type Vario LF+ (35 seats).

333	338	343	348	353	358
334	339	344	349	354	359
335	340	345	350	355	360
336	341	346	351	356	364
337	342	347	352	357	365

PRAGOIMEX VARIO LF2/2 IN

Built 2013–14. New 100% low-floor bi-directional trams. 44 seats.

361	362	363	366

HERITAGE/MUSEUM FLEET

The heritage fleet is based at Slovany depot except car 195 which has been donated to Strašice museum. Car 18, part of the original tramway fleet, is described by PMDP as "the oldest functioning electric tram in Central Europe".

No.	Type	Built	Status	Notes
18	Křižík & Brožík 2-axle motor car	1899	A	Wooden-bodied tram.
121	Tatra T1	1956	A	
133	Tatra T2R	1958	A	Ex-Ostrava 612/Liberec 23.
192	Tatra T3	1975	A	
195	Tatra T3	1975	M	Museum of Transport, Strašice

9.1.7. PRAHA (PRAGUE)

www.dpp.cz   **Network:** 142.4 km.   **Lines:** 30.   **Depots:** 7 + works & museum.

Standard livery: red & cream, or red, black & grey.   **Tramway established:** 1891.

Depot codes:

HL	Hloubětín	KO	Kobylisy	ST	Strašnice
HO	Hostivař Ústřední Dílny	MO	Motol	VO	Vokovice
	(Central Workshops)*	PA	Pankrác	ZI	Žižkov

* There is no operational allocation at Hostivař apart from two works cars.

In addition the Museum fleet is maintained at Střešovice depot (an operational depot until 1992) which is part of the tramway museum (opened 1993).

Praha's fantastic tramway is one of the largest in Europe, with its 30 lines covering most parts of the Czech capital, which has a population of around 1.2 million. Beautifully situated on the River Vltava the city has become one of the most visited in Europe since the fall of communism, with tourists drawn by the well-preserved central area, Praha Castle, the classic and unspoilt Baroque architecture and its river setting.

As well as serving the city centre, via various different routes, the tramway also serves Praha's extensive suburbs. Although there were a small number of closures when some Metro lines opened, the tramway has slowly expanded in recent years, with the impressive Hlubočepy–Sídliště Barrandov extension opening in 2003 (replacing an express bus line). A more recent short extension opened to Radlická (for the Metro station) in 2008. There are many highlights, including the eight river crossings, Vyšehrad tunnel, the aforementioned Barrandov extension with its "hooped" overhead supports and new tram viaduct and a number of segregated express routes (one of the best examples is Line 17 to Levského (Modřany) in the south of the city).

DPP has invested heavily in both track rebuilding and fleet replacement in recent years. The extensive fleet once comprised more than 1100 T3 trams but in more recent years many of these have been replaced by longer articulated vehicles. Most remaining T3s have received replacement traction equipment. There are also KT8D5s (49 originally delivered and now fitted with low-floor centre sections) and T6s (150 originally delivered). The first of the new era low-floor cars were the 14Ts from Škoda, which despite success in Wrocław, Poland and also in Brno were not successful in Praha and most are currently stored, although they are slowly being returned to traffic. More successful and now forming the backbone of the fleet is the 15T, also from Škoda. 250 of these will be in traffic by 2018. The T3, T6 and articulated Tatra trams still form an important part of the fleet as well, although many redundant T3s have been exported to Ukraine and Russia in recent years. Even though they are younger than some of the T3s, the T6s also started to be withdrawn in 2015.

Use of tracks by multiple routes is the norm in Praha. Trams operate 24 hours a day, with daytime operation from 05.00 to midnight. On core routes such as Line 22 trams operate as frequently as every 4 minutes in the peaks, and most routes run with a frequency of at least every 8–10 minutes. There are a number of good locations to observe trams within the city, at some busy junctions it is possible to observe more than 250 vehicles in a "rush hour". The best junctions for observations include Hradčanská, Karlovo náměstí, Anděl, I.P. Pavlova, Masarykovo nádraží, Strossmayerovo náměstí and Palmovka.

As well as the daytime routes there are nine night tram routes, Lines 51–59 operating to a half-hourly frequency between midnight and 05.00 and serving most of the city. All lines converge on Lazarská in the city centre. The night services are usually operated by single T3s or T6s.

The large museum at Střešovice (open weekends and public holidays late March–late September) is well worth a visit and museum trams can regularly be seen operating special tourist Line 91 at weekends and on public holiday afternoons late March–late October, to a half-hourly frequency through the city centre (special tickets required). See www.dpp.cz/en/nostalgic-tram-line-no-91 for more details. Museum trams are also available for private hire.

Praha's trams are operated by Dopravní Podnik hlavního města Prahy (DPP). Day tickets are available covering the trams, metro, buses and local trains in the city (within the PIT – Praha Integrated Transport area). In 2016 these were 110czk for 1 day (24hr) and 310czk for 3 days (72hr). Time-based (90 or 30 minute) tickets are also available and all tickets can be purchased at an outlet at the Airport or from ticket machines. DPP also operates the funicular from Újezd to the top of Petřín Hill (PIT tickets are valid) and the chairlift at Praha Zoo.

PRAGOIMEX EVO1

Built 2015. Pragoimex demonstrator vehicle being used in Praha on a trial basis. 30 seats.

0033   ST

WORKS CARS

Converted from various T3 versions. Each depot has at least one works car, whilst the staff training cars are based at Pancrác depot.

Original T3 design unless stated.   m   T3M (5550/51 have been rebuilt).   r   T3R.P.

*   cut-down for use as a greasing tram with the aim of reducing track noise from the newer trams.

5411	m	HL	5417	m	VO	5516	r	HL	5523	r	HL	5550	m	HO
5412	m	KO	5418	m	ZI	5519	m	PA	5524	r	HL	5551	m	HO
5413	m	MO	5419	m	PA	5520		PA	5525	r	PA	5572	m*	PA
5415	m	ST	5502		PA	5521		KO	5526	r	HL			

TATRA T3/T3 DESIGN

Original vehicles built 1966–89, some rebuilt with new bodies 1996–2009. All of the remaining T3SU and T3SUCS (7xxx number series) trams and the T3M trams (80xx series) are to be withdrawn as more new 15Ts enter traffic.

c   T3SUCS (24 seats).   m   T3M (24 seats).
d   T3M2-DVC (24 seats). Rebuilt 1996.   r   T3R.P (24 seats).
f   T3R.PLF (low-floor centre section,   s   T3SU (24 seats).
     22 seats). Rebuilt 2006–09.   v   T3R.PV (24 seats). Rebuilt 2002–07.

Livery variation: 8251–8283 and 8564–8579 are in a retro-style maroon & silver livery.

7001	s	ZI	7153	c	HO (S)	7262	c	ZI	8076	d	HL	8174	v	ST
7002	s	HO (S)	7160	c	ZI	7267	c	ZI	8077	d	HL	8175	v	ST
7014	s	HO (S)	7161	c	ZI	7269	c	ZI	8079	d	HL	8176	v	ST
7020	s	HO (S)	7165	c	ZI	7270	c	ZI	8080	d	HL	8177	v	ST
7021	c	HO (S)	7172	c	HO (S)	7271	c	HO (S)	8082	d	HL	8178	v	ST
7027	c	HO (S)	7174	c	ZI	7273	c	ZI	8083	d	HL	8179	v	ST
7041	c	HO (S)	7175	c	ZI	7275	c	ZI	8085	m	HL	8180	v	ST
7047	c	HO (S)	7187	c	HO (S)	7282	c	ZI	8087	d	HL	8181	v	ST
7049	c	HO (S)	7188	c	ZI	7283	c	ZI	8088	d	HL	8182	v	ST
7064	c	ZI	7189	c	ZI	7285	c	ZI	8089	d	HL	8183	v	ST
7065	c	ZI	7191	c	ZI	7286	c	ZI	8151	v	ST	8184	v	ST
7071	c	HO (S)	7192	c	ZI	7287	c	ZI	8152	v	ST	8185	v	ST
7077	c	HO (S)	7193	c	ZI	7289	c	ZI	8153	v	ST	8211	r	PA
7079	c	ZI	7201	c	ZI	7290	c	ZI	8154	v	ST	8212	r	PA
7081	c	ZI	7202	c	ZI	8009	d	HL	8155	v	ST	8213	r	PA
7082	c	HO (S)	7203	c	ZI	8013	m	HL	8156	v	ST	8214	r	PA
7083	c	ZI	7205	c	ZI	8014	m	HL	8157	v	ST	8215	r	PA
7086	c	HO (S)	7215	c	ZI	8015	d	HL	8158	v	ST	8216	r	PA
7087	c	ZI	7217	c	ZI	8016	m	HL	8159	v	ST	8217	r	PA
7100	c	ZI	7224	c	ZI	8021	m	HL	8160	v	ST	8218	r	PA
7115	c	HO (S)	7225	c	ZI	8029	m	HL	8161	v	ST	8219	r	PA
7117	c	HO (S)	7232	c	ZI	8038	m	HL	8162	v	ST	8220	r	PA
7121	c	ZI	7234	c	ZI	8042	m	HL	8163	v	ST	8221	r	PA
7122	c	ZI	7235	c	ZI	8043	m	HL	8164	v	ST	8222	r	PA
7123	c	ZI	7245	c	ZI	8049	m	HL	8165	v	ST	8223	r	PA
7127	c	ZI	7246	c	ZI	8051	d	HL	8166	v	ST	8224	r	PA
7128	c	ZI	7247	c	ZI	8053	d	HL	8167	v	ST	8225	r	PA
7134	c	HO (S)	7250	c	HO (S)	8057	m	HL	8168	v	ST	8226	r	PA
7142	c	ZI	7252	c	ZI	8063	d	HL	8169	v	ST	8227	r	PA
7143	c	ZI	7255	c	ZI	8067	d	HL	8170	v	ST	8228	r	PA
7144	c	ZI	7256	c	ZI	8068	d	HL	8171	v	ST	8229	r	PA
7145	c	HO (S)	7258	c	ZI	8072	d	HL	8172	v	ST	8230	r	PA
7152	c	HO (S)	7261	c	HO (S)	8074	d	HL	8173	v	ST	8231	r	PA

8232	r	PA	8317	r	VO	8381	r	ST	8445	r	KO	8509	r	PA
8233	r	PA	8318	r	VO	8382	r	ST	8446	r	ST	8510	r	KO
8234	r	PA	8319	r	VO	8383	r	ST	8447	r	ST	8511	r	KO
8235	r	PA	8320	r	VO	8384	r	ST	8448	r	KO	8512	r	KO
8236	r	PA	8321	r	VO	8385	r	ST	8449	r	KO	8513	r	KO
8237	r	PA	8322	r	VO	8386	r	ST	8450	r	KO	8514	r	KO
8238	r	PA	8323	r	VO	8387	r	ST	8451	r	KO	8515	r	KO
8239	r	PA	8324	r	VO	8388	r	ST	8452	r	KO	8516	r	KO
8240	r	PA	8325	r	VO	8389	r	ST	8453	r	KO	8517	r	KO
8241	r	PA	8326	r	VO	8390	r	ST	8454	r	KO	8518	r	KO
8242	r	PA	8327	r	VO	8391	r	ST	8455	r	KO	8519	r	KO
8243	r	PA	8328	r	VO	8392	r	ST	8456	r	KO	8520	r	KO
8244	r	PA	8329	r	VO	8393	r	ST	8457	r	KO	8521	r	KO
8245	r	PA	8330	r	VO	8394	r	ST	8458	r	VO	8522	r	KO
8251	f	ST	8331	r	VO	8395	r	ST	8459	r	VO	8523	r	KO
8252	f	ST	8332	r	VO	8396	r	ST	8460	r	KO	8524	r	KO
8253	f	ST	8333	r	VO	8397	r	ST	8461	r	KO	8525	r	KO
8254	f	ST	8334	r	VO	8398	r	ST	8462	r	KO	8526	r	KO
8255	f	ST	8335	r	VO	8399	r	ST	8463	r	KO	8527	r	KO
8256	f	ST	8336	r	VO	8400	r	ST	8464	r	ST	8528	r	KO
8257	f	ST	8337	r	VO	8401	r	ST	8465	r	KO	8529	r	KO
8258	f	ST	8338	r	VO	8402	r	ST	8466	r	KO	8530	r	KO
8259	f	ST	8339	r	VO	8403	r	ST	8467	r	KO	8531	r	KO
8260	f	ST	8340	r	VO	8404	r	ST	8468	r	KO	8532	r	PA
8261	f	ST	8341	r	VO	8405	r	ST	8469	r	KO	8533	r	PA
8262	f	ST	8342	r	VO	8406	r	ST	8470	r	KO	8534	r	KO
8263	f	ST	8343	r	VO	8407	r	ST	8471	r	KO	8535	r	KO
8264	f	ST	8344	r	VO	8408	r	ST	8472	r	KO	8536	r	PA
8265	f	ST	8345	r	VO	8409	r	ST	8473	r	KO	8537	r	PA
8266	f	ST	8346	r	VO	8410	r	ST	8474	r	KO	8538	r	KO
8267	f	ST	8347	r	VO	8411	r	ST	8475	r	KO	8539	r	KO
8268	f	ST	8348	r	ST	8412	r	ST	8476	r	PA	8540	r	PA
8269	f	ST	8349	r	ST	8413	r	ST	8477	r	PA	8541	r	PA
8270	f	ST	8350	r	ST	8414	r	KO	8478	r	KO	8542	r	KO
8271	f	ST	8351	r	HL	8415	r	KO	8479	r	KO	8543	r	KO
8272	f	ST	8352	r	HL	8416	r	KO	8480	r	KO	8544	r	PA
8273	f	ST	8353	r	HL	8417	r	KO	8481	r	KO	8545	r	PA
8274	f	ST	8354	r	HL	8418	r	KO	8482	r	KO	8546	r	KO
8275	f	ST	8355	r	ST	8419	r	KO	8483	r	KO	8547	r	KO
8276	f	ST	8356	r	ST	8420	r	KO	8484	r	KO	8548	r	PA
8277	f	ST	8357	r	HL	8421	r	KO	8485	r	KO	8549	r	PA
8278	f	ST	8358	r	HL	8422	r	KO	8486	r	PA	8550	r	PA
8279	f	ST	8359	r	HL	8423	r	KO	8487	r	PA	8551	r	PA
8280	f	ST	8360	r	ST	8424	r	KO	8488	r	KO	8552	r	KO
8281	f	ST	8361	r	ST	8425	r	KO	8489	r	KO	8553	r	KO
8282	f	ST	8362	r	HL	8426	r	PA	8490	r	KO	8554	r	KO
8283	f	ST	8363	r	HL	8427	r	PA	8491	r	KO	8555	r	KO
8300	r	PA	8364	r	ST	8428	r	KO	8492	r	PA	8556	r	HL
8301	r	PA	8365	r	ST	8429	r	KO	8493	r	PA	8557	r	HL
8302	r	PA	8366	r	HL	8430	r	KO	8494	r	KO	8558	r	HL
8303	r	PA	8367	r	HL	8431	r	KO	8495	r	KO	8559	r	HL
8304	r	PA	8368	r	ST	8432	r	VO	8496	r	KO	8560	r	HL
8305	r	PA	8369	r	HL	8433	r	VO	8497	r	KO	8561	r	HL
8306	r	PA	8370	r	HL	8434	r	KO	8498	r	KO	8562	r	HL
8307	r	PA	8371	r	HL	8435	r	KO	8499	r	KO	8563	r	HL
8308	r	PA	8372	r	HL	8436	r	KO	8500	r	KO	8564	r	ST
8309	r	PA	8373	r	HL	8437	r	KO	8501	r	KO	8565	r	ST
8310	r	PA	8374	r	ST	8438	r	KO	8502	r	KO	8566	r	ST
8311	r	PA	8375	r	ST	8439	r	KO	8503	r	ST	8567	r	ST
8312	r	PA	8376	r	ST	8440	r	KO	8504	r	KO	8568	r	ST
8313	r	PA	8377	r	ST	8441	r	KO	8505	r	KO	8569	r	ST
8314	r	PA	8378	r	ST	8442	r	KO	8506	r	KO	8570	r	ST
8315	r	PA	8379	r	ST	8443	r	KO	8507	r	KO	8571	r	ST
8316	r	VO	8380	r	ST	8444	r	KO	8508	r	PA	8572	r	ST

8573	r	ST	8575	r	ST	8577	r	ST	8578	r	ST	8579	r	ST
8574	r	ST	8576	r	ST									

TATRA T6A5

Built 1995–97. Two types of seating layout: 8601–8680 have a 1+1 seating layout (25 seats) and 8681–8750 have a 2+1 seating layout (31 seats). 8702 now forms part of the Museum fleet.

Withdrawals of these trams have already started and 20 have been sold for export to Sofia (Bulgaria) (identities to be confirmed), whilst in early 2016 8631 was exported to Kharkov, Ukraine. A number of other T6s have already been scrapped after accident damage.

8601	MO	8632	MO	8661	MO	8691	ZI	8722	ZI
8602	MO	8633	MO	8662	MO	8692	ZI	8723	ZI
8603	MO	8634	HO (S)	8663	MO	8693	ZI	8724	ZI
8604	MO	8635	MO	8664	MO	8694	ZI	8725	ZI
8606	MO	8636	MO	8665	MO	8695	ZI	8726	ZI
8607	MO	8637	MO	8666	MO	8696	ZI	8727	ZI
8608	MO	8638	MO	8667	HO (S)	8699	ZI	8728	ZI
8609	MO	8639	MO	8668	MO	8700	ZI	8729	ZI
8610	HO (S)	8640	MO	8669	MO	8701	ZI	8730	ZI
8611	MO	8641	MO	8670	MO	8703	ZI	8731	ZI
8612	HO (S)	8642	MO	8672	MO	8704	ZI	8732	ZI
8613	MO	8643	MO	8673	MO	8705	ZI	8733	ZI
8614	HO (S)	8644	MO	8674	MO	8706	ZI	8734	ZI
8615	HO (S)	8645	MO	8675	MO	8707	ZI	8735	ZI
8616	MO	8646	MO	8676	MO	8708	ZI	8736	ZI
8617	HO (S)	8647	MO	8677	MO	8709	ZI	8737	ZI
8618	HO (S)	8648	MO	8678	MO	8710	ZI	8739	ZI
8619	MO	8649	HO (S)	8679	MO	8711	ZI	8740	ZI
8620	MO	8650	MO	8680	MO	8712	ZI	8741	ZI
8621	MO	8651	HO (S)	8681	MO	8713	ZI	8742	ZI
8622	MO	8652	MO	8682	MO	8714	ZI	8743	ZI
8623	HO (S)	8653	MO	8683	MO	8715	ZI	8744	ZI
8624	MO	8654	MO	8684	MO	8716	ZI	8745	ZI
8625	MO	8655	MO	8685	MO	8717	ZI	8746	ZI
8626	MO	8656	MO	8686	MO	8718	ZI	8747	ZI
8627	MO	8657	MO	8687	MO	8719	ZI	8748	ZI
8628	HO (S)	8658	MO	8688	MO	8720	ZI	8749	ZI
8629	MO	8659	MO	8689	ZI	8721	ZI	8750	ZI
8630	MO	8660	MO	8690	ZI				

TATRA KT8D5.RN2P

Built 1986–90. Rebuilt from KT8D5 with low-floor centre section 2004–13. At the same time cars were fitted with new TV3 traction equipment. Cars were renumbered by adding 50 to their fleet number, ie 9001 became 9051 on rebuilding. In 2014–15 two KT8D5 cars were bought from Strausberg, Germany (both originally being ex-Košice), becoming 9056 and 9098. The original 9006 had been withdrawn, whilst 9048 was not rebuilt and is part of the Museum fleet. In 2016 two further cars were purchased from Miskolc, and are being overhauled to become 9099/9100. It is understood that there are options to purchase further KT8D5s from Miskolc. 50 seats.

* Originally ex-Košice. 9056 rebuilt ex-Košice 505/Strausberg 23, 9098 ex-Košice 527/Strausberg 21, 9099 ex-Košice 539/Miskolc 200 and 9100 ex-Košice 522/Miskolc 204.

9051		HL	9061	HL	9071	HL	9081	HL	9091	HL
9052		HL	9062	HL	9072	HL	9082	HL	9092	HL
9053		HL	9063	HL	9073	HL	9083	HL	9093	HL
9054		HL	9064	HL	9074	HL	9084	HL	9094	HL
9055		HL	9065	HL	9075	HL	9085	HL	9095	HL
9056	*	HL	9066	HL	9076	HL	9086	HL	9096	HL
9057		HL	9067	HL	9077	HL	9087	HL	9097	HL
9058		HL	9068	HL	9078	HL	9088	HL	9098	* HL
9059		HL	9069	HL	9079	HL	9089	HL	9099	* HL
9060		HL	9070	HL	9080	HL	9090	HL	9100	* HL

▲ The classic sight of a pair of T3s on the streets of the Czech capital will still be seen for a number of years. The T3R.P was the standard refurbishment of the 2000s, and boasts new digital displays. On 14 May 2014 8389+8391 leave the Bohemians stop with a Line 7 service to Radlická.   **Robert Pritchard**

▼ A pair of Tatra T6A5s – 8621 and 8622 – emerge from the tunnel under Vyšehrad with a Line 3 service to Lazarská on 12 May 2014.   **Robert Pritchard**

ŠKODA 14T

Built 2005–09. These Škoda trams were nicknamed "Porsche". Reliability has been poor at times, not helped by a number of accidents, and some trams have spent long periods out of traffic. 9165 was written off in an accident in 2011 and heavily stripped to provide spares for other cars before being scrapped, whilst 9112 and 9163 were scrapped in 2015. All others were withdrawn in 2014 and put up for sale after excessive problems with frame cracking in the harsh Praha street environment. However there were no takers and the fleet is now slowly starting to be returned to traffic (initially on Line 17) after extensive repairs to their chassis. Some cars are also being refurbished, with a revised interior layout, 9148 being the first to be done. 69 seats.

9111	HO (S)	9124	HL (S)	9136	KO	9147	KO (S)	9158	HL (S)
9113	HL (S)	9125	KO	9137	HL (S)	9148	KO	9159	KO (S)
9114	HL (S)	9126	HL (S)	9138	HL (S)	9149	HL (S)	9160	HL (S)
9115	HO (S)	9127	KO	9139	HL (S)	9150	KO	9161	MO
9116	HO (S)	9128	KO	9140	HL (S)	9151	KO (S)	9162	MO (S)
9117	HL (S)	9129	HO (S)	9141	KO (S)	9152	HL (S)	9164	KO
9118	HO (S)	9130	HO (S)	9142	HO (S)	9153	HL (S)	9166	HO (S)
9119	HO (S)	9131	HO (S)	9143	KO (S)	9154	HL (S)	9167	HL (S)
9120	KO (S)	9132	HO (S)	9144	KO	9155	HL (S)	9168	KO
9121	HL (S)	9133	HO (S)	9145	KO (S)	9156	KO (S)	9169	HL (S)
9122	HL (S)	9134	KO (S)	9146	HL (S)	9157	HO (S)	9170	HL (S)
9123	KO (S)	9135	MO (S)						

ŠKODA 15T

Built 2009–14. 250 100% low-floor 15T trams were ordered from Škoda in 2008, with delivery scheduled between 2009 and 2018. The new trams are fitted with a new type of fully rotating articulated bogie better suited to Praha's streets that the rigid bogie used under the 14Ts. The 15Ts were also much more powerful to cope with Praha's hills.

The first 15T entered service in 2011 and they can now be found on most routes. At the time of writing all 125 of the initial 15T trams are in traffic, and the 15T4 (second variant) trams are being delivered. DPP is taking 32 new 15T cars per year until 2018. 60 seats.

9201	PA	9226	PA	9251	PA	9276	VO	9301	VO
9202	PA	9227	PA	9252	PA	9277	VO	9302	VO
9203	PA	9228	PA	9253	MO	9278	VO	9303	PA
9204	PA	9229	PA	9254	PA	9279	VO	9304	VO
9205	PA	9230	PA	9255	MO	9280	VO	9305	VO
9206	PA	9231	PA	9256	MO	9281	VO	9306	VO
9207	PA	9232	PA	9257	MO	9282	VO	9307	VO
9208	PA	9233	PA	9258	MO	9283	VO	9308	VO
9209	PA	9234	PA	9259	MO	9284	VO	9309	VO
9210	PA	9235	PA	9260	MO	9285	VO	9310	VO
9211	PA	9236	PA	9261	MO	9286	VO	9311	VO
9212	PA	9237	PA	9262	MO	9287	VO	9312	VO
9213	PA	9238	PA	9263	MO	9288	PA	9313	VO
9214	PA	9239	PA	9264	MO	9289	VO	9314	VO
9215	PA	9240	PA	9265	MO	9290	VO	9315	VO
9216	PA	9241	PA	9266	MO	9291	VO	9316	VO
9217	PA	9242	PA	9267	MO	9292	VO	9317	VO
9218	PA	9243	PA	9268	VO	9293	VO	9318	VO
9219	PA	9244	PA	9269	VO	9294	VO	9319	VO
9220	PA	9245	PA	9270	VO	9295	VO	9320	VO
9221	PA	9246	PA	9271	VO	9296	VO	9321	VO
9222	PA	9247	PA	9272	VO	9297	VO	9322	VO
9223	PA	9248	PA	9273	VO	9298	VO	9323	VO
9224	PA	9249	MO	9274	VO	9299	VO	9324	MO
9225	PA	9250	MO	9275	VO	9300	VO	9325	VO

ŠKODA 15T4

Built 2015–18. The second batch of 125 15Ts started to enter service in autumn 2015 and all should be delivered by the end of 2018. Following customer feedback a number of changes have been made – the trams are fully air-conditioned, they have wi-fi and plastic moulded seats. A revised livery is also carried. The first trams in this series are being delivered to Motol depot, whilst later batches will be delivered to Žižkov depot in 2017–18. 60 seats.

9326	MO	9351	MO	9376		9401		9426	
9327	MO	9352	MO	9377		9402		9427	
9328	MO	9353	MO	9378		9403		9428	
9329	MO	9354	MO	9379		9404		9429	
9330	MO	9355	MO	9380		9405		9430	
9331	MO	9356	MO	9381		9406		9431	
9332	MO	9357	MO	9382		9407		9432	
9333	MO	9358		9383		9408		9433	
9334	MO	9359		9384		9409		9434	
9335	MO	9360		9385		9410		9435	
9336	MO	9361		9386		9411		9436	
9337	MO	9362		9387		9412		9437	
9338	MO	9363		9388		9413		9438	
9339	MO	9364		9389		9414		9439	
9340	MO	9365		9390		9415		9440	
9341	MO	9366		9391		9416		9441	
9342	MO	9367		9392		9417		9442	
9343	MO	9368		9393		9418		9443	
9344	MO	9369		9394		9419		9444	
9345	MO	9370		9395		9420		9445	
9346	MO	9371		9396		9421		9446	
9347	MO	9372		9397		9422		9447	
9348	MO	9373		9398		9423		9448	
9349	MO	9374		9399		9424		9449	
9350	MO	9375		9400		9425		9450	

▲ Carrying the Czech national flag on what was a public holiday (Liberation Day), 8 May 2015, Škoda 15T 9276 arrives at Hradčanská with a Line 20 service to Sídliště Barrandov. **Robert Pritchard**

HERITAGE/MUSEUM FLEET

The varied Praha heritage fleet is based at Střešovice museum or in the museum depository and workshops alongside. Almost the whole fleet is kept in operational condition, and most vehicles are available for private hire, although some trams are normally limited to static display in the museum. In recent years more "modern" trams such as T3s and even a T6 have joined the fleet. The whole Praha museum fleet is listed here, apart from horse trams and trailers.

No.	Type	Built	Status	Notes
88	Ringhoffer 2-axle motor car	1900	A	Wooden-bodied tram
109	Ringhoffer 2-axle motor car	1901	A	Wooden-bodied tram. Ex-4063
200	Ringhoffer 2-axle motor car	1900	A	Wooden-bodied tram
240	Ringhoffer 2-axle motor car	1908	A	Wooden-bodied tram
275	Ringhoffer 2-axle motor car	1908	A	Wooden-bodied tram
297	Ringhoffer 2-axle motor car	1909	A	Wooden-bodied tram. Ex-4091
349	Ringhoffer 2-axle motor car	1915	A	Wooden-bodied tram. Ex-4022/4212
351	Ringhoffer 2-axle motor car	1915	A	Wooden-bodied tram. Ex-4023/4213
357	Ringhoffer 2-axle motor car	1915	A	Wooden-bodied tram. Ex-4029
412	Ringhoffer 2-axle motor car	1920	A	Wooden-bodied tram. Ex-4037/4225
444	Ringhoffer 2-axle motor car	1923	A	Wooden-bodied tram.
500	Ringhoffer 2-axle open motor car	1913	A	Wooden-bodied tram (open-sided)
2110	Ringhoffer 2-axle motor car	1928	A	Wooden-bodied tram. Ex-4214.
2172	Ringhoffer 2-axle motor car	1929	A	Wooden-bodied tram.
2210	Ringhoffer 2-axle motor car	1930	A	Wooden-bodied tram. Ex-4209/4210.
2222	Ringhoffer 2-axle motor car	1930	A	Wooden-bodied tram.
2239	Ringhoffer 2-axle motor car	1930	A	Wooden-bodied tram.
2272	Ringhoffer 2-axle motor car	1931	A	Wooden-bodied tram.
2294	Ringhoffer 2-axle motor car	1932	A	Wooden-bodied tram.
3062	Ringhoffer/Tatra 2-axle motor car	1942	A	Wooden-bodied tram.
3063	Ringhoffer/Tatra 2-axle motor car	1942	A	Wooden-bodied tram.
3083	Ringhoffer/Tatra 2-axle motor car	1948	A	Wooden-bodied tram.
4002	Ringhoffer/Tatra 2-axle motor car	1942	R	Wooden-bodied tram. Ex-3068/4101
4049	Ringhoffer 2-axle motor car	1923	S	Wooden-bodied works tram. Ex-447
4053	Ringhoffer 2-axle works car	1917	A	Wooden-bodied works tram. Ex-2053/4001
4092	Schörling grinding motor car	1966	A	Rail grinder.
4100	Ringhoffer/Tatra 2-axle motor car	1948	S	Wooden-bodied tram. Ex-3098
4206	Ringhoffer 2-axle motor car	1929	R	Wooden-bodied tram. Ex-2196
4217	Ringhoffer 2-axle motor car	1915	A	Wooden-bodied tram. Ex-355/4027
4218	Ringhoffer 2-axle motor car	1915	R	Wooden-bodied tram. Ex-356/4028
4223	Ringhoffer 2-axle motor car	1929	S	Wooden-bodied tram. Ex-2170
5001	Tatra T1	1951	A	
5002	Tatra T1	1951	A	
5419	Tatra T3M	1975	A	Ex-6928/8058
5500	Tatra T4YU	1966	A	Ex-Beograd 111
5602	Tatra T3	1964	A	Ex-6400
6002	Tatra T2	1955	A	
6102	Tatra T3	1962	A	
6149	Tatra T3	1962	A	
6340	Tatra T3	1964	A	Ex-works car 5511
6892	Tatra T3	1973	A	
6921	Tatra T3	1973	A	
7292	Tatra T3SUCS	1989	A	
8084	Tatra T3M	1976	A	Ex-6960
8702	Tatra T6A5	1996	A	
9048	Tatra KT8D5	1990	A	

9.2. SLOVAK TRAM SYSTEMS

9.2.1. BRATISLAVA

www.dpb.sk **Network:** 40 km. **Lines:** 9. **Depots:** 2.

Standard livery: All over red. **Tramway established:** 1895.

Depot codes: KR Krasňany JU Jurajov Dvor **Gauge:** 1000 mm.

The tramway of the Slovak capital was in limbo for a number of years whilst a decision was taken on whether to completely regauge the system, or retain and modernise the metre gauge network. Eventually a decision was made to modernise the existing network, and also invest in an extension to cross the River Danube to the massive Petržalka estate (home to around a third of the city's population and said to be the most densely populated residential district in central Europe). The first part of the extension, 2.4 km to Jungmannova, is due to open in spring 2016. The second part of the extension will be to Janíkov dvor (3.8 km) by 2020. The initial section has been constructed as dual-gauge as one idea was to integrate the extension with a tram-train style operation, but this has since been dropped.

The line to the main railway station, closed in 2011 owing to deteriorating track, has also been rebuilt and reopened in late 2014 whilst the rest of the system is now slowly being modernised with new platforms, replacing rudimentary stops built into pavements.

Bratislava has a population of around 430 000 and is less than an hour by train from another European capital – Wien (Vienna) in Austria. Highlights of the tramway include an 800 m tunnel that takes trams under the castle to reach the long line to the west of the city and multiple routes operating along a busy shopping street (Obchodná ulica).

Bratislava has been playing catch-up with other nearby systems in terms of low-floor vehicles – there were no low-floor vehicles in Bratislava's fleet until late 2014 when the first of 60 Škoda 29T and 30T trams were delivered. By early 2016 30 bi-directional 30Ts and 30 single-ended 29Ts were in traffic, for use on the new extension and also to replace many of the ageing T3s. The 29T and 30T are based on the 26T supplied to Miskolc in Hungary. As well as the T3s, the tramway has 58 T6s and just over 30 K2s, almost all rebuilt by Pars nova in the late 1990s and 2000s. The T3s and T6s usually run in consecutively numbered pairs (they are not normally used singly). The main works is located at Jurajov Dvor depot, which also maintains most of the T3s and the new Škoda trams, whilst the other depot at Krasňany is the home depot for the K2s and T6s.

A new all over red livery was adopted by operator Dopravný podnik Bratislava (DPB) in 2010, with the city's slogan "Little Big City", although many trams still carry the original red & cream livery. There is also a trolleybus network of 12 lines. Day tickets are available for travel on the trams, trolleybuses and motor buses, and also on ZSSK regional trains within the Bratislava area.

TATRA K2S

Original vehicles built 1974–83. K2S rebuilt with new bodies 1998–2009. 46 seats.

g K2G. Rebuilt with replacement body to classic K2 style in 2001.

7085	g KR	7108	KR	7115	KR	7122	KR	7129	KR
7101	KR	7109	KR	7116	KR	7123	KR	7130	KR
7102	KR	7110	KR	7117	KR	7124	KR	7131	KR
7103	KR	7111	KR	7118	KR	7125	KR	7132	KR
7104	KR	7112	KR	7119	KR	7126	KR	7133	KR
7105	KR	7113	KR	7120	KR	7127	KR	7134	KR
7106	KR	7114	KR	7121	KR	7128	KR	7135	KR
7107	KR								

TATRA T3S/T3MOD

Original vehicles built 1975. Rebuilt with new bodies 1999–2001. 22 seats.

o T3MOD. t T3S.

7301	t KR	7302	t KR	7303	t JU	7304	o JU

ŠKODA 29T

Built 2014–16. New single-ended trams all delivered by early 2016. 69 seats.

7401	JU	7407	JU	7413	JU	7419	JU	7425	JU
7402	JU	7408	JU	7414	JU	7420	JU	7426	JU
7403	JU	7409	JU	7415	JU	7421	JU	7427	JU
7404	JU	7410	JU	7416	JU	7422	JU	7428	JU
7405	JU	7411	JU	7417	JU	7423	JU	7429	JU
7406	JU	7412	JU	7418	JU	7424	JU	7430	JU

ŠKODA 30T

Built 2014–15. New bi-directional trams all delivered by the end of 2015. 52 seats.

7501	JU	7507	JU	7513	JU	7519	JU	7525	JU
7502	JU	7508	JU	7514	JU	7520	JU	7526	JU
7503	JU	7509	JU	7515	JU	7521	JU	7527	JU
7504	JU	7510	JU	7516	JU	7522	JU	7528	JU
7505	JU	7511	JU	7517	JU	7523	JU	7529	JU
7506	JU	7512	JU	7518	JU	7524	JU	7530	JU

TATRA T3

Built 1975–89. Many are being replaced by new 29T and 30T. 22 or 29 seats.

c	T3SUCS.	g	T3G.	m	T3M.	p	T3P.	s	T3SU.	
7602	m KR	7739	c JU (S)	7767	c JU (S)	7795	p JU	7821	c JU	
7610	m KR	7740	c JU (S)	7768	c JU (S)	7796	p JU	7822	c JU	
7703	p JU	7741	c JU (S)	7769	c JU (S)	7797	c JU	7823	c JU	
7704	p JU	7742	c JU (S)	7770	c JU (S)	7798	c JU	7824	c JU	
7706	p JU	7745	c JU (S)	7773	c JU	7799	p JU	7825	c JU	
7715	p JU	7746	c JU (S)	7774	c JU	7800	p JU	7826	c JU	
7717	p JU	7747	c JU (S)	7775	c JU (S)	7801	c JU	7827	c JU	
7718	p JU	7748	c JU (S)	7776	c JU (S)	7802	c JU	7828	c JU	
7719	p JU	7749	c JU	7777	c JU	7803	c JU	7829	c JU (S)	
7720	s JU (S)	7750	c JU	7778	c JU	7804	c JU	7830	c JU (S)	
7721	s JU	7751	c JU (S)	7779	c JU	7805	c JU	7831	c JU	
7722	s JU (S)	7752	c JU (S)	7780	c JU	7806	c JU	7832	c JU	
7723	s JU (S)	7753	c JU	7781	p JU	7807	c JU	7833	c JU	
7724	s JU (S)	7754	c JU	7782	p JU	7808	c JU	7834	c JU	
7726	m KR (S)	7755	c JU (S)	7783	p JU	7809	c JU	7835	g KR	
7727	s JU (S)	7756	c JU (S)	7784	p JU	7810	c JU	7836	g KR	
7728	s JU (S)	7757	c JU	7785	p JU	7811	c JU	7837	g KR	
7729	m KR (S)	7758	c JU	7786	p JU	7812	c JU	7838	g KR	
7731	s JU (S)	7759	c JU	7787	p JU	7813	c JU	7839	g KR	
7732	s JU (S)	7760	c JU	7788	p JU	7814	c JU	7840	g KR	
7733	m KR	7761	c JU	7789	p JU	7815	c JU	7841	g KR	
7734	m KR	7762	c JU	7790	p JU	7816	c JU	7842	g KR	
7735	s JU (S)	7763	c JU (S)	7791	p JU	7817	c JU	7843	g KR	
7736	s JU (S)	7764	c JU (S)	7792	p JU	7818	c JU	7844	g KR	
7737	c JU (S)	7765	c JU	7793	c JU	7819	c JU	7845	g KR	
7738	c JU (S)	7766	c JU	7794	c JU	7820	c JU	7846	g KR	

TATRA T6A5

Built 1991–97. 7901/02 were originally prototypes built for Praha. 30 seats.

7901	KR	7906	KR	7911	KR	7916	KR	7921	KR
7902	KR	7907	KR	7912	KR	7917	KR	7922	KR
7903	KR	7908	KR	7913	KR	7918	KR	7923	KR
7904	KR	7909	KR	7914	KR	7919	KR	7924	KR
7905	KR	7910	KR	7915	KR	7920	KR	7925	KR

7926	KR	7933	KR	7940	KR	7947	KR	7953	KR
7927	KR	7934	KR	7941	KR	7948	KR	7954	KR
7928	KR	7935	KR	7942	KR	7949	KR	7955	KR
7929	KR	7936	KR	7943	KR	7950	KR	7956	KR
7930	KR	7937	KR	7944	KR	7951	KR	7957	KR
7931	KR	7938	KR	7945	KR	7952	KR	7958	KR
7932	KR	7939	KR	7946	KR				

WORKS CARS

Converted from Type K2, T3 or T3SUCS.

Original T3 design unless stated.   c   T3SUCS.   k   K2.

8133	k	KR	8137	c	KR	8434	c	KR	8437	JU	8438	JU
8135	c	KR									

HERITAGE/MUSEUM FLEET

The museum fleet is based at Krasňany depot. At least two cars are normally used to operate special services during the annual "Bratislava Rendez" event in June every year.

No.	Type	Built	Status	Notes
18	BMEŽ Štvorokeňák	1937	A	Wooden-bodied tram.
31	BMEŽ Páťokeňák	1938	A	Wooden-bodied tram. Ex-101
38	DPMB 2-axle motor car	1958	A	
104	Ganz II/Typ I 2-axle motor car	1910	A	Converted from Ganz trailer 124
215	Tatra T2	1959	A	Ex-230/7230
275	Tatra T3	1964	A	Ex-7509[I]/works car 8136
317	Tatra K2	1971	A	Ex-7009
7086	Tatra K2YU	1983	S	

▲ K2S 7108, a Tatra K2 rebuilt with a new body by Pars nova in 2000, is seen near Bratislava's old town – close to the Kapucínská stop – with a Line 9 service to Karlova Ves on 11 June 2014.

Robert Pritchard

9.2.2. KOŠICE

<u>www.dpmk.sk</u> **Network:** 34 km. **Lines:** 7 (+ R1–R8). **Depots:** 1 (Bardejovská).

Standard livery: Blue, white & yellow. **Tramway established:** 1891.

Košice, in the east of Slovakia, is the second largest city in the country with a population of around 240 000. It has an interesting tramway that is roughly the same size as Bratislava's, but at standard (1435 mm) gauge. The network essentially has six separate lines radiating from the city centre, one of these serves the main railway station that is to the east of the city centre. Other lines have been built on reservation to serve high density residential areas. The highlight of the network is the 11 km line to the US Steelworks to the south of the city. Built in 1964 this inter-urban line runs through open countryside and is served by a half-hourly limited stop service at off-peak times. However many more trams run to and from US Steel in connection with shift change times on weekdays – around 06.00, 14.00, and to a lesser extent 18.00 and 22.00. There are as many as 14 departures from US Steel in the hour from 14.00 to 15.00, on a number of different routes (all prefixed "R").

In the well-preserved city centre, although there is no longer a tramway, there is still a section of non-electrified tram track that sees horse trams on certain days in the summer.

Until recent years the tram fleet consisted of T3s, T6s and articulated KT8D5s. Originally 40 KT8D5s (500–539) were delivered but in the 1990s some were sold to other systems to raise funds, including ten to nearby Miskolc in Hungary and three to Brno. Some of the 19 KT8D5s remaining in Košice have been fitted with low-floor centre sections.

From 2014 tram operator Dopravný podnik mesta Košice (DPMK) started to invest heavily in the future of the tramway. Extensive track relaying has been taking place and the tram fleet is being renewed. One of the Pragoimex Vario LFR.S trams was taken as a trial in 2011 and in 2014 the operator placed an order for 28 new articulated Vario LF2+ trams (like those already delivered to Ostrava) for delivery between August 2014 and September 2015. The order was later increased to 33, and then to 46 (834–846 were ordered spring 2016). These trams now form the backbone of the system, having replaced most of the T3s, which now only see occasional use.

▲ Carrying the latest livery, KT8D5 525 has just left the Vstupný areál US Steel terminus with a route R7 service to Amfiteáter on 5 June 2014. All routes serving US Steel are prefixed "R" and run to different termini, although some of the "R" routes only have one or two services a day.

Robert Pritchard

TATRA T3

Built 1964/1970 (101/100) and 1982–89. 23 seats.

c   T3SUCS.   s   T3SU.   w   works car.

100	s w	363	c (S)	385	c (S)	395	c (S)	405	c	415	c
101	w (S)	364	c (S)	386	c (S)	396	c	406	c	416	c
112	s w	367	c (S)	387	c (S)	397	c	407	c	417	c
336	c (S)	376	c (S)	388	c (S)	398	c (S)	408	c	418	c
337	s (S)	377	c (S)	389	c (S)	399	c (S)	409	c	419	c
349	s (S)	378	c (S)	390	c (S)	400	c	410	c	420	c
356	c (S)	380	c (S)	391	c (S)	401	c	411	c	421	c
357	c (S)	381	c	392	c (S)	402	c	412	c	422	c
359	c w (S)	382	c (S)	393	c (S)	403	c	413	c	423	c
361	c (S)	383	c	394	c (S)	404	c	414	c	424	c
362	c (S)	384	c (S)								

TATRA KT8D5

Built 1986–91. 54 seats.

*   KT8D5.RN2. Rebuilt with low-floor centre section 2003–09. 56 seats.

500		512	*	521	*	528	*	531	*	536
501		513		523		529	*	534	*	537
508		517	*	525		530	*	535		538
509	*								

TATRA T6A5

Built 1992–93. Missing tram 618 was scrapped after accident damage. 30 seats.

600	605	610	615	621	626
601	606	611	616	622	627
602	607	612	617	623	628
603	608	613	619	624	629
604	609	614	620	625	

PRAGOIMEX VARIO LFR.S

Built 2011. 22 seats.

701

PRAGOIMEX VARIO LF2+

Built 2014–16. 834–846 are on order. 44 seats.

801	809	817	825	833	840
802	810	818	826	834	841
803	811	819	827	835	842
804	812	820	828	836	843
805	813	821	829	837	844
806	814	822	830	838	845
807	815	823	831	839	846
808	816	824	832		

HERITAGE/MUSEUM FLEET

No.	Type	Built	Status	Notes
10	Ringhoffer 2-axle motor car	1920	S	Wooden-bodied tram. Ex-Praha 371.
103	Ringhoffer 2-axle motor car	1920	S	Wooden-bodied tram. Ex-Praha 4031/364
104	Ringhoffer 2-axle motor car	1920	A	Wooden-bodied tram. Ex-Praha 4030/363
203	Tatra T1	1957	A	Ex-Ostrava 683
212	Tatra T2	1960	A	Ex-Ostrava 619

APPENDIX: COMMON TERMS IN ENGLISH, CZECH, SLOVAK & GERMAN

ENGLISH	CZECH	SLOVAK	GERMAN
train	vlak	vlak	Zug
express train	Expresní vlak (Ex)	Expresný vlak (Ex)	Schnellzug (Ex)
fast train	Rychlík (R)	Rychlík (R)	Schnellzug (D)
regional speeded train	Spěšné vlak (Sp)	Zrýchlený vlak (Zr)	Eilzug (RE)
passenger train	Osobní vlak (Os)	Osobný vlak (Os)	Personenzug
unscheduled train	Mimořádný vlak	Mimoriadny vlak	Sonderzug
special train	zvláštní vlak	osobitný vlak	Sonderzug
freight train	nákladní vlak	nakladný vlak	Güterzug
works train	montážní vlak	montážny vlak	Arbeitszug
railway	železnice	železnica	Eisenbahn
standard gauge railway	normalnerozchodna železnice	normalnorozchodna železnica	Normalspurbahn
narrow gauge railway	úzkorozchodná železnice	úzkorozchodná železnica	Schmalspurbahn
broad gauge railway	širokorozchodná železnice	širokorozchodná železnica	Breitspurbahn
rail	kolejnice	koľajnica	Schiene
track	trat	trat	Strecke
platform track	kolej	kolaj	Gleis
platform	nástupište; perón	nástupište; perón	Bahnsteig
station	nádraží; stanice	stanica	Bahnhof
main station	hlavní nádraží	hlavná stanica	Hauptbahnhof
halt	zastávka	zastávka	Haltestelle
locomotive	lokomotiva	lokomotiva	Lokomotive
loco	stroj	stroj	Lok
locomotive depot	lokomotiva depo	rusenove depe	Bahnbetriebwerk
diesel locomotive	dieselová lokomotíva	dieselová lokomotíva	Diesellok
diesel electric	dieselelectricka	dieselelectricka	Dieselektrische
diesel hydraulic	dieselhydraulická	dieselhydraulická	Dieselhydraulische
diesel mechanical	dieselmechanicky	dieselmechanicky	Dieselmechanische
tractive effort	tažná síla	tažná síla	Zugkraft
electric locomotive	electrická lokomotiva	electrická lokomotiva	E-lok
alternating current	střídavý proud	striedavý prúd	Wechselstrom
direct current	stejnosměrný proud	jednosmerný prúd	Gleichstrom
steam locomotive	parní lokomotiva	parní lokomotiva	Dampflok
diesel motor coach	motorový dieselový vůz	dieselový motorový vozeň	Dieseltriebwagen
electric multiple unit	elektrická jednotka	elektrická jednotka	Elektrische Garnitur
carriage	vůz	vozeň	Wagen
sleeping car	lůžkový vůz	lôžkový vozeň	Schlafwagen
couchette car	lehátkový vůz	ležadlový vozeň	Liegewagen
route diversion	odklon	odklon	Umleitung
closure	výluka	výluka	Sperre
ticket	lístek; jizdenka	lístok	Fahrkarte; Fahrschein
crown (currency)	koruna; Kč	koruna; Kč	Krone
supplement	doplatok cestovného	doplatek jízdného	Zuschlag
First Class	1. třídy	1. třídy	1. Klasse
Second Class	2. třídy	2. třídy	2. Klasse
arrival	příjezd	príchod	Ankunft
departure	odjezd	odchod	Abfahrt
timetable	sešitový jízdní řád	cestovný poriadok	Fahrplan
timetable book	jízdní řád	cestovný poriadok vlakov	Kursbuch
diagram	oběh	oběh	Umlauf
train number	číslo vlaku	číslo vlaku	Zugnummer
hello/good day (formal)	dobrý den	dobrý deň	Guten Tag
goodbye (formal)	na shledanou	do videnia	Auf Wiedersehen
thankyou	děkuji	dakujem	danke
Do you speak English?	mluvíte anglicky?	hovoríte po anglicky?	Sprechen Sie Englisch?
drinking water	pitna voda	pitna voda	Trinkwasser
beer	pivo	pivo	Bier